THE LIFE OF
SIR WALTER SCOTT

Borgo Press Books by S. FOWLER WRIGHT

*Arresting Delia: An Inspector Cleveland Classic Crime Novel * The Attic Murder: An Inspector Combridge & Mr. Jellipot Classic Crime Novel * The Bell Street Murders: An Inspector Combridge & Mr. Jellipot Classic Crime Novel * Beyond the Rim: A Lost Race Fantasy * Black Widow: A Classic Crime Novel * The Blue Room: A Novel of an Alternate Future * The British Colonies: No Surrender to Nazi Germany! * The Capone Caper: Mr. Jellipot vs. the King of Crime: A Classic Crime Novel * Cortéz: For God and Spain: An Historical Novel * Crime & Co.: An Inspector Cleveland Classic Crime Novel * David the King: An Historical Novel * Dawn: A Novel of Global Warming * Dead by Saturday: An Inspector Cleveland Classic Crime Novel * Deluge: A Novel of Global Warming * Dream; or, The Simian Maid: A Fantasy of Prehistory (Marguerite Cranleigh #1) * Elfwin: An Historical Novel of Anglo-Saxon Times * The End of the Mildew Gang: An Inspector Cauldron Classic Crime Novel (Mildew #3) * Four Callers in Razor Street: An Inspector Combridge & Mr. Jellipot Classic Crime Novel * Four Days' War: The Alternate World War II, Book Two * The Hanging of Constance Hillier: An Inspector Cleveland Classic Crime Novel * The Hidden Tribe: A Lost Race Fantasy * Inquisitive Angel: A Novel of Fantasy * The Island of Captain Sparrow: A Lost Race Fantasy * The Jordans Murder: An Inspector Combridge & Mr. Jellipot Classic Crime Novel * The King Against Anne Bickerton: A Classic Crime Novel * The Last Days of Pompeii: An Historical Novel * The Life of Sir Walter Scott: A Biography * The Lord's Right in Languedoc: An Historical Novel * Marguerite de Valois: An Historical Novel * Megiddo's Ridge: The Alternate World War II, Book Three * The Mildew Gang: An Inspector Cauldron Classic Crime Novel (Mildew #1) * Murder in Bethnal Square: An Inspector Combridge & Mr. Jellipot Classic Crime Novel * The Ordeal of Baratá: A Political Fantasy * The Police and the Public: Some Thoughts on the British System of Justice * Post-Mortem Evidence: An Inspector Combridge & Mr. Jellipot Classic Crime Novel * Power: A Political Fantasy * Prelude in Prague: The Alternate World War II, Book One * Red Ike: A Novel of Cumberland (with J. M. Denwood) * The Return of the Mildew Gang: An Inspector Cauldron Classic Crime Novel (Mildew #2) * The Rissole Mystery: An Inspector Combridge & Mr. Jellipot Classic Crime Novel * The Screaming Lake: A Lost Race Fantasy * The Secret of the Screen: An Inspector Combridge & Mr. Jellipot Classic Crime Novel * Seven Thousand in Israel: A Novel * The Siege of Malta: An Historical Novel * The Song of Songs and Other Poems * Spiders' War: A Novel of the Far Future (Marguerite Cranleigh #3) * Three Witnesses: A Classic Crime Novel * Too Much for Mr. Jellipot: An Inspector Combridge & Mr. Jellipot Classic Crime Novel * The Vengeance of Gwa: A Fantasy of Prehistory (Marguerite Cranleigh #2) * Was Murder Done? A Classic Crime Novel * Who Murdered Reynard? A Classic Crime Novel * The Wills of Jane Kanwhistle: An Inspector Combridge & Mr. Jellipot Classic Crime Novel * With Cause Enough?: An Inspector Combridge & Mr. Jellipot Classic Crime Novel * The World Below: A Novel of the Far Future * Wyndham Smith: His Adventures in the 45th Century: Science Fiction Novel*

THE LIFE OF SIR WALTER SCOTT
A BIOGRAPHY

S. FOWLER WRIGHT

THE BORGO PRESS
MMXII

BORGO BIOVIEWS
ISSN 0743-0628
Number Eleven

THE LIFE OF SIR WALTER SCOTT

Copyright © 1932 by S. Fowler Wright
Copyright © 2012 by the Estate of S. Fowler Wright

FIRST BORGO PRESS EDITION

Published by Wildside Press LLC

www.wildsidebooks.com

THE LIFE OF
SIR WALTER SCOTT

CONTENTS

FOREWORD 9
THE LIFE OF SIR WALTER SCOTT 11
ABOUT THE AUTHOR 759

FOREWORD

"I shall proffer you large proffers," said Sir Lancelot, "that is to say I shall unarm my head, and the last quarter of my body, all that may be unarmed, and I shall let bind my left hand behind me, so that it shall not help me, and right so I shall do battle with you."

A life of Walter Scott requires no apology. He is by far the greatest figure in Scottish literature, and has only one rival in the English tongue.

Without making any claim to finality, this volume is intended to represent that life in clearer outline than Lockhart's voluminous records succeed in doing, and with greater accuracy than they attempted to reach.

In particular, it endeavours to give an equitable and intelligible account of business transactions which were often much simpler in themselves than are the interpretations which have been loaded upon them—and to be equitable, not only to Scott himself, but to others who by the accident of association with him were drawn into the light of the same publicity.

In the presentation of the closing years it has been possible, through the courtesy of Messrs. Douglas & Foulis of Edinburgh, to quote from Sir Walter Scott's Journal as it was edited by Mr. David Douglas, and is published by them.

—S. FOWLER WRIGHT

SIR WALTER SCOTT

CHAPTER I.

In the early April days of 1758, a young Edinburgh lawyer, Walter Scott, married Anne Rutherford, the eldest daughter of Dr. John Rutherford, Professor of Medicine at the University, and they set up house-keeping together at the end of the narrow sunless alley of the College Wynd, as the residential deficiencies of the Scottish capital, and their slender income permitted.

Walter Scott had not been born in Edinburgh. He was the eldest son of a Roxburgh farmer, Robert Scott of Sandy-Knowe, one of the Harden branch of that once-turbulent Border family, and he had come to the metropolis to make his way in the only form of civil warfare which survived the pacification of the Lowlands, and the English Union.

Anne Rutherford, though we meet her as the daughter of a city doctor, was of a kindred breed. Her father, like Walter Scott, had come to Edinburgh from an ancient moorland home, half fort, half farm, where the Rutherfords had held their own (and sometimes a few trifles to which the word was not originally applicable) through the bickering of centuries, while the law lay more lightly upon the land than the weight of a Border sword.

Her mother (dead now, and her father married again) was Sir John Swinton's daughter, bringing in another ancestry conspicuous for some previous centuries in Lowland politics, and civil and national warfare.

Perhaps, as we look backward, we should not omit a glance

at Walter Scott's mother also—Barbara Haliburton, of whom we know little beyond the fact that Robert and she were the parents of a large family whose after-records speak well for their upbringing in the rather primitive and strenuous life of the bleak moorland farm. The Haliburtons were a Berwickshire family of good repute, but somewhat quieter character than Scotts or Rutherfords or Swintons were ever likely to be. Still, like the Rutherfords, they had held their own, which had become a considerable area around Dryburgh and elsewhere, and it was an operation difficult to sustain without a good wit, and some toughness of fibre, through the disorders of the two previous centuries.

Such were the ancestries of the Edinburgh lawyer and the girl he brought to the narrow house at the corner of College Wynd. Our tale is not of these two, entering the romance of marriage under a shadow that they could not foresee, and would find difficult to understand, but they are necessary to know, and worth knowing.

Walter had been apprenticed by his father to George Chalmers, a Writer to the Signet, which is a professional description equivalent to that of an English solicitor, the Scottish legal fraternity having split into two branches, similar to those which have become so profitable to themselves and so oppressive to litigants in the Southern country. At this period, Writers to the Signet commonly took from one to several apprentices, of whom a minority only could establish themselves in the profession which they, or their parents, had chosen. But Walter Scott had shown character and ability which had caused him to be retained in George Chalmers's office when his apprenticeship ended, and to appear as a partner not very long afterwards.

At the time of his marriage, he had built up a good and growing practice, having the confidence of many clients among his numerous and important relatives in the Lowland counties. As the years passed, he became known as an expert conveyancer, adept in the intricacies of ancient title-deeds, a student of ecclesiastical history also, and one who, while advocating individual freedom, was yet conservative in his desire for the retention of old-established customs which were of the spirit of feudalism.

A strict Calvinist in religion, having the type of mind which would delight in the difficult intellectual gymnastics by which such systems of theology are sustained and defended, he yet appears to have been without bigotry or intolerance, and to have ruled his life by the broader and more vital principles of Christianity. Popular among his contemporaries, of a personal austerity towards physical indulgence which was conspicuous against the manners of the times rather than extreme in itself handsome in person, with a gracious kindliness of manner which tended somewhat to formality as the years passed, he stands out well in the white glare of enquiry which the light of his son's genius was to cast backward upon him.

His fault (if such it were) was one which might be anticipated when a man of generous mind, and of such combative ancestry, engaged in the civil warfare of litigation. His clients' interests would become his own, even to financing their quarrels personal to himself. His clients' honour would be interpreted by his own standards, so that those who left their funds in his hands, though they could be very sure that he would not apply them to his own use, could have less certainty that they would not be diverted to vicarious generosities toward some needy relative, whom (Mr. Scott had no doubt) they would have been prompt to relieve, had there been convenient opportunity to consult them before the urgent disbursement had to be made.

Those clients who instructed him in their quarrels would find that they would be ably and pertinaciously defended, and that the growing bill of costs, paid or unpaid, would not be allowed to check disbursement or weaken advocacy. It must take its time and its chance.

Had such a man been a fool, among such clients as the times would bring to his door, or had he been without a scrupulous personal integrity, he would have been speedily discredited in his profession, and ruined in his finances.

As it was, he made many bad debts. His opponents might find it hard to outwit him, but to an unscrupulous client it would be an easier thing. Yet his practice and reputation grew.

In his wife he seems to have made a very fortunate choice. Lockhart says that Anne was superior to her husband "in talents as well as tastes". We can believe that or not as we will. The praise would be equally convincing without the comparison. The fact seems to have been that they were different in details of intellectual interests, with strong outlines of similarity. It is of such diverse similarities that the most successful marriages may be made, and the best children come.

Anne had an equally deep-rooted religious faith, but we have her son's testimony that she wore the theological cloak with a considerable difference, which tended to mitigate the severities of the Sabbatarian tradition which would lie heavily, even then, upon the children of such a home.

She was a wide reader, of poetry in particular, a lover of old ballads, a skilful story-teller, and had the sense of humour which is almost the first necessity for successful motherhood, or successful marriage.

She was of a natural gaiety also, and had a stubborn and buoyant courage, of which she was to have need enough in the first years of married life, as we shall soon see.

She was 'short of stature, and by no means comely, at least after the days of her early youth'. Lockhart again. He could not have seen her, except at an advanced age, when her vivacity survived, but little else of the attractions of earlier days. You have to know Lockhart first to judge how much, or how little heed to give to his confident oracles. Standards of beauty differ. It is hard to imagine that Anne Rutherford—or Mrs. Walter Scott—was unattractive. Obviously there was one man—and he of a rather fastidious temper—who thought differently, and whose means of judging were much the better of the two.

It is curious to consider how greatly our conception of an individual depends upon the age at which he or she becomes an object of observation.

Keats and Shelley survive in the glamour of perpetual youth. Dr. Johnson was born a rather slovenly and obese old man. It is the penalty of those who produce genius that they are cast in the pageant of history for the parts of parents, who are usually elderly when they attract the biographer's notice. Yet they had their youth too.

CHAPTER II.

We need not doubt that Walter and Anne Scott set up housekeeping together very happily in College Wynd, having, many common interests, and a bond of love which would endure, but across the natural course of their marriage an inexplicable shadow fell—fell, and would not lift.

They were themselves in vigorous youth, and of an abundant vitality. They were of healthy stock, and their lives had been continent and well-ordered. Anne had children. They came rapidly. Babies that were strong at birth, as the children of such parents should be. But yet, after a few months, one after one, they tailed and died. It seems that love could not save them, nor any care. Family counsels were of no avail. The Professor of Medicine, with his grandchildren's lives at stake had no sufficient wisdom to give.

The fact seems to have been that these children, of such entirely moorland ancestry, could not thrive in the smoke— and germ-laden city atmosphere. There could be no enduring life for them in the sunless rooms of that narrow ungardened house, at the end of the College Wynd. They could not resist the infections which the slum-bred child, of weaker vitality, was adapted to overcome. But who was to know that? The bitter lesson which industrial England was to learn in the following century was still unguessed.

Other children of seemingly weaker stocks thrived well enough; or lived, if they did not thrive. But prayers and tears were of an equal vanity here. There must have been many prayers. There is nothing surer than that. But it seemed that they prayed to a deaf God.

Pregnant again, and near the time of a fifth birth, Anne folded up four little packets of hair. She was arranging her private drawer, as a woman should who is approaching the ordeal of childbirth, so that it should be left neatly if anything should go wrong, as we know it may, though we are not so cowardly as to talk of that. She wrote on the packet in her slanting Italian hand: *All these are dead.* With what thoughts or tears she wrote we cannot tell now. She knew herself a failure among mothers. Four times. Was there any value in those short frustrated lives? Immortal futures, as she would have said with confidence, in her darkest hour? Nothing but a physical failure, and the folly of unspaced births, as some of us, with an equal confidence, would assert today? Well, God knows.

But this time she was to be rewarded with a child that would not die. Robert they named him, after his grandfather, still farming at Sandy-Knowe. That was to be his name, and his destiny was a naval life. There was a Scottish obstinacy about this programme—or was it a joke?

If it were so, we must go back a generation or two to understand its subtlety, for the elder Robert, life-long sheep-farmer at Sandy-Knowe, had been bred for the sea also, and that by a father of very obstinate disposition.

Robert's father had been another Walter by the christening rite, but it was as "Old Beardie" that he was remembered, the nickname earned by a flowing beard that he had vowed not to shave or trim till the Stuarts should be re-established on the Scottish throne.

But the Covenanters had held their ground, and the beard thrived.

Old Beardie, a man not to be lightly crossed, had destined his second son, Robert, to the sea, and to the sea he went. His first voyage was on a ship of which we know little more than that it took a northerly course, possibly for Scandinavia or the Baltic ports. But the North Sea was unkind. Robert's ship must have met a tempest from north or east, for it ended as a broken wreck on the Dundee coast. Robert got to the land alive, and on the land he would remain. He had a long walk home. When he arrived he said he had come to stay. He was emphatic about that. Old Beardie was emphatic too. He should go back to the sea, or he should never have another bawbee from him, or another meal at his board.

Robert agreed very cheerfully. He demonstrated his independence by turning Covenanter on the spot. It must have been a lively discussion.

He walked out, and went to John Scott of Harden, who was the chief of the clan. He asked for the lease of Sandy-Knowe, which was vacant. Sandy-Knowe was a high moorland farm with a poor soil. The ruins of Smailholm Tower stood at its centre—one of those small square-built Lowland holds, which had been so numerous in the Border counties.

Perhaps the fact that Robert had quarrelled with his father was no bad credential to bring. Certainly Old Beardie's political activity must have been an embarrassment to the family. It had cost him the forfeiture of some ancestral lands. It had led him (he was a man of scholarly repute) to a club in Edinburgh where the members talked treason exclusively in the Latin tongue. It had once led him into the folly of active rebellion, from which he had escaped unhanged through the intervention of the Duke of Monmouth, which his wife, the Duchess of Buccleuch, had influenced in favour of this misguided member of her own clan.

Anyway, Robert got the farm.

As it must be stocked if it were to be of any profit, he next made a bargain with an old shepherd named Hogg, doubtless an ancestor of James, the Ettrick celebrity of that name, though the exact pedigree might not be easy to trace.

Hogg was to lend Robert the thirty pounds which he had accumulated in a life of penurious saving, and Robert was to appoint Hogg head-shepherd of a yet sheepless farm. Together, they were to buy sheep.

On this errand they journeyed to a Northumbrian fair, Robert carrying the money-bag. They separated on arrival and Hogg made a tour of the sheep-pens. When he had matured his opinions upon the prices and qualities that the market offered, he rejoined his master, who was now on horseback. There was no need to worry further about the price of sheep. The horse was bought, and the thirty pounds were gone.

Tradition says that there was some difficulty in explaining matters to the satisfaction of the ancient shepherd. As to that we may think what we will, and that Robert had to face a second interview of a lively kind is a very probable thing, but if we go on to suppose that this is no more than a tale of youth indiscretion we are miles out.

Robert could ride. In fact, he liked riding as much as he disliked having to swim. He rode that horse after the hounds when he got home. He was a judge of a good horse, and he knew how to take a fence. In a few days' time the horse was sold for a doubled price. After that, he bought sheep.

Robert settled down on the moorland farm, married Barbara Haliburton, and reared a numerous family. It was land from which a Welshman might have wrung a meagre living, and on which an English farmer would have promptly starved. But Robert had some uncommon qualities, beside the thriftiness of those who are reared on a shallow soil. Where he was, his success would be. He became a dealer in cattle, his operations extending from the Scottish Highlands to the midland counties of England. Shrewd, sagacious, quick of thought and speech, of a tireless activity, and with a name for scrupulous honesty, his reputation grew, and his business with it. We may think of him as sheep-farmer and cattle-drover, for such he was; but we must regard him also as a Harden Scott, whose name entitled him to meet the gentlefolk of the countryside on an equal footing, and whose thriving finances enabled him not only to establish his eldest son as an Edinburgh lawyer (as we have seen) but to provide on a similar scale for other members of the rather large family that he and Barbara raised beneath the shadow of Smailholm Tower, including a boy named Robert who was sent to sea!

He found time also for the games and field-sports in which he delighted, and in which he had a cultivated proficiency, not only in their exercise, but in their rules and traditions, as he had in other questions of country rites or usage, so that he became widely reputed as an arbiter of dispute. At the period to which we are coming, we must think of him as a white-haired man, of medium height, and a spare activity, the sporting proclivities of earlier years still symbolised in the jockey cap which is his usual head-gear. Barbara is alive also. She will outlive him, and with an activity and capacity which will carry on the farm when he is dead; but it is the gentleness of her disposition which is most impressive to those who meet her. When we remember the 'sweetness' which was remarked in more than one of her children, and particularly in the Walter with whom we have been concerned, which was hardly discernable as a characteristic of the earlier Scotts, we may confirm our thought that the Haliburtons must not be overlooked when we consider his ancestry, and that of his greater son.

CHAPTER III.

We have seen that there is a child at last in the corner house at the College Wynd, who is not destined to an infant's grave. He is to be named Robert, and, in defiance of the record of a previous holder of that name, he is also to go to sea.

Another son, John, followed after a short interval, and then—three years later—a third boy, who was named Walter after his father and Auld Beardie, and it would be hard to say how many other ancestors. It was not the first attempt to continue the name which Walter's parents had made. It is significant of a stubborn fighting quality which is persistent in the Scott family, generation after generation, that the living children repeated the names of those who had died in infancy before them.

The second Walter throve (in spite of an unfortunate experiment with a tuberculous foster-mother), and shortly after his birth the Scotts removed to a larger and lighter residence in George's Square. The shadow of those four children's deaths was a receding thing in a nursery which was made noisy by three vigorous boys, to which a baby girl had just been added when it threatened again in a new way.

Walter, now eighteen months old, had been very lively one night, as was remembered afterwards, and resisted capture when bed-time came, but the next morning he was in a state of fever. The wisdom of the nursery authorities attributed this to a coming tooth, but upon the fourth day it became an insufficient explanation of the fact that he could not move his right leg.

Anxious family consultations followed. The medical faculty of Edinburgh congregated around the child's cot—Alexander Wood, the grandfather, Dr. Rutherford, and other names of repute at that time. Many treatments, blistering among them, were suggested, and tried in vain. The fever went. The child was otherwise well. But he crawled on the floor with the dragging weight of a useless limb.

A chicken, being vigorous at birth, may run about very cheerfully for the first fortnight, even if it be badly fed and worse housed. It is when the down moults, and the growth of feathers makes the first call on its strength, that the effects of previous damp, or lack of exercise or sunlight or vitalising food are shown in weakness and death; while another, that was no stronger at birth, but which has had its necessities better supplied, will grow feathers as easily as it will swallow a worm. A child should grow its teeth in the same way, and it is a poor standard of rearing which anticipates trouble. But if there be any lack of initial vitality, or if there have been any serious deprivation of air or light or essential food, it is then that Nature will present a bill which the child must pay.

Dr. Rutherford, if he failed with those four children before, has the credit of having spoken the right word now. "Try Sandy-Knowe." The proposal was quickly adopted by parents who remembered those four tiny graves of children who had been strong at birth, and then so soon, so inexplicably failed.

Walter was consigned to his grandparents' care. Mrs. Scott sent him to Sandy-Knowe in the charge of a maid in whom she must have felt that she had cause for sufficient confidence, but it was badly placed. The girl was mentally unstable. She was in a lunatic asylum soon afterwards.

She may have had good reasons of her own for desiring to return to Edinburgh. It may have been no more than a general dislike of a quiet country life, which often affects the town-dwellers whose minds are badly developed in our own day. For their own peace they require a surrounding clamour. They are dependent, almost for existence, upon that which happens outside themselves. Anyway, she conceived a longing for the city streets, and hatred of the child who was the unconscious cause of her detention from them. Concealing a pair of scissors, she went out with the baby in her arms. She climbed the crags with a purpose of cutting his throat, and burying him in the moss. Even if suspicion should fall upon her, there could be no proof. The child would have disappeared. After a few days, she would be allowed to go home. Her need to do that appeared more to her than the life of a deformed baby.

Had she carried out her purpose, there would have been a short trouble in George's Square; a crime, whether discovered or not, too unimportant for any permanent memory; and Robert Burns would have continued to be the greatest of Scottish poets. The English-speaking race would have lost one of its major intellectual impulses during the succeeding century, Tom Purdie would have gone to jail for poaching, Miss Charpentier would have found a different husband, and J. G. Lockhart a different wife. But the future development of English poetry (though Macauley would not have written the *Lays of Ancient Rome*) or of the English novel, would not have been very different, for reasons which we must not turn aside to consider here.

But, fortunately for many besides the child who was most concerned, the young woman altered her mind. She went back, and the peak of full insanity must have been very near, for she mentioned the unusual use to which she had thought of applying her scissors to Alison Wilson, the housekeeper, with the result that she was sent back to Edinburgh by the next coach, as her heart desired. Shortly afterwards, the wretched creature disappeared within the sinister silence of asylum walls.

It is a curious duplication of the exceptional that Walter Scott's life was again threatened many years later by a man who was crossing the threshold of lunacy. On that occasion (as we shall see in its place) he owed his safety to his own courage and self-control: on this one, his own part in the incident though it may not have been without importance, must have been of an unconscious kind.

So the child of pure Border blood is back in the farmhouse where his father was born. He is in his grandfather's charge. Alison Wilson, the old housekeeper, takes him into her care. The baby happy-tempered, very loving in baby ways, alert of mind, healthy but for the dragging limb, becomes the common pet of the farm. There is no nurse to restrain his activities, nor (by Heaven's mercy) and baby-carriage to confine him further. Tibby Hunter and the other farm-girls compete for the privilege of carrying 'the darling' on their backs when they go ewe-milking among the crags. Better than that, when Sandy Ormiston goes out to the flocks, he is on the old man's shoulder. He is laid down to roll and crawl in the heather as he will, or as he can with that dragging limb. He raises baby hands to pull the fleeces of the friendly sheep. He lies out in sun and rain and wind as the lambs lie.

Sandy has a whistle that he can blow at need from the crag's height on a note which will be heard in the kitchen at Sandy-Knowe, and one of the maids will come running to carry him in; but for the most part he is left in the heather's care, and once at least is forgotten, and must be sought through the torrent of moorland storm.... It was his Aunt Janet who found him at last, looking up at the lightning with laughing eyes.

So, significantly enough, after half a generation of city life (or more on the mother's side) the child of Border blood, of

Scotts and Rutherfords, Haliburtons and Swintons, is back on his native crags, the child who is to interpret, to the world's end, that Border country in itself, in its history, and its people, as it never otherwise would have been known; transfigured somewhat, if you will, by a valour and nobility which was of himself, and which to him must be in every tale for it to be worth the telling, but always with the breadth of the only roof which closed the vision of his waking hours, the wide sanity of the moorland sky.

CHAPTER IV.

For the next three or four years the younger Walter saw little of his parents' house in George's Square, where there was an ever-growing family, from which the curse of infant weakness seemed to have permanently lifted, but whether through the change of residence or the superior vitality which is frequently observable in the younger children of a large family might be hard to decide. Tom and Daniel are added to Robert and John and Anne. It seems to have been a happy, noisy family, in spite of the strict routine of its Calvinistic Sabbath. Its mother ruled it with a sympathetic gentleness. She had humour as well as courage and wisdom. Its father was absorbed in his growing practice. He was often absent on visits to his country clients. His reputation for chivalrous integrity, separating him somewhat from the practise of his brother lawyers, increased his clients, and in spite of some consequences of that quality, his income and status grew.

We shall see more of these children later, and of the mother of so many, dead or living, of whom our Walter (who, of course, ought not to have been born at all) was to write nearly forty years later that she "is, I am glad to say, perfectly well."

May there not be something to be said after all for the old gallant ignorant days? The days before we were so very sure that consumptives ought not be allowed to marry, or women to stake the risks of pregnancy, or a straightened income, against the gain of a child's life, and—in short, that we should always accept defeat without battle, unless we are quite sure of victory, and that we shall take no wound?

However that be, Walter lives, by whatever precedent folly, for which we may unite to be thankful. The year was young when they brought him to Sandy-Knowe, and as the summer came, and he lay through the long hours under the moorland sky, the curiosities of childhood, and of an exceptionally alert and adventurous mind, joined the vitalising influences of sun and wind, in the unhurried impulses by which he crawled, and then stood uncertainly on the shrunken limb, and then began to run upon it with an increasing freedom.

When the young woman of the scissors had brought him to Sandy-Knowe, it had been hard to rouse him to any activity. One of his first recollections was of his grandfather, with the jockey-cap on his short grey hair, still alert and active, though very near to his life's end, wrapping him in the skin of a just killed sheep, which was supposed to impart some mysterious vitality. And there was another old man there whose portrait was to be fixed indelibly on the child's abnormally retentive mind. Sir George MacDougall of Mackerstone his grandfather's cousin, once Colonel of the Greys, in "a small cocked hat, deeply laced, an embroidered scarlet waistcoat, and light coloured coat, with milk-white locks tied in a military fashion." So he knelt, not guessing that he was winning for himself a curious immortality as he dragged his watch along the floor, and the boy struggled to follow the bright attraction, beneath the weight of the heavy skin.

The boy who would have grown up a crippled invalid in the city streets, gradually found it possible to engage in many robust activities. He would be able to ride well: to take long walks, though his progress might not be rapid. Determination can overcome much. Later, at Edinburgh High School, the difficulty of fighting on equal terms would be overcome in the same spirit, when he would chastise an enemy with the legs of both of them tied beneath the bench on which they fought. It is an arrangement which might well be considered by the promoters of boxing contests in our own day, with a view to prolonging their exhibitions of professional heavyweights, whose passion for the horizontal so often brings them to abrupt conclusion.

Walter who, by the attraction of his own loving and generous nature, was throughout his life to have very many and loyal friends, owed much to Janet Scott during the years that followed.

He had been about two years at Sandy-Knowe when someone suggested to his parents that the waters of Bath would be of benefit to the shrunken limb. The idea proved to be of no value, and the change was probably detrimental if weighed in a purely physical scale, but it seemed to the family to be a chance worth trying, though it was a more portentous and relatively expensive enterprise than it would be today. Coaches were slow. Roads were bad, and sometimes dangerous. Janet volunteered She was not young, as a woman's youth was reckoned at that period. She was over thirty. But it was a time when even mature women did not readily adventure such expeditions, with no company but that of a young child.

Walter, watching with a child's comprehending silence, and storing everything in a memory the range and accuracy of which have been rarely equalled, thought that she was reluctant to face the ordeal. But, if it were so, her affection for him was strong enough to dominate her weaker fears, or her private plans. Indeed, it is hard to see who else could have gone, unless it had been a younger aunt in Edinburgh, Christian Rutherford, for which, had she been willing, there might have been a score of difficulties which can only be guessed today. Rather than that he should miss an opportunity of being healed, or pass into the charge of strangers, Janet said she would take him.

It is an illuminating comment on the state of the Northern roads that it was considered safest to go to London by sea, and then complete the journey by the famous age-old thoroughfare of the Bath road.

So Janet, with her three-year-old charge, faced the primitive conditions of a voyage in the small sailing-vessels that traded between Leith and London at that period, and made an eventless passage in the *Duchess of Buccleuch*—a name which suggests that some members of the Scott family may have been among its owners—leaving us no record either of hindering storm or the sight of a pirate's sails, and landed safely in London, where they delayed their journey sufficiently to visit its most famous buildings, and other places of interest. Walter records that when he inspected the Abbey and the Tower of London twenty-five years later, he was surprised to find how accurately he had remembered them through the intervening years, and that this experience increased his confidence in other infant memories which could not be checked in the same way.

They remained at Bath for about a year, Walter going through the routines of the pump-room without any apparent benefit, and attending for three months at a dame's school which was near their lodging, where he learned to read.

He owed his most vivid memory of this period to Janet's sailor brother, Captain Robert Scott, (for though the first had jibbed, the second Robert, like the third, had been sent to sea, as though in propitiation of Auld Beardie's still-indignant ghost!) He visited Bath while they were there, and took them to a performance of *As You Like It*. It was Walter's first experience of the theatre; an intoxication of poetic pageantry which he could never forget.

To Captain Robert he owed a debt of another kind. He was already voracious in demand of tale and legend, and with an imagination which preferred such as were of a sombre horror or tragic magnificance. To his temperament, coming from the moorland scenes which were all that his memory knew, it is not very surprising that the sight of carved statuary, particularly such as portrayed the human form in grotesque or distorted shapes, impressed his childhood's imagination as a sinister and dreadful thing. Even the angels of Jacob's ladder, sculptured at the Abbey church, were a spectacle from which he drew back in horror.

Learning of this imaginative fear, his uncle patiently introduced him to a statue of Neptune, till he could approach it without dread, and by this familiarity enabled him to overcome what might have remained as a permanent obsession. We see here, as we shall see many times again, that he was very fortunate in his friends, and not least in those who were of a kindred blood.

Beyond these, his after-memories of Bath were no more than disconnected visions—of a toy-shop near the Orange Grove, and of looking across the Avon to cattle lowing upon the opposite hill.

He returned from Bath to a brief stay in Edinburgh in his parents' home, and then back with Janet to Sandy-Knowe, where he lived almost continuously for the next three or four years.

CHAPTER V.

In considering these early years of the town-born child we may observe a curious duplication of experience, such as can rarely be paralleled.

Scott's ancestry on all sides are of farming, cattle-raising, border stock: they are of the land, not the city. But his immediate parents have changed their environment, though they have not diluted their blood. Their experiences are those of the city schools, and the city streets. Walter begins on the land, as his race began. He looks up to a country sky, his infant hands pull the fleeces of living sheep, his infant ears hear the country legends) the country songs. But this is not the environment in which he completes his development. He will go also to the life of city schools and streets, and be informed by the same duality of experience which had been overlaid to form him before he was born.

This duplication of duality is of a vital significance. The breadth and sanity of the country-side is to become articulate, and not merely in self-interpretation. Its spirit is to inform and to interpret the whole panorama of human existence.

But widely though Walter Scott's interests were to reach, and universal as his sympathies were to be, it is worth observation, and has a lesson for some theorists of today, that their roots struck deeply into the tradition of the past, and their trunk was nourished with the artistic consciousness of his own race, and the local literature of its creation. He did not abandon his roots, as a means of enabling him to produce a new flower....

A cold-blooded criticism may admit that Robert Burns is a grossly over-rated poet. Yet a sympathetic understanding will comprehend why he is so dear to the Lowland Scotsman. His poems were not written by one man; they are the songs of a nation: their distinctive lyric note, passionate and plaintive, was the creation of unrecorded names. In his aspirations and nobilities, he interpreted the spirit of the people of whom he came, as, in his vices, he exposed them upon their weaker side.

There is a degree in which, though on a higher plane, the earlier work of Walter Scott was of the same kind, and there is a sense in which it also is not an individual achievement, but the work of many.

His grandmother, Barbara, has her share, as have the authors of a score of forgotten ballads which she repeated to the eager child. So has Janet. So, then and later, have a dozen others, his mother prominently among them, who fed his imagination and stored his memory from the resources of their own minds. For much of that which he was to give to the common knowledge of men was not singular to his own conception. It was to he an interpretation, rather than a creation of genius...

Janet's father, Robert Scott, was dead when she brought Walter back from Bath. Her mother carried on the farm, not without help from more than one of her children. Her eldest, Walter's father, was able to relieve her of any care for the legal aspect of her late husband's affairs. Her second son, Thomas, who had the management of the Crailing property for Mr. Scott of Danesfield—a relative, of course, though not of the closest—helped her with the farm in matters which were beyond the capacity of her advanced years and failing health. He came over once a week, and might be the only one who would visit them for such an interval. Walter would listen eagerly for the news he brought. The English settlers in America were fighting for independence of the Home Governments and Walter longed for news of the defeat of Washington, which he was not destined to hear.

It was only later in life that he observed the inconsistency of this desire with a hatred of the Hanoverian ruler, probably fiercer and less discriminating than Washington's own, which had developed in his infant mind, largely from listening to the tales of cruelty which followed the defeat of Culloden. One or two distant relatives of the family had been among those who were executed at Edinburgh or Carlisle, and it was all so recent that Mr. Curle at Yetbyre, who had married Janet's sister, and was an occasional visitor at the farm, had been present, and seen them die.

Walter lived for about four years in the quiet peace of the moorland farm, with his grandmother and Janet, having no regular tuition, and seeing no one outside the household, except for the visits of relations, and that the parish clergyman, Dr. Duncan, a 'tall thin emaciated man' of over seventy, wearing clasped gambadoes on his legs, would call occasionally, and impatiently damn (but not using that word, of course,) the noisy ballad-shouting child who interrupted his sedater conversation.

Sixteen years later, Walter, then a young Edinburgh lawyer, called on Dr. Duncan, a fortnight before the old man's death, and recorded his wonder at the mental vigour and fortitude of this writer of a forgotten *History of the Revolution*, who had once been impatient of a child's noise....

But though he had no set tuition during these years, his mind found material on which to feed, perhaps with the greater vigour because it was at its own freedom to take or leave.

There were a few books in the farmhouse of a congenial kind. *Ramsey's Tea-table Miscellany* was to be favourably remembered in later years. Josephus was so much loved, and Janet was so patient to repeat the reading of "favourite chapters" that the boy gave early evidence of prodigious memory by repeating long passages from memory before his own reading was sufficiently advanced to render him independent of his aunt's assistance.

His grandmother, sitting quietly by the fireside in the evening of a long life, with thoughts that went back beyond her dead husband and scattered family, may have found as much pleasure in telling, as he in hearing, the tales which her own childhood had known.

Tales which were fading into a doubtful tradition, and which were to be restored by the immortality of his own genius, had been near and vivid to her. She may have talked more of others than of the Scotts of Harden and Buccleuch, for we must remember that she was a Haliburton herself, from the next county. Her favourite tales were of the Deil of Littledean, an outlaw of much repute and many exploits, who had married her mother's sister, and might almost be regarded as one of the family.

But she told also of Watt of Harden, and of her husband's father, Old Beardie Walter's great-grandfather—and of much else which was to be the foundation of future knowledge.

And so the time passed, till the boy was in his eighth year, and he would run about, vigorously though awkwardly, on the shrunken limb, taking any comfort that he could from the fact that two of the ancestors of whom he had heard had (curiously enough) been lame too, and had overcome that obstacle to self-assertion, even in the days when the argument of physical fitness had been a first necessity for those who would come out on top in the rough struggle of Border life. Going far backward along the ancestral tree there was John Scott the Lamiter (circa 1300) who, while avoiding the discipline of the monasteries, appears to have taken up a life of scholarship with sufficient success to marry and leave children and a good repute at his death, though how he contrived this is beyond saying. And six generations later there was a Scott of Harden, commonly known as William

Boltfoot, who boldly recognised that a man on horseback maybe none the worse for a lame leg, and became of a widely dreaded reputation as a fearless rider, and one whose spear a prudent man would prefer to shun.

Walter, by his own account, must have been nearly eight (he was born in August) in the summer when Janet went with him to Prestonpans. His leg (he was told) was to benefit from sea-bathing, and the decision to send him there may have been taken with this hope, but there are indications of other adjustments. Changes at Sandy-Knowe may have rendered it necessary for him to leave that hospitable roof, to which he did not return. Prestonpans may have been chosen—if Janet chose it—because it was there that she could meet George Constable, as, in fact, she did.

George Constable was a friend of Walter's father. They had studied law together, but George had not practised, retiring to his own property, which was near Dundee. He was under fifty at this time. He seemed old to the child.

Yet it was clear that he was not only his father's friend. He was the friend of his father's sister also. They were constantly together, and Janet was not one to endure an uncongenial companionship. Yet it was a friendship which does not seem to have ended in discord, nor to have gained fruition in a closer intimacy. They both died unmarried. It is their matter, not ours.

Walter saw much of George Constable at a later date when, residing in Edinburgh, he used to be a regular guest at the Sunday dinner-table in George's Square. He observed his licensed tendency to lead the conversation from his father's Calvinistic austerities to subjects of history or antiquity, in which he more greatly delighted. He had humour, and was rich in anecdote, often drawn from his own experience. He remembered the '45. He professed a hatred of women, and the memories of the young man, while he sat respectfully silent, went back to those childhood days at Prestonpans, when he had .observed Mr. Constable and his aunt together—and he was not sure.

Afterwards, he reproduced some of Constable's peculiarities

in the character of Jonathan Oldbuck, but without intending to give a recognisable portrait, and was surprised when George (Chalmers, a London solicitor who had known both Constable and his father, affirmed that he must be the author of the *Antiquary* as he recognised the original of that character.

But we are looking ahead. At Prestonpans, George Constable earned a grateful memory by finding intervals in his attentions to Janet in which he talked to the precocious child of Shakespeare's characters, being apparently unable to contribute to the supply of ballads and local traditions which were his first demand upon every friendly acquaintance.

At Prestonpans, he also made the acquaintance of a retired veteran 'Captain' Dalgety, from whose memories he took the toll which he was already practised to extract from all whose reading or experience could add to the stores of his own mind.

By his own account, it was the summer of that campaign which ended in the disaster of Saratoga. Cornwallis, coming down from Canada, was to march through the wilderness of the backwoods, and take the rebel army in the rear. What would become of Washington then, already defeated and driven out of Long Island?

It was one of those ideas that are strategically sound, but inadequately operated. The old man and the child leaned over the map together. The veterans' military pride clashed with the imagination of his young companion as they gazed upon it. The old soldier foretold the military triumph of England. The child's eyes gazed upon the map, with its suggestions of wooded wilderness and rivers and entangling lakes, and the vital imagination and invincible sanity of judgement which would always enable him to see the strength and quality of the opposition darkened his mind with foreboding. The two disputed as to whether the news would be of disaster or triumph, and when the tale of Saratoga came, there was a cooling of this intimacy, for the veteran sulked.

That is Scott's own account; but there is a difficulty here, which we must explain as we can. He was born on August

15, 1771. The surrender of Saratoga took place on October 15, 1777. At this date he was not 'in his eighth year'. His age was six years and eight weeks. If we allow for the interval which must have elapsed—anything from six weeks to ten before the news could have reached Prestonpans—he will have been a few weeks older, and the season proportionably less propitious for sea bathing on the North Sea coast.

There is not only the difficulty of the increased precocity of the child's understanding, which is implied by the alteration of date, there is the fact that, if we accept his statement as it stands, it alters the length of his stay at Sandy-Knowe, and the date at which he returned permanently to his parents' home, which seems an improbable mistake for him to have made, for several reasons. But there must be *some* error in his statement. It is chronologically impossible.

Was the whole episode imaginary? It seems extremely unlikely. He had remarked, in other connections, on how accurate he found his memory of the events of his early years, when he was able to check it.

Is it not more probable that there was more than one visit to Prestonpans? More than one occasion for Janet and George Constable to stroll on the sea-shore, while Walter played with shells on the turf, and sailed boats on the tidal pools, as he remembered doing so clearly when he revisited the scenes in his closing years...?

There is another memory of these early years which came back to him, and was recorded at the other end of his life, when he attended the funeral of his uncle Raeburn. That was a recollection of when he was four or five, and was staying at his uncle's home, Lessudden House. Under whatever circumstances, he must have been there for a considerable time, for he remembers half-taming a starling, which his uncle ruthlessly killed. He never forgot this, and though his uncle did, the two never liked each other afterwards. Scott did much for his family, and Raeburn showed no gratitude, taking it as being done for his wife and children rather than for him, and Scott, in his scrupulous justice, admitted the fairness of this in his own mind.

CHAPTER VI.

It was in the autumn following his eighth birthday, if we follow his own recollection and a balance of probabilities, that Walter returned to his parents' home in George's Square, which was to be his permanent residence until his marriage about eighteen years later.

Up to then he had been, in his own phrase, "a single indulged brat," and his first experience as an unimportant member of a large family left a recollection of misery which time did not obliterate, though he could analyse it without bitterness, and met it at the time with a measure of good sense and good temper which showed that character is something more than the product of its own environment.

Robert, the naval officer to be, and John, who was to take up a military life, were from three to five years older than himself; Anne was about a year his junior: Tom, destined to succeed to their father's practice, and Daniel, destined to nothing better than a life of failure, completed the family.

It was about this time than Anne suffered from the almost fatal accident which physically wrecked her life. She is one of those tragedies of human existence of whom no biographies are written, and whose lives are only regarded when they obtrude upon the stage of some more dominating personality. Yet had the scales of fate tilted a different way, as Walter might have remained at home to die of infantile paralysis, or might have been buried in moorland moss with the wound of a mad woman's scissors in his throat, so she might have used her gift of imagination to a purpose as great as he. We can do no more than guess, and perhaps, if we could see with clearer eyes, the difference would be no more than a little thing.

She was a child who walked blindly in a world of dreams. It was a quieter world than we know today, when such a one would end promptly beneath a lorry's wheels, but its dangers were too many for her. Her hand was badly crushed in a wind-swung door: her halt-drowned body was dragged out of an old quarry-hole in the open ground, known as Brown's Park, which was then on the south side of George's Square: before she was six, her clothing had caught fire when she was in a room alone. She survived this last catastrophe, after a long illness, with a broken constitution and a disfigured face. She died before she was thirty. She was devoted to Walter, the lame brother who was so near in age to herself, and who dreamed to such different ends. She lived long enough to give swift friendship and loyal advocacy to Charlotte Charpentier, when Walter brought her, a gay, courageous, foreign, frightened girl, to be his wife in the cold Edinburgh atmosphere.

Looking at it as a whole, there seems to be a Divine cruelty in such a life as Anne's, which opens with a brightness of morning dreams, and is so quickly clouded. A barren, physically frustrated life, with an inward bitterness which was sometimes bitter to others. Yet the thought may be no more than the folly of ignorance. *Are not five sparrows sold for two farthings, and not one of them is forgotten of God?*

Robert bullied the new-comer, to whom the experience did no harm. Indeed, the balance may have been in the other scale. But to Robert, his disposition being as it was, it was misfortune that he was the eldest of the five brothers.

He was a boy of many fine qualities rather floridly worn, but of an overbearing disposition. Afterwards, as a young naval officer, he did well. He was in 'almost all' Rodney's battles, and came safely through. Walter says that he was a lover of literature, music, and the mechanical arts, could sing a good song, tell a good tale, and even wrote a good elegy in the then-conventional manner on the April night of 1782, when he was a midshipman of sixteen, and the English fleet was cleared for the action of the following day.

And for these things? in spite of his "capricious tyranny", Walter 'loved him much'. But he was barely eighteen when the peace of 1782 apparently ended the prospects of rapid naval advancement, and so he resigned his commission, and joined the East India Company's service. That, at least, was the argument, but it was complicated by the fact that he considered that he had been badly treated by a superior officer. We know nothing of the rights and wrongs of this quarrel. The naval discipline of those days could not have been easy to endure, and the East may have called to Robert's imagination, as it has done to thousands of others before and since. But it was a fatal decision for him. He made two voyages, and contracted some tropical disease of which he died.

Walter held the belief that had Robert continued in the navy he would have made a name in the great wars that were soon to follow. Like Anne's, it is the record of a frustrated—perhaps we should say self-frustrated—life. The boy's adventurous, too-impatient spirit was soon quietened in its Indian grave. But before we call such a life vain, we might do well to define the standards of vanity by which we judge.

And as we trace the history, one by one, of the children of any numerous household, and watch the impact of character and circumstance, and the accidents of mortality, we may pause to consider the modern theory of the advantages of the limited family, the sheltered existence, the 'best' schools, the concentration of every approved stimulus upon a single life, and wonder, by several standards, whether its premises are quite sound.

Robert, who died young, has yet left a clear impression of personality, John, who lived longer, is a less emphatic figure in the family picture. He went into the army, and at the age of forty he held the rank of Brevet-Major in the 73rd regiment. So far, merit and seniority neither of much avail without influence at that period—appear to have been responsible for such promotions as he had gained; then the intervention of Mr. Canning secured his commission as major of the regiment's second battalion. But his health broke down almost at the same time. He retired from the army, lived an invalid's life with their mother for a few years, and died before he was forty-eight.

Of Walter's younger brothers there may be more to be seen, bad or good, at a later time.

Whatever hardship there might be for an indulged and sensitive child in adjusting his egotism to the routines and dominations of family life was mitigated by his mother, who gave him the understanding sympathy without which love itself may be vain. She found space for his bed in her own dressing-room: she found time to guide his reading, and to listen while he read aloud—from Pope's *Iliad* in particular—and to discuss what was read. The child noticed the exertion of a gentle pressure: to divert his mind from the grotesque and terrible, in which at that time it most delighted, to the consideration of nobler and serener things. That he was not influenced by his mother's intellectual and moral standards would be too emphatic an assertion. His love and admiration for her continued to her life's then distant end, and with such relations prevailing, some influence there must have been. But his own personality, both in character and intellect, was too strong to be widely diverted either by the pressure of circumstance or the dominations of other minds. He might suffer 'internal agony' from the first impacts of unkindness, when subjected to his brother's capricious and bullying moods, but it did not blind him to that brother's more admirable qualities, nor alienate his natural affection from him; he was conscious of his mother's moral or literary preferences, but she could not lessen his own delight in tales of wonder or terror, about which he wrote many years after "I have remained a child, even unto this day".

But the sanctuary of his mother's dressing-room, in which he slept, through her protective partiality or the exigences of a rather crowded household, gave him the full advantages of all that her own mind could offer to his eager intellectual appetite, with access to the Shakespearean plays which she kept there for her own reading.

His own witness is that he owed more to his mother than to any other, more even than to his grandmother or Janet Scott, for the power to realise vividly and to accurately reproduce the incidents and characters of the legendary history of Scotland which were to provide the substance for so many future romances both in verse and prose.

It is with this return to his parents' home that the formal ritual of education began. It is customary to represent it as having been delayed by the ill-health of his early years, and to have been distinguished by some subsequent deficiencies both of conduct and opportunity. An examination of the facts gives little support to these impressions, for which he is himself partly responsible, by his deprecatory allusions to lack of scholarship, and which is partly due to Lockhart's more conventional prejudices.

His own statement is that he returned to Edinburgh from Prestonpans sometime after his seventh birthday (August 1778) and that he accompanied his brothers to the Edinburgh High School before the end of that year, where he was put into the second class, and found himself rather behind his class-mates, both in age and studies. Previously, he and his brothers had received home lessons in Latin from a private tutor. The possible interval for this private tuition appears short, and the suggestion occurs again that he might have had a period of home life during the earlier winter, but, in any event, his systematic education commenced before he was at an advanced age. But we must not overlook two facts if we are to assess his own and Lockhart's references justly. Education at that period meant primarily a knowledge of the Latin and Greek languages and literatures. If you had received that teaching you were educated: if you hadn't you weren't. Also, it was customary to commence this education at a very early age. The age (we might almost say the childhood) of his brother Robert when he became a midshipman in Rodney's navy is illuminating. Rodney himself had entered the navy when he was twelve. It is true that midshipmen of that age were expected to continue their studies—more or less—when they were not commanding a boat's crew, or carrying powder up from the magazine. More or less—and in times of active service less rather than more. It is evident that if you wished to make sure of acquiring the classical languages it was the safest way to commence young.

The conventional definition of education might have been worse, but lacked breadth. Walter Scott gained a good knowledge of Latin, and several other languages, but he never learned Greek. That was regrettable, as all ignorance is. But to obtain a correct perspective we must recognise that if he had learnt more Greek he must have learnt less of something else. The human mind cannot be occupied with two things at once. He was of an immense intellectual industry. His mind worked best on subjects which interested it most, as is the common experience. He had an extraordinary memory. He reached a prodigious scholarship. It was his gain and ours that it was not entirely on conventional lines. Lockhart appears to recognise this possibility in one luminous sentence. *"As may be said, I believe, with perfect truth of every really great man, Scott was self-educated in every branch of knowledge which he ever turned to account in the works of his genius."* The crowding superlatives of this sentence are an example of Lockhart's style at its worst, and its over-statement approaches nonsense, but it shows that he saw the truth for a moment, though (as often) he lacked the self-confidence and independence of mind that would have enabled him to do justice to his own perceptions. Lockhart constantly overestimates the influence of environment, and overvalues the conventional standards of the moment. Conversely, for all his admirable compilation of details, he fails to appreciate, though he sometimes mentions, the independence and force which may often be obscured by the tolerant breadth of Scott's emotional and intellectual sympathies.

Anyway, if we accept Scott's own memory, at the age of seven-and-a-half he was in the second class of the Edinburgh High School, studying Latin with about eighty other children, most of whom were rather older, and knew more. The boys were not seated alphabetically, but were arranged according to their real or estimated ability, and he found himself near the foot of the class with some dull-witted seniors. He accepted this position and companionship very cheerfully. His mind was full of many things beside the study of Latin. It was occupied with romantic imaginations, and the intoxicating music of words. The fascination of the art which weds emotion and imagination to verbal melody caused him to love the reciting aloud of the poetry which he memorised so readily. But he had learned already that this might arouse derision in minds incapable of its appreciation, and he would prefer to recite in solitude, being sensitive to ridicule at this time, as children are.

That he did not advance more rapidly in the study of a dead language was owing to no lack of parental effort. His father supplemented the High School teaching of his sons by engaging a tutor, a Mr. James Mitchell, who assisted them in the preparation of their home tasks, and taught writing and arithmetic also. He had been the minister of a sea-port kirk, and had quarrelled with his congregation on the question of whether their fishing-boats should set sail on the Sabbath. They thought it brought them luck, and he thought that damnation would be more likely to follow. Rather than surrender his opinion, he resigned his living. Scott says drily that "the calibre of this young man's understanding may be judged of by this anecdote". But the stubborn honesty of his character may have seemed a more important recommendation to the elder Walter, who may also have agreed with him upon the theological aspects of the point on which he wrecked his worldly prospects. For though, in other ways, the household at George's Square seems to have been driven on a light rein, and with wisdom as well as love, the Sabbath observance was a strict rule, strictly enforced; "and in the end" Scott gave his deliberate tolerant judgement in after years, "it did none of us any good."

But even Mr. James Mitchell was able to contribute something more than a teaching of arithmetic, and the hearing of lessons in Latin and French. He was a student of the early history of the Church of Scotland, and Walter discovered that knowledge, and took the toll that he extracted from the mental stores of all with whom he came in contact during these early days.

And so life went on for the next three years, during which he developed physically in a manner which enabled him to engage in many active exercises, in spite of the difficulty of a lameness which was now recognised as permanent. And the spirit in which he strove to overcome this physical handicap united with that which caused him to be quicker to help a companion's task than to excel in his own, to win him a general popularity among his school companions. The experiences of his boyhood contrast with those of many poets of more morbid or egotistic moods during this period of life, and, characteristically, looking back, he attributed his popularity to the natural nobility of the nature of the youthful male. "Boys," he reflected, "are uncommonly just in their feelings, and at least equally generous." It is not a proposition to which Shelley would have given a ready assent. It may be doubted whether the idea would have occurred without qualification to Byron, Coleridge, or Wordsworth. Yet it may have at least as much truth as would be contained in a meaner judgement. He offered the courage and generosity of his own nature, and he found ready response.

He gained a reputation also among his companions in those early years for the skill with which he could narrate his 'inexhaustible' tales, and there was emulation among them for the privilege of sitting nearest to him at the winter fireside on such occasions....

At the age of ten, he was promoted to the class over which the head of the school, Dr. Adam, himself presided. Dr. Adam may have magnified his office, and his own importance. Watching the careers of the many boys who passed through his class, he may have been disposed to attribute their successes too much to his own exertions, and their failures to an excessive measure of original sin. But it was a fault of zeal, if fault it can be called, and the after-records of his scholars were a legitimate source of pride. He recognised the ability of a sometimes-indolent sometimes-inattentive boy, and succeeded in making him realise that knowledge was worth a disciplined effort to win. During the next two years, Walter gained a proficiency in the construing of the Latin classics which took him into the higher form of the two over which Dr. Adam presided. For the first time, he felt the confidence of scholastic ability, and a new pride of proficiency in studies which he had previously regarded as a boring interference with the independent activities of his own imaginations.

For the first time, also, he owed and recognised a clear debt to the deliberate influence of another mind. Not that he had previously gained nothing from others. But when he had plundered such stores as he considered worth the carrying away from the memories and imaginations of Janet Scott, and Barbara Haliburton, of his mother, Anne Rutherford, and of a score of others, he had done it of his own free will, as a corsair will empty hulls. But he allowed Dr. Adam to lay a hand on his mind's helm, and to deflect its course. The importance of this was not that he learnt more Latin, though there was gain in that, but that he was induced to discipline his mind, which he found difficult to his life's end. As is frequent with those of strong imagination, he could not easily concentrate on a set task. His mind was not idle, but of a prodigious activity. It had a restless waywardness which hated harness. Dr. Adam succeeded in convincing him that his mental powers should be subdued to be tools rather than tyrants, and he recognised the importance of this lesson in later years.

When he had been two years under Dr. Adam's tuition, Lord Buchan called to inspect the school.

We know Lord Buchan best as an old man, a fussing busybody, of a conceit which sometimes achieved unconscious comedy. Scott, with a rare contempt, alludes to him in his journal as 'a trumpery body'. But, like the rest of us, he had been young once. He was a young man when some whim of self-importance took him on this visit of inspection to the Edinburgh High School. Walter Scott, in disgrace for an aggravated negligence, was seated near the foot of the class, as the custom was under such circumstances. But Dr. Adam forgot that his pupil was exiled from the seats of honour in the desire to show the best ability of his school. He called him out to repeat the passage from the

Aeneid in which Hector's ghost appears. The recitation was a success, and was warmly applauded. It was the first time that his passion for poetry had met a stranger's approbation, and it became an enduring memory. Many years after, it inclined him to patient endurance of the tiresome follies of Lord Buchan's declining years.

CHAPTER VII.

During the four or five years that Walter was at the Edinburgh High School, he had made frequent visits, for the length of the school vacations, to his Aunt Janet, who was now living in a house in Kelso, which was at that time his father's property, the farm at Sandy-Knowe having been given up when her mother died. Kelso is a village delightfully situated where Tweed and Teviot meet. "The most beautiful, if not the most romantic village in Scotland," Scott called it in later years. His health benefited by these visits, and they cultivated his passionate love for that locality which was to be one of the inspiring and controlling influences of his life, both for good and evil.

It was springtime, in the course of his thirteenth year, when his term at the High School ended, and in the natural order he would have gone on at once to the greater freedom of college tuition. But he was growing fast, and a suggestion that he should spend the summer at Kelso was readily adopted, doubtless to his delight, and not at all to the detriment of his education. For the Kelso schoolmaster, Mr. Lancelot Whale, was one of those men, so commonly met in the records of a period in which ability exceeded opportunity, who are too good for the positions they fill. An arrangement was made by which Walter read Latin with Mr. Whale and the other senior scholars, and helped in the school by teaching elementary subjects to the junior class. He has recorded that Mr. Whale gave him more than his fair share of attention, and he looked back on that summer as a time when he learnt much, and in many ways. It was during these months at Kelso that he became consciously aware of the beauty of his surroundings, and that the romantic pageantry of creation captured his imagination through a medium other than the printed page.

For he had become an insatiable and (to his own memory) an indiscriminate reader, and this notorious appetite had found its own means of gratification. A free lending library—a subscription library—his mother's volumes of Shakespeare, (wickedly devoured after he was supposed to be in bed, by the light and warmth of her bedroom fire, with an apprehensive ear for the ascending footsteps which would send him scuttling back to his dressing-room bed)—these, and the school-book classics, had been magically supplemented by the fact that Dr. Blacklock—a name deservedly honoured in the Edinburgh records of that time—had noticed the boy's omnivorous appetite, and given him the freedom of his private library. He gave him wise guidance also, introducing him, in particular, to the poetry of Edmund Spencer, which became probably the strongest single influence upon his own creations in later years.

Edmund Spencer is regrettably neglected today, and his place is only grudgingly recognised in the front rank of English poets. But to Walter Scott, even in boyhood, the *Fairie Queen* had nothing to offer to which he could not respond with the high quality of an equal appreciation. The rich and seemingly-inexhaustible varieties of verbal melody, the luxuriance of imagination, the continually changing wonders of light and colour, the high chivalrous conception of the purpose of life in which nobility is normality, and 'No service lothsome is to gentle kind', all these were of the substance of the reader's own intellect, and of his own character. It is no wonder that the poem which is to many a forbidding wilderness, and to others a magic forest in which they cannot tire to wander, became to him an intoxication, till a "really marvellous" number of its myriad stanzas became part of the enduring furniture of his own mind.

With the autumn opening of the College term, he returned to Edinburgh, and commenced to take the Greek and Latin

University courses. Under the laxer college discipline, students were not compelled to application. They could work or not as they pleased. It was their own choice, and their own (or their parents') loss, if they neglected to do so. With this freedom, Scott is emphatic in self-condemnation. So far as the Greek class is concerned, he didn't please in the least. He had learnt no Greek up to that time, and he found himself among boys who had already mastered the rudiments of the language. His mind was full of other interests, and (he says) he asserted an obstinate opinion that Greek wasn't worth learning. His classmaster, Professor Dalzell, an enthusiastic classical scholar, expostulated in vain. Being required to write an essay upon the comparative merits of the authors they had studied, Scott perversely infuriated the Professor by producing an ingenious comparison of Homer and Ariosto, to the detriment of the earlier poet. The "quality of out-of-the-way knowledge" which the essay displayed surprised Professor Dalzell, but was impotent to soothe his anger at this audacious heresy.

Protest came also from a fellow-pupil, an innkeeper's son, who came to George's Square to argue in favour of the language and literature to which he was himself devoted. He offered to give free help in the evenings to assist in its study, but it was a rejected kindness. Scott blamed himself afterwards very severely for this attitude, which was foolish enough, and, looking back, he had an uneasy self-contemptuous fear that the boy's social inferiority may have influenced the repulse. If so, it was as unlike himself to have acted from such a motive as it was characteristic that he should make public acknowledgement subsequently.

But the fact is that he was attracted rather by the living cargo which the world's literature carries than by the dry bones of scholarship. It was noticed by his first Latin master that he might be slower than some others on points of construction or syntax, but that he would be the first to extract the vital meaning of the passage with which they dealt.

There may have been another reason why his neglect of the

Greek classes met with less opposition than would otherwise have been the case.

It was his father's purpose that he should enter his own profession, though it was not resolved whether he should follow the 'higher' branch, or succeed to the management of the business which his father had built up. He accepted this programme with complacence, if without enthusiasm. The legal profession had much use for Latin, but little for Greek. Had the elder Walter heard that his son was treating the Latin tongue with contempt, there might have been more said. As a fact, his father seems to have shown no dissatisfaction at this period either with his abilities or application. The abortive attempt upon the Greek tongue ended of itself in the second term, when another breakdown of health resulted in a second prolonged visit to Kelso, and to the desultory reading which may have been of far greater value than his own assessment allows. Subsequently, on returning to Edinburgh, he took courses in Mathematics, in History, in Moral Philosophy, and in Ethics, in which last he had the honour of being chosen to read an essay before Professor Robertson.

The subjects appear to have been of his father's selection, and he attributes the fact that they were not more numerous to the parental desire that he should have ample leisure for legal studies. He took the University courses in Civil and Municipal Law.

His father wisely considered that, even if he were destined for the Bar, he would gain much by a detailed knowledge of the routines of a solicitor's work, and early in his fifteenth year he commenced a five-years' apprenticeship in his father's office.

To the ideas of today, he had left College at an absurdly early age. He had acquired a wide range of knowledge, and had a keen appetite for acquiring more, which school teaching does not always give. His time had not been wasted, as the sequel showed.

His own judgement of these years of study was afterwards given in these words: "it is with the deepest regret that I recollect in my manhood the opportunities of learning which I neglected in my youth; that through every part of my literary career I have felt pinched and hampered by my own ignorance; and that I would at this moment give half the reputation I have had the good fortune to acquire, if by so doing I could rest the remaining part upon a sound foundation of learning and science."

It is a severe judgement, in which humility weights the scale. Conscious of what he might have gained, he may have undervalued that which he would have lost to acquire it.

"Few ever read so much," he says of those years, "and to so little purpose." It is an opinion with which few will be likely to agree.

CHAPTER VIII.

Although we may dissent from Scott's modest estimate of his own scholarship, it is evident that he expressed genuine feelings of regret and deficiency in the quotations given in the previous chapter.

Even a century ago, the world of knowledge was not considered beyond the travelling capacity of a single mind. Either you had taken the grand tour of its dominions, or you had not. It was a question of fact, about which there could be no ambiguity. If you had, you were educated, even though you had forgotten half you had seen: otherwise you were not.

The same idea is still dominant in the practice of giving a University degree for a minimum proficiency in a group of subjects, instead of a certificate of proficiency for each or any. The most profound knowledge of ancient languages will not avail a man who declines or is unable to attain a set standard of mathematical ability. Nor will the most profound knowledge of mathematics be honoured in another, if he persists in disregarding all languages but his own.

These composite standards of judgement may be condemned as stupid and inequitable—as they are—but they are based upon the sound principle that we have not mastered any subject unless we understand it in its relations to others. We do not know a continent because we have separately explored its countries, unless we know their relations to one another, and where their boundaries meet. The effect of a furnished room is something more than the sum of the effect of its items of furniture; and if we are conversant with only half its contents, and regard them separately, no closeness of scrutiny will alter the fact that we are of an inferior knowledge to one who sees the whole, even though it be in a poor light.

We have warning examples of this result of specialisation today in men who have attained eminence in one branch of knowledge, and have then made public demonstration of some childish credulity by which they mislead the simple, who fail to see that their concentration upon physics or anthropology may have resulted in a peculiar ignorance of other subjects, and that a reputed proficiency in one branch of research does not demonstrate exceptional soundness of judgement, and may be consistent with an amazing absence of common-sense. So that wide publicity is given to authoritative nonsense such as that fishes do not learn from experience, that the ghost of Napoleon can be summoned by an illiterate medium to chatter "roses, roses all the way," or (from a scientifically-omniscient bishop) that there was a recent period during which women commonly produced twelve children, of which only three survived. Such people, whatever their reputation or degrees, may properly be described as uneducated, not because they are ignorant, as we all are, but because they are unaware of their limitations.

To be truly educated—it is the most we can hope, and should be the least at which we should rest content—is to be aware of the nature and extent of the realms of knowledge which we do not explore, and to be prepared to enter them so far as time allows and occasion calls. All knowledge is then at our disposition, and may be used to good purpose so far as we have trained ourselves to the logic and toleration which are necessary to that end. To burden memory with endless accumulations of detail is as foolish as to endeavour to carry all our material possessions continually on our backs.

This was as true a century ago as it is today, and by such standard Walter Scott was far better educated than most of those whose claims he would have readily conceded to be superior. But he had no inclination to magnify his own attainments or creations, as men of less genius are apt to do. He looked high and far, seeing all that he was not, and could never be. Seeing himself as he was, he thanked God for a small thing. By his own vision he may have been right, but if we agree with him we convict ourselves....

Having entered his father's office, he took on the work which it required with a conscientious diligence, which brought its own rewards. He hated the confinement, but on his own testimony, which certainly did not err in leniency of self-judgement, he was no 'idle apprentice'. His statement on this point might be worth consideration by all who plead the "artistic temperament" as an excuse for inability to undertake their fair share of the prosaic work of the world, and those who condone the shallow egotism of such an attitude. "The drudgery of the office I disliked, and the confinement I altogether detested; but I loved my father, and I felt the rational pride and pleasure of rendering myself useful to him. I was ambitious, also; and among my companions in labour the only way to gratify ambition was to labour hard and well."

He had his ultimate reward in becoming a more than competent lawyer: his immediate incentive in a system of copy-money which was the apprentices' slender remuneration for the clerical work they undertook, and which enabled him, whose shillings had been infrequent and few, to indulge in an occasional visit to the theatre, or the acquisition of some otherwise inaccessible book. With such incentives, he remembered once fair-copying 120 folio pages without interval either for food or sleep....

We must not linger unduly over these years of legal apprenticeship, but there are a few recorded incidents which are of intrinsic interest, and illuminating quality.

It was about at this period that he met Robert Burns for the first time and the last, except for casual street-encounters when he was (quite naturally) not recognised by the older man. There is kindness and admiration in his memory of this event, and its cruelty is without intention. It was at Professor Fergusson's, amid a group of several of those who were of literary reputation in Edinburgh at the moment, Dugald Stewart among them. It was Burns' first visit to Edinburgh, and he was the centre of the gathering. He was shown a print of one of Bunbury's pictures, with some lines of Langhorne's ('Cold on Canadian hills, or Minden's plain') beneath it. The sloppy sentimentality of the lines are rivalled by the bathos of the print. Dead soldier in snow—faithful dog howling beside him—widow also punctually present, with (need it be said?) a baby on her mourning breast. Burns 'seemed much affected by the print. He actually shed tears.' He wanted to know who wrote those pathetic lines about

"—her eye dissolved in dew,
The big drops mingling with the milk he drew."

The literary gentlemen looked at each other, but were unable to supply the information. Scott, modestly in the background as became his youth, whispered Langhorne's name to a bolder companion, who spoke it for him. Burns "rewarded me with a look and word which, though of mere civility, I then received, and still recollect, with very great pleasure". It is a curious fact that Langhorne's name was printed under the lines, but the eyes of all the company may have been blurred with tears.

Scott makes no criticism of Scotland's national bard. He probably believed to his life's end that he had stood in the presence of a greater man than himself. He says: "Among the men who were the most learned of their time and country, he" (Burns) "expressed himself with perfect firmness, but without the least intrusive forwardness; and when he differed in opinion he did not hesitate to express it firmly, yet at the same time with modesty."

It is a good witness. But what judgement it is on the man that such testimony should be considered worth putting on record...!

Wishing to read the old French romances in the original, this boy of fourteen, who is so dissatisfied at his neglect of his early opportunities, had already mastered their language, and now, with the lure of Ariosto and Tasso—he had only seen the latter in the 'flatness' of Hoole's translation, not, it seems, having encountered Fairfax's livelier version, or the real poetry of Carey's fragment—he determined to learn Italian. The cost of two evening classes a week became a first charge upon the shillings which his penmanship earned.

But in spite of the confinement of office hours, the learning of Italian, and his insatiable reading, his life at this time was far from sedentary. Lockhart hints that his fellow-apprentices were a rather boorish lot. He could not have known them, and there is some explicit contrary evidence. Scott's special friend, both at High School and subsequently, John Irving, was certainly not of that description. The two boys lived near to one another, and had found a congenial fellowship from a very early age, taking Song walks together, and narrating romances to one another, which they composed in turns. It was an occupation kept secret to themselves, lest it should provoke ridicule, but Walter had discovered that his friend's mother was a preserver of ancient ballads, both in her own head and their original printings, and Mrs. Irving was added to the list of those upon whom he made distraint to store the resources of his own mind.

As the years passed, and his strength grew, these walks increased in length, his eager vitality overcoming the reluctance of the shrunken leg, as it had done when he first crawled among the sheep in the heathered moorland of Sandy-Knowe.

It appears to have been at a later period of his fifteenth year—probably in the summer of 1786 that he was able to visit the Highlands for the first time. He went on the invitation of one of his father's Highland clients—for the firm's practice had spread far beyond the original relationships in the Lowland counties, an accession of business which may have originated with grandfather Robert's cattle-dealing connections; and when we probe the origins of this invitation we come upon another of Walter's childhood memories.

Alexander Stewart of Invernahyle was a Jacobite patriarch who had survived participations in the '15 and '45, and would visit Edinburgh in connection with various litigations which had superseded more primitive and congenial methods of settling differences with his Highland neighbours. Walter's first memory of him was at the time when Edinburgh was expecting attack from that picturesque Yankee 'pirate', Paul Jones, and the ancient claymore-girded warrior was volunteering assistance in defence of his country's capital. That was in September 1779. Alexander can scarcely have been under eighty, and Walter was just eight. The incident must have occurred at his father's home or office, and Walter cannot have been at Sandy-Knowe or Prestonpans at that time.

Seven years later, Mr. Stewart still flourished, and his legal business still necessitated visits to his attorney at Edinburgh. Here he renewed acquaintance with the younger Walter, and joined the goodly company of those who had contributed to the wealth of legend and reminiscence which were being stored in the young law-student's mind. Such conversations led to an invitation to visit the Highland chieftain in his own home, and so the first materials were made available for the future *Waverley*.

It was probably in the spring after this visit, or in the following year—the exact date is again in doubt—that Walter's health broke down seriously. His own statement is that it had become 'uncertain and delicate' from rapid growth 'and other causes', and that a blood-vessel broke. The medical treatment which was considered suitable for his condition was of a drastic kind, with some surprising features, but it was justified by its results. He was bled and blistered 'till he had scarcely a pulse left'. He was starved both of warmth and food. It was northern spring weather, cold and raw, but it was part of the remedial treatment that his bloodless body should shiver beneath a single blanket. He had a meagre diet of vegetables, which did little to satisfy a hunger which had become ravenous. He was not even allowed to talk. He might play chess and he might read.

He lay thus for several weeks. An arrangement of mirrors enabled him to watch troops exercising on the promenade. His own exercise was of the imagination only. He read military history, and set out its battles in childlike games with shells and pebbles and seeds, with toy cross-bows for artillery, and with a wooden fortress which a friendly carpenter—when was he ever to lack the friend of his need?—had helped him to model.

He says that he was afflicted at this time by a nervousness which he had never experienced before, and from which he never subsequently suffered. His inclination was to attribute this condition to the hated vegetables, which continued to be his sole diet during the convalescence of the following summer, though he is fair enough to say that it may very possibly have been the result of the disorder, and not of the cure.

Anyway, cured he was, and he recovered to a more robust and vigorous health than he had previously known. For the next thirty years he was clear of the doctors' hands, and pains and remedies were alike forgotten.

During the remaining years of his apprenticeship he took much riding exercise. He rode well. He resumed and lengthened his pedestrian wanderings. He was not easily wearied, and the lame leg "disfigured rather than disabled" him in these activities.

Once he walked with three fellow-apprentices to breakfast at Prestonpans, spent the day in wandering among the Seton ruins and the adjoining battlefield, and back to Edinburgh in the evening (after a dinner of haddocks, and two bottles of port for the four) without any toll of fatigue for the thirty miles he had covered.

Such walks were frequent at that period, and though the half-bottles of port may have been less so, they also have their significance. Walter, like his father, was then, and at all times of life, of abstemious habits. But the word must be used comparatively. At the period, and among his own social order, the taking of large and steady quantities of alcohol was a routine, which on convivial occasions became a ritual also. To many of those who led robust open-air lives it appeared to do little harm till they approached or passed their fiftieth year, but during the following decade they aged very rapidly, and apoplexy, gout, and diseases of liver and kidneys, were almost as general among them as the indulgences from which they came. To those who had abandoned the healthier and more active country life for the occupations of the city courts, offices, colleges, and consulting-rooms, a companion habit of gluttony appears to have been regarded too-frequently as the natural condition of their later and more leisurely years. Of Scott's three closest business associates, two became of such bulk in the days of their prosperity that their deaths were more probably hastened by their physical appetites than their business troubles.

Scott himself was too active in habits, as he was too strong in self-discipline, to surrender to such indulgences, and if he did so at times it was rather from the claims of good-fellowship than a physical craving. To suggest that at any period of his life he ate or drank excessively would be an overstatement which would have the effect of falsehood. Yet it is no more than he would have freely admitted to say that if he had drank less than he did he might have lived longer and died differently....

But this love of long rides and of wandering walks—mainly he says, for the delight he experienced in discoveries of romantic scenery—developed until they were protracted beyond the limits of single days, and his parents were first alarmed and then reconciled to his irregular absences. Remonstrance went no further than his father's irritable remark that he must have been born to be a strolling pedlar, and the circumstance throws a kindly light upon the relations of parents and son, and the confidence that must have been felt that these all-night absences were not the indications of any serious escapade.

He set out on one occasion, not alone, but with a party of other lawyers-to-be, to fish the lake above Howgate. They got there in time for breakfast, fished all day, stayed the night, and started back early next morning. His constant friend, John Irving, was one of the party. General Abercromby's son, George, was another. A third was William Clerk.

Pennycuik House, the residence of Sir John Clerk, lay a little off the track of their return. William Clerk took the opportunity of introducing his friends. They were warmly received, William Clerk and John Irving for themselves, "and I for their sakes," as Scott modestly says. They were "overwhelmed with kindness" and persuaded to stay for a day or two. But the remainder of the party had gone on, without noticing those who had turned aside, and there was alarm at George's Square that night, while Walter's mind was obliviously occupied with the beauty of his surroundings, the "fine pictures" that the house contained, and the pleasant hospitality that he was experiencing.

William Clerk must have more than a passing reference, for he became an intimate and life-long friend. Scott's own statement is that John Irving was his closest friend at this period. Lockhart puts Irving quietly aside, and installs Clerk in that position. Indeed, Lockhart will have it that Clerk was a guiding influence over a weaker man. The question of who was his closest friend is one on which Scott himself is the best authority. Whether he or Clerk would be likely to have the stronger influence on the other is a point of opinion which we must decide as we will, looking at the characters and records of the two men. Scott had a readiness to recognise the force of an opponent's arguments, an unselfish generosity, a willingness to yield ground on nonessentials, that combined to give an impression of his being far more pliable than he really was.

But there was a difference between the social status of the two friends which could not fail to influence Lockhart's mind, though its effect on that of Scott would have been nothing at all. Clerk was to become a barrister. Irving's home was near that of the Scotts in George's Square. He could not introduce his friends to a country seat with the dignity of Pennycuik House. Lockhart's class-consciousness was constant and unashamed. When he met Constable he was moved to wonder that a bookseller could behave like a gentleman. He felt it natural, if not necessary, to record this astonishment, and the evidences on which he felt that Scott might be excused for such an association.

But we must not tip the scale to the other side. Scott's friendship with William Clerk was a close one, which endured as the years passed. Clerk was one of those men who are content to be, rather than to do. Life came easily to him, and he ruled it with a negative wisdom, leaving a record without achievement, and free from folly. Scott said of him in later years that he was unsurpassed in strength and acuteness of faculties by any man he had conversed with familiarly. It is high praise, even from Scott, who praised generously, but not loosely. Clerk is (more or less) portrayed as the Darsie of Redgauntlet.

So much is true; but Lockhart's suggestion that "it was Clerk who first or mainly awakened his social ambition: it was he that drew him out of the company of his father's apprentices, and taught him to rise above their clubs and festivities, and the rough irregular habits of all their intervals of relaxation," is simply silly.

It is needless to consider what ground, if any, Lockhart had for this general inditement of the office apprentices, because Scott had always shown an aptitude to chose congenial friends, and however sociable he might be with men of every type and class, he walked in his own ways. Indeed, in his whole account of this friendship, Lockhart shows a profound ignorance of Scott's character, and his own unfitness to be his biographer. We owe much to Lockhart. He was a diligent collector of facts. He was an acute observer of the events that came under his own eyes in later years. But his witness cannot be trusted, even when his prejudices are not aroused, unless we are careful to distinguish between observations and deductions therefrom. There were sides of Scott's character which he was unable to interpret because they were too alien from his own nature. He did not adequately interpret his romantic ideality, his love of jeopardy for its own sake, his essential democracy, because he did not understand them—and, had he done so, he would have felt that they were for excuse rather than admiration.

CHAPTER IX.

Scott's apprenticeship lasted from his fourteenth year to his nineteenth. Before it closed, his decision had been made to adopt the profession of advocacy rather than that of an attorney, and even this choice is ascribed by Lockhart to the influence of William Clerk, with which "another influence must have powerfully co-operated". There is neither evidence nor inherent probability that either of these influences—to the second of which we have still to come—were exerted in such direction, or would have been decisive upon it. It is more reasonable to suppose that the decision came from Scott's own inclination, and his father's counsel.

At this time, his younger brother, Tom, had also entered the office. It was a business which might have found occupation for both, apart from which, Walter, as the elder may be said to have had the first claim. But it was not a matter, the Scotts being what they were, which was likely to be settled on such a point. Walter may have seemed to his father, and may have been, the more likely to succeed as a barrister. It had some obvious advantages for the brothers to divide their energies between the two branches of the profession. Tom was anxious to be an attorney, though he was certainly not of the temperament to object to Walter as a senior partner. There was a close and genuine affection between the brothers which would outlast the days of a common prosperity. Would Walter have succeeded as a solicitor? Would he have done better than Tom? It is hard to guess. Neither father nor sons were typical of the successful lawyer. They lacked the narrow cautious selfishness which is the lawyer's safeguard. In spite of personal probity, and far more than average abilities, they had characteristics which might be more advantageous to their clients than to themselves and which might even threaten possibilities of final disaster in which client and attorney would have suffered together. It is a frequent paradoxical fact that (defaulting solicitors are not the worst of their kind. Not that there was any question of default here. The elder Walter was nearing the time when he could gradually withdraw himself, as his health weakened, from a long record of honourable practice. He had built up a flourishing business. If he had made some bad debts on a large scale, he had yet made good provision for a numerous family; he had lived in a state or increasing comfort, though without ostentation; and he had acquired considerable property.

Incidentally, he had at last brought to a triumphant conclusion certain litigation on behalf of Mr. Stewart of Appin (a brother of Alexander of Invernahyle of whom we know) against certain Maclarens, his insurgent tenants in the neighbourhood of Loch Katrine. There had been a legal process to be served personally by the Courts order upon these defeated litigants. Someone from the office must go. It is easy to imagine that Walter was an eager applicant for this rather perilous enterprise, which his father allowed him to undertake. The Highlands had become comparatively quiet since they were subdued after the '45, but that the bearer of such a document would have a friendly reception was not a likely thing. Walter rode to Stirling alone, and obtained an escort of a sergeant and six men from the regiment stationed there. He found the sergeant to have a fund of anecdotes in which Rob Roy and himself were about equally prominent, and he picked his brains in the usual way. So, at eighteen, he rode into the Trossachs pass, which he was afterwards to immortalise as the scene of perhaps the best imaginary skirmish that the world's literature contains, not with a twilight forest of southern spears, but with the glitter of six bayonets behind him to enforce his will.

The 'other influence' which Lockhart thinks may have inclined him to adopt the profession of the Bar, was the determination which he formed to marry Williamina Stuart, the daughter of Sir John Stuart Belches of Invermay. Lockhart appears to be impressed by a social gulf which he supposed would be lessened by the adoption of the higher branch of the legal profession. But here prejudice ignores fact. The obstacle (apart from the question of the girl's own inclination) was not social but financial. Williamina was one of the richest heiresses in Scotland, but, even so, her parents did not oppose the intimacy. His decision involved two further years of unprofitable study, to be followed by the precarious income of those who commence to practice at the Bar. Had he adopted the attorney's profession, he might have felt in a position to make a formal proposal of marriage two or three years earlier than he actually did, and very many things might have developed and ended differently.

But there is another reason why Lockhart's suggestion that his desire to win Williamina Stuart influenced his decision on this matter cannot be regarded seriously. It is clear from Scott's own account that the decision was taken before—and probably a considerable time before—the termination of his apprenticeship. His articles began when he was just over fourteen, and terminated shortly after his nineteenth birthday. Williamina was born in October 1776. She was a full five years younger than Walter, being just fourteen years old when his articles ended. It is certain that they were both young when they met, but it is, at least, improbable that he fell in love with her when she was thirteen. It is more probable that the acquaintance began when he had already commenced his studies for the Bar, and that it was the incentive which (as we shall shortly see) was to drag William Clerk out of bed a good deal earlier than that indolent gentleman had been accustomed to rise.

This probability is increased by Scott's own statement that he had "three years of dreaming, and two of awakening". Williamina married Willie Forbes on Jan. 19, 1797, her age then being twenty years and four months. If we conclude that the acquaintance began when Walter returned to Edinburgh after the vacation which followed the completion of his articles in the autumn or winter of 1790-91, everything else falls into line, and only Lockhart's inherently improbable suggestion that she influenced his choice of a profession has to go to the scrap-heap.

He met her first, as the tale goes, in the porch of the Greyfriars Church. She had no umbrella and was faced by a sudden storm, so he offered his, and they went home together. That may have been the occasion on which they first spoke, but how long he may have desired such an opportunity of acquaintance is another matter. Sir John's Edinburgh residence was near to George's Square. They found (they may have known it before) that they went the same way home.... But they are not usually alone. Their two mothers come to church also. The elder ladies recognise each other. Thirty years ago, more or less, they were school friends, though they have not met since. They have common subjects of conversation. The Edinburgh pavements of that time were not adapted for four people to walk abreast. We may guess how the pairing went.

So far, all went well. The mothers did not oppose, and Williamina did not repulse. In fact, she gave a willing friendship at this time, if not more. She was observed to sit out dances with a boy whose lameness withheld him from that diversion. Walter's father knew nothing of the growing intimacy. We may deduce that he had given up going to Church. He had the excuse of weakening health, though he appears to have been able to attend to his professional work for several subsequent years.

But the time came when Sir John and his family went back to Invermay, and Walter found that a holiday in that neighbourhood had become an urgent necessity. The obstinacy of his selection of the locality intrigued his father's mind, and explanations followed.

His father did not directly oppose the acquaintance, but he was disturbed by doubts. Did Sir John know what was happening? It appeared that Sir John didn't. Like Mr. Walter Scott he stands convicted by this ignorance. He also must have given up the habit of going to Church. Well, he must know Without telling his son, who, in fact, was in ignorance of the event until many years afterwards, he wrote to Sir John? telling him what his son's position and prospects were. It led to nothing, for Sir John declined to interfere. We may conclude that it was the women—the two elder women—who had their way. There came a time when the younger woman had her way also—but that is looking ahead.

CHAPTER X.

Fortunately, we are not dependent upon Lockhart's surmises for the reasons which led to Scott's choice of the advocate's rather than the attorney's profession. Against his suggestion of exterior influences we have Scott's own statement, which is clear and explicit. He says: "My father behaved with the most parental kindness. He offered, if I preferred his own profession, immediately to take me into partnership with him, which, though his business was much diminished, still afforded me an immediate prospect of a handsome independence. But he did not disguise his wish that I should relinquish this situation to my younger brother, and embrace the more ambitious profession of the Bar. I had little hesitation in making my choice—for I was never very fond of money; and in no other particular do the professions admit of a comparison. Besides, I knew and felt the inconveniences attached to that of a Writer; and I thought (like a young man) many of them were '*ingenio non subounda meo.*' The appearance of personal dependence which that profession requires was disagreeable to me; the sort of connection between the client and the attorney seemed to render the latter more subservient than was quite agreeable to my nature; and, besides, I had seen many sad examples, while overlooking my father's business, that the utmost exertions and the best-meant services do not secure the *man of business*, as he is called, from great loss, and most ungracious treatment on the part of his employers. The Bar, though I was conscious of my deficiencies as a public speaker, was the line of ambition and liberty; it was that also for which most of my contemporary friends were destined.

And, lastly, although I would willingly have relieved my father of the labours of his business, yet I saw plainly that we could not have agreed on some particulars if we had attempted to conduct it together, and that I should disappoint his expectations if I did not turn to the Bar. So to that object my studies were directed with great ardour and perseverence during the years 1789, 1790, 1791, 1792."

A careful examination of this statement will show that Lockhart's picture of the youth diverted from boorish companionships and an attorney's desk by the impulses of ambitious love and the influences of a mentor of superior social position is not merely conjectural, but of a demonstrable falsehood. The decision was taken at least as far back as 1789—when he was no more than eighteen, at no very great distance from his illness. It is also worth notice that he mentions that he was influenced (though it can be no more than a very subordinate consideration) by the fact that the Bar was the profession to which "*most* of his contemporary friends" were destined. We may transform this into the singular, and take it to refer exclusively to William Clerk, if we will, but it would be an unreasonable perversity. So far as we have any authoritative evidence, his closest friends at this time, apart from Irving and Clerk, were George (afterwards Lord) Abercromby, David Boyle (afterwards Lord Justice Clerk) Thomas Grierson, the Hon. Thomas Douglas (afterwards Earl of Selkirk), Adam Fergusson (Professor Fergusson's son), and James Ramsey. Judging by the careers of these men, it is not a boorish list.

The fact is that, while no man would be more sympathetic to human weakness, or tolerant of human folly, Scott was always honest with himself and others in seeing failures for what they were, and calling them by plain names. Through all his life, in the highest sense of the word, he was the neighbour of those around him. He was helpful to thousands. But he chose his friends with discrimination.

His suggestion that, while he would have felt competent to take over his father's practice entirely, he saw the elements of probable friction if they should have been in partnership, is interesting, and may have been a well-founded fear. They were 'both men, in spite of the "sweetness" of disposition which was attributed to them, of strong opinions and strong wills. The elder man was in gradually failing health, and relaxing energies. The practice, though it could still have spared an ample income for an incoming partner, tended to contract as old clients died or drifted away. There were probably many leakages which a younger man could have stopped: debts which he would have been more energetic to collect: parasites which he would have brushed away. Youth is intolerant, and not always wise. Values would have differed. He may have seen his father's weaknesses more clearly than he would see his own at a later day. They were both capable of romantic perversities, which a prosaic wisdom cannot defend.

There is an earlier incident, authenticated in after-years by a still existing saucer, which illuminates the characters of both—and of Mrs. Scott also.

The lawyer did not talk about his clients' business at home. Not even to Anne. That was understood. But when a closely cloaked stranger came to George's Square, night after night, to hurry with a muffled face from his sedan chair to her husband's private room, and to remain there in conferences which sometimes lasted long into the night-hours, and when Anne's natural questions as to the identity of this mysterious visitor were turned aside, her curiosity was aroused. That can be understood too.

A direct answer being refused, Anne did not badger her husband, or make it a cause of quarrel. Neither did she watch surreptitiously, nor abandon her resolution to know who the secret caller might be. She waited up till the ringing of a bell from her husband's room announced that his visitor was about to leave, and his sedan-chair must be summoned to the door. Then she appeared on the scene with a hospitable tea-tray, and the suggestion that the gentleman would be glad to have some refreshment after so long a conference.

The stranger thanked her, and drank. Walter Scott sat silently before his untasted tea. When his client had gone, he rose and took up the emptied cup. He opened the window. The night-air came in, and the precious china was flung out. He turned to his indignant wife to say that he did not blame her curiosity, but neither he nor his should put lip to cup where Murray of Broughton drank.

The name means nothing to us today. Fame and infamy go down to the same oblivion. This was the man who had been secretary to Charles Stuart in his invasion of England in '45, and had afterwards bought his own life by giving evidence through which others died.

The lawyer had no use for the Stuarts. He looked for an ordered government which would bring even the wilder northern counties to the benefit of a settled peace. He might feel also that Murray, in these last shameful years, had troubles to which he could not refuse his professional aid. But his inward scorn of the man was of an intensity to give birth to that illogical destruction. For the cup would have washed. The china of that day was a treasured thing. A sentimentalist might have washed it twice. But the incident is profoundly significant of the strain of unpractical ideality which is observable in the Scott family from generation to generation. If spiritual and material values clash, the material goes carelessly to the gutter, or is flung there to the flinger's loss.

We are reminded of the younger Walter's refusal (afterwards bitterly repented) to stand by his brother Daniel's dis-honoured grave, or of his conception of the parting of Douglas and Marmion. When Murray entered the lawyer's room, we may be sure that he was not met with an outstretched hand.

At the time, the boy reacted differently, though in an equally characteristic way. Awake in his mother's dressing-room, or reading surreptitiously by the light of her bedroom fire, he may have heard the cup scatter its fragments upon the pavement of the silent Square. Anyway, he learned what had occurred. He discovered that his father's picturesque indignation had not extended to the saucer from which the cup had been lifted to desecration. He added it to the accumulation of his private relics. The same ironic fate led the saucer to a prolonged existence and the cup to a violent end.

Did Murray of Broughton hear the cup crash on the pavement as he entered his sedan-chair? Did he understand its significance? It would be pleasant to think he did.

CHAPTER XI.

The Faculty of Advocates required, as a condition of admission to the Bar, a course of study which could not be less than two years, the first being occupied with Roman and the second with Scottish Law. Walter Scott's twentieth and twenty-first years were almost entirely occupied with these studies, and on July 6th, 1792, about a month before his twenty-first birthday, he passed the final examination with honours, as did William Clerk at the same time, the two friends acquiring the right to practice, and assuming the gown in public, five days later together.

Walter may have seen little of Williamina during these two years, and she may have given him no very decided encouragement, but the determination to win her, distant as it might be, and doubtful as it might seem to others, had become the strongest motive that ruled his life. For the first time, he bears witness of himself without qualification that he had applied himself to study "with stern, steady, and undeviating industry". It was a discipline which cannot have been easily self-imposed, to one of his alert mind and varied interests. It was not only poetry and literature which must be repressed. He had been making obstinate attempts to paint (William Clerk painted with ease and skill) and would not readily admit that he could not reach artistic expression through this medium. He had endeavoured to understand music, for which he had not more than an elementary appreciation. He had actually had a singing-master at one time, (if Robert could sing, why not he?) and, curiously enough, the singing-master was better satisfied with his efforts in this direction than were his other auditors.

There was a reason for that. Alexander Campbell, who taught him, had some private financial troubles which, Scott recorded afterwards, "I could relieve, if I could not remove". What he was able to do at that early age, by monetary or legal assistance, is not clear, but it won a measure of gratitude which would not admit that the young man was unable to sing if he wished to do so.

Lady Cumming, who lived next door at George's Square, was under no such obligation, and her opinion differed. She sent in a jocularly sarcastic note of expostulation. Would Mr. Scott kindly cease flogging his sons at precisely the same hour each day? She had no doubt the punishment was deserved, but the noise was dreadful..... After that, we may suppose that the songs ceased.

But now poetry and history, painting and music, were alike discarded, at the call of ambition, and the memory of Williamina's eyes. And Williamina at Invermay, though she might give some thought to the young lawyer-lover, whom her mother favoured so strongly, was giving others to Willie Forbes of Pitsligo, the heir of the banker-baronet, Sir William Forbes, who also loved, or might be persuaded to love her. And far south, born in a French town, and now living in London) was a dark, vital, vivacious girl, who had her own dreams, and who could give Walter love and loyalty of a good kind, if they should ever meet, which it was millions to one that they never would. Is it all law? Or all chance? Call it as we will, we may still ask, do we weave it ourselves, or is it the dancing pattern of a Creator's dream? Seeing no more of the future than others do, Walter Scott followed a lying light, and toiled at the law.

To give him quiet time for his studies, it had been found possible to allot a semi-basement room at George's Square to his sole use. The home was already breaking apart. Robert had gone by the sea's way. John could only be home on rare occasions. Walter need not sleep in the dressing-room now. His father's health no longer permitted the entertaining which had done so much for the business, and brought so many diverse people in earlier years under a child's all-observant eyes. Only intimate friends now enter the quieter rooms. There is Dr. Rutherford—not Anne's father, who came once to give the wisdom of his advice to save the life of a palsied child—it is Anne's brother who is the Dr. Rutherford of today. And Christian Rutherford comes rather frequently: she is Anne's half-sister, the child of her father's second wife, a clever, even brilliant girl, so much younger than Anne that she is like a sister to Walter, though he must call her aunt.

Tom and Daniel complete the family, with the invalid sister who has her mother's name, and who now has difficult moods, which call for the patience of others. She is passionately attached to Walter, her favourite brother, and the one (as it is easy to guess) who is most understanding of the tragic isolation in which her spirit still survives in the fire-wrecked body....

Walter found a natural pleasure in the first living-room that he could call his own. It was here that Francis Jeffrey came to visit him, after hearing him read an essay on ballads at the Speculative Club, and found it crowded with 'dingy' books which overflowed the shelves and must be piled on the floor, and ornamented with Broughton's saucer, and an old Lockaber axe and claymore that Alexander had given him, a cabinet of collected coins, and other accumulations. It is significant of the growing freedom of Walter's life, and the atmosphere of the quietening home, that he took this unexpected and welcome visitor out, and gave him a dinner at a neighbouring tavern.

The fact that William Clerk and he commenced the two years' study for the Bar at the same time, drew them into a closer intimacy at this period, as Walter's absorption in his work tended to loosen the ties which he had formed with others. William lived at the end of Prince's Street, about two miles away, and they made a compact to meet alternately at each other's house in the early mornings (Sundays excepted) to undergo a system of mutual examinations upon an agreed portion of the range of study that was before them. Walter did his part, but he waited vainly on the mornings when his friend should have appeared at George's Square. Lockhart's paragon would not leave his bed. They did not fall out over the discovery of these "fetters of indolence", neither did the plan fall through. It was characteristic of the mingled determination and complaisance of Scott's character that he agreed to do all the walking. Before seven every morning, be the weather what it might, he would be hammering on the door in Prince's Street, prepared to examine his friend, and to be himself examined, upon the self-set reading of yesterday. The severe discipline of this method endured (apart from the usual vacations) for the two years of study. It is not surprising that they both passed with honours. We have nothing beyond Lockhart's imagination to support the suggestion that William persuaded Walter to undertake these examinations. There is better evidence of the debt which was owed to Walter by his lazier friend. The fact may still be that William brushed his clothes better than Walter up to the close of Walter's nineteenth year, after which there was a dead heat in the measure of this activity. It may even be true that, at the earlier period, William was rather uppish to Walter in allusions to his superior neatness. The evidence is not easy to find, but it is a point on which we may be content that Lockhart shall have his way. Had this tireless biographer understood how to thin out the forest of facts amid which he wandered, some of his best trees might have been better grown.

There can be no doubt that Lockhart had a sincere admiration for Scott, both for his literary genius, and his personal character. He had a real affection also for an older man of most lovable attributes who was his wife's father, and his own friend. In intimacy, in admiration, in many personal qualifications, he was particularly suited to be his biographer, and his work remains a mine of information and a monument of literary industry. But though he is not sparing in adjectives of laudation, and sometimes acute in criticism, we feel that he was writing of a man whom he had observed from the outside, but whom he could never know.

And this ignorance concentrates itself in one fatuous amazing paragraph in which he assures us that during the period of his studies for the Bar, and the first years of legal practice, when he was concentrating his energies to hasten the day when he could make a formal offer of marriage to the girl he loved, he was not consorting with prostitutes, nor seducing housemaids.

Lockhart gravely tells us that he does not bear this witness without careful enquiry. Before venturing to give such an assurance he collected the "concurrent testimony of all the most intimate among his surviving associates"!

The letters which Scott wrote at that period, or at least those which survive, are not numerous, but Lockhart had access to a large quantity which had been addressed to him, and which obviously were not meant for publication. He remembered Southey's idea that such letters reveal the character of him who receives, as much as those who write them, and lest there should be anything which the "concurrent testimony" had failed to expose, he went through them diligently in search of any "coarse or even jocular suggestion" which might reflect by implication upon the recipient. Naturally he failed to find that which he should have known without looking would not be there.

It may be suggested—it may be likely enough—that a physical licentiousness in the conduct of his own life would have broken down the deep reticence with which Scott always treated the emotional contacts of lovers, both in verse and prose. Had that been so, it would not have been a gain to literature, but an incalculable loss.

His conception of a love which is worthy of song or tale is one in which the spiritual element dominates. It is not that physical passion is weak or absent, but that there is something which transcends it, of which it is no more than the carnal garment.

> "It liveth not in fierce desire
> With dead desire it doth not die."

We may observe that he did not refuse to look at any of the facts of human life with steady, tolerant, and understanding eyes. But he knew obscenity for the comparative triviality which it is, and his work was always free from the defect which reduces so much of modern fiction to a diseased sterility. He was neither under the necessity of asserting, nor the folly of supposing, that the lowest gutter gives the broadest view....

On the day following that on which the two friends assumed the dignity of the barrister's gown (Scott's first guinea fee having been received that afternoon) the Court of Session rose for the Autumn vacation, and he was able to escape to Kelso, and indulge in a holiday well earned by the two years of successful study. He stayed there for a short time—on this occasion with Captain Robert Scott, who will be remembered as having visited Bath when his sister Janet was there with their infant nephew, and who demonstrated the harmless nature of statuary by introducing the child to a familiar intercourse with a sculptured Neptune, which was a very natural selection for a mariner to make.

Captain Scott had now retired from the East Indian service, and followed Janet's choice of Kelso as a residence for his declining years. He was easily persuaded by his nephew's youthful impetuosity that he would enjoy a holiday in Northumberland, and they adventured as far as Hexham together.

The holiday was without recorded incident, and is of no separate significance. But Scott's wanderings during this and succeeding years have an importance which cannot be overlooked.

His life from this time divides itself conveniently into five periods.

First, there are the five years of legal practice and wandering holidays which preceded his marriage.

Next there are the ten careless years—probably the happiest of his life—of assured and growing income and reputation, of congenial occupations which could be carried on without haste or weariness, and of quiet and happy domesticity—the years of

Lasswade and Ashestiel.

Then there are the ten years during which he had the reputation of the greatest living poet: the succeeding ten years during which he had the reputation of the greatest of living novelists, ending with that sudden absolute disaster which left him widowed, bankrupt, broken in health, and loaded with a fantastic total of liabilities: and finally the five years during which he camped stubbornly upon the field of battle where he would not admit defeat.

During the first ten or fifteen years of this period, it is common to represent him as one who had not 'found himself', and who was unaware of the potentialities of his creative powers. But there is little evidence to support this judgement, and there is much to oppose it. He did not, of course, see the details of his successes—he could not have known that his work would win its immense popularity, and bring him an income such as he could have obtained in no other way. In these first years he looked, naturally and necessarily, to the profession he had adopted to support his home, and he gave it the major portion of his time and energies. He had the broad sanity of judgement which told him that home-making is more important than the rhyming of couplets, and if anyone had advised him that he could improve the prospects of a literary career by deferring marriage, he would not have thanked him for the suggestion, nor delayed the ceremony.

But it seems clear, from the evidence of a hundred details, and his own most definite statements, that his ambitions were directed from an early age to the distinction of literary achievement. He was so tireless in these years in the collections of material upon which his published work was afterwards constructed, that it is, at least, difficult to suggest how he could have employed his energies to more direct advantage, had he foreseen the future in detail.

It is also to be considered that creation must precede publication, and that this precedence is of uncertain length in the absence of direct evidence of the period of composition. *The*

Lay of the Last Minstrel is founded upon the traditions and ballads which were his earliest learning. *The Lady of the Lake* centres round Loch Katrine and the Trossachs, to which we have seen him make a spectacular journey in his nineteenth year. *Marmion* is a tale of Flodden Field. The visit to Hexham was his second expedition into Northumberland. He had found means and opportunity to visit Flodden at an even earlier age.

When we come to the novels, we find similar evidence. It is not only that *Waverley* is known to have been partly written at a period much earlier than that at which it was published. *Guy Mannering*, which was the next to follow it, was produced with such celerity, under the stress of financial need, as to support its internal evidences of having been largely designed and possibly written at a much earlier date.

It is true that there are records of the actual composition of some of these works, both verse and prose, which date them definitely at later periods, (Waverley was *completed* at a known time, and an amazing speed,) but the doubt remains as to whether there may have been considerable drafts or partial compositions in previous existence: flowering which is profuse and sudden could come only from nourished roots and buds in which the petals were shaped already.

At this time, he had only been back in Kelso for a few days of pleasant idleness when he started out for Jedburgh, and though he may have gone in search of legal business at the Michaelmas head-court there, his introduction to Mr. Robert Shortreed, the Sheriff-substitute of Roxburghshire, led to another of those profitable friendships which he was so adept at forming. They had scarcely made each other's acquaintance before they were setting off together into the wilderness of Liddesdale. The young barrister had expressed his desire to explore its desolate uplands, and the sheriff had volunteered to guide him!

The county of Roxburghshire, with which Scott is so peculiarly identified, had endured the stress of almost continual border warfare from the tenth century, when the Saxons surrendered it to the Scottish king, with other Lothian territory, to-the date of the English Union, nearly eight hundred years later. Its surface was strewn with half-ruined castles and peels which had once protected the lives of its hardy scanty population, or had been sacked and burned when the English raiders had been too strong for successful resistance. The bleak moorlands of its southern portion, rising at times to mountainous heights, and broken by narrow stream-filled hollows, were better adapted to discourage or resist invasion than to support a numerous population; but in its northern valleys—that of the Tweed, the Esk and Teviot dales—the twenty miles, more or less, which separated their inhabitants from the English border had allowed time for the beacon-signals to give warning of hostile invasion, and for men to gather in formidable strength. It resulted that it had been possible to follow the pursuit of agriculture in relative security, and some urban industries, such as the weaving of 'tweed' cloth, had grown up to a modest extent in Hawick, Kelso and Jedburgh, with populations of some thousands at each of these centres. There were fields of barley and oats stretching beneath the wooded slopes of the valleys; and the orchards around Melrose and Kelso were justly famed.

But further south, the moors, the high hills, green to their rounded summits, had been no better than precarious sheep-walks for the best part of a thousand years. Their spare population had depended for its security upon the rude poverty of its existence, as much as upon the strength of the walls behind which it sheltered when the beacons flared. A small force would turn back, baffled by the strong-walled towers, with their narrow windows, and single room on each storey: a large force would pass them by, seeking for richer spoils in the further valleys.

Of all this barren desolate southern portion of the county, the wildest and most desolate was the district of Liddesdale in the extreme south, where the moors slope downwards to Cumberland, and the Liddell flows to join the Eden and the Irish Sea.

When Walter Scott came to Jedburgh, Liddesdale—twenty to thirty miles to the south—was still as wild and little known as the remotest Highlands. Here and there, was a sheep-farmer's isolated house. Less frequently, a little church might be found, or a lonely manse, or the ruins of a deserted tower. It had no roads—no inns. No wheeled vehicle had ever attempted the roughness of its mountain tracks. It was a country where few dwelt, and to which no one came.

Here, it seemed to Scott, there might be treasure of old ballads and old tales to be gained by one who would take the trouble to seek them, and who could win the friendship of its lonely inhabitants. Old Border riding-songs might still be sung.

He could have no better guide than the Sheriff-substitute, the one man of his own status who knew the country, who knew the Elliots and Armstrongs who occupied its lonely farms, and who was known and trusted by them. The new friends set out on horseback together, and by night-time they were sleeping in the same bed (as they would have to become accustomed to do) at the farm at Millburnholm, and between fatigue and Willie Elliot's toddy, we may be sure that they slept well.

There followed for Scott a very happy and successful week. They spent nothing, being received at manse and farm with a free and equal hospitality. Scott was introduced by Shortreed with the strange and frightening dignity of being an Advocate of the Edinburgh Court, such as had never been known to visit the dale before. They found him to be a tall, handsome, attractive boy, very active, in spite of a shrunken leg, very willing to be 'just a cheild like ourselves', very quick to make friends with every dog that he met, full of inexhaustible anecdotes, and with a smile that charmed the confidence of the shyest of these lonely dwellers on the moors. For he was at home here as much as ever he would be in the streets of Edinburgh. The hardy Cheviot sheep might have been those among which the baby with the dragging leg had crawled above the crags of Sandy-Knowe. It was the same moor, and the same sky.

With his usual luck (if that be the word to use) he found a friend of the right kind in a doctor at Cleughhead—an Elliot like the rest, who had been collecting manuscript ballads for some previous years for his own satisfaction. Dr. Elliot, under the impetus of the enthusiasm of the younger man, undertook this work with a new energy. For many years after, he made an occupation of seeking out these dying traditional songs, oral or written, and sending them as a willing tribute to the young Edinburgh lawyer whose genius would put them to immortal use.

It was only the first of many 'raids' which Scott was to make upon the Liddesdale country in the same company during succeeding summers, but Shortreed remembered and told long afterwards the intoxications (mental and too-nearly physical) of that first excursion. "Eh me!" he said, "sic an endless fund o' humour and drollery as he then had wi' him. Never ten yards hut we were either laughing or roaring and singing. Wherever we stopped, how brawlie he suited himself to everybody! He ay did as the lave did—" Scott's mind reacted buoyantly from the hard self-imposed discipline of the two previous years, that had brought him with honours through the examinations of a month ago. He was released from that ordeal, and, for the moment, free. He had the genius of sympathetic imagination which made him all things to all men. But he took their confidences rather than gave his own. All his life he would be the willing confidant and helper of those around him. They would sometimes think him pliable. Where they would think to constrain him to a mile they would sometimes find that he would go two. But it would be of his own will.

Only occasionally would he give emphatic rebuff to some too-impudent liberty. But his sympathies would seldom deflect his judgement. His own soul would remain apart, almost aloof,

in a reticence only to be partially broken at last in the Journal of his closing years, when he would write *'God help us: earth cannot'*, and find the help for which he looked was there....

The farmers of Liddlesdale had two occupations which relieved the healthy monotony of the sheep-walks, otherwise only varied as the seasons changed, or by the occasional visits to Hawick, or Jedburgh, or Hexham fair. They had the stimulus of alcohol; and the emotional exercise of their religion, with the intellectual acrobatics of the theological guise it wore. The young lawyer appears to have avoided, as far as courtesy would permit, the excesses of convivial hospitality. Shortreed remarked that he was rarely 'fou' and never showed any of the usual symptoms of drunkenness, but it was not always easy to be abstemious at that time, if one would mix sociably with all conditions of men. There came a day when they reached a remote hill-farm where they were relieved to find that the warmth of their reception was not immediately interpreted in terms of alcoholic refreshment. But it was a respite only. The eager host had sent at express speed to a smuggler on the Solway Firth, when he heard of his approaching visitors. A sober supper, at which the home-brewed elderberry wine was the only beverage, was followed by the customary religious ceremony, through which the light of Christianity was maintained in these scattered homes. A young 'student of divinity', who was of the party, was conducting the solemn service when there was a sound of horses' feet on the stony road. Two herdsmen burst into the room with the keg of brandy for which the anxious farmer had been listening ever since his visitors had arrived too soon. Religious habit and self-control gave way at the joyful sound. He leapt up from his knees. "By God, here's the keg at last!" Scott would always remember the look of despair on the face of the young clergyman, as he closed the book.

He rode back to Jedburgh with a Border war-horn slung around his neck, the gift of Dr. Elliot, and found (it is said) at the ruins of Hermitage. It is not clear whether he actually visited the relics of that sombre isolated castle, the outpost of the Scottish borders, which the Douglases had held so stubbornly against the raids of Cumberland, on this occasion, or in the following year. He had resolved that he would return to Liddesdale at the first chance he had, but, for the time, he must turn his mind to the profession from which his income must be earned. In November, the Court was sitting again at Edinburgh, and Walter Scott was in regular attendance at Parliament House.

CHAPTER XII.

Lockhart came on two of Scott's notebooks dated 1792, and evidently written in that year. He gives a list of the contents of one of them, which is an illuminating criticism of those who depreciate him for a lack of pedantic scholarship. There were first seven closely-written quarto pages containing *"Vegtain's Kvitha*, or the *Descent of Odin*, with the Latin of Thomas Bartholine, and the English poetical version of Mr. Gray; with some account of the death of Balder, both as narrated in the Edda, and as handed down to us by the Northern historians—*Auctore Gualtero Scott."* The Norse original, and the two versions follow. The whole is obviously an essay to be read before one of the Edinburgh literary or debating societies to which he belonged at this period. The book also contained these miscellaneous jottings:

A transcript of a receipt for some plate lent to King Charles I.
A copy of Langhorne's *Owen of Carron*.
The verses of Canute on passing Ely.
The old English cuckoo-lyric, which has since become part of the common furniture of most Anthologies.
A translation by "a gentleman in Devonshire" of the death-song of Regner Lodbrog.
One of the quatrains of Gray's Elegy,
"There scattered oft, the earliest of the year"
which he omitted from the published version.
An Italian canzonet praising blue eyes (Williamina's colour).
Several pages of etymologies from Ducange.
Several pages of notes on the Morte D'Arthur.
Abstracts from the books of Adjournal, about Dame Janet Beaton, Sir Walter Scott of Buccleuch (Wicked Watt), and his wife, who was to appear as the
real heroine of the *Lay of the Last Minstrel*.
Other abstracts concerning witches and fairies.

Some couplets from Hall's Satires.
A passage from Albania.
Notes on Second Sight, with abstracts from Aubrey and Glanville.
A 'list of Ballads to be discovered or re-discovered'.
Abstracts from *Guerin de Montglave*.
Many more 'similar entries.'
A table of the Maeso-Gothic, Anglo-Saxon and Runic Alphabets. Beyond these, the book had a section headed *German*, and left blank.

Such was one of the note-books of a young man, who stands self-accused of neglecting his opportunities of study, and of whom Lockhart himself writes as though his defects of education need to be leniently explained away. The fact is that he was self-accumulating the stores of the erudition he needed, which none of the professional scholars of the University would have been competent to supply. There was a time when his mind, excited in a score of other directions, declined to engage itself in the study of Greek, which he afterwards regretted, but not sufficiently to induce him to repair the omission. It was regrettable, as all ignorance is. Had he felt sufficient occasion, he would doubtless have mastered the language, as he did Spanish about this time, or earlier) and German during the coming year....

The first year of an advocate's life in the Edinburgh of that period, as is that of a young barrister of London today, was one of waiting for irregular opportunities, with many dissultory intervals which he would use or waste as his disposition led him to do. There were occasional briefs to be handed out by the Court for those who must be defended *in forma pauperis*, which were usually allotted to the junior advocates. The fees were small, but they gave opportunities of showing abilities which might be recognised by the watching attorneys from whom briefs of a more valuable kind would then be likely to follow. There was chamber practice in the preparation of "informations", and kindred work, from attorneys, and busier advocates, which was ill-paid, but gave similar opportunities of showing ability where it would be valued, and establishing contacts, which might be of subsequent profit. Steadily, though not rapidly, Scott's practice and income grew.

The younger advocates, idling for their opportunities around the door of the Court, formed themselves into a loosely organised club, which became known as the *Mountain*, of which Scott was a very popular member. He still carried the nickname of his college days—*Duns Scotus*, in recognition of his antiquarian zeals. William Clerk was a member also. His airs of indolent superiority had won him the good-humouredly-ironic title of Baronet, in evident allusion to Sir John Clerk, of the honour of which relationship he appears to have been sufficiently conscious.

With his genius for the right friendships, Scott added to his intimates at this time, Thomas Thomson, who became later a leading antiquarian authority; and William Erskine (Lord Kinedder), with whom he established a close and enduring friendship. Lockhart gives his opinion that Erskine had an important influence at this time in persuading Scott of the "extravagances both of thought and language" which disfigured the German literature which he was endeavouring to master. "His friendly critic" (Lockhart says) "was just, as well as delicate—and severity as to the mingled absurdities and vulgarities of German detail commanded deliberate attention coming from one who admired not less enthusiastically than himself the sublimity and pathos of his new favourites."

William Erskine was one of the weaker members of a brilliant family. He was Scott's contemporary, not his grandfather, nor his tutor. Lockhart calls him his 'monitor', but it is difficult to understand why, unless we regard it as axiomatic that one who knows Greek is the monitor of one who is ignorant of that language.

In fact, Scott, Erskine, Thomson and Clerk agreed to learn German together in this winter of 1792-3. They found a good teacher in Dr. Willich. It was the fashion to be interested in

German literature. English literature was hesitating towards a new florescence. French literature was regarded as contaminated by the anarchistic activities at which Europe shivered. Interest in the work of Goethe and Schiller was a natural consequence. Scott took what it had to offer, learning, as did his companions, to read its poets in the original. He took what he wanted, as he did from his neighbours' brains. That Erskine's estimate of it was more accurate or more critical than his own, that their estimates differed, that Erskine influenced him rather than being influenced by him, that such influence materially altered Scott's own poetry—these propositions may appear to be of a mounting improbability. Still, Lockhart appears confident. He writes not as one asserting an opinion, but as recording a fact. We may think as we will....

The first legal business of importance for which Scott was briefed, and of which there is any detailed record, was not a pleading before the Civil Court, but a matter of Ecclesiastical discipline. There was a certain minister named McNaught, of the kirk at Girthon in Galloway, who was charged with various scandalous proceedings, and the brief for his defence came into the hands of Mr. Scott, with a fee of five guineas marked upon it. It was a hopeless cause. He went down to Girthon, when the rising of the Edinburgh Court in March 1793 released him from attendance there, and marshalled such evidence and arguments as the nature of the case permitted. But the fact was that the reverend gentleman was not easy to defend. It appeared that he was most often drunk. That his songs were lewd and profane. That he danced with gingerbread-sellers of an improbable chastity. Robert Burns had done no less, and remained the hero of the national life, but while a poet may indulge in promiscuous familiarities with "the maids that make the bed for him", and be thought of none the worse by his fellow-countrymen, the ethical standards of the manse are somewhat different, and the Scottish conscience was stirred.

Scott appeared in due course at the Bar of the Church Assembly, and argued McNaught's case at considerable length, at which the Venerable Court was not pleased. He showed some ingenuity in establishing that there is an important legal distinction between 'ebrius' and 'ebriosus'—between being drunk (which might happen to anyone) and being drunken, which is less capable of defence. He quoted one of the obscene phrases alleged to have been used by the reverend gentleman, and was rebuked for repeating such language with unseemly boldness. When he had occasion to quote a song of the same pattern, which was also at issue, he spoke so low that his legal friends, who crowded the gallery, and who may not have regarded the Kirk Assembly with as much respect as the Civil Court, shouted to him to speak up, and were promptly turned into the street by the order of the indignant Elders.

Such, at least, is the tale. It may be of as much truth, or as little, as such tales usually are. Scott probably did what was possible in a hopeless case.

But he was less fitted by temperament to be a barrister than a judge. He saw both sides. He would be a poor advocate of a poor cause. All his life, his tendency was to advise against litigation: to make peace where he could.

It is true that he went on to Jedburgh, and secured the acquittal of a poacher, which was no mean feat of advocacy in those times, but he had a kindness for this class of miscreant, as Tom Purdie found on a later day. Scott told the man that he was a lucky scoundrel, to which he agreed very cheerfully, and added that he would send him one of the hares when he got home, as no doubt he did.

But when the Jedburgh Court session was over, Scott was on the way to Liddesdale once again.

CHAPTER XIII.

However vague Scott's ultimate ambitions may have been to his own mind, or however privately he may have kept them there, his literary interests were becoming increasingly evident to those among whom he associated, and may have done actual harm to his professional prospects. Men are seldom willing to credit their neighbour with two separate excellencies. Of the Speculative Club, he had before this time accepted, one after another, the triple offices of librarian, secretary and treasurer. In fact, it pivoted upon his personality.

To suggest that he neglected any opportunity of engaging in the profession he had adopted, or that he failed to give good service to those who briefed him, would go not merely beyond evidence, but beyond probability, remembering the capacity for self-discipline that he had shown in his legal studies, and his stubborn resolution, now known to many, that he would marry the heiress of Invermay. But briefs came irregularly, the passion for poetry, for history, for antiquarian research—they were always with him. While legal practice halted, as, in the experience of most young barristers, it is apt to do, what could he do better than pursue them? The Advocates' Library was in the vaults beneath the Parliament House. It had many old and curious manuscripts which he was expert in deciphering. He became one of its Curators, which was an honour reserved for Advocates who were conspicuous for literary rather than forensic triumphs. During the considerable portions of the year when the Courts were not sitting, he resumed his wanderings with a systematic diligence against which his now-invalid father protested even more vigorously than he had done in earlier days. To him, at least, it appeared a dissipation of energy which militated against the legal career of a brilliant son. It was a view for which some argument could be urged. Probably the older man was disappointed that his progress was not more rapid during these first years. He had expected much. Now he looked rather irritably for the cause, if not of comparative failure, of delayed success. His son kept steadily on the track of a destiny which may—or may not—have been clear to his own mind. He was not insensitive of his father's feelings, but he held to his own course. Christian Rutherford was a sympathetic confidant.

As his father's health failed, the house at George's Square

took on a tone of increased austerity. Tom left it—marrying Elizabeth McCulloch, a Galway girl, with one of the usual ancient Scottish pedigrees. She lived to survive him, and Walter's children. 'One of the best and wisest and most agreeable women I have ever met', Lockhart called her, writing from the standpoint of the generation that followed. We may notice again that the Scotts chose their wives well.

So Tom, doubtless drawing a larger income from the attorney's office than Walter had yet in sight, set up his own housekeeping, and the only two others who were still at home were the youngest brother, Daniel, not very anxious to be doing anything in particular, nor likely to succeed at it if he did, and the half-invalid, Anne.

Whenever the Court was not sitting in Edinburgh, it would be certain that Walter would not be at home. He might be at Tullibody, the seat of George Abercromby's grandfather, Sir Ralph, listening to that resolute old gentleman's tale of how he once visited Rob Roy in his own caravan. (He went on the track of his missing cattle, saw them hanging by the heels where they had been slaughtered for the nourishment of the robber gang, was hospitably allowed to share the meal which his meadows had provided, made a blackmail bargain which protected him from a repetition of such calls, and came back safely.) Or he might be at Newton, hearing tales of the '45; or with Buchanan at Cambusmore; or with Lord Kaines at Blair-Drummond, or with John Ramsay at Ochtertyre.

Or he might have joined William Clerk at Craighall, where the Rattrays, who were Clerk's relatives, would entertain them together. He wandered far in Highlands and Lowlands, and everywhere he went he gathered local colour, character, or anecdote which would appear in the publications of later years.

During the period that he was in attendance at the Edinburgh Court he gained another reputation, not characteristic of most barristers, or lame or literary men. It was a time of political unrest, and Scott's interests were too catholic and too keen for him to remain outside its resulting turmoils. The Bolshevism of those days was not at a comfortable distance, so that men could be coldly and remotely curious as to whether it had murdered millions, or engage in academic discussions concerning its five-year plans. It was at the door of England, looking over the narrow seas. It shook Europe. It seemed to many to open a pit of anarchy into which Christianity and civilisation must go down together: must go surely down, unless it could be saved by English courage—and English gold. To others, it was the dawn of a new hope. Liberty and equality, comfort and affluence, were offered to a world of slaves.

To appreciate the bitter controversies of those times, to be fair to those who took part in them on whatever side, we must; wipe out from our minds all knowledge of the events that followed. We must look at the blackness of the approaching storm, not knowing that we shall outlast it, or that it may drift away.

It is common to misrepresent Scott as a bigoted Tory, whose politics were of a reactionary obtuseness; one who would have been called a "die-hard" had he lived today. It is a judgement which is profoundly stupid. His attitude toward political questions was consistent from youth to age, because it sprang from certain basic conceptions of the nature of man, and the nature and purpose of human life, which he may or may not have analysed, but which were fundamental in character. He believed in liberty. He believed in order, as a condition of its existence. He believed in the inequality of men. He believed in nobility, concrete as well as abstract. *But it must be a nobility of service always.* No other is worthy to endure. No other will endure. That was the political creed of a man whose genius may have been more widely and sanely sympathetic than that of any other European poet except Dante—Shakespeare certainly not excepted. It was the creed of one who sympathised with and understood equally the feelings of the hunters and the horses, the dogs and the deer. Ellen Douglas, carelessly emptying her purse in the guardroom—

"with the grace
And open bounty *of her race*"

—symbolises this ideal, as does De Vaux, who

"of gold had never need
Save to purvey him arms and steed.
The only gold he ever stored
Inlays his helm and hilts his sword."

It may be no more (and no less) than the ideal of feudalism, from which feudalism fell away. But when it fell away, itself fell. Its central truth is the kernel of Christianity: "If any man would be first among you, let him be the servant of all."

When in his later years he would give entertainment to the villagers congregated beneath the shadow of Abbotsford—who if we probe the position deeply enough we find to be living mainly at his expense, on the proceeds of the Waverley novels—he would have no pride in what he did, but only a humility of wonder that others could be grateful for so light a cause.

And when confronted by the certainty of his own ruin, his first thoughts will be for others, and almost his first for the protection of those humbler dependants who had—

"Found shelter underneath his shield."

When, in his last years, he will drive through the industrial districts of Lancashire, and observe the "stern sullen unwashed artificers", thrown out of work by the financial crisis of the time, crowding frowningly around the vehicle, his sympathies will not be with his own class. He will write that night in his Journal, 'God's justice is requiting, and will further requite—' not those who were threatening England with revolution, but those, of whatever class, who could make wealth out of the poverty of their fellow-men.

His ideal of aristocracy was not one of wealth, but of conduct.

An aristocracy of *noblesse oblige*, and by that motto he believed that it could be established impregnably.

It was with such instincts, such beliefs, such ideals, and with an observation of the state of all grades of the society around him which few, if any, of his age and time can have equalled, that Walter Scott faced the political disorders and listened to the conflicting theories which were discussed around him.

CHAPTER XIV.

Looking back, we observe that the horrors of the French revolution did not extend to this island. We observe England as the guide and comforter of all who opposed, from whatever motive, the effort which the French Directory made to impose its political doctrines upon the rest of Europe. So, in retrospect, the fact stands. But to those who lived through the years of strife, the issue was not so clear. The civil difference was acute, bitter, and often violent. The revolutionary element in Edinburgh was so strong that there was at one time a plot to seize the castle, and defy the government. To a superficial view it might not have seemed surprising if the young lawyer, hungry for adventurous living, full of anti-Hanoverian sympathies, might have been drawn into participation in such disorders. But his reaction was different.

In the theatre, treason had found expression until it was louder than loyalty. An actor's phrase which could be misconstrued into a seditious meaning would bring a roar of applause. Such sentiments might have more weight than any artistic merit in deciding between the success or failure of the play. The first bars of the National Anthem would be the signal for an outburst of cat-calls, hisses and howls. An Irish element, led by some medical students of that nationality, was blamed primarily for this rowdyism. They came, shillelahs in hand, overawing the quieter and more loyal elements of the audience.

There was a night, after a number of minor disturbances,

when a young man rose up in the stalls and announced that he and his friends were determined not merely that the National Anthem should be played in silence, but that it should be sung by the audience. Anyone of a different mind had better leave. Should he interrupt, he would be thrown out. A howl of derision answered from the pit. It flourished defiant sticks. But the warning was no idle threat. There were ready clubs among the group of youthful barristers and attorneys in the stalls from which the challenge came. Conflict roared and did not cease till the last disloyalist had fled or been ejected from the theatre doors. Law and medicine had fought, and the law triumphed. They sang the National Anthem to their own satisfaction.

Proceedings followed in the Magistrates' Court. With some lack of humour, the defeated party appealed to the law to which it had professed its defiance. One of the defendants was Walter Scott. He was accused of having led the attack. Three complainants showed broken heads, and identified him as the one whose cudgel had knocked them out. With four others, he was bound over to keep the peace, and ordered to find bail for his good behaviour in future. His opponents got little satisfaction from that. There were sureties to be had in plenty. He could have had half the town.

It was at this time—as early as 1794—though he was unable to effect his purpose till a later date, that he conceived the idea of the formation of an Edinburgh regiment of volunteer horse, which his lameness would not prevent him from joining. Drilling was becoming general over the country. The fear of invasion grew. The regular army was required for foreign service. Loyal citizens must learn to defend themselves. Before breakfast, in the summer days, his brother Tom drilled as a grenadier. But even the volunteer army had no use for Walter Scott, though Nelson's physical weakness had not kept him out of the navy. Today, we know better. We should have rejected both.

CHAPTER XV.

It was in the course of 1796 that the five-years dream of marrying Williamina Stuart came to the end which mutual friends appear to have anticipated, though they were reluctant to express their doubts to the one who was most concerned, or found him unwilling to be convinced.

By this time he was doing considerable ill-paid work at the Bar—his fee-book for the previous year showed payments of £84. 4. 0d., a much more considerable sum then than it would be today—and he was busily occupied in the translation of German ballads, not yet published, but having some private circulation.

Two new friends come on the scene here—George Cranston (afterwards Lord Corehouse) and his sister Jane Anne (afterwards the Countess of Purgstall). Jane was in his confidence, and actively corresponding and intriguing on his behalf. It was she who wrote about this time, in the random course of a personal letter, "Upon my word, Walter Scott is going to turn out a poet—something of a cross, I think, between Burns and Gray". It was a shrewd judgement on the material that she then had on which to form it. As a lyric poet, it probably defines what he became as accurately as a chapter of criticism would be likely to do.

When he went to Invermay early this April, Miss Cranston had an idea. She shared it with William Erskine, and together they had his translation of *Leonore* set up in type, and one beautifully-bound copy followed and surprised him a few days after he arrived at Williamina's home.

Miss Cranston seems to have had some hope at the time that her little scheme had advanced his interests, but, in fact, it was a wasted effort. There may have been girls who would have considered the fact that a man could translate a German ballad a sufficient reason for marrying him, but Williamina thought differently. What her mother thought was revealed long after (when Williamina herself was dead and most of those who were busy now with intrigue and speculation concerning her) but she had the wisdom to let her make her own choice.

In the autumn, Scott was again at Invermay, and appears to have had a disappointing reception, for Miss Cranston writes to him, after he had left the house "—to trot quietly away, without so much as one stanza to Despair—never talk to me of love again—never, never, never...! Heaven speed you, and hope to the end."

But Scott knew that the end had come. Early in October it was public knowledge that Miss Stuart was engaged to William Forbes, and that the marriage would promptly follow. His friends, by the evidence of correspondence that still remains, appear to have had some apprehension of the way in which he would take the shattering of his five-year dream. But they did not know him. He spent a few days riding in solitude in the Montrose district. He came back, seeming his usual self, and saying nothing to anyone. He was never one to expose his feelings lightly. But the wound remained unhealed to his life's end. Characteristically, his friendship with his successful rival remained unbroken.

Lockhart professes to identify Miss Stuart both with Margaret of Branksome and Matilda of Rokeby. He may be right about one or other, but not both. Margaret had yellow hair, and there is evidence that Williamina (whom Lockhart calls Margaret, in evident error) had hair of the same colour. Beyond that, there is no description of Margaret's appearance by which comparison can be made. As to character, all we are told of Margaret is that, at a time of acute grief, she neglected to dress properly, that she could rise early and tread lightly at the call of love, and that she bolted like a hare at the approach of danger to her lover's life. Those who knew Williamina may have recognised her immediately from these incidents, but it seems unlikely.

Matilda was not physically heroic, but she lacked Margaret's pleasantly putty-like qualities. She managed her two lovers with some adroitness, and she did manage to "seize upon their leader's rein" and give the troopers commendably brief and accurate directions, which saved her lovers' lives. Had Margaret been placed in Matilda's situation we feel that the singing of

> "Let our halls and towers decay"

would have lacked spirit.

There is some evidence that the plot of Rokeby was suggested by the triangle of Scott himself and Williamina and Willie Forbes; and Matilda may have been as like Williamina as he was like the consumptive Wilfred—which would not be much. But if we accept these comparisons, we must entirely acquit Miss Stuart of any measure of deceit or inconstancy. It is the central idea of Rokeby that love neither overcame honour nor destroyed friendship in those who were of sufficient nobility to equal the assault of circumstance.

Lockhart, with more reason, regards the following passage from the twelfth chapter of *Peveril of the Peak* as having been written with its author's own experience in mind:

> "The period at which love is formed for the first time, and felt most strongly, is seldom that at which there is much prospect of its being brought to a happy issue. The state of artificial society opposes many complicated obstructions to early marriages; and the chance is very great that such obstacles prove insurmountable. In fine, there are few men who do not look back in secret to some period of their youth, at which a sincere and early affection was repulsed, or betrayed, or became abortive from opposing circumstances."

There is an interval of a quarter of a century, but the constancy and strength of Scott's affections, and his enduring memory of this thwarted passion, make it almost impossible that he should have written such a paragraph without consciousness of his own experience.

Late in life, he said that he had never faced any serious

trouble without being vexed in dreams by memories of this emotional disaster of earlier days. He also expressed a wish that its details should not be probed, though he feared that that was too much to hope. There is a border of decency in the investigation of the intimacies of those who are dead which it is easy to overpass, and which is passed very frequently. That they should be less protected than the living cannot be readily allowed by any logical or generous mind, and this applies more particularly to those who are related to, or who come into some contact with men of an enduring celebrity, but who have done nothing themselves to challenge publicity, or deserve its penalties. It is equally true that a biography which is insincere, or deceptive, is about as worthless, if not actively pernicious, as a book can be. Most biographies should not be written at all. The material does not exist, or cannot properly be brought into evidence. It is as though we were to stage a trial at which some essential witnesses would be absent, and the evidence of others would be abruptly terminated before its climax; at which no one could be cross-examined and no one would be on oath; and then bring in a casually-confident verdict, which a bench of experienced judges might decline to do.

Scott showed a truer sense of historical responsibility when he refused to write a life of Mary Stuart, at a time when money was a vital need, and though he must have known that it would have an enormous popularity, because he did not feel that he understood sufficiently the events of that gallant and tragic life. Possibly, had anyone suggested to his mind that the Casket letters were forgeries, he might have come to a different conclusion, and the result would have enriched our literature.

The character of most authors is sufficiently (and always most reliably) indicated by the work they leave us. The excuse (if it be needed) for considering the life of Scott is that which he would have applied himself to any theme that might come before him—that it is of an explicit nobility; a tale that it is worth while to tell.

The suggestion that he had a cause of grievance against Miss

Stuart does not come from him, and there is no evidence to support it which endures critical examination.

It is her abiding honour that Walter Scott loved her with that quality of love which will survive hope, and which endured to his last hour, and we can be content to leave her name untarnished.

He was too great of soul to suppose that this love was inconsistent with that which made sunlight in his life for many after years: too great either to conceal it from Charlotte Charpentier, or any who had his confidence, or to make it cause of complaint, or excuse for bitterness. And it was not without its reward in the control and conduct of his own life. However we may estimate the extent or directions in which it impulsed his literary work, there can be no doubt that the thought of Williamina Stuart inspired his determination to enter the Faculty of Advocates within the minimum possible period, and that when he put aside a score of contending interests for the steady uncongenial study of those two strenuous years

"'Twas she for whose bright eyes was won
The listed field at Askalon."

CHAPTER XVI.

The same October (1796) that saw the final defeat of Scott's effort to win Miss Stuart, saw his first published attempt at victory in the field of literature.

He published a thin quarto volume containing the version of *Leonore* ("William and Helen") which Jane Cranston caused to be set in type six months earlier, and *The Wild Huntsman,*. both being translations from Burger, a copy of whose ballads in the original had been presented to him by a German lady who had married Hugh Scott, the chief of his own (Harden) branch of the family.

This brings us to another of Scott's innumerable friendships, and to another of Lockhart's alleged 'influences'.

That Walter Scott would visit Hugh Scott at Mertoun was a certain thing. That Mrs. Hugh, the daughter of Count Bruhl, the Saxon ambassador in London, should take an interest in a young kinsman of her husband, who had learnt the language of her native country, and was translating its literature, was natural also. And it was absolutely certain that Scott would use the opportunity to learn from her all that the stores of her own mind, the experiences of her own life, could supply. He appears to have had the gift of pillaging the minds of others in such a manner that they were left with a pleasant satisfaction in the thought of how much they knew, and how much they had been able to help the pleasant and diffident young man with whom they had been conversing. It is curious, but not unnatural, that Scott seems to have shared their belief quite frequently. It had some truth. The mental wares which had been spread on the table between them had been those of their own minds. They did not realise that those which he had already accumulated were a hundred times more than theirs would ever be. They asked nothing from him. He asked information from them so deferentially that we are reminded of ants gently stroking aphidian abdomens, so that their milk shall flow freely.

Mrs. Hugh Scott, daughter of the Dowager-Countess of Egremont (think of that! Lockhart asks us to do so), met Walter Scott when he was twenty-five, and thought him very young for his years. She knew English better than he. They agreed about that. She could correct his bad rhymes; the Scotticisms of his conversations, which would otherwise (doubtless) invade his youthful efforts at literary expression. He once spoke about the "little two dogs" and she was able to explain that "two little dogs" was preferred in the best society. He was duly grateful. She spread her tail in the sun.

She did more than this. She "set him right in a thousand little trifles," as she naturally could, being the "first lady of fashion" to "take him up". It is an unconscious comedy as Lockhart tells it, but he may do justice to neither.

When we think of the verbal loveliness of *Rosabelle* and other lyrics which must have been written at or very soon after this period, and all the experimental beauties of *The Lay of the Last Minstrel*, we may smile a little at this picture of uncouth diffidence being instructed by this German-born lady in the elements of the English tongue; but Scott doubtless did learn something from her, and the lady was happy. It is more blessed to give than to receive.

Lockhart has supplied his hero with a "mentor" in Will Clerk, a "monitor" in Will Erskine, and now a "lady of fashion" to complete the preparation for his exalted destiny, after which he should go far.

But, for the moment, he didn't.

Friends who knew him in Edinburgh talked of the book and gave it generous praise, which may not have exceeded sincerity, because they regarded it in relation to the riches of his own mind, of which they already knew. But London literary circles declined to be excited. In fact, they declined to buy it at all. Lockhart is sure that "real lovers of poesy" saw that "no one but a poet could have transfused the daring imagery of the German in a style so free, bold, masculine, and full of life." Perhaps it was so, and perhaps they did. Lockhart's team of adjectives are somewhat of the same colour, and go no further than to suggest that the translations were of a vigorous quality. So they were. They had energy, and showed some skill in craftsmanship. But they were not his subjects: they were not his inventions: vitally, they were not *his*. They were more or less capable exercises in verse: they were not poetry at all. It was a time at which everyone was translating Burger. Some did it better than Scott, and most could have been better occupied. If he could do no better than that, he might give up trying, and it would be no loss to the world.

He took the failure with serenity. Beaten, for the moment, both in love and literature, he made no complaint. He went on practising the art of verse: he went on with his legal business: he redoubled his efforts to organise a regiment of volunteer horse.

And in this same Autumn of 1796, while the preparations for Williamina's wedding were being pushed forward at Invermay, Scott commenced another of his life-long friendships. A young man, James Skene of Rubislaw, who had just come back from Saxony, where he had been staying for several years, no doubt first attracted his attention owing to his interest in German literature. He wanted to know many things that James should be able to tell him. The fact that Skene was some years the younger of the two may explain Lockhart allowing Scott to have a friend who is not a monitor, but for the extent and quality of the resulting intimacy we may take Mr. Skene's ultimate statement that it continued for "nearly forty years"—that is till one of them should be buried in Dryburgh Abbey—"without ever having sustained a casual chill from unkind thought or word."

For the moment they talked of chargers, of the fear of French invasion on the northern coast, of the regiment of Light Horse that had been raised in London, and of the possibility of a similar enterprise being successful in the Scottish capital. During the winter, Scott worked so hard at this project that he was able in the middle of February to send a petition to the Government in London, signed by a sufficient number who would be willing to serve in a regiment of volunteer cavalry, to secure the necessary authority; and with such energy was the recruiting pressed that the regiment was an established fact when the spring came. It pledged itself to serve, in case of invasion, in any part of the United Kingdom. It was commanded by Charles Maitland of Rankeillor. Scott was "Paymaster, Quartermaster and Secretary." Its cornets were James Skene, and William Forbes of Pitsligo. The last name is an incidental evidence that no shadow of hostility had fallen between Walter Scott and his successful rival.

As most of the members of the corps had business or professional duties that filled their days, the hour for drill was fixed for five A.M.—an hour which recalls Scott's early-morning energies in his legal studies, and suggests that the secretary of the corps had some responsibility for this arrangement.

James Skene's account of him in this connection deserves quotation:

> "The part of quartermaster was purposely selected for him, that he might be spared the rough usage of the ranks; but, not withstanding his infirmity, he had a remarkably firm seat on horseback, and in all situations a fearless one: no fatigue ever seemed too much for him, and his zeal and animation served to sustain the enthusiasm of the whole corps, while his ready "mot a rire" kept up, in all, a degree of good-humour and relish for the service, without which the toil and privations of long daily drills would not easily have been submitted to by such a body of gentlemen. At every interval of exercise, the order, Sit at ease, was the signal for the quartermaster to lead the squadron to merriment; every eye was intuitively turned on 'Earl Walter', as he was familiarly called by his associates of that date, and his ready joke seldom failed to raise the ready laugh. He took his full share in all the labours and duties of the corps, had the highest pride in its progress and proficiency, and was such a trooper himself, as only a very powerful frame of body and the warmest zeal in the cause could have enabled any one to be."

The triple offices which Scott held at the first organisation of the regiment, for the existence of which his persistent energy was responsible, reminds us of the similar multiplicity of his official services to the Speculative Club. On this occasion, he found that he had undertaken more than it would be possible to continue permanently, and an arrangement was made for the paymaster's duties to be transferred to Mr. Colin Mackenzie. But it is amazing at this, as at every subsequent period of his life, to observe how much of his time (and often of his money also) was given to the service of others, or to occupations that brought no remuneration. It is obvious, from Skene's account, and from much other witness, that he was the life and inspiration of the regiment, though he had no thought to press for its higher dignities. At this time it seemed as though he would allow himself no time for solitary or introspective thought. He rose early: he read late. On a charger fitted for his unusual height and weight, which he had named Leonore, and the purchase of which had presented such difficulty that he had seriously thought of selling his collection of antique coins to acquire it, he appeared among his brother volunteers as of an inexhaustible vitality, and a good temper that nothing could overset.

It was so that he would appear to others through the vicissitudes of many future years. As they passed, it would become almost a routine with him to give his time and money to assist the troubles of others, and to keep his own to the privacy of his own heart. There would even be those in later days (but not who had known him) who would suggest that his passions were of no more than a moderate temperature. It is true that in the immense volume of his writings the allusion to periods—

"When on the weary night dawned wearier day,
And bitterer was the grief devoured alone,"

are very brief and few. But shallowness is a more talkative and more selfish thing.

CHAPTER XVII.

In the latter days of the reign of Louis XVI, there had been living in Lyons, with his wife and two young children, a M. Jean Charpentier, a government official of some wealth and position. Among his friends had been the Marquis of Downshire, who had stayed at his house for some time when travelling on the Continent. When the revolution broke out, M. Charpentier did not fly—he may probably have been in no condition of health to do so—but he prudently sent some of his money to England, about £4,000 in all.

The Marquis of Downshire was his good friend in the matter. He appears to have arranged its investment, part of the money being secured by a mortgage on his own estate. When her husband died, as he did shortly afterwards, Madame Charpentier left Lyons for Paris, and then fled with her two children to London, as the murderous horrors of the revolution darkened around her. Lord Downshire gave the fugitives shelter in his own house. The mother died almost immediately, and he acted from that time as the guardian of the two orphans who had been left on his hands. He appears to have acted throughout with kindness and probity. He educated the children wisely, and conserved their property. In due time, he procured for the boy, Charles Charpentier, an appointment under the East India Company, who in 1797 already held a good position as a commercial resident at Salem. It is probable that some of the children's original capital had been invested in connection with this appointment, subject to Charles contributing to his sister's support, for at this date we find that Charlotte Charpentier (or Carpenter, as she had now taken to writing it, in the English style) reckoned her income at £500 a year, part of which was from interest on secure investments, and the remainder dependent upon the regularity of her brother's remittances.

Charlotte's education had been entrusted to Miss Jane Nicholson, a daughter of the Dean of Exeter, and grand-daughter of William Nicholson, Bishop of Carlisle. The Bishop of Carlisle was dead, but Jane Nicholson still had friends or relatives in Carlisle with whom she kept up acquaintance. Charlotte's education was over, but Lord Downshire still retained Miss Nicholson's services as a companion for the lonely girl.

It followed from these circumstances that when Charlotte and Miss Nicholson took a holiday together in August of this year, Carlisle was the selected spot, from which they went to Gilsland, to spend some summer weeks among the beauties of the English lakes.

At the same time, the legal session at Edinburgh having closed in July, and the new yeomanry regiment having suspended its drills (after three weeks in camp at Musselburgh), John and Walter Scott, with Walter's friend, Adam Fergusson, came southward on a wandering holiday, stopping at several places before they put up their horses at a Gilsland hotel. The next morning Walter and Adam took a long ride together to explore the district in Walter's usual manner. Charlotte Carpenter was fond of riding. She had a slim figure, which looked well in a riding-habit, as she doubtless knew. There is no evidence that Miss Nicholson had a similar figure, or a similar liking for a horse's back. There is no evidence either way, beyond the fact that next morning Charlotte rode out alone. She was a dark girl by English, and still more by Scottish, standards. We have her son-in-law's testimony that her complexion was "of the clearest and lightest olive"; that her eyes were "large, deep-set and dazzling, of the finest Italian brown." The two young Scotsmen who reined up their horses to watch her ride must have seen more of her figure, and of jet-black hair that blew loose in the wind. From that hour Charlotte's fate was a settled thing.

Etiquette did not permit that the girl should be accosted on the lonely moorland. But she could be discreetly followed, and her dwelling marked down for a more circumspect approach. We do not know whether she knew that she was stalked, or disliked the experience, but they rounded her up satisfactorily in Gilsland; which prevented any necessity for changing their own location. There was a dance that night, at which, by whatever combination of chance and swift contriving, they were all present together.

John had found time to change into the scarlet splendours of his lieutenant's uniform. Adam had put on that of the volunteer regiment which Walter had founded. Walter was content with a more civilian aspect.

John danced with Charlotte. Adam danced with Charlotte. The lame Walter waited his time, and took her in to supper, as his patience gave him a claim to do.

A week or two later, he addressed his mother in the following letter.

"My dear Mother,

I should very ill deserve the care and affection with which you have ever regarded me, were I to neglect my duty so far as to omit consulting my father and you in the most important step which I can possibly take in life, and upon the success of which my future happiness must depend. It is with pleasure I think that I can avail myself of your advice and instructions in an affair of so great importance as that which I have at present on my hands. You will probably guess from this preamble that I am engaged in a matrimonial plan, which is really the case. Though my acquaintance with the young lady has not been of long standing, this circumstance is in some degree counterbalanced by the intimacy in which we have lived, and by the opportunities which that intimacy has afforded me of remarking her conduct and sentiments on many different occasions, some of which were rather of a delicate nature, so that in fact I have seen more of her during the few weeks we have been together than I could have done after a much longer acquaintance, shackled by the common forms of ordinary life. You will not expect from me a description of her person—for which I refer you to my brother, as also for a fuller account of all the circumstances attending the business than can be comprised in the compass of a letter. Without flying into raptures—for I must assure you that my judgement as well as my affections are consulted upon this occasion—without flying into raptures, then, I may safely assure you, that her temper is sweet and cheerful, her understanding good, and, what I know will give you pleasure, her principles of religion very serious. I have been very explicit with her upon the nature of my expectations, and she thinks she can accommodate herself to the situation which I should wish her to hold in society as my wife, which, you will easily comprehend, I mean should neither be extravagant nor degrading. Her fortune, though partly dependent upon—her brother, who is high in office at Madras, is very considerable—at present £500 a-year. This, however, we must, in some degree, regard as precarious—I mean to the full extent; and indeed, when you know her, you will not be surprised thatI regard this circumstance chiefly because it removes those prudential considerations which would otherwise render our union impossible for the present. Betwixt her income and my own professional exertions, I have little doubt we will be enabled to hold the rank in society which my family and situation entitle me to fill. Write to me very fully upon this important subject—send me your opinion, your advice, and, above all, your blessing."

The letter seems formal to the ideas and practices of today, but a consideration of the circumstances under which it was written, and the difficulties which had to be overcome, reveal it as a very diplomatic document. It does not palter with truth: its statements of fact—as far as they go—are explicit and exact. Neither does it suggest difficulty. Yet there is argument in every line. There is menace also, of a kind. For while it asks advice and even 'instructions', it has a tone of resolution which his mother knew him too well not to be able to understand. That it was addressed to her has been explained, perhaps rightly, as being due to the weakness of his father's health. But it might have been more natural to address it jointly, even under such circumstances. As it stands, his father is not ignored. The minimum of the filial deference of the period is observed. He would "neglect his duty" if he should omit to "consult" both parents upon a step so important to his own welfare. The girl's nationality is not mentioned. Her religion—by Heaven's mercy she was not a Catholic, but it is equally sure that she was not a Presbyterian—is only vaguely indicated. These things are left for John (who carried the letter) to explain.

For Walter did not go home himself. Neither did Charlotte return to London. She went to her friends in Carlisle. Walter found a lodging in the same place. He meant that there should be no mistake on this occasion. Neither mistake nor delay. And he had a double difficulty to overcome. He had to persuade Charlotte to a willingness to face life with him under the strange and perhaps repellent conditions of the cold northern capital, and he had to persuade his own relatives, not merely to a passive consent to the marriage, but to give his wife the reception that he was resolved that she should have. In the meantime he would neither risk leaving Charlotte, nor introduce her to Edinburgh without invitation, and assurance of welcome there.

In the result, he stayed in Carlisle till the end of September, when the opening of the Jedburgh court called for his presence. Charlotte stayed, too, treating her guardian in the same way. The matter must be settled by correspondence, unless he should come to her. Miss Nicholson doubtless stayed also, and made her own representations. There might be doubt in London and perturbation in Edinburgh, but there were two young people in Carlisle who meant to have their own way.

We may suppose that, in spite of the delays and expense of correspondence at that time, Walter's post-bag was heavy during those six weeks. The idea that he should marry a foreign woman whom he had only just met could not be well received in Edinburgh's rigid Calvinistic atmosphere. John may have said what he could in his brother's cause. He was a man of slow brain, but the women must have questioned him more than enough. He may have mentioned that her speech had a foreign accent; that her pronunciation was imperfect. She would always say 'dat' for 'that'. It was very different from the type of English which was spoken in George's Square.

People may admire such a girl's looks, but they don't marry

her if they are wise. They know too well what the French are.

In any case, what kind of wife would she be likely to make? With no common interests or sympathies, knowing nothing of the customs or conventions of the society to which she would be introduced? Probably she would waste, or quarrel, or sulk, or mope. She might even be faithless or run away.

Is it surprising if Mr. Walter Scott senior intimated that any rash and sudden step would incur his severe displeasure? If others, even Christian Rutherford, even Jane Cranston (now busily preparing for her own marriage), wrote in remonstrance, or with a hesitation that was too easy to understand?

There are families in which marital disaster is a frequent incident, and is regarded as an almost normal mischance upon the journey of life. There are others in which you may search in all their branches, and for many generations, and find no matrimonial troubles, though they may have their share of crime and follies of other kinds. The Scotts had always been of the latter category. We have seen already that they chose their wives well.

All the correspondence which passed has not been preserved, and we must guess with equity, if at all; but one fact stands out in unmistakable significance. There came a point when Walter wrote that he intended to marry Miss Carpenter, and that as soon as he could prevail upon her to attend the ceremony. But he would not bring her to Edinburgh unless he were assured that she would be received in the right way. Otherwise, he would go with her to the Colonies, and make a career there.

He could not have written this unless he had ascertained her willingness to adventure with him. In fact, she may have thought the programme at least as attractive as that of settling down in that dull northern atmosphere, among people who were so plainly reluctant to make her one of themselves.

The moment was critical, both for those most concerned, and for a large part of the world's reading during the succeeding century. But courage and resolution conquered, as they most often do. Edinburgh answered with a flag of truce, if not of surrender. Walter, who had emphasised his determination by returning from Jedburgh to Carlisle, instead of proceeding to Edinburgh in the normal course of his legal procession, now agreed to come home. He fulfilled his usual attendances at the Court during the latter part of the autumn session, and returned to Carlisle at its close, in time to marry Charlotte Carpenter in St Mary's Church on December 24, 1797. He had successfully carried out his purpose without the risk that would have been involved in a meeting between Miss Carpenter and the Edinburgh ladies before the event had become irrevocable, and he had the promise that she should be received into the family when he brought her home.

CHAPTER XVIII.

It has been too customary to write of Charlotte Scott in a tone of disparagement, as though a prosaic marriage had followed flatly after a romantic love. But the evidence is overwhelmingly contrary to this ungenerous fiction.

It is obviously true that Charlotte could not have her husband's interest in the antiquities of Scotland, or the rude spirit of its Border ballads. She was of another tradition, another race. Coming to Edinburgh, as she did, to live the life of his own people, she risked more, and surrendered more, than he had occasion to do.

It may have been a fact, when he waked her up during the night in the excitement of discovering the meaning of a burn's name, that she failed to duplicate his own emotion; but the evidence that they were good comrades and devoted lovers to the hour of her distant death is both direct and indirect, and the indirect evidence is of the strongest kind.

It is a fact of the highest significance that, from the date of his marriage, Scott's genius asserts itself in his verse as it had never done previously. The advance commences almost at once, and is continuous. There was promise before: there is to be performance now. Whatever other effects his marriage may have had, it did not stifle his ambition, nor divert his mind from his old pursuits, nor reduce the quality of his imaginative work.

During the five previous years, he had planned and dreamed and accumulated. Now plans became actions, dreams realities, the accumulations of yesterday were to be the building materials of tomorrow. Marriage brought happiness: it was also to bring success.

When they first came to Edinburgh, they went into a temporary lodging in George Street, the impetuosity of Scott's assault upon the citadel of the position not having allowed sufficient time for the preparation of a home to which he could take his bride. Not that he had neglected this aspect of the enterprise he had undertaken. He had rented a little house in South Castle Street during the few weeks that he had been in Edinburgh, and some furnishing preparations had been made, but it was not ready for occupation—a circumstance about which Charlotte may have been well content. She had her own ideas as to what a home should be, which she might prefer to Walter's, and certainly to that of the female members of his family, however kindly their help may have been given. The quickly-captured girl had shown some disposition to protest already against the strength and swiftness of the stream on which she was carried. 'I will give you a little hint—that is, not to put so many *musts* in your letters—it is beginning *rather too soon*.' So she wrote during those brief weeks of November separation. She may not have minded those musts very greatly, coming from him, but she would be less complaisant to the interference of others. By his evident unwillingness to take the risk of her meeting his family before the irrevocable ceremony, she was coming to a home that she had not seen. She must have been well content that the completion of its arrangements should be left to her.

Some of the means of its ultimate furnishing probably came from her own resources. It is certain that her money provided the larger and more certain part of the joint income on which their housekeeping was commenced, though it did not long continue to do so. There had been negotiations with London as well as

Edinburgh, the success of which had been vital to the celerity of the impetuous marriage, in which Charlotte must have done her own part. But it is certain that Walter had substantial assistance at this time from his father's purse, such as he might fairly expect to receive when once the main point had been conceded. John was not living on his regimental pay. No officers did at that period. He must have drawn on his father with regularity. Tom had an income from the business. He was already married. He had not furnished his home from the savings of his apprentice years. Walter had remained at home. He had lived without cost to himself. His legal fees had been for his own pocket. All his life he was without personal extravagances. But his income had not been sufficient to allow of saving, except for immediate objects. Three or four years ago he had written to Shortreed that he was saving fees so that he could have his next Liddesdale holiday on the back of his own horse, instead of having to borrow from a friend in Jedburgh, as he had done previously. In the spring of this year, he had considered the sale of his precious collection of coins when he had been in difficulty for the price of a military charger.

But his father had substantial resources in these days, and for some help he could fairly look. Nor can we doubt that it was readily given. Love and pride would unite to see that, in the carefully-worded phrase with which he had opened the negotiations, the conditions to which he should introduce his wife should be "neither extravagant or degrading".

It says much for Charlotte that she succeeded in conforming to the customs and prejudices of the strange city into which she had come sufficiently to establish friendly, if not intimate associations with her new relatives. There must have been forbearances on both sides. Lockhart says quaintly that she had "some little leaning to the pomps and vanities of the world," but she "made up her mind to find her happiness in better things." It is unlikely that either she or Walter would have described the position quite in that way. She had been used to spending her money more freely than she could now afford to do, and she showed the practical sense and economy of her own nation in her control of expenditure in the new circumstances of her life. Frugal, critical Scottish eyes watched, and approved.

When they were able to move from the George Street lodging, and she became the mistress of her own home, she scandalised Edinburgh by living in the drawing-room, which should only have been entered (except to dust it) on Sunday afternoons, and some occasional ceremonies. Such are the pitfalls yawning for the feet of those who marry into strange lands. Yet if we give sympathy, it may be misdirected. She met the position with some courage, some gaiety, some concessions to the opinions of others, and some occasional stubbornness when she felt that a limit should not be passed. She would meet the later troubles of life with the same resolute spirit (Scott was to write of her, on the day after her death, as "the sharer of my thoughts and counsels, who could always talk down my sense of the calamitous apprehensions which break the heart that must bear them alone"); she would meet that death ("You all have such melancholy faces!") with the same laughing eyes.

She made many friends. Walter's invalid sister extended her passionate love for her favourite brother to include his wife.

His own friends received her with enthusiasm. The legal fraternity of the Mountain had just been deprived of the two ladies who had been most closely associated with it. Jane Cranston had married, as had William Erskine's sister. They found that Mrs. Walter Scott would entertain them gladly. The officers of the Cavalry regiment which he had done so much to create were another circle of acquaintance to which she was welcome. They formed a club, meeting weekly for dinner at each others' houses. The two circles (several belonged to both) consisted of young men of limited means, of busy days, of high ambitions which were realised in a surprising proportion of instances. Broadly considered, they were of good characters and an exceptional intellectual standard. Charlotte was fortunate in her husband's friends.

They went often to the theatre, usually with William Erskine for company. It had been one of Walter's pleasures ever since, and as often as, his means permitted. It was an amusement of which Charlotte was passionately fond. Swiftly and happily the winter passed, and when spring came they found a cottage at Lasswade, six miles out in the Esk valley, and Scott forgot his disposition to wander over the country, as he tamed its garden to order, and Charlotte made its single living-room suitable to entertain their friends.

CHAPTER XIX.

In the spring of 1797 there were few men whose literary reputation stood higher than that of Matthew Gregory Lewis. Time has shortened that stature, as it has laughed at his own diminutive proportions. To do him justice, we must look at what he did in relation to his own time. He had written a romance, *The Monk*, which was of a universal popularity. It had given him the nickname of Monk Lewis, by which he became more generally known. He was a lover of poetry, and, if not a great poet, he had a sound technique, and he did not attempt more than he was capable of doing, which is not a universal wisdom among men of literature. He was an enthusiastic collector of ballads. He had a design of bringing out a volume of such pieces which was to be entitled *Tales of Terror*, for which he was collecting materials. William Erskine went up to London, and met him there. He talked about his friend, Walter Scott, and showed the two translated ballads which had been so abortively printed. He said there were others to be obtained from the same source.

Correspondence followed. From the cottage of Lasswade, there came a packet of manuscript ballads, complete or in draft, such as Scott had written at the time, and considered suitable to offer for such a collection. Lockhart, as is usual, is unfair to both men in the relations that followed. He first sneers at Lewis's literary status, depreciating it below its actual level, and then makes the absurd suggestion that Scott owed him a heavy debt because the reading of Lewis's *"Ballads of Alonso the Brave* etc., had rekindled effectually in his breast the spark of poetical ambition." If Scott had needed a 'spark' to be 'rekindled' by such means he would not have been a poet at all. But, as in other instances where Lockhart represents Scott as a weak vessel whose course is steered by stronger wills, or who is inspired by stronger creative impulses than his own, examination shows it to be no more than random assertion, as entirely without external evidence as it is without inherent probability.

Scott was the younger, though the abler man. When Lewis came to Edinburgh in the autumn, and asked him to dinner at his hotel, he was naturally pleased, or even excited at the opportunity. To have responded differently would have shown an absurd conceit, which Scott never had. That he was generous in his estimate of the abilities of others, sometimes to excess, was true throughout his life. But in this case he was in the position of a young officer, inexperienced and unproved, who is noticed by a famous and victorious general, and invited to join his staff.

Lewis stayed for some time in the neighbourhood of Edinburgh, and Scott and he saw much of each other. Lewis visited him at Musselburgh, lodging with him in narrow quarters, while he was in training with his regiment there. They were together (probably on an invitation of Scott's procuring) at Dalkeith House. The Scotts had improved acquaintance, during the summer at Lasswade, with the young Duke and Duchess of Buccleuch, Dalkeith House being only two or three miles down the Esk valley, as they had with the Clerks at Pennycuick, about twice as far in the opposite direction, and with other of Scott's numberless friends whose country houses were within riding distance. It was on this occasion that Saunder's caricature of Monk Lewis, representing him as a dark-lanterned, cloak-muffled cut-throat was passed round, with exclamations of appreciation at the likeness achieved. The Duke of Bucclench objected "Like Mat Lewis! Why that picture's like a man," and was disconcerted on turning round to find that Lewis was standing beside him. The remark was, of course, in derision of one who Scott describes as "the least man I ever saw, to be strictly well and neatly made."

Lewis went back to London before the end of the year, taking with him a translation of Goethe's tragedy, 'Goetz,' which Scott had now completed. His friendly interest was successful in placing it almost immediately with a London publisher, and actually inducing him to give £25 for the first edition. This was in January. The play appeared in the following month, Lewis making a better bargain for the unknown author than he would have been likely to be able to do for himself, had stipulated for a further £25 if a second edition should be required. "I have made him" (the publisher, Bell) "distinctly understand that, if you accept so small a sum, it will be only because this is your first publication," Lewis wrote, when sending on the offer of the first payment. So it was, on the London market.

There was no call for a second edition. Lockhart suggests the explanation to lie in the change of literary fashion which was tiring of some of the absurdities of contemporary German literature, and rejected all indiscriminately in its revulsion of feeling. So it may have been, but no explanation is really needed. Scott's pre-eminence was not in the translation of German drama, and the demand for such a work from a new author was not likely to be large.

Still, its acceptance and publication was a success, through whatever influence it had been negotiated. The friendship of Mat Lewis had borne an early fruit, and it may have been the deciding argument in the resolution to visit London which was almost immediately taken. *Goetz* was published in February. In the following month, Mr. & Mrs. Walter Scott were in London together, sharing M. Dumergue's hospitality. It was the first time he had been there since Janet had stopped with him on the road to Bath. He had a short period of exploration among its historical and architectural treasures; some pleasant meetings, on Lewis's introduction, with London literary circles; others, doubtless, among Charlotte's earlier friends. But the visit was quickly and abruptly terminated by a letter which brought the news of his father's death.

He had sent to Lewis, or left with him a play, *The House of Aspen*, which had also been written during the first year of his married life. It is said to have been brought to Kemble's notice, and actually reached the point of rehearsal, though it was never acted in public. It is unlikely that it would have had any popular success. Its chief interest is in its lyrics; and their importance is of a negative kind. They show that the almost flawless perfection of form which Scott ultimately attained in this class of composition, a perfection which is so complete as to appear effortless, was not reached without practice, by the path of comparative failure, which is the common experience.

CHAPTER XX.

Walter Scott senior died of apoplexy in his seventieth year. He had survived several strokes, beneath which body and mind had gradually given way, and the task of nursing him had been a heavy strain upon his wife and invalid daughter during the previous winter. The manner of his death was that which was most usual at that time in the class to which he belonged. The fact that he survived to the completion of the seventh decade, particularly when consideration is given to the sedentary life he lived in contrast to that of his Border ancestors, gives some support to the abstemious reputation that he enjoyed. His widow, as is common in the family records of this period, survived him for nearly twenty healthy and happy years, modern prejudice would say in spite of the large family that she had borne in her youth. We must explain that as we please; but the habit of taking alcoholic refreshment in large and continual quantities appears to have been masculine rather than feminine, and paralytic deaths among the women were proportionately infrequent.

Mr. Scott left a sufficient capital sum to provide his widow with an income of about £300 a year, on which she lived in a quiet and comfortable independence, refusing resolutely to have it supplemented in the days of her son's prosperity. Beyond this, Tom had the business, and though the residue which remained for division among the other children was less than had been expected, it doubtless eased the position of all at the time, though with a finality which closed any future expectations from the source on which they had been used to rely.

The home of a generation in George's Square was closed and dismantled. Walter and Charlotte offered his mother and sister the hospitality of Lasswade, in which narrow quarters they remained together till the autumn came, and the cottage was abandoned for the winter months in the usual way, though somewhat later than usual, for it was here in October that Charlotte's first baby—Charlotte Sophia—was born.

It was natural, during a summer in which Mrs. Scott and Anne were with them at Lasswade, and Charlotte was approaching motherhood, that Walter did not wander far from his own home. He reduced his annual Liddesdale raid with Sheriff Shortreed to the limit of a single week—the conditions of life in the desolate moorland country being too primitive for Charlotte to have been his companion on that occasion—and they improved acquaintance with many friends in the Eskdale district. There was a short visit to Robert Scott at Kelso, during which a printing order was given to James Ballantyne, of which more must be said. There was a visit also to Bothwell Castle, at the invitation of Lady Frances, the Duke of Buccleuch's sister, who had just married Lord Douglas, and who did not allow her marriage to break the friendship which had been formed during the previous summer. There was even a proposal during this visit that the Scotts should give up the Lasswade cottage, and accept the free tenancy of a little house which had been built within the ruins of Craignethan Castle, which was the property of Lord Douglas. The offer, and the fact that it was not rejected, show how close and cordial was the friendship already established with the Buccleuch family. That it was afterwards abandoned was due to other developments to which we must come in due order. It was a year of many events, and in which the seeds of the future were freely sown.

It was a year of importance also in Scott's literary history, for it saw an output of original ballads in which we may observe him gradually evolving the forms of creative art in which he was to show himself as a pioneer of literature, doing that which had never been done before, and which subsequent imitations have not approached to equal. They are of sufficient importance to deserve some detailed consideration, which it may be convenient to give before coming to the events of the autumn months.

These ballads, or some of them, were sent to Lewis, either for his opinion, or as possible contributions to the *Tales of Wonder*, which had still not materialised. They resulted in correspondence between the two poets, in which Lewis took the stand of a prosodic purist, and was severely critical of Scott's looser or more experimental constructions. He was partly right and partly wrong; and so far as he was right, Scott showed himself receptive to his ideas, and may have consciously modified his methods of composition in consequence. The difference may be briefly summarised by saying that Lewis attached too much importance to metrical and rhythmical regularity, and Scott, his poetical appreciation nurtured on old ballads which were often crude and irregular in construction, was too complaisant to defects of form, which are not beauties in themselves, though their tatters may disclose a loveliness which better garments might hide.

The first of these ballads to reach a complete and final form appears to have been *Glenfinlas*; the most interesting and significant were *The Eve of St. John* and *The Grey Brother*: and the most technically satisfying was *The Fire King*.

Glenfinlas begins well;

"O hone a rie! O hone a rie!
The pride of Albin's line is o'er."

but there is little more to be said in its favour. It is far too long, and its horror is diffused and elaborated, where its presentation should be swift and simple. The fault is partly one of construction, and partly a defect of the subject itself, which has not sufficient length or variety of incident to supply material for a ballad. It is fit rather for use as a poetic reference, or allusion, of the length of a few lines, in the course of a longer poem.

Scott made the mistake here that he and Wordsworth made together at a later day. A man died on Helvellyn, and a dog was found long afterwards watching beside his skeleton. The subject was utterly unsuitable for a poem, because anything worth saying about it could be said in a single stanza. They both tried, and they both failed. They wrote the kinds of verse which were natural to either when he had nothing to say. Scott climbed the dark brow of the mighty Helvellyn, and Wordsworth asked anxiously, What is the creature doing here? Neither poem is worth reading, and, had they been the work of unknown authors, neither would have been remembered for a week. They are not so much examples of how not to do it, as what not to attempt to do.

Glenfinlas is a ballad of the same brand. Scott must have felt that he hammered on cold iron, though he may have blamed himself for the poor craftsmanship that resulted. There is one stanza that lives in the reader's memory—which must have been a moonlight memory to himself of when he had wandered in the Highland night, and seen the solitary expanses of lake and mountain outstretched beneath a cloud-crossed moon.

> "The moon, half-hid in silvery flakes,
> Afar her dubious radiance shed,
> Quivering on Katrine's distant lakes,
> And resting on Benledi's head."

The stanza is profoundly significant of Scott's genius, and to consider it is to understand why his descriptions of scenery mean so much to some, and so little to others.

His great contemporaries, Coleridge, Shelley, Wordsworth, and Byron, are all conscious of the natural beauty around them, and all have the skill to draw it. But, in their different ways, they make it reflective of their own moods. Scott loved it simply and utterly for what it was. There is less ego in his cosmos. Where they question, or pose, or fret, he accepts and is satisfied. It may be difficult to consider this difference and remain in doubt as to which is the saner or nobler attitude.

There are people who are not content with a picture of lake or woodland unless the foreground is disturbed by the obstruction of a human figure. They will be likely to agree that Wordsworth is the greater poet. There are others who admire Wordsworth also, but who keep him apart in their minds, lest he should appear dwarfed by too close a comparison with a loftier stature.

The Gray Brother is deformed in another way. Its opening and closing stanzas are effective, and could not easily be bettered. Its abrupt close is excellent. It would have been a better ballad if two-thirds had been lopped away.

> "Who knows not Melville's beechy grove,
> And Roslin's rocky glen,
> Dalkeith, which all the virtues love,
> And classic Hawthornden?"

The answer to this question is obvious, and not worth giving. But—and that is the real criticism—it has nothing to do with the subject of the ballad. Scott was simply inserting the addresses of the good friends he visited during the summer months at Lasswade, the beautiful situations of which, and their romantic traditions, he admired and loved. His method is emerging, but his genius has not yet fully controlled it to successful ends.

The Fire King is a ballad of a different kind. It has no local background. It is pure imagination throughout. It has a dramatic theme, competently and completely handled. It is not Scott at his greatest, but of its kind it would not be easy to equal, and of itself it would not be easy to improve. It has a separate interest in the fact that Scott is seen for the first time handling a popular metre with the originality of a prosodic genius which was still only experimenting. The anaepest has a treacherous habit of inopportune levity. It gives the impression that it would dance on its mother's grave. In Scott's time, when poetic style was struggling to escape from the formalism of the previous century, the anaepest was used by almost every poet, major and minor, with disastrous consequences. There were few solemnities on which it did not obscenely or absurdly dance, in utter ignorance of its own grotesqueness. Scott controls it to his own mood in this ballad:

> "The battle is over on Bethsaida's plain.—
> Oh, who is yon Paynim lies stretched mid the slain?
> And who is yon Page lying cold at his knee?—
> Oh, who but Count Albert and fair Rosalie!
> The Lady was buried in Salem's blest bound,
> The Count he was left to the vulture and hound:
> Her soul to high mercy Our Lady did bring;
> His went on the blast to the dread Fire-King."

It is the same metre that he was afterwards to use in a new way, a kind of heroic levity, in *Lochinvar*, in *Hail to the Chief who in triumph advances,* and in *When the dawn on the mountains*:

> For the rights of fair England that broadsword he draws,
> Her King is his leader, her Church is his cause;
> His watchword is honour, his pay is renown—
> God strike with the gallant that strikes for the Crown!

Scott's innovations gave the anaepest a new place in English poetry: they blaze the trail for Swinburne's intricate cadences: in Kipling's ballads their defiant note was sounded again.

This is not an essay on prosody, and it would be too long a diversion to probe the subtle vowel uses and points of accentuation on which the successful use of the anaepest depends, if it is to avoid being a jog or a jerk—they depend primarily upon the facts, which are not always recognised by teachers of prosody, that English accents do not always fall upon the centres of the syllables which they stress, and that those syllables are not merely long and short, but of many differing lengths—but it is impossible to do justice to Scott as an artist in the music of words without recognising how numerous were his successful experiments, and how much he broadened the bases of English verse.

The Eve of Saint John stands apart from the other ballads which we know to have been written during this year, not only for itself, but because of the method of its production, which is worth some detailed examination. Its genesis was casual. The ruins of Smailholm Tower rose from the rock which overlooked the farm of Sandy-Knowe. They were one of the earliest memories of Scott's infant years. They were dear to him for their romantic memories, and for the associations of his own family. He saw signs of dilapidations which he asked his Harden kinsman, Hugh Scott, who owned the property, to repair. The reply, not perhaps seriously meant, was that a ballad must be the price. Scott accepted the condition, and *The Eve of St. John* was the result. Lockhart says that he actually wrote it at Mertoun House, but this should not be taken too literally. It is not off-hand work. It is not only that it is of very skilful dramatic construction, nor that it has varieties of melody in the changing forms of its stanzas, such as do not appear in a too hasty composition: it is that the tale itself is a made thing. Scott did not know any legend of the tower suitable for such purpose. For the first time, we can watch him collecting from the stored resources of his own mind to make a new tale, and to supply the incidents and background which it requires.

The central idea—that of the return of the murdered lover—is from an old Irish tradition. The idea of the nun of Dryburgh who 'ne'er looked upon the sun,' had an actual and recent parallel there. The placing of the event in the middle of the sixteenth century gave a plausible reason for the Baron's absence: an opportunity to use the call of war for the settlement of a private quarrel. The battle of Ancrum Moor, an historic event dimly indicated in the background, gives a suitable atmosphere, and verisimilitude to the supernatural tale. And the fact that it is left as a mere background shows that Scott was finding by practice the importance of form, even in the apparent looseness of the construction which this ballad wears, and which Mat Lewis, printing it afterwards in his *Tales of Wonder*, must have regarded as evidence that Scott was beyond his teaching, in spite of the courteous deference of the letters which acknowledged the advice he gave.

And the temptation to extend the references to Ancrum Moor must have been a strong one. Scott had been over the ground in the course of his Liddesdale 'raids'. It was a battle in which his own clan—the Scotts of Buccleuch and Harden—played an honourable and decisive part. It held none of the bitterness of the memory of the time when Teviotdale and Liddesdale had been engaged in the civil strife which was to be recorded deathlessly in the *Lay of the Last Minstrel*.

> When Home and Douglas in the van
> Bore down Buccleuch's retiring clan,
> Till gallant Cessford's heartblood dear
> Reeked on dark Elliot's Border spear.

For at Ancrum Moor, Teviotdale came to the support of Liddesdale, and they fought and conquered together....

Lord Evers had a dreaded name in the Border country. It was not his first raid into Scotland when he came at the head of a little army in which there were 3,000 foreign mercenaries, and 700 renegade Scottish borderers, including the broken Armstrong clan, supporting his own English followers, who were estimated at 1,500 men. He penetrated as far north as Melrose, which he sacked for the second time in two years, and retreated, heavy with spoil. Too weak to attack, too bitter to let him go, Earl Douglas hung on his rear.

Lord Evers did not want to fight. He had nothing to gain by

that. He had done all that he came to do. His eyes were turned towards the Cheviot Hills, and the safety of Cumberland. But he halted on Ancrum Moor, as though hesitant: no one will ever know why. It was his business to get home. It does not follow that he was wrong. He may have thought it too great a risk to descend to the Teviot ford with Douglas around his rear. He offered battle upon the moor. He commanded a force which evidently did not want to fight, and he had a difficult choice.

While he halted, Douglas was joined by Sir Walter Scott of Buccleuch. He rode in with his own Scotts and those of Harden. The force was not large, but the Scotts had a name that gave confidence. It also appeared that the Sir Walter of that time was a man of brains. He proposed a plan of action to Douglas, which is not very clear, as Lesley gives it, but it was common talk that it won the battle, for which Sir Walter had the praise at the last.

There was to be going on and off hills, and a pretended flight, and Lord Evers was to do most of the running about (particularly uphill) and at last, when he was quite blown, and had the sun in his eyes, he was to find that the battle wasn't over, but just about to begin.

The event worked out according to plan, which such tactics very seldom do, and when they saw how things were likely to go, the 700 renegade Scots settled matters by changing sides once again. That was the end. The mercenaries bolted: the Scots turned their coats: the English died where they stood, Lord Evers and his son heading the list.

Even a quarter of a millennium later, it was a good tale for the Scotts to tell. Liddesdale and Teviotdale had joined forces and triumphed together, and it was Teviotdale that had the honour in the mouths of men. That was better than when Teviotdale had gone down in battle before the Liddesdale spears

> "Till Mathouse burn to Melrose ran,
> All purple with their blood."

It was a good thought on Scott's part to use this muster for Ancrum Moor as an excuse for the Baron to arm himself and ride off on an errand of private vengeance, but the temptation to allow the battle to invade the foreground of the tale must have been great, and it shows a growing skill of construction that he kept it in the exact place that it ought to occupy.

He used the old flexible ballad metre, with its optional internal rhymes, which can be so poor or perfect a thing according to the handling it receives, and he did this with an independence of Lewis's theories of regularity which showed that, however courteous or even deferential he might be to the opinions of the older man, he had sufficient independence to develop his own work on his own lines.

The stanzas, considered separately, have individual beauties, and single lines that remain in the memory. The whole ballad has vigour and dramatic intensity, though it is less perfect, at almost every point of judgement, than some others—notably *Alice Brand*—that were to follow.

But it is in the selection of materials of fact and fiction from diverse sources out of the stores he had accumulated, and blending them into an artistic unity, that this ballad is not only an achievement in itself, but an indication of the method by which he would go on to much greater triumphs.

CHAPTER XXI.

The year 1799, which witnessed the death of Scott's father (too soon to know the justification of those early wanderings which had vexed his mind), the publication of the Goetz translation, and the birth of his first child, was momentous in two other directions.

During that week in the early autumn which was spent with Captain Robert at Kelso, Mr. Walter Scott had a visitor. The Editor of the *Kelso Mail*, Mr. James Ballantyne, a young man of his own age, called to request an article from him on a legal subject of topical interest, with which he was particularly competent to deal. Scott agreed to write it, and to bring it in to the *Mail* office on completion. The importance of this incident may be exaggerated. The two men had known each other from boyhood, James having been a pupil of Mr. Lancelot Whale when Walter had attended his school during the summer that intervened between his High School and College courses. After that, James had come to Edinburgh, continuing his studies there, his father (a "decent shopkeeper" Lockhart calls him, which is praise by implication, though it holds a sneer) intending him for the legal profession. But this plan was abandoned, and James on his return to his native town, founded the *Kelso Mail*; laying down his own plant, and being proprietor, printer and editor of this local weekly.

Scott, as we know, was a frequent visitor at Kelso, first with his Aunt Janet, and then at Rosebank with Captain Robert, and the schoolboy acquaintance had been kept up.

In the light of after-knowledge, James Ballantyne's call at Rosebank may seem to be of a decisive importance to many lives, but this may be an appearance only. Had he not called, Scott might have called upon him. Anyway, when he did so, he not only had the promised article in his pocket, he had some of his ballads also, to which the talk turned. Lockhart's hearsay account of this interview derived from James Ballantyne, is the best we have. He says:

> "Scott, carrying his article himself to the printing-office, took with him also some of his recent pieces, designed to appear in Lewis's Collection. With these, especially, as his Memorandum says, the 'Morlachian fragment after Goethe,' Ballantyne was charmed, and he expressed his regret that Lewis's book was so long in appearing. Scott talked of Lewis with rapture; and, after reciting some of his stanzas, said—"I ought to apologise to you for having troubled you with anything of my own when I had things like this for your

ear."—"I felt at once," says Ballantyne, "that his own verses were far above what Lewis could ever do, and though, when I said this, he dissented, yet he seemed pleased with the warmth of my approbation." At parting, Scott threw out a casual observation, that he wondered his old friend did not try to get some little booksellers' work, "to keep his types in play during the rest of the week." Ballantyne answered that such an idea had not before occurred to him—that he had no acquaintance with the Edinburgh 'trade'; but, if he had, his types were good, and he thought he could afford to work more cheaply than town-printers. Scott, "with his good-humoured smile," said—"You had better try what you can do. You have been praising my little ballads; suppose you print off a doze copies or so of as many as will make a pamphlet, sufficient to let my Edinburgh acquaintances judge of your skill for themselves." Ballantyne assented; and I believe exactly twelve copies of William and Ellen, The Fire-King, The Chase, and a few more of those pieces, were thrown off accordingly, with the title (alluding to the long delay of Lewis's Collection) of "Apology for Tales of Terror—1799". This first specimen of a press, afterwards so celebrated, pleased Scott; and he said to Ballantyne—"I have been for years collecting old Border ballads, and I think I could, with little trouble, put together such a selection from them as might make a neat little volume, to sell for four or five shillings. I will talk to some of the booksellers about it when I get to Edinburgh, and if the thing goes on, you shall be the printer."

It is improbable that this account of a conversation which is based on James Ballantyne's recollection at a much later date has more than an approach to accuracy, but it is clear that Scott did not give him a printing order merely because he admired his types. It is clear that since his hurried, prematurely-ended visit to London, he had been steadily occupied in the production of ballads such as might (he hoped) be accepted by Lewis for inclusion in the *Tales of Terror*. He had worked systematically to complete those that had been in draft, and he had written others. His correspondence with Lewis shows that he had the definite aim of producing such as would be acceptable for the projected book, the delay of which was prolonged.

It is clear also that since the date of his marriage (if not earlier) he had fixed his mind upon winning honours in the field of literature. Ballantyne may have got a contrary impression, but he was not on terms of intimacy with him at this period, and allowance must be made for Scott's habitual reticence where his personal feelings or projects were concerned. Lockhart recognises this as a probability, in spite of his tendency to represent Scott as a more or less plastic centre of surrounding influences. If he goes widely wrong, it is in the assumption that his ambition was not known among his inner circle of friends. He produces some evidence to support this conclusion, but it may be argued that it should be placed in the opposite scale.

There is the letter from Mr. Kerr, which congratulates Scott upon some increase of business this autumn at the Jedburgh Court, and continues:

> "Go on: and with your strong sense and hourly ripening knowledge, that you must rise to the top of the tree in the Parliament House in due season, I hold as certain as that Murray died Lord Mansfield. But don't let many an Ovid, or rather many a Burns (which is better), be lost in you. I rather think men of business have produced as good poetry in their by-hours as the professed regulars; and I don't see any sufficient reason why Lord President Scott should not be a famous poet (in the vacation time), when we have seen a President Montesquieu step so nobly beyond the trammels in the *Esprit des Loix*. I suspect Dryden would

have been a happier man had he had your profession. The reasoning talents visible in his verses assure me that he would have ruled in Westminster Hall as easily as he did at Button's, and he might have found time enough besides for everything that one really honours his memory for."

Lockhart recognises that this letter expresses an opinion on which Scott had so far acted, and continued throughout his career, but Lockhart may have been less ready to accept its wisdom. He was himself a professional literary man, who doubtless regarded his occupation as too exacting to be shared with other business interests. This may be true in many instances, and of literary work of diverse kinds. But so far as poetry is concerned, Kerr expressed a truth which many professional poets might have learnt to their own benefit, and that of their art. The writing of poetry cannot be a full-time occupation for any lifetime, nor a legitimate excuse for continued idleness; and if it be used in that way the results may be of a deplorable kind.

Chaucer, Dante, Spencer, Shakespeare, Milton—they were all men of affairs, who could show records of careers of honour, apart from the art they loved; and the influence of those activities is evident in the quality of the work they left. Those who make the writing of poetry an excuse for standing aside from the adventure of life, or for failing to take its fences properly, may produce work in consequence which is of an inferior beauty or a lessened authority. The best "professional" poets have usually buried their excellencies amid quantities of versifying which are not worth reading, and which a busier man would not have written at all.

Kerr states a more disputable opinion when he asserts that Scott was likely to rise to 'the top of the tree' in Parliament House. It is improbable that he would ever have made a great name as an advocate, but the qualities which unfitted him for that occupation would have made him an excellent judge. He was a sound lawyer. He was sympathetic. He had a profound knowledge of human nature, and an exceptional capacity for judging character; and he would never have allowed his sympathies to deflect his judgement.

Had he not turned from poetry to fiction, and found it a more time-absorbing occupation, it is more than likely that Scotland's greatest poet would also have been known as one of her greatest judges; but his promotion would, in the first instance, have been by patronage, rather than as the reward of forensic triumphs.

This letter of Kerr's, whatever be thought of the advice he gives, shows rather that Scott was already regarded by his friends as destined for a literary career, than that it was a future which even he himself had not begun to contemplate seriously.

He went to Ballantyne with the ballads in his pocket—and it is difficult to avoid the conclusion that he had the thought of ordering them to be printed before he entered the door. The title shows what was in his mind. They were an apology for the non-appearance of the book to which he was to have been an important contributor, and which had been a subject of expectation among his friends ever since Monk Lewis had visited them nearly twelve months ago....

The other event which belongs to the close of this year, and which was to have many after-consequences, arose from the unexpected death of Mr. Andrew Plummer, another antiquarian-scholar with whom Scott had established a familiar intimacy, and who held the office of Sheriff of Selkirkshire. The duties of such an office were not heavy, and it was a life-appointment, carrying a salary of £300 a year. There was no doubt of Scott's suitability for the position, in ability, in character, and in legal knowledge. It was such a position as was often found in those days (and still is in the United States) to provide means of livelihood for men of literature, leaving them the leisure which their work requires. Joined to Charlotte's income, which was being regularly paid, the money he had received at his father's death, and his earnings at the Bar, it might seem sufficient to secure him from financial anxiety as long as his life should last. It would be congenial work, and the appointment would be very opportune now that his first child was born, and the question must arise of how long the Lasswade cottage would give sufficient accommodation for the summer months.

An appointment of this kind was, at the time, in the gift of the Crown, and its vacancy was the occasion of a political scramble, in which it was likely to fall to the man who had the most and the loudest friends. It is a method of appointment which is, at least, superior to that of a competitive examination, and though some scandals resulted, it was unusual for a man obviously unsuitable to be able to secure sufficiently numerous and powerful nominations. In Scott's case, though he felt an enduring sense of obligation to a large number of people for the result of their concentrated activities, it must have been a walkover from the first. His services in promoting the formation of the Yeomanry regiment were alone sufficient, with his personal qualifications, to give him a claim which it would be difficult to ignore. He was widely known among the most influential in political, legal, and military circles in Scotland, and universally popular. The Duke of Buccleuch, the young Earl of Dalkeith, Lord Montague, and a dozen others united their efforts. It is an incidental evidence of Scott's numberless friendships that Mr. Henry Dundas (Viscount Melville) who had control of the Crown patronage in Scotland, found the nomination supported by his oldest son (who had known Scott at the High School), and his two nephews, Robert Dundas, the Lord Advocate, and William Dundas, the Secretary to the Board of Control.

With this din in his ears, Mr. Henry Dundas, who had himself (of course) met Mr. Walter Scott previously, and been favourably impressed, made the recommendation, and on December 16th, 1799, the patent of appointment was formally issued, and Scott was in office as Sheriff.

The appointment necessitated the refusal of the offer of the summer residence at Craignethan. Strictly, it required that there should be actual residence in the county for not less than four months in the year, but it was not until the Lord Lieutenant of Selkirkshire had made a formal protest, about three years later, that Scott fulfilled this condition. Until the summer of 1804 he continued to reside at Lasswade so far as he was at home during the summer months. He visited Jedburgh regularly in the autumn, maintaining his practice at the Head Court there. He spent the winter in Edinburgh during the legal terms. The house which had been rented in South Castle Street was exchanged for one of a similar size in North Castle Street, which he was now able to purchase, and which would continue to be his winter home for the next twenty-five years. For the rest of his life, circumstances would require or enable him to divide his year between a city and country life, as it would be divided between professional and literary work.

He found a little inn at Clovenford on the road to Selkirk, at which he made a habit of putting up, when the duties of his appointment required his presence in that neighbourhood. He made (needless to say) new friends in that district. Two of them William Laidlaw and James Hogg, will require more than a passing mention, as will John Leyden, whom he met at Edinburgh at about this time.

The winter of 1799-1800 was a time not only of its own successes but of far greater dreams, many of which were to be the facts of the future, and yet none of which may have been audacious enough to forecast how great that future was soon to be.

In April 1800, Scott wrote to Mr. Ballantyne suggesting that he should leave Kelso, and set up a printing business in Edinburgh. He thought that he saw an opening for "a man of talent and education". He, and a friend, were prepared to influence business to such a firm, and some capital might be found in return for a share of the profits, if that were necessary. There was business to be done in the printing of legal documents. Beyond that, why should not Ballantyne succeed with a weekly newspaper in Edinburgh, as he had established the *Mail* in Kelso?

Why not a monthly? Why not an Annual Register?

Vaguely, if not definitely, Scott had the vision of a press which should be under his own control.

CHAPTER XXII.

Before suggesting to James Ballantyne that he should remove his business to Edinburgh, Scott had given him expectation of an order for a book which could be printed at Kelso, *The Minstrelsy of the Scottish Border*, a project which may have been in his mind for a long previous period, and was now taking definite shape.

For the past ten or fifteen years he had been collecting Scottish ballad poetry with a tireless energy, and with the assistance of every friend he could discover who had a kindred interest.

Now, if not earlier, this work was being pursued with the definite object of ultimate publication, and Scott was anxious that the date should not be long deferred.

He had new helpers during this winter. Mr. Richard Heber, a scholar who specialised in the literature of the Middle Ages, and who sat in Parliament as representative of Oxford University, spent some months in Edinburgh, and was of assistance, not only by his own knowledge and the resources of his own library, but indirectly to a greater extent by his discovery of John Leyden.

John Leyden was a literary phenomenon, who, like so many of the numberless friends whom Scott accumulated, deserves a central stage rather than the passing reference which is all that there is space to give.

Born in poverty, in a cottage hovel in Roxburghshire, he was at this time a self-taught youth whose exact and various scholarship could confound those who were of greater repute in a dozen branches of learning. Rough and uncouth in speech and manner, he is said to have united the characteristics of boor and scholar in a way which was as bewildering as his own attainments. He had no money to purchase books, but Archibald Constable, a young man who had started a small second-hand store in a side-street of Edinburgh, would let him come to his shop, and read as long as he would.

Mr. Heber, searching for worm-eaten treasures, came to

Constable's shop also, and his attention was attracted by the uncouth visitor, and the recondite nature of the volumes with which he would observe him to be sitting absorbed, either on stool or ladder. Conversation followed, and when Heber discovered that Leyden's miscellaneous learning included an exceptional knowledge of, and enthusiasm for the old ballad-poetry of the country, he told Scott, and Scott came quickly on the scene.

From that time, for the two years that they were working together, the assistance which John Leyden gave to Scott's enterprise was of a primary importance, and was not overpaid by the fact that their friendship opened many doors of social or literary eminence to the poorer man.

John Leyden had already contributed for several years under the semi-anonymity of his own initials to Jeffrey's Edinburgh Review. He had shown himself to be an expert translator of the poetry of several languages. Now he contributed an original ballad to Lewis's slowly-growing collection. His suggestions enlarged the intended scope of Scott's own scheme of a Border Minstrelsy volume. It was now to be two volumes or more, with an original section, to which Leyden would contribute three ballads. The work of preparation went on during these spring months with a two-fold energy.

Heber went back to London when the spring came, and was followed by a letter from Scott, asking him to look out for a phaeton, which Mrs. Scott was very anxious to have. It was to cost no more than £31. 10. 0 and was to be "strong, low, and handsome". There is significance in this combination of qualities. Doubtless the handsome aspect was for Charlotte's contentment, and it must be strong and low because they had planned that she should be with him on his next summer's raid into Liddesdale, which was therefore to be undertaken with more thought for comfort than had been his custom. The phaeton was destined for many spring-straining jolts on pathless hills and moors, where no wheeled vehicle had ventured previously.

The difficult commission appears to have been successfully executed. Anyway, there was a phaeton in the Lasswade coach-house when the summer came, a phaeton that found its way over the hills to Hermitage, where Lord Dalkeith had made timely provision that its occupants should have a welcome somewhat more liberal, if not more kindly, than the moorland farmers would have been able to give.

It was during this summer that Sir John Stoddart, touring Scotland, paid a visit to Lasswade, to which he made reference in an account of his wanderings which he published in the following year. He had a pleasant memory of the encounter, and gushed accordingly. It appears that he observed Scott to be engaged *inter alia* in 'the daily exercise of the most precious sympathies as a husband, a father, and a friend'. His fatherhood was "daily exercised" at this time upon one baby girl of about nine months. No doubt Sir John was well entertained, and saw the interior of a happy well-ordered home, but there would be more cause to thank him had he recorded a single fact, instead of a paragraph of vague superlatives.

Scott was an excellent father, showing love and sympathy, and a discreet wisdom, tolerant yet without weakness, as the years passed. His attitude towards small babies was that to which a large number of men would plead guilty, if they had the courage to do so, as is shown by a note in his Journal, nearly thirty years later, when that nine-months baby was herself a mother, and he was in London inspecting his own grandchildren. "My name-son, a bright and blue-eyed rogue, with flaxen hair, screams and laughs like an April morning; and the baby is that species of dough which is called a fine baby. I care not for children till they care a little for me."

It was during this summer of 1800 that Scott also made the acquaintance of the Laidlaw family, and of the "Ettrick Shepherd," James Hogg.

He came on the Laidlaw household when he was making one of the sojourns in Selkirkshire that his office required, and rode out from his lodgings at the inn in Clovenford to explore the upper part of the Yarrow valley. Up Douglas-burn, fifteen miles or more from Clovenford, at the further end of the county, he halted at Blackhouse farm, and was well received by its in-mates. Among them was William Laidlaw, the son of the house, little more than a youth at that time, but one of kindred tastes to his own, of exceptional intellectual abilities, united to a very gentle and loveable character. Scott's genius for choosing and making friends asserted itself again, and a few weeks of meeting and correspondence laid the firm foundations of a life long intimacy.

William Laidlaw introduced him to a shepherd who had been in his father's employment for nine previous years, but had recently left to take service with a neighbouring farmer, and to the man's aged mother, Mrs. Hogg (herself a Laidlaw), whose mind proved to be another of those wells of ballad-treasure which Scott's ceaseless diligence was continually discovering. Her son, James, was a ballad-maker in his own right. Like Leyden he was self-educated, but, unlike him, he cared little for knowledge: for its own sake, and he was content with a very elementary standard of scholarship, which was probably all that he was mentally fitted to reach. But he was an exceptional poet, who never became more than half articulate; though, under the influence of praise and patronage, he became voluminous at a later time. He was of the Burns order, but without the coarse vitality or exuberance of that more popular poet. After a lifetime of effort, he was to leave one poem, *Kilmeny*, which, had he not written it, no one would have believed that he could ever write. He was an incomparably better lover than Burns, and a worse farmer. His father's methods had been to save money penuriously as a shepherd, which was difficult, and lose it as a sheep-farmer, which was quite easy to do. James pursued this sequence with the regularity of routine. At this time he was saving carefully for the first disaster.

He was about nine months older than Scott, and had already got some occasional magazine publicity. His contact with Scott at this time, and the generous recognition of his ability which he received from him, may have their shares of responsibility for the hurried publication of a first volume of his verses a few months later, which was admittedly premature. Later, he did better. With childlike vanity, he professed that his birthday was that of Burns, which was a mistake. He gradually rose to the opinion that his poetry was equal to that of Scott, which was another. But there are many worse and smaller men in the records of Scottish poetry, in which his own place is one of honour, and stands secure.

CHAPTER XXIII.

The winter of 1800-1 saw the belated appearance of Lewis's *Tales of Wonder*, to which Scott had made substantial contribution. It fell flat, having been talked about too much in advance, and published a year too late. In fact, Lewis was a setting star. But it is unlikely that Scott was greatly concerned about a book that was not his. He was too fully and hopefully occupied with his own affairs. *The Minstrelsy of the Scottish Border* was now something more than a dream. It took shape. Two volumes were in an advanced state of preparation. Arrangements were made with Ballantyne to print it at Kelso. A London firm of publishers, Cadell and Davies, were to bring it out. It was first intended to include an old mutilated metrical romance, *Sir Tristrem*, attributed to Thomas of Erchildoune, and certainly of Border origin, but the accumulation of material had been too great. Something must go overboard. *Sir Tristrem*, if flung out, would make space for a dozen ballads. Scott decided to complete it in imitation of the old form, and print it later as a separate book.

In this and similar work, the result of which was to be seen later, the first year of the new century passed.

There is little record of summer wanderings for this year, which may be explained by the fact that in October Charlotte had a second child, a boy this time, to add another to the many generations of Walters that the Scott family showed.

It was in this year also that Scott's sister died, after a twenty-five-year struggle to maintain courage and sanity of spirit in the body which fire had disfigured and injured, "living in an ideal world," as he recorded, "which she had framed to herself by the force of imagination".

The Scotts spent Christmas in Lanarkshire, on the invitation of the Duke of Hamilton. It gave an opportunity of inspecting the ruins of Cadyow Castle, and the remains of the old Caledonian forest, which are in the neighbourhood of Hamilton Palace. The Ballad of Cadyow Castle was a result of this visit. Lockhart implies that Scott was anxious to include it in the two volumes of Border Minstrelsy which were now in the press, but that Ballantyne vetoed it, on the ground that the volumes were already full enough. The possibility of this seems doubtful. The ballad could not have reached Kelso much before January 1st, 1802, and that date is improbably early. The two volumes were *published in London* during that month. They had to be printed, and Ballantyne's machinery was limited, and its processes would seem slow today. He had done his work well, which does not suggest haste. After printing, binding must follow. Delivery to London would take about a week at that time. That Scott proposed an insertion of additional matter at such a stage, simply to include something that he had just written, is an improbable thing. The point is of no great importance, except as showing how careless in assertion Lockhart can be, and that is of some moment, in view of more seriously controversial matters which are before us. 'Does it matter?' he might have asked, as he did when he was convicted of a worse inaccuracy. But, if not, why say it at all?

That it would have been politic to include the ballad there can be no doubt. It had a right to be there, for its author was certainly a Border minstrel. But it was a Clydeside ballad, glorifying the House of Hamilton. It would have called on Glasgow and Paisley, and all the Hamilton interests, to support the book. There may possibly have been a promise to Lady Anne Hamilton that it should be included. But the third volume remained.

Apart from such arguments, the thing was good in itself. There were points—there were stanzas—in which it surpassed any of Scott's published, if not any of his written work.

The Hamilton estate included a fragment—perhaps the only remaining fragment—of the old forest of Caledon. The enormous girth of its dying oaks showed that they had flourished when that forest extended unbroken from the Atlantic to the North Sea. Up to ten years ago (about 1790) the ancient wild white cattle had still roamed in its shade.

The ballad begins, as it ends, with a graceful compliment to the peaceful beauty of the present scene, and to her who had asked that it should be written:

"For chiefs intent on bloody deed,
And vengeance shouting o'er the slain,
Lo, Highborn Beauty rules the steed,
Or graceful guides the silken rein."

And then it proceeds very skilfully to call up the past in such a way that the chase of one of the great white mountain bulls in the sixteenth century and the assassination of the Regent Murray at the same period are blended into a single tale.

The description of Murray's entrance into Linlithgow, when,

"From the wild Border's humbled side,
In haughty triumph marched he,"

is ballad poetry, but it is ballad poetry raised to a new plane of artistry:

Dark Morton, girt with many a spear,
Murder's foul minion, led the van;
And clashed their broadswords in the rear,
The wild Macfarlanes' plaided clan.

Glencairn and stout Parkhead were nigh,
Obsequious at their Regent's rein,
And haggard Lindesay's iron eye,

That saw fair Mary weep in vain.

'Mid pennoned spears, a steely grove,
Proud Murray's plumage floated high;
Scarce could his trampling charger move,
So close the minions crowded nigh."

These stanzas are not flawless. The repetition of 'minion' must have passed unnoticed; and the first line of the second requires careful accenting, if it is to be read well, but their melody is still of the highest order, with subtle uses of assonance and alliteration and accenting which it would require a chapter to analyse. And defects are as significant as excellences. They show Scott, not as a laborious artificer, but a careless master. It is the distinction which we recognise when we attempt to differentiate between talent and genius. And yet careless is a word which may imply more than the fact. It is Scott's distinctive quality as a poet that he would always put what he had to say before how he said it. He would paint a scene as he saw it to be. Parkhead *was* one of the two who were closest to Murray when he was shot (the bullet that killed the Regent went on at a downward slant into Parkhead's horse), and the stanza had to put up with the accenting of the man's name as best it could.

Scott approached the temple of song by the ballad-path. All his life he wrote ballad-poetry, in which the subject matter was the first consideration. What has to be said must be said, and you must dress it, however roughly, in the best garments that its shape will wear. But he brought to their composition an understanding and control of the music of words which raised such poetry to the highest technical level. Miss Cranston judged well when she foretold a cross between Burns and Gray. Gray himself, most patient of craftsmen, and most severe in self-criticism, never produced anything more flawless than were the lyrics which Scott would write for the ornamentation of his longer poems.

Cadyow Castle, though it was not immediately printed,

obtained a prompt circulation in manuscript form. It came into the hands of Thomas Campbell (who, like everyone else, had met Scott in Edinburgh, two years earlier). Campbell, (it is his own witness) could not get it out of his head.

"Where, mightiest of the beasts of chase
That roam in woody Caledon,
Crashing the forest in his race,
The mountain bull came thundering on."

He recited audibly in his morning walks, and with such gesticulations that the line of coachmen he passed regarded him as an entertaining lunatic.

Has the art of verbal music reached new heights in the subsequent century, or is it a cause for satisfaction that we are less alert to hear it?

CHAPTER XXIV.

The first two volumes of the *Minstrelsy of the Scottish Border* appeared in January 1802, and were an instant success. The literary public were quick to appreciate a work of comprehensive character, the editing of which had been done by one who had mastered the subject with which he dealt. Those who knew most of the traditional ballad poetry of the Scottish borders were the readiest to recognise its quality. In the lucid authoritative prose of the introductions and notes, they admitted a knowledge that surpassed their own. The volumes were, indeed, the product of almost twenty-five years research and labour, in which the aid of scores of others had been enlisted, and ungrudgingly given. Scott was to overshadow himself more than once in the coming years, and, looking back, these volumes seem a minor incident in his literary career. But, had he done no more, they would have stood out in a different light, and been sufficient to give him an enduring reputation, which he himself was to convert to a relative obscurity.

The ready sale of the first edition was not caused, but was certainly assisted, by the manner in which the volumes had been produced by Ballantyne at his Kelso press. It was fitting that a book of this kind should be printed in its own district, though it was expedient that it should be published in London. But such a production might reasonably have been expected to be inferior to that which would have been issued by a London firm. Such a difference would have needed little apology. Deficiencies of plant, and lack of experience, would have been valid in explanation. But there was no need for excusing anything. Instead of that, there was praise. So far, Scott had made no mistake. He had chosen his printer well. Lockhart is so frequently unfair to James Ballantyne, and (by an implication which he was far from intending) to Scott also, through the whole course of the development of this printing business, that the point deserves emphasis.

Scott chose a small country printer, one of his boyhood friends, in preference to an established Edinburgh firm, and his judgement was justified by the result. Ballantyne had an opportunity to show that he was capable of good work on a large scale, and he rose to take it.

When he heard of the success of the book, and that not only the editor but the printer had won praise in the capital city, he went himself to London to discuss the possibility of obtaining orders from publishers there. He must have been well received, for he wrote a letter of warm gratitude to Scott on his return to Kelso. He regarded the opportunity which Scott had given him to print the *Minstrelsy* as "one of the most fortunate circumstances" of his life. He added, "I can never be sufficiently grateful for the interest you unceasingly take in my welfare." He mentioned that he was now sure of a profit on the enterprise, which implies that he had agreed to take some share of what must, in its inception, have been an adventurous risk for all concerned.

Mr. Longman, an enterprising London bookseller, journeyed

to Edinburgh. He came to negotiate for the copyright. The edition which had been first printed at Scott's or Ballantyne's risk appears to have been one of 500 copies. Scott's agreement with the publishers provided that he should receive half the net profit on the venture. They ultimately paid him £78 10. 0. in settlement of this obligation. Longman came to terms with Scott for the copyright, including the volume which had yet to be issued. He paid him £500. He gave Ballantyne an order for a further 1,000 copies, and for 1,500 of the third volume when it should be ready.

Editor and printer had good cause to be satisfied with the result of their first venture together. Scott looked ahead, planning boldly, with the confidence which success gives. Ballantyne's letters to him show that the project of moving his business to Edinburgh was becoming more definite. It was 'when' now rather than 'if'.

It is a general experience that we are more pleased by a small success in an art for which we have no natural genius than by a much greater in one at which we are really proficient. Scott had wished the *Minstrelsy* to include a sketch of the sombre ruins of Hermitage. There was no drawing in existence, nor any artist who would be willing to take the journey which would be necessary to make one. Scott thought (or wished) he could draw, and when his mind was resolved he was hard to turn. Shortreed and he had made an expedition to Hermitage to get the drawing. It was a time of deep snow on the hills. Scott said that he stood sketching for an hour 'up to his middle' in snow. He may have been a few inches wrong about that. Anyway, it was not too deep for him to move his arms.

He took the result back to William Clerk, who made from it another drawing of a more conventional kind. This went to the artist who was illustrating the book, and he made a third.

When the book appeared, those who knew the ruins said they could have guessed right without the help of the name which was printed beneath the sketch. Scott felt the pride of a child who has drawn a quadruped on a slate and finds it recognised for the cow which he had meant it to be. As a poet, he was well aware of his own deficiencies: even as a lawyer, it might be possible that he had his defects, though they were less obvious: but as an artist he was justified by the sketch he made when he was 'up to his middle' in snow.

With the encouragement he had received, it may be supposed that the summer of 1802 saw the third volume of the *Minstrelsy*) and other literary projects, pushed rapidly on. Seeking fresh materials, he made a journey into the remotest districts of the Ettrick forest, this time with John Leyden for company. Charlotte stayed at home, which was well for her. They slept on peat-stacks. They were fed on mutton which had died from such a cause as is commonly called an "act of God", but in which no butcher had intervened. They came back no worse for that, and with results which they regarded as sufficient compensation for these experiences.

Before this time, John Leyden had confided to Scott his desire to get out to the East, and to add a study of Oriental languages and literatures to his omnivorous learning. By the beginning of the year, the interest of Scott and his friends had been active on his behalf, and William Dundas had 'obtained the promise of some literary appointment in the East India Company's service'. At midsummer he had the disconcerting news that the patronage possibilities of the season had been exhausted. The only vacant post which could be placed at the disposal of Mr. Dundas was that of an assistant surgeon, and that would be useless to Mr. Leyden, as it could only be given to a qualified man. At least, that was assumed. Mr. Leyden thought differently. How soon would he have to qualify? He must be ready in six months. Very well. That would do for him. He took instantly to medical study, and was a qualified surgeon in time to join the ship to which he had been appointed. He went out with a letter of introduction from Scott to Charles Charpentier, and doubtless with others which Scott's interest had secured. In Scott's letter, he makes some mention of his own circumstances, and of the success of the *Minstrelsy*, without boasting, but with some natural elation.

John Leyden had seven years in India, becoming famous, in that brief period, for Oriental scholarship, before the climate killed him.

Scott laid a wreath of verse on his friend's grave when he wrote of

> "Scenes sung by him, who sings no more:
> His brief and bright career is o'er,
> And mute his tuneful strains;
> Quenched is his lamp of varied lore,
> That loved the light of song to pour;
> A distant and a deadly shore
> Has Leyden's cold remains."

But this is looking too far ahead. In the autumn of 1800, John Leyden was concentrating upon preparation for his medical examination, and the Scotts gave him the quiet hospitality of Lasswade in which to study. We know enough of Leyden's circumstances to suppose that it was an unrequited kindness: enough of his character to know that it would be received with gratitude.

Scott had more money this year than had been under his control at any previous period, and we see that it is already being used for the benefit of those around him. In 1808, before the time of his greatest prosperity, he wrote with truth that he had never cared overmuch for money. There would never be a time when he would have that which his friends (and some others) would not be free to share.

Joseph Ritson was a visitor to Lasswade while Leyden was staying there. Ritson was a man of strong and difficult individuality, the nature of which must not be taken to have been fairly drawn by Lockhart, whose prejudice is too strong to avoid caricature. Ritson was a scholar, an antiquarian, a loser of old poetry. He was best known for his assaults upon Bishop Percy's editing of the *Reliques*. It is a controversy which does not concern us now. The right was not all on one side. Lockhart evidently preferred that of the bishop. He calls Ritson a 'narrow-minded, sour, dogmatical little word-catcher', who was 'utterly incapable of sympathising with any of Scott's 'higher views'.

It is hardly judicial language, and must be justified, if at all, by the further damnations that Ritson was a vegetarian, and did not like Scotsmen. He was certainly a man of difficult temper, and it was regarded as a triumph of Scott's diplomacy in correspondence that he had enlisted his help. It surprised George Ellis, with whom Scott had also been in correspondence, since their mutual friend, Richard Heber, had returned to London.

Ritson came to Lasswade, and, on Lockhart's own statement, it was Leyden who played the clown, having a plate of raw meat brought in from the kitchen, and eating it, not from choice, but with the intention of horrifying his hosts' visitor. This exhibition, according to Lockhart, produced glances of "exquisite ruefulness" from Ritson, which is an improbable reaction.

Gillies, in his *Reminiscences of Sir Walter Scott*, recounts a somewhat similar scene. He called at Lasswade, and found Scott and Will Erskine starting out for a walk, which he joined. They left John Leyden and Mrs. Scott in the house, where Ritson was expected. They came back to find that he had both come and gone. Mrs. Scott, in a forgetful moment, had served him with some cold beef. Ritson had rejected it in a way which Leyden thought rude, and a violent quarrel had followed, as a result of which Ritson had left the house. Scott heard the tale, and did not look pleased, but on Leyden becoming excited in self-justification, he put it aside with a jest.

As Lockhart tells it, Leyden is justified by the fact that vegetarians should not expect to be treated with ordinary courtesy. They are *non compos mentis*. Had not Leyden 'first tried to correct him by ridicule'? To which 'the madman's' only response was to become more violent, instead of showing the gratitude which such an attitude should arouse? After that, if Leyden threatened to wring his neck, and didn't do it, it only shows how mild-mannered he really was.

These anecdotes show Leyden on his worst side, as one

who was born a boor, and may raise a doubt as to what was the atmosphere of the thatched cottage at Lasswade, which could give hospitality to such inmates. But Gillies, who tells the tale, and who looked with the eyes of a brother barrister, and a scholar accustomed to the amenities of city life, gives us this picture also: "In approaching the cottage I was struck with the exceeding air of neatness that prevailed around. The hand of tasteful cultivation had been there, and all methods employed to convert an ordinary thatched cottage into a handsome and comfortable abode."

But the decision that it must be left, whatever amount of loving care had been spent upon it, would soon have to be reluctantly taken. It was during the next summer that the Lord-Lieutenant of Selkirkshire addressed a formal complaint to Scott that he was doing less than justice to the duties of the official post he held. The remonstrance was not of an urgent character, but it was not of Scott's disposition to disregard it. During these years his absorption in the preparation of the *Minstrelsy* for the press, his other literary and his legal work, and the military duties which he had undertaken, must have left little time for those of a sheriff to be performed. He replied, very properly, with an expression of regret, and an assurance that there should be no cause for future complaint.

To fulfil this undertaking, the natural course was to arrange that, as he must still remain in Edinburgh during the winter months, his summer residence should be in the county where his duties lay.

Besides, the two babies grew, and there would be a third by the time that this correspondence took place. (Anne was born in February 1803). Yet, to the Scott's, to leave Lasswade would not be a welcome decision. It was the first country home that they had had. It had been theirs for six very happy years of a growing prosperity. They had spent much upon it, having made it the home it was. But it was a step which could not be much longer deferred....

When Gillies called at the cottage, on the occasion already

mentioned, and went walking with Scott and Erskine, they took him to see the ruins of Roslin, and he has recorded his memory that Scott's foot slipped on the crag-top, and that he "must have been killed" but that he dislodged a hazel-tree which went down with him, the two arriving safely at the foot of the cliff together. He rose, he says, "with a hearty laugh," and called from below to know whether they would dare to descend in the same way.

Such incidents tend to be exaggerated in reminiscence, but there is a large body of testimony to Scott's physical and sometimes almost reckless daring, and the buoyant attitude with which he faced mischance or danger. Gillies says that, at this point, "he retained in features and form an impress of that elasticity and youthful vivacity which he used to complain wore off when he was forty, and by *his own* account was exchanged for the plodding heaviness of an operose student. He had now something of a boyish gaiety of look, and in person was tall, slim and extremely active."

Doubtless, as the years passed, he insensibly lessened, little by little, the strenuous activities of his earlier years. Doubtless he sat longer at his desk, or, by insensible degrees, longer at the table while the wine passed and the talk went on. Doubtless, his weight insensibly increased, and his steps shortened. But those who saw him long after his fortieth year noticed the same buoyancy of temperament, the same tireless activity, the same readiness to take the risk, on foot or horseback, either of leap or fall.

CHAPTER XXV.

In the beginning of April 1803, Mr. and Mrs. Scott went up for a second time to London together. John Leyden had now taken his medical diploma, and gone up at an earlier date, awaiting his sailing instructions. Dates of sailing were, in those days, of a vague uncertainty. They were anxious to see him before his departure, and they probably started as soon as Charlotte felt equal to the long coach journey, which was at that time a rather formidable enterprise, her third child having been born only five or six weeks previously. But, in fact, Leyden had sailed when they arrived.

They went to stay with M. Charles Dumergue as before. He was a French refugee who had known Charlotte's parents intimately, and who was always ready to give them hospitality when they came up to London together.

Scott brought with him, among other things, the incomplete manuscript of a long poem, which had at first been no more than a ballad, intended for the third volume of the *Minstrelsy*, but had grown to a size which had made that an impossible medium of publication. It had been written—more or less—during the previous year: may, indeed, be said to have been the principal work of that period, while he appeared to be fully occupied with other things.

James Skene had seen him writing busily when they had been in barracks together at Musselburgh in the autumn, and Scott had received a kick from a horse which had laid him up for three days, and after that he had shown him the first canto of the poem in a fairly complete condition. But we must accept the idea of hasty composition with important reservations, if at all. To a large extent they are contradicted by circumstantial evidence as to the way in which it developed: they are rendered extremely improbable by the internal evidences of the poem itself.

But it must have been either in the course of the journey to London, or after his interviews with booksellers there, that he came to a definite decision as to the title and form which it should take, and the manner of publication, for it was shortly after his arrival that he wrote to James Ballantyne with instructions that he wished an advertisement to be included in the third volume of the *Minstrelsy* which was to be worded thus:

> "In the press, and will speedily be published, the *Lay of the last Minstrel*, by Walter Scott, Esq., Editor of the *Minstrelsy of the Scottish Border*.

Also *Sir Tristrem, a Metrical Romance*, by Thomas Ercildoune, called the Rhymer, edited from an ancient MS., with an Introduction and Notes, by Walter Scott, Esq."

No doubt, when Scott drafted that announcement (giving James Ballantyne authority to alter it at his discretion) he anticipated that its forecast would be realised, and that, when the third volume of the *Minstrelsy* should appear, the two volumes would be actually "in the press". He must have looked on the completion of the "*Lay*" as a thing to be lightly and swiftly done. The third volume of the *Minstrelsy* was in an advanced condition of the proof-sheet stage. Scott's letter would stimulate Ballantyne to renewed efforts, with the news that the first two volumes were going well, and that Longman was well pleased with the quality of the 1,000 extra copies of them which he had ordered last year, and which had been already delivered.

Ballantyne had moved to Edinburgh. He had not sold his business at Kelso. He had come up to the capital city carting his machinery with him. He had taken premises of a very limited size in a side street near Holyrood, and put up a sign, *The Border Press*. He had done this only three months ago—a bold, it might be a ruinous step, relying upon Scott's encouragement, and upon the quality of his own work. They had each shown confidence in the other, and their first venture together had been a success, in which each had won praise of its own kind.

James Ballantyne had founded the *Kelso Mail*, and built up his printing business, on a very limited capital. He had neither wealthy relatives, nor powerful friends. He had known and overcome financial difficulties enough, to reach the measure of success, of reputation, which he had won when he set out for Edinburgh. Lockhart regards these circumstances as though looking down from a height. It is an attitude which has the absurdity of one who would disparage the victory of a chess player because it had been won with fewer pieces than are usually allotted, or than an opponent held.

It had been won, in part, because James Ballantyne was something more than a commercial printer—or less, if you will. He was an artist in type.

There was danger in that, as well as strength. But Scott and he were both confident of the future, and of themselves. Wordsworth, meeting Scott in the following year, was amazed at the audacity of the plans he made. It was as though Napoleon, Consul of France, had spread maps of continents which he planned to win. But the anticipations at which Wordsworth wondered were less than the facts of the years to be. It was a battle of giants to which we are coming, great with incredible victories, with a final tragedy when world-forces shall bear it back, and almost bear it down at the last; and Lockhart could look at it without understanding, without imaginative sympathy, as a "painful," ignoble thing: only remembering complacently that, at the battle's crisis, he had refused the (possibly worthless) help that Constable asked him to give...

As to how the *Lay* was written, let us have dates. When we come to consider it in detail, we shall be able to connect its opening stanzas with the summer of 1800. Skene observed Scott to be busy upon its first canto in the autumn of 1802. Now, in the spring of 1803, he has its title fixed, and anticipates that it will soon be finished. Going back from London, and stopping with George Ellis for a week at Sunninghill, with Heber and Douce in their company, a considerable part of the first two or three cantos was read aloud while picnicking in Windsor Forest. It is a reasonable presumption that the later cantos, if they existed at all, were too embryonic for production. In the following autumn, Wordsworth speaks of the first four cantos as having been read to him. The third volume of the *Minstrelsy*, which was first to have included the *Lay*, and then announced that it and *Sir Tristrem* were separately "in the press", was published in May 1803. *Sir Tristrem* was published in May 1804. The *Lay* appeared in January 1805. So far from there being strong presumptive-evidence to support the common assertion that it was hastily written, the evidence is circumstantially and overwhelmingly opposite, and it is just what anyone with experience of writing poetry would expect. It has abundant internal evidences of being an experimental work that was neither swiftly nor completely born. It sprang first from a seed in the mind of Samuel Taylor Coleridge, who begot something which he could not have conceived. It groped blindly for shape, and grew to a final form and a final beauty, which its beginnings had not shown. Had the same years of careful work been spent (for instance) upon the *Lord of the Isles*, it would have been a more excellent thing. We cannot assess fairly the importance of the work of these years 1800-04, without realising that Scott was continually preoccupied with the construction or composition of the *Lay* during that period, but what it was we must leave to be dealt with later.

CHAPTER XXVI.

The Scotts travelled back to Lasswade by way of Oxford, in the company of Richard Heber, who was going to his own place, and they stayed there long enough to make the acquaintance of his brother, Reginald, who was not then a Calcutta Bishop, nor the world-known author of a missionary hymn, but had just won the poetry prize of the year at Brazenose College, and brought the manuscript with him to the breakfast table for Scott to see.

We might linger pleasantly at Oxford with the Scotts, or at Blenheim which they also visited, making new friends continually, but the difficulty is that to be introduced to all the friends that they made as the years passed is to stop to look at everyone of literary, most of political, and many of those of social or military reputation in the United Kingdom over a period of thirty or forty years. They crowd into the picture, each with his own individuality, his own background. To look at them once, is to be tempted to look again. The sentence becomes a paragraph, and the paragraph a chapter.

Unless we would have a universal biography of the period, we must turn resolutely aside. We have glanced at the group in Sunninghill, and beneath the oak trees in Windsor Forest, but we have avoided being introduced. We have not even looked at the 'indefatigable and obliging' Douce; and the London conversations with Rogers, and Mackintosh, and William Stewart Rose, have passed unheard.

After Oxford, there is no record of any further break in the return journey. The whole visit had been very short for so expensive and laborious an expedition as a journey to London was at that period. But Charlotte must have had many thoughts of the three small children that she had left in the Lasswade cottage, including a baby that was still only ten weeks old, and Scott had many interests to which to look forward on his return. In fact, he got back to Edinburgh in time to see the third volume of the *Minstrelsy* published at the end of May.

It was during this summer that there came the remonstrance from the Lord-Lieutenant of Selkirkshire to which allusion has been made already, and that it was recognised that the leaving of Lasswade could not be much longer deferred.

Following the completion of the *Minstrelsy* publication, Scott first appears as a contributor to the Edinburgh Review, which Jeffrey was editing. He reviewed Southey's *Amadis of Gaul*, for which he was particularly well qualified. His subsequent articles cover a wide range of subjects, but have the common quality of being those with which he was specially conversant. He never cultivated the journalistic habit of being promiscuously omniscient.

The summer passed without any climax of incident, in work on the *Lay* and *Sir Tristrem*, and in the usual routine of visits, and legal and military duties. The last had become of more than perfunctory character. While the Scotts were on their way back from London, the war in Europe, after a short pause of exhaustion had broken out with a renewed and increasing fury. The fear of invasion was far more real and reasonable than when, a century later, an English government lacked either the courage or the military insight which would have used its full strength on its foemen's ground. Now, people were told that the army was for use abroad. If they did not join it, they must be prepared for the defense of their own homes. The camp at Musselburgh had become an active military centre. A letter to Miss Seward, written at that time, and quoted by Lockhart, deserves reproduction, but, in reading it, it is well to remember that the regiment that owed its first inception to Scott's imagination and practical energy was not a peacetime plaything of the pageantry of war. It met and trained with the knowledge that, at any moment, it might have to oppose its inexperienced valour to the war-hardened legions of France, that would have landed upon the British coast with the prestige of having strewn the map of a ruined Europe with the sites of a hundred victories. It was the year when Collingwood, after the few months of home-life that the brief peace gave, put to sea once more, never to see his wife and infant children again. He died at sea *seven years* later. England fought for life with an extremity of effort for which there is no parallel in the war of a later century. Her fleets, watching the French ports, must beat backwards and forwards, in all seasons and any weather, as the winds allowed. The partial relief of Trafalgar was still two years ahead.

Scott wrote:

> "We are assuming a very military appearance. Three regiments of militia, with a formidable park of artillery, are encamped just by us. The Edinburgh Troop, to which I have the honour to be quartermaster, consists entirely of young gentlemen of family, and is, of course, admirably well mounted and armed. There are other dour troops in the regiment, consisting of yeomanry, whose iron faces and muscular forms announce the hardness of the climate against which they wrestle, and the powers which nature has given them to contend with and subdue it. These corps have been easily raised in Scotland, the farmers being in general

a high-spirited race of men, fond of active exercises, and patient in hardship and fatigue. For myself, I must own that to one who has, like myself, *la tête un peu exaltée* 'the pomp and circumstance of war' gives, for a time, a very poignant and pleasing sensation. The imposing appearance of cavalry, in particular, and the rush which marks their onset, appear to me to partake highly of the sublime. Perhaps I am the more attached to this sort of sport of swords because my health requires much active exercise, and a lameness contracted in childhood renders it inconvenient for me to take it otherwise than on horseback. I have, too, a hereditary attachment to the animal—not, I flatter myself, of the common jockey cast, but because I regard him as the kindest and most generous of the subordinate tribes. I hardly even except the dogs; at least they are usually so much better treated, that compassion for the steed should be thrown into the scale when we weigh their comparative merits. My wife (a foreigner) never sees a horse ill-used without asking what the poor horse has done in his state of pre-existence? I would fain hope that they have been carters or hackney-coachmen, and are only experiencing a retort of the ill-usage they have formerly inflicted. What think you?"

The joyous courage which could be optimistic enough, but which did not allow any optimism to take the place of the hard work by which safety is gained, or success comes: the universal sympathy with all around him, extending as he wrote to the cavalry horses for the welfare of which it is a quartermaster's duty to provide—do they not make easy explanation of the fact that Wordsworth noticed when he and Dorothy visited the Scotts during this autumn, that "I believe that, in the character of the sheriff's friends, we might have counted on a hearty welcome under any roof in the Border country"?

William and Dorothy, walking from Roslin, where they had

left the carriage in which they were touring Scotland, called at Lasswade so early that Mr. and Mrs. Scott were still in bed, but they got no worse reception for that.

"We were received," Wordsworth said to Lockhart long afterwards, "with that frank cordiality which, under whatever circumstances I afterwards met him, always marked his manners; and, indeed, I found him then in every respect—except, perhaps, that his animal spirits were somewhat higher—precisely the same man that you knew him in later life; the same lively, entertaining conversation, full of anecdote, and averse from disquisition; the same unaffected modesty about himself; the same cheerful and benevolent and hopeful views of man and the world. He partly read and partly recited, sometimes in an enthusiastic style of chant, the first four cantos of the *Lay of the Last Minstrel;* and the novelty of the manners, the clear picturesque descriptions, and the easy glowing energy of much of the verse, greatly delighted me."

We notice that the *Lay* was advancing. There were four cantos now. And Wordsworth listened with an intelligent appreciation. It was not his kind of poetry, but, of its kind, it was quite good. And, so far as he praises, it is intelligent praise. He may have noticed—he may have remarked—a very curious similarity between the opening lines and those of an unfinished poem called *Christabel,* that his friend Coleridge had written, and which had already had some manuscript circulation; but, if he did, there is no record that he spoke aloud.

Later in the day, Scott walked back with the Wordsworths to their carriage at Roslin. He recommended the little inn at Clovenford, where they stayed the night. He was starting to ride to Jedburgh in the course of the next day, and if they cared to pause at Melrose he would catch them up, and show them the ruins there.

So he did, and they went on to Jedburgh together. He introduced William Laidlaw, who was very anxious to meet a poet whose verses he already knew. He rode with them to Hawick on the next day, and would have taken them into the wilder

Liddesdale country, "where," he said, "I have a home in every farmhouse". But he had his sheriff's duties in Jedburgh, and it was time that they should be back in their Westmorland home.

He gave Wordsworth the impression that he did not take literature or literary success very seriously, and yet that it was in his easy reach. He said casually that he did not make much money at the law, and added that "he was sure he could, if he chose, get more money than he should ever wish to have from the book-sellers".

Wordsworth, having less reason for a similar confidence, was puzzled, but not alienated by this remark. They parted with cordiality, and he doubtless regained his usual intellectual altitude, making a disquisition to Dorothy, as they rumbled onwards to Westmorland.

Wordsworth was about eighteen months older than Scott. He was physically and intellectually about at his best at this time. He had recently married, having left a wife and a new-born baby when he set out with his sister on this Highland tour. He had lost something of the neurotic temperament of earlier years, and the pontifical was not yet at its worst. They met with the common consciousness that Wordsworth was the greater man, about which both were content. They had a common love of poetry, but little else to draw them together. Wordsworth was a powerful young man, well-made, with no lameness to hold him back, but there was no thought of a saddle in his mind, no sword in his hand. He went on a Highland tour.

That Scott's multitude of activities shamed him in any way is an unlikely thing. They are the occupations of the herd, from which genius stands apart. When we remember that Wordsworth had neither sense of humour, nor spark of romance, that he actually attributed the failure of *Lyrical Ballads* to the fact that he had reluctantly agreed to the inclusion of the *Ancient Mariner*, we may consider him to have been one of the most difficult friendships that Scott ever made.

As to Scott's measure of legal success at this time, his fee-book shows a steady advance from year to year, and its total for

1802-3 had reached £228 18. 0. This could not have been the case had he failed to give good service to those whose briefs he accepted. But it is evident also that he had many more engrossing occupations, and a note in his journal, written twenty-two years later, shows how little he had the temperament which successful advocacy requires.

"Was engaged the whole day," (he noted) "upon Sheriff Court processes. There is something sickening in seeing poor devils drawn into great expenses about trifles by interested attorneys. But too cheap access to litigation has its evils on the other hand, for the proneness of the lower class to gratify spite and revenge in this way would be a dreadful evil were they able to endure the expense. Very few cases come before the Sheriff Court at Selkirk that ought to come anywhere.... I try to check it, as well as I can...."

CHAPTER XXVII.

The publication of *Sir Tristrem* was not placed with a London firm. It was entrusted to Archibald Constable, the young bookseller at whose shop Richard Heber had met John Leyden two or three years earlier.

Archibald Constable's book-selling business increased, and he had already made one or two successful publishing ventures. As to *Sir Tristrem*, he had a clear opinion as to how it should be produced, and sufficient force of character to have his own way.

It was not a book from which substantial profit could be reasonably anticipated. The edition should be limited to 150 highly-priced copies. So it was agreed, not without reluctance. They were sold at £2. 2. 0. each. The cost of paper and printing was covered. The production of the Border Press was admired. The author's pocket may not have benefited, but his reputation grew.

It was at the beginning of May 1804 that *Sir Tristrem* appeared, and the decision to leave Lasswade was already definite, and the new home had been found.

Hesitant search in other directions had been abruptly ended by the death of an uncle, Colonel Russell, who had had a house on the Tweedside, a few miles from Selkirk. Colonel Russell had married one of Anne Rutherford's sisters, one of the elder family. He had children of his own—cousins of Walter Scott, of whom we may hear again—but his death broke up the home, his eldest son being in India. The house was not for sale, but was offered to Scott on lease. There was a small farm beside it, which he also took.

While these negotiations were approaching completion, Captain Robert Scott died at Kelso. He left Rosebank, and thirty acres of fertile land around it to his favourite nephew. There was some temptation to Scott to live in a house that was his own freehold, and Kelso was a place of pleasant memories, and delightfully situated. But it was not quite where he wished to be, and the rural qualities of Rosebank were being reduced by surrounding building. It was neither country nor town. On the other hand, it would sell well. The final decision was to sign the Ashestiel lease, and to let Rosebank go. Later in the year, it was sold for £5,000, and Scott found his finances substantially improved

As an alternative to Ashestiel, there was a small estate called Broadmeadows, on Yarrow-bank, which it was known would be put up for sale during the summer, and the idea of using the proceeds of Rosebank to acquire this property had an allurement which was not easily put aside. Lockhart considers it "in one point of view, the greatest misfortune of his life" that Scott did not do this. He points out that he now had an income, jointly with Charlotte, of about £1,000, without any great personal exertion. He could have avoided the "mere" commercial direction in which the bulk of the money was ultimately invested.

It is a point of view with which many will sympathise. It is possible that poems and novels such as he afterwards gave to the world might have been written in a retirement of quiet peace. It is possible, but much less than sure. It is certain that Scott, being what he was, would not have accepted such a scheme of life in his thirty-fourth year. Besides, he had an obligation to Ballantyne in honour, if not in law, and it was in that direction, a few months later, that a large part of the money was to be invested, as we shall see when we come to the events of the next year.

It is useless, at any stage of his life, to represent Scott as being driven by stronger forces, which Lockhart will continually attempt to do. Because he spoke with a smile to those among whom he moved: because he was always ready to give help to the extent of his own wisdom or his purse's depth, with the understanding sympathy which is more than wisdom or gold, Lockhart fails to see that he dominated, though he may not have domineered, and in doing this he reduces an epic to the dimensions of his own mind.

He does not see that Scott was a born adventurer, whether in life or art. He would have been of this disposition at any time, in any circumstances, in any occupation. Born at any period of the world's history, whether on a conspicuous stage or in some village obscurity, he would have played high, whether to success or disaster.

Ballantyne may have made many mistakes, he may have committed many imprudences—follies—neglects—he may have been of a doubtful honour, he may have eaten and drunk to excess as the years passed. He may—or he may not. But it was Scott's audacious dreaming which loaded up the Kelso printing-presses on the road to Edinburgh: it was Scott's genius which made those audacious dreams come true. Scott planned the campaigns. Ballantyne, at the most, was no more than Soult to his own Napoleon. If it be said that Ballantyne commanded on the commercial wing, and it was that wing, at the last, which was driven in, the reply is not only that, time after time, as the years passed, and some crisis of financial battle came, Scott was in personal control of the operations; it goes beyond that to ask what Napoleon have we here, who is alleged to have appointed a muddle-headed, incompetent, slothful field-marshal, and continued to entrust him with that position for nearly thirty years?

It is also to be remembered that defeat does not always imply incompetence in those who sustain it. Twenty years later, in an extremity of world-wide financial crisis, similar to, but more acute than that of 1931-2, the great book-distributing firm of Hurst & Robinson went down. That disaster involved the ruin of Archibald Constable, and his ruin involved that of Ballantyne & Co., which involved that of Walter Scott, who was a partner in the printing business. These events caused the exposure of many financial transactions and circumstances which would otherwise have been private to the parties concerned. Lockhart recounted them in some detail, and with the implication that Scott was deserving of serious condemnation, which he would have avoided if he could, had not the facts been too plain. He uses the curious adjective "painful". He says explicitly in the course of the subsequent controversy which he provoked, that he made "no such ridiculous attempt" as to show that Scott was "without blame in the conduct of his pecuniary affairs". He assumed, as those who only understand commercial matters from the outside are apt to do, that failure and disgrace are synonymous. But he represented Scott's position as being due mainly to over-confidence in James Ballantyne and his brother John, by whom, and through whose incompetence, that confidence was abused and betrayed. He also represented that Scott was imprudent in investing the very large profits that his novels made in the purchase of land. And though this may sound somewhat remote as a cause of failure, popular imagination, which likes its explanations to be simple and picturesque, has seized upon this idea, and, rightly or wrongly, Scott is now commonly believed to have overreached himself through an inordinate and rather vulgar ambition to become a great landowner, and to have contrived his own ruin in consequence.

The friends of James Ballantyne did not accept Lockhart's account of these events with complaisance. They issued a pamphlet, which they entitled *Refutations of the Misstatements and Calumnies contained in Mr. Lockhart's* Life of Sir Walter Scott, Baronet, *by the Trustees and Son of the late James Ballantyne.*

The title of this pamphlet is indicative of its authors' style. It pours words. It makes explicit accusations of mendacity against Lockhart, some of which cannot be dismissed without serious examination. It asserts that James Ballantyne was ruined entirely through having placed his confidence in Sir Walter Scott, that he had made large profits which he had left in the business, and that, through Scott's reckless speculative follies, all the accumulations of a life of successful industry had been swept away.

Many of its assertions were extremely disputable, and some were palpably false. Lockhart replied, in a spirit of contempt, and with far greater controversial skill. He carried war into the enemies' country, showing the weakness of their positions rather than the strength of his own.

It is proverbially easy to be wise after the event, but it is less so to judge precedent events with equity when we know what the end will be. With the knowledge that we now have it is difficult to regard the varied fortunes of the next twenty years without the consciousness of this advancing shadow. But we should endeavour to regard each event at its separate value, though with the added care of those who know that there is a judicial process to come. It may end in storm, but we are now at the dawn of a splendid day.

CHAPTER XXVIII.

It is the Sheriff's Court at Selkirk. We have a glimpse of Scott sitting there in the local dignity of his magisterial office. A poacher is in the dock. He gives the name of Tom Purdie. The case is proved beyond cavil. He has, in fact, been convicted before. The Sheriff looks at him keenly. The Sheriff may be the most popular man in Selkirkshire, but those who come before him when he is on the bench do not always like the experience. "Anything to say, Purdie?"

It appears that the man has. Quite a lot. He is out of work. He has a family who need food. There are grouse on the moor.

The Sheriff listens, but is unmoved. He points out that it is not a first offence. It is a bad case, and poaching has got to stop. He imposes a heavy fine, with a jail sentence as an alternative. Tom Purdie has no money with which to pay fines. He goes from the dock to his own place.

But, in fact, Tom Purdie went home. When the Court rose he was told to do so. "Sherra," they told him, had paid the fine.

So it might have ended, an incident of which no one would know today, had Tom Purdie been content that it should be left there. But he asked where the Sheriff could be found. He wished to thank him for that unexpected freedom.

But the Sheriff had left the town. He had gone home to the new house he had taken on the other side of the Tweed, three or four miles away. Tom set out to walk.

In the evening he came to Ashestiel. It was built in a woody place, a meadow's breadth from the Tweed bank, with a little gorge at the side, where a mountain stream came downward to the wider riser. Behind, the hills rose, with Yarrow valley on their further side.

Tom had a talk with the Sheriff and went home to tell his wife that he had got a job.

Scott had added another—indeed several others—to the endless list of his life-long friends. We may think, as the years pass, that money will leave his hands rather freely at times, but he never made a better investment than when he paid a poacher's fine.

How often he acted in the same spirit to others who faced him over a space of twenty-five years in the same dock, can be a matter of conjecture only, but there is a letter still in existence, casually discovered in 1928 by Mr. M. Kliman of Manchester, which deserves reproduction.

"George and John Brown—You have paid into my hands one guinea being the amount of a fine imposed on you by my sentence of that date for disorderly proceedings at Galashiels on the night of the eighth current, of which fine you are hereby discharged, and I shall transmit the same to the proper quarter.

Recommending to you over circumspection in future.

I am, etc.,

WALTER SCOTT."
Abbotsford,
10th April.

The year is not inserted, and though there is a probability that it was written about 1824-5, there is no certain proof. Under what circumstances the two men came to send their fine to Abbotsford, instead of to the Court, can be a matter of conjecture only. It was not usual at that period to allow men convicted of disorderly conduct to go free with a fine unpaid. But if there had been any leniency in the treatment they had received, there is a cold warning in the communication which has neither the ordinary courtesies of a letter, nor the neutrality of an official receipt.

They may have had mercy now, but if they presume upon it—if they forget to be 'over circumspect' in future, they will be exceptionally foolish men....

We must not suppose that Scott invented work for Tom Purdie's benefit. Tom had, in fact, called at a lucky time. There had been no regular outside staff at Lasswade, where the garden was small, and the land no more than two or three acres; of grass, on to which a horse could be turned at need. Ashestiel was a small farm. Tom was engaged as a shepherd at first, and was soon promoted to be in general charge of the place, taking a position which had been discussed for the Ettrick Shepherd. How James Hogg would have filled it may be difficult to imagine. Scott had a way of getting the best out of those he employed, and of controlling and reconciling difficult characters, either as guest or servant, but we may conclude that it was best as it was. It was a position of some responsibility, as house and farm would be left in Tom Purdie's charge during the winter months. But we shall find that Scott made few mistakes in his judgements of men, which may be worth remembering when we come to James Ballantyne once again.

He found a job for Tom's brother-in-law also, Peter Mathieson, about this time. Income has increased, and the larger house must be run on a larger scale. Charlotte wanted the dignity of a closed carriage, and that meant a coachman, for which Peter would do. The phaeton being an open vehicle, Scott had driven it himself. In fact, he had driven it where phaetons were not adapted to go. There had been more than one spill, in which Charlotte and he had been thrown out together. To overturn a phaeton, especially one that had been purchased on the specification sent to Richard Heber, does not sound easy to do. Lockhart attributes it to Scott's "awkward management", and hints that Mrs. Scott thought she would like a change in her charioteer. But to argue that is to ignore some known facts. That Scott drove a vehicle awkwardly is very improbable. But the phaeton had been intended to venture on the hill-tracks of Liddesdale, where no vehicle had ventured before. It may be believed that it had some spills. The closed carriage was not intended for such exploits, and would have rolled over with more disastrous frequency had they been foolish enough to test it. In fact, Lockhart attempts a comparison that does not arise. The closed carriage was to drive into Selkirk, with Mathieson on the box, in the state which a Sheriff's wife may be expected to show. Scott preferred his own saddle, and his own horse.

But that there had been some perilous driving in the course of the Liddesdale raids may be believed without difficulty. They had definite destinations to reach, and they were attempting them in a new way. It was an adventurous enterprise. Scott, who knew the hills, may have been sanguine, and Charlotte, who didn't, may have been trustful, when it was planned. Still, they came safely home. She could thank his driving for that.

That he would take risks for himself with a light heart is the testimony of many witnesses. Archibald Park, a neighbouring farmer, who was sheriff's officer, used to ride with him much at this time in that capacity. He had the name of a good rider himself, but he used to exclaim at the way in which Scott took the chances that the rough country gave. He helped the Sheriff in the arrest of a gypsy who was wanted for murder, when they came on a gang of them in a lonely place, and Scott recognised the man and was determined to have him, as, in fact, they did.

Archibald's brother, Mungo, knew Scott also, and also slept at Ashestiel just before the call of Africa took him back on that last journey from which he did not return. He was about to leave his family on a pretext of visiting Edinburgh, not having courage to tell them that he was leaving Scotland again, and (of course) Scott was the confidant to whom he disclosed his plans.... But the resolution to avoid mention of Scott's friends, where they stand aside from the main course of the narrative, must be better kept, for it is an endless list....

Beside the farm at Ashestiel, Scott had undertaken the care of the plantations on the estate, not renting them, but supervising on his absent cousin's behalf. The fact that his mind was turned upon this duty may have originated a remark in a letter to George Ellis about this time. The Ellises must have had a thought of visiting Scotland, and Scott is anxious that Mrs. Ellis should not expect too much of literal forest in the Ettrick valley. "Ettrick Forest," he writes, "boasts finely shaped hills, and clear romantic streams; but, alas! they are bare to wildness, and denuded of the beautiful natural wood with which they were formerly shaded. It is mortifying to see that, though wherever the sheep are excluded the copse has immediately sprung up in abundance, so that enclosures only are wanted to restore the wood wherever it might be useful or ornamental, yet hardly a proprietor has attempted to give it fair play for a resurrection."

From a quite different cause, there is a similar process of

denudation on the moors of Yorkshire today, where the heather advances and the birch-woods dwindle, and it is equally disregarded. But we may conclude that if Scott shall come to the owning of land in the time to be, it will be a good day for the land.

In the autumn of this year, on a sudden impulse, born of James Ballantyne's importunity, Scott ceased the alterations and additions to the *Lay* on which he had been engaged since he got settled at Ashestiel, and gave it to him to go to press. He could not foresee the success it would win, but he knew it to be a greater thing than the ballads with which he had gained the position he already held. For these years, while it had been taking gradual shape, he had felt like a general who sees the fight go well, but knows that his best troops are still held back in reserve. He may well look with confidence to the hour when they will sweep forward across a field which is already won.

It is an axiom of prosody that a long poem cannot sustain its highest notes either of emotional intensity or verbal melody. There must be flat stretches between the hills. The prosodic standard for the long poem differs from that of the lyric, and is, in some respects, lower. We do not look for continuous gold. If a line sparkle here and there, we have our reward: the gold flashes amid the quartz. But it is the distinctive quality of the *Lay* that the lyric level is sustained, in which respect it did not conform to the accepted standards, or limitations, of epic, narrative or lyric poetry. It was a new thing.

Its lyric qualities support the evidences of substance and construction to prove that it was not hastily written. James Skene, having no experience of the writing of poetry, might believe that two cantos were the work of as many idle days. But, if it were so, it was not an act of genius: it was an act of God.

CHAPTER XXIX.

Lockhart explained Scott in his earlier years, as being the product of a mentor, a monitor, and a "lady of fashion," to which trinity we should be proportionately grateful for what they gave us. In his thirty-fifth year, he can load him with laudatory adjectives, but he is still unwilling that he should stand alone. William Erskine, the monitor, is still beside him, and is still able to give the literary advice and guidance which he so obviously needs. He had two monitors now. William Erskine—and James Ballantyne! They are the joint reasons why he may prudently publish the *Lay* without sending it to Sunninghill for George Ellis to put it into shape. *"With two such faithful friends within his reach, the author of the* Lay *might safely dispense with sending his MS. to be revised, even by George Ellis."*

That George Ellis would have had the stupidity (or the impudence) to attempt to revise the poem, had it been sent to him in MS., is an improbability which has no documentary support beyond the fact that he wrote proposing that Flaxman might illustrate it. Scott, with better judgement, thought Flaxman to be an unsuitable artist, and declined the suggestion. He did this by a letter written in the tone of deferential courtesy which he always used to those friends whom he admitted to an intellectual intimacy, and which often obscured the fact that, on essential points, he continued his own course. He added politely that he would have been pleased for Ellis to see the MS., and to have his "opinions and corrections"—but it had already gone to press.

That William Erskine ever altered as much as two words of the *Lay*, or attempted to do so, is an improbability unsupported by anything but Lockhart's guessing, and when he guesses he is a very dangerous guide.

As to James Ballantyne, his position was different, and throughout the whole of Scott's literary life, from this date almost to the end, he acted a very natural and necessary part.

The days of typewriters, of stenographers and dictaphones, had not yet dawned. Scott wrote with his own hand, at first on folio, but afterwards always on quarto sheets, in the small, neat, rapid script which he had practised as a copyist in his father's office. He sent these sheets to the printer, to be set in type, and for the proofs to be returned for his own correction. For many years the output of Scott's pen was the main financial support of the Border Press, and its greatest activity. James Ballantyne made the oversight and correction of these proofs his personal concern. He corrected obvious clerical errors in the rapidly written script, which were not frequent: he referred back to the author anything which was not clear to the compositor or himself.

When poetry gave place to fiction, this might be one of Ballantyne's main occupations. There were times when Scott was writing incessantly—writing against time in the endeavour to get a novel rapidly through the press. It was being set in type, day by day, as its composition proceeded. Day by day, the new script went to the press, and the proofs of the previous sheets would come back for correction. Scott struggled to keep up with the press, or the press struggled to keep up with him.

At such times, it is more than possible that some of the "mere" commercial interests of the printing business—it is Lockhart's adjective, not mine—may have been subordinated by both Ballantyne and Scott to their literary preoccupations, or they may have been delegated to less competent hands. If this were done to their own ultimate loss, we have no cause for complaint. It was to our gain, and it was they who suffered, not we. And, even by mere commercial standards, they might have shown some justification, for they laboured at the most vital point, either for attack or defence.

In these ways, the services that James Ballantyne rendered, though not of a monitorial kind, approached those of a secretary, and their value, within their natural limits, is beyond reasonable challenge. He was such a secretary as any author should be glad to have.

He took a keen interest in the advancing narrative of a novel, as its proofs passed through his hands, and if the author's rapid writing left any point of incident or character obscure, he would naturally call attention to it, in the fourfold capacities of friend, partner, proof-corrector and printer. There were occasions, as the years passed, when he ventured expostulation in respect of features of plots which he thought would be unpopular. In the two instances of which we know, because Scott gave way to his importunity, and that of others—the weakening of the tragedy in *St. Ronan's Well,* and the resurrection of Athelstan in *Ivanhoe*—Ballantyne was clearly wrong, as it might be expected that he would be. It is a distortion of fact to represent that Scott depended upon him, or anyone, at any time, for revision of what he wrote, and it would be absurd to discuss such a point, did not Lockhart imply it from time to time with a quiet persistence which gradually destroys the perspective in which Scott should be regarded, particularly in respect of his literary creations, in relation to his surrounding friends.

It is true that, in separate sentences, Lockhart states explicitly that Scott went his own way in these matters. (Yet, if so, why say it at all? Most authors do.) But, having done so, he will, in the course of a single paragraph, be as explicit in contradiction of his own assurance as when he says that Ballantyne "conveyed his mind on such matters with equal candour and delicacy during the whole of Scott's brilliant career. In the vast majority of instances he found his friend acquiesce at once in the propriety of his suggestions.. Mr. Erskine was the referee whenever the poet hesitated about taking the hints of the zealous typographer; and his refined taste and gentle manners rendered his critical alliance highly valuable."

Lockhart, though he wrote some forgotten novels, was a critic rather than an originator, of literature. He did not understand that great poets and great novelists usually write their own books.

CHAPTER XXX.

The Lay of the Last Minstrel was published in London in 1805, and had an instant success, on a scale which was beyond anticipation or precedent. A century later, it had become fashionable in literary circles to depreciate the genius of Scott, particularly as a poet. Smaller men, of meaner ideals and baser instincts, moved restlessly beneath so great a shadow. Literary neurotics questioned the possibility of great art taking on serene or courageous forms. Literary decadents were equally sure that art and obscenity were inseparable friends. Scott, they told each other, was in eclipse, and those who regarded them as intelligent guides repeated the clap-trap phrases in which they dismissed him to a decent obscurity. But it may be doubted whether the eclipse had much reality even then. He gave a light which did not penetrate to their own minds, but it was visible to a million others. And, today, the tide turns. Even the cant formula in which he is said to have been a greater novelist than poet is not repeated with the old assurance, though its echoes have not yet died.

In textbooks of literature, it had become the fashion to say that he was not Homer or Shakespeare, which is obviously true. Neither was Homer Shakespeare, nor Shakespeare Scott. But of what other figures in modern literature would it occur to any mood of criticism to make either of such comparisons? still less, to make both of the same man? The fact is that, even while they disparage his stature, they are aware of a giant form, as their comparisons prove. Homer—Dante—Shakespeare—Scott—we may give precedence as we will, but they are names that are at home together, and there are no others with which to compare them except themselves.

Each of these great poets took the material that lay around him to weld it into forms of immortal beauty. Each of them would surely have done the same, with whatever differences, had they been born in each other's places. Scott had his first material in the traditions of Border chivalry, and it is hard to imagine that any poet could have transformed it to a greater thing.

Something (though not the most) of the novelty of the *Lay* came from the metre in which it was written, for which Coleridge had a responsibility of unintentional suggestion, and must have his recognition or praise.

It will be remembered that Sir John Stoddart called at Lasswade Cottage in the summer of 1800, and had a reception that pleased him well. Sir John was a friend of Wordsworth and Coleridge. He was an admirer of the latter poet, and in the course of conversation he mentioned a narrative poem, unpublished and incomplete, which Coleridge had written. It was in octosyllabic lines, instead of the decasyllabic which were usual for such poetry—indeed, for any which was beyond lyric length. He quoted from memory of the manuscript he had read.

The Lay of the Last Minstrel is written in the same metre. Its first canto contains one line which is almost identical with one in *Christabel*.

The *Lay* has:

Jesu Maria, shield us well!

Christabel has:

Jesu, Maria, shield her well!

Beyond that, there is no similarity in subject, idea, or context.

Christabel has:

The night is chill; the forest bare;
Is it the wind that moaneth bleak?

The *Lay* has:

> Is it the roar of Teviot's side,
> That chafes against the scaur's red side?
> Is it the wind that swings the oaks?

Again, there is no similarity of theme or treatment. The two poems approach verbally at these points, and then go their separate ways.

Neither are they of comparable qualities. There is magic in *Christabel*, but the narrative is hesitant, unsure of itself. It wanders blindly about, and that it should have been left unfinished seems a most natural thing. Some suppose that Coleridge had no idea, any more than anyone else, what the end should be. He said he did, and he was in the best position to know. Yet, in fact, he did not finish it. His difficulty probably was that his conclusion lacked substance. He could have ended it in a few lines, but he failed to end it in as many hundreds, which he had intended to do. The thought was too thin.

Neither will the two poems endure comparison on the prosodic level on which they meet. *Christabel*, again, has its magic lines, and to praise the *Lay* does not require their depreciation. But they have not the richness, the profuse variety, of the new verbal melodies that the *Lay* contains. Neither Coleridge nor Scott originated the octosyllabic metre. Yet comparing the cadences of the early lines of the two poems, and the verbal similarities mentioned, it is bare justice to recognise that the seed of the *Lay* came from the mind of the English poet. It grew, in its new sowing, to such foliage and flower as it could never have produced in its native soil...

It is difficult to write of the *Lay* without enthusiasm. Criticism which is unenthusiastic must be unintelligent also.

Its originalities and varieties of verbal music are alone sufficient to lift it into the front rank of the poetic literature of the world. In this aspect of its originality only Spenser with *The Fairie Queen*, and Swinburne with the first series of *Poems and*

Ballads, the one before and the one after, made a comparable addition to the cadences of English song.

There is a curious illumination in these comparisons, because these three poets are the three great solitary peaks in the procession of English poetry. They are of separate grandeurs, without ancestry or descendants. The continuous stream of English literature can be traced intelligently without noticing them at all. And, however separate and different from each other they may appear, they have their deep-rooted affinities. Spenser and Swinburne approach closely to Scott, though from opposite sides, and Scott reaches out to both of them, filling the great space between....

It is one of the comedies of pedantic criticism that this poem which abounds in lyrical ornament should have been used to support an argument that Scott had a defective ear for the elementary metrical patterns which do not constitute the beauty of poetic form, but are the looms on which its colours are woven. The line usually quoted on this inditement is:

"Saw a terrier and lurcher pass out."

This line is obviously experimental, and does not succeed, because it needs to be read with a change both of time and inflexion of the concluding syllables.

The only subsequent attempt to establish it of which I am aware is that of Mr. Chesterton in the *Ballad of the White Horse*.

"His fruit trees stood like soldiers
Drilled in a straight line."

In this ballad, the construction is repeated several times, showing that it must be deliberate, but its defect is still that it is too unexpected for its rhythm to be recognised at a first reading.

A full slow equal value may be given to two sequent monosyllables at the commencement of a line of English verse, but the idea will not readily be caught by a reader if the construction be at the end of a line in which the cadence falls. So we may allow that the line first quoted is no better than an experimental failure, because, for reasons too technical to analyse here, it cannot be used in English verse with sufficient regularity to render it an expected thing. But for those who can read the *Lay* without being intoxicated by its verbal melodies, there is no more to be said—to them.

The instantaneous success of the poem was not won by its lyric beauty only, nor by the glamour of its reconstruction of a rudely-chivalrous manner of life which had then left the world more recently than it has today. It had the vigour of sympathetic imagination which would vitalise all that Scott would write in whatever form; and with it there was a bias towards nobility which is like the constant tug of an undercurrent, drawing us to the contemplation of "whatsoever things are lovely, whatsoever things are of good report".

It was the poetry of action, written as it had never been written before, and perhaps will never be written again; but it was not of the order of imagination which exalts the physical. It was occupied with spiritual issues continually. Conduct is not three parts of life; it is the entire whole. As Scott said to his son-in-law on his death-bed, "nothing else matters".

It is not by supremacy of strength, but "through good heart, and our Lady's grace," that horse and man struggle upward from the midnight ford. Valour, in Scott's romances, never achieves impossible physical feats. Having been up all night, Deloraine goes down before Cranston's lance, as a weary man on a weary horse might be expected to do, but he does not become smaller by the fall, for we had been made aware of the spirit which forgets its weariness "when he marked the crane on the Baron's crest".

The vital issue of the poem is not whether the kidnapped child will be carried away, or the castle stormed, but in what spirit the Lady of Branksome will meet the threats which are made against her: whether she will barter her honour to regain her child. When she has replied

> "For the young heir of Branksome's line,
> God be his aid and God be mine;
> Through me no friend shall meet his doom;
> Here, while I live, no foe finds room,"

the real battle has been fought and won.

After the death of Scott, the pursuit of physical science led mankind into a pit of materialism from which it is scarcely emerging, bewildered as from an evil dream, and the majority of our novelists, and some self-called poets, have followed it into a darkness from which they assure us, quite truthfully, they can see no stars.

It is in estimation of the relative importance of spiritual and physical or material issues that Scott is out of sympathy with modern fiction and modern criticism. Generous and tolerant though he was, he would have dismissed most of the "sex" novels which Mr. Gerald Gould reviews each week with such portentous solemnity, as too trivial and shallow, if not too base, for the wasting of a word upon them.

"Sexual" is a harmless necessary word, but it is not necessary, nor without significance, that it should be used in contemporary literature (and contemporary journalism) perhaps a hundred times more frequently than in any previous period. The novelists of our time, and some who have professed to be our own poets also, have concentrated on the degradations of physical passion, and observing that the older novelists painted on a wider canvas, and with a different perspective, they bring a humourless accusation against them that they portrayed only half of the panorama of life. The accusation is untrue; but were it of a literal accuracy, the honour would still be theirs, for how many of their successors could claim a breadth of view which would extend to such percentage of the total area?

Scott was of the tradition of Homer, who saw that there was a higher poetic value in the despairing sorrow of Helen over the dead Hector, than in the way in which she had previously surrendered herself to the arms of his younger brother.

Like Dante, he would have sorrowed over the tragedy of Francesca—and placed her in the hell to which she belonged.

We could trust most modern novelists that they would go wrong in either of these instances, and some of those who call themselves our poets would be lost on the same road. To them, the poetic value of Helen and Francesca would be in contemplation of their adulteries, but, like Homer and Dante, Scott preferred greater things....

The enthusiasm with which the *Lay* was received is easy to understand. It was not only that it was a very beautiful thing. It was beauty in a new form—new both to the popular mind, and to the student of literature of any time, or in any tongue.

Beyond that, it was alive; and, being alive, it had the qualities of living matter. It was not carved out of stone, but built of living cells. It was not fashioned, it grew. It had the qualities of its spontaneity; and the defects, if we will. There were those who criticised its structure when it first appeared, and these depreciations have never been entirely silenced, nor are they entirely groundless. A work of outstanding originality is almost always assailed by such criticism. It will differ from the requirements of ordered form, as a river differs from a canal, and for the same reasons. It has not been carved; it has flowered.

And yet the accusation of defective form cannot be left without qualification. The six-cantoed structure, with its breaking interludes, was regular enough—regular, indeed, as the severest form of the classical epic. And it, also, like the substance of the poem, had the charm of a new thing. It was its author's invention, admirably adapted to his own genius, and which he was to repeat several times to successful ends, though no subsequent poet would be able to give it the same vitality. It was of the content that the charge of lack of balance and structural unity could be most plausibly urged. It might be compared to a plant which the gardener confines to limited boundaries, within which it can grow at its random will.

In its final form, it had a well-defined plot, well handled, and reaching a sufficient climax. To a close examination, it may appear that the goblin-dwarf is a needless intrusion, or even an excrescence upon it. In its first form, it had been no more than a ballad of *diablerie,* in which the dwarf had been a central figure. To have ejected him at a later stage, and made the poem a more literal account of one of the major raids which periodically devastated the Borders in the Middle Ages, would have involved such radical changes that it would have been a different poem, and whether the gain would have outweighed the loss must be hard to guess. But if the excision of the supernatural element had involved that of Deloraine's midnight ride, and the opening of the wizard's grave, probably most lovers of English poetry will be well-content that Scott used his genius for the blending of the various elements that he drew together as the years passed, and the poem lengthened, rather than to discard that to which a more prosaic standard of criticism might object as having become incongruous to the poem in its final form.

CHAPTER XXXI.

The first edition of the *Lay* had consisted of 750 quarto copies, elaborately printed. The bulk of this quantity went to Longmans, in London, and was sold immediately. The publication in Scotland was entrusted to Constable, who had a similar experience. The basis of the agreement with Scott was that the profits of this edition should be shared equally, the copyright remaining his property. Ultimately he received £169 as his share of the proceeds of these 750 volumes.

But the reception of the book showed Mr. Longman that he had found a poem which could be largely—no one could do more than guess how largely—sold. Again, he hurried to Edinburgh. He proposed to bring out a larger and less expensive edition in octavo size. He offered Scott £500 for the outright sale of the copyright, which was accepted, and was one of the worst bargains Scott ever made. A subsequent present of £100 to buy a horse to replace one that went lame when publisher and author were riding together, did little to adjust the balance of advantage, for the sales of this book, during Scott's own lifetime, approached 50,000 copies. But, indirectly, the *Lay* was the source of some further profit in which Scott participated, for the printing orders were to be placed with the Ballantyne Press.

Up to this time, Scott had had no proprietary interest in Ballantyne's printing business, though it was on his own persuasion that it had been brought to Edinburgh, and he had assisted that migration with a substantial loan. Since then, he had been able to place so much work in its way that the growth of its prosperity could be attributed directly to his own patronage. On the other hand, Ballantyne had done his part well. The event has justified Scott's encouragement of the migration, both by orders which had been secured, and the manner in which they had been discharged.

Now Ballantyne approached Scott with a statement of his financial position. He was embarrassed by his own success. He was not in a position to execute the amount of orders he was receiving, both for the *Lay*, and from other directions, unless further capital were available. Scott had a large sum of money awaiting investment. His heart was in the Ballantyne business, and he had the responsibility of those who give advice which is taken. Friends who looked to him for help under any circumstances were not sent empty away. He agreed to invest about a third of the money which Captain Robert had left him. There is no reason to suppose that he did this with reluctance. But he declined to go further as a mere creditor. He required a partnership, to which Ballantyne agreed very willingly. A deed was signed, under which the profit was to be divided into three parts. One was to be paid to James Ballantyne in recompence of his work as manager, the others were to be drawn by the two partners equally. Scott, it will be noticed, had no responsibilities of management at this time. He was to be a sleeping partner. The division of profits may be considered equitable if Ballantyne's capital were substantially equal to that of Scott, or generous if it were less. Lockhart failed to find that any Balance Sheet was drawn up as a foundation for this partnership, and suggests that it was arranged so loosely that there was no such document, which has been assumed as a fact by some later writers. The negative evidence that no such document could be found thirty years later is not convincing, and the improbability that it was not drawn, if the nature of the agreement required it, is extreme, as any accountant will recognise. What basis, in the absence of such a document, could there be for the calculations of future profits, which were certainly made? But the financial circumstances of this partnership, even from its inception, have been the subject of acute controversy, and must be treated in a separate chapter.

It was subsequently suggested that Scott's action, as a practising barrister, in entering a commercial partnership, was a breech of etiquette, if not of honour, and that this explained an alleged secrecy in which the arrangement was shrouded. It is a suggestion which will not endure examination either in fact or theory. There was, at this period, no law of limited liability. Capital could not be invested in shares or debentures by those who sought to use it in commercial channels, nor could commercial firms obtain it by means of such issues. Scott's legal training had taught him that arrangements for sleeping partnerships, such as this, were the routine business of any attorney's office at that period, and the suggestion that barristers were debarred from such investments requires to be supported by some affirmative evidence, which is wholly lacking. It is said that "only" William Erskine, among his friends, was taken into his confidence at that time, a method of stating an admitted fact which appears to place it in the opposite scale to that to which it belongs. Even if it be literally true, surely the fact that Scott informed a friend who would have been fully aware of the nature of what he was doing, and who was himself a lawyer, should absolve him from the suspicion that he was aware of impropriety. But, in fact and in spite of, or perhaps because of, the endless number of his friends, Scott was not randomly confidential with them about his personal affairs. Even with the pen, he had a habitual reticence, which was only partially abandoned at a later period of life. There is no more than a casual significance in the fact that the attempt at autobiography which he made three years later, and which covered his youthful years with a detailed fluency, broke off abruptly at the time when Williamina Stuart must have come upon the scene, and he could not have continued a frank and sufficient narrative without disclosing matters which he was too sensitive to discuss.

Lockhart attempts a subtler point when he suggests that the fact that Scott's partnership was not generally known was unfair to publishers who might be influenced by his proposals as to books which they should produce, without knowing that, if they placed the printing with Ballantyne & Co., it would be financially advantageous to himself. The argument will not endure examination, and the more explicitly it be stated, the more dubious it becomes. It could be argued with at least equal force that he would have been better able to influence business toward the Border Press if it were known that he had a financial interest in it. He might have expressly stipulated that the printing should go to his own firm in cases where he was editing the proposed volumes, which he could hardly do without implication that he was financially interested. At the most, the inditement amounts to an argument that Scott was in a position to act unfairly to others, had he been of a disposition to do so. It is not only disputable in its premises, it is unsupported by any evidence that such breaches of equity occurred, and confronted by an immense improbability, Scott's character being what it was, that he could have allowed it to happen.

But was the partnership so close and unguessed a secret in commercial circles? There was not, at this time, the publicity of shareholders' registers, there was no system for the registration of partnership names, such as the freer atmosphere of those days would not easily have endured. But, in the absence of the limited liability Acts of later years, such partnerships were extremely common. The closeness of Scott's interest in the Border Press, and his associations with it, could not easily have been concealed from those publishers who were doing regular business with it, and there is no evidence that there was any attempt to conceal them. Had they asked themselves, as they most probably did, if they were not explicitly told, whether Scott had any partnership stake in the printing business, nine out of ten might have made the correct guess, and all must have known that it was a very probable thing.

Beyond that, there were the type-makers, the cloth and paper merchants, and others from whom, as the business developed, large credits were obtained. There were the banks which gave ever-increasing overdrafts, and discounted customers' bills, by which, in that period of fevered war-finance, the publishing business was almost entirely carried on. Did they never ask for the names of the partners with whom they dealt? Were they never told? The contrary supposition is without proof, and is entirely improbable.

It does not follow that there may not have been many of Scott's literary and social friends, and more of his acquaintances, who remained ignorant of the details of his investments, and, in particular, of his financial interest in the Ballantyne Press. Any large commercial failure in those days might lead to anxious speculation as to whom it would ruin, and often resulted in the disclosure of unexpected names.

In the investigation of these matters, Lockhart had the enormous advantages of being closer to the period with which he dealt, having access to more documents than are now available, and having been in personal contact with many of the people concerned. He showed industry in searching among the facts, and some skill in presenting such as he thought most appropriate for exhibition. He had the disadvantages that he was without commercial training, or commercial sympathies. He was biased in Scott's favour as his son-in-law and biographer, and as one who had received much help and affection from him: he was biased against him by personal limitations and prejudices. Frequently, he makes apology where only explanation is needed. He accuses by excusation....

CHAPTER XXXII.

In the beginning of this year (1805), and before the success of the *Lay* could have been more than anticipation, Scott was contemplating a step which would define and limit the claims of his legal profession upon time and thought, and give clear spaces of freedom for literary work, into which no briefs would intrude: this was to obtain an appointment as Clerk of Session at the High Court of Edinburgh, at which he was now a practising barrister. The office, which was closely similar to that of an Associate to a High Court Judge today, was honourable, but not exalted. Such positions were usually granted to barristers of good character and sound legal knowledge, who had lost hope or ambition of attaining to higher legal distinctions. They were life appointments, and those who took them rarely emerged from their honourable obscurity to take up more important offices.

The duties of a Clerk of Session consisted in watching the course of the cases which were on his list, seeing that they were technically in order, placing them before the officiating Judge, and reducing his judgement to writing in legal form at the conclusion of the hearing. To perform such duties efficiently required legal knowledge and intelligent observation, but they were free from the advocates' anxieties, or the uncertain claims upon time and thought which might be made by cases in preparation before they came into court.

These appointments were made by Crown patronage, and there were instances of slack or inefficient holders delegating their duties to subordinates, who shared the salary of the office. But most of the Clerks of Session were lawyers of good repute, whatever may have been the nature of the intrigues, or bribery, or direct purchase, by which their appointments had been obtained.

That Scott should have fixed his mind on the obtaining of such an office at so early an age may be regarded as conclusive evidence that he had decided to regard his legal profession as subordinate to his literary ambition.

The matter was not actually arranged till the end of the year, and Lockhart, with a surface plausibility, suggests that Scott's decision was taken in direct consequence of the success of the *Lay*, and of the commercial partnership into which he had entered. What he says is:

> "The first notice of this affair that occurs in his correspondence is in a note of Lord Dalkeith's, February 2nd, 1805, in which his noble friend says: 'My father desires me to tell you that he has had a communication from Lord Melville within these few days, and that he thinks your business in a good train, though not certain.' I consider it as clear, then, that he began his negotiations about a seat at the clerks' table, immediately after the *Lay* was published; and this in the strictest connection with his trading adventure."

But when we remember that the *Lay* was not published till the beginning of January in London, the state of the posts at that period, and the other circumstances of the position, including James Ballantyne's explicit statement that it was after the publication of the *Lay* that he first opened the financial negotiations with Scott that led to the partnership being arranged, we may be so far from "considering it as clear" that Scott's decision followed the success of the *Lay* and the partnership negotiation as to observe with equal clarity that it must have been formed at an earlier period.

Four weeks after the *first day of publication* in London, Dalkeith was writing that his father (who did not live in his immediate neighbourhood) had heard some days earlier from Lord Melville in reply to a communication that must first have been sent to him, and which was not likely to have received his instant attention; and prior to this communication being sent, Scott must have made his request to the Duke of Buccleuch, sometime *after* he had heard from London of the success of the *Lay*, which the first purchaser would scarcely have had time to read when the news must have been dispatched to him!

This is only one of many instances in which Lockhart fails to appreciate accurately the implication of the dates he gives; and this looseness of deduction is emphasised by his further reference, at the time at which the appointment was made—nearly a year later. He then says:

> "Meantime, the affair of the Clerkship, opened nine or ten months before, had not been neglected by the friends on whose counsel and assistance Scott had relied. Whether Mr Pitt's hint to Mr William Dundas, that he would willingly find an opportunity to promote the interests of the author of the *Lay*, or some conversation between the Duke of Buccleuch and Lord Melville, first encouraged him to this direction of his views, I am not able to state distinctly."

The suggestion that the success of the *Lay* was so instantly realised, and that Scott so instantly decided thereupon to apply for a Clerkship that the negotiation had been well advanced within a month of that publication, may be no more than an extreme improbability, but it becomes an absurdity when it is developed into the supposition that Scott may have been first "encouraged" to "this direction of his views" by the communication to him of a remark said to have been made in London by William Pitt some time after he had read the poem.

It is a careless, and may seem in itself to be no more than a trivial error, but it had more than a surface significance. Lockhart has, in fact, made it clear that Scott had decided upon this course before he could have known of the success of the *Lay*: and before there would have been any suggestion of a Ballantyne partnership, unless the design had been formed in advance of Ballantyne's application, through foresight of probabilities, and in the privacy of Scott's own mind. But he comes to an opposite conclusion from that which his own evidence indicates, because he is imputing his own disposition to the man whose biography he is writing.

Lockhart allowed himself to be influenced by the pressure of circumstance, and relied upon the advice of others, in ways, and to an extent, which Scott never did, but which he imputes to him continually. When Lockhart discusses Scott's character in the abstract, he is not sparing of laudatory adjectives. Indeed, he may use half-a-dozen when a less number would be sufficient. But when he deals with events he constantly represents him, not merely as being driven before the gale of circumstance, but as one who is constantly looking around for stronger shoulders on which to lean, as he instinctively supposes that men most naturally do.

Here he represents him as impelled by the circumstances of a great literary success, and a commercial investment, to seek the comparative ease of an official appointment, and as being guided thereto by the "counsel" of his friends, whereas the date he himself gives is the strongest evidence that Scott had planned this development at the time he launched the *Lay* upon the world, and before the partnership had been even discussed or suggested: and there is not the faintest reason to suppose that he sought or received anyone's counsel in the matter, though he naturally sought the assistance of those who were able to influence the appointment which he desired.

There was actually no vacancy among the Clerks of Session at this time, and to await the death or retirement of one of them would not have suited his purpose, nor could he have been sure that he would have obtained the prize in the scramble which would have taken place on the occurrence of such an event. He therefore entered into an arrangement which was usual at the period. George Home of Wedderburn was an old man, who had held a Clerkship for thirty years, and would be glad to retire. They agreed to make application for the office to be held jointly while they both lived, and then by the survivor alone. While he lived, Home was to draw the entire salary, and Scott was to do the entire work. By this bargain, Scott avoided the necessity of making any capital payment to Home, such as would otherwise have been necessary to purchase his retirement. At a later date, the custom of such arrangements was superseded by a pension system, and the sums which had been found by individuals came out of the public purse.

The matter, as we shall see later, was not completed until the end of the year, but it could be anticipated with some confidence, and may have relieved his mind from the obligation of further effort to improve a practice at the Bar which would so soon be ended, and there must have been advantage in this, for it was a year bright with victory and with the anticipation of others to follow, and full of many activities which must have consumed the time and strained the energies even of Scott's amazing and unexhausted vitality.

He wrote to Ballantyne in April telling him that he had an idea for a complete edition of British poets in one hundred octavo volumes, which he would edit and annotate. He would ask a fee of thirty guineas per volume for his trouble, and the copyright would be theirs. It would have been money well-earned, judging by the editorial standard of the *Minstrelsy*, and his subsequent work in other directions, and the plan might have resulted in a standard edition of British poetry such as we are never likely to have, but it was rejected by the London publishers, in view of a smaller scheme of the same kind which was already on the commercial horizon. It is difficult to regret this, for it must have been, even to Scott, a labour of many years, and would have meant that we should have lacked some better things that we now have. But Scott made proposals for other new editions in the same letter, a complete one of Dryden among them, and this proposition bore immediate fruit. It had Constable's approval, and he was already becoming a voice of some authority in the world of books. It was destined to be published, just three years later, by William Miller of London, a gigantic venture in eighteen octavo volumes. The publisher paid forty guineas a volume for Scott's editorial work upon them, and money has seldom been more hardly or more capably earned. The commercial success of the venture had been regarded dubiously in the trade, and even by Scott's own friends, but the event justified Constable's judgement and Miller's courage. The sale, though not rapid, was steady. A dozen years after publication, the whole edition was exhausted, and a continued demand justified the issue of another.

For the next three years—till the close of 1807—we must regard all Scott's activities as carried on with this work in the background, and in continual progress, for it was undertaken in no perfunctory manner. He did not think it sufficient to concentrate upon the text of Dryden, but must familiarise himself with all the literature, politics, and personalities that environed him. He wrote, in this autumn of 1805, that he had already read completely over a hundred pamphlets of the period. The bulk of Dryden's writings in verse and prose, and the fact that so much of it was politically or topically directed, and is full of obscure allusions to forgotten things, made the work an immense labour to one whose mind was preoccupied by so much else of original work, nor does Dryden seem to be one to whom his genius would be naturally sympathetic; but the work, being undertaken, seems to have been finished without weariness or regret. There is little evidence in his other writings of this three years concentration upon it, beyond the brief allusion, in the introduction to the first canto of *Marmion* (written while the editing of Dryden was actually still on hand) to Dryden's never-realised ambition to have given some adequate poetic interpretation of the Arthurian legends for which our literature still waits, when

"Dryden in immortal strain
Had raised the Table Round again,
But that a ribald King and Court
Bade him toil on to make them sport;
Demanded for their niggard pay,
Fit for their souls, a looser lay,
Licentious satire, song and play;

The world, defrauded of the high design,
Profaned the God-given strength, and marred the lofty line.

In this same year, Scott made one of his first—possibly his first serious—attempt at prose fiction. He showed William Erskine a fragment—probably about the first seven chapters—of *Waverley*. They may have been commenced earlier, but the title, which was ultimately used, *'Tis sixty years since*, supports the probability that they were the actual work of this year.

William Erskine was not enthusiastic, which showed good judgement. Scott's own mind may have supported his friend's criticisms. That he deliberately abandoned the attempt may be doubted, but he hesitated, and the idea was smothered for the time amid other activities. It may have been well for him, and for us. His work in poetry was not yet done.

As to that fragment of *Waverley,* a prophetic genius might have been able to see the potentialities which it did not contain, but no ordinary critic could be expected to do so. In that preliminary fragment, a great vessel is struggling to get out of harbour. It has not spread its wings to the wind. Or it may be compared to the effort of some gigantic bird that is too heavy to rise. Shown those first chapters, and asked whether there would be a public eager to read them, any critic might have replied in hesitant words. Remembering the gigantic success that the *Lay* had just attained, any critic might have replied that poetry was the better medium for the next attempt. But Scott, though he listened to all, had a habit of going his own way in the end. It was not the opinion of William Erskine that caused the *Waverley* fragment to be laid aside; it was the doubt, and still more the contending activities, in his own mind.

He wrote also, during this year, an almost regular series of articles, on very diverse subjects, for Constable's Edinburgh Review, which Thomas Jeffrey was editing. From this time, Constable advances steadily toward the front of the stage, a young man, of Scott's own age, whose commercial genius, joined to a genuine love of literature for its own sake, and a faculty of criticism which was sometimes superior to that of the professional writers, was advancing him to a position in the trade with which few, even of London publishers, could compare. Looking back now, it may appear that he owed this position largely to the huge sales of Scott's own writings which he was to control in the days to be. To say that would be no more than to recognise that he seized the opportunities which came his way, but, even so, it would do less than justice to his own position. He had already acquired the Edinburgh Review, when it was in its infancy, thinking of it primarily as an advertising gesture, and had made it the foremost literary magazine of its time. That may be attributed partly to Thomas Jeffrey's editing. But who chose Jeffrey for the position?

He had adventured, with little capital, on the perilous sea of publishing, and had shown the fine discrimination of judgement, both as to the literary value and commercial possibilities of an author's work, which a publisher needs, and so few appear to have.

We find Scott being drawn by the caprice of circumstance into the orbits of Constable and Jeffrey, but we must observe a difference between them and the James Ballantyne connection. James was his own choice. James had to the last, and through all vicissitudes, a personal loyalty to himself, which Constable certainly never felt in the same way.

Jeffrey, a somewhat older man, like Scott a barrister, and unlike him having found that a literary career did not interfere with success at the Bar, was not one whom Scott would naturally have chosen for friendship; but he was one who, in his editorial capacity, was in a position to accept or reject the articles which Scott offered for the Review. He might criticise, as from a height: he might even patronise with his pen. He was often a shrewd, and may always have been an honest critic, but he was never able to see Scott's work in a correct perspective. They were too close together.

Not that Scott was sensitive to adverse criticism. He lost no sleep over that. But Jeffrey, in his political views, and in points of character, was antipathetic to him in many ways. The political differences were, indeed, an evidence of their fundamental discords, rather than the cause that divided them.

Constable also, though Scott recognised and appreciated some of his greater qualities, was never admitted to a close confidence, or to the inner circle of his friends. They were business acquaintances, united by common interests, and, at one time, by great successes; but all the justice and generosity of Scott's character did not enable this bond to reach real cordiality, or the future course of events might have been somewhat different.

Had Scott been of the easily-influenced amiability that Lockhart attributed to him, their relations might have reached a closer intimacy. But they were both men of strong wills, and of different audacities, and their wills clashed. There were occasions when Constable was in a position to enforce his own, and had the courage to do so, and was probably right. But the position was such that the issue could never be proved. Scott was not one to let rancour dwell in his mind, but opposition was always a latent possibility between them, of which both were conscious. We must not exaggerate this quality of their association, which had other, and more dominant aspects, but it is necessary to observe it.

CHAPTER XXXIII.

As the spring advanced, and Scott would naturally have retired from Edinburgh, with the close of the legal session, to his Ashestiel home, he had a further call upon his time and energies in the increase of military duties which the crisis of the year required. Lockhart, using one of the most unfortunate words that his biography contains, says that it was a year of 'mania' in volunteering. It was a year of crisis in the fate of the United Kingdom, and men of good courage looked into the gloom ahead with steady but not sanguine eyes. Italy lay at the feet of Napoleon. Prussia gathered her armies, but delayed to say to what purpose they would be used. The French army lay at Boulogne. Spain had joined France, and her splendidly equipped, though unpractised, fleet was suddenly added to the naval strength of our foes. It was known in March that the French admiral was out of port, and that Nelson was in pursuit; but beyond that there was silence. They had disappeared into the Atlantic together. Any day the news of Nelson's defeat, or even that Villeneuve had evaded him successfully, might mean the instant landing of Napoleon's mightiest army upon the English shore. Only Austria, Russia, Sweden—furthest removed from the centre of the common danger—still had courage or capacity to unite with England in open hostility to the European conqueror. A ruined continent was a sufficient warning to English and Scottish men to array themselves in defence of their threatened homes.

As men had laboured to rebuild the walls of Jerusalem with trowel in hand, but a sword at an arm's reach, so men went about their business in Edinburgh in such a guise that volunteer uniforms were more common than civilian clothes. To prepare themselves, as well as they might, to meet the battle-practiced veterans of the Grand Army of Napoleon, sham fights were planned on a scale that the Scottish capital had not seen, nor imagined previously. It may be supposed that the regiment of cavalry which owed its creation to Scott's foreseeing energy was not backward in these manoeuvres.

Yet it is in this summer that he had another editorial scheme in his mind—a uniform series of the old English Chronicles, to which he was striving (with no final success) to bring his correspondents to an equal enthusiasm.

And when he retires at last, as the summer advances, to the remote quietude of Ashestiel, he is inundated with many visitors, Robert Southey among them, who distract him from his work, and from many time-requiring duties of the country life on which the half of his heart is fixed. And there is a constant influx of correspondence, sent on the easy basis that the heavy postage must be paid by him who takes it in, which he receives, and to which he replies with an amazing patience, and a courtesy that will continue to his life's end, only rarely ruffled to a moment's protest by some exceptional impudence, or too-persistent boring.

It was in August that John Skene first visited Ashestiel. He was a man of many sides, and particularly associated with Scott in connection with the regiment he had helped to form. He was fond of open-air sports also, and these summer visits became an almost regular occurrence during the coming years. They rode back together from the camp at Edinburgh, and reached the north bank of the Tweed, looking across to Ashestiel, which stood at a little height, half-hidden in trees, on its further side. Ashestiel lay in a wild quiet land. Even the country houses that were scattered all over the Lowland counties, were few and far in that neighbourhood. Only Selkirk, the small county town, scarcely more than a village, that was the centre of the Ettrick dale, lay over the wooded hills a few miles to the south.

There was no bridge to Ashestiel. You went through the river as best you could, calling it a ford. But it was a poor ford at the best, and now the river was swollen with heavy August rains. Scott made no difficulty of that. He put Captain to the water, going first, as a host should. The horse lost his footing almost at once. They swam safely through the flood. Skene tells the tale as an instance of Scott's somewhat reckless courage in taking untested risks. He was a great taker of fords, either on horse or foot. Skene does not say how he got over himself. We may conclude that he went by the same way.

The Scotts showed him round the little farm together. There were Charlotte's fowl-pens, into which the wild-cats from the woods had so persistently broken. There were the horses, more than a few. Besides the carriage-horses, Scott had three for his own riding. He fed them himself, when he was at home, before his own breakfast. Besides Captain, there was Lieutenant, and Brown Adam, a dangerous brute who had broken one groom's arm, and another's leg: and whom no one but Scott would ride.

But if the stable-door were opened, Brown Adam would trot to the stone that Scott required to use when he mounted, in consequence of his shrunken leg.

All his life, Scott had a marvellous control, and understanding of animals. His friendships with them were almost as numerous as with his human associates, and there were some curious unsolicited advances from them to him. There is a tale of a young pig which strains credulity, and another of a hen, of a similar colour.

There were the dogs, too. First of these was Camp, a large fierce house-dog, but of a trusted gentleness with the children. These children had become a noisy lively nursery now. Sophia was nearly six; Walter was nearly four: Anne, still the baby, was in her third year. Charlotte was expecting another child before the year should close.

There were the greyhounds, Douglas and Percy, whose gambols, if they were admitted to the study, Camp would ignore with a grave contempt, but who came into their own when their master would take them out to show their skill in the chase.

Skene had a good time, shooting and coursing in such directions as the season allowed; exploring the wild beauties of the district; and spearing salmon by torch-light over a boat's gunwhale, or wading middle-deep into the Tweed.

He noticed a change in Scott's habits, which continued as long as his health lasted. He was methodical, as all men who get through exceptional quantities of work, and especially those who do so with an appearance of leisure, are obliged to be: and he had now changed a practice of working late, after others had retired, to one of early rising, and doing about three hours work before breakfast. He had been subject during recent years to a series of nervous headaches which a doctor whom he consulted attributed to the late night-hours at which he worked, and who gave him the advice on which he always afterwards acted. He got up at five, lit the fire if the weather were chilly, and dressed in a careful methodical manner, allowing himself an hour for these processes. Probably that mentally leisured hour held the secret of the ease with which he wrote subsequently. It gave time for unhurried thought, and should be added to his hours of work, if we would total them truly. From six to nine, he wrote steadily. Skene was impressed by the orderly arrangement of manuscripts and books of reference in a study from which the children were never excluded, and to which the three dogs were admitted as to their own kennel.

Breakfast gave an interval between nine and ten, after which two hours of further work would be enough for the day, if the weather were fine. On a wet day, he might continue for further hours, the extra labour constituting a fund on which he would draw if some day-long expedition in which he joined should prevent his after-breakfast work on another occasion.

Under this routine, he would be free for outdoor sports or wanderings, or for social intercourse, while the day was still young, and so long as he held to his rule of retiring early, it was a healthy and well-ordered regime.

The radical defect in his habit of life, of which he only became fully aware when it was too late to avert its consequences, and which, even then, he could do, or at least did, little to alter, lay in the difference between the manners of his summer and winter occupations and exercises. This difference was to be accentuated by the Clerkship for which he had now applied. For about six months of the year he would live in the North Castle Street house, taking little exercise, and making daily attendances at the Court (excepting on Mondays, when only criminal cases were taken, in which he was not concerned). During the remaining six months he would live a country life of a particularly active kind, in which long rides or walks, and violent field-exercises, were a regular feature. These periodic changes became a strain upon his constitution which increased as the years passed. That he would live intensely, in whatever form, was of his nature, and an unavoidable thing. But probably he would have lived a longer and healthier life either as a city or country dweller for the entire year than in this regular alternation of violent change.

But at thirty-five he thought as little of his health as young and vigorous manhood will. He was conscious only of an abundant vitality....

When Skene left, Scott set off with Charlotte on a visit to Westmorland. Her days of horse-back riding may not have been over, but at this time, on a journey of such length, and with a baby expected in three or four months' time, there was no question of how it must be undertaken. Peter Mathieson climbed on to the box of the closed carriage, and Charlotte got inside. But Scott, who had been willing to drive his wife in an open phaeton over wilder ways, was not disposed to be driven. He got on Captain's back, and rode at the carriage-side.

They called at the Wordsworths' Grasmere cottage, and the cordiality of their reception was a pleasant memory for many after-years. Wordsworth was glad to show the beauties of his own country to one who had once introduced him to those of Melrose and the Lowland hills. In the company of Sir Humphrey Davy, whose many-sided personality made him a welcome addition to the party, they climbed to the Helvellyn summit, and saw much of a country which has many similarities to that of the Scottish lakes, and is yet of a different beauty.

But the real objective was to revisit the Gilsland scenes where they had wandered together in the days when love was new, and the only anxiety had been as to the nature of the letters which the post-bags brought.

Leaving the Wordsworths, they went on to Gilsland together. In Lockhart's queer pre-Victorian phraseology "Scott carried his wife" there. We know nothing as to which of them first proposed the expedition, which must have been a pleasure to both, but we may assume that the carriage continued to carry her, and Captain to carry him, and the phrase implies nothing beyond the subjection of wives to their husband's authority: it strikes an attitude of propriety.

However that be, it was a pleasure quickly and abruptly ended. They had been at Gilsland for a few days only when there was a report that the French army was embarking for England. Beacons flared from a hundred summits, as they had done in the Armada warning two centuries earlier. Scott lost no time in leave-taking. He mounted his horse, and in twenty-four hours he was at the Dalkeith muster, a hundred miles away. We may assume that Mr. Wordsworth made another disquisition to his wife and Dorothy, dealing with the possible consequences of such invasion, in his Grasmere cottage. Or it may have been about primroses.

But the alarm died down. A few weeks later, it had passed away for a century with the smoke of the guns of Trafalgar. Scott did not wait for Charlotte's return. He mounted his horse again, and rode back to meet her at Carlisle, and, as Lockhart would say, to "carry her" home once more, as he had done after their marriage there, nearly eight years ago.

CHAPTER XXXIV.

In the early days of 1806, Scott paid a hurried visit to London. Charlotte, for the first time since their marriage, did not accompany him, the reason doubtless being her own state of health, their fourth and last child, Charles, having been born a few weeks before.

The journey was taken in connection with an appointment of Clerk of Session, of which the Patent had now been issued. It would have been open to him to pay the fees, and take over the office without further trouble, but an examination of the document had disclosed an error immaterial to himself, but which might be disastrous to the man he was superseding. The Patent gave Scott the appointment in his absolute right, without reciting the circumstances under which he obtained it, or asserting the pecuniary interest which Mr. George Home was to retain. This would have been of no consequence while they both lived, in view of the agreement between themselves, but if Scott should pre-decease the older man, he might, on the face of the document, be left without continuing income, or any effectual remedy. An examination of the practice of the time suggests that it would not have been beyond legal ingenuity to devise a further agreement between the parties which would have overcome the difficulty, in view of the fact that the estate of a holder of such office was, up to some years after this date, held to have a financial interest in its reversion. But Scott determined that he could not honourably accept it in the form in which it had been drawn, and that he must apply for a new Patent to be correctly issued. Lockhart does not blame him for this decision, but thinks his journey to London was not only needless, but that he should have realised how causeless it was, and suggests that he would have done this but for an ignorant provincialism, which attributed the petty meannesses and intrigues of Edinburgh politics to the finer spirit of a metropolis to which he was still a stranger. What Lockhart actually says is:

> "It seems wonderful that he should ever have doubted for a single moment of the result; since, had the new Cabinet been purely Whig, and he had been the most violent and obnoxious of Tory partisans, neither of which was the case, the arrangement had been not only virtually, but, with the exception of an evident official blunder, formally completed; and no Secretary of State, as I must think, could have refused to rectify the paltry mistake in question, without a dereliction of every principle of honour. At this period, however, Scott had by no means measured either the character, the feelings, or the arrangements of great public functions, by the standard with which observation and experience subsequently furnished him. He had breathed hitherto, as far as political questions of all sorts were concerned, the hot atmosphere of a very narrow scene—and seems (from his letters) to have pictured to himself Whitehall and Downing Street as only a wider stage for the exhibition of the bitter and fanatical prejudices that tormented the petty circles of the Parliament House at Edinburgh: the true bearing

and scope of which no man in after days more thoroughly understood, or more sincerely pitied. The seals of the Home Office had been placed in the hands of a nobleman of the highest character—moreover, an ardent lover of literature—while the chief of the new Ministry was one of the most generous as well as tasteful of mankind; and there occurred no hesitation whatever on their parts. In communicating his success to the Earl of Dalkeith, whose warm personal kindness, without doubt, had first animated in his favour both the Duke of Buccleuch and Lord Melville, he says (London, February 11th); 'Lord Spencer, upon the nature of the transaction being explained in an audience with which he favoured me, was pleased to direct the commission to be issued, as an act of justice, regretting, he said, it had not been from the beginning his own deed. This was doing the thing handsomely, and like an English nobleman.'"

Now for the facts. The position of Clerk of Session might be purchased by bargain with a predecessor, as Scott had done, but the formal assent to the arrangement—the issuing of the Patent—was a matter of Crown Patronage. It had been obtained for Scott by the interest of his political friends from the Government of the previous year, and with the death of Pitt on January 23rd, that Government was utterly fallen. The Government which succeeded it was not merely one of bitter hostility to those who had obtained the appointment, it was its declared intention to impeach Lord Melville for maladministration of public funds—and it was Lord Melville who had been Scott's especial friend in the matter.

The fact that Lord Spencer willingly and promptly adjusted the error may be a tribute to his own character, as well as to Scott's high literary reputation, but the suggestion that London political circles were freer from intrigue and corruption than those of the Northern capital would require more evidence than

Lockhart's assertion, and Lord Spencer's very proper conduct.

If Scott made any miscalculation, it was in failing to realise the popularity he had attained, and that it would enable him to ask with confidence for that which might have been refused to an unknown man. The wisdom of his decision to go to London, as soon as he heard that the new Government was in office, is not challenged by the fact that he succeeded in that which he set out to do. And it may be observed that a prompt adjustment of the difficulty, or a refusal to set it right, were not inevitable alternatives. Such a document, with the growing correspondence concerning it, might lie on a Whitehall table for an indefinite period.

Probably most people will agree that Scott took the right course in making a personal application for an amended Patent, and that Lockhart's stricture is baseless. Scott's sense of the delicacy of the position is shown by the fact that he would not visit at Holland House, lest it should be misconstrued. He came to ask an act of justice from his political opponents, but there must be no possibility of supposing that he was buying it with the sacrifice of the principles which he held.

Lockhart himself records that, in spite of Scott's personal popularity, there was some political outcry from the Whig party, when the appointment was gazetted in the following month; and that alone is sufficient justification of the prompt and energetic manner in which Scott dealt with an unforeseeable emergency.

Having obtained what he came for, Scott was soon on his way back to Ashestiel, but his visit gave him opportunity for the brief renewal of many friendships, and for the beginning of several new ones. Among these, his introduction to Joanna Baillie, a dramatist who was then at the height of a fame which proved to be no more than a fading light, must be noticed, because, though this first interview was a little disappointing to the anticipations of both, as such meetings most often are, it led to an enduring friendship, and a correspondence which was maintained on both sides, with little interruption, for many years.

The impeachment of Lord Melville resulted in his acquittal a few months later, and Scott, ever faithful to his friends, and recognising, truly enough, that the prosecution had resulted from party rancour, rather than any serious belief that Lord Melville's standard of honour was below that which commonly prevailed at the time, wrote a song for a dinner which was given in Edinburgh to celebrate the event, which James Ballantyne sang. The incident would not be worth recording had not W. S. Landor subsequently got hold of the tale in a malignantly muddled way, and committed himself to the statement that Scott, after flattering Fox during his life-time, sang a song at a public banquet to deride him after he was dead. It would be hard to cram more falsehoods into one libellous sentence. Scott never wrote any song about Fox, after his death or before. He never sang anything in public, at any time, being aware that he was unable to sing in tune. The lines that he wrote to "flatter" Fox are in the introduction to the first canto of *Marmion*, which was published in 1808, Fox having died eighteen months earlier:

> "For talents mourn, untimely lost,
> When best employ'd, and wanted most;
> Mourn genius high, and lore profound,
> And wit that loved to play, not wound;
> And all the reasoning powers divine,
> To penetrate, resolve, combine;
> And feelings keen, and fancy's glow,
> They sleep with him who sleeps below:
> And, if thou mourn'st they could not save
> From error him who owns this grave,
> Be every harsher thought suppress'd
> And sacred be the last long rest.
>
> Here, where the end of earthly things
> Lays heroes, patriots, bards, and kings;
> Where stiff the hand, and still the tongue,
> Of those who fought, and spoke, and sung;

> Here, where the fretted aisles prolong
> The distant notes of holy song,
> As if some angel spoke agen,
> "All peace on earth, good-will to men;"
> If ever from an English heart,
> Oh, here, let prejudice depart,
> And partial feeling cast aside,
> Record, that Fox a Briton died!
>
> When Europe crouch'd to France's yoke,
> And Austria bent, and Prussia broke,
> And the firm Russian's purpose brave
> Was barter'd by a timorous slave,
> Even then dishonour's peace he spurn'd.
> The sullied olive-branch return'd,
> Stood for his country's glory fast,
> And nail'd her colours to the mast!"

It is obvious that these lines were not only published, they were written after Fox's death, and they are not the words of a man who would sing ribaldry over a political opponent's grave.

But it is quite separately true that Scott regarded the Whig ministry as of the nature of a national disaster, for reasons which are clear enough if we understand his ideals of conduct and character, and consider the political issues at stake. He appears to have given an unusual amount of time to active political work during the brief period that this ministry remained in office.

He was also particularly stirred by certain proposed "reforms" of legal procedure which he considered to be designed to reduce the independence and prestige of the Northern capital. There was a meeting of the Faculty of Advocates to debate these proposals, at which he spoke against them at such length, and with such emotional eloquence, that Jeffrey, walking away with him from the meeting, and who had taken the other side, jested at the earnestness with which he could regard such questions, and was surprised to notice that he turned away, but not quickly enough to hide his tears.

The anecdote might be dismissed as a probable exaggeration—as most of such anecdotes are—were there not other occasions in later years, when he showed the same passionate jealousy of any attempt by the Government in London, or the Crown Officers, to centralise administration at the expense of Scottish independence and prestige, which would rouse him more easily than any question of personal interest.

During the same year—1806—he found time to edit *The Original Memoirs written during the Great Civil Wars; being the life of Sir Henry Slingsby; also the Memoirs of Captain Hodgson*. Ballantyne printed these memoirs, and Constable undertook their publication. They were off his hands in October, and immediately afterwards he commenced another poem, which was to be of the length and manner of the *Lay*, and he was soon tentatively negotiating with more than one publisher concerning it.

The *Lay* had grown into its final form from an uncertain beginning, and the time of composition was no guide to that which would now be necessary when he commenced with a clear intention as to the shape which the new poem would take, and with a plot which (from the substance of the opening stanzas) must have been outlined already. He appears to have anticipated that its composition would be rapid; but, in fact, it was the work of twelve months—or fifteen with its final revisions. Not, of course, of twelve months of continuous work, but it is obvious that it was a constant preoccupation during that period, which is not surprising when we consider the nature of the result.

He was attempting a high test of his own capacity, and its issue must be momentous for his literary future. For the *Lay* seemed to many to be a thing that could not be done twice. Saturated as he was with the spirit of Border chivalry, having his mind stored with so much of Border ballad and Border lore, knowing the history and topography of the subjects with which he dealt, he had extended a ballad of ancient raiding until it had assumed an unexampled length, and sparkled with unfamiliar beauties. But it might not appear to be a thing that could be repeated successfully. Was there not danger, even probability, that there would be staleness, repetition, signs that the materials were no longer fresh? Would not the public, now that the novelty had gone, be more critical, harder to please, even if he could rival the first with a second effort of equal brilliance?

Scott, at least, was sure of himself. While the idea of the poem was still new, while it was little more than an unwritten dream, he had made a bargain with Constable that he should pay him One Thousand Guineas for the copyright, and that this payment should be immediately made, before there could be delivery of a manuscript which, as yet, did not exist.

That Scott should have proposed, and succeeded in obtaining these unusual terms, arose from a combination of converging circumstances. First, he found himself needing money in an urgent and unexpected way. Second, Constable had already formed a shrewd opinion that Scott's work would be a good commercial speculation for any publisher who could obtain it. He was on the spot. He was doing other publishing for him. He was in the best position to close a deal. But it was still true that London was the natural centre for publication of an important book. Longmans had made a great success of the *Lay*. Miller had made a liberal bargain about the Dryden. Others were willing to deal. Constable was well content to close the bargain on the best terms he could. The risk that Scott would die before the completion of the poem, or that it would be a worthless effort, was less than that another publisher would be before him if he should be slow to close.

We observe Constable as a man prepared to take a bold risk where his judgement urged it. The Lockharts of the world stand aside from the dust of the commercial arena, looking only to results, and equally ready to give their facile condemnation or their worthless praise. Had Scott never delivered the poem, there would have been many who would have said that it showed the Edinburgh publisher as a proved fool, and the same voices would applaud the success which his boldness won.

Actually, having taken the plunge, he re-insured a proportion of the risk in a very prudent manner. For some reason, he either did not approach Longmans, or they stood aside from a bargain which they may have felt should have come entirely into their own hands. But he sold a fourth of the risk to Miller, and another fourth to John Murray, both of Albemarle Street, so reducing his own stake, and securing the active interest of the London market.

With such a bargain, and such an amount received, it was not surprising that, as the months passed and the poem remained unfinished, Scott sent it, canto by canto, to Ballantyne to be set up as an earnest of the progress that was being made.

The urgent necessity for a substantial sum of money which had constrained Scott to conclude this sale, had no connection with the Border Press, nor with any personal enterprise. It was a trouble of the business which their father had built.

In plain words, Tom was ruined. He was Scott's favourite brother, and there was no question that, to the limits of his ability and his financial resources, he would help him now. His own account of the trouble, written years afterwards in selected words, was that Tom "was unfortunate from engaging in speculation respecting farms, and matters out of the line of his proper business". Anyway, the trouble was acute, and must have been a matter of substantial sums, or the family resources and dispositions would have averted any open disaster. But, for the time, until matters could be adjusted, Tom retired to the Isle of Man. In fact, he never returned to Edinburgh, and provision for himself and his family would be an intermittent—even a constant—care for the rest of Scott's life, without any shadow of division entering into the close friendship of their correspondence in consequence. Tom, in the Isle of Man, did not resign himself to despair, nor waste his time in idleness. He was active in connection with the raising of a volunteer regiment there. In the end, he had his reward in an offer of a position as paymaster to the 70th regiment, which was afterwards gazetted to Canada.

There he went, and there he remained till his death, seventeen years later.

Now Scott had need of money on behalf of his brother's honour; even a personal need there may have been, for he had become surety for him in connection with an estate with which he had been dealing. The thousand guineas for an unwritten poem was a very welcome sum.

CHAPTER XXXV.

In the early part of 1807, Scott again visited London, this time for a stay of several weeks, during which time his days were spent with regularity at the British Museum, as he had felt the need of utilising its resources in connection with the preparation of the Dryden volumes. Charlotte did not come with him on this occasion, the uncertain length of his absence, and the claims of her growing family, being the probable hindrances to an expedition she would not lightly miss.

Naturally, he used the evenings to improve his London acquaintances; but the quietness of mind, and opportunities of solitude which his manner of life allowed, were utilised to put the earlier half of *Marmion* into form for the printers. The first three cantos were sent to Ballantyne, a few sheets at a time, in a series of envelopes which Lord Abercorn franked for his use, and the post-marks showed that the week-end habit was practised at that period, the packets being dispatched at those times from Lord Abercorn's Stanmore residence, or that of George Ellis at Sunninghill.

But though the winter had seen the first three cantos developed to this stage, at which, though they might be subject to some final revisions, they were fit to be set in type, there is evidence that the completion of the poem was not only unwritten, but could have been no more than vaguely outlined in the author's mind—which is not, of course, suggesting that he had not worked from the first on a fixed plot.

His brother Thomas had handled the legal business of the Abercorn family, and while visiting Lord Abercorn in London, Scott successfully recommended another Edinburgh attorney, Mr. Thomas Gurthie Wright, who was of the circle of youthful lawyers around which the Light Horse regiment had first been founded, to take over the business, but there was probably more than friendship in this arrangement, and it may have been only one of many negotiations which Scott undertook to realise the goodwill of his father's firm.

However that may be, he made arrangements to travel to Dumfries with Mr. Guthrie Wright during the summer, to meet Lord Abercorn, who would pass through that city on his way to Ireland, and give him the benefit of a personal introduction to his new client.

Such meetings could not be arranged in those days with the exactness of a railway time-table. Not wishing to risk being too late, they arrived at Dumfries some days too soon. Scott probably did not mind that overmuch. They explored the ruins together in his usual manner. Sweetheart Abbey and Calaverock Castle were added to the countless list of such places that he already knew. While they explored, they talked. At least, Scott did, according to Guthrie Wright, almost incessantly, as he would on such occasions when his mind was free, and he had a congenial companion, whom he knew that he did not bore. He talked delightfully, with wit and humour, shrewd observation, and endless anecdote. He was not self-centred, or self-absorbed on such occasions, but occupied with matters outside himself. A good listener also, and ready at any moment to be interested in the pre-occupations of a companion's mind.

He had the proofs of the first three cantos of *Marmion* with him, and perhaps the next in some form, and he read these to his companion. Gurthrie Wright listened with care, and was critical. He said the route by which *Marmion* travelled to Scotland had a startling originality. Scott said it would do well enough. Did Gurthie think he ought to have travelled by mail-coach? Gurthie said no to that, but why come by Gifford, Crichton

Castle, Borthwick, and Blackford Hill, there having been no such road since the world began?

Scott said, no doubt truly, that he had made him come that way because he didn't mean to miss the view from Blackford Hill, and that way it had got to be. Anyway, what did Gurthie consider the better route to have taken?

Gurthie said if he'd come by Dunbar and the coast road he might have met fewer bogs; besides, he would have come to Tantallon Castle, and why shouldn't he have spent an interesting evening with old Archibald there?

Scott answered that he shouldn't change the route. Marmion must come to Scotland by the way he was told, and get through as best he could. He may not have troubled about the better surface of the coast road, but the idea of a visit to Tantallon Castle allured his mind, for he went on talking about it, and, as we know, it was by the Dunbar route that Marmion made his return journey, Douglas undertaking to show him the best way home.

We may conclude that, if Mr. Thomas Scott had been more prudent in his investments, the sixth canto of *Marmion* would never have been written in its present form. We should have had something else which will never be, but the situation which ended in the dramatic parting of Marmion and Douglas would not have arisen in Scott's mind, though the battle of Flodden might have been much as it now is. But this is, of course, an observation which might be made about anything. As one seed out of a million bears, so we live one out of a million possible lives that are before us at birth.

As it was, Thomas Scott, safely entrenched from Scottish legal process in the island kingdom of Man, watched for posts to arrive on the weekly mail-boat, with news of Walter's battles on his behalf; and Walter, using his legal knowledge, and all the resources of his endless friendships, to transfer the derelict practice, gets an idea for *Marmion* as he loiters with a brother lawyer in the ruins round Dumfries....

In the later summer, we get another glimpse of the composition of this poem. The regiment was in its autumn training at Musselburgh, and Skene remembered how Quartermaster Scott would ride out with a party of their companions to Portobello, and how he would pace the great black horse he rode backwards and forwards along the sand at the tide's edge, in periods that would be broken suddenly by short reckless gallops that scattered spray from the charger's heels.

Afterwards as they rode back to barracks, Scott would rein up to his side, and repeat the stanzas of the Flodden battle that he had composed. And so, month by month, the work grew.

Many years after, when Scott wrote an introduction to this poem, he made the explicit statement that it was "finished in too much haste to allow me an opportunity of softening down, if not removing, some of its most prominent defects".

He wrote in similar reminiscence of other of his longer poems and there can be no doubt that they left that impression on his mind. There is an immense technical labour in producing a narrative poem of such length? of the standard of lyric excellence which his own judgement required. As Gray laboured for half a life over a few dozen stanzas of his *Elegy*, so would Scott labour to produce the faultless beauty of the songs with which these poems are strewn, and so, had he had leisured time from a dozen other contending interests, had he not had the thought (as he says himself) of that thousand guineas already paid ever before his mind, he would have liked to labour till every stanza of *Marmion* should have been of a kindred excellence. Whatever years he might spend on these poems, circumstances would still hurry them to the press in the end, leaving him with a sense of frustration, of having parted with that which he should have made into a better thing.

This idea of the hasty careless composition of these poems has grown until it is not unusual to depreciate them as of an obviously low or facile standard, and this error of judgement is easier because there is so little in English—indeed, in any—poetry with which to compare them. It is an error grown in an error's soil. They read so easily because they were so hardly written.

These long periods of composition had another result, which the author did not consciously aim to reach by that path. They are, in fact, romances in lyric form. There is no difference between *Marmion* and *Ivanhoe*, except in the method of presentation. There may be a resulting difference, as there is in the same tune played on the violin and the organ: but the substance is similar. Sooner or later, it was almost certain that Scott would be drawn to the swifter, freer medium of the novel, the larger canvas that it allows. But the assumption that it was better adapted, even for his own purposes, does not sustain examination undamaged. The subsequent novels were more hastily imagined, more hastily composed. They were usually begun without knowing how they would end (which might not be a bad way), and they were written about as swiftly as a pen moves.

The longer poems (except the *Lay*) did not merely differ in having carefully constructed plots; the time which was spent upon them was so much longer than on the novels that the characters were often more clearly defined, and were drawn with an almost miraculous economy of words. Anyone may observe this by considering the crowded characters of *Marmion* or *The Lady of the Lake*, and observing how few words are given to each, and how surely every word tells. In the same way, this concentration of powerful imagination upon a few stanzas produced descriptions of vivid beauty which the novels do not frequently challenge. Scott might have described a stag-hunt in prose, and would have done it well, but would it have been comparable with that on which his mind dwelt for the period which was required to narrate it in the vivid brevity of octo-syllabic stanzas?

> The stag at eve had drunk his fill
> Where danced the moon on Monan's rill,
> And deep his midnight lair had made
> In lone Glenartney's hazel shade."

Would a paragraph of Scott's fluent picturesque prose have made more vivid the wide silence of the solitary Highland night, and the shadowy stag that stooped his head beside the moving, moonlit waters? Could it have held the mind so that, to many of us, having read it once in youth, the whole canto is an enduring memory, for which we could still thank God, though all else but the heavens fell? For which we would lightly barter all the disquisitions (which is not saying all the lyrics and sonnets) that Wordsworth ever wrote under the delusion that he was his Deity's right-hand man?

That Scott should have converted to prose was, sooner or later, a natural, almost an inevitable thing. That it had some advantages over verse, and enabled him to do some things which would have been impossible in the more difficult medium, may be true also. But it was a difference which bought its gains at a great price. And those who say that Scott "found his vocation" when he became a prose novelist, do not understand the matter on which they talk, for his vocations were never changed. He was a great romancer from the day when he constructed the plot of *The Eve of St. John*, and he was a greater poet to his life's end.

The lyrics in *Ivanhoe* alone would have been enough to establish the first-rank fame of a separate poet. *Allan-a-dale*, and *When Israel of the Lord beloved*, would have been in every standard Anthology; but the results of his genius are obscured by their own profusion.

CHAPTER XXXVI.

The closing months of 1807, when *Marmion* had been completed (if we regard it, as we should, as a separate and greater thing than its introductory epistles, the last of which was written in the Christmas atmosphere of Mertoun House), are not of remarkable incident, though there was no relaxation of Scott's multifarious activities. He had added to his other occupations—for a meagre honorarium, and a vague expectation of future political patronage, which bore no visible fruit—that of Secretary to a Parliamentary Commission for the improvement of Scottish Jurisprudence, over which Sir Ismay Campbell had been appointed President, and found its duties more onorous than he may have expected; and he was still writing articles for the Edinburgh Review. More than that, he was actually in correspondence with Robert Southey, in an endeavour to enlist him under the same banner, so that the Constable alliance must have had an outward aspect of stability, which (it might be thought) would be further strengthened, should the publication of *Marmion* justify the large sum which had been advanced upon it. But Southey would not join the circle of Edinburgh Review contributors. The Review had said that he was a poor poet, and that Wordsworth was rather worse, which was making three errors about two men, one of which Southey did not forgive. If Constable had seen Scott's part of this correspondence he would not have been pleased, though Jeffrey might not have minded at all. Jeffrey was an editor who went his own way, caring for few, and not much for them; but Constable was a bookseller, and a business man. He believed that Walter Scott was a good investment to have on his list, and he would go far to keep him. Southey would have nothing to do with the politics of the Edinburgh Review, and Scott would say nothing in their defence. The fear of invasion which had roused men of all parties to a common determination, had lessened after the naval strength of France had been broken at Trafalgar, but on the continent Napoleon was at the height of his power. Having all the great nations of Europe under his heel, he was now picking up crumbs. He overran Portugal. He occupied Rome, taking the shadow of Papal authority that was still there, to use it to his own ends. Only England remained, unbeaten and unafraid. What use was there, there were those who asked, in continuing such a war? Were we to meet the whole world in arms? It was a war we could never win. That was the line taken by the Edinburgh Review. The tide was high, and it still rose.

Who could say that it neared the turn, as, in fact, it did? Such articles as appeared in the Edinburgh Review—defeatist rather than pacifist—weakened the courage of men, when fortitude was the greatest need. Scott hated them, and to see his name on the same cover. But Jeffrey cared nothing for that.... And, at last, toward the end of February, *Marmion* came out.

The success of the new poem, both in literary circles and general popularity, was instant and beyond any precedent—if we except the one by the same author which had been published three years earlier. To have achieved such a triumph once, by whatever combination of merit and fortune, was marvel enough: to repeat it was a more unparalleled feat. It placed Scott at once in a more secure and permanent position, as a poet who could maintain the standard that he had once reached. The fact that the poem had substantial differences from the *Lay*, and was yet of the same order, increased the sense of capacity which the achievement gave. After this, it would be hard to say what its author could not do. There was general disputation as to which was the greater poem; and that such a point should be regarded as doubtful, after the reception of the earlier one, was praise enough for a second venture, which is always judged with greater severity, and especially so when the success of the first has been of an extraordinary kind. In the first poem he had utterly outdistanced the popularity of all contemporary poets: in the second he had to contend with the record he himself had set.

The reception of *Marmion* by his brother-poets was generous, both in private correspondence and the public press; and their criticisms were sometimes more intelligent and discriminating than is much of that which it receives a century later.

Leyden, it is true, wrote in an excitement of protest when the poem reached him in India. Leyden was an easily excitable man. He thought it out of focus that a statesman and a military leader of the sixteenth century should be a party to forgery. Others had said the same before he had the opportunity to do so. Scott, who was usually ready to agree when told that there were defects in what he wrote, allowed that he might have improved the plot, if he had had more sense—more time. He had, in fact, anticipated that this criticism would be made. The "gross defect ought to have been remedied, or at least palliated," 'he wrote in amiable agreement at a later date. But he adds that he had decided to let the tree lie where it had fallen. In fact, he allowed his own artistic judgement to override his anticipation of a criticism which is ill-founded, being based on errors both of logic and fact. For why should *Marmion* have been a typical rather than an exceptional character? And was forgery really an invention of a later century? It was not long after the period of *Marmion* that an Edinburgh tradesman would supply forgeries of the signatures of all public men at a reasonable tariff, or complete letters to those who could make profitable use of such documents. The date of the forgery of the Casket letters is not very much later, and these were procured, if not actually indited, by men of the half-political half-military class to which Marmion belonged.

To forge letters, is, of course, against the spirit of chivalry; and this view, with its own intolerance, is well expressed by the aged Douglas:

"A letter forged! St. Jude to speed!
Did ever knight so foul a deed!
At first in heart it liked me ill
When the King praised his clerkly skill.
Thanks to St. Bothan, son of mine,
Save Gawain, ne'er could pen a line:
So swore I, and I swear it still,
Let my boy-bishop fret his fill."

Forgery is a crime of which there are instances in every age, and in all ranks of society that have been able to commit it, and Lord Archibald was right about there being only one absolute safeguard.

The poem was more justly criticised in respect of the "introductions" which were interpolated between the cantos, and which introduced nothing but irrelevant matter, with a perfunctory tag at the end of each. To suggest that such intrusions relieve the concentration of the mind upon the principal subject is as absurd as it would be to say that such a book can be enjoyed best by those who are interrupted by constant callers. Its logical issue would be to print two books together in alternate chapters.

It is true that the *Lay* was in a superficially similar form, but in that case there was a definite relation between the introductions and the main stream of the narrative, and there were natural transitions. Even so, they may be thought to be less than a certain gain. That Scott had been doubtful of the effect of these interjected epistles is shown by the fact that he had considered, and at one time half-resolved, to give them separate publication under the title of *Epistles from Ettrick Forest*. Issued in such form, they might have had considerable semi-private, and a limited public circulation, partly on their own merit, and partly on the author's reputation, and the biographical details which they contain. That Scott did not carry out this idea may be attributed to that thousand guineas that he had received for Tom's assistance a year ago. The bargain had been for a poem similar to the *Lay*. To remove these introductions would shorten it substantially, and reduce the measure of its superficial similarity, and if they had once been talked of, or intended, for it, to publish them separately would be open to the construction of attempting to obtain a profit on that which had been already sold. Mr. Ellis, with some knowledge of these circumstances, and with a decided opinion that the introductions were in the wrong place, suggested in subsequent correspondence that it might have been possible to lengthen the *Marmion* narrative to its own advantage. Perhaps it would. It is evident that it contains sufficient matter for a longer tale. We can suppose, from what Scott did subsequently, in what manner he would have enriched and extended it, had it been produced in a prose form. But poetry is not prose. To write good poetry is a work of time, and good narrative poetry, of the standard which Scott had set to himself, may be of every kind the most difficult, though to write it badly may be an easy thing. To have lengthened it substantially would have meant another year's work, to Constable's natural irritation, and a doubtful gain.

As it was, Constable came out well, as did his partners in London. There was solid profit for them. It meant no further cash to Scott: nothing more than a present of a hogshead of claret from publishers who could afford to be generous. The first edition of 2,000 copies, published at £1. 11. 6., was sold out immediately. Larger, less expensive editions were to follow rapidly until a total of 30,000 copies had equalled the record of the *Lay*.—A total which was doubled with the next forty years, and remains an amazing circulation for such a poem, when the population of the United Kingdom, and the limits of education and reading habits at that time are remembered.

And if the publishers had the gold, Scott had the reputation, which might, with judicious marketing, be turned into kindred coin.... He had not only got *Marmion* off his hands at this time, and so cancelled his debt with Constable in a way very greatly to that publisher's satisfaction, the long labour of the Dryden was also completed. It was actually published in London before the end of April, and already his part was over, as were the pleasant receipts of forty guineas per volume, which had become due to him eighteen times in the last two years.

He was looking round for new worlds to conquer, and planning some intervening relaxation when the Court Session should end, and he could escape to the active leisure of Ashestiel, when, on returning from Court one midday to his study in the North George Street house, he found his copy of the April number of the Edinburgh Review on his desk, with this letter:

"Dear Scott,

If I did not give you credit for more magnanimity than other of your irritable tribe, I should scarcely venture to put this into your hands. As it is, I do it with no little solicitude, and earnestly hope that it will make no difference in the friendship which has hitherto subsisted between us. I have spoken of your poem exactly as I think, and though I cannot reasonably suppose that you will be pleased with everything I have said, it would mortify me very severely to believe I had given you pain. If you have any amity left for me, you will not delay very long to tell me so. In the meantime, I am very sincerely yours—F. Jeffrey."

Mr. Jeffrey had remembered that he had a dinner engagement at the Scotts that evening, and had sufficient prudence or good manners to inform his host before coming of the nature of the article he had written. It was an attack on *Marmion*. Appearing in the Review to which Scott was a regular contributor, and from the editor's own pen, it was an extraordinary article. Lockhart thinks that it was honestly written, and, to an extent, he may have been right. He says that Jeffrey, feeling as he did, acquitted himself on this occasion in a manner highly credible to his "courageous sense of duty". In a limited sense, that may be true too. It was Jeffrey's nature to attack, to cavil. He was always prodigal of censure, but would measure praise with a meaner hand. Prejudice is not dishonesty, though they may arrive at the same place. Yet there are things in the review which are barely sane. Scott is actually accused of neglecting Scottish feeling and characters. It would be a waste of words to discuss such a proposition as that.

Scott read the letter. He read the article. He wrote a short note to Jeffrey, and sent it to him by hand. He was quite right to say what he thought, though Scott hoped the booksellers wouldn't agree. He was to come to dinner, and put it out of his mind.

Scott showed in sign that he cared. Probably he didn't. He was conscious of being sated with praise. He was of deliberate watchfulness at this time, lest he should lose his sense of proportion from this cause. He received Jeffrey with his usual cordiality. The position is different today. No one now but a fool absolute could be conceited about writing a best-seller of any kind. If he should feel in danger of such an emotion, he would read a best-seller by another author, and understand what they are. But if Scott didn't care, Mrs. Scott felt differently. She was no more than coldly polite. She would not be rude to a guest, but her usual laughter was stilled. When she wished Mr. Jeffrey good-night, she made one cryptic reference. She said that she had heard that he had abused her husband in the Review...she hoped Mr. Constable had paid *him* well for writing the article.

It was one of those remarks which have no obvious meaning, but which provoke thought. Constable had paid Scott very well for the poem. He paid Jeffrey's salary. There was comedy in the fact that he should be paying him to attack the poem, and possibly reducing its sales. Mrs. Scott's remark shows not only that she was more sensitive to any attack on her husband than he was himself: it shows that she saw how significant the incident was of that deep division which underlay the surface friendship which brought Jeffrey so frequently to the North Castle Street dinner-table.

She might not share all her husband's enthusiasms. There might be some with which she was barely in sympathy. She was a French refugee, who had found asylum in England, and, for a husband, perhaps the greatest Scotsman of any time. As it has become fashionable with many to disparage Scott's poetry, so it has become fashionable to disparage his wife with indifferent, halting praise. But her pride in him, and her passionate loyalty, stand out too clearly to be ignored.

The April number of the Review went on to London. A copy came, in due course, to the desk of Mr. John Murray, the London publisher who had ventured his money in a share of *Marmion*. He read that attack on the poem in Constable's own periodical with a puzzled wonder. He turned the pages to read one of those defeatist articles which were so alien from Scott's politics and temperament. He wondered thoughtfully how long the connection could last....

The attack on *Marmion* led to no immediate breach. Scott made it no cause of quarrel. With his usual magnanimity, he appeared to put it out of his mind. The danger of those who deal with such generosities is that they may suppose that they have no limit at all. The incident was, indeed, rather a symptom than a cause of division. But Scott's name ceased to appear on the cover of the Edinburgh Review. He offered Jeffrey no more articles, being, doubtless, sufficiently busy in other ways.

What was Jeffrey's antipathy to *Marmion*, which broke out in this unmeasured way? Perhaps we need go no further than the introduction to the first canto to understand it, for in those two hundred and fifty lines Scott includes professions of his own literary and political faiths to which Jeffrey would react coldly, or with an active hostility.

It is true that they contain the passage concerning Fox, who was the just-dead hero of the party to which Jeffrey gave his support, but even that would be read with a very moderate satisfaction. Fox is praised for various virtues, but most of all because, 'when Austria bent and Prussia broke', he had not counselled surrender to the common foe. It was as though you were to praise Ramsey McDonald for having joined the National Government, and expect a Communist to be grateful.

Then there were the lines on Pitt. He and Fox had both died during the previous year, and Scott's appeal for charity over the one grave might equally be applied to the other. But the nature of the praise he gave was a challenge to all those who saw the salvation of the land to lie, not in the shattering of the sinister continental power, but in the granting of a wider measure of internal freedom.

They felt no thrill of admiration on being assured that Pitt,

> "when the frantic crowd amain
> Strained at subjection's bursting rein,
> O'er their wild mood full conquest gained,
> The pride he would not crush restrained,
> Showed their fierce zeal a worthier cause,
> And brought the freeman's arm to aid the freeman's laws."

Or the suggestion that his fortitude had saved the land from the horrors of invasion, for which he deserved a universal gratitude while

"on Britain's thousand plains
One unpolluted church remains."

Nor would Jeffrey respond very readily to Scott's creed as to the inspirations through which great poetry is written

"Pure love, that scarce its passion tells,
Mystery, half-veiled and half revealed,
And Honour, with his spotless shield."

He might have said that Alexander Pope wrote some (to his mind) excellent poetry without being overmuch impelled by any of these inspirational forces....

And the whole spirit of *Marmion*, apart from these introductory epistles, was alien from his natural sympathies. It was less his intellect than his character which impeded an intelligent appreciation.

Marmion is a poem of action. To a superficial glance, it may show no more than a glitter of steel and a sheen of silk; but it has the spiritual quality that is dominant in all Scott's romances, whether in prose or verse. It is always implicit that it matters little what is achieved or obtained, but that what we are and how we act matter much. In fact, no one in *Marmion* does anything worth boasting about, Marmion least of all. We see him overthrown through moral cowardice by a weaker man: we see him go into battle, and then "dragged from among the horses' feet" in a dying condition. We believe in his battle-courage and battle-wisdom simply because Scott tells us it was so, and he can tell such things in a convincing way.

The central theme of the *Lay* was that opposition can be overthrown by a service rendered. That of *Marmion* is magnanimity toward an enemy by those who were most deeply wronged.

That of the *Lady of the Lake* was to be a king's surrender of the woman he loved to a successful rival. That of *Rokeby*, that rivalry in lose need not overcome friendship. That of the *Lord of the Isles*, the self-sacrifice of Isabel ("Then by the cross the ring she placed"). That of the light-hearted *Bridal of Triermain*, the overcoming of the temptations "spread by avarice, lust and power". *Harold the Dauntless* failed mainly, and as far as it did fail, because there was no sufficient nobility of theme to hold Scott's mind in concentration upon it. He tired, feeling that it was all about nothing.

He is at his best on a battlefield, not because men are taking lives, but because they are giving their own.

It is impossible to say how much he infected others with the heroism of his own mood, through the years of national calamities during which these great poems were written, and the whole nation read them. But if we weigh the moral forces which held the heart of Britain steadfast through the unslackening strain of the greatest struggle she has ever known, the inspiration of him who was a truly national poet will not be least in the scale.

Carlyle could see no edification in the poetry of Scott, and those who think that their lives should be preoccupied in the saving of their own souls may find that he has little to offer. Scott is not often a conscious teacher, or a conscious prophet. He simply directs our minds to such things as are worth observing. He interprets his own ideals. If we would be of his standard, we must not only have love to live, we must have strength to die. Particularly, we must have strength to die.

He shows us the dusk falling over the Flodden Field, where

"The stubborn spearmen still made good
Their dark, impenetrable wood,
Each stepping where his comrade stood
The instant that he fell,"

and we may be content that he shows us a good thing. Or we may like Mr. Jeffrey's counsels in the Edinburgh Review to surrender while we can still make terms, however ignoble they may be, and leave Napoleon in possession of a prostrate Europe, and ourselves in such freedom as he would be likely to allow us.

We may like one or other of these—but not both.

And if we would understand the political atmosphere of that time, we must dismiss from our minds any comparison with the war of a later century, when the tests of endurance and courage, however severely they may have fallen upon some individuals, never came upon the nation with any severity. Or if we compare at all, we must imagine what it would have been if the long battle-line of France had been broken through: if the Italian armies had been shattered on the Venetian plains: if the German flag had been flying over a captured Paris, and the Austrian over a surrendered Rome: if the Germans had added to their own the strength of the French and Italian fleets, and menaced us with the invasion of a war-hardened army which might be ten times the number of any opposition which we could muster against it—if we make such comparisons, and remember how, in our own day, if the line of battle in France should appear to falter, our own politicians would falter too, we may understand something of the shadow that lay over the Britain of an earlier century: a shadow that grew as the years passed, till it seemed to many that it would never lift; and something also of the valour of those who governed during those perilous years, facing a world of enemies abroad, and disaffections at home, with a resolution that never broke.

It was this extremity of national tension which both inspired and responded to the patriotic outburst in the *Lay*—"Lives there a man with soul so dead," and it is implicit in Marmion's defiance of the threatened Scottish invasion:

"But Nottingham hath archers good,
And Yorkshire men are stern of mood,
Northumbrian prickers wild and rude.
On Derby hills the paths are steep;
In Ouse and Tyne the fords are deep;

And many a banner will be torn,
And many a knight to earth be borne,
And many a sheaf of arrows spent,
Ere Scotland's king shall cross the Trent."

And it inspires the dignity of Marmion's reply to the scornful attitude of Douglas,

"And first I tell thee, haughty peer,
He who does England's message here,
Although the meanest in her state,
May well, proud Angus, be thy mate,"

and it rises to intenser flame as it describes how "groom fought like noble, squire like knight," when the out-manoeuvred Scottish army refused to admit defeat.

It explains the final plea for a merciful judgement over Marmion's nameless grave:

"When thou shalt find the little hill,
With thy heart commune, and be still.
If ever, in temptation strong,
Thou left'st the right path for the wrong;
If every devious step thus trod
Still led thee further from the road;
Dread thou to speak presumptuous doom
On noble Marmion's lowly tomb;
But say: 'He died a gallant knight,
With sword in hand for England's right.'"

The plea is as old as Christianity: 'Let him who is without sin among you cast the first stone'. But is there not a familiar sound in the concluding reflection? Was not the plea of war-service urged in the law-courts of our own times, even after peace had returned, and even for offences which were subsequently committed?

The same consciousness of the war-atmosphere, and the same attitude toward it, are shown in the allusions to Edinburgh in the Epistle to George Ellis which introduces the fifth canto.

There is more than a perfunctory patriotism in its comparison to the warlike chastity of Britomart, and the allusion to the 'dauntless voluntary line' of the regiment which Scott had done so much to gather for its defense.

The advocates of peace at any price must have found the tone of *Marmion* a distasteful thing....

The Introductory epistles, apart from the first, do not merit any extended reference. Their poetic level is not high. The third, addressed to William Erskine, is interesting for its reminiscences of the author's own childhood, and concludes with an intimation to Lockhart's "monitor" that he preferred to write his poems in his own way rather than that which Erskine considered most admirable,, and proposed to continue to do so. The decision is no less emphatic because it is conveyed with the politeness which publicity required.

The sixth, written to Richard Heber amid the Christmas festivities of Mertoun House, after the main poem was finished, and this addition only needed to complete the structure, has the vivacity of the atmosphere in which it was composed, and contains a vision of an old-time Christmas which deserves quotation, in spite of its length, both because it gives a picture of such forgotten scenes which is never likely to be surpassed, either in prose or verse, and because it is informed by Scott's instinctively democratic sympathies, and explains why, at the period of his ultimate prosperity, and surrounded by those who were dependent upon it, he was said by one of his servants to treat them all as though they were his blood-relations.

"And well our Christian sires of old
Loved when the year its course had rolled,
And brought blithe Christmas back again,
With all his hospitable train.
Domestic and religious rite

Gave honour to the holy night:
On Christmas Eve the bells were rung;
On Christmas Eve the mass was sung:
That only night, in all the year,
Saw the stoled priest the chalice rear.
The damsel donn'd her kirtle sheen;
The hall was dress'd with holly green;
Forth to the wood did merry-men go,
To gather in the mistletoe.
Then open'd wide the Baron's hall
To vassal, tenant, serf, and all;
Power laid his rod of rule aside,
And Ceremony doff'd his pride.
The heir, with roses in his shoes,
That night might village partner choose;
The Lord, underogating, share
The vulgar game of 'post and pair'.
All hail'd, with uncontroll'd delight,
And general voice, the happy night
That to the cottage, as the crown,
Brought tidings of salvation down.

The fire, with well-dried logs supplied?
Went roaring up the chimney wide;
The huge hall-table's oaken face,
Scrubb'd till it shone, the day to grace,
Bore then upon its massive board
No mark to part the squire and lord.
Then was brought in the lusty brawn,
By old blue-coated serving-man;
Then the grim boar's head frown'd on high,
Crested with bays and rosemary.
Well can the green-garb'd ranger tell,
How, when, and where, the monster fell;
What dogs before his death he tore,
And all the baiting of the boar.

> The wassal round, in good brown bowls,
> Garnish'd with ribbons, blithely trowls.
> There the huge sirloin reek'd; hard by
> Plum-porridge stood, and Christmas pie;
> Nor fail'd old Scotland to produce,
> At such high tide, her savoury goose.
> Then came the merry maskers in,
> And carols roar'd with blithesome din;
> If unmelodious was the song,
> It was a hearty note, and strong.
> Who lists may in their mumming see
> Traces of ancient mystery;
> White shirts supplied the masquerade,
> And smutted cheeks the visors made;
> But, Oh! what maskers, richly dight,
> Can boast of bosoms half so light!
> England was merry England, when
> Old Christmas brought his sports again.
> 'Twas Christmas broached the mightiest ale;
> 'Twas Christmas told the merriest tale;
> A Christmas gambol oft could cheer
> The poor man's heart through half the year."

CHAPTER XXXVII.

It may be convenient at this point to turn somewhat aside, and somewhat backward, to consider the position of Scott's partnership in the printing business, and the nature of the commercial association into which he had entered.

While Lockhart allowed that James Ballantyne might have many excellent qualities, which he spasmodically attributed to him, his presentations both of him and his brother John are of the nature of caricatures rather than portraits, and it is always necessary to examine his statements very narrowly in any matters into which they intrude; and if these be verified, it is still necessary to maintain an attitude of caution toward his inferences therefrom.

While he represents John Ballantyne as having been of an habitual financial imprudence, he is content to paint the elder brother as financially incompetent; indolent; extravagant; and indifferent, if not hostile, to exact accounting.

The trustees of James Ballantyne, after his death, resenting these presentations, set up the proposition that James was not merely innocent of such faults, but that he had lost a prosperous business, and a lifetime's savings, even including his wife's fortune, which he had been too trustful to protect, through Scott's reckless extravagance, and the levity of his financial expedients.

Lockhart retorted, not merely by re-asserting the truth of the picture he had already drawn, but with the suggestion that there was much more which might have been said to James Ballantyne's detriment, which he had suppressed in a spirit of kindly reticence. He said that, from the very commencement of the partnership, James had drawn all, and more than all, the business profits for his private use, and that it was a matter for amazement that Scott, who was a good business man in many ways and kept careful control and account of his personal expenditure? should have been so blindly trustful of his business partner. He did not confine himself to general assertion. He gave figures. With the partners' capital accounts actually before him, bearing the joint signatures of Walter Scott and James Ballantyne, he stated that 'between Whitsuntide 1805 and Martinmas 1807, it appears that Scott's drafts on the business came to £306. 4. 3—James Ballantyne's to £3,966. 4.1!!!" The marks of exclamation are his, and as the total capital of the business was only a few thousand pounds, they would appear to be justified. Both the amounts and proportions of these drawings appear to show that both partners were guilty of an excess of folly, though of widely different varieties. If Scott allowed the business to be drained in this manner of all the money he invested, it would be hard to imagine any subsequent foolishness of which he might not be capable.

The Ballantyne Trustees replied by giving Lockhart the lie direct regarding these figures. They made a new counter-charge of their own that Scott had lent money to the business at an exorbitant interest.

The controversy is curious, because the charges on both sides, asserted with confidence, and often supported with explicit figures, were entirely baseless. They are broadly refuted by the facts that Scott gave James, with some clearly expressed qualifications and occasional admonitions, a continued confidence through many financial vicissitudes, and that James wrote of him after his death as having been his lifelong benefactor.

But fortunately, on this point at least, we are not limited to a weighing of probabilities, and an inferential judgement. We have the material for a final analysis, which acquits both Scott and James Ballantyne with an equal completeness, and leaves only Lockhart and the Ballantyne Trustees with their reputations for good sense or accuracy severely damaged in the course of the controversy.

It appears, in the first place, that when James made his migration to Edinburgh toward the end of 1802, bringing his plant with him, he raised fresh capital to the amount of £1,000, half of which was a loan from Scott, and the remainder was in the form of an overdraft from the Royal Bank of Scotland for which Scott, and the Rev. Robert Lundie of Kelso, became "cautioners," or, as we should say, guarantors.

With this capital, James continued to finance a growing business until the early part of 1805, when, following the successful printing of the *Lay*, he approached Scott with the information that the orders he was receiving were beyond his capacity to execute without further assistance, and a partnership was arranged in consequence.

The basis of the partnership is quite simple, and disposes finally of Lockhart's suggestion that the absence of a Balance Sheet indicated financial laxity on either side. The existing plant and stock, together with a house in Foulis Close, being James

Ballantyne's property, were valued at £2,090. 0. 0. It was agreed that this should be his contribution to the partnership assets, and that the outstanding book-debts should remain his property. He was also to discharge the liabilities up to that date. Scott cancelled the promissory note for £500 which he held, which was now valued at £580, including something over two years' interest which had accumulated upon it, and advanced £1,500 in cash. In this way, his capital was made up to a total of £2,080, being approximately equal to that of James.

On this basis, it was agreed that James should have one third of the profits as remuneration for his management services, and that the remainder should be divided equally, in accordance with the amounts of their partnership capital.

It will be observed from these particulars that the business was commenced without liabilities of any kind: with plant and stock and other property of an agreed value of over £2,000, and with £1,500 cash in the bank.

It may be observed also that Lockhart, in his first allusion to this partnership, was inaccurate in representing, as he does, that Scott invested at this time the bulk of his inheritance from his uncle's estate. He had sold Rosebank for 5,000 guineas. He benefited beyond this sum as a residuary legatee. He invested £1,500. There is a wide margin between these figures.

Beyond this, it may be observed that the principles of financial equity had been somewhat strained in James's favour, to arrive at a basis which would provide adequate additional capital, and yet enable him to appear as an equal partner. His overdraft with the Royal Bank of Scotland was not brought into account, and remained his private liability, the Bank being satisfied with the guarantees which they held. The cancellation of the promissory note which Scott had been holding was not precisely what it appeared to be. Had James repaid the money in cash to Scott, as he was entitled to claim, and had Scott then invested it in the business, his own capital outlay would have been precisely the same, but there would have been £2,080 instead of £1,500 in the partnership bank account. The method of the adjustment was therefore equivalent to the gift of £290 by Scott to his new partner, and had he insisted upon this being dealt with by a more severely logical method, and to the Royal Bank overdraft, for which he was already jointly responsible, being brought into the capital account, James would not have been able to sustain his claim to an equal partnership. Neither Lockhart, nor the Ballantyne trustees, chasing red-herrings of each others' imaginations, appear to have appreciated this difference. But while it is certain that an impartial accountant, had it been left to his decision, would have arranged the figures in a way less satisfactory to James Ballantyne's interests, there can be no doubt from the clear grasp which Scott shows, in letters which are still extant, of far more complicated financial settlements, that he knew what he was doing, and acted with an intentional generosity.

The position resulting was that if Scott, having an independent income, did not draw his third share of the profits from the business, his capital interest would continually increase, and Ballantyne could only remain on a level footing if, or so far as, he could keep his own personal expenditure within the limit of the third part of the profits which was his remuneration for his services as manager. This must depend primarily upon how large the profits would be; and he had therefore the utmost incentive both to make such profits, and to keep down his private expenditure, if he desired to maintain an equality of interest in the business. In theory, he could have insisted upon his partner drawing out his own share of profits, but in practice this would not happen. A business growing as rapidly as this one did would be in continual need of additional support, and it was no doubt a substantial relief that Scott did not require to draw heavily upon it.

The circumstances being as they were, Lockhart's charge that James drew so exorbitantly during the first two-and-a-half years is an attack equally upon his honour and his business capacity. It is made worse by the fact that Scott, as we shall see later, was giving it additional financial support, and if it were true, it might be hard to decide which partner it convicted of the greater folly: the one who wasted the money, or the one who allowed him to do so, and went on filling the hole.

The fact is that Lockhart's charge was false; and though it would do him injustice to suppose the falsehood deliberate, it is impossible to acquit him of the grossest carelessness; nor can we avoid the conclusion that, if the figures had appeared at a first glance to reflect upon Scott in the same way, he would have given them a second (which was all that was necessary) before founding similar conclusions upon them.

It is of minor importance that the amount that he states was drawn by Scott during the period, £306. 4. 3., is inaccurate, though it must be corrected, for if we have figures at all they should be the right ones. Scott's capital account, as it was finally signed by both partners, shows that he drew these amounts—

1805 £s,d

Oct. 10th—To Cash 2000
Nov. 8th"—"3000
1806
May 13th"—"5000
June-Nov."—"7500
1806-7
Dec.-Mch."—"7500
Sept."—"13143

£38143

It will be seen that there is a discrepancy of £75, Lockhart having, apparently, made a hasty abstract, and overlooked one of the two £75 items.

During the same period, on May 13th, 1806, Scott had invested a further sum of £1,000. The profit had been calculated half-yearly; his third share for the two-and-a-half years had .amounted to a gross total of £1,142. 15. 1., and his capital interest in the business had risen to £3,702. 17. 6. The apparent discrepancy of £66. 13. 4. is one third of the salary of James's younger brother, John, who, as we shall see, was employed in the last year of the period with which we are dealing, under a bargain that two-thirds of his salary should be paid from James's share of the profits.

Now for James. It will be remembered that he neither transferred the book-debts due to himself to the new partnership, nor did it undertake his prior liabilities, but, under a method which is most common in such circumstances, and of an obvious convenience, these book-debts were collected by the partnership business, and the liabilities were discharged through its bank account, the totals of such receipts and payments being set off against one another by the usual method in James Ballantyne's capital account. The total £3,966. 4. 1. which Lockhart gave as the amount which James drew out of the business during the period with which we are dealing includes the payment of the liabilities which were outstanding when the partnership commenced. It is true, and it is only fair to Lockhart to say, that the totals carried to James's capital account do not show these payments separately from his personal drawings, but it is a poor defense to an error of this nature and magnitude, in view of the fact that the account shows on the opposite side for May, 1805, a credit of £1,668. 9. 11. for book-debts collected up to that date, and entries for much smaller amounts, but of kindred character, occur during subsequent periods.

The gratuitous charge brought by Lockhart against James Ballantyne that he drew improperly for his personal use, or any other cause, *during the early years of the partnership*, must be dismissed as groundless, and condemned as having been recklessly brought. The counter-charge made by the Trustees against Scott that he had loaned money to the business at extortionate interest will be found on examination to be equally baseless.

We may observe, as the years passed and the business grew, that James Ballantyne was confronted by a double difficulty. He had to ask Scott to increase his capital investment, and he had to endeavour to raise his own to a similar figure, so that his claim to a full two-thirds of the profits should not be jeopardised. Looking ahead, we find that on the 13th December, 1809, the partners met and signed a joint memorandum, the substance of which was that Ballantyne agreed that he would draw in future £900 annually, and Scott agreed that he would draw £450, and they mutually agreed that whatever profit there should be beyond these sums should be added to the business capital. At this time it was agreed that Scott's partnership capital amounted to £3,842. 9. 8., and that James's was so closely similar that they could be accepted in future as identical figures. How had this equality been reached? In the first place, the profits were good. They were now from £1,500 to £2,000 a year. In the second, Scott had somewhat increased his drawings and had received £700 during the last annual period with which they were dealing. In the third, it was due to the method of bookkeeping which had been applied to additional capital which had been brought into the business from various sources.

Scott had found £2,000. Of this, £800 had been his own money, and £1,200 had been lent by his elder brother, Captain John Scott. It was agreed that this £2,000 should not be added to Scott's capital account, but should be credited with interest at the rate of 15% per annum.

James had also obtained further capital from among his own friends. There was £500 from Mr. Creech, £500 from Miss Mary Bruce, and £600 from his brother, Alexander Ballantyne. These monies were not treated by the same method that was applied to the extra capital supplied by or through Walter Scott. They were added to James Ballantyne's capital, the origin of the sums being frankly stated in the ledger, but the transactions being treated as monies personally lent to James, and re-lent by him to the firm.

The effect of this method was that the firm was not properly responsible for the interest due to the lenders of these sums, for which James had to provide out of the profits which he drew, (as he was still doing for the £500 which had been advanced to him by the Royal Bank), whereas an agreed 15% interest—£300—was charged upon the profits before they were allocated to the partners on account of the £2,000 which had been found by Walter Scott and his brother.

It was this difference of method, and the rate of interest agreed, which caused Ballantyne's Trustees to retort to Lockhart's attacks that Scott had acted harshly in his financial transactions with the firm. There was ignorance of accountancy and lack of expert advice on both sides of the controversy, and a common folly of supposition that they could do good to their own side by discrediting the other, which was the actual reverse of the truth, and for which attitude Lockhart was initially responsible.

There is a passage in his first reply to the Ballantyne Trustees, which explains, though it does not justify, the attitude he adopted:

> "Had the reader been left to take his ideas of these men from the eloquence of epitaphs—to conceive of them as having been capitalists instead of penniless adventurers—men regularly and fitly trained for the calling in which they were employed by Scott, in place of being the one and the other entirely unacquainted with the prime requisites for success in such callings—men exact and diligent in their proper business, careful and moderate in their personal expenditure, instead of the reverse; had such hallucinations been left undisturbed, where was the clue of extraction from the mysterious labyrinth of Sir Walter's fatal entanglements in commerce? It was necessary, in truth and justice, to show—not that he was without blame in the conduct of his pecuniary affairs—(I surely made no such ridiculous attempt)—but that he could not have been ruined by commerce, had his partners been good men of business. It was necessary to show that he was in the main the victim of his blind overconfidence in the management of the two Ballantynes. In order to

show how excessive was the kindness that prompted such overconfidence, it was necessary to bring out the follies and foibles, as well as the better qualities of the men."

This is an example of how a good case may be ruined by bad advocacy, for it is evident that the attempt to represent lames Ballantyne as a ' penniless adventurer,' or even as a man without ordinary business abilities, will not survive examination, and if even a partial defence of Scott's business or financial activities must depend upon such premises being established, it is no better than a lost cause. In fact, the 'clue of extrication' does not primarily concern the character of the Ballantynes, in his relations with whom Scott was a dominant rather than a dominated partner, nor should a biographer assume, in advance of examination, as Lockhart evidently did, that it must be ' ridiculous' to suppose the possibility that a man who loses money should not be blamed.

The bad advocacy was not all on one side. The Ballantyne Trustees could have made out a much simpler and stronger case in James Ballantyne's defence if they had avoided the random counter-attacks upon Scott's character and business methods which were natural enough under the provocation they had received, but which sustain examination no better than those which had aroused their wrath.

The capital arrangements which they attacked show no more than a natural effort on the part of James Ballantyne to maintain his own interest in the business on an equality with that of his partner, and a generous willingness on the part of Scott to facilitate this position.

The gathering of capital from various sources for the assistance of a growing business was done in the manner which was customary at the time, before the principle of limited liability had been legally recognised, and we may best appreciate the equities of the position if we compare it with that which would almost certainly have developed under similar circumstances today.

Assuming that the business had been registered as a limited company when James came to Edinburgh, to enable him to obtain from Scott and others the capital which he required; that the same investments had been made subsequently by all parties; that he had received the same remuneration as managing director that he drew under that heading from the partnership profits; and accepting the total capital figure which was agreed over the signatures of Walter Scott and James Ballantyne on Dec. 13th, 1809, the Shareholders' Register would have shown the following holdings:

Walter Scott...4650
John Scott...1200
James Ballantyne...2250
Alexander Ballantyne...600
William Creech...500
Mary Bruce...500

9700

The above position is subject to some more or less counterbalancing qualifications, an analysis of which will show that any differences would almost certainly have been to James Ballantyne's disadvantage. These are (a) the Company might have taken over the overdraft at the Royal Bank of Scotland, in which case his shareholding would have been £500 less than is shown above, (b) he would probably have received a progressive salary as Managing Director, which might or might not have exceeded the proportion of profits which he drew under this heading, but (c) he would not have been receiving so much in the final division of profits, out of which the capital holding shown above was sustained through the intervening years. Finally, part of the capital might have been invested in the form of debentures or preference shares, at fixed rates of interest, which would have been to the relative advantage of James Ballantyne and other ordinary shareholders while the business showed good profits. But, subject to these minor qualifications, the position would have been substantially as is shown above. The profit for the year ending September 29th, 1809, after providing for the management remuneration, but before deducting the interest credited to the Scott family, was £1,400. 3. 4. which is equal to 14½ % upon the invested capital. This amount, whether drawn in dividend, or left in the business, would have been the property of the shareholders in proportion to the amount of their holdings, so that John Scott would have benefited to almost exactly the same percentage, with the important difference that he would have had a proprietary interest in the business, and that, instead of Ballantyne remaining an equal partner, he would have been in the position of holding less than a quarter of the capital, and, even if he had had the undivided support of the shareholders whom he had introduced, they could still have been outvoted by Walter Scott alone, even without his brother's support.

Scott had, in fact, by 1809, a preponderating financial stake in the business, and the arrangements made show that he refrained from emphasising this position to his partner's detriment.

It is due to James Ballantyne to notice also that during the preceding four years he must have lived within the limits of the two-thirds profit which he received, out of which he had also provided whatever rate of interest he had undertaken to pay to William Creech, Miss Bruce, and his brother, as these successive investments were received, together with the interest upon the £500 overdraft which remained in his own name; for the amount of his capital, after all deductions had been made, remained somewhat larger than at the commencement of the partnership.

It has seemed desirable to state these facts in careful detail, because of the reckless nature of Lockhart's allegation that James Ballantyne had wasted in personal extravagance the capital which Scott provided, which was made with these figures before him. It must have been from James's capital account that he abstracted the figure of £3,966. 4. 11. which he used to support the charge, and it seems to be no more than a fair conclusion that his evidence is unworthy of acceptance on any financial question, unless it can be confirmed from independent sources.

The allegation that James was a 'penniless adventurer' doubtless seemed a more serious one to Lockhart's mind than Scott would have recognised it to be, and it is obviously less serious than that of wastefulness when the control of capital came into his hands, but, serious or not, it is of a demonstrable falsity. A close analysis shows that he must have been substantially solvent when he left Kelso, and came to Edinburgh at Scott's urgent suggestion. He had done work at his Kelso press which was the admiration of London publishers, and which justified the removal. His character and reputation were such that a prominent Kelso resident was prepared to guarantee his bank account at that time. The business which he established in Edinburgh, with Scott's assistance, was consistently profitable during the period, 1802-9, with which we are now dealing.

There is not a shred of evidence that Scott and James Ballantyne had a word of difference, or that either gave the other cause of complaint during all these years. Long afterwards, when misfortune had done its utmost to part them, Scott still wrote and spoke of James Ballantyne as of a valued and trusted friend. After his death, James wrote of him as his "dear friend and benefactor" toward whom his emotions had been to the last those of "respect and love".

Lockhart thought he did service to Scott by making proofless assertion that during these early years James Ballantyne had been robbing him by what would have been an almost crazy scale of extravagance, and that Scott had shown himself to be a blindly confident fool; to which we have seen that Ballantyne's Trustees retorted with counter-charges of a similar quality.

'Save me from my friends,' might be a common cry from Dryburgh Abbey, and from a humbler grave.

CHAPTER XXXVIII.

Enter John Ballantyne. He was a younger brother of James. He had been in London, but returned to Kelso in 1795, when his father took him into partnership. He married in 1797, after which his father transferred the tailoring branch of the Kelso business entirely to him. In 1805 he closed this business and migrated to Edinburgh, where his brother gave him a situation as bookkeeper, with Scott's consent, at a salary of £200 per annum. So far, the facts are agreed.

As to how he came to Edinburgh, Lockhart's first account is this:

> "John Ballantyne a younger brother of Scott's school-fellow, was originally destined for the paternal trade of a merchant—(that is to say a dealer in everything from fine broadcloth to children's tops)—at Kelso. The father seems to have sent him when very young to London, where, whatever else he may have done in the way of professional training, he spent some time in the banking-house of Messrs. Currie. On returning to Kelso, however, the 'department' which more peculiarly devolved upon him was the tailoring one. His personal habits had not been improved by his brief sojourn in the Great City, and the business, in consequence (by his own statement) of the irregularity of his life, gradually melted to nothing in his hands. Early in 1805, his goods were sold off, and barely sufficed to pay his debts. The worthy old couple found refuge with their ever affectionate eldest son, who provided his father with some little occupation (real or nominal) about the printing office; and thus John himself again quitted his native place under circumstances which, as I shall show in the sequel, had left a deep and painful trace even upon that volatile mind.

He had, however, some taste, and he at least fancied himself to have some talent for literature; and the rise of his brother, who also had met with no success in his original profession, was before him. He had acquired in London great apparent dexterity in book-keeping and accounts. He was married by this time; and it might naturally be hoped that with the severe lessons of the past, he would now apply sedulously to any duty that might be entrusted to him. The concern in the Canongate was a growing one, and James Ballantyne's somewhat indolent habits were already severely tried by its management. The Company offered John a salary of £200 a year as clerk, and the destitute ex-merchant was too happy to accept the proposal.

"James had serious deficiencies as a man of business, and John was not likely to supply them. A more reckless, thoughtless, improvident adventurer never rushed into the serious responsibilities of commerce; but his cleverness, his vivacity, his unaffected zeal, his gay fancy always seeing the light side of everything, his imperturbable good-humour, and buoyant elasticity of spirits, made and kept him such a favourite, that I believed Scott would as soon have ordered his dog to be hanged, as harboured, in his darkest hour of perplexity, the least thought of discarding 'jocund Johnny'."

The Trustees of James Ballantyne, though mainly concerned with the reputation of the elder brother, disputed the accuracy of this statement in numerous particulars: Regarding the position of the parents, and the circumstances under which John came to Edinburgh, they gave Lockhart the lie direct. They said that John did not arrive in Edinburgh in a destitute condition, nor was it true that his goods had ever been "sold off". They said that he disposed of his Kelso business deliberately, after it had been arranged that he should occupy the position of book-keeper in Edinburgh, and went there to take up an appointment which he had already received.

It is fair to notice that most of Lockhart's statements in the above quotation are of a nature which, after the lapse of a quarter of a century, it would be impossible to refute. Who could disprove (or how could Lockhart have known?) that James had been 'rather indolent' at that remote period? But the points on which he was challenged were capable of some verification. Being asked to justify them, he made this reply:

> "The Pamphleteers speak of the father of the Ballantynes as a man 'in easy if not affluent circumstances'. At some period of his life he may have been so, with reference to the scale of things at such a place as Kelso, and his station there. His shop was one of a kind still common in little country towns—the keeper of such a shop is vulgarly styled a 'Johnny Allthings'.
>
> "The second son (Rigdumfunidos) was on his return from London 'entrusted', says the pamphlet, with one department of the business. This 'department' was the tailoring one—and I have been told that Rigdum was considered as rather an expert snip among the Brummells and D'Orsays of Kelso.
>
> ...I inferred—from John's language about his 'goods and furniture with difficulty paying his debts'—that at the time he was 'left penniless', the shop at Kelso was shut up altogether, and that, as happens almost always in similar cases in Scotland, the 'goods' etc., were disposed of by auction. The Pamphleteers may or may not be right in contradicting me upon these particulars—but of what consequence are they?"

Perhaps they were not of much consequence, but it is a poor defence coming from the man who thought them to be sufficiently so to "infer", and then write them down as facts, with the evident intention of disparaging the man of whom he wrote.

Even when convicted of something approaching invention, he has not the grace to apologise. He endeavours to turn the point of the attack by emphasising that John had been a tailor—even that he had had the reputation of being a good tailor is the occasion of a sneer.

The name 'Rigdumfunidos' was given by Scott to John Ballantyne in a spirit of good-humoured intimacy: it is repeatedly used by Lockhart in one of sustained contempt.

He appears to suggest that you cannot libel a tailor—not to matter, that is. He had been painting a picture of Sir Walter Scott. If John Ballantyne could be a useful figure in the background, should he not be of any colour which the picture required?

There remain a number of allegations in the first-quoted paragraph which may be true or false, and are beyond testing; but what claim has Lockhart to be believed, as a result of examining statements which can be verified?

It is a fact, of whatever significance, that John lent £300 to the firm shortly after the date of his arrival in Edinburgh.

Lockhart is discredited as a biased and inaccurate witness, impulsed on his own confession by a curious delusion that it was to the benefit of Scott's reputation to discredit those whom he trusted in a lifelong business association. It does not logically follow that the Ballantynes were free from human frailties or human faults. We have to ask Lockhart to stand down from the witness-box, and judge the panorama of events as it unfolds before us, with unprejudiced minds.

CHAPTER XXXIX.

In the spring of 1808, the plant of the Border Press—substantially increased since the day when James carted his presses to Edinburgh—was working at its utmost capacity to meet Constable's orders for *Marmion*, while fulfilling the requirements of its other customers. James was "rather indolently" (?) managing this busy and successful business, and maintaining his reputation for beautiful and accurate work. He may have sat too much in his own office, giving more attention to the care of his proof-correcting, and the style of his bindings, and less to the oversight of his work-people, than a man of meaner or less artistic temperament would have been likely to do. But to suggest that he neglected these requirements of the business he had built up would go beyond the evidence or the probabilities. He liked a good meal when he got home at night. He showed some tendency to increase his weight.

John, a small alert man, whom no one would ever accuse of indolence, was dealing with the accounts, with the knowledge of finance and bookkeeping which he was said to have acquired in London.

Scott was working, as even he may never have worked before. The London booksellers—the two in Albemarle Street, Murray and Miller, in particular, and Murray most of all—were competing eagerly for his editorial services, and he had taken on a quantity of work suggestive of an audacity of enterprise outweighing judgement, but that, as we look back, we see that he had not overestimated his own capacity. He was editing three volumes of the Sadler State Papers: he was editing a huge accumulation of the Somers Tracts—a labour of four years and thirteen ponderous volumes, which Ballantyne was already commencing to print as they were prepared for his hands. He had undertaken with Murray to complete in its original style a novel (Strutt's Queeny-hoo Hall) which the author's death had left unfinished.

Also, for Constable, he was editing Carleton's Memoirs of the War of the Spanish Succession, and the Memoirs of Robert Cary. He was still friendly with the Edinburgh publisher, but he did not take him into his confidence as to his general undertakings or plans.

Constable went up to London himself to convoy the second delivery of *Marmion*, and superintend its distribution. Doubtless, he had other business there. Naturally, he talked to Murray and Miller, his partners in the *Marmion* venture. He learnt the extent to which they were employing Scott's energies, which he had not previously guessed. He went back to Edinburgh a frightened man.

Constable at this time appears to have felt that he had a first claim upon Scott's output, for no reason that is easy to discover, unless it were that the circumstances under which he made the advance on Marmion placed Scott under an obligation to him. If so, it would be the kind of plea which Scott would be very quick to recognise, even though inclination might pull in other directions. Now Constable felt that it was no use to grumble at what was already fixed up: he must find something to occupy Scott's time in earnest. He knew that he had talked of a new edition of Swift as a congenial enterprise. He went back and made a munificent offer. Scott was to edit Swift's complete works in the style in which he had done the Dryden volumes for Miller, but the remuneration was to be increased. Sixty guineas per volume. Fifteen hundred for the complete work. Scott signed the contract with a light heart. It was a happy, strenuous time.

Early in May, letters were going out right and left from Ashestiel soliciting material for the life of Swift, and the editing of his works. The new enterprise was started with as much energy as though other occupations did not exist. It is hard to visualise the study at Ashestiel, to which the dogs came, and to which the four children were always licensed intruders, and which appeared so neatly ordered to other visitors. It must have had a crowded appearance at this period. But Scott had an extraordinary capacity for organisation and method. He made a rule at this time that every letter he received should have a reply on the same day, unless the nature of its contents should render this impracticable, and he held to this till health and energy failed. It was already no light burden, for strangers wrote from all parts of the country: admiring letters on which he must pay postage and answer courteously: letters for advice and guidance on literary matters which he would not refuse; begging letters in endless variety which had suitable but generous responses: letters enclosing manuscripts (on which the postage would be heavy at that time) which he was expected to read, and to advise on their publication. He sent some of these to Constable, and more that were brought to him by needy authors in person, for which Constable was less than grateful. He said that he cared more for Scott's own bairns than for his adopted children.

There is another direction for which some credit may be given for the ordered state of the study and the smoothness of Scott's life in this and subsequent years of over-strenuous labours. He was not one to pose, or to treat his work as of a portentous seriousness, as lesser artists may be inclined to do. He would not be late for meals, and is said to have been the easiest author with which to live of which there is any record for comparison. But Charlotte was always near, with a loving uninterfering watchfulness. It was only during her last illness, many years later, that he realised that a study fire does not put on its own coal.

It may have been owing to the extent and variety of the editorial work he had undertaken that he appears to have spent this summer almost entirely at home, but there was a constant succession of visitors, who found him to be of an apparent leisure, at least after the midday meal, and ready for the active outdoor sports and expeditions for which the literary labours of the earlier day seem to have left him in a condition of undiminished vitality.

Joanna Baillie came from London to spend a short holiday at Ashestiel, and to talk to Sophia of the day when, if her parents would bring her with them, she would show her the sights of London. Sophia was eight now, and had learnt to ride out with her father, and to get as few bruises as possibly when tumbling off a mountain pony. All the children were taught to ride as soon as their walking lessons were over. Scott, who found miraculous leisure for everything, gave much time to his children. He gained the understanding and confidence which is so difficult between one generation and another, and which so many parents fail to reach. He seemed never to lack time to talk with them, or to join their games. He ruled them with a gentle firmness, and a word of displeasure meant more than a blow would have done in many households of that period. He would never hear of boarding schools. A child's place should be with its own parents, in its own home. He thought conduct even more important than education. Hardihood must be learnt, at whatever risk.

He appears, at this time, to have had only one intolerance, which his width of understanding, and sympathy with the weaknesses of human nature, did not enable him to overcome. He could not endure cowardice, though a man might fall short in almost any other way, and still ask for his aid. His brother Tom's financial disaster did not weaken the bond of friendship between them. Rather he exerted himself on his behalf as though those difficulties were his own. His brother Daniel had disgraced the family name and strained its patience in various ways before Scott used his friendship with George Ellis to get him an appointment on a Jamaican estate. But Daniel failed to act with ordinary courage in some emergency of disorder, and came home, having been dismissed with contempt. He came home broken with dissipation, and his mother took him in and nursed him till he died, as he did soon after this date. She had had dead babies enough, but she had to learn that there may be worse sorrows for motherhood than an infant's grave. She must do what she could for the child she bore, but Walter would not forgive this last episode. He would not see Daniel again while he was alive. He would not go to his funeral when he died. He would not wear mourning for him, though he usually conformed to that ugly custom. Many years afterwards, he expressed a deep regret for this attitude. He wrote the *Fair Maid of Perth* to illustrate his realisation that even cowardice may be uncontrollable. Daniel left a child, illegitimate and derelict, when he died. His mother took it into her home, and Scott showed it kindness from the first, and provided for it subsequently as though it had been his own.

It was during this summer that he established another enduring friendship of momentous consequences—that with John Morritt, of Rokeby. Mr. Morritt came on a visit to Edinburgh, travelling further north. He was a friend of the Hamiltons. He knew George Ellis. He had introductions to Scott, who met him in Edinburgh. There was an immediate and mutual liking. Scott gave him the time which he seemed always to possess in such miraculous quantities. He took him (walking) to see his friends at Dalkeith. He turned aside to see how the new tenants were keeping the cottage at Lasswade. He told Morritt of the happiness of those first married years of limited income and many activities, which had been spent in the earlier home. He recalled how he had made the dining-table with his own hands.

Morritt had no time then to visit Ashestiel, thirty miles to the south, but promised to do so on his return journey, which in the later summer, he did.

He retained vivid memories of that visit. He spent a happy week with a man of great literary fame who knew that life is more important than literature. He was shown Melrose, and St. Mary's Loch, in the usual routine. He observed that Scott was the "cherished friend and kind neighbour" of all the inhabitants of the district. He was taken "to dance with Border lasses on a barn floor" at Farmer Laidlaw's harvest-home. This Laidlaw was a (distant) kinsman of Scott's friend of that name. His farm stretched up to the garden at Ashestiel, separated only by the gorge and stream that bounded the eastern side. Morritt observed Scott's entrance to this convivial gathering. He says: "His wife and happy young family were clustered round him, and the cordiality of his reception would have unbent a misanthrope."

His visit extended over Sunday, and he had the different experience of seeing Scott read prayers at the morning service, which he held in his own drawing-room. The parish church was eight miles away. Roads were rough in those days. Scott let it be known that all who would could attend on these occasions. Presbyterian neighbours gradually overcame their antipathy to the English prayer-book till the "parlour-chapel" was inconveniently crowded.

After the morning prayers, it was customary on Sundays for the whole family to go walking together at this time of year, and picnic in the summer woods. The dogs came, but no one might ride, for Scott had made it a strict rule that all domestic animals must have a day of rest. In other ways, he drove the Scottish customs of Sabbath observance with a light rein, remembering the severity of his own childhood experiences, and the conclusion he had formed that "it did none of us any good".

There were happy days in this summer of 1808, and while they passed, John Murray, in London, had been thinking hard.

CHAPTER XL.

John Murray had a bold plan. He had dreamed for some time that it might be possible to establish a periodical which would rival the Edinburgh Review, and now the idea took shape. He had decided that, if he could obtain Scott's support, it would be a practicable scheme. He noticed that Scott had ceased to contribute to Constable's magazine. He remembered that extraordinary attack on *Marmion* which it had contained, even while Constable and he had been busy marketing the poem. He read articles in it clamouring for peace at any price, exalting the prowess of the French armies as of an invincible quality, and threatening revolution in England if the war should continue. What would Scott think when he read them? Murray saw much, and he guessed more.

Having resolved to open the campaign, he acted with his characteristic caution and circumspection. He decided that Scott could best be approached through the Ballantyne connection. He wrote to James, discussing printing orders. His action raises additional doubt as to whether Scott's interest in the firm was the close secret that Lockhart represents it to have been. Anyway, that is what Murray did, and James rose to the bait.

Murray conducted his approach with skill. Having suggested business of sufficient importance to justify an interview, it would have been natural for James to come to London, which he was evidently willing to do. But that would not have suited

Murray at all. He wanted to meet Scott. Yet he would not go to Edinburgh, nor disclose his plans, till he was better acquainted with the position. Printer and publisher agreed to meet each other midway. They chose Ferrybridge in South Yorkshire, where the coaching-road crossed the Aire, and, when they met, Mr. Murray mentioned a project that he had in mind of a new Novelist's Library of a comprehensive kind, such as would be dear to any printer's heart. They discussed paper and types. But, beyond that, Murray kept his thoughts to himself. He said nothing of the Quarterly Review that he had in mind. He let James Ballantyne talk, drawing him out. James may have been no less circumspect than he, though he may have talked more. He made no secret of his opinion that Scott was becoming less friendly with Constable. It was Constable and Hunter now, and Scott and Hunter had exchanged angry words. He believed that Scott would need little persuasion to set up a publishing house in Edinburgh in competition with Constable, particularly if he had a good connection in London (such as Murray would be). What did Mr. Murray think of that? Mr. Murray was not discouraging. Ballantyne became detailed. He mentioned Scott's idea of an Edinburgh Annual Register, which he had suggested when the Border Press was first set up. Constable had discouraged) but Scott had always persisted in that idea. He hinted that Scott was already thinking of another poem in the *Marmion* style. There was the possibility of a novel.... Did not Mr. Murray think that it might be worth while to come to Edinburgh, and talk things over there? Mr. Murray did. They went back together.

Murray arrived in Edinburgh in October. The autumn term had begun, and the Clerk of Session had left Ashestiel for his home in North Castle Street. Scott received him with cordiality. Murray talked of the Edinburgh Review, and Scott told him not only that he had ceased to contribute to it, but that he regarded an article in the current number with so much dislike that he had decided to cancel his subscription. During the following month, Constable received a note from Scott with this intimation: "The Edinburgh Review *had* become such as to render it impossible for me to contribute to it.—*Now*, it is such as I can no longer continue to receive or read it." Constable must have received this clear though ungrammatical letter with more annoyance than surprise. He scrawled "Stop!!!" against the name of Walter Scott on the subscribers' register.

Murray went back to London having given James Ballantyne, in addition to the prospect of substantial orders, a promise that if a publishing business should be started in competition with Constable he would act as its London agent. He had received a promise from Scott to give his support to the projected quarterly, and to enlist the aid of George Ellis, Morritt, Heber, and other literary friends of their political sympathies.

Rumours of the projected competition must have reached Constable, and Scott's part in the matter may have become known to him. In any event, he could not doubt that Murray would solicit, and would receive his support.

Good relations must have been strained to breaking-point by this development, under whatever circumstances, but the actual breach came through the intervention of Constable's partner. Mr. Hunter was an almost fanatical Whig; and Scott's politics were particularly obnoxious to him. He was also a competent business man. He had introduced capital to Constable's business, and valuable connections. He meant to make it pay. He examined the Scott contract relating to Swift with a critical and disapproving eye. There was no time-limit. He decided that it was a most unsatisfactory document.

But after reflection he reached the conclusion that, while it imposed no time-limit during which the work must be completed, there was an implied obligation that Scott would not take on any further contracts of the same kind in the meantime. He saw Scott, handling the situation in a firm and business-like manner, to which he found that the author did not respond in the right way. He appears to have had more than one interview, ending without cordiality on either side. The work was, in fact, making good progress, but Scott was never easy to drive, and his courtesy of manner may have misled Mr. Hunter as to the nature of the man with whom he was dealing. In any case, the moment was inopportune. On Jan. 2nd, 1809, Scott wrote a formal letter to Constable & Co., offering to cancel the deed relating to the Swift edition, if they thought on reflection that they had committed themselves too hastily.

Constable was in a state of consternation at this development, but there is pride as well as anger in his reply. He would not cancel the contract. Scott had attached too much importance to an "unguarded expression". He suggested that 'the misrepresentations of interested persons' were keeping them apart.

Lockhart thinks, and may be right, that this is an allusion to John Ballantyne, but, even if so, it may not have been a well-founded imputation.

Scott's reply speaks for itself.

> 12th Jan. 1809
>
> "Gen
>
> To resume *for the last time* the disagreeable subject of our difference, I must remind you of what I told Mr. Constable personally, *that no single unguarded expression, much less the misrepresentation of any person whatever, would have influenced me to quarrel with any of my friends*. But if Mr. Hunter will take the trouble to recollect the general opinion he has expressed of my undertakings, and of my ability to execute them, upon many occasions during the last few months and his whole conduct in the bargain about Swift, I think he ought to be the last to wish his interest compromised on my account."

Apart from the Swift, which went on to completion in due course, the break was now absolute, and had an appearance of finality. From the wording of the letters above quoted, it is clear that Scott had a personal interview with Constable between their dates, and the nature of some of the differences which had accumulated to part them is shown in a letter written to Miss Seward at Lichfield a couple of months later.

Miss Anne Seward was a poetess whose reputation has not survived. She had more words than ideas, and her feelings were not controlled by an adequate intelligence. But she was sentimentally fluent, took herself seriously, and had established her own valuation in many minds. She had a voluminous correspondence with those of literary prominence in her own time. She had written effusively admiring letters to Scott from the date of the publication of the *Border Minstrelsy*. They were letters of the kind that he intensely disliked, but he had replied with politeness. When he had been returning from London in March 1807—two years earlier—she had prevailed upon him to travel through Lichfield, and pay her a call.

After that, she wrote to Cary, telling him *inter alia* that the "proudest boast of the Caledonian muse" had expressed an absurd opinion about the Divine Comedy, which we may believe if we will.

Now, in March 1809, Scott wrote to her in these terms:

> "Constable, like many other folks who learn to undervalue the means by which they have risen, has behaved, or rather suffered his partner to behave, very uncivilly towards me. But they may both live to know that they should not have kicked down the ladder till they were sure of their footing. The very last time I spoke to him on business was about your poems. I understood him to decline your terms; but I had neither influence to change his opinion, nor inclination to interfere with his resolution. He is a very enterprising, and I believe a thoroughly honest man, but his vanity sometimes overpowers his discretion."

In most of these remarks Scott is simply expressing his own feelings. They have no direct relation to the publication of Miss

Seward's poems, but it is clear that she had sent them to Scott with a request that he would use his influence with Constable to publish them, and that Constable was not grateful for the opportunity. It is a position in which we can sympathise with both men—and with the lady also. But that is not the end of the tale, for Miss Seward had made a will, of which we shall hear more. She might have altered it, with better opportunity, after reading this letter, but it can scarcely have reached her hands, for it is dated March 19th, and on the 25th she was dead.

It is curious that Constable spoke of Scott very much in the tone in which Scott wrote of him, and with kindred metaphors. 'There is such a thing as rearing an oak until it can support itself.'

There is exaggeration in both metaphors. Constable certainly had not reared the oak. Scott had put profits into Constable's pockets, and had done important editorial work for which he had refused to charge, which made Hunter's complaints more unreasonable and hurtful than they might otherwise have been, but the ladder by which Constable had climbed was primarily his own business ability, and the success of the Edinburgh Review.

Lockhart suggests that the breach had been engineered by John Ballantyne. But there is no shred of supporting evidence. It is clear that political differences underlay it; and, individually, Hunter, Jeffrey, and Murray each played a hand in the game. But, primarily, it appears to have been Scott's own decision and his own plan. With an audacious self-confidence, and with the supporting knowledge that he had, so far, carried to success every plan he had made, he had decided that, as he had already fostered a successful printing business, he would be a publisher also. He would found a publishing house to rival Constable in Edinburgh. Murray should be his London agent, and Murray should have his support in the London Quarterly, which, under Gifford's editing, might be of as high a literary standard as the Edinburgh, and of a different political complexion.

Immediately after he wrote the letter to Constable signifying that the correspondence was closed, he developed his plans with characteristic energy. A publishing house was started in Hanover Street under the style of John Ballantyne & Co., of which John was to be manager, and Scott and James Ballantyne the remaining partners.

Lockhart condemns this enterprise as a mad folly from the start, which is saying no more than that it was not permanently successful. Lockhart wrote with a knowledge of following events, which he used in place of the business judgement which he did not possess. Anything which succeeds will be "sagacious" at its inception: anything which fails will be "rash," and probably condemned with more contemptuous adjectives. Constable advanced Scott a thousand guineas on an unwritten poem without incurring Lockhart's sarcasm, because he finally got what he paid for, and everyone came off well. Where facts are lacking, confident assertion will be sufficient to fill the gap. It is difficult to find, in all Lockhart's endless pages, any intelligent sympathetic appreciation of a business position *as it then was*, without reference to a future which could not have been foreseen at the time.

Now he wanted a culprit for the foundation of this publishing business, and he selected John Ballantyne. As we have seen? he is always inclined to attribute Scott's actions to outer influences, rather than his own decisions. He now represents that Scott embarked upon a disastrous publishing venture under the urgent influence or John Ballantyne, who was to be given its control, and whom he describes as 'a person without capital, and neither by training nor by temper in the smallest degree qualified for such a situation.' The degree to which John was suitable for such a position must he a matter of opinion, but the question of whether the inception of the business was due to his urgency is one of fact. The causes already shown appear sufficient, and John's name is not even mentioned in any surviving correspondence or other documents in this connection. The Trustees of James Ballantyne challenged this account of the venture, in which they said that Scott had been the initiating as well as the dominant spirit, and Lockhart replied that he had drawn the conclusion that John was at the bottom of the business because "he was an exceedingly vain, presumptuous and aspiring little fellow." He added: "Was I to forget the old rule *Cui fuit bonum*? But the point is of no consequence."

In plain English, he had made the suggestion without an ounce of evidence, and replies with abusive language, and the ' Does it matter?' which is he usual retort when convicted of inventions which are at least as disparaging to Scott as John Ballantyne, and which, fortunately for the memories of both, have no foundation of fact or even of probability. If Lockhart meant no more than that John was glad to get the opportunity of serving Scott's plans and justifying his own abilities in the management of a new business, and that he may have over estimated what those abilities were, it is not a serious accusation in itself, the sting lying in the sneer with which it is said. But Scott had known John for a considerable time at this date, and if he made the egregious blunder of selecting one who was utterly unsuited for the position, it would reflect upon himself, even without the added suggestion that he was a tool in the 'little fellow's' hands. (The utterly irrelevant allusion to John's stature is an unfortunate, but characteristic, example of Lockhart's controversial methods.)

There is absolutely no evidence as to John having any part in the matter until the deed of partnership was executed in January, but James kept a diary, and some entries in it are creditable to him, and supply strong confirmation of the course of events having been as is suggested by the evidences already given. There was an occasion in December when he called to see Constable, was well received, and booked a substantial order, but he shortly afterwards left the shop hurriedly when Constable and Hunter were together, because he did not want to quarrel, and would not listen in silence to Hunter's abuse, *not of himself but his friends.* He records Constable's irritated suspicions as to the reason of Murray's visit to Edinburgh, and his own realisation that the political gulf between Scott and Hunter and the Edinburgh Review were rendering business relations increasingly difficult to maintain, but he appears to have been concerned to lessen friction rather than to create it.

There was one curious point of dispute between Constable and himself, about which they argued vainly, but on which we know that Constable must have been wrong. We know that Scott had had the idea of an "Edinburgh Register" in his mind ever since he persuaded James to set up business in the capital city. It appears that James and Constable had had a conversation about the possibilities of such a publication when they had been travelling together earlier in the year. Now it was being talked of again, and Constable, wishing to discourage the project, put to James the disconcerting suggestion that he could not honourably have anything to do with it without his consent, because he (Constable) had originated the idea! Constable was evidently in a state of self-delusion on this point, and lames shows in his diary that he was worried by a suggestion which he knew to be untrue, but might find it hard to disprove. This was in December.

We get a glimpse in the diary also of Scott's house in North Castle Street, as the storm-centre upon which other parties converge. Scott sends to James to come to him to discuss the position. As he is leaving, Constable is at the door, probably for that final interview, and James turns aside into the dining-room, lest they should meet in the hall....

The deed of partnership, which the partners agreed to leave in Scott's custody, provided that the new firm should start with a cash capital of £2,000, half of which was to be found by Scott, and £500 each by the other two. James had no free capital outside the printing business, which certainly could not afford to lose that amount even if James could have drawn it without reducing his capital below the partnership level. For the time, Scott lent him the money, finding £1,500 in all. That is as far as the documentary evidence goes. Lockhart says this: "Scott appears to have found all the capital, at any rate his own, half share, and one fourth, the portion of James, who, not having any funds to spare, must have become indebted to someone for it. It does not appear from what source. John acquired his, the remaining fourth." It will be observed that the first part of this statement is false, by its own conclusion. But John had been cast for the part of impecuniosity. It is true that he had advanced £300 to the printing business some time previously, and that £600 of James's capital had been found by Alexander, another brother, who was still trading in Kelso, but Lockhart will have it that they were a penniless family, and this idea must be sustained. Now John (appears to have) invested £500 without difficulty. It does not matter to us how such sums came into his hands. He may have burgled. He may have forged. Quite possibly, he may have borrowed, though a clerk with a family to provide for, and earning £200 a year, would not easily obtain such an advance unless he were of better character than Lockhart will allow. He may have done any of these things, but there is not a shred of evidence that he did, and, if that does not matter to us, Lockhart's method of presenting the case, if we are to go forward in his guidance, certainly does.

CHAPTER XLI.

Some premises in Hanover Street were promptly taken for the accommodation of the new firm or John Ballantyne & Co. and John himself, the 'vain, presumptuous, and aspiring little fellow', said goodbye to his wife, and climbed on to the London coach we may suppose with what high dreams, to interview John Murray and others in the important capacity of the Edinburgh publisher who was to control the Scottish distribution of the new Quarterly Review (of which the first number was to be published in April), and who had Mr. Scott's support in the endeavour to establish an Edinburgh business which would challenge the somewhat autocratic monopoly which Constable now held in the northern capital.

He was not to be left to his own unsupported efforts. Mr. and Mrs. Scott were following by sea, so soon as the Court should rise. They stayed, in fact, for about two months, renewing associations with old friends and forming new ones in political and literary circles, in which Scott now had a securely founded reputation. He saw the new Review successfully launched with three articles from his own pen, and went back very confidently to resume control of the increased responsibilities to which he had committed himself. We may suppose that James Ballantyne, who had been left to hold the fort alone, without even the help of John's bookkeeping abilities in the always more or less complicated finances of the printing business, and without Scott's financial aid to be called upon in emergency, would be glad to see him return. But, for the moment, there was little cloud in the financial sky.

John Morritt had been in London while Scott was there, and tells one anecdote which is sufficiently characteristic to be worth recording. There was a gathering at which Scott and Coleridge were present, and poems, published and unpublished, were being recited and criticised. It was the kind of assembly that Scott tolerated rather than liked, though he would play the game in a good-tempered and very capable way.

On this occasion there was an element present which was disposed to exalt the compositions of the English pot, in comparison with those of his Scottish rival, which Scott took with his usual good humour; but when after a time he was asked to favour the meeting with an example of his own occasional poetry, he replied that he had nothing which it would be worth their while to hear. But he had read some verses recently in a provincial paper which he would repeat as an example of what good poetry should really be.

This he did, and the verses he gave were criticised somewhat mercilessly, until, when a member of the company pointed out that one line which he admired was sheer nonsense, and Scott was exerting himself to defend it, Coleridge exclaimed in desperation: 'For Heaven's sake, leave Mr. Scott alone. *I wrote that poem myself.*' It was 'Fire, Famine, and Slaughter,' on which Scott performed this feat of casual memory, and incidentally exposed the hollowness of the critical judgements in which such coteries indulge.

For the most part, he regarded the lionising which is? perhaps, the worst penalty of successful authorship, as a part of the game which, if it gave pleasure to others, it would be bad manners to decline. He would ask his hostess at times if he were expected to roar, or if he could consider himself among friends, and would lead the conversation accordingly. He endured, in the same spirit, the endless and ever increasing crowd of travellers who brought introductions or framed excuse to call upon him at Ashestiel or in Edinburgh; only showing a rare resentment if he thought that visitors failed to show sufficient courtesy to his wife, and to remember, in his own phrase, that it is possible to become an author and remain a gentleman.

The Scotts travelled back by road in the company of Mr. Morritt, who was returning to his Yorkshire home, and who persuaded them to break the journey at Rokeby, where they fell in love—as who would not?—with the beauties of Rokeby Park, and the wooded hills among which the Greta joins the Tees. Scott heard the traditions of the Civil War which are associated with the district, and talked of a poem to be—which was the almost customary reward of those who entertained him in hall or castle. He may have been already framing some of the songs which will make the name of Rokeby famous while the language endures, but, for the moment, he had another poem on hand, which he expected to occupy all the time that other engagements would leave him till the year should end. He had planned that *The Lady of the Lake* should be ready by the end of the year, and, for once, he was to prove approximately equal to his own forecast. He had fixed its locality in that wild region into which he had penetrated as a youth with a file of bayonets behind him, and he had probably outlined its plot, and, imagined its characters, for none of all his poems was to show clearer conception, or superior artistic unity. It gives the impression throughout that the last line was foreseen before the first was written. But his immediate requirement was to renew and correct his memories of the region of Loch Katrine and Ben-ledi. Almost as soon as he and Charlotte arrived at Ashestiel, they left again. Scott had a short and busy period in Edinburgh, during which we may suppose that James had something to report as to the progress of the printing business, and John to receive many instructions as to the development of the publishing enterprise, and then Charlotte and he spent July in the district which was to be the scene of the new poem, making their headquarters mainly at Buchanan House, from which centre, in the company of Mr. Macdonald Buchanan, Scott explored the locality. He wrote the first canto while in the midst of the scenery which it describes, actually riding the whole course which the chase was supposed to take, that he might verify its possibility, and reading this part of the poem to Lady Louisa Stewart and others before leaving the district....

But we must turn aside at this point to give brief attention to a matter which has been mentioned already—that of Miss Seward's will.

This lady had been a voluminous writer of letters. She had met most of the literary celebrities of the times, and she used to write about them to each other, and elsewhere, usually, though not always, in terms of very fulsome praise, and with detailed descriptions. The letters were full of personalities, and she appears to have regarded them as of sufficient importance to preserve them in duplicate, for she had approached Scott during the previous year, and asked him to undertake to edit them after her death.

But this he had explicitly declined to do, telling her in plain though courteous language that he did not think that such letters should be published at all. However, he had undertaken to use his influence with Constable to induce him to print her collected poems, with a result which we have seen already.

Knowing that Scott had refused to have anything to do with the letters, but had been more complaisent toward the poems, and not knowing that Constable had refused publication of the latter, which must have failed to please her, she made a will shortly before she died, leaving her letters to Constable and her poems to Scott, with injunctions that they should be published after her death. She even directed that Scott was to have the honour of writing a biography to preface the poems, and it is characteristic of Scott's weaker side that he does not appear to have thought of declining the monstrous obligation which had been thrust upon him. But, in a letter to Joanna Baillie, he exposed his feelings:

> "The despair which I used to feel on receiving poor Miss Seward's letters whom I really liked, gave me a most unsentimental horror for sentimental letters. I am now doing penance for my ill-breeding, by submitting to edit her posthumous poetry, most of which is absolutely execrable. This, however, is the least of my evils, for when she proposed this bequest to me, which I could not in decency refuse, she combined it with a request that I would publish her whole literary correspondence. This I declined on principle, having a particular aversion at perpetuating that sort of gossip; but what availed it? Lo! to ensure the publication, she left it to an Edinburgh bookseller: and I anticipate the horror of seeing myself advertised for a live poet like a wild beast on a painted streamer; for I understand all her friends are depicted therein in body, mind, and manners."

What availed it, indeed? What will it ever avail to protest in the name of decency against the publication of random or poisonous gossip, if and when it can be done with profit and legal impunity? Yet, for the moment, Scott had his way. The provisions of the will led to correspondence between Constable and himself. They parleyed courteously from their opposite camps. It appeared that Constable accepted the lady's legacy. He saw money in those gossiping letters, being right on that point, as he usually was. But he offered Scott an opportunity of going over them, and striking out the numerous references to himself, which he very gladly did. It was left to Lockhart to publish both the above letter, and one of the silly effusions to which Scott objected so strongly. It is not the only occasion on which we are left to wonder whether it was Lockhart's skull or his skin which was of an unusual thickness.

Mr. James Ballantyne learnt that he would have the pleasure of printing Miss Seward's poems, and Mr. John that he would have the profit of publishing them. There is no record of what they said.

CHAPTER XLII.

Scott had a good deal of correspondence with Joanna Baillie during this year, when we are confronted with another of his multifarious activities. He was using money and influence—not unsuccessfully—to bring one of her plays on to the Edinburgh stage.

He had always loved the theatre, and it will be remembered how, in earlier youth, he had given broken heads to those who disturbed its peace. Charlotte loved it also, with the passion of her own race. They had made many theatrical friendships while in London together, particularly with Mrs. Siddons, and John Kemble. Now Scott exerted himself to arrange that Kemble's nephew, Henry Siddons, should acquire the lease of the Edinburgh theatre. He purchased a share himself, becoming an acting trustee. He stipulated that Joanna Baillie's play *The Family Legend* should be the first to be presented under the new management. He was always true to his friends.

He threw himself into the preparations of this play with the energy of an unoccupied man. He attended the rehearsals: he arranged the costumes: he wrote a prologue. Whether through his efforts and popularity, or on its own merits, it had an unusual success for an author whose plays were less acted than read. Scott, writing to London, could exult in the good news that he was able to send.

There was at least one direction in which we may be sure that the play would be kindly treated. For at this time James Ballantyne had won a recognised authority as a dramatic critic in Edinburgh—an 'authority', Lockhart says, with his inevitable sneer, 'supremely gratifying to himself '. But a man does not become an authority in dramatic criticism without some other qualities than a capacity for self-congratulation.

It was as an actor in the company that produced this play that Scott made the acquaintance of Daniel Terry. Lockhart records of this actor, famous for himself, and of a more famous name, that 'he and the Ballantynes were constant companions', and it is, perhaps, for this reason that he presents his admiration of Scott in a spirit of impossible caricature. Though he is generous enough to allow, with an amusing subtlety of distinction, that the actor "had the *manners and feelings* of a gentleman."

Amid these extraneous activities, the *Lady of the Lake* made steady progress, and was raising high expectations among those who heard parts of it read as its composition proceeded: the Swift editing was substantially advanced: the Sadler papers went to the press, and were finally off his hands: several volumes of the Somers tracts, a huge labour by which he ultimately earned a total of £1,300, were completed, and the Memoirs of Robert Cary was also a finished thing.

Financially, the publishing business must have brought in little, and required much. But this is usual with publishing businesses in their first year. What it owed would be mainly to the printing house, which would not be an oppressive creditor, and, by the methods of finance which were usual at this period, of which an extended explanation will be required, this position would not be quickly felt.

Anyway, there was the new poem to come, concerning which it had been arranged that Scott's price should be 2,000 guineas. A fourth of this was to come from Miller, who would purchase the same proportion of the copyright that he had done previously from Constable (at a smaller figure) when *Marmion* was published. By this means, his distributing facilities would be enlisted. Murray would act as agent for John Ballantyne & Co., on the terms of the general agreement existing between them. The poem would be published through the previous channels, and (in London) with all the previous advantages, but the John Ballantyne Company, after paying Scott the agreed fee, should have a large and continuing profit—if the success of the *Lay* and *Marmion* could be achieved for a third time, and those who had seen parts of the new poem were inclined to think that it would.

Scott had done a graceful thing in instructing John to ask Constable for the benefit of his advice as to the quantity which should be printed for a first impression, and on other details, and Constable gave some generous help. Both Scott and he may have felt a recovered goodwill since that exchange of courtesies over the Seward letters. Constable may have looked ahead. Scott may have reflected that to confer a favour may make an enemy, where to ask one will make a friend. Few men object to know that their advice will be valued. Scott once said that wherever he had lived he had always been on good terms with the most difficult of his neighbours. He had found that, with sufficient patience, a side could always be found from which a man could be approached successfully. Certainly, he had acted with wisdom now.

All this year, as earlier, he had been fulfilling the duties of Clerk of Session without remuneration, as he must expect to do while Mr. Home lived. But Home was an old man. He might not wish him to die, yet when he totalled his growing income, and weighed against it the responsibilities which he was undertaking, he might reasonably consider that a further £1,000 or £1,500 a year would be his at no distant date.

The beginning of 1810 was a happy time. Scott felt that his many activities were well under control. There was little at this period that he did not feel equal to undertake or to overcome. *The Lady of the Lake* went to the press.

CHAPTER XLIII.

The Lady of the Lake was published in London early in May, and met with a chorus of approbation louder and more united than had been those which welcomed the earlier poems.

That George Ellis would write of it enthusiastically in the *Quarterly* might be expected, but, surprisingly, in the *Edinburgh,* even Balaam blessed.

Those who read it then had not done so when they were young. It came to them as a new thing, this poem that made music of Highland names. They read the chase in the first canto, and knew, if they knew English poetry, that it could offer nothing to put beside it. Probably it never will. They read the following cantos, and found them to be of a kindred freshness, though with different excellences. There were passages in *Marmion*, even apart from the battle canto, which rivalled anything in the later poem, but here was a more sustained, a more equal altitude. The magic of the *Lay* might never be recaptured, but here was a different beauty, and a more perfect whole. The annoying interludes of *Marmion* had been wisely abandoned for the briefer beauty of opening and closing lyrics. The octosyllabic metre, while less varied, less experimental, than that of the *Lay,* was now handled with a practised ease, which had the narrative quality of concentrated and cadenced prose. Those who would not be easily converted from their traditional respect for the decasyllabic line, as the necessary medium for English narrative poetry, made some protests in public against Scott's continued adherence to the shorter metre, and his correspondence shows that these views were expressed more freely and urgently in private letters, though usually with the argument that he who had done marvels already would do miracles with a better tool.

He replied, without taking the correspondence over-seriously, that it was inclination rather than judgement which had controlled his decision. Yet he offered sound argument in its support. The ten-syllable line may be incomparable for many purposes, but for narrative—is it quite so sure? He instanced a passage from Pope's *Iliad* in which there is a two-syllable padding in every line. He might have asked whether his own verse would have gained in any material prosodic quality had he lengthened it in the same way:

> The stag at eve had drunk his *something* fill,
> As *something* danced the moon on Monan's rill,
> And *something* deep his midnight lair had made,
> *Something* in lone Glenartney's hazel shade.

It is possible that such a poem would have been equally admired: it is less probable that it would have been equally read.

The wizardry of Scott's poetry is an undissectible secret, and no one except Macaulay, and he only partially, and with obvious plagiarisms, has been able to put his tools to a kindred use. Yet we may see that his own imagination, the particular quality of knowledge which he had gathered, a universality of sympathy which has been seldom equalled except by the greatest poets, a prosodic skill which tends to conceal itself—all these things are informed by an instinctive ideality, a love of noble living, which made his poetry a separate individual thing. And we may observe something of the prosodic principles, conscious or unconscious, on which he worked, and by which his results were reached.

There is the quality which we have observed already, in which his subsequent prose romances as a whole were to be markedly inferior—the direct and often monosyllabic force and concentrated brevity of the narrative, especially in its conversational parts.

Having an enormous vocabulary under control, he was able to produce such results with a delusive aspect of ease, and sometimes even of carelessness, the latter appearance arising from the fact that however great might be his care to achieve beauty of form, he always put matter first, if there were a conflict between the two which he was unable to reconcile.

On this point, he may be contrasted with Tennyson, who, in the same difficulty, would always make the opposite choice, with the result that he would pile ornamentation upon his narrative poetry until the tale itself would sink beneath its burden, as where he concluded with the statement that—

> "he that told the tale in older time
> Says that Sir Gareth wedded Lyonors,
> But he that told it later says Lynette."

—and if you care which it was, it is something which (for several beautiful pages) the author had ceased to do.

An equal contrast of method, in which the same poets are at the extremities of difference, may be observed in their use of metaphor or simile. Tennyson frequently interrupts his narrative to insert metaphors, often of great beauty, and sometimes of a length of several lines. They may be good in themselves, but they weaken the force of the narrative, distracting the reader's mind. For example:

> "But at the flash and motion of the man
> They vanish'd panic-stricken, like a shoal
> Of darting fish, that on a summer morn
> Adown the crystal dykes at Camelot
> Come slipping o'er their shadows on the sand,
> But if a man who stands upon the brink
> But lift a shining hand against the sun,
> There is not left the twinkle of a fin
> Betwixt the cressy islets white in flower;
> So, scared but at the motion of the man,
> Fled all the boon companions of the Earl."

Scott *never* does this. His metaphors, whether hackneyed or of an original beauty, are always brief, and always tend to concentrate attention, and intensify imagination.

Consider the subtlety of contrast, and the force of the illustration as showing the bearer's fixity of purpose in the five-word simile—

" But still, *as though with parting life,*
Firmer he grasped the cross of strife."

Consider the rising intensity of the three-fold simile which prepares us for Roderick's dying effort to revenge his wound:

"Like adder darting from his coil
Like wolf that dashes through the toil,
Like mountain-cat who guards her young,
Full at Fitz-James's throat he sprung."

Here, as always in situations of emotional intensity, Scott puts the simile first: the act itself is the culmination. But if it be a moment when we are to pause and watch, it will come afterward, delaying the mind upon the scene to which it has been directed, as in—

"So forth the startled swan would swing:
So turn to prune his ruffled wing."

And we may learn something of the art of poetic narrative by the skilful economy of the sustained metaphor of the ' forest' of spears, made darker by contrast of the bright sunshine in which the battle is fought.

"Their centre ranks, with pike and spear
A twilight forest frowned

How shall it keep its rooted place
The spearmen's twilight wood?
Like reeds before the tempest's frown,
That serried grove of lances brown

At once lay levelled low.

As illustration of Scott's terseness of diction in these poems it may be observed that when Macaulay borrows, *he always lengthens*. For examples, we need go no further than the page from which the above abstracts are taken, for Macaulay's borrowings were of a routine frequency.

Scott has:

"I see," he cried, "their column shake,
Now, gallants, for your ladies' sake,
Upon them with the lance."

Macaulay lengthens the last two of these lines into:

"Now by the lips of those you love, fair gentlemen of France,
Charge for the golden lilies, upon them with the lance."

Scott has:

"So did that deep and darksome pass
Devour the battle's mingled mass."

Macaulay lengthens to:

"And fliers and pursuers are mingled in a mass
And far away the battle goes rolling through the pass."

Comparing these paraphrases it may be agreed that there is something to be said for the superior narrative vigour of a shorter line.

There is one point in these narrative poems at which Scott achieved a success which is unique in the literature of our civilisation.

The accurate and adequate description of a battle has always been a matter of almost insurmountable difficulty, both to the poet and the historian.

Even its geography, however limited, its chronology, however short, are difficult to rescue from the confusion over which the cloud of battle rose into a blinded sky. A man who emerges whole from that ordeal may have no certain memory of his own part, and still less of what others may have done, or when they did it in relation to the other confusions around him. Or should memory avail, courage and cowardice may unite in an equal silence. Men may be slow to say 'I was first over the wall', or 'I lay flat in the ditch', and their comrades, having their own activities or preoccupations, may have failed to observe either of these incidents. The reconstruction of the battle-drama is the work of many tongues, among which flattery finds its voice, and envy strikes from behind.

The poet, aiming to recreate it emotionally, in a unity of portraiture, has an added difficulty—that of separating the individual from the crowd, and yet not giving him a grotesquely disproportionate stature.

In the old days of hand-to-hand fighting, the leaders did stand out in an individual prominence. They were usually better horsed, better armed, and better trained, than were those they led into battle, and they were often of exceptional physical strength. The rank-and-file of the opposing force would be inclined to give way before them, or would try to win fame at their life's price. Such men must be opposed, if at all, by those of equal eminence in the opposing ranks, and the fall of one might mean a local rout, or even a decisive turn in the whole tide of the battle.

The oral traditions, or even the written records of great conflicts, would centre round the meeting of such champions, and its songs would be of a similar substance. The Iliad fighting is all of this character, and resembles the distorted perspective of a primitive painting, in that the contending armies are reduced to the vagueness of surrounding shadows. For many centuries, epic and ballad poetry followed the Homer tradition. The impressionist method, of which Campbell's *Hohenlinden* may be considered a classic example, is much harder to do well, and is of quite recent origin.

It may be scarcely an exaggeration to say that only Scott, in the whole range of the world's literature, has described these old battles in a correct perspective, and with the emotional intensity which such a subject requires, though the crude vigour of Drayton's *Agincourt* approaches actuality by the same path.

Thus, the urgent message of the dying Marmion to his brother-leader does not say that he has been outflanked, or has lost a hill. Stanley will understand the desperation of the position when he learns that—

> "Tunstall lies dead upon the field,
> His lifeblood stains the spotless shield.
> Lord Howard is down: my life is reft:
> The Admiral alone is left."

But around this strife of leaders, Scott keeps the roar of the whole battle constantly in our ears.

> "The Border slogan rent the sky
> A Home! A Gordon! was the cry
> Loud were the clanging blows.
> Advanced—forced back—now low—now high—
> The pennon sunk and rose."

The roar of the Border slogan is the index of the desperation of the English position. Before the era of uniforms, friend and foe were not always easy to distinguish on a broken field. Men shouted of who they were. Men who were outnumbered by their foes had a natural tendency to keep quiet. Badge or armlet, if worn at all, could easily be cast aside. A Staffordshire billman, who could save his life by shouting 'A Gordon!' for ten minutes in a lusty voice till he got to a safer part of the field, might think it well worth the price. At the least he would move with a quiet mouth.

So the fight slackens, as the English right wing gives way, and the victorious Borderers, shouting and plundering, close in toward the English centre, until the English left under Stanley, which had already broken the Highlanders to which it was opposed, curves inward upon the Scottish centre, upon which the whole battle line pivots round, as the strife bursts into a fresh intensity.

> "The war that for a space did fail
> Now trebly thundering swelled the gale,
> And Stanley was the cry."

But is not the coming of an individual warrior that turns the tide of the battle. It is because he can "With Chester charge and Lancashire" that the success of the Scottish right has been won in vain.

The description of Flodden was an imaginative re-creation of a real battle, and as such may always keep its place, unequalled even by Scott's subsequent description of Bannockburn, but in the skirmish at the entrance of the Trossachs pass Scott was using his unhindered imagination, and its perfection is of a different kind. Clearness of conception, vivid brevity of description, and that all-including imaginative sympathy without sentimental weakness which is Scott's peculiar excellence, combine to give it a solitary eminence, to which it is difficult to discover a seriously-competing poem. We are at one in a dozen lines with the feelings of the flying archers as "For life, for life, their flight they ply", with the exultant rush of the Highlanders, and with the anxious doubt of Mar, as he watches the approaching charge. We understand the necessity for the ruthless order by which he saves his command from annihilation.

> "Down, down," cried Mar, "your lances down!
> Bear back both friend and foe,"

(We do not understand Scott unless we understand that he would have given the same order under the same circumstances, and would have expected those who died by it to approve the decision), and we feel apprehension give place to confidence the spearmen as now 'closely shouldering side by side' they await the confused rush which is bearing down upon them.

We may depreciate Scott's poetry if we will, by that shallow method of criticism which condemns it for not being many things at which it does not aim, as we may condemn an elephant for the absence of airy grace, or complain that a butterfly has no bulk, but it remains secure in its own wizardry, an unmatched and unapproachable thing.

CHAPTER XLIV.

Having finished the *Lady of the Lake*, and even before the success of its publication, Scott was looking round for the inspiration of a new poem. He was drawn in three directions at once, an invitation from the Laird of Staffa, Macdonald Buchanan's brother, to visit the further Highlands suggesting the possibility of another Scottish poem with wilder and more desolate backgrounds: he had in memory the promise he had given to Morritt that he would make the district of Greta Bridge the scene of a major poem: and, perhaps strongest of all, he had the desire to make some memorable literary use of the Peninsular struggle which he had been watching since its commencement with an interest that nothing would avert. Charlotte found cause for protest in the size and variety of the maps which accompanied their coach journeys together, and the difficulty of diverting Walter's attention to her more important self when he was engaged in studying them. Now he proposed that he should pay a visit to the seat of war, to gain the local colour which he required. Charlotte thought that he would be more likely to get other less desirable things. She thought of diseases, bullets, drownings at sea. He was much better where he was. She may have been right about that. It is hard to imagine Scott under such circumstances in the discreet rear. Anyway, she had her way. Scott says that he felt it would have been wrong to gratify his own curiosity at the cost of Charlotte's distress.

So John Miller, a young barrister friend of Lincoln's Inn, with whom he might have sailed, set out alone to spend the long vacation in Portugal, and came back safely, and lived to become a K.C., which may be taken to indicate that Scott might have done the same, but the details make it less sure.

John Miller said he had had a good time. He had landed in Oporto, and travelled through a silent land, desolated by the ruins of war, on the track of the English army, and had then very unexpectedly met it face to face, for it was in full retreat. In fact, it was just turning to bay upon a pursuit which had become inconveniently close. As Mr. Miller was on the spot, he could lend a hand. There was a rifle to spare. He took an amateur's part in the battle of Busaco on the next day.

Charlotte, when she heard the tale, may have felt even more satisfied with the result of her own tears than she had done previously. So Scott never landed in the Peninsular, though he was to pass Gibraltar in a King's frigate before he died, and must take such satisfaction as he could from the letters of his friend Fergusson, now an officer in Wellington's army, telling how he would read Scott's battle-poetry to men who lay flat while the bullets passed.

When John Miller set sail for Oporto, Scott started off in the opposite direction; for the call of the Highlands had proved stronger than Mr. Morritt's pressing invitation, and Charlotte's barouche had set out from Ashestiel with a pair of good horses, to take the risks of the Highland roads, loaded with Scott and herself, and Miss Hannah Mackenzie (a sister of Scott's friend, Colin, of whom we should have seen more than we have—but his friends were so many), and another close family friend and distant relative, Mrs. Apreece at this time, to be Lady Davy later, and Sophia, who was now in her eleventh year, and judged old enough to come, and last, but by no means least, there was Wallace, the dog. It is Wallace now, not Camp; for Camp died in that January a year ago when Constable was making his last effort for peace and James was turning into the dining-room to let him pass, and he had been buried by winter moonlight in the little garden behind the house in North Castle Street, amid the tears of the household, and leaving a memory in a child's mind that she had never seen her father looking so sad.

There are many records of this journey, in recollections that were written afterwards, and long letters that were written at the time, and if we go with them at all we must go to a book's length, so, as we have other matters with which to deal, it may be better not to start at all. It is a long tale of the wild scenery that they saw, and the new friends they made, and how Scott would leave the carriage during the day, and wander his own ways, and come up with them again at night, having walked far; till they came to Oban, and put to sea. And after that there were the wilder Hebrides, and long rowing against strong tides, and warm, primitive hospitalities, and the adventure in which Sophia lost her peebles and shells, and Charlotte lost her shoes.—It is a long tale, and we must be content that they were safely back at Ashestiel in September, and to observe Walter Scott, now resuming the morning work at his desk and the active physical exercises of the later day with a recruited energy, searching an old desk for fishing-flies, and coming on those chapters of a projected novel which he had once shown to William Erskine, and more or less forgotten as the result of his doubtful criticism, or, more probably, through the pressure of more congenial or more urgent work.

Now he hesitates again. His desk is loaded with work. He has three new poems dimly outlined in his mind, either of which may be a goldmine if he can bring it to a good end. It is near the time when he must go back to Edinburgh to add the Court attendances four or five days a week to the other claims upon his time.... Yet he is tempted to try.... It might be a success.... Anyway, there will be no harm in letting James Ballantyne have a look at it, and seeing how it strikes him....

So James had those commencing chapters of *Waverley*, read

them carefully over, and sent this reply:

Edinburgh,
Sept. 15th, 1810.

Dear Sir,

What you have sent of Waverley has amused me much; and certainly if I had read it as part of a new novel, the remainder of which was open to my perusal, I should have proceeded with avidity. So much for its general effect; but you have sent me too little to enable me to form a decided opinion. Were I to say that I was equally struck with Waverley as I was with the much smaller portion of the *Lay*, which you first presented to us as a specimen, the truth would not be in me: but the cases are different. It is impossible that the small part of a fine novel can equally impress one with the decided conviction of splendour and success as a small part of a fine poem. I will state one or two things that strike me.... The account of the studies of Waverley seems unnecessarily minute. There are few novel readers to whom it would be interesting. I can see at once the connection between the studies of Don Quixote, or the female Quixote, and the events of their lives; but I have not been able to trace betwixt Waverly's character and his studies such clear and decided connection. The account, in short, seems to me too particular; quite unlike your usual mode in your poetry, and less happy. It may be, however, that the further progress of the character will defeat this criticism. The character itself I think excellent and interesting, and I was equally astonished and delighted to find in the last-written chapter, that you can paint to the eye as well in prose as in verse.

Perhaps your own reflections are rather too often mixed with the narrative—but I state this with much diffidence. I do not mean to object to a train of reflection arising from some striking event, but I don't like their so frequent occurrence. The language is spirited, but perhaps rather careless. The humour is admirable. Should, you go on? My opinion is clearly—certainly. I have no doubt of success, though it is impossible to guess how much...."

From this point the letter diverted to business matters. The criticism asked for, and candidly given, seems to have been very similar, but perhaps less discouraging, than that which had been received from William Erskine several years earlier. Scott had made an enormous reputation as a poet: to foretell that he would duplicate it as a novelist would be more than James could be expected to do—certainly not from those chapters of *Waverley*. Yet he was definite in advising the continuation of the work. He had "no doubt of success". It seems a straining of probabilities, even though we suppose Scott to have been more easily influenced by others than he may actually have been, to attribute the fact that he did not continue *Waverley* with immediate energy to the receipt of this letter.

In any case, it is sound criticism, honestly and clearly stated. The pace of the opening chapters of Waverley is extremely slow. It is like a study in still life. From the method by which Scott had won success, it was not merely an alteration from verse to prose. It altered swiftness of presentation to a leisurely stroll. To say not merely that it was good in itself but that it would have the immense popularity of the poems would be an unreasonable audacity, even had a complete book been under consideration. And, as we know, when *Waverley* was completed later, the pace quickened, though the literary style may not have improved.

The letter went on to report and advise on business matters. It is admirable in construction, as James Ballantyne's letters usually are, and its contents are worth some consideration in view of Lockhart's assertion that Scott was not treated frankly in business matters, on points on which it was essential that he should be informed correctly. Lockhart appears to have made this assertion under the impression that it was essential to Scott's reputation that he should have been deceived. Scott would have given Lockhart no thanks for the attempt to defend him in such a way, and, in fact, there appears to be no evidence to justify the assertion, nor need to have made it. Scott's reputation is founded on firmer grounds, and the truth, for all concerned, is a better thing.

If James did not discourage the continuation of *Waverley* in explicit words, it is possible that the next paragraph in his letter may have tended to turn the mind of the reader back to the poems he already had in embryo in his mind, and it may even have been deliberately intended to do so, for he went on to report that he had just got the eleventh edition of the *Lay* off his hands that week, and that while he was completing the fifth edition of the *Lady*, the orders had exhausted it, so that a sixth must be put in hand immediately.

Here, at least, was a gold-mine of certain yield. And the remainder of the letter showed that gold might soon be ;a needed thing. For it discussed the publishing business, which, apart from the success of the *Lady*, and the routine control of the Scottish distribution of the new Quarterly, and other agency business for Murray, was not doing well. Indeed, several of the major enterprises which had been undertaken threatened serious loss. As to the responsibility for their inception, there is no doubt. It belonged to Scott. They were his ideas. On such points he was clearly the driving force of the firm, as well as the partner with the greatest financial interest. There is no evidence that the other partners had differed, when the books had been put in hand. It is possible that a more experienced publisher than John would have made better sales. Constable might have done so. He probably would. But it is fair to remember that the principal of these projects had been condemned and refused by him. It is fair to observe also that the success of these books largely depended upon Murray and other London booksellers, and that it was they who were unable, or unwilling, to sell. Of the restless energy of John's efforts, of his desperate struggle to reach success, there is no more doubt than of his personal devotion to Scott, which was of an almost dog-like quality, and lasted to his life's end. He might be more sanguine than James, less ready to admit the approach of failure, more fertile of excuse and expedient, more capable of the self-deception which may deceive associates without the deliberate intention of doing so, and these qualities may have acted under the strain of future difficulties in their natural directions, but for the present position of the publishing business he had a very limited responsibility.

Now James is explicit and detailed in his report. He mentions first that the Sadler publication (in the success of which they were less directly interested, John Ballantyne & Co., not being the publishers) was not going well. He attributed this to a hostile review in the Edinburgh. He thought it had killed the book.

Then there was the Beaumont and Fletcher. This was an edition which was being edited by an otherwise impecunious German named Weber, who was under Scott's patronage. The man's poverty did not condemn him, nor (in itself) did his nationality. But the latter raises a suspicion that he may not have been particularly well qualified for the task he had undertaken, and the former that Scott's kindliness may have warped his judgement, as it was apt to do. Constable had declined this expensive enterprise in emphatic words. John Ballantyne found that his brother's excellent printing did not enable him to sell the volumes that were now coming through the press at regular intervals.

Next, there was the History of the Culdees by Dr. Jamieson. Scott considered it a most capable work, and was probably right. Few others put themselves into a position to dispute this judgement, or seemed likely to do so. The Culdees were a section of the ministers of the Kirk of Scotland, of an earlier day. There was an absence of excitement concerning them during the progress of the Peninsular War.

Worst of all (at the moment) appeared to be the 'Tixall Poetry?' about which James wrote with no lack of clarity:

> "I hope you will agree with John and me that this Aston business ought to be got rid of at almost any sacrifice. We could not even ask a London bookseller to take a share, and a net outlay of nearly £2,500 upon a worse than doubtful speculation is surely 'most tolerable, and not to be endured."

It is not to be understood from this protest that a sum of £2,500 had been already expended. It was the direction in which they were going unless a prudent decision should cut the loss. But the total outlay upon the various publications put in hand during the past year must have been very large. Miss Seward's poems may have seemed a safe investment beside some of these others, but that also had been consuming wages, and incurring debts at the paper mills, for which the returns would prove a very inadequate set-off.

And, overshadowing all, there was that mighty project of the Annual Edinburgh Register—an idea which seems to have been as vague as its name, and which was never even annual in its production, though two volumes were now about to be issued, and it was destined to be continued for many years, and to include much good material, and contributions by many famous writers—at a loss which James Ballantyne estimated at not less than £1,000 annually. It was well both for printing and publishing houses that Scott's own works went as they did.

The publishing business benefited only from the *Lady of the Lake*, but, though Scott had sold the copyright of the earlier poems, the printing orders still came onto James's desk, and a very valuable separate printing connection had been built up by Scott's influence, and the quality of James's productions, which was helping to balance the scales. But a point has come at which the finances of these two business enterprises, in which Scott was the senior partner and the directing spirit, though his other activities might divorce him from them for long periods, must have a separate chapter.

Now Scott read this letter with the knowledge that he would be back in Edinburgh almost immediately: questions of policy might well wait till he could have James and John together in his North Castle Street study. Those who came to these conferences in doubt or despondency usually separated in better spirits when Scott's vigorous optimism and practical sagacity had been applied to their confronting difficulties. It must all wait its time.

Two months later he wrote to Joanna Baillie from Edinburgh. He spoke of his deficiencies as a practical farmer. He could overwork himself, but to drive others was less congenial. The difficulty of making farming pay was as great then as it usually is. But the land at Ashestiel had not been sufficient to make its farming a very serious issue. He had given more thought to coursing hares than to ploughing land.

Now the lease of Ashestiel would soon be over, and he was already thinking of removal, though his letter does not make direct allusion to such a possibility.

But it has one significant sentence. He did not care overmuch for farming, but "planting and pruning of trees I could work at from morning till night, and if ever my poetical revenues enable me to have a few acres of my own, that is one of the principal pleasures I look forward to".

So he dreamed: and, so far he had found that he could make his dreams come true....

It must have been about this time that young Walter, now entering his tenth year, came home from the Edinburgh High School in a battered condition, the result of a furious onslaught upon certain boys who had called him "The Lady of the Lake," probably intending no insult; but he had not heard of the poem, and supposed that they accused him of some girlish quality? to which blows were the best reply. One of Scott's friends asked the boy if he were not conscious that great people congregated round his father more than others, and why he thought it was, and Walter thought, and answered that he supposed that his father could see a hare on its form more quickly than anyone else.

The story is linked with that of James Ballantyne, who asked Sophia about this time what she thought of *The Lady of the Lake*, and received an answer that she had not read it, as her father had told her that there was 'nothing so bad for young people as reading bad poetry'.

Sophia, two years older, and with a girl's observation, would no doubt have passed a better examination than Walter on her father's occupations, but the trivial anecdotes reveal a healthy freedom from the atmosphere which makes an absurdity of so many literary households.

They gain in force from the intimate relations which Scott always maintained with his children. He would not ever part with them to boarding-schools. They appear to have accompanied almost every transit between Edinburgh and Ashestiel, however short. Walter went to the High School when they were in Edinburgh, and Scott found time to give him regular lessons in Latin himself. A Miss Miller had been engaged as governess for the younger children. She had been chosen with Scott's usual success in judging character, and continued in the household for many years.

CHAPTER XLV.

Lockhart states that "between 1805 and the Christmas of 1809, Scott invested in the Ballantyne firms not less than £9,000," and that there had probably been a further demand on his purse during the following year, which was now drawing to its close.

There is no doubt that the amount of his advances was increased during 1810—there is a specific credit of £1,500 to the publishing business in June, which has a suggestive resemblance to the amount which he was to have received for the three-fourths interest in the *Lady of the Lake*, which the firm had agreed to purchase. This may be no more than coincidence, but it is evident that if the firm paid him for the copyright, they received a loan to an equal amount, so that the whole profit of the poem was available to assist in financing the other ventures they had undertaken.

But the accuracy of the figure which Lockhart gives is, at least, questionable. It appears probable that he made up the figure by including this £1,500 advanced six months later, and the £500 lent to James Ballantyne when the publishing, business was formed. By the inclusion of these figures we can arrive at approximately £9,000 thus:

Partnership capital as agreed with £ s. d.
James Ballantyne on Nov. 25th, 1809 3,842 9 8
Loan capital—ditto—including £1,200 from Captain John Scott) 2,000 0 0

Capital first invested in John Ballantyne & Co. 1,000 0 0

Loan to James Ballantyne re same 500 0 0

Further Capital advanced in June, 1810. 1,500 0 0

£8,842 9 8

But it will be noticed that this total includes the amount advanced by Captain John Scott, and it must not be understood from these figures that Scott was out-of-pocket to such an amount—or anything approaching it—over the period in question. If he had invested substantial capital, he had received (at least from the printing business) substantial income against it. His drawings since 1805, after deducting Captain John's interest, cannot have been less than £1,500, according to detailed evidence which is still available.

On balance, the net amount which he was out of pocket during the whole period must have been substantially less than that which he had inherited from Captain Robert Scott. Of course, the drawing of profits should not be regarded as a set-off to capital investment, and his capital stake in these enterprises can be correctly given as £9,000 at this period, but, if we are to have a correct perspective, we must recognise that his investment had (so far) justified itself. The printing business

had been consistently profitable. On the other hand, it had grown at a rate which had caused it to suffer from lack of capital almost from its commencement, and for this reason, and owing to the methods by which it had been financed (which were quite usual at that period) Scott was probably liable for substantial sums in addition to the capital which he had actually invested, and which might have embarrassed him seriously had he been required to find them at short notice.

To enable this to be understood, and to appreciate the developments of later years, it is necessary to give some explanation of the business methods by which a firm in good credit would commonly over come any temporary financial stringency. The usual, almost the routine expedient under such circumstances was to discount a bill, either with your own bankers, or with professional bill discounters, who did a large, and quite reputable business of this kind.

By the same method, immediate cash was obtained upon transactions for which long credit was given. The printer would give a long-dated bill for the paper he purchased, and the paper-merchant would discount it with his bankers for immediate cash: the printer, having made delivery to the publisher of the books ordered, would draw a long-dated bill upon him, and realise upon it in the same way. Practically, they assigned their book-debts to the banks, who advanced money upon them by which fresh trade could be financed in its turn. In the event of such bills falling due before provision could be made to meet them, they could often be renewed for further periods with the goodwill of all concerned; but this was a delicate operation, depending upon mutual confidence, so that the greater the necessity the more difficult it might be. It was sometimes done quite openly:

sometimes in such ways that the banks concerned could regard it as a fresh transaction if they cared to do so, but were, in fact, well aware of its actual nature, at which they thought it well not to look too closely: and sometimes, when credit tottered, with elaborate evasions, to prevent the real nature of the arrangement becoming evident to those who would have declined to support it.

So far as these documents represented actual trading transactions, and were supported by the solid assets of those who signed them, they were of an evident utility in facilitating and extending credit. But they were capable of being, and were in fact, used more extensively and in more dangerous ways, though these might also be recognised by the commercial customs of the time, and with the tacit consent of the banks, which was liable to be withdrawn at any sign of financial weakness, often with immediately disastrous consequences.

Bills of Exchange are said to have been invented by some Hebrew genius in the Middle Ages, with the recondite object of making it difficult for a ruler to seize a financier's wealth without incurring the risk that he might be emptying the pocket of his best friend. But the idea is so simple, and is of such obvious utility to any commercial system founded on the practice of usury, that it is difficult to suppose that it had not been operated in earlier periods.

For purely financial purposes, and especially in transactions of international magnitude, it is evident that these documents could be used to conceal the actual ownership of wealth, to transfer it from one country to another, and to make it difficult to alienate it, with any certainty as to where the loss would fall. But with such uses we are not concerned. These documents, of whatever origin, had been found to be of general commercial utility, and it is the ways in which they were so used, in connection with the affairs of the firms with which we are dealing, which it is necessary to understand.

It is evident from what has been said already, that a Bill of Exchange is of the nature of a post-dated cheque, but, unlike a cheque, for which funds should normally have been provided when it is issued, because it is intended for immediate payment, it is not a business necessity, nor a requirement of honour that a man who 'accepts'—that is, signs—a bill should have means at that time to meet it. There is, indeed, an opposite presumption, or why should he select this manner of discharging his obligation? But there is an obvious presumption that he has a reasonable certainty of having sufficient funds available when the date of payment shall arrive.

This must depend in part upon the prudence and sagacity with which his transactions are arranged, but it is evident that, under any circumstances a business which is largely dependent upon such financing is in a precarious position. While trade is good, all may go well, but if a change should come, it may not only he faced with the difficulties of the moment, but if its customers fail to meet the bills which have been received from them, which have been discounted months before, and are regarded as closed transactions, it may be called upon with an unexpected suddenness to make good such obligations—to return the money borrowed upon bills which it had every reason to regard as good, but which have proved to be worthless.

It is also evident that much larger credits may be given and received under such a system than would be possible, or than would be considered prudent, if the whole account remained open and increasing, with no payment being received upon it.

Yet, if it he soundly based, it facilitates trade, and to the bankers, who provide and risk the capital involved, it has the attraction that all the parties whose names appear upon the bills are equally liable to them, and their risk of final loss is reduced accordingly.

The position may be compared to that of a number of mountain climbers who are roped together. They may climb farther than they otherwise could, and with an increased security, but each member of the party is dependent upon the discretion of others, as much as upon himself, for his own safety, and should an accident come it may be of a greater magnitude.

So much for the use of bills in connection with actual trading in which substantial value is given. But at the period with which we are dealing (in which, it is necessary to remember, the system of limited liability, with its encouragement to the private investor to support commercial enterprises had not been instituted) it was a common practice to raise capital by the discounting of bills which were of a purely financial kind. It was, indeed, a method of investment which was clearly understood and extensively practiced. In moderation, and providing that the capital so obtained could be profitably utilised, it might be argued that it was not only sound in itself, but the cheapest and best way in which such financial support could be obtained.

The Balance Sheet of James Ballantyne & Co. at the end of the first partnership year shows that in addition to the capital which James had brought in the shape of plant and stock (and a house in Foulis Close), and the cash which Scott had provided, a sum of £450 had been obtained by this method. It is possible that it had been obtained at a lower interest than was paid (for instance) to William Creech for the £500 which he lent in a more permanent way. It is possible that James obtained it by signing a bill in the name of the firm without disclosing that Scott was a partner, which he was under no obligation to do. It is more probable than anyone discounting such a bill would enquire, and would have been truly informed as to who the partners were. It is about equally likely that Scotts name actually appeared on the bill—that Scott accepted it in favour of the firm, in which case it would have been easy to discount, and the rate of interest might have been lower. In any event it was a partnership liability, which, in the event of financial crisis, Scott would have been called upon to pay.

So far, the printing business had prospered. It had brought in a substantial income, and it was now doing better than ever. Yet its obligations must have been heavy in proportional to the moderate capital on which it was supported.

During the past five years Scott had been making a large income from his literary work. He was in easy, if not affluent circumstances. But it is improbable that he had made substantially more than he had spent, and any capital resources which were at his disposal at the time that Thomas's difficulties became acute would certainly have been used in that direction. We shall see during the following year that, when a round sum was needed, financial arrangements were necessary for the raising of the whole amount.

The home at Ashestiel had not been carried on very economically. It was roomy, and often had many guests. To suggest extravagance would be inaccurate. Scott, through his whole life, maintained a severe economy in his personal expenditure. He commenced at an early date to put down everything which he spent on himself, and he continued his practice through life. But, as fortune came, he bought books, old armours, and the kinds of curiosities in which he delighted with a free hand, and he was not one who would bargain prices in a niggardly way.

Charlotte ran the house much in the same spirit. It was certainly well ordered. It is improbable that the tradesmen's accounts were closely examined, or that questions of overcharges were often raised. It might be said that the management was good if no question of finance entered into it. And it was a house of wide charities; if there were any within walking distance who did not benefit from it, it was because they were in no need of its help.

Indeed, Scott's gifts and loans were a continual drain upon his resources. The total which he paid out in such ways during his life must have reached an almost incredible figure. Not that he was reckless or indiscriminate in his generosities, but if he saw a need—and there were many in these war-time years—it was his instinct to help, which was only restrained in cases where his judgement told him that it would be a vain thing.

It is clear that during these years there had been numerous, and sometimes sudden calls from the printing business for his financial help—or for the use of his name on a bill, which (for the moment) might be nearly the same thing, and that the capital investments which are credited from time to time, or the amounts shown to be drawn against profits, are not solitary payments, but represent the balance of more or less numerous payments and repayments during the period. So far, he had mastered circumstance, but he was not one whose life would ever glide on in a smooth way.

In this autumn his correspondence shows signs of restlessness which may have had other causes than the fact that a removal from Ashestiel was an approaching necessity. *The Lady of the Lake* had done well. He had told Miss Baillie that if his poetic ventures were ever sufficiently profitable he would buy a place of his own. But was that likely? Such a poem as that was could not be produced in less than a year, or perhaps two. It might bring him £2,000. But how long could he expect to continue such successes? How many times? It was a precarious hope. Now, amid the three poems he had in view, he was concentrating upon *The Vision of Don Roderick*. It would have a topical interest, that of Spain and the Peninsular War. It would have the variety of being written in the Spenserian stanza. It might be a great popular success—or it might not. And just now he had a chance of going to India, and the excitement of a new life.

Lord Melville's son, Lord Dundas, who was his personal friend, was likely to go out as Governor-General to India. If Scott wished for an appointment with him, it would be easy to get. It would mean throwing up the prospects of the Clerkship, about which he was rather tired of waiting for the income of a man who did not die. It would mean selling out his interest in a good printing business, and in a publishing one about which he was already realising that it might be difficult to carry it on, and more so to end it without ruinous loss. It would give him some more important occupation than that of Sheriff of Selkirkshire. He could still write, if he would. He wrote to Tom, still in the Isle of Man, and relying upon him for news of many things in his native town, to which he could not safely return:

"Were Dundas...willing to take me with him...I would not hesitate to pitch the Court of Session and the booksellers to the

Devil, and try my fortune in another climate".

That was in November. It was in the following month that Lady Forbes—Williamina Stuart—died. It is possible that this brought the events of fifteen or twenty years ago back to his mind with a new vividness, and was responsible for the plot of *Rokeby*, and for the fact that he now put the composition of that poem definitely before the one for which the background was to be supplied by the Hebrides that he had just visited.

But almost immediately after this date, there came an improvement in his financial circumstances in an unlooked-for way.

It will be remembered that he had been acting as Secretary to a Government Commission which had been considering reforms in Scottish Judicial Procedure. That Commission had now completed its work, and reported upon it. Scott disliked some of its recommendations, which were intended to bring Scottish and English practices into closer harmony. He was jealous of Scottish independence and prestige, and he thought the English procedure was likely to be adopted in directions in which it was inferior to that of the Northern Kingdom. He wrote an article for the first number of the Edinburgh Annual Register to this effect.

He may have been right or wrong, but there was one point of reform which they recommended, which was put into operation almost immediately, to his personal benefit.

The whole system by which Clerks of Session were paid by fees, and allowed to sell or delegate their positions, was swept away. They were to be paid salaries while in office, and pensions when they retired. Mr. Home was of an age at which he could claim a pension, which was granted to him. Scott was an acting Clerk. He received an immediate salary of £1,300 a year. With this substantial addition to his income of a permanent character, not conditional upon public favour or the profits of commercial enterprise he felt that he would be justified in buying himself a home.

The idea of India, if he had ever entertained it seriously,

faded away.

CHAPTER XLVI.

The Vision of Don Roderick was published in July, 1811. It had been very hastily completed, at the call of charity. Early in the year a committee had been formed in London to raise a fund in aid of the Portuguese whose homes had been burned and desolated during Massena's campaign. Massena was in retreat when the spring came, with Wellington on his heels, but he withdrew from a wasted land. The cause was one which would be sure to arouse Scott's sympathies, and he had promised to subscribe the whole profits of the first edition of his new poem. The edition sold readily, and the fund benefited accordingly, but the poem never reached nor deserved the popularity of its predecessors. It was well constructed, competently written, and contains a few memorable lines, if not stanzas. But it is of a commonplace texture, even if its commonplace be of a superlative kind. Those who had said that Scott would do better if he should use a longer line may have thought their argument refuted by this poem, but it really proves nothing beyond the facts that Scott could use any length of line with an easy mastery, and that he could not write as good poetry when he was in a hurry as when he had ample time for the work. If we look at the *Vision* , it is easy to give it praise: it would have made the name of a smaller man. But if we compare it with such a poem as the *Lay*, then the praise dies. Scott himself seems to have been little concerned for the fate of this poem. It was scarcely off his hands before he was concentrating again upon the unfinished *Rokeby*. He had also found the place that he was resolved to buy—a stretch of land on the south bank of the Tweed, which was of no great beauty, and a house that was poor enough; but they were the raw material that he thought to mould to his own liking. The raising of the necessary purchase money was a difficulty which he felt equal to overcome. But it would be necessary that James should know and assist his plans. On May 12th—before the *Vision* was actually published—he wrote to him:

> "My lease of Ashestiel is out. I have, therefore resolved to purchase a piece of ground sufficient for a cottage and a few fields. There are two pieces, either of which would suit me, but both would make a very desirable property indeed. They stretch along the Tweed, on the opposite side from Lord Somerville, and could be had for between £7,000 and £8,000—or either separate for about half the sum. I have serious thoughts of one or both, and must have recourse to my pen to make the matter easy. The worst is the difficulty which John might find in advancing so large a sum as the copyright of a new poem; supposing it to be made payable within a year at farthest from the work going to press—which would be essential to my purpose. Yet the Lady of the Lake came soon home. I have a letter this morning giving me good hope of my Treasury business being carried through: if this takes place, I will buy both the little farms, which will give me a mile of the beautiful turn of Tweed above Galafoot—if not, I will confine myself to one. It is proper John and you should be as soon as possible apprised of these my intentions, which I believe you will think reasonable in my situation, and at my age, while I may yet hope to silt under the shade of a tree of my own planting. I hope this Register will give a start to its predecessors; I assure you I shall spare no pains. John must lend his earnest attention to clear his hands of the quire stocks, and to taking in as little as he can unless in the way of exchange; in short, reefing our sails, which are at present too much spread for our ballast."

We may suppose that James became thoughtful after reading this letter. A new poem which would have the success of

Marmion or the *Lady* would be good for his own presses, and for the publishing business, which, in the end, should be well able to pay the author £2,000 from the resulting profits. But it could not find such a sum in advance. That was a sure thing. Not, at least, in cash.

The concluding sentences were reasonable enough, yet they held an intimation of an ominous kind. The 'quire stock' was the quantity of the various books they had published for which there was no present demand. They would not be bound until ordered, or might be sold to the London trade in that condition, and sent to be bound there. John was to struggle to improve the financial position by reduction of the publishing stock. It was the right policy under any circumstances, but, coming in this letter as it did, it could be taken as an intimation that Scott wished the business in future to stand on its own legs. It shows also how clearly he realised that his own peace and fortune were also in that 'reefing of sails' of which he saw the necessity, but which John might find it hard to contrive.

Finally, there is the promise of special effort to make the next number of the Register attractive. It is to be so good that it will not only sell itself, but give a spurt to the demand for the earlier volumes, of which so many are still on the Hanover Street shelves: a hard thing for any periodical volume to do.

Lockhart remarks sagely that Scott would have been more prudent to delay his purchase until the poem was written, and the Clerkship salary a settled thing. Perhaps he would, but Scott did not play the game of life in that spirit, or he would not have been Scott at all, nor been able to write poems which would bring in £2,000. Lockhart's paragon of prudence, who would yet have been Scott, having his splendid successes, but never taking a splendid risk, is a monstrous impossibility. Besides, the event justified itself.

We may observe also that the lease of Ashestiel would not extend itself till the poem should be complete. The Scotts must have somewhere to go. We may observe further that Scott, practical in his audacities, only bought half the land on which his heart was set. He paid £4,200, of which £2,000 was found by his brother John, on a mortgage which was well secured, and the bulk of the remainder raised on the security of the unwritten poem. Scott entered into a contract with John Ballantyne & Co. to sell the copyright of *Rokeby* for £2,000. The firm gave long-dated bills for that sum, which Scott endorsed and discounted. It is a transaction at which a bank would look doubtfully today, but methods of finance were somewhat different at that time, and, besides, Scott was Scott an author with an enormous reputation, and a record of sustained successes. He was also a man of many friends, including those who were at the head of the Edinburgh banking world, and he had a character that inspired confidence. If James Hogg, or any other Scottish poet, had attempted such a transaction he might have faced a bank manager who gazed at him with stony eyes.

The leaving of Ashestiel must have occasioned some regrets, but they appear to have been expressed by others rather than those who were most concerned. Miss Baillie wrote that she hoped to come to Scotland to see the new home when it should be ready, but she would never forget, and would hope to visit that which she had first known: she alluded to the affection a man must always feel for his first love. But the first love of the Scotts was not Ashestiel, but the Lasswade cottage. They may never have thought of the former as a permanent home. It was where they would be for the lease's length. After that had not Scott always dreamt of walking on his own land? He had thought of buying Broadmeadows when Lasswade had to be given up, and had put the idea aside so that the printing business might be established. Now he looked forward to larger prospects, standing on surer ground. Regrets at leaving Ashestiel faded before the excitement of the idea that they would own their own home, and that it would be formed to their own will.

Yet they had done much to Ashestiel, and James Hogg, prosaically practical in his verbal wisdom as he was unpractical in his life, expressed a thought which would be common to many when he wrote that he had been sorry to read the news of the removal in the papers, after Scott had been "at so much trouble and expense" in making Ashestiel "a complete thing". No doubt Ashestiel had been improved while the Scotts lived there. So had Lasswade before. So, doubtless, would be any place to which they should go next. Scott was a dreamer, no doubt. But he was of those who make their dreams come true.

The place he had bought was called Cartly Hole, (Commonly written Clarty Hole, which is wrong.)—an opprobrious name. That was easy to change. The land had once belonged to the Abbot of Melrose: it faced a ford in the Tweed. Abbotsford would be a good choice.

The house itself would be more expensive to change. So would the land. The place, though no longer an abbot's property, had still been in ecclesiastical hands. It was bought from the Rev. Dr. Douglas, holder of the living of Galashiels, who had not resided on the property, nor given it any care. It was a small and dirty house, with a midden on one side, and a foul pond in front. The land was ill-fenced, and ill-drained. Some of it was rough, furze-covered, never brought under cultivation. It was bare of trees, except for one narrow ridge of unsightly firs, which had won for itself the name of the Haircomb. Scott looked at it with contented eyes. He could plant here to his own will. What did it matter if the price were two hundred pounds above the market value, or a hundred below? Or that there had been a rather heavy price to pay for the discounting of those *Rokeby* bills? Scott was never one to care for money for its own sake. He had the thing that he would.

At this time, though there might be an occasional flutter of trouble in the finances of the Edinburgh firms, if we will ignore the prophetic visage of Lockhart, shaking his head in a prudent doubt over everything which is done, we must see Scott as he was, one of the most enviable of the millions of living men. He had robust health, an unexhausted and seemingly inexhaustible vitality; he had a loving wife, who gave ready co-operation and found her happiness in the same life as himself; he had healthy and happy children; he had varied and congenial occupations; he had a great reputation, and many friends. If he wrote of self-sacrifice, and noble living, was it not an easy thing to do? He stood on the safe shore, giving high counsels to those who struggled against the tide. He had no use for a coward. He would not wear mourning when Daniel died. But who knew that he would have done better in the same place? What test of courage or faith had he ever had?

CHAPTER XLVII.

Cartly Hole might be a bare and unattractive property when Scott first walked upon it, but it was rich in traditional associations, and it was a spot to which he had already given immortality in the *Lay*. Readers will remember the repeated allusions to the historic feud between the Kerrs (or Carrs) of Cessford and the Scotts of Buccleuch, which had caused so much bloodshed, and left so many place-names in Roxburghshire.

In 1529, in an effort to stay the continual bloodshed of a feud in which murder was repaid by murder in an unending sequence, the heads of the two houses signed a bond of amity in which each undertook to perform regular pilgrimages to pray for the souls of their fallen enemies, but even this effort for peace proved futile. It is to this abortive "bond" that allusion is made in the first canto of the *Lay*.

> "Can piety the discord heal,
> Or stanch the death-feud's enmity?
> Can Christian lore, can patriot zeal,
> Can love of blessed charity?
> No! vainly to each holy shrine,
> In mutual pilgrimage, they drew;
> Implored, in vain, the grace divine
> For chiefs their own red falchions slew;
> While Cessford owns the rule of Carr,
> While Ettrick boasts the line of Scott,

> The slaughter'd chiefs, the mortal jar,
> The havoc of the feudal war,
> Shall never, never be forgot."

The feud had commenced in a fierce political Border quarrel for the possession of the person of the boy-king, James V. It had culminated in a struggle known as the battle of Melrose, in which the Scotts and their allies had been badly beaten. They had been chased by their victorious enemies, Carr of Cessford heading the pursuit, until one of Buccleuch's retainers (an Elliot, curiously enough, for the Elliots were a Liddesdale clan, and supporters of the Douglas faction) had turned upon the pursuers, and given Cessford a mortal wound; and his death had put an end to the chase.

It is a result of this feud which is the theme of the *Lay*. Margaret's lover was unendurable to her mother, because he

> "against her father's clan
> With Carr in arms had stood
> When Mathouse burn to Melrose ran
> All purple with their blood."

And it is the dark memory of this conflict which comes to the night-riding Deloraine:

> "Now Bowden Moor the march-man won,
> And sternly shook his plumed head,
> As glanced his eye o'er Halidon;
> For on his soul the slaughter red
> Of that unhallow'd morn arose,
> When first the Scott and Carr were foes.
> When royal James beheld the fray,
> Prize to the victor of the day;
> When Home and Douglas, in the van,
> Bore down Buccleuch's retiring clan,
> Till gallant Cessford's heart-blood dear

Reek'd on dark Elliot's Border spear."

The spot where Cessford was killed and the pursuit ended became known as Turnagain, and was on the actual ground that Scott now bought. He would look over the Tweed to Melrose Abbey, which he had immortalised in the same *Lay*.

CHAPTER XLVIII.

Either the completion of the purchase of Abbotsford took place too late in the year for the alterations which the house urgently needed to be put in hand before the following spring, when Ashestiel must be left, and residence, under whatever conditions, taken up there, or it was a deliberate decision not to incur any considerable expenditure until it could be personally superintended.

However that be, little appears to have been done during the autumn, and when the winter came, there was the usual migration to North Castle Street, and Tom Purdie was left in charge of house and stock at Ashestiel in the usual way.

Perhaps the position may have been influenced by the fact that the Clerk of Session's salary did not commence until January, 1812. After that date there would be a quarterly payment of £325, which would be a clear addition to Scott's previous income, and could be relied upon with a regularity which is not a feature of the profits of literary work.

Anyway, so it was. The migration to Abbotsford took place at Whitsuntide. The distance was about five or six miles, which family and effects must traverse by road, as was the only way at that time. There was the carriage for Mrs. Scott, Miss Miller, the two younger children, and as much else as it would hold. There were ponies for Sophia and Walter to ride. Scott had his horse. The cows and dogs came on their own legs. The establishment provided one or two other horses and farm vehicles, and sufficient additional ones had to be hired or borrowed. Of course, Tom Purdie and his household came. So did Peter and his. It was a patriarchal procession. Banners and fishing-rods, muskets and spears, swords, bows, and targets, were among the endless details that were brought forth to be loaded on the over-burdened carts, or distributed among a dozen 'rosy ragged peasant children' who were eager to carry them. An old helmet provided safe transit for a brood of turkey chicks.

So they forded the Tweed....

Lockhart's financial prudence might have delayed the purchase of Abbotsford, but a prudence of another kind might have said that provision for the necessary migration had been left till too late a day. The place was hardly large enough as it stood to take in those who came. What would it be when the windows were out, and the roof being raised, and the cottage which was to take in the household staff still only half built?

Scott's intention was not at this time to build a great house, nor to incur any heavy expense. But he must have it large enough to entertain his friends. He had written to Joanna Baillie, with whom he kept up a regular correspondence, that his intention was to enlarge it till it could accommodate his own family and still have two spare bedrooms, with dressing-rooms attached, each of which could 'on a pinch have a couch bed'. He said he could not give up his rule of 'accommodating all the cousins and duniwastles, who will rather sleep on chairs, and on the floor, and in the hayloft, than be absent when folks are gathered together'. But a limited space would provide for many by that method. He remembered once when there had been thirty-two persons under the roof of Ashestiel, which ten were enough to fill....

Between Whitsuntide and July the family lived at Abbotsford as they best could, and Scott spent five days of each week in Edinburgh, and two there. Then he was able to put in full time on the spot. The alterations were of his own design. He did much labour with his own hands. There was one room in which everyone was obliged to live. He had his desk in the window, overlooking the Tweed. Charlotte nailed up a curtain behind his chair to give him such privacy as she could for his morning writing. Miss Miller and the four children did lessons at the other end.

He had twelve men employed on the house at this time, and after lunch he left his desk, and did a man's share.

He had been working on *Rokeby* in Edinburgh during the earlier year, and must now press it forward with the knowledge that it was to earn the money for the house he had already bought, and that James was anxiously enquiring for a date at which he would be able to bring it out. Apart from that, he was less pressed than usual with miscellaneous work. The Swift, to which he had given a large portion of time during the previous year, was still on his hands, and the Annual Register was a more or less constant preoccupation, but there was little besides these, and another poem which had seized his imagination, and for which he had again pushed aside that of the Highlands which had been intended for precedence two years ago.

This was *The Bridal of Triermain*, the genesis of which is of interest, as showing the slow growth of these poems which have been supposed to be so randomly written. A year ago, in an effort to invent attractive features for the Register, he had inserted a passage of verse which was entitled 'In Imitation of Walter Scott'. (In the present year, with the same object, he inserted the whole of *Don Roderick*, instead of using it in a popular edition, when the quarto one was exhausted.) These stanzas, which appeared to be an abstract from a longer poem, remained of ambiguous authorship, but Scott had encouraged an idea that they were an attempt by William Erskine to imitate him. They show that the idea of the poem must, even at that date, have taken form, and some substance. Now, in the midst of his other occupations, he had revived it in earnest, and its composition went forward when that of *Rokeby* halted, as it was too much inclined to do. For he had an idea respecting the *Bridal* by which his sense of humour and of adventure equally gratified. He would complete and publish it anonymously. It should be the common rumour (with Erskine's assent) that he (Erskine) was the actual author. What public would it gain, apart from the prestige of his own name? How would Jeffrey review it? The idea of mystifying Jeffrey was particularly attractive.

Erskine lent himself to the joke. He wrote a foreword, purporting to be by the anonymous author, containing some Greek quotations, which Scott would be unlikely to use.

The deception of the poem itself is a very skilful thing. Scott did not parody or imitate his own style: he varied it, as only a master of prosody would have been able to do. He introduced new cadences. He adopted a lighter, gayer tone than he was accustomed to use in such poetry.

> "Where is the maiden of mortal strain
> That may match with the Baron of Triermain?"

Anyone could see that it was like Scott, but those who were good judges would see the difference too. They would see that it was the work of another mind, which had been influenced by Scott's poetry. There was the difference in tone, which was unmistakable: a gay, gallant tone that at times approached flippancy:

> "Within trumpet sound of the Table Round
> Were fifty champions free,
> And they all arise to fight that prize—
> They all arise but three.
> Nor love's fond troth, nor wedlock's oath,
> One gallant could withhold,
> For priests will allow of a broken vow
> For penance or for gold.
> **
> And still these lovers' fame survives
> For faith so constant shown,—
> There were two who loved their neighbours' wives,
> And one who loved his own."

Scott pushed on with it with a light heart.

But *Rokeby* moved with more difficulty. He wanted it to equal, if not excel, anything he had done previously. He had evolved a good plot, with some excellent situations. He was ornamenting it with some of the best lyrics he ever wrote. He felt that it would be good—in parts. But the Yorkshire scenery, the locations of the incidents, were not as clear in his mind as were the Highland mountains or the Lowland moors of his earlier poems. He had not the same richness of material on which to draw. He wrote to Morritt, asking for detailed descriptions and topographical detail to refresh his own memory.

Morritt wrote back urging him to come himself. Surely it would be worth while to spend a month in the district which was to be the scene of the poem? He knew how welcome Mrs. Scott and he would be to spend as long as they would.

Scott was frank in reply. He did not see how he could come. He was short of money as well as time. He was superintending the work at Abbotsford, doing what he could with his own hands. It progressed well enough, but as the work advanced his funds diminished alarmingly. No. He must stay where he was. What he wanted to know was whether there were any old ruins near Rokeby such as would suit the topography of the poem. He wanted an old church, which should be easy to find. If possible, a robber's cave....

Morritt replied with fresh urgency. A written description would be a poor substitute for a personal inspection. As to any financial occasion for having the poem out by Christmas, it was a pity that haste should mar it. He had five or six hundred pounds at the Bank for which he had no present use—if a loan of such amount would render Scott independent of the booksellers, it would be very willingly made. Morritt added, with an adroit courtesy, that it was no great merit to offer such accommodation now that Scott had got rid of his 'Old Man of the Sea'—the undying Home.

The offer and invitation in combination were irresistible. The loan was accepted on the security of some of James Ballantyne

& Co.'s bills, and a week later Abbotsford was left to the workmen and Tom Purdie's care, only Miss Miller and the two younger children remaining at home.

Scott set out on horseback. Charlotte came in the carriage. Sophia and Walter mounted their ponies.

They rode through Flodden, to find a landlord grateful for the increased custom that *Marmion* had brought to his counter, and Scott gave him a parodied quotation from that poem—'Drink, weary pilgrim, drink and PAY' to hang over his door.

They stayed a week at Rokeby, Scott finding the cave he wanted in the Brignall quarries, and the church in the ruined abbey of Egglestone. He showed the *Bridal* to Morritt—now more than half done. But that was under a promise of confidence. It was to be 'a trap for Jeffrey', of which no hint must leak out. No one else in England, not even George Ellis, was taken into this confidence. Scott planned that the two poems should come out on the same clay, to increase the improbability that they were by the same hand, and to invite reviewers' comparisons. But that proved impracticable. *Rokeby* had to be published at the first possible moment, and the *Bridal* was not ready on that date. The trap for Jeffrey failed also, for that self-confident critic chose this time for visiting America, but, apart from these details, the plan worked as Scott had meant that it should....

There are two anecdotes of about this period which are of little importance, except as showing the sensitiveness to his personal honour which contrasted with Scott's indifference to literary reputation. The one relates to what is probably the only occasion on which he cut a man publicly, Lord Holland being the individual who had this unexpected rebuff. He was introduced to him when on a visit to Edinburgh, and had the unpleasant experience of meeting a man who looked without response at his outstretched hand, and turned silently away. A reconciliation ultimately followed, and there was cordial correspondence in later years, but the occasion of this episode was a matter on which Scott must have felt deeply, though few would have done so by the political ethics then prevailing.

The fact was that, as Clerk of Session, he had the patronage of several minor offices, which, as they fell vacant, he could bestow upon whom he would, and, some years earlier, he had given one of these to his brother Tom. This was no breach of custom, and he afterwards instanced it as evidence of his scrupulous integrity that it was an office bringing in only £250 a year, while another of a much more lucrative character he had bestowed on a stranger, as the more suitable applicant.

The office, like many others at that period, was one which could be, and commonly was, delegated by the actual holder, who paid a substitute for discharging such duties as it entailed. Tom had done this, and when, as Lockhart says (with a discretion of speech which he would not have used regarding one of the Ballantynes, had they ever been in similar difficulties,) he 'soon after found it convenient to withdraw for a time to the Isle of Man,' it did not affect the continuance of the office—a point on which Scott had no longer either responsibility or control.

But a Bill was brought in shortly afterwards to abolish this, and numerous other similar offices, which included compensating those who held them. Under the provisions of this Bill, Tom would become entitled to a small annuity. But when the measure went into Committee in the House of Lords, the Earl of Lauderdale had protested against this payment, alleging that it was an instance of political jobbery, as Scott had known, when he appointed his brother to the office, that it was about to be abolished, and that the appointment had been made with the sole object of entitling him to claim compensation under such circumstances.

The accusation was certainly false, and had no substance of probability. It was probably forgotten as soon as the debate was over. It was not even a serious one, by the political standards of the time. Had Scott acted in that spirit, it would have been, on all sides, regarded as a natural thing, and it is doubtful whether actual proof would have made any difference to the practical unanimity with which the Lords approved the terms of the Bill. But when Lord Lauderdale moved his amendment to eliminate the provision respecting Mr. Thomas Scott's compensation, one solitary peer—Lord Holland—spoke in its support. Scott took this as an attack upon his personal honour, and it was unfortunate that Lord Holland should have encountered him only a few weeks later.

"I remembered his part in your affair," Scott wrote to his brother, "and cut him with as little remorse as an old pen." Jeffrey, standing by, was surprised to observe the incident. He had never known Scott personally rude to anyone, nor did he again in many years of later acquaintance. It was an occurrence that he would not easily have believed, if he had not seen it. It showed that hidden core of inflexibility in Scott's character, which was so rarely, and then so disconcertingly bared.

The other incident is of a different kind, and belongs to the summer of 1812, when Lord Byron was introduced to the Prince Regent, and that peculiar gentleman confided to him an admiration for Scott's poetry which seems to have been of a very genuine kind. Byron told his publisher, Murray; and Murray thought that the incident could be used to heal the offence of Byron's attack three years before, in *English Bards and Scotch Reviewers,* upon the senior poet.

It was, in fact, mild and good-tempered in comparison with some of the gibes which were included in that impish poem, and had it been merely an attack upon Scott's literary standing, it would have been disregarded or long-since forgotten. But the concluding lines had asserted a charge of a different kind:

"And thinkest thou, Scott! by vain conceit perchance,
On public taste to foist they stale romance,
Though Murray with his Miller may combine
To yield thy muse just half-a-crown a line?
No! when the sons of song descend to trade,
Then bays are sear, then former laurels fade.
Let such foregoe the poet's sacred name,
Who rack their brains for lucre, not for fame.
Still for stern Mammon may they toil in vain,

And sadly gaze on gold they cannot gain!
Such be their meed, such still the just reward
Of prostituted muse and hireling bard!
For this we spurn Apollo's venal son,
And bid a long 'goodnight to Marmion'."

The attack had Byron's usual glittering shallowness, and deserved no answer but silence. The poet who is not pleased to get a good price from his publisher (unless he be of independent wealth) may be still unborn, though it is a form of trouble which afflicts few. That a desire for gain was the inspiration of Scott's genius was, of course, an absurd suggestion. Yet it was a fact that he had needed money when *Marmion* was written—for a purpose which he was not likely to make widely public. It was known to his friends that he had resented Byron's imputation, though he had restrained himself from any public reference. Now Murray's efforts succeeded in healing the breach.

Scott wrote:

> "The poem, my Lord, was not written upon contract for a sum of money—though it is too true that it was sold and published in a very unfinished state (which I have since regretted), to enable me to extricate myself from some engagements which fell suddenly upon me, by the unexpected misfortunes of a very near relation. So that, to quote statute and precedent, I really come under the case cited by Juvenal, though not quite in the extremity of the classic author—
>
> *Esurit, intactam Paridi nisi vendit Agaven*
>
> As for my attachment to literature, I sacrificed for the pleasure of pursuing it very fair chances of opulence and professional honours, at a time of life when I fully knew their value; and I am not ashamed to say that in deriving advantages in compensation from the partial favour of the public, I have added some comforts and elegancies to a bare independence. I am

sure your Lordship's good sense will easily put this unimportant egotism to the right account, for—though I do not know the motive would make me enter into controversy with a fair or *unfair* literary critic—I may be well excused for a wish to clear my personal character from any tinge of mercenary or sordid feeling in the eyes of a contemporary of genius Your Lordship will likewise permit me to add, that you would have escaped the trouble of this explanation, had I not understood that the satire alluded to had been suppressed, not to be reprinted. For in removing a prejudice on your Lordship's own mind I had no intention of making any appeal by or through you to the public, since my own habits of life have rendered my defence as to avarice or rapacity rather too easy."

Lord Byron answered in a spirit of unreserved apology and withdrawal, such as could not fail to remove any feeling which Scott might have had up to this time. He said that Scott's explanation was "too kind not to give pain". The relations of the two alien-natured poets were always afterwards of a cordial character. However diverse were the characters of the poets of the day, and however bitterly they might differ among themselves we may observe that Scott made friends of them all. Southey, Hogg, Byron, Wordsworth, Coleridge, Campbell, Moore and a host of others of equal differences, but lesser fame—he was the friend of each, and the substantial benefactor of more than one of the number.

It was in the early August of 1812 that he received a letter at Abbotsford from James Ballantyne, in which he alluded to an accumulating pressure of financial difficulties which were worrying his brother, about whose health he was concerned, on receipt of which Scott wrote:

"Dear John,

I have a letter from James, very anxious about your health and state of spirits. If you suffer the present inconveniences to depress you too much you are unjust to us all. I am always ready to make any sacrifices to do justice to engagements, and would rather sell anything or everything, than be less than true men to the world."

James was looking forward to the new poem for substantial aid to the finances of both firms, which, mainly as the result of the heavy stock of publications on hand, were being supported by the discounting of bills to an extent of which, even now, Scott may not have been fully aware. Yet the Balance Sheets, and other financial statements which were supplied to him on his own instructions at short intervals, must have given him a view of the position which was broadly accurate, though John's valuations and forecasts might be of a more sanguine complexion than would have been endorsed by an impartial accountant.

Still, they all knew what was wrong. They had too much stock. The position would gradually right itself, if they could maintain credit in the meantime. That was the vital thing.

Scott had promised James that *Rokeby* should be finished in time for publication to take place at the beginning of the year. He supposed that to be the way in which he could give the most efficient help. He kept his word about that.

CHAPTER XLIX

Rokeby was published on January 12th, 1813, and the first quarto edition of 3,000 copies was sold immediately (This is the figure Scott gave Morritt at the time. Writing seventeen years later, when his memory was not always exact on dates and figures, he puts it at half the quantity. Anyway, the total sale, including octavos, was ten thousand within three months of publication). So far so good. Scott was anxiously aware of how much the security of his commercial interests was staked upon the success of this poem. On that date, as he sat in Court, and some long-drawn case gave him the leisure for correspondence, he scribbled a note to Morritt to give him the good news. He added: "I am heartily glad of this, for now I have nothing to fear but a bankruptcy in the Gazette of Parnassus; but the loss of five or six thousand pounds to my good friends and school companions would have afflicted me very much." He goes on to talk of a christening dinner which James Ballantyne was giving in the usual custom of celebrating the birth of these poems, at which many friends, including the Duke of Buccleuch, would be present. (The Duke died during the month, and we must think of Scott's lifelong friend, The Earl of Dalkeith, by that title henceforward.)

The letter shows that, since his return to Edinburgh, Scott has become sufficiently conversant with the affairs of the publishing firm to realise that a failure to sell out the first edition of this poem must have disastrous consequences. The amount he mentions need not be taken too literally; it probably included his brother's capital in the printing firm, and Scott's "friends and school companions" were so numerous that it would be hard to arrange an overdraft, or discount a bill, or buy a few score reams of printing paper, without taking or receiving an obligation from them. Yet the amount is some indication of the extent to which the two firms were now financed from sources supplemental to the partners' capital. Morritt, as we know, had been added—may be said to have added himself—to the list of those who had Ballantyne bills in their safes. It would be good news to him that the commercial skies cleared, though he would care even more about the success of the poem on other grounds, for, the scene being laid in his own estates, he regarded it almost as a personal thing. He would care very much for Scott's welfare also, being a friend of a good kind.

The news was good—yet it was not good enough. The sale of

3,000 copies would bring in a retail price of 4,500 guineas. The publishing and printing houses would receive about two-thirds of this sum, of which more than half would be gross profit. But they had given Scott £2,000—in bills—to purchase the copyright. In the end, it would be worth more than that. But the bills would soon be due—and numerous others, which had nothing to do with this poem.

If Scott had staked much on the sale of the first edition, he may not have been unduly rash, for in view of the popularity of his previous poems, that was an almost certain thing. It was the demand for the cheaper octavos which were to follow which would make the difference between a moderate and a great financial success. And these—as Scott was to find during the following weeks—did not go off as he had hoped that they would. There was an immense sale. For any other poet it would have been of a phenomenal kind. But it was not equal to any of his three previous experiences. There was a definite turn of the tide.

The reason for this may have lain in the poem itself, or in the competition of Byron's new popularity, to which it is usually attributed, but the fact was one that the Ballantynes had to face in anxious conference. Indeed, it is evident that no sale, however phenomenal, either of this poem, or of the *Bridal* which followed two months later, would have enabled them to vanquish the difficulties that were now before them.

Lockhart accuses the Ballantynes of having deliberately concealed the true position of both businesses at this time from their senior partner. The accusation, at least as far as John is concerned, may not be entirely without foundation, but some of the evidences which he offers do not go as far as the inferences which he asks us to make.

The winter of 1812-13 was a period of severe depression and restricted credits. England, for twenty years, had been engaged in almost continuous and exhausting war. Looking back, we can see that there were, even then, signs that the peace for which Europe longed would not be much further deferred. Napoleon was back in Paris, leaving the skeletons of his army on the frozen plains of Russia. In the Peninsula, Wellington had done well. The signs to us seem unmistakably clear. But if France were exhausted, she was facing exhausted foes. Napoleon would hear of no surrender: no compromise. In Paris, he gathered strength again. Even the sailors were fetched out of the fleet to swell the ranks of the new army that he would raise. On the Vistula, Murat recovered the fragments of the Grand Army, as best he could. By the spring, Napoleon would take the field again with 350,000 men. On the 2nd of May he would shatter once again at Lutzen the allied strength of his foes.

The financial history of this period is closely similar to that of a century later. During the last stages of the European struggle, national debts rose to what appeared to those who endured them to be fantastic heights. Finance appeared an impossible nightmare, from which men would wake at last to they knew not what frightful reality. All Europe owed debts to England which it was never likely to pay. Like the later experience, the financial crises of the war were less acute, and less disastrous in their consequences, than was that which came after a few years of recovered peace (which we shall also encounter in a later chapter), but they seemed bad enough at the time. In the publishing trade, failures were numerous during the early part of 1813. Every one that occurred made it more difficult for those that remained to continue trading. If a firm were rumoured to be doing badly, and depended for its existence upon renewing its bills, its chance of survival would be small indeed.

Interpreting such facts as we have in the light of probabilities, the position of John Ballantyne & Co. at the time when Scott was writing cheerfully to Morritt, may be stated thus:

During the first period of its existence it had ordered large quantities of its new publications from James Ballantyne & Co. for which, at first, it had made some cash payments, but for the bulk of which it had given bills, which had been discounted by the printing firm. Had it been able to dispose of sufficient quantities of its stock it should have been able to pay these bills as they fell due, but its sales had never reached such an amount. So far as credit was as available, the bills were renewed, and their amount grew.

At this time the printing business was (on paper) still prosperous—indeed, increasingly so, if these obligations of John Ballantyne & Co. would ever be met. It had established a valuable connection. It was doing work on a large scale for several London publishers. (Southey's *Kehama*, for instance, was printed by the Ballantyne press.) The large editions of Miss Seward's poems, the huge Beaumont & Fletcher, the History of the Culdees, the successive volumes of the Annual Register—all these and a dozen other publications, large and small, were extra work for the printing business, and would swell its legitimate profits—if John Ballantyne & Co. ever paid.

When it became evident that the sale of these editions would be slower and more difficult than had been anticipated, the putting in hand of new books was severely restricted. To that extent the policy of "reefing sail" had been adopted at least a year ago. But that restriction did not sell the large quantities already printed. It did not pay John Ballantyne's salary, nor all the weekly expenses of the Hanover Street premises: the wages of the Hanover Street staff. If sales were made beyond the requirements of these recurring expenses, it is improbable that they reduced the outstanding liability as much as it was increased by the deliveries of the successive volumes of the Beaumont and Fletcher and the Edinburgh Register, which were still coming through the press.

And all this time it will be observed that John Ballantyne & Co. need be incurring no liabilities except to the printing business, to which firm it gave its bills as the stock was delivered. It was James Ballantyne & Co. that had to pay out the wages, that had to buy the paper and types by which these books were produced, and that had to discount the bills it received in order that these liabilities might be discharged. So long as John Ballantyne & Co.'s credit were maintained, and the amount of these bills were not increased, they might steer through the storm, and find calmer water at last.

But John Murray had withdrawn his agency. The Quarterly Review was an established success. No one could alter that now. The arrangement had served its purpose. He had tired of trying to sell stock which no one wanted to buy. He may have decided that John Ballantyne was less successful as his Scottish agent than a more experienced publisher would be likely to be. He may have had more specific cause for complaint.

Anyway, so it was. Scott does not seem to have felt that there was anything to resent. His personal relations with Murray were as friendly as before. But it must have been an almost fatal wound. It removed the most reliable source from which those weekly expenses at Hanover Street would be met. It was a thing that could not be concealed, that must have damaged the credit of the business beyond even John's ingenuity to explain away.

Even so, a superficial consideration might conclude that, for the moment, it should be able to hold its own, with the help of these 3,000 copies of *Rokeby* which were delivered from the printing works as the year closed, and for which such satisfactory payments in drafts, and good, discountable bills, would be coming in from the London trade. So Scott evidently thought. But suppose that it was by anticipation of the publication of *Rokeby* that James and John (particularly John) had been putting off payments already due? Suppose it were in anticipation of this time of abundant money that they had been persuading bankers or trade creditors to renew bills?

James had told Scott plainly that it was vital that the poem should be out by the end of the year, and Scott had done his part. So had James. It had been set up as it reached his hands. His preparations had been made. It came out of the press promptly and well. But how many were watching for this event, and in what mood?

It might actually have been easier to carry on if the publication of *Rokeby* had been delayed. They might, on that pretext, have been able to persuade creditors to renew their bills to a larger total than the cash that they now received. But creditors might ask today—if you do not pay us now, how will you in six months' time? From the later editions of *Rokeby*? But there would soon be a rumour in the trade that the cheaper editions of *Rokeby* were going somewhat slowly.... That is, compared with anticipations.

John may have made promises to the firm's bankers, also, that when this money came in from the *Rokeby* sales there would be a reduction in the accommodation they had been receiving. That is a very probable thing. For as to the relations of John Ballantyne & Co. with its bankers we have one sinister fact recorded in John's fragmentary autobiography, which he wrote many years later. It reads:

> "1811.—Bills increased to almost fearful degree. Sir Wm. Forbes & Co. shut their account. No bank would discount with us, and everything leading to irretrievable failure."

It is practically certain here that the date is an error. For 1811 we should read 1812. It seems most probable that the trouble with Forbes & Co. occurred in the autumn of 1812, and John must either have concealed it from Scott entirely, or given some explanation which minimised its importance at the time.

And, under all, we have to keep steadily in mind, there moved this adverse current of world finance which no man could foresee, or control. It was a tide in which many stronger swimmers than these two firms would go down; which two, indeed, apart from the imponderable element of Scott's character and resources, had no chance at all.

Fighting for their lives, they carried on until the *Bridal* was published with some success, in spite of its anonymity, in the early part of March, and shortly after that a position developed in which it became evident that considerable money must be found at once if they were to continue trading.

It appears certain that the active partners had struggled to overcome their difficulties without worrying Scott with all the details of the position; and that he now felt that if he had been informed earlier, he could have dealt with it more competently than they had been able to do, for he was not one to express such feelings, and with the indignation which he certainly showed, without some substantial reason. He blamed John Ballantyne particularly. In fact, matters might have gone further on the downhill grade, had not demands been made upon him direct of such nature and amount that concealment, even had it been desired, was no longer possible, at which, with his customary energy, he lost no time in investigating and facing the crisis that had arisen.

On March 16th, John sent him, in accordance with his instructions, a very long and detailed statement of the financial position, with particular reference to those liabilities which had become of a critical urgency.

Lockhart, having the whole of this statement before him, gave two abstracts, the second of which is obviously of the nature of a personal footnote:

> "This business has always been more or less difficulted by all its capital, and £3,000 more, being lent the printing office, and the necessity of keeping up this advance by discounting it from time to time. The profits of the office being nearly commensurate to the drafts made on it, and the supplies of materials from year to year, this debt, once constituted, has never been reduced...."

> "Dear Sir
>
> I have read over this melancholy statement, and have in truth nothing to add to it. Amidst my vexation and apprehension, it is some consolation that I cannot charge myself with undue negligence in my department. I have nothing to add but my hope that I may not

wholly lose your countenance and regard, which has for many years been the pride of my life."

Four days later, John wrote to Scott again, saying:

> "I know for my part that I have lived upon the £300 allotted, and can live...on much less.... I think any money you choose to raise should be applied in liquidation of the printing office's debts, as it seems to me impossible that it can continue to maintain, even for a period, a loan to the office of £5,000."

Lockhart selected these abstracts as evidence that the printing business was in debt, without legitimate excuse, to the publishing office for a huge sum, which position he attributes to the reckless private expenditure of James. He discredits John's assertion that he had lived within his salary. He says he had met people (twenty years later) who thought that John had spent four times as much.

In fact, John's evidence is never to be believed unless it can be used to discredit James, when he at once becomes a reliable witness! But do these passages from John's statement really bear the implication that Lockhart places upon them?

When the publishing business was started it had a substantial sum of cash in the bank. The printing business was straining its resources to finance the orders it already had. The publishing business placed very large orders with it, entailing heavy expenditure in wages and other directions long before there could be actual deliveries of goods. The publishing firm would naturally make advances, under these circumstances, first in cash, and afterwards in bills, against the orders in hand. To the extent at any date at which these payments on account exceeded actual deliveries, the printing firm would appear to he 'in debt' to the publishing firm on the books of both. It is a position which might almost have been assumed, without evidence, and is supported by a Balance Sheet of the publishing business which John drew up for Scott's information in 1810, which shows the printing business as in its debt for £928 at that earlier period.

These transactions are quite consistent with the normality of the position and would not require or deserve such detailed analysis, were it not for the accusations of personal extravagance and deception which Lockhart made against the Ballantynes, and of blind credulity against Scott himself, which degrade and obscure the simpler truth of the mistakes which were made, and the characters of those who were associated in these difficulties.

John Ballantyne did *not* conceal from Scott that the printing business was indebted (on paper) to the publishing office. He set it out plainly and periodically. If Scott did not understand, and did not trouble to enquire, as to the nature of the transactions which produced that position, if all the capital which he provided for the publishing business were really being transferred to the printing firm, so that it could be wasted by James in extravagant living, and Scott did not understand or enquire as to what was happening with these figures before him, then he deserves such sympathy as an imbecile should receive, but not more.

To recognise that is not to suggest that John Ballantyne or anyone else was impeccable in character, or infallible in judgement. John's correspondence suggests that he was something of an opportunist, he is sometimes more plausible than convincing, but the underlying causes that produced the position are clear enough, and are not radically disparaging to anyone of the three most concerned. Whatever be thought of John's correspondence, that of Scott and James Ballantyne is about equally creditable to both, and James, in particular, has a gift of clarity which few business men would equal.

On March 22nd, a few days later than the letters above quoted, he sent Scott his own statement of the position of the printing business, and concluded his letter with this paragraph:

"It is thus evident that the bookselling could be supported only by credit: and the best mode would have been for us to have limited it as much as possible. But, unfortunately, as it now appears, we did not. We embarked upon various speculations, some of which—those in which you were concerned as author or editor—had great success—others the fair average the bookseller expects; but a third class, and that class unfortunately the largest in amounts though not the most numerous with no success at all corresponding to the expense laid out upon them. Of these, Beaumont and Fletcher, and the Register, have been the heaviest hitherto. By these adventures nearly £15,000 (perhaps more) of stock has been created without any capital whatever; and therefore that sum must be due by us to sundries.... Having said all that occurs, I shall conclude with assuring you that you will find in John and me the most implicit compliance with whatever you shall propose, either for the general welfare of the business, or your own security. Whatever you propose I am confident it will be proper for us to agree."

That seems to put the position with a clearness and equity which Lockhart certainly fails to reach. James does not defend himself from any charge of personal extravagance, and it is evident that none has been made against him. Without imputation against anyone, he goes to the root of the trouble, and takes his share of the blame. He recognises that the whole enterprise owes its success, almost its existence, to Scott, as well as that its embarrassments arise from projects that he initiated, and which they had all approved.

It was a position in which quarrelling and recrimination would have been a likely issue. The temper in which the crisis was faced was highly creditable to the characters of all concerned: it was left to Lockhart, twenty years later, to introduce posthumous imputations of bad faith and folly, which the evidence does not support, and Scott's reputation did not require.

CHAPTER L

On investigating the position with which he was now confronted, Scott found that the one hope of saving it, so far as the resources of the two firms were concerned, lay in an immediate realisation of the publishing stock. There was only one man in Edinburgh who might possibly be willing, and who had the means or credit, for such a speculation. That was Archibald Constable. Scott suggested that they should approach him at once. His partners said that they had already done this, and negotiations proceeded. Scott said he would deal with that matter himself. He went to see Constable. Fortunately, the obnoxious Hunter had left the firm. He found that, though Constable might not have shown a disposition to come to brisk terms with the Ballantynes, he was quite ready to deal with him.

By May 18th, when the news of Lutzen was spreading consternation through Europe, and the financial crisis in England was at its height, he was able to feel that, for the time at least, he had saved the position. Constable had bought one-fourth share in the remaining *Rokeby* copyright for £700. He had picked out a quantity of stock that he was prepared to buy, of which some 800 copies of *Don Roderick*, 300 sets of the Annual Register, and a large quantity of De Foe's novels have the appearance of being the most saleable items. He gave £1,300 for these, making £2,000 in all. Scott calculated that Constable would make a large profit on the transaction, which he did not grudge him, but a young man, Robert Cadell, whom Constable had just taken into partnership in place of the obnoxious Hunter, bore witness subsequently that it was sold off at a heavy loss, and this is more probably true.

The amount received, though a mere fraction of the total liabilities that had to be faced, was sufficient to discharge such obligations as were of a critical urgency; and it was now definitely agreed that the publishing business was to be given up. It was the right decision to take, and Scott had shown wisdom as well as courage in the way in which he had faced the crisis. John was to make it his sole occupation to market the heavy quantities of stock that would still be on the Hanover Street shelves. He was to collect the outstanding accounts as quickly as he could. Beyond that, there was to be no more trading. As accounts were collected, or stock sold, the remaining liabilities were to be paid off. Scott could feel that he had done the right thing, though it was a confession of failure, and likely to mean very heavy loss to himself. He had at least turned the helm toward a quiet harbour, though he might still be steering through stormy seas. By itself, the printing business should be able to recover its position.

It might be clear that it was the right course to take, but it had one danger. For this decision to wind up the business, and the bargain with Constable, would become known to the trade, and the credit of John Ballantyne & Co. would be a dead thing. Henceforward, it would be a race between the rate at which John could collect accounts and sell stock, and the dates at which the now-floating bills would fall due, with such help as the printing business could give, or Scott, at the worst, provide. It was a struggle in which the odds were against John Ballantyne. He may have calculated how many thousand pounds worth of that stock he would have to sell before the year ended, and no one knew better than he—perhaps no one knew quite so well—how difficult it would be. But on this 18th day of May, he, too, may have felt the relief of a crisis past. He was in London, where he had gone to collect accounts and endeavour to renew some credits there, when he received a letter from Scott of that date: "For the first time for many weeks," he read, "I shall lay my head on a quiet pillow,"—and then in its concluding words:

> "Adieu, my dear John. If I have ever expressed myself with irritation in speaking of this business, you must impute it to *the sudden, extensive, and unexpected embarrassments in which I found myself involved all at once*. If to your real goodness of heart and integrity,

and to the quickness and acuteness of your talents, you added habits of more universal circumspection, and, above all, the courage to tell disagreeable truths to those whom you hold in regard, I pronounce that the world never held such a man of business. These it must be your study to add to your other good qualities. Meantime, as some one says to Swift, I love you with all your failings. Pray make an effort and love me with all mine. Yours truly W.S.

P.S. James has behaved very well during this whole transaction, and has been most steadily attentive to business. I am convinced that the more he works the better his health will be. One or other of you will need to be constantly in the printing-office henceforth—it is the sheet-anchor.

They are words written in a mood of relief: at an ended crisis, generous in what they allow, and, for that very generosity, the more serious in what they impute. Yet, at their most serious implication, they are not such as Scott would have written to a man with whom he had been associated in business for several years, and who had finally been revealed as a proved knave or a proved fool....

Something of the condition of the country, the business atmosphere, in which these "heavy skirmishes"—it is Scott's phrase—had taken place, may be judged from a letter which he wrote to Southey in the previous June, when he was living during week-ends in a "gardener's hut" at Abbotsford, and doing his duty as Sheriff to keep order in Selkirkshire. It is the letter of a man who held no brief for the master against the workman, whose sympathies were always for the under-dog, but who saw his country threatened with foes abroad and revolution from below, and who saw also that such revolution, at such a time, would bring a thousand times more miseries to the world than it would be likely to cure. It must be remembered that, for good or evil, there was no police force as we understand it in those:

days. Men lived freer lives than we can easily imagine, or are soon likely to experience again. Order depended, in the country districts, almost entirely upon the energy of the Sheriff and, indirectly, upon his personal popularity, and the readiness with which voluntary helpers would come to his call. And Scott was determined that, while he was Sheriff of Selkirkshire, there should be order in at least one county in Scotland.

Southey had been expressing his fear that unrest and misery and misrule might bear fruit in a revolution, before which all ordered government would be swept away; and Scott replied from Edinburgh on the 4th June, 1812:

> "You are quite right in apprehending a *Jacquerie*; the country is mined below our feet. Last week, learning that a meeting was to be held among the weavers of the large manufacturing village of Galashiels, for the purpose of cutting a man's web from his loom, I apprehended the ring-leader and disconcerted the whole project, but in the course of my enquiries imagine my surprise at discovering a bundle of letters and printed manifestos, from which it appeared that the Manchester Weavers' Committee corresponds with every manufacturing town in the South and West of Scotland, and levies a subsidy of 2/6 per man (an immense sum) for the ostensible purpose of petitioning Parliament for the redress of grievances, but doubtless to sustain them in their revolutionary movements. An energetic administration which had the confidence of the county should soon check all this...."

We are not, of course, to understand that a single 2/6 was an 'immense sum', even by the standards of those days, but that such a levy would accumulate one far greater than the promotion of any petition could require. The fact that the half-starved weavers could be induced to contribute so largely was also an ominous sign of the strength of a discontent which had no outlet to express itself at the polling-booth.

Scott, it may be said, took the standpoint of the traditional Tory, but that is disputable, unless, indeed, we place a high interpretation upon what that standpoint is. It may be doubted whether he would have seen any prospect of social salvation in placing equal voting power in all adult hands. It was an experiment which had not been tried, and even some of those who are best satisfied with its results today might have hesitated to prescribe it as an immediate remedy for the conditions, and for the population, of that period. But, primarily, Scott blamed the Government, not the mob, if disorders came. Had the power been in his hands, he would have attacked every social evil with the same practical ideality with which he was now planning to drain and ditch and plant fair woodlands on that derelict Abbotsford land.

In his fullest, most prosperous days, when his dream of Abbotsford had come true, and the whole world was at his feet, he had not only the care to order that the boot-boy should be allowed free time to continue his studies, but to have him once a week in his own room to instruct and encourage him in the efforts he was making to improve his mind. Had the government of the day consisted of such as he, there would have been no fear of revolution among the weavers of Manchester or Galashiels.

CHAPTER LI.

The financial crisis in the affairs of the Ballantyne firms was sufficiently severe to oblige Scott to put other plans out of his mind, until the treaty with Constable gave a respite to the sharp pressure of immediate anxiety. But with his successful conclusion of this bargain his thoughts reverted immediately to a project which had been stayed by this disagreeable interlude. Side by side with the production of the two poems which had just been published, he had, as we know, been maturing the plan of another, the scene of which was to be the remote Highlands. Parts of it were already written. As the two others were dismissed from his mind, he had concentrated immediately upon the one that remained, and had formed a confident hope that he could make it equal to—perhaps that it could even surpass—his previous triumphs. He was not discouraged by the comparative failure of *Rokeby*. He thought that that could be attributed in part to the scene and character of the poem, and in part to Byron's competing popularity. The first objection would not apply to the new one, the scenes of which would be in the Scotland where he felt that his strength lay; as to the second, he was resolved not to be driven from the field without an effort to retain his championship. He felt that he had an attractive plot. He would introduce a description of Bannockburn, Scotland's most famous victory. He read over the parts of the poem already drafted and felt that they had a good sound. He would call it the *Nameless Glen*....

The idea that this poem should win back any ground that *Rokeby* had lost was linked with another project which he hoped rather than expected to carry through. Behind the land which he had bought along the Tweedside there was a hilly, treeless waste, stretching southward to a desolate mountain lake, known as the Cauldshiels Loch. The owner was willing to sell—at a price—and Scott was keener to buy. He saw the possible beauties of those barren hills, if they were planted in his own way. With some difficulty, they had arrived at a tentative price—£5,000. Constable had once given him a thousand guineas for an unwritten poem at a time when his reputation had not been as firmly based as it was now. Why should he not try again for a higher price?

Doubtless, when he had been negotiating with Constable to save himself and his partners from the shadow of an impending bankruptcy, he had mentioned that he had another poem in hand. Doubtless, Constable had had the thought of an ultimate bargain concerning it. But, even in that extremity, Scott had not thrown it into the scale. He had another use for that. He might have sleepless nights, but he held to the ultimate purpose he had in view with the tenacious courage which had brought him through so many previous adventures of life, physical and commercial, and of other varieties.

Now he lost no time in opening the negotiation. He told Constable frankly why he wanted the money. £5,000 he must have. That, therefore, was the poem's price. Constable thought not. It was far too high. They argued in correspondence. Each of them wished to deal, and neither would give way.

It has been used as an evidence of Scott's financial recklessness that he should have attempted such a deal within three weeks of the experience through which he had passed, but it is difficult to see any logical basis for this accusation. Audacious it may have been. But to exchange a few sheets of verse for the title deeds of a freehold property does not decrease the financial stability of the man who is able to pull it off. Freehold land is usually regarded as an investment of a rather conservative kind. Now suppose that Constable had had £5,000 worth of freehold land, and had sold it to buy a poem, and the poem had turned out a dud? What would Lockhart have said to that?

But, in fact, the deal was not made. Scott, with the knowledge of the continued profits of the *Lay* and *Marmion*, in which he had no further copyright interest, and on the *Lady of the Lake*, in which he had, would not give way. The price was £5,000. Constable would not give way either. In fact, it is almost certain that the figure, though he did not say so, was beyond his means. Of course, he could have given bills. Almost certainly the settlement would have taken that form, had it been made at all. Even in the financial atmosphere of those days, bills with Constable's name, and Scott's, upon them, might have been good enough to obtain the money—at a price.

But bills have to be met. Constable would sometimes take a bold risk, but he was far from being reckless in his financial adventures. Otherwise, he would not have weathered the commercial crisis of this period, and been able to give help to others, while so many publishing firms were failing in London.

But Scott meant to have the land, and though he would not give way concerning a price that he had once named, he may have felt a scruple of honour in offering the poem elsewhere after the help which Constable had just given. In the end, they came to an amicable bargain, but that is part of a later tale. The name had been changed as the correspondence proceeded. It was to be *The Lord of the Isles.*

Scott found other means of buying the land. After all, there was a good deal of money in the family. Land is not a bad security on which to lend. In July, he had got what he would. All the way from the Tweed to Cauldshields Loch, he could walk over his own land.

Whatever trouble there might have been during the last few weeks, it is evident that Scott did not regard himself as a poor man, nor the future with any fear. He had an assured income of £1,600 a year from his official appointments. If he were willing to give a sufficient proportion of his time to articles and editorial work he could get something like a further £1,000 a year from the publishers. Probably more. He might hope for further large sums for future poems. He could hope that when Hanover Street was finally closed he would again be in receipt of profits from the printing business, from which from £500 to £750 had been accruing due to him in the past with approximate regularity. But even without that, even it he lost the £9,000—or whatever it was—that he had invested in these enterprises, he was not a poor man. And there was Charlotte's smaller separate income, as a last ditch in the rear.

As to the publishing business, the arrangement was clear and simple. John was to realise all he could, and endeavour to meet liabilities as they fell due, without troubling Scott further. But if he could see that he might be short, there was to be no more loss of credit. No more discreditable episodes such as those in which Court processes and attorneys had figured in the immediate past. No more dishonoured bills. He was to let Scott know in good time, and the needed amount should be made up.

Scott left Edinburgh for Abbotsford on July 12th, the Session being over. On the evening of July 23rd there was a messenger with an urgent letter from John at the door. He was short of £350 which must be banked tomorrow if credit were to be saved. The youth had ridden thirty miles with that letter: he would have to ride thirty miles back. Scott allowed him a few hours' sleep and started him of at dawn with the 'order'—the cheque, as we should say—that the situation required.

The next day he wrote to John Ballantyne—

"Dear John,

I sent you the order and have only to hope it arrived safe and in good time. I waked the boy at three o'clock myself, having slept little, less on account of the money than of the time. Surely you should have written, three or four days before, the probable amount of the deficit, and, as on former occasions, I would have furnished you with means of meeting it. These expresses, besides other inconveniences, excite surprise in my family and in the neighbourhood. I know of no justifiable occasion for them but the unexpected return of a bill. I do not consider you as answerable for the success of plans, but I do and must hold you responsible for giving me, in distinct and plain terms, your opinion as to any difficulties which may occur, and that in such time that I may make arrangements to obviate them if possible."

A sharp note, but not unreasonable. It was evident that these calls for help were becoming rather frequent. Scott must derive what consolation he could from the thought that the liabilities of John Ballantyne & Co. were getting less with each payment that was made.

John might have said that, if he did not call out till the eleventh hour, it was because he did not want to trouble Scott at all. In this case he had thought he could obtain a renewal of bills which Sir William Forbes had refused. He had been too sanguine, it may be said, but it may be a good fault, and he was careful in his own way. We have seen how James represented him as being ill with anxiety a year ago. But the fact was that banking credit was being restricted in all directions. It may have been a necessary consequence of many failures. It was producing more. Friendly firms, holding Ballantyne bills, might promise John that they should be renewed, perhaps with a small reduction of the amount, and then find at the last moment that their bankers would veto the promised accommodation. It was a tempest in which many strong ships were foundering. What chance was there for John Ballantyne & Co., damaged and ill-equipped, and self-doomed to an early end? If we have any imagination, any knowledge of business under such conditions, we may spare a thought of sympathy for John Ballantyne at the daily helm; and for James also, inextricably entangled with the other firm by that nightmare of bills that seemed always to be falling due, and the wages to be found every Saturday morning, and those uncertain London remittances....

As we watch the course of these events, as they will develop during the following months, we may also ask ourselves whether, or how far, it could have been a continuing secret that Scott was a partner in these labouring firms. The more closely we examine the facts the stronger the suspicion may grow that to discuss the ethics of the position on that assumption is to waste time on a baseless myth.

The fact was that John had an almost impossible task. A publishing business depends mainly, for current income, upon the new books which it is bringing out. To sell the old stock fast enough to pay off all those thousands of pounds of accruing liabilities, now that credit was lost, and bills were almost impossible to renew...well, John was finding that it couldn't be done.

Perhaps Scott understood this well enough. He may have felt that the burden of disposing of that stock would fall on him in the end. There would be no use in saying that now. Let John do what he could, without discouragement. But these last-minute appeals *must* be stopped. Had that messenger come a few days later, Scott would have been away in Nithsdale. What would have happened then?

The Scotts were going to Nithsdale, to Drumlanrig Castle, on the invitation of the Duke of Buccleuch, who had just inherited that estate, in addition to those that came to him when his father died. They were to have a week there, and then Scott was to meet the Marquis of Abercorn at Carlisle, on that old business of Tom's administration of the estate. But he had given John his Drumlanrig address, and there were two more urgent messengers there during the week.

One concerned some renewal bills on which Scott's name was imperative. The other was a cry for help concerning the rates on the Hanover Street premises, for the recovery of which legal process was threatened.

When the second came, Scott decided that he could not safely go on to Carlisle without knowing more of the position in Edinburgh. He wrote to John to meet him at Abbotsford, and set out for home.

The interview that took place there was sufficiently reassuring to allow him to go on to Carlisle with a quieter mind than he might otherwise have had, and to transact his business there, which was of a personal importance, for there was a large sum of money due to his father's estate, which had been in Tom's hands, or invested in the Abercorn property—we need not turn aside to probe the details of that—which by Scott's or Gurthie Wright's exertions, or by the process of time, was to be repaid at the end of the year. Scott was to benefit personally to a substantial sum, and he would have no difficulty in discovering a direction in which it could easily be used. It was already evident that the winding up of John Ballantyne & Co. was going to be a worrying and expensive business.

John's optimism had given Scott such immediate reassurance that he had decided to carry out a previous purpose to go on to Rokeby, being so near, and have a few days with Morritt. At Penrith he found another letter had been sent forward by John to await him there. Another cheque went to Edinburgh. Scott rode on to Brough, and there had found a letter from Morritt, telling him of the serious illness of his wife. It was doubtful whether it would prove a well-chosen time for such a visit; it was certain that the affairs of the publishing business required his attention. This condition of being asked for cheques by express messenger about twice a week was intolerable in every way. Besides, look at the cost. The plan of realising the stock while the creditors sat round and waited was not going to prove a success. Scott turned his horse, and rode back to Edinburgh, determined to cut the knot.

Once again, Constable was taken into confidence, and far more completely than before. Scott may have been too ready to anticipate that the efforts of the Ballantynes would be equal to maintaining their floating credits while the slow realisation of stock reduced the total. He may have acted as most men would have hesitated to do in buying those barren hills behind Abbotsford a few weeks after the first extremity of crisis had been overcome. But when he came on the scene it was in no hesitant mood, nor as one whom circumstance would find it easy to overwhelm. John's optimistic assurance at Abbotsford, followed almost immediately by the letter to Penrith, had decided him that the position could not continue. A cheerful optimism may be a very valuable quality for a partner to have. John had been fertile—possibly even too fertile—of expedients in the days while it had been possible to screen with a bold front of prosperity the financial exigencies of the hour, and when it may have seemed almost as important that the sleeping partner should not be dissatisfied or disturbed as that there should be no cause for such feelings, if the truth were bare. But John's expedients were about done.

Now Scott had two schedules prepared, and laid before Constable. One was a complete list of the stock. The other was the liabilities of John Ballantyne & Co., including obligations to bankers, and the bills on which, either as drawers or acceptors, its name appeared. These figures may not be available now, but it is evident from the subsequent facts that the stock would have been more than sufficient to discharge the liabilities if it could have been realised at anything like its nominal wholesale value. Unfortunately, that was a large 'if'.

Constable studied the list of stock. It was a huge total. He studied the list of floating liabilities with experienced eyes. He considered his resources. He said he was sorry. The problem was beyond his means.

Scott's plan appears to have been that the whole stock should have been handed over to Constable's control, against which he should have made himself responsible for the liabilities, for which, with the support of his name, extended times of payment might have been arranged, and Scott in turn would be responsible to him. In future, Scott and Constable would have dealt direct. John was to be eliminated entirely. He must seek other employment. Scott meant to put an end to those twice-weekly expresses. Or, at the worst, that they should come in future from James rather than John.

Alternately, he would doubtless have been glad to sell the whole stock to Constable outright, and face the position with a finality which could be secured in no other way. It contained much that was of value, if it could be marketed without haste, and there was probably no one in the trade, either in London or Edinburgh, who could have done it better than he. But Constable was firm in refusal. It was too large a risk for him to take.

Yet he would do what he could. He earnestly desired to secure Scott as an author. There was that new poem *The UnKnown Glen*, or whatever it was called, which was to be the greatest that Scott had written, on the horizon. Beyond that, he seems to have acted in a spirit of genuine goodwill. The idea that John was to go out of the trade would not make the proposals any less attractive. It is probably that he never liked John, and certain that John disliked him, and would not hesitate to do him an ill turn if the wheel of circumstance gave opportunity at some future time.

Constable said that he would do what he could. He would

take a substantial portion of the stock, at his own price, but, if Scott wished to feel that the position was relieved with any approach to finality, there must be provision of a much larger sum than he would be able to undertake.

Scott saw that as clearly as he. He wrote a letter to his friend the Duke of Buccleuch, who had now returned home. It was mainly about an offer of the Poet Laureateship which he had just received. It was an honour which he did not particularly covet, and there was the fact to consider that there were many greater poets alive than he, who got less reward. It would bring in (he was told) about £300 a year. He was already receiving £1,600 from official sources. Was it fair to take more, while other poets had none? His inclination was to refuse it, and suggest Robert Southey as the more suitable.

On the other hand, was it a discourtesy to the Crown to reject the offered honour? It was a question of etiquette, and, in that aspect, an affair of the clan, of which the Duke was the head. What did Buccleuch think?

He mentioned, in a brief opening paragraph, that he was in financial difficulty with the printing business, and must ask for his friend's help. He thought the actual finding of money could be avoided if the Duke would guarantee his account for £4,000, and that he could manage matters in such a way that there would be no risk of ultimate loss. Otherwise, he must sell his copyrights, which he was anxious to avoid.

The Duke replied promptly. His letter was also mainly occupied with the Laureateship question, on which he agreed with Scott. Let Southey have it. It could be done without breach of etiquette, if it were done in the right way.

So Southey, instead of Scott, became the English Laureate. There was correspondence, in which Southey said the right things as we may be sure that he would. Scott put the matter as one of poetic merit. "I am not such an ass," he wrote, "as not to know that you are the better in poetry." Probably Southey observed, in the discreet rear of his mind, that Scott was a good judge.

As to the bank guarantee, the Duke made nothing of it at all. He was a wealthy man. As the Earl of Dalkeith he had been Scott's life-long and intimate friend. So, almost equally, was the Duchess. Scott may probably have told something of these troubles when he received those two unwelcome letters at Drumlanrig, and made hasty change of his plans to return to Abbotsford. Buccleuch merely said that he didn't quite know how these things were done, so would Scott oblige him by drawing up "the paper" himself, and sending it to him to sign?

Within two or three days the whole matter was completed. Scott insured his life for the amount of the guarantee, that the Duke should not lose if he died. If he lived, he felt confident that no one need lose through him.

Consequences, says the proverb, are God's comments. Scott was one who had acted from boyhood as the friend of all around him, from most of whom he took little, while he gave much.

We may observe, through all the changes of his life, that he never lacked friends of the right kind.

Between most men, after the past differences of Constable and himself, there would have been an established enmity. Now Constable was carting stock that he did not want over to his own warehouse, and giving bills to supplement the assistance of that £4,000 guarantee. It may have been a business transaction. No doubt it was. But would that deal have been carried through if John Ballantyne had been the negotiator?

The bulk of the stock was still on the shelves and in the cellars at Hanover Street. Seeing how little difference even these wholesale disposals to Constable appeared to make, Scott must have realised how much difficulty was still before him. He may have called himself fool as he thought of the sanguine spirit in which he had edited those books, and allowed their printing. He was not one to deceive either himself or others. Yet we may observe him as one who gave battle to difficulties in a bold and confident way. In May he had first known the truth of the financial dangers in which the two firms were involved. Promptly and energetically, he had taken such steps as overcame the immediate crisis. In July, he had put these troubles aside to acquire the land at Abbotsford on which his heart was set. In August, he was back in Edinburgh facing the new difficulties there in a spirit that had conquered again.

He rode back to Abbotsford, where Tom Purdie was planting trees, with the confidence that he had mastered circumstance, as Charlotte had been so very sure that he would. In whatever difficulty they might be, she was always sure about that.

It was no more than a detail that he had used all the £4,000, and all Constable's money, to relieve the position in Edinburgh, and that he rode back with an empty purse. Nor was he one to care that the planting of trees is not an immediately remunerative occupation. Looking at those desolate barren hillside fields, it was so obvious that it was the right thing to do....

It was during the extremity of the Ballantyne crisis that the Rev. C. R. Maturin, being in urgent financial difficulties, wrote to Mr. Walter Scott for help, and received a kind letter and a cheque for fifty pounds.

CHAPTER LII.

The suggestion that Scott, in these business difficulties of the Ballantyne firms, was the duped victim of unscrupulous and incompetent men, will not bear investigation, nor would he ever have set up such a contention, nor (we may confidently presume) would he have thanked anyone for presenting him in such a guise of credulity. But the particular accusation of duplicity as advanced by Lockhart against John Ballantyne is one of those lies which are made more deadly by a percentage of truth. Scott *did* consider that John had shown a lack of frankness in regard to earlier difficulties. He thought that, if he had been earlier informed, he could have dealt with them in different and better ways, and that, if he had done so, the later troubles would have been entirely avoided, or would have been of minor dimensions.

On August 20th, 1813, when he was receiving those too frequent calls for instant help, to which he objected so strongly, he wrote:

> "The evil of this business is having carried on the concern so very long—until its credit was wholly ruined—*before* having recourse to my assistance; for what I have done ought to have cleared it, if the business had been in a situation to help itself. But I will not do in my own case what I have condemned in others—this is, attempt to support a falling business beyond the moment when it appears rational to hope for its being retrieved. I have no debts of my own of any consequence, except such as have been incurred in this unlucky business."

And two days later:

> "I have every wish to support the credit of the house—but if we are to fall behind £1,000 every month, over and above what has been calculated and provided for, who can stand it?"

There is here a specific statement, and a definite charge in letters addressed, not to third parties, but to John himself, that Scott's financial trouble was entirely due to the publishing business, and that this trouble could have been avoided had John been franker at an earlier date. Scott would not have been likely to make such a charge without grave reason, and the known facts support it.

But Lockhart, having this basis on which to build, has gone far beyond anything that Scott suggested at any time. He is specific and detailed in his accusation that John had been deceiving Scott with faked Balance Sheets from the first—with accounts that criminally and even transparently false, and that Scott was so infatuated, so blindly foolish, that even this terrible experience did not open his eyes to the real character of the men with whom he was dealing, so that James still went on his career of incompetent, indolent extravagance, and John continued to hoodwink him with faked accounts till the end of their respective lives.

It is evident that Lockhart made this charge in a spirit of honest prejudice, because, as with that grotesque tale or James's reckless drawings during the early years of the printing business, he betrays himself by the accounts which he puts forward in evidence, in a manner in which no one who understood what he was writing about would have had the audacity to do.

The first of these accounts appears to have been supplied in June 1810, and was probably made up to the previous Whitsuntide.

Engagements—£ 7,549 11 0 Sundry Credits.
Book Debts,
Stock, etc.—£11,45540
Balance in Trade
in favour of
J. B. & Co—£3,905130

£11,45540 0151—£11,45540

This Balance Sheet, as we should call it, was, of course, set out in more detail, but that is how Lockhart states it, and I am following his figures, and his argument. He might have given details, and urged that the valuation of the stock was too high, and that reserves should have been made which were not there, and he might have been right, but he does not do this, because he is advancing a much more serious charge—that the account was faked, and was faked deliberately to deceive his partner, which it succeeded in doing. This is what he says:

> "Now how is this 'balance of trade in favour of John B. & Co.' constituted? Read and wonder.

Original stock—£2,000
Loan from Mr. Scott—£1,500
Profit (besides supporting
the establishment)—£405 13 0

£3,905 13 0

"Both the £2,000 original stock, and the loan of £1,500 ought, so everybody sees, to have figured on the debit side of the page; and the £405. 13. 0., and no more, should have stood as balance of trade.

"I am sorry to bother you so much with figures, but it is really necessary to pause a moment on this audacity. This bookkeeper wishes to persuade Scott that the Company is flourishing, and he bravely claims for the *credit* side of his sheet, first the original stock of £2,000, and then Mr. Scott's loan £1,500. Why, according to this mode of computing, the more the Company borrowed, the more was the balance of trade in its favour!.... How Sir Walter could have shut his eyes to anything so plain—or seeing it, why he did not draw back from the desperate hazard in which he had already invested the bulk of his capital with such managers—may be matter of wonder, and of deep regret."

The answer to the first paragraph of this amazing nonsense is that the amounts *do* appear on the debit side, which, as Lockhart says, in the only sane phrase which the comment contains, is the place where they ought to be.

The answer to the second is that John does not claim them for the credit side, and if we are to conclude that Lockhart does not know the difference between debit and credit, and is only trying to say that which ever side they are on, they ought to be on the other, then it does not help him, for they are on the right side, and the only side on which they could be in any account prepared by a man who understood what he was doing.

The account was prepared and worded according to the manner which was customary among Edinburgh accountants at the time, and could neither have deceived an intelligent partner, nor an intelligent child, on the point on which Lockart's comment is concerned. The 'balance of trade' is the amount of capital invested in the business *plus* the profit, or *minus* the loss subsequently incurred. Scott knew that £3,500 had been invested in the business, and if it now showed a favourable balance of £3,905, the profit was £405. Had the capital been stated separately on the same side of the account, and had there *also* been a balance of £3,905, then there would have been net profit of that amount, but that is not the case. The capital is shown nowhere else on the account. What had become of it, if it were not in this item? If Scott couldn't find his own capital on such an account, or observe its absence, it would have not been worth while to show him any figures at all.

But had John been knave enough (or perhaps fool would be a better word) to put the capital on the other side, as Lockhart would have had him do, the balance of apparent profit would not have been £405 but £7,405!

In fact, the charge is grotesque, and it is waste of words to discuss it further.

But Lockhart gives a subsequent account (Whitsuntide 1811) in more detail, and bases upon it a more plausible charge.

This is the account, as he has it:

Engagements—£10,453; Book Debts—£4,718
Balance in Trade—£4,364; Stock at sale Prices £10,800
Less 10% 1,080—£9,720

Cash in hand—£379

£14,817—£14,817

With this account John sent a sanguine letter, suggesting that it would allay Scott's uneasiness, as it showed a substantial improvement in the capital figure, It will be observed that it is in the same form as that of the previous year, and Lockhart appears not to have observed that the capital figure is in the same place as before, but he now objects (a) that a large part of the book debts were probably bad, as to which there is not a shred of evidence, nor much probability, nor do we even know on what basis they were valued, and (b) that the stock is grossly overvalued, because a mere 10% from the sale price is an absurdity for any publisher to deduct. So it is. And as the whole basis of this account is the value of the stock in question, if Scott really asked anxiously for an account, and then didn't trouble himself as to how it was valued, or why, then he was an absolute fool. There is no more to be said.

But there are abundant evidences that Scott was not such a fool as that, as, indeed, few men are; and a moment's thought suggests a probable explanation of what this valuation is, and why it is stated in that form.

The books of which this stock consist were all printed by James Ballantyne & Co., and sold by them to John Ballantyne & Co., who resold them to the retail trade. John was a partner in the second firm, but not in the first. Almost the first question to be discussed when the publishing firm was formed would be the basis on which the printing firm would transfer stock to it, as the possibility of John showing a profit would depend primarily upon the margin on which he had to work.

The probability is that this margin was agreed at 10%; the 'sale price' is the wholesale figure at which John is to sell to the trade, and the 10% is the agreed margin between that price and that at which the printing firm charges in to him. The questions of whether that was a well-considered basis on which to value the stock, and whether the account was calculated to allay anyone's fears are quite separate ones. The charges which Lockhart makes are that the accounts were fraudulent, were made up with the intention of deceiving the senior partner, and did so deceive him, and these charges utterly fail. They must have been quite clear to Scott, and they gave him the information for which he asked in an absolutely straightforward way.

It is due also to John Ballantyne to notice this, that if the stock were, in fact, charged to his firm by the printing firm less 10%, and he valued it in his accounts on that basis, then it did not improve those accounts by a single penny while it remained unsold. So far was it from a case of writing up the stock to deceive his partner, that if he had had £5,000 of stock in from the printing business the day before, his item of 'engagements' would have been increased by exactly the same amount, and his balance would remain the same. It is also due to him to recognise that this interpretation supports his argument that the publishing business was paying, to this extent, that he could not have shown an appreciation of capital unless the amount of the stock which he actually had sold had been sufficient for the 10% margin upon it to cover his salary and the other Hanover Street expenses, and to leave a balance on the right side. That is what he means to make clear on the earlier account when he claims a profit "besides supporting the establishment". That result he had achieved. The weak point was that the printing firm was manufacturing stock beyond his capacity to sell, and beyond the capacity of either firm to finance, and was constantly delivering and charging it to him, and drawing bills upon him for it, and that is plain enough on his account for a child to see. That was the mistake which was realised on all sides when it was too late to avert its consequences. Having no experience of publishing, they had overestimated their selling capacity. It was a bad mistake, for which a heavy price had to be paid. James puts the case clearly and fairly and without recrimination, in his letter quoted on p. 309.

For that first mistake, it may be agreed that Scott had the largest share of responsibility, and there is no evidence that he would have denied it. His one complaint against his partners, and particularly against John, was that when they found difficulty in renewing the bills by which the capital was largely provided they should have informed him *before* untoward incidents happened, through which the credit of both firms was permanently damaged; and that if they had done this he contended that he would have made the necessary provision, which would have been a vastly smaller sum than was needed after the damage had been done.

That was his one steady complaint, and it appears to have been the sole grievance he had. It was left to Lockhart, when all the three partners were dead, to invent tales of extravagance and fraud, which have no foundation in fact, and which the circumstances do not require.

The stock, which should certainly not have been manufactured in such quantities, was not bad in itself, and a more experienced firm, with a better selling organisation, might have shown better results. Having been printed, Scott showed a determination that it should be sold, rather than pulped, in which we shall see that he succeeded in the end, in his own way. It consisted of such publications as these:

Hume's History of England with Smollett's continuation (16 Vols)
Jamieson's History of the Culdees
Kerr's Voyages (17 Vols)
Edinburgh Annual Register
"Popular Romances"
Beaumont & Fletcher (14 Vols)
Tales of the East (3 Vols)
Seward's Poems (3 Vols)
Grahame's British Georgics
Castle of Otranto
De Foe's Novels

They were mostly works of solid value, but they were not readily marketable in the quantities in which they had been produced.

CHAPTER LIII.

The Duke of Buccleuch's guarantee, and the sales to Constable, had enabled substantial reductions to be made in the liabilities of the publishing company, but did not prevent there being great difficulty in dealing with those that remained. There were two things that had become clear in commercial circles: it was a dying business, and it was one the creditors of which could get paid if they made themselves sufficiently troublesome. The wonder is not that there was a good deal of worry under these circumstances, but that (even allowing for the fact that the printing business was still being carried on) the major liabilities could be kept floating at all.

The position is sufficiently indicated by a letter from Mr Morritt which reached Scott by express messenger when he was in Edinburgh in November. There was a rumour in London that John Ballantyne & Co had failed, and that Scott was heavily involved. It was a detailed report. The liabilities were put at £20,000. Morritt hoped it was not true, but he evidently thought that it was. If it were not too late, would Scott without delaying for further correspondence, draw upon him for any amount—*any* amount—that the circumstances required?

We may observe again that Scott had some good friends. We may doubt anew whether Scott's partnership in these firms was the closely-guarded secret that it has become customary to allege.

Scott was able to relieve his friend's mind with an assurance that the rumour was false, but that it was true that the firm was being liquidated as fast as possible. He was aiming to get clear of these commercial entanglements. He did not mention the Duke's guarantee, but he alluded vaguely to the fact that he had insured his life for £4,000, which would be to the advantage of his family if he should die before such matters were straightened.

So it would: for it would pay off an overdraft which had taken the place of £4,000 of debt. He was sincere, too, in his intention of retiring, both from the printing and publishing firms. He had not allowed the relief which came from the guarantee to alter the programme regarding the publishing business. John was to become an auctioneer. Scott had written several weeks earlier offering to retire from the printing firm, if James could find a new partner, even though it would mean sacrifice of all the capital he had invested in that concern. But he had said that he would do nothing to damage James's interests, and the new partner did not appear.

Scott thanked Morritt with a good will, but did not accept the offer for further assistance. For the moment, he felt that he had the position sufficiently under control....

It is at this time that Mr Weber comes to the front of the stage for a brief hour. He may be remembered as the German refugee scholar whom Scott had first befriended ten or more years ago, and who had edited the Beaumont & Fletcher which Constable had refused to publish, and which now constituted a substantial proportion of the Hanover Street stock.

No doubt, Scott had anticipated that the edition would sell. He may even have hoped for a substantial profit. But it is equally certain that he would never have thought of financing a new edition of those Elizabethan dramatists if he had not wished to find congenial occupation for a German refugee. Neither is there any doubt that, during those years of editing, Weber had been living at Scott's expense. When that work was over, Scott still found him occupation. In fact, by this time, he had become almost one of the family at North Castle Street. He was a man of many amiable qualities, and might have been supposed to be of a very harmless disposition. But lately he had degenerated. He had taken to drinking heavily. Scott appears to have made a serious effort to pull him up. He did not want to turn him adrift. He could not have a drunken man about the house. He warned him that there must be a change, and, at the same time, with characteristic kindliness, he took to keeping him for dinner when his work was done, lest he should employ his time in a worse way. That was the position when the Scott family left Edinburgh as usual to spend Christmas at Mertoun House.

On the afternoon of the day that they returned, Scott sat in his library. He was working on the Swift that he had been editing so long for Constable. It was nearly complete now. Weber sat at the other end of the room, engaged on some labour of transcription. The short January afternoon darkened, and Scott paused in his work to ring for candles. He looked up, and saw that Weber was not writing. His eyes were fixed upon him with the fierce menace of insanity. "Weber," he asked, "what's the matter with you?"

They were divided by the breadth of the table which filled the centre of the room. Scott had had it made in imitation of one that he had admired at Rokeby. Massively built, it had a desk at each end, all in one piece, and small drawers round it down to the floor.

The broad table was covered with bundles of letters and legal documents, proofs and manuscripts, all neatly tied in the redtape which his father's office had taught him to use. There was a small movable table at his side, bearing the works of reference which his occupation required. All round, from floor to ceiling, except where the French windows opened on to the tiny lawn, there were shelves of books, well-bound, well-ordered, numbered and indexed. If one were lent, there would be a wooden blank in its place, bearing the record of where it was.

Besides those tables, and the chairs on which they sat, there was one chair for the use of any invited visitor, and the heavy well-railed ladder-steps which Scott must use if he would climb to the higher shelves, and there should be no one at hand to help.

There was no other furniture in the quiet soft-carpeted room.

Comfort, competence, order—above all, order. The room expressed and explained the immense industry of the man who had formed it to what it was. A man who was not often hurried by circumstance. *"Weber, what's the matter with you?"*

Weber got up, and crossed the room. He had two loaded pistols in his hands. He laid one before Scott. He said he had been accused of insobriety. There was only one way in which such an insult could be avenged. He wanted them to exchange shots—at once.

Scott did not rise. If he recognised the deadly peril which confronted him, his nerves were equal to the occasion. He said, Yes, of course. But they mustn't do anything to alarm Mrs Scott or the children? Weber could see that? Suppose they walked out after dinner together, and found a quiet spot in which they could fight it out? And suppose they put the pistols away safely in the meantime? As he spoke, he pulled open a drawer in the desk. He put into it the pistol which Weber handed to him. Weber made no protest. He laid his pistol beside it. Yes, he said, that would be the best way. Quietly, the drawer was locked. Weber went back to his desk. The lights were brought, and the two men resumed their work in the silent room.

When Scott went to dress for dinner, he took the opportunity to send a note to a friend of Weber to come at once. Weber was quiet at the meal. Everything seemed normal, until Scott, who had kept the whisky decanter near to his own hand, instead of passing it over in the usual way, mixed two weak glasses, and handed one to Weber. The man started up in a burst of anger, controlled himself with difficulty, and sat down, as Charlotte asked whether he were feeling unwell. No, he said, he had spasms. He emptied the glass, and pushed it back to Scott to be filled again. As he did so, the friend for whom Scott had sent entered, and Weber rose and rushed from the room, and hatless into the street. He was put into a strait-jacket that night, according to the ghastly custom of the time, in a condition of raving lunacy.

So we have the tale. It has an aspect of truth, except that Weber's reaction to his friend's appearance needs explanation, and suggests that there may have been previous outbursts, and that it had an implication of restraint, which he was instant to understand. He was placed in an ;asylum at York, where he died four or five years later, Scott, of course, paying the bills.

Punctuated by this brief but lively incident, Scott worked

with his customary energy during these winter days. He had received additions to his private resources, which had assisted a step further in the reduction of those endless Hanover Street liabilities, and the clearing of the political horizon had given its indirect help to business conditions. Leipzig had been fought and lost, and a half-incredulous Europe had seen the invincible arms of France flung backward across the Rhine.

Resolute for success, Scott planned in a clear mind. He was pushing on with the *Lord of the Isles* (it was decided that that should be its title now) with a determination to hold his ground against Byron's growing popularity. But, while he did this, he planned another line of attack if he should be defeated there. At last, he was working on *Waverley* with the definite purpose of publication. But he was resolved that it should be an anonymous effort. The reason for this decision may not have been entirely clear, even to his own mind. There is no doubt that he liked these adventures in anonymity.

"Yet why a second venture try?"
"A warrior thou, and ask me why!"

There is a fundamental element of Scott's character implicit in those two lines. All its strength, its love of hazardous living—its weakness, if you will. All the chivalrous audacities which Lockhart thought so splendid when they went right, and so 'painful' it they went wrong. There may be many who dream, as Scott dreamt, but he had found that he could make his dreams come true.

Yet there may have been good sense, as well as the spirit of adventure, in this decision. *Waverley* might succeed or fail, but if the new poem were as great a success as the best of its predecessors, it would not matter much either way, nor would Scott have complicated the greatness of his reputation by the writing of an indifferent novel.

He may have thought of Lord Howard's argument in the *Lay*

"for if he gain
He gains for us, but if he's crossed
'Tis but a single warrior lost."

He could always acknowledge it afterwards if he would.

But probably stronger than any of these arguments, certainly more consciously operative in his own mind, would be the desire to see how the novel would be received on its own merits, without the prestige of his name to influence its regard.

How many—or how few—must the secret include? There was William Erskine. He had seen the first chapters already. There was no escape there. There was, of course, Charlotte. It would go no further with her. He could always rely on Charlotte to play any game that he would, in his own spirit. It was less certain that she would read the book when it appeared. Neither of them worried about that.

There was James Ballantyne. He, also, had seen the earlier chapters. He must know. So must John. It would be the simplest way in the end. Besides, someone had got to copy the MS. Scott's hand was too well known in the publishing offices. It was before the era of typewriters. John could do that. He was not yet finding a gold-mine in the business of auctioneering, and Scott was resolute that he should not be a charge on the publishing firm, beyond his services in regard to any stock he could actually sell. He must work on commission now, it at all, for that business.

All the same, he had got to be provided for. Scott regarded that as naturally as that he should pay for Weber in the York asylum. He could not let John Ballantyne, or his family, want. He would as soon have let one of his dogs starve. Let John copy the book.

Beyond these, he made one confidant, though not till after publication. Then he wrote to John Morritt, sending him the book and asking his opinion concerning it. Morritt was far enough removed from the gossip of Edinburgh, and of a character that made it a safe thing to do.

The first volume was completed, and John had copied it by the time at which its author's life was at the jeopardy of Mr Weber's pistols. It was set up in the printing office, and John was commissioned to offer it to Constable as an anonymous work. It may have been recognised that he could lie better than James.

Constable listened. What he thought he kept to himself. He said he would take a few days to consider it. At the end of that time he offered £700 for the copyright of the complete novel. According to the sales of fiction in those days, it was an extraordinarily liberal offer. John conveyed it to Scott, who was not content. He said shrewdly that it was either too much—or too little. "If our fat friend had said £1,000, I should have been staggered."

Constable, like James, was laying on flesh as the years passed, and, unlike James, had a large framework on which to build. John went back to their fat friend, and talked again. Finding the offer was not accepted, Constable must have known who was the author with certainty, if he had doubted, to think which would go very nearly to calling him a fool. But he was a man who would not readily bid up from a price he had once named. It was because of that that the bargain about the *Lord of the Isles* was still in suspense. He may have thought that it would be difficult for John to maintain the fiction of anonymity, and get such an offer elsewhere.

If Scott meant it to be understood that his figure was £1,000, it led to nothing. Constable would not go above £700. Scott was equally firm in declining it. In the end, it was agreed that there should be no payment at all. Publisher and author should share the profits equally. Constable would have done better for himself had he given way.

Having no prospect of immediate money to come from the *Waverley* MS., Scott did not put it aside, but he finished other things first. He got the *Swift* finally off his hands. It had been an immense labour, carried out with his usual thoroughness, annotated extensively, and including much of the Dean's work which his own industry had discovered. He must have been glad when it left his desk. He earned £200 by writing articles on *Chivalry and the Drama*, for Constable's supplement to his *Encyclopaedia Brittannica*. Then he turned to *Waverley*, and finished it in a few weeks. The many-volumed *Swift* appeared in June. On the 4th. of that month, he commenced upon the two remaining volumes of *Waverley*, which were set up in type as they were written. He reckoned that his own work upon it was finished on July 1st., and with such celerity did the printing-office proceed that it was actually published within a week of that date. Morritt's three volumes were mailed to him on the 9th. For an indolent, unbusiness-like man, as Lockhart will have him to be, James seems to have managed his printing-works with considerable ability. The speed with which publication was carried through is often as remarkable as the quality of the work which was done under such conditions. It is not surprising that James Ballantyne & Co. had a good reputation in the trade.

The time in which Scott said that he wrote the major portion of the book—about twelve pages a day—is surprising, but not incredible. It is modified by a remark in an earlier letter to Morritt in which he mentions that, in the early days, in addition to writing the opening chapters, he had 'sketched other passages'. It is supported by the tale of the convivial gentleman in an adjoining house, who had to change places with his host, because he could overlook a window in which he saw a hand write. Through the length of the summer evening it never stopped. Page after page was written and laid on the heap beside the hand, but it still went on. His host said that was Walter Scott's house. You could see that hand every night. That was in June 1814. Young Lockhart, then a student for the Scottish bar, was one of that drinking-party. He could fix the date afterwards because he had only been in Edinburgh on a short visit on that occasion. Scott had his legal duties to attend to at that time of year. He wrote *Waverley* in the evenings, when his work was done.

It may have been no more than a natural haste to get the book out as fast as possible, or it may have been one of those experimental audacities in which Scott delighted, which caused it to be published in the "dead season". Publishers were even more sure then than they are now that all books ought to be published in one congested spate, as far as possible at the same time of year. An anonymous novel would not then be smothered by the out-pouring flood, it would be hurried forward with them on the tide of success. Publishers were as sure of that then as they now are that the sale of a book ought not to continue for more than six or eight weeks.

Had Scott given *Waverley* to a London publisher, he would have held it back till September. He would have said that he was not fool enough to get it out at the wrong time of year.

But Scott was doing his own publishing (with Constable's co-operation) on this occasion. It came out in July.

The first edition was 1,000 copies. Three small octavo volumes at £1. 1s. 0d. the set. In five weeks they were sold out. In August, a bolder policy printed 2,000 more. But before then indeed, before he had had time to learn more than the local Edinburgh opinion of this anonymous novel—Scott had gone off on a holiday where, for a few weeks, he would hear little of such events. He had joined a Commission to Inspect the Northern Light Houses. This Commission consisted of William Erskine (now Sheriff of the Orkneys) and three other good friends, who found it to be a duty of their office to sail once a year around the northern coasts and islands of Scotland to survey their charge.

Scott was glad to join such a party, for now that *Waverley* was off his hands he meant to finish the poem without more delay. If the novel failed, it would be a needed thing, and if it succeeded—well, it would be no worse for that.

He had a good two months holiday in the narrow quarters of the little ship that wound its way among the Hebrides' thousand islands and round the Orkneys and Shetlands, and must give a passing glance at every lighthouse on the mainland coast. He got the local colour he wanted for the new poem (for he had found his first Hebrides holiday had given him sufficient material), and he gained a knowledge of the Orkneys which would make a novel of a future day.

The head of the expedition was an engineer, Stephenson, already of a growing fame, with whom he was specially glad to talk. He said you could gain more from these "professional men of talent" than from the wit of more conventional celebrities. The party came back with the record of six weeks which had passed without a word of discord. "Each," Scott made record, "seemed anxious to submit his own wishes to those of his friends. The consequence was that, by judicious arrangement, all were gratified in their turn, and frequently he who made some sacrifices to the views of his companions was rewarded by some unexpected gratification calculated particularly for his own amusement. We had constant exertion, a succession of wild and uncommon scenery, good humour on board, and objects of animation and interest when we went ashore:—*Sed fugit interea—fugit irrevocabile tempus*."

It was a condition of good-natured kindliness which seems to have been natural among company of which Scott formed a part.

Owing to the wandering nature of the expedition, and the localities visited, it had been impossible, as the posts were then, to receive any regular correspondence, and even Scott's own letters must have been dispatched irregularly, though it was his rule, on the few occasions when their holidays were not together, that Charlotte should not be disappointed of her expectation of a letter by every post.

Yet one piece of news reached him a few days before his return, to be confirmed as he landed in the Clyde by a heart-broken letter from his friend, the Duke of Buccleuch, to say that his wife was dead. *Fugit irrevocabile tempus*, indeed. It was a friend's sorrow, and his own too. The two families had been on terms of very close intimacy in the old days of visiting between Lassswade and Dalkeith House. The Duke did not survive this bereavement for many years. His young son would reign in his place.

Long after, Scott, a ruined widowed man, of broken health, walking with such difficulty that he would notice, with a gallant smile at the absurdity, that a flock of sheep could pass him, would visit the boy-duke at Drumlanrig, and old memories would return of when he had taken his young wife to visit the boy's parents there, and he would write that night in his diary:

> "God bless him! His father and I loved each other well, and his beautiful mother had as much of the angel as is permitted to walk this earth. I see the balcony from which they welcomed poor Charlotte and me, long ere the ascent was surmounted, streaming out their white handkerchiefs from the battlements. There were four merry people that day—now one sad individual is all that remains."

But he had other thoughts as he drove post-haste from Glasgow to Edinburgh, where he must pause for a few hours to see Constable and the Ballantynes, before he rode on to Abbotsford. He came back to triumph. Anonymous, out of season, it might be, but the novel was a sure success. Critics, hesitating, differing, cancelling each other out in the usual way, were yet agreed about that. *Waverley* was a new thing, as the *Lay* had been nine years ago. The 3,000 copies were gone. Constable said the book was still in demand. If James would print another 1,000, he would take a third. So it was agreed. They were large figures in those days. In November they would be printing again.

Constable wanted to talk about the new poem also, and, at last, he found Scott ready to meet his terms. Refusing Scott's price £5,000, he had finally offered £1,500 for a half-share. That had been some months ago. Lockhart says it might have been settled then, but for Ballantyne's efforts to add a condition about taking over more stock, concerning which Scott now gave way. He adds "It may easily be believed that John's management during a six weeks absence had been such as to render it doubly convenient to the poet to have this matter settled." If we take John Ballantyne at Lockhart's valuation it is easy to believe anything, or at least anything bad; but, otherwise, it is rather puzzling to imagine what he had done. He was in business now as an auctioneer. The sign of John Ballantyne & Co., Booksellers, was kept up for many years, but, in fact, the firm was dead. There was only stock to be realised, and floating bills to be paid off. In another place Lockhart hints that Constable had given help in some financial difficulty during Scott's absence, and, if this were so, we can understand that Scott would feel an obligation of honour not to delay further in closing the deal. But then, Lockhart hints that John, from whatever despicable motive, had concealed Constable's friendly services from Scott's knowledge. In fact, Lockhart attacks John from so many angles that when he knocks him off the bench with a blow on one side of his head, he is apt to knock him back with a blow on the other, as Mr Squeers did with his hopeful son.

John can do nothing right. It is his duty to sell a huge stock, for the existence of which he has a minor responsibility, and to assist in keeping afloat a ghastly list of liabilities, for which his share of responsibility is about the same. Neither of them is a simple matter to undertake. If he fails to sell the stock—isn't it just what you'd expect from a man like that? If he is persistent in his efforts to get Constable to buy it—doesn't it show what sort of a man he is? If he can't keep the liabilities afloat any longer—hasn't Lockhart told us from the first that he is no good? If he wriggles along, with a renewal here, and an instalment there, isn't it just the sort of thing with which you would expect such a man to be occupied? But even Lockhart admits that he had one virtue, if such we call it. He loved Scott like a dog, and for that we might forgive him for more than there may be occasion to do. At least, Scott, who was most concerned, seems to have found forgiveness easy.

Lockhart allows that John was a good auctioneer. Scott used to be a frequent visitor at his new auction-rooms in Princes

Street on sale days when in Edinburgh. He helped the bidding, and sometimes bought. That, Lockhart suggests, is why John was "really one of the most plausible and imposing of the Puff tribe". He gives praise with a sneer. John hesitated, in Scott's presence, to develop his propensity to be a bad auctioneer to its natural dimensions!

When Lockhart gives us facts, we need to examine his inferences with care, as they are not always logical. When he gives us inferences without facts, we need to be more careful yet. We shall never know what happened in Edinburgh while Scott sailed in the Northern seas. We may think what we will.

CHAPTER LIV.

There might be many to guess correctly who the author of *Waverley* might be, but a guess, however confident, is different from a known thing. Other rumours, other speculations, had place. Some even suggested that the author might be Tom Scott, now in Canada with the 71st. Scott wrote, telling him this. Of course, he didn't wish to saddle him with a book that he had never seen, but still—Tom might keep a shut mouth. And why shouldn't Tom write a book? Why not, at least, the outline of a Canadian tale, with local scenery, local dialect, local customs marked out, and Scott would "cobble" it into shape, and it would be published in Tom's name, and confusion would be worse confounded than it was now. Anyway, it might put money into Tom's pocket. Possibly £500. And, anyway, he shouldn't do it for nothing. Let Tom send on such notes, such skeleton of a tale, as he would, and he could draw on Scott for £100 at the same time, at fifty days from sight, and he would find that it would be met.

But unfortunately for the possibility of a good book, and the certainty of a good joke, Tom didn't rise to the bait.

Scott had other letters to write almost immediately that he got back to Abbotsford, of a different character from that which he dispatched to Canada.

The settlement in Edinburgh had left his own pocket empty, as such adjustments were apt to do. But he thought that he had, at least, arranged so that he would escape further financial demands from that direction for some months to come, while he would be finishing the poem, and writing a second novel which was already projected in his mind, and he was even wrong about that, in an unexpected way. And, for the first time, there was a serious difference, and a sharp correspondence with James Ballantyne.

If we take these troubles in exact chronological order, James must come first. It may be remembered that, in the first years of a growing business, he had borrowed several amounts to supply capital which had been urgently needed, and it had been treated on the books as though he had himself provided it, so that his stake in the business should appear equal to that of Scott. These amounts were liable to be called in at agreed notice, to his obvious embarrassment, or that of the firm—or, more probably, both. In fact, more than one of these items had been called for, and—more or less—repaid. The difficulties with the John Ballantyne bills, and the persistent rumour of failure which had attached at one time to the name of that firm, could not fail to affect the credit of one that was allied to it so closely. And this damage to its credit had come, as we know, at a period of national financial crisis, when all business had been difficult to carry on. James had had a bad time. It is to his credit—and that of his partners in different ways and degrees—that he had pulled through as he had. He had shown a bold front to the world, had continued to turn out good work with regularity, had been supported with good orders both from London and Edinburgh, and had survived while many concerns of far greater original resources had fallen beside the way. The firm had had a good deal of banking accommodation, largely, no doubt, through Scott's influence, and had strained it to the utmost, as is inevitable under such conditions. Its London customers, like those in its own city, paid almost entirely by long-dated bills, as was the general trade custom at that time. When the amount of these bills got too large, and the state of the publishing trade in London too precarious, for it to be easy to discount them separately, an arrangement had been made with Sir William Forbes & Co. to pool them in one account, which could be drawn on to a percentage only of the total deposited, and to an agreed maximum. As bills matured and if they were met, about which there would be a constant anxiety, new credit would be released. To estimate the resources of a coming month under such circumstances would be a matter of elaborate calculation, and partial guesswork. The liabilities that would have to be met, and the wages that would have to be paid, would be much easier to work out.

Through these difficulties, with many anxious arguments at the bank, many expedients and evasions, many last-minute borrowings, James had carried on and pulled through. He appears to have avoided, in the main, troubling his senior partner with the details of these worries, though John knew them well enough, and doubtless gave what help he could.

James may have been influenced in his reticence mainly by the knowledge that Scott had his hands overfull already with the affairs of the John Ballantyne bills, and a loyal desire not to worry him further. He may otherwise have been restrained by the fact that the difficulties were increased through his own capital being diminished, by the forced return of the borrowed items of which it had been partly composed. He made new borrowings where he could, but this had become harder to do, partly because credit was shaky, partly because people had less to lend.

He had also committed an irregularity of procedure in relation to those early borrowings, the nature of which he never appears to have been able to appreciate properly, and concerning which he defended himself strenuously when Scott became aware of it, and took the view which any lawyer, and any competent business man (and Scott was both) would be inclined to do.

Although these monies had appeared on the books as James's

personal capital, he had given the lenders the firm's bills in acknowledgement.

He said he had done it in good faith, never thinking of concealment. If Scott had not known, it was only because he had not asked.

He said (with probable truth) that he could never have got these amounts at all if he had refused the firm's signature, and that, at the time, the money had been so much needed that he had only been conscious of the importance of getting it. Scott had seen the need for the additional capital as clearly as he at the time, and if he had mentioned that the firm's acknowledgement was required he was sure that he would have raised no difficulty.

All these things may have been true, even including James's contention that he had acted with absolute good faith; but they did not touch the real point at all. If these amounts were loans to the firm, for which it was responsible, they should have been entered on the firm's books, and should not have gone to James's capital account. They had enabled James to claim a proportion of profit which may have been more than the interest he paid for them. The fact that that interest was paid by him, not by the firm, so far as his own book-keeping showed, was conclusive on this point. He had treated them, and had the benefit of them, as though they were personal loans to himself. He couldn't have it both ways.

Among these items, there had been a sum of £600 which he had borrowed from his younger brother, Alexander, now in business at Kelso, to which there had been some more recent additions. Now Alexander had his own difficulties, and while Scott had been inspecting lighthouses, he had asked for the return of the money, which James had told him that he couldn't have. Alexander didn't wish to embarrass his brother, but he had his own need. He held the firm's bills, on which he could have sued. Being brothers, they wouldn't talk about that. But, being brothers, Alexander did expect that James would do what he could. There was the property at Foulis Close. Could he have a mortgage on that? So he had asked, or so James had offered to him. James thought it a good plan. He would not give it without Scott's consent, but he seems to have thought that he would get that without difficulty. Instead of that, Scott met the request with an emphatic veto. He went further. He said that James had no right to have given his brother the firm's bills. He must get them back at once, and substitute his personal paper—which was not easy for James to do. But Scott was firm, and in the end, he had his way, Alexander abandoning the legal position which he certainly held for the more precarious one of a personal claim on his brother, rather than be the cause of an acute quarrel between Scott and James which seemed otherwise unavoidable.

James sent Alexander copies of his letters to Scott and Scott's replies, so that Alexander might see how serious the position was. He wrote covering letters to Alexander, in which he invites him to notice how clearly he has the best of the argument, and how unreasonable Scott can be. It is a point on which few who read them will be likely to concur.

But James brought forward one argument which was ingenious, though not convincing. It may be remembered that Scott had made a loan of £3,000 to the firm in its early days, of which £1,200 had been supplied by his brother John. It appears that when that £1,200 was advanced Scott had stipulated that (if his brother required) it should be secured by a mortgage upon the plant, to which James had agreed. There had never been such a mortgage, but there was the fact. Scott had wanted to protect his brother, and James had agreed at once! James had wanted to protect his, and there was all this row!

The reply was obvious. The whole of Scott's £3,000 had been a loan to the firm in addition to the capital he had invested level with James. The amount found by Alexander was part of the capital credited to James. But James would not see that.

It may have been the stubbornly illogical nature of James's correspondence on this subject that roused Scott to extremities of expression very unusual in his own letters. On September 24th we find him writing:

> "All those who advanced money to me would be equally glad, I promise you, to be paid, and I can hardly keep some of them quiet. Yet their money *to five times the amount* was equally advanced to the concern...."

He added a footnote:

> "I wish to God that you could send me £25 or £30 just now, as I am almost penniless. You know where my last quarter from Exchequer went.

The allusion to the amounts which had been advanced by Scott's own friends points to the fact that Morritt was not the only one who was now holding renewals of the John Ballantyne bills. These bills had been given by John Ballantyne & Co. to James Ballantyne & Co. in payment for printing of that wretched stock. James Ballantyne & Co. were still responsible for them. As it had become impossible to renew them in banking or commercial quarters, Scott had placed some of theme with his own signature upon them, among his friends, till the stock could be sold.

Within three weeks of the letter quoted there was a new trouble arising from Abbotsford, 'Charles Erskine wishes his money, as he has made a purchase of land—paid he must be forthwith, as his advance was friendly and confidential'.

It appears that Charles Erskine had not actually discounted bills. He had lent £500, and some long-dated bills had been deposited with him as collateral security. Scott goes on to instruct John to obtain the money by a further sale of stock. If Constable jibs, he must negotiate it with Murray or Longmans in London. He can offer them a new novel, if necessary, from the unknown author of Waverley. He is to get to work at once, and let Scott know what he can do. One way or other, the money has got to be found.

John acknowledged the letter promptly. He would carry out his instructions. He had another subject on which to write. There had been a poinding in Edinburgh. In other words, the bailiffs had been in on James Ballantyne's premises. It was an affair of taxes. James had been away in Kelso (probably to argue with Alexander) and John had been sent for, to pay them out.

It was the kind of incident which Scott found it hard to endure. In his personal transactions he paid promptly. He might run risks, but even his audacities had order, method, and foresight. He knew that it was such incidents which destroy credit. It might mean another £1,000 to be found during the next few months. Was he not always telling both James and John to let him know in good time, and he would see that such incidents did not occur? People talk in Edinburgh. He may have felt a personal sensitiveness, for it is almost impossible to think that his connection with the firm was not very widely known. It is significant that in the controversy with James and Alexander's loan, James never appears to have suggested that there was a secrecy about Scott's partnership, though it was an argument which would have been useful, if it were true; and he writes to his brother without reserve, or suggestion of confidence, treating it as a known thing.

Under all the circumstances, Scott's reply to John may be described as mild:

"17th Oct. 1814.

Dear John,

I received your letter with the astonishing news of James's utter disregard to his own credit. He promised to let me have account of his prospects, and consult me upon the management of his cash affairs, but he has kept his word but lamely. He is even worse than you, for you generally give a day or two's notice at least of the chance of dishonour, and this poinding is little better. His Kelso expedition has proved a fine one."

He may have written to James with added vigour, for we have James's reply, which is more agitated than coherent, and far worse constructed than his letters usually are. He says to Scott in effect: "I am in the trenches. You are at headquarters, thirty miles away. What do you know of wounds?"

"23rd October 1814.

Dear Sir.

I received your packet containing the preface to Waverley, and copy for the poem. It is quite needless to say anything more of the poinding. It is one of fifty things which happen to sour the temper, and I by no means wonder that you see the matter under an aspect different from that in which I regard it, and apply to it epithets which do not strike me as justly belonging to it. Meantime, I trust the printing will cease to be that burthen which hitherto it has been. As to my own expenditure, I have not yet been able to take the funds for it with anything like regularity. On the contrary, often when I had appropriated a sum to pay my own little accounts, have I been forced to turn it into the channel of wages or bills. To this irritation I have no other hope than to be long subject. One glance will show that it cannot be otherwise. But as to despondency, I once more say that I know nothing about it; and as to these taxes, they figured in my mind as no more than fifty other equal difficulties that at this moment press upon it equally. Had I ever had it in my power (I mean since I took up these affairs) to have a little before me, the case would have been different. In the way of retrenchment, I do whatever I can. There are some objects which I do not retrench, simply because it is likely my mother has not long to live, and because I have not the fortitude to make her last days less happy than they have been. This, I must confess, compels me, to one or two extravagances, particularly my gig and my horse.

...There is another claim for £25, made up of old taxes due four years back on a place I had at Newhaven. I could just as soon pay the national debt at present, poind where they will. 'A poor thing, Sir.—Poor, miserable poor!' As to borrowing, I have pretty well got the better of shame but really I don't know anybody that would trust me. The cause of all this is, to myself at least, perfectly clear and sufficient—*beginning in debt, without capital, and always heavily in advance.*"

Knowing Scott, we may easily guess that this letter had no ungenerous reply. Perhaps he paid the penalty of his irritation in the settlement of the Newhaven tax! These matters were over now, but the £500 for Charles Erskine remained to be found, and as to that John had an idea.

He had failed with Constable, with whom he most often did fail. Constable was a man who could only be got to say yes with great difficulty, if he had once said no. He was sometimes almost too quick to say no to John. He may have preferred to be asked by Scott himself. He may have thought that the slower he was in taking over that wretched stock, the more good bargains for poems and novels it would enable him to make. He may have thought that if he didn't, no one else would. Anyway, he said no now, and John loved him even less than before.

He wrote to Scott suggesting that while an unwritten novel by the author of *Waverley* would be a good bait for the London publishers, a new edition of *Waverley* itself (which was now needed) would be even better. So, no doubt, it would; and there was no legal obstacle. The deals with Constable had been for each separate edition as it came out. But neither Scott nor Constable had really understood the bargain in that spirit, whatever might be its strict legal interpretation. It had been a joint adventure, in which they shared the profits by a percentage agreed at the start.

It was understood to be Constable's book in the trade. Had a rival firm brought it out, he would probably have had apoplexy, for he was getting to be a heavy, full-blooded man. Was he not known in London as the Napoleon of the book-trade? In Scott's own circles, was he not called the Czar? That a rival firm should publish one of his own books!

John chuckled to himself, thinking that he would please Scott with an unexpectedly good sale of Culdees, and the Eastern Tales, and other treasures which the trade would not appreciate at their true worth, and do Constable one in the eye at the same time. And then he got Scott's reply, and his face fell:

"Dear John,

> Your expedients are all wretched so far as regards me. I never will give Constable, or anyone, room to say I have broken my word with him in the slightest degree. If I lose everything else, I will at least keep my honour unblemished; and I do hold myself bound in honour to offer him Waverley, while he shall continue to comply with the conditions annexed."

So there was no use in saying any more about that. John approached Longmans, they bought the required stock, and Charles Erskine had the £500. Longmans were to have the London publishing of the next novel, and Constable was to have it in Edinburgh. Constable, though he had refused the stock, was brought into the deal to that extent by Scott's wish. The whole matter had to be arranged through John, for, if Scott had not written *Waverley*, what concern was it of his?

CHAPTER LV.

The *Lord of the Isles* was finished on Christmas Day, 1814, and published about three weeks later. It had not been easily written—had, indeed, in its later stages, been a matter of forcing, rather than spontaneous growth. Yet Scott thought well of it, and expected success. He meant it to be the last of these long narrative poems, but he meant the curtain to fall upon a final triumph. On January 19th before he could know anything of its reception, he wrote to Morritt: "It closes my poetic labours upon an extended scale".

It was true that he had another such poem—*Harold the Dauntless*—on hand. It had been on hand for some time. But that—if it were ever finished—was to be published as by the author of the *Bridal of Triermain*. He had begun it in the same light, lilting, flippant rhythm that made the most serious things sound rather like a joke of a new kind:

"Woe to the realms that he wasted! For there
Was shedding of blood, and rending of hair,
Rape of maiden, and slaughter of priest,
Gathering of ravens and wolves to the feast.

When he hoisted his banner black,
Before him was battle, behind him wrack,
And he burned the churches, that heathen Dane,
To light his band to their barks again."

Quite a cheerful note. But somehow, it wasn't easy to keep it up. Perhaps in another mood—at a later day.

But the *Lord of the Isles* was a different matter. He had put all his best into that poem. It was true that the sales of *Rokeby*, large as they were, did not nearly reach those of the earlier poems, but he had a theory about that. He said that the *Lay* was a poem of style, *Marmion* of description, the *Lady of the Lake* of incident, and *Rokeby* of character. And people did not care for character in a poem.

The distinctions hold some truth, though not much. But the comparative failure of *Rokeby* was not because it was a poem of character, nor because Byron had a growing popularity. It was because it was of comparatively poor quality.

Rokeby, separately considered, is a poem which it is easy to praise. It contains splendid scenes. The burning of Rokeby Castle, the interrupted execution—they are Scott at his (almost) best. But the general level is not merely unequal to such parts as these, it is definitely below that of the earlier poems. Its failure is not because it is a poem of character, although it is true that character is portrayed in a new way. In the *Lady of the Lake*, it is indicated with a brevity which is genius. It is clearly drawn with few lines. Here is character more consciously filled in. It approaches nearer to the style by which, in the prose novels, Scott was to win a different success. But there were large parts of it which lacked the old spontaneity, which were more or less mechanically written, which suggested that, like Southey and Wordsworth and other of his contemporaries, Scott was in danger of degenerating into a professional poet.

Rokeby was little more than a good novel in rhyme, and Scott's earlier romantic poems are much greater than that. It is redeemed by one or two scenes of the old wizardry, and by its incomparable lyrics, in which Scott excelled himself. It has nothing like that first of all literary ballads, *Alice Brand*, which was thrown carelessly, as a kind of extra, into the *Lady of the Lake*; but otherwise its lyrics compare with those of any of the previous poems. Apart from the lyrics, it is inferior, particularly on its technical side: it is inferior in the melody of words.

Had Scott seen more clearly that the comparative failure of *Rokeby* was not a fault of fickleness on the part of the public; nor of character replacing incident (it has plenty of that); nor of Byron's competition; but resulted from the inferior texture of the poem itself, there might have been a better prospect of the new victory at which he aimed. And yet, perhaps—in part—he did see it. And he certainly made a deliberate effort to recover the old freedom and the old power.

That was just what was wrong. It was a deliberate effort of genius, and the spontaneity of genius is a better thing.

Yet it was far from failure. It is a much better poem than

Rokeby: there can be no doubt of that. Its plot is at least equally good. In some respects the two plots are complementary. *Rokeby* is a tale of two men who could still be of a mutual generosity, although they were rivals in love. *The Lord of the Isles* is the even less probable one of two women who could show the same spirit to one another, though they loved the same man. They both illustrate the wide gulf there is between Scott's ideality, and that of our contemporary novelists. They would have us understand that love is a force before which all barriers should go down. It is Scott's continual theme that honour is more than love.

The plot is so good, and so adroitly handled, that we may be tempted to regret that Scott did not give it the length and freedom of a prose presentation. The idea of a woman disguising herself in a page's dress is one of which Scott, like Shakespeare, was always fond, but it has never been better handled than it is here, perhaps because Edith never shows any masculine attributes. She is still a timid girl, and when she shows courage, it is in a woman's way.

The conception of her being sentenced to be hanged by her own brother, and holding back from the word that would save her life lest it should betray, not her lover, but the man she loves, is one of the finest in romantic literature. But the whole poem is splendid in imagination. The scene of the interrupted wedding: the Abbot's curse that was changed to blessing: the night-scene in Cormac's hut: the scene in Isabel's cell: the interrupted execution: the description of Bannockburn:—if these be failure, what should we require to call it success? And yet if we compare it with the earlier poems, all the nobility, all the high qualities of imagination may be here, but something of the old magic is gone. It is a splendid effort: but the others were not efforts; and—significantly—it has only one lyric. There is nothing of song, except the *Brooch of Lorn*.

The description of Bannockburn is something which only Scott could have done. It is immaterial that he was probably misled by tradition as to the actual tactics of the battle. He gives us battle-poetry which is incomparable, except for one other—his own Flodden, and before that it must recede to a second place.

And yet—it has its own excellence, and its closing scene is of a good kind. Let Wordsworth (having finished the writing of great poetry) write rhymed prose for thirty years if he will. Scott prefers to make his exit in a different way. He shows us Argentine riding back to die, and his own song dies on that most tender note of mourning for his dead friend, the Duchess of Buccleuch.

CHAPTER LVI.

A week after the publication of the *Lord of the Isles*, Scott sent to James Ballantyne to call upon him at North Castle Street. Scott sat at his desk in the library, and James took the visitor's chair.

"Well, James, I have given you a week. What are people saying about the *Lord of the Isles*?"

James was not quick to reply.

"Disappointment?" Scott queried.

The printer's silence was sufficient answer. He says that Scott looked 'rather blank for a few seconds'. It was not what he had expected to hear. Then he recovered his cheerfulness. "Well, well, James, so be it. But you know we mustn't droop, for we can't afford to give over." He said goodnight to James, and turned back to the third volume of *Guy Mannering*. If the poem had failed, he must have the novel out all the sooner. It was published within three weeks of that night.

A month later, after an interval of six years, he set out for a visit to London. (Charlotte came with him on this occasion, and Sophia also (on an invitation from Joanna Baillie, with whom she would stay, and who would show her the sights), for he came on holiday now. Not to work at the Museum, or to visit booksellers, but to take the respite that a man may who can look back on a long warfare that has ended in victory. For he was now as sure of his position as of himself. In the financial sky there might still be clouds, but they were breaking apart. For *Guy Mannering* had duplicated—had even exceeded—the success of *Waverley*. Published anonymously, without the prestige of his name, they had won for him the assurance of a second fortune, and a second throne. To write poetry is a precarious thing. A wayward, difficult art. To need money, and to depend on poetry to bring it, is to be doomed indeed. The public could have two novels a year if they wanted. Or three. But he would take a holiday first.

They stayed as usual with M. Dumerge, Charlotte and he. They had a brilliant reception. He might know that the *Lord of the Isles* was not selling as the earlier poems had done, but it had an immense sale, none the less. During the six years of his absence, his fame had grown, had matured. Everyone had read him now. The mystery of the novels—to which the answer was not hard to guess—gave an added glamour to the poet's name.

And it was a different London from that of six years ago, when it had been under the shadow of prolonged and unvictorious war. Last year it had been gay with triumph. Napoleon was in Elba. The voices in the Edinburgh Review that had counselled surrender and foretold defeat had become silent then. In Vienna, where men divided the world anew, England had the first voice.

Now, before Scott reached London, there was a new excitement. Napoleon had escaped from Elba. No one doubted what the end would be. But would he be able to fan the ashes of strife to a new flame? News had not been awaited with such eagerness in the darkest days of the war.

It was not only in literary circles that the Scotts were feted. Ministers of State were glad to welcome the famous author who had used his great influence consistently through times of critical unrest on the side of established order: the highest of social circles sought to recognise the poet whose flame of patriotism had been an inspiration to England in her war-weariest hours.

Byron sought opportunity to meet him: the Prince Regent delighted to do him honour.

In this atmosphere, those past difficulties about the Ballantyne bills shrunk to their true insignificance: the provision of the money for that Kaeside land to the east of Abbotsford did not seem likely to be difficult to arrange....

He met Byron in John Murray's drawing-room in Albemarle Street. There had been doubts, in Scott's mind at least, as to whether there were common ground on which they could meet congenially. Not that he failed in generosity of appreciation. James Ballantyne had found him reading the *Giaour* a few nights after he had conveyed the news that the *Lord of the Isles* was a comparative failure in the view of the trade. Byron had sent the book, with a graceful inscription: *To the Monarch of Parnassus, from one of his subjects.* James asked if he might borrow it, and it had been handed over with the reflection: 'James, Byron hits the mark where I don't even pretend to fledge my arrow'. But they differed widely in politics, in religion, and in ideals of the conduct of life.

Yet, in fact, when they met, they were good friends. Scott's sympathetic tolerance, which forgave all, and yet conceded nothing, conquered, as it so often did. They talked of many things, and he concluded that Byron had no very fixed opinions either in religion or politics. He told him that he thought, in the end, he would 'retreat upon the Catholic faith', and become austere in his penances. Byron showed Scott his best side, as most men did. Scott wrote afterwards that he had 'Always continued to think that a crisis of life was arrived, in which a new career of fame was opened to him, and that had he been permitted to start upon it, he would have obliterated the memory of such parts of his life as friends would wish to forget'.

The Prince Regent entertained him more than once. He had an incongruous, but obviously genuine admiration for Scott's poetry. Scott's opinion of the Regent may be understood from the fact that he declined to give it. But he thought of two things which it would be possible to say when he was asked, and he said them both.

An absurd tale got into circulation that the Prince had asked him explicitly whether he were the author of *Waverley* and that he had given a solemn denial. James heard it, and when Scott got back to Edinburgh, he asked him if it were true. Scott said no. He did not know what he should have said in such circumstances, but 'I was never put to the test'. He added that the Prince had a reputation for good manners: which is in itself enough to dispose of such a tale, yet it lives on to this day.

Scott's duties as Clerk of Session took him back to Edinburgh, and he was there when Waterloo was fought. He was eager to visit the continent, and that battle having been sufficiently decisive in its results to quieten Charlotte's objection, he set off as soon as the Court rose in the company of three of his younger Abbotsford neighbours, John Scott of Gala, Robert Bruce. and Alexander Pringle.

They took coach to Harwich, travelling through Cambridge, where two of the party had recently taken their degrees, stayed there overnight and preserved Scott's incognito successfully, but he was recognised by the master of the Harwich packet, who drank his health so often that they felt it was due to Providence, rather than to him, that they landed safely on the quay at Helvoestleys.

Scott had taken a holiday of several months—almost the only one of his adult life—from any serious literary work, and he now recommenced it in earnest. He had a contract with Constable to write an account of his experiences and impressions abroad, and he did this in the form of daily letters, which it was his habit to send to Charlotte when they were parted. He wrote them as a series supposed to be sent by an elderly bachelor to various relatives and friends. They all went to Charlotte first, and then to whoever was afterwards intended to have them, Captain John, or Christian Rutherford, Lord Somerville or Dr. Douglas of Galashiels, (from whom Abbotsford had been purchased), on the understanding that they would be passed on to William Erskine and James, who were entrusted with the excision of private matter, and any other changes which might be needed in preparing them for the press. They were published in the following January under the style of *Paul's Letters to his Kinsfolk*, and had a sale of eight or nine thousand copies. That paid for the tour, with a good margin. Scott also wrote a rather long poem, *The Field of Waterloo*, for charity. The proceeds were to go to the families of the men who had been killed in the battle. Its only justification is the object for which it was written. It has a vigorous passage descriptive of the repulse of the Old Guard, apart from which it is worthless. It shows the kind of thing that he would have done frequently if he had degenerated into a laureate, or any other form of professional poet. Scott could not write a good poem (other than a brief lyric) without years of working upon it. No one can.

On this tour, Scott met most of the monarchs, soldiers, and statesmen, who had been most prominent in the later years of the war, and were now looking after the interests of their countries or themselves in the settling of a peace which was giving them almost equal anxieties. He met the Duke of Wellington, to whom he offered something as near to hero-worship as he did to any living man. He was introduced to the Czar of Russia at a dinner given by the Earl of Cathcart. The Czar may have heard of him before, or he may not. The Earl had done his best to explain Mr Scott's many excellences before the introduction. He had presumably said something about Scott's energy in raising that Yeomanry regiment which had (in fact) never been any use, unless its existence had encouraged the Government to send other troops abroad. The Earl may not have made himself very clear. Many languages met in Paris in those days, and mistakes were common. The Czar understood that Mr Scott was a vaguely important, vaguely valiant man. He was anxious to be polite. Mr. Scott wore the official uniform of the Sheriff of Selkirkshire. He was splendid in red and blue. He was plainly lame. The Czar enquired in what action he had taken his wound? Scott replied that he had not been wounded: he had been lame from childhood. The Czar said that the Earl had already informed him of Mr Scott's distinguished military career. Scott looked at the Earl, and the Earl looked worried. He tried to assist the situation by saying that he had served in a sense—in a Yeomanry regiment—a kind of landsturm. The Czar observed that he had at last encountered a modest man. "Under what commander had he served?" "Under M. le Chevalier Rae." "In what actions had he been?" Scott said gravely that he had been present at the battle of the Cross Causeway, and the affair of Moredun Mill. The Czar was politely impressed. If he did not know the names of all the glorious victories of his gallant allies, he was not likely to reveal his ignorance.... Scott caught sight of Lord Cathcart's face, and realised that the conversation had better change. Laughter might have been hard to explain.

But Scott's great conquest was Platoff, the Cossack Hetman, whom he met at the same dinner. They could not speak a word in common, and who or what he supposed Scott to be is beyond guessing. Someone may have told him that he wrote *Mazeppa*. Anyway, he jumped off his horse next morning in the Rue de la Paix, and left his escort staring, while he ran to Scott, kissing his cheeks. With an interpreter's help, he invited him to see his Cossacks reviewed, which Scott was pleased to do. The Hetman would lend him a most quiet horse. So the Hetman did, and Scott saw the review, but he had no idea what it was all about.

Scott came back through London with Scott of Gala, while their two friends went on to Switzerland. He met Charles Matthews and Daniel Terry there, and there was probably a good business reason for this, for Terry produced a play next spring called *Guy Mannering*, which had a long run, and was revived frequently for many years afterwards, to the probable profit of the author of that anonymous novel.

He stopped at Kenilworth, among other places, on the way back, and examined the castle ruins with care, and arrived home at the Abbotsford cottage (it was still a cottage in these days) somewhat later than he had been expected. He found James Skene there, having come on a friendly call, supposing that he had been already back, and James Ballantyne, who had brought particulars from Edinburgh of how business had gone during his absence, and whom Charlotte had kept till he should arrive, and between business and friendship, and all the domestic chatter, he sat down in the drawing-room without noticing that Charlotte and the girls had renovated it, and newly upholstered the furniture to surprise him on his return, till the maddened women couldn't keep silence any longer. And after that he was so full of apologies that he couldn't talk of anything else..

And in the morning there was trouble of another kind, for since it had become plain that the Yeomanry regiment was never likely to see active service, Scott had sold his chargers, except Daisy, a pure-white horse of which he was particularly fond, partly because he would stand so absolutely still to be mounted and his lameness caused him a particular awkwardness in getting on or off a horse, though, when he was once up, we was a better rider than most.

But now Daisy put his ears back, and reared and threw him when he had one foot in the stirrup. He was as quiet as ever when Tom Purdie mounted him, and he had been well-conducted in his master's absence. Peter had ridden him regularly into Melrose with the post-bag, to give him exercise. But he was determined that Scott should not ride him again, and after a week of abortive trials, even of experimenting with Tom Purdie in some of Scott's clothes, to which Daisy made no objection, the fact had to be recognised and the horse sold.

It was an inexplicable puzzle, and Scott sold the horse with lasting regret. He felt that he would never have—would never have occasion to have—another blood-horse of that quality again. Henceforward he would be riding a cob. It was as though the chapter of his youth had closed.

But he bought the Kaeside land, on which his heart was set, and he wrote to Joanna Baillie that Walter (who was fourteen now) could ride well, and he went into Edinburgh and made a contract with Constable for another novel, which was to be called the *Antiquary*, and on which he could get to work at once.

And then there came an opportunity for "Master Walter

Scott, younger of Abbotsford" to make a public show of the skill in horsemanship of which his father had boasted, for the old feud between Selkirk and Yarrow—between Buccleuch and Home—was revived in a solemn football match which was made occasion for a semi-military pageant, at which Walter carried the banner of Buccleuch. And Scott wrote a ballad for the occasion, and James Hogg wrote another, and probably thought (and may have been right) that his was the better of the two.

It was on this occasion that the more distinguished members of the company were invited to dinner at Bowhill, and the Ettrick Shepherd, who was included in that category, would have sat down at the children's table in error, but that Scott took his arm, and explained that that one was reserved for the 'little lords and ladies', and unfortunately Hogg didn't hear the word 'little' and thought indignantly that there was a table there at which he was not considered good enough to sit. And though Scott put him between himself and Scott of Harden, the Shepherd sulks audibly in his autobiography at the fancied insult. But he did not quarrel with Scott on this occasion, because he had done so only last winter, about a similar misunderstanding, so that, when he had fallen ill, Scott had been obliged to help him with an elaborate obliquity through a hatter on the North Bridge; and Hogg had afterwards written in abject apology, never hoping to be forgiven, and Scott had told him to drop it, and come to breakfast. So it would have been rather soon to start quarrelling again, especially when it had to be all on one side, because Scott never would quarrel with the Ettrick Shepherd, let him behave as he would.

CHAPTER LVII.

It is at the close of 1815 that James Ballantyne appears on the stage in a new part. The fact that a printer is associated in business with a man of genius is no sufficient reason why his private affairs should be subsequently exposed, and his letters, though obviously of a most confidential and personal character, published after his death. Having said this, it is bare justice to Lockhart to add that it was the Trustees of James Ballantyne who were primarily responsible for this publicity. It is a fact that, in February 1816, Scott took over the entire ownership of the printing business, and James became his manager, and this position continued for about five years. The Trustees held certain accounts which were agreed at the time, and thought that their publication would disparage Scott. Lockhart was easily able to show that this idea was baseless, and he had some justification for publishing certain private letters of James to Scott, which was an indecency which he had not previously intended to commit. He was foolish enough to retort, with some provocation, and with his usual incapacity to understand figures, making charges against James Ballantyne which are nearly as groundless as those which the Trustees made against Scott, and he was provoked to expose an incident which occurred during James's subsequent management of the business which is detrimental to his memory, though there is something to be said on James's side which Lockhart was not careful to observe. When recriminatory charges have been flung backwards and forwards it is better to examine the facts, of whatever nature, rather than to pass them in silence, if only because the truth is most often the cleaner thing. In this case the circumstances in which James resigned his partnership are entirely creditable to all concerned.

James, a shy middle-aged man who had never married, had fallen in love with a girl much younger than himself. She was a Miss Hogarth, one of six children. Her father, a gentleman farmer, had a considerable fortune. He intended to provide substantially for his girls when they married. When he observed that his daughter was receiving James's attentions with some complacency, his son, Mr George Hogarth, who was a Writer to the Signet, had a business talk with the Canongate printer, and James told him straightforwardly about the financial difficulties of the firm, and, particularly, about those John Ballantyne bills, for the whole of which he was responsible, even including those for which Scott had provided through the Duke of Buccleuch's guarantee. It does not appear that he made any secrecy of the fact of Scott being a partner, nor that Scott expected him to do so.

Mr Hogarth took the position very seriously. He did not forbid the marriage. He even allowed a date to be tentatively fixed. Both he and his daughter (unlike Lockhart) seem to have liked James.

But on one point Mr Hogarth was firm. He was not going to give his daughter money which might be used, sooner or later, to pay John Ballantyne bills. James said that he reckoned that his capital in the business was practically gone. Very well. There would be no question of paying him out. Let his partner release him. Mr Hogarth did not ask that James should have a fortune of his own, but only that he should be clear of these business complications. Let Mr Scott say that he would accept sole responsibility for the liabilities of the printing and publishing firms, and James could marry the girl. Otherwise not.

James wrote to Scott, laying the position before him. He wrote with great frankness about his own feelings, and all that the decision would mean to him. He was writing an intimate letter, addressed to a man of his own age, whom he had learnt to trust and respect, and of whose sympathy he was sure. He could have had no thought that it would ever be exposed to strangers' eyes.

He said frankly that he had no right to that for which he asked, but it was Mr Hogarth's request, not his. As he had no means outside the business, Scott could not, by releasing him, increase the real responsibility that he already had. He would work for the business as manager with the same energy as in the past, and his remuneration—in fact, everything, if the main point were conceded—could be as Scott thought best. There would be no argument about that.

We have no record of Scott's reply. It is clear that it was not a refusal. James had said that Scott, being a lawyer, would best know how such an arrangement could be carried out. Anything which Scott prepared he would be ready to sign. But, being a lawyer, Scott may have seen difficulties which did not occur to James's mind. Difficulties of giving James the effectual release which both James and Mr Hogarth were so ready to trust him to do. And accounts must be prepared. From whatever reason, the matter dragged. The date first fixed for the wedding had to be given up. It was put forward to February 1st. As that day approached, James wrote to Scott a somewhat pathetic letter. He was a middle-aged man, without means, or personal attractions to offer a women so much younger than himself, who had a fortune (if not a large one) to bring to him. He had a fear that, if the date of the marriage were postponed again, it would never take place.

It appears to have been in response to this appeal that Scott wrote a memorandum in which he said, so far as the John Ballantyne bills were concerned:

> "the burthen must be upon you and me—that is, on the printing office. If you will agree to conduct this business henceforward with steadiness and care, and to content yourself with £400 a year from it for your private purposes, its profits will ultimately set us free. I agree that we should grant mutual discharges as booksellers"—(we should say publishers)—"and printers. I agree farther that the responsibility of the whole debt should be assumed by myself alone for the present—providing you, on your part, never interfere with the printing profits, beyond your allowance, until the debt has been obliterated or put into such a train of liquidation that you see your way clear, and voluntarily assume your station as my partner, instead of continuing to be, as you now must consider yourself, merely my steward, bookkeeper, and manager in the Canongate."

Having agreed the principle, Scott entrusted the preparation of the necessary deed, and the details of the arrangement, to Mr George Hogarth, a conclusive evidence both of the spirit in which he met the call which had been made upon his generosity, and the direction from which it came.

The condition which Scott himself made, for which James had not stipulated—for which he could not in decency have asked—that he could claim to be reinstated as a partner at any time should he think it to his advantage, is equally conclusive in its evidence that Scott was not himself aiming to acquire the sole ownership.—And five years later, James invoked this clause, and was admitted to partnership again.

But the conditions of the dissolution, though broadly generous, were not flabby. Scott was always definite in these matters, both in what he gave, and what he required. James was to do certain things within his capacity, and he was, in particular, to remain responsible for the £3,000 which Scott and his brother had advanced to the firm in addition to Scott's partnership capital. This amount was to be left over indefinitely, but James was to insure his life in Scott's favour, so that it would be adjusted at his death—if the premiums were kept up.

So far good. It might be thought that there is nothing in these events about which Scott's friends could subsequently attempt to disparage James, or James's friends to disparage Scott. But naturally, and indeed inevitably, accounts were prepared showing the liabilities with which the agreement dealt. Even in these figures there was nothing surprising or inconsistent with the events of which we already know. A competent accountant might have examined them, and said: "If the parties most concerned are agreed, how can human ingenuity contrive to make trouble here?"

But a time came when James's Trustees and then Lockhart examined these figures with an equal determination to make trouble, and an almost equal incompetence to understand them. Lockhart had given the first provocation by a series of almost reckless libels, and frequent sneers in his *Memoirs of Sir Walter*

Scott, and the Trustees were anxious to hit back with any weapon that they were able to find. In this account, the John Ballantyne bills which were still outstanding, and the acceptances of the printing business, were grouped together in one figure, and entered as Scott's liability. That, as he was assuming sole responsibility, was the correct, and may be said to be the only possible way in which they could be entered at all, but the Trustees leapt to the absurd conclusion that this figure represented accommodation bills which Scott had obtained for his own use, and became hysterical in denunciation of the way in which a prosperous printer had been exploited by his unscrupulous partner. It was sheer nonsense, as an accountant's pupil would see at once in his first year, and Lockhart ridiculed it as it deserved. Unfortunately, he went further. He fastened upon that £3,000 which it had been agreed should be continued as a liability, however dormant, from James to Scott, and boldly asserted that it justified his previous assertion that James had ruined the printing business by a wild extravagance of personal expenditures. But he forgot the length of time that the business had been established. Even assuming that this £3,000 represented personal expenditure, which it did not, it would still have done little to support Lockhart's previous charges, for, if they were substantially accurate, James would not have been likely to have owed the business such a sum at the end of twelve years. It would have been more nearly £25,000.

But James was married to Miss Hogarth and the date arranged, and no doubt Scott went to the wedding, and James was proud of the presence of the 'life-long benefactor' whom he 'loved and honoured', whose generosity had made the marriage a possible thing: and Scott went with the happy consciousness of having done that which was equally wise and right, and they had a merry time, untroubled by the thought that they had given subject for the slanders of smaller men.

The other matter which Lockhart discovered and exposed in somewhat natural retaliation against the quite groundless accusation that Scott had used the credit of the partnership business for his own accommodation, is of a different substance.

It appears that shortly after James ceased to be a partner in the firm it became absolutely necessary to his younger brother, Alexander, that he should have back the money that he had lent to James, which had been part of James's original capital in the business, and for which he, with an irregularity which he never appears to have been able to appreciate clearly, had given the firm's acceptances in the first instance.

When Alexander pressed for the return of the money now, Scott was not informed of a matter which did not strictly concern him, and which had been the cause of the single instance of friction between them in the past, but James went to John, who undertook to raise the amount on bills which James gave again in the firm's name; which John succeeded in doing.

When the first of these bills became due, being for £200, it was dishonoured.

Scott, probably through his legal associations, appears to have had channels through which he was almost instantly aware of anything which might happen detrimental to the credit of the printing business. He heard that one of its bills had been dishonoured, at a time when the credit of the business was being solidly re-established, and when he was the sole proprietor. It was a bill of which he had no knowledge, which he had neither signed nor authorised, which ought not to exist. He sent for James, and learnt that he was out of town. He sent for John, and found John knew all about it, though the knowledge had been kept from him. John made as little of it as he could. He said the bill was now paid. His clerk had been to the bank, and put it right. James could explain about the existence of the document, and it was just bad luck that it had been dishonoured, for which no one was really to blame.

Scott wrote to James for an explanation, and received a long written reply, in the course of which he made a frank admission of the whole circumstances:

> "The £200 bill lately dishonoured was given by me for an equal sum advanced by him, and paid by me to Alexander. The remainder of the sum was made up in the same manner, and I have the absolute promise of the persons through whom I raised it (Manners & Miller) that they will aid me in retiring the bills granted to them till it shall be convenient to me to retire them finally....
>
> "I was aware that the bill was due on Monday last. I had a letter from John on the morning of Friday, saying that he was to be at Abbotsford on that day on his way home, and that he would be in Edinburgh on Saturday. I left Edinburgh for Carfrae on Saturday morning, leaving £200 enclosed in a letter for John to pay the bill, in the event of his failing to procure the cash in another quarter. In place of arriving on Saturday, John staid till Wednesday—a circumstance wholly out of my contemplation. The bill, of course, was dishonoured, to my *unspeakable vexation* and sorrow. John's man, however, got scent of the money which I left, and proffered it at the bank, *just too late to save noting*."

James's letter, both in its admissions and explanations, is clear and explicit. John assumed a somewhat different attitude. He attempted to take the blame on to himself, but in such a way as to suggest that there wasn't much to take. He said it had all been done on his own advice, and he had been as completely unaware *as James himself* of there being any irregularity in drawing such bills, or he wouldn't have suggested it. He added:

> "In truth, his own name would have done as well, for this bill was paid to Cadell, not for value received, but as additional security over other assets, under which he took on himself the payment of claims on me while I was absent. Of course, the circumstance will never occur again. I am sure the Bank are entirely

satisfied that the money lay for payment from the Saturday preceding."

The lucidity of these explanations is not absolute, and they include one or two statements the exact accuracy of which it is possible to doubt, but so far as James was concerned, they did show that he had not neglected the bill. It had not been renewed, because he had been prepared to pay it. It appeared that he had raised the money with great difficulty, actually borrowing a final amount from his father-in-law to make it up.

Scott considered these circumstances, and in the end his anger cooled. But he felt that he had been badly treated, and he used some straight words. Suppose that he had died, and that James had had to give his explanations to strangers? Did he realise that he had issued a forged bill; There being this series, of which he had only learnt by a mischance, how many more might there not be?

As to that, James gave assurances, which were believed, and were true. Beyond that, he merely protested that he had had no dishonourable intention, which was plain enough from the way in which he had been dealing with the obligation, and that he had not realised the serious nature of the irregularity.

In considering this defense, it is only fair to observe that James had not only been a partner, but in sole control of the business for many years. He still had the right to sign on the firm's behalf. We can see how it appeared to him. In the end, the cloud passed, and Scott and he were as good friends as before. It is incomprehensible to Lockhart. When words fail, marks of exclamation must take their place. Yet Scott may have been the better judge of his fellow-men.

CHAPTER LVIII.

The *Antiquary* was begun in the last weeks of 1815, and published in the following May. Its first success was even greater than that of the two previous novels. It had an immediate sale of 6,000 copies. But this sale was a tribute to its predecessors rather than its own merit. Criticism, when it came, hesitated in praise. Scott had his own doubt. He had written to Terry 'It wants the romance of *Waverley*, and the adventure of *Guy Mannering*, and yet there is some salvation about it for if a man will paint from Nature he will be likely to amuse those who are daily looking at it.'

But the hesitation did not last. Steadily and surely the current of its quieter excellence carried it to its deserved place. For of the three novels, it is, as a whole, the most satisfying: the surest in delineation of character: the most natural in its dialogues: the smoothest in continuity: the most consistent in tone.

These distinctions may be the result of a more practiced art, or they more probably had another, or an additional cause. *Waverley* was written at different times, with long intervals. It shows differences of texture, and cracks where it is joined. Memory strove to revive old imaginations, and imagination works best at its free will. Scott had a belief that his best work was done swiftly, which was only partly true, and, so far as it appeared to be so, the swiftness was a quality rather than a cause. But when he threw aside a work that was half done, he found it difficult to continue it afterwards on the same note, and the new imagination moved less freely, hampered by the memory of the old, which was of a diminished vitality.

The genesis of *Guy Mannering* is more doubtful. It appears certain that it owes material parts of its plot to a ballad sent to Scott by Mr Joseph Train, a Supervisor of Excise at Castle-Stewart, with whom he formed a friendship while inspecting lighthouses, and this ballad did not reach him till November 1815, by which evidence it would appear that the book was written within a very short period. But the scenery which it describes is that which Scott visited early in 1793, when he was preparing the defence of the too-lively McNaught, and it is a curious fact that some of the names in the novel correspond with those of the witnesses in that trial. It seems at least probable that some materials for, or portion of, the book had been in existence from an earlier period. We know that Scott had expressed to James Ballantyne an intention of following *Waverley* with a historical novel of earlier date, and it seems more probable that Train's ballad would have changed his intention if it offered additional plot for some existing material, than if it brought an entirely new idea to his mind.

However that be, it seems clear that the *Antiquary* was written continuously, and, although rapidly enough, at a period of comparative mental leisure, and with little editorial or other work in competition.

The only incident that punctuates this period is the death of Captain John Scott, which cannot have been a very sharp grief, for the brothers had little in common, though they were always on terms of mutual goodwill. John left about £6,000—half to Walter, and half to Tom, they being his only surviving brothers.

Tom, in Canada, must have found such a sum a very welcome addition to his limited resources. Scott would find it almost equally welcome. It did not come to him in cash, but it cancelled the mortgage on the first purchase of Abbotsford land, and the £1,200 loan to the printing business, which the recent arrangement with James had transformed into his private responsibility. The relief which the removal of these charges made must have increased both his capacity for, and confidence in, the acquisition of further patches of the land around Abbotsford, on which his heart was set.... He wrote to Tom, advising him of the amount by which he would benefit under their brother's will. He added that there was a further £3,000 which would fall due to Tom at their mother's death. These things being so, would not Tom like to come home? He would do all that a brother could to find him a good position. But he added that such positions were now hard to get. The government was enforcing economy in all directions. It was not like it had been during the war.

As he got the *Antiquary* off his hands, Scott decided upon another adventure in anonymity. He had in mind the writing of the novel of which he had talked to James before he decided to put *Guy Mannering* first. It was to be a historical romance of Claverhouse and the Covenanters, and the battle of Bothwell Bridge. This would be different from the tales of more or less contemporary manners with which the name of the author of *Waverley* was associated. Why not project a series of such historical tales to be linked under a common title, *Tales of my Landlord*, and try whether a separate and third anonymity would win a fourth success? That would best be done through a publisher other than Constable, and, as far as the author could contrive it, a change in his own style. With this object, John was instructed to approach Mr. Blackwood, a young Edinburgh bookseller who was now acting as Murray's Scottish agent, and suggest that they should undertake this new anonymous series, which, they were informed in confidence, was by the author of *Waverley*, but of which connection they were to make no public announcement. The terms offered, and readily accepted, were that the author should receive half the profits, and that Murray should take a £500 parcel of the unending Hanover Street stock. So far, the facts appear to be simple, natural, and requiring no further explanation. But to Lockhart's mind they supplied fresh evidence of the villainy of John Ballantyne, and the charges which he makes against him in this connection are so gross, and their foundations appear to be so extremely flimsy, that it seems best to state them in his own words:

> "After the first and more serious embarrassments had been overcome, John was far from continuing to hold by his patron's anxiety for the total abolition of their unhappy co-partnership. He, unless when some sudden emergency arose, flattered Scott's own gay imagination, by representing everything in the most smiling colours; and though Scott, in his replies seldom failed to introduce some hint of caution—such as 'Nullum numen abest si sit prudentia'—he more and more took home to himself the agreeable cast of his

Rigdum's anticipations, and wrote to him in a vein as merry as his own—e.g.—'As for our stock,

"'Twill be waring awa', John,
Like snaw-wreaths when it's thaw, John'," etc.

John could never have forgotten that it was to Constable alone that his firm had more than once owed its escape from dishonour; and he must have known that, after the triumphant career of the Waverley series had once commenced, nothing could have been more easy than to bring all the affairs of 'backstock, etc.' to a close, by entering into a distinct and candid treaty on that subject in connection with the future works of the great Novelist either with Constable or with any other first-rate house in the trade: but he also knew that, were that unhappy firm wholly extinguished, he must himself subside into a clerk of the printing company. Therefore, in a word, he appears to have systematically disguised from Scott the extent to which the whole Ballantyne concern had been sustained by Constable—especially during his Hebridean tour of 1814, and his Continental one of 1815—and prompted and enforced the idea of trying other booksellers from time to time, instead of adhering to Constable, merely for the selfish purposes—first, of facilitating the immediate discount of bills—secondly, of further perplexing Scott's affairs, the entire disentanglement of which would have been, as he fancied, prejudicial to his own personal importance.

It was resolved, accordingly, to offer the risk and half profits of the first edition of another new novel—or rather collection of novels—to Mr. Murray of Albermarle Street, and Mr. Blackwood, who was then Murray's agent in Scotland; but it was at the same time resolved, partly because Scott wished to try another experiment on the public sagacity, but partly also, no question, from the wish to spare Constable's feelings, that the title-page of the 'Tales of my Landlord' should not bear the magical words 'by the Author of Waverley.'"

It reads speciously enough, but there is hardly a sentence in this page of poisonous nonsense which does not contain or suggest a lie, and the accusations made against John Ballantyne with such careless levity—that he 'systematically disguised' Constable's conduct to his own principal, and that he acted with the 'selfish purpose' of 'further perplexing' Scott's affairs, are of the standard of conduct for which Dante placed the most despicable of human sinners with Judas in the lowest hell. Scott was his benefactor, his employer, his friend. Human degradation cannot go much lower than in the deliberate betrayal of a trust created by such relations. This is not a life of John Ballantyne (who had his faults) and it might be inopportune to turn aside, even to relieve him of a transparently baseless charge; but a large measure of misconception as to Scott's character and business capacity has been built upon this fiction of Lockhart's that he was continually hoodwinked by the knaveries of those to whom he gave a life-long confidence, and for this reason it may be worth while to tabulate some of the errors of fact or logic which this accusation contains:

First, there was no excessive optimism in foreseeing that the stock would be cleared. (Lockhart recognises this himself, in a later sentence). In fact, it was cleared entirely, at no distant date.

Second, it is not clear that it could be dealt with to the best advantage through a single channel. There is an opposite presumption. By placing parcels of a stock which consisted of large quantities of a comparatively few books now with Constable, now with Longman, and now with Murray, the widest channels of distribution were opened.

Third, it is not obvious that it would have been a sound business proposition to negotiate a forward contract for further Waverley novels, on a basis which would have entirely cleared the Hanover Street stock, even if Constable would have agreed, which cannot be assumed with confidence. He was always difficult to drive. The contracts which were ultimately made for further novels, and the final bargain regarding the stock, suggest a directly contrary conclusion.

Fourth, it was not a fact that the conclusion of the sale of this stock would automatically cause John to subside into the position of a clerk to the printing firm, nor would occasional large transfers of stock, which took place at intervals of months or years, have been sufficient to save him from such a fate. The suggestion ignores the fact that he was now engaged in business as an auctioneer.

Fifth, the strength of John's position with Scott was not, at this time, based upon these occasional disposals of stock, but upon the fact that he was acting as his literary agent. Most authors find it an advantage to have such a representative, and Scott's complicated anonymities, both in prose and verse, rendered it an absolute necessity to him.

Sixth, it is difficult to know what is meant by the vague accusation that John concealed Constable's services in sustaining "the whole Ballantyne concern" during Scott's absences. It is extremely unlikely that Constable did anything of the kind. It is equally improbable that the Ballantynes could have concealed such a circumstance from Scott on his return, even had they had any adequate reason for desiring to do so. Scott and Constable frequently met.

In fact, the whole accusation proves on examination to be devoid not only of proof, but of any basis of probability. It is wildly unlikely that the idea of a separate series of anonymous novels originated with John Ballantyne, rather than with Scott, and if there were to be such a series, it was an obvious advantage to find a separate publisher, which Scott doubtless told John to do. He may have told him to use the opportunity to get rid of some more of that difficult stock, or John may have mentioned it first. It is a point of no importance, because it would be in both their minds. It is certain that there was not any intention of throwing Constable overboard, for he had already been taken into the secret of the authorship of the Waverley novels; and Scott was not foolish enough to start a new anonymity with the intention of dropping the one which he had already made a success. That would have been a pointless stupidity. Obviously, he intended to carry on both, side by side.

Nor is it likely that Constable would be more difficult to manage because another channel had been opened through which novels could be published. But at this time Constable was so far from being willing to agree to everything that was asked, that he was showing his own strength, and his own independence in an unexpected way. He was cold-shouldering James Ballantyne & Co., and placing his printing orders in other directions. Even with the novels themselves, he had taken up the position that it must not be assumed that they would be printed at the Canongate works. It was a matter for estimate and negotiation.

He was entirely within his right in this attitude, which may have had several significances. He may have thought that the importance of the orders which he placed with James had been insufficiently appreciated, and that it should be made clear that favours were not all on one side; or he may have found that prices had been raised against him as orders had come to be regarded as matters of routine rather than negotiation, and it may have been no more than a skirmish between James and himself as to what type-setting is worth; or it may have been that the change was less in Constable's policy than in surrounding circumstance. For twelve months, the war to end war had been over. Expert statesmen were re-partitioning Europe into new areas of enduring peace. In England, everyone was going to work less in future, and enjoy more. What else is peace, what else is victory, for? It is a recurring insanity, when the discords of battle cease. There was no statesman of sufficient wisdom to sound a warning note: none to propose that the nation shall be organised for peace, as it had been for war: to call for an effort which it might have been willing to make. They told it to slumber now, with a promise of pleasant dreams.

Perhaps this casually-mentioned trouble, the fact that Constable was distributing his orders more widely than he had done during the war, is the most portentous fact which emerges from these negotiations. It is the cloud, small as a man's hand, rising in the skies of post-war—prosperity, that ten years hence will be black with financial storm.

But as to the random charge against John Ballantyne that he was bent on prolonging the publishing business even to Scott's detriment, or that he must otherwise subside to the position of his brother's clerk, they may be refuted from Lockhart's own pen, for when he subsequently wrote his pamphlet to Sir Adam Fergusson in reply to the Ballantyne Trustees (p.55), being busy with a different argument, and forgetting what he had written before, he says, of the time of James's marriage:

> "Johnny's separate business as an auctioneer was now in a promising state, and all concerned were equally desirous of finally closing the bookselling and publishing adventure."

And the idea that Scott was a puppet in John Ballantyne's hands is sufficiently refuted by his own letter of instructions dated April 29th 1816, addressed to John Ballantyne, while the negotiations proceeded, in the course of which he says: "James has made one or two important mistakes in the bargain with Murray and Blackwood," and goes on to give minute instructions as to the number of copies on which they shall have copyright, the length of credit which may be given, and other details, and adds:

> "If they agree to these conditions, good and well. If they demur, Constable must be instantly tried; giving half to the Longmans, and *we* drawing on *them* for their moiety, or Constable lodging *their* bill in our hands.... I do not limit you to terms, because I think you will make them better than I can do. But he must do more than others, since he will not or cannot print with us. For every point but that, I would rather deal with Constable than any one; he has always shown himself spirited, judicious and liberal. Blackwood

must be brought to the point *instantly*; and *whenever* he demurs, Constable must be treated with, for there's no use in suffering the thing to be blown on. At the same time, you need not conceal from him that there were some proposals elsewhere, but you may add, with truth, I would rather close with him.

Yours truly, W. S.

P.S. I think Constable should jump at this affair; for I believe the work will be very popular."

In this, as in all his correspondence with the Ballantynes, and generally in his business letters, Scott shows himself to have a clear grasp of affairs, and a will to control the negotiations in which his agents are occupied. He is capable of large deliberate generosities, but he handles even these with a firm hand. We may notice how, in the letter just quoted, in dealing with a contingent negotiation which it was never necessary to open, he safeguards himself in advance against the possibility that Constable, as the intermediary with Longmans, might have retained their bills, and given Scott his own for the whole amount—thereby depriving him of the security of Longman's name, and retaining discountable paper which would have given Constable the use of the money until his own bills to Scott should have become due for payment.

CHAPTER LIX.

Scott's original contract with Murray was to write four tales, each of a single-volume length, and he supplied *The Black Dwarf* to this pattern, but his tale of Claverhouse expanded till it sufficed for the other three.

John Murray read *The Black Dwarf*, and felt dubious. He showed it to Gifford, the Quarterly editor, who said whoever had written it had written a poor thing. Murray sent this discouraging opinion on to Blackwood, who agreed, with an increased emphasis. He went to see James, who was secretly, if not openly, of the same opinion. Blackwood wanted James to induce the unknown author to write the latter part of the book again. He even sketched what he thought that ending should be. James said he would see what he could do. But what about the cost of resetting? Blackwood said he felt so strongly about it that he was willing for that to be charged to him. James went to see Scott, who resented Blackwood's suggested alterations. He said he would see them damned before he would change a word. With an author's proverbial perversity, he thought the *Black Dwarf* to be an example of his best work. Not like—? Of course, it wasn't like anything else he had written. Wasn't it understood that he was to write in a new way? James said diffidently that everyone agreed that it began well. The trouble was that it became lifeless before it died.

But Scott still answered after the manner of Pilate. What he had written, he had written. It was a very powerful study No, he wouldn't change anything.

So that was that, and there was no more to be said. Fortunately, Murray read *Old Mortality*, and felt better. In spite of its dull-sounding title, he saw that he had got a good thing. A historical novel of a new kind. Was there no end to Scott's wizardry? He wrote to him with congratulations.

Scott was not to be hooked with that bait. What were the *Tales of my Landlord* to him? If Murray liked, he would demonstrate his independence of them by writing a review for the Quarterly. Everyone would recognise that a man would not cut up his own children. Even Solomon knew that.

There was laughter in Albermarle Street when this letter came. Gifford was taken into consultation. Then Murray replied. Why should Scott confine himself to reviewing the *Tales of My Landlord*? Why not deal with the Waverley novels?

Scott wrote back, and agreed, on condition that William Erskine, who thought better of those novels than he did himself, should lend a hand. So, in a short time, it was done. No one who engaged in the correspondence could doubt the authorship of the novels. Scott might admit nothing, but he did not write in the tone and manner in which he would certainly have done had he been dealing with work which was genuinely not his. People were agreeably mystified rather than deceived. Everybody said that they *knew*—and yet there was just that little pleasant flavour of doubt, which the review helped to maintain when it had been a dying thing. The novels were not over-praised, but Scott (or Erskine in his name) discussed them intelligently. It was excellent advertising. Excellent copy for the Quarterly also. The money for the article was well-earned, and doubtless Erskine had a liberal share.

And the second experiment in anonymity was as great a success as the first. The position of *Old Mortality* relatively to the whole gallery of Scott's romances has been a matter on which differences of opinion have been expressed at later periods, but its first reception was a chorus of praise, in which the only note of discord came from those who asserted that the Covenanters were not represented fairly. It was a contention which an impartial judgement will hardly sustain. Indeed, as a work of pure imagination, the book suffers from Scott's desire to be historically accurate, and exactly fair. It may be said that it is too romantic for history, and too historical for romance. The character of Claverhouse is well drawn, but Scott is too anxious to draw it. Instead of leaving it to reveal itself, a method in which he had an almost incomparable ability, whether in prose or verse, it must be explained, even self-explained at times, and there are occasions when Claverhouse talks like a stuffed dummy in consequence. Yet in narrative power, in force and realism, the book was a new thing in historical fiction: it had humour also, which is the one added excellence in Scott's prose romances, which his lyrical ones rarely attempt. It is no wonder that it had high praise, and a large sale.

Almost immediately after the publication of *Old Mortality* and the *Black Dwarf*, the anonymous author of the *Bridal of Triermain* issued another poem, *Harold the Dauntless*. Constable published it. It had been hanging about for years. It contained parts which lovers of Scott's poetry would be sorry to lose. It contained others that he could have had little pleasure to write. He must have been glad to have it off his hands. Its sales were not such as to induce the kind of boasting that gives exact figures. It is enough to say that they were quite good.

CHAPTER LX.

Enter Boswell. It is the spring of 1817, and a public dinner of farewell is being given to John Henry Kemble, who has completed a series of Shakespearian performances at the Edinburgh theatre. Jeffrey is in the chair, Scott and John Wilson are the after-dinner speakers. Lockhart is a young lawyer among the guests. All his life he could not remember anything 'more impressive' than that dinner, though he does not say why or how. Doubtless Scott spoke well, as he would when he was among friends, and *con amore* to the subject with which he dealt. Doubtless, he said the right word to the young lawyer, as he to him. He had good spirits. He did not seem an ill man. Yet he had been ill all the winter, at intervals, with attacks which might seize him at any moment. One had been so severe that he had been laid up for a month, and 'as weak as water' when he wrote to Morritt afterwards to explain why he had not done so earlier. There had been intense pains, culminating in inflammatory symptoms 'about the diaphragm', for which he had been bled and blistered with great severity, and burnt with hot salt, and he believed that these measures, 'under higher assistance' had saved his life. It was a condition which would be met by prompt operation today. It would have been cure or Will. In those days doctors fought it with such knowledge as they had, and by such methods as experience warranted or tradition required, which are disparaged now. Yet it is fair to observe that their patient lived. His remaining blood continued to course through his body, and it was a body in which the spirit was unbroken and unafraid. Friends might be anxious for him, and in correspondence he might admit that the symptoms were of a dangerous kind—Baillie had been frank about that—and his own account is that when the severe symptoms had subsided: "I could neither stir for weakness and giddiness, nor read for dazzling in my eyes, nor listen for a whizzing sound in my ears, nor even think for lack of the power of arranging my ideas. So I had a comfortless time of it for about a week." Yet as he lay, he had dreams. He would win more with his pen from those neighbours who had no love for the land they owned. He would yet make fair woodlands of those barren neglected hills. And he would build a house more fitting than this cramped cottage to be the centre of the loveliness that would one day surround it. "I will pull down my barns and build greater." And no voice answered him with "Thou fool" in the night, for another dream was to come true.

So when he was strong enough to walk, and before the pain returned, as it surely would, he marked out the foundations of Abbotsford.

It was at this time that William Laidlaw came to Kaeside. Farming had been difficult during the war. It became impossible afterwards, except for those who had stored capital which they could afford to lose. William Laidlaw gave up the fight. His farm was sold up. Scott, in the midst of his illness, had another worry on his mind, more acute than any question of how matters were going at the Canongate works, or with the bill-discounting account at Sir William Forbes and Co's bank. With whatever may be happening in those directions, he can deal when he gets about again. And, as a matter of fact, things went well enough. The prestige that those anonymous novels had brought made credit easier: the money they brought made it less necessary to obtain: their printing kept the works busier than ever before, and brought a humble prosperity into many homes. But Scott's worry was of a different kind. How, without appearance of charity, could he help Willie Laidlaw, as helped he must surely be? It was by the mercy of Heaven that he had bought that land at Kaeside, with the little house upon it which the tenant, Moss, was due to vacate at Whitsuntide. So he wrote to Moss to know whether it were really convenient to him to leave (for we cannot turn a man out of his home simply because his lease is over), and on receiving a reply that Moss had arranged to go, he used his diplomatic persuasion to induce William Laidlaw to bring his family there.

So it was arranged, and Scott, thinking to aid others, gave good help to himself in the end, as men often do. In Edinburgh, Constable watched with an angry contempt while Blackwood started a magazine. Pringle, Blackwood's new editor, asked Scott for his help. Scott was too busy for that—and too ill. But he could get his friend Laidlaw to write a good article on gypsies for the first number, with others to follow. So it was agreed. The article was written in Scott's bedroom, Scott dictating anecdotes, as the intervals of pain allowed, from his memory's endless store. He discovered thus that he could write by dictation, and that Laidlaw was a sympathetic amanuensis, which he put to a good use at a future time.

He got better as the summer approached. He designed a new Waverley novel, concerning which he instructed John Ballantyne to open negotiations with Constable. Constable proposed that he should come to Abbotsford, and discuss the contract with Scott himself. Scott agreed to that, but preferred that John should be present. He sent this note to Hanover Street:

"Abbotsford.
Saturday, May 3, 1817

Dear John,

I shall be much obliged to you to come here with Constable on Monday, as he proposes a visit, and it will save time. By the way, you must attend that the usual quantity of stock is included in the arrangement—this is £600—for 6,000 copies. My sum is £1,700 payable in May—a sound advance, by'r Lady, but I think I am entitled to it, considering what I have turned off hitherto on such occasions.

I make a point of your coming with Constable, health allowing.

Yours truly,

W. S."

On the following Tuesday, John sent this letter on to James, with another note scribbled upon its foot:

"Half-past 3 o'clock Tuesday.

Dear James—I am this moment returned from Abbotsford, with entire and full success. Wish me joy. I shall gain about £600—Constable taking, my share of stock also. The title is *Rob Roy, by the author of Waverley!!!* Keep this letter for me.

J. B."

James did keep the letter and returned it to John, for the latter pasted it into a book in which he kept correspondence of importance, and he wrote beneath it at a later date: "N.B. I did gain about £1,200. J.B."

Many years later, Constable still had a clear recollection of that Monday evening at Abbotsford, and of how they sat together in the garden after dinner, when their business was done. He did not often find Scott so genial to him in his attitude, so readily confidential about his plans. He even gave way about the title, which he rarely would. The book was to be about Rob Roy. Constable, with a sound commercial instinct, said that its subject should be its title also. You couldn't do better than call the book by the Highland bandit's name. Scott always liked titles which meant little until the book had been read. But on this occasion he gave way.

John proposed bringing Rob Roy's old gun out of the house, and firing a salute in honour of the christening of the new book. Scott vetoed that, saying it would explode. Constable jibed at John: 'What put drawing at sight into your head?'

Constable's pleasantries were apt to be of that kind. He once spoiled a business deal by mentioning that he had named five geese after Longman and his four partners. He knew something about long-dated bills himself, and was destined to know more.

Scott saw that John resented the jest, and was quick to interpose a request that he should give them the *Cobbler of Kelso*. John was famous among his friends as an entertainer, having a quick wit, and an exceptional power of dramatic mimicry. Scott and he had watched this cobbler when they were schoolboys together. He had a favourite blackbird, to which he would talk while it sang. John could imitate his high cracked voice and the blackbird's song about equally well. Lockhart says that he could do these imitations 'with wonderful skill'. It is the witness of a man who disliked John, caricatured him without mercy, and libelled him without scruple, and he is not likely to be overgenerous in his praise.

So peace was restored, and, in the morning, Constable and John travelled back to Edinburgh together.

As to John's £600 of estimated commission—which became £1,200—we may agree that he was well paid, without accepting Lockhart's comment that 'he had no more trouble about the selling or publishing of *Rob Roy* than his own *Cobbler of Kelso*.' He adds that 'one must admire his adroitness in persuading Constable, during their journey back to Edinburgh, to relieve him of that fraction of his own old stock, with which his unhazardous share in the new transaction was burdened. Scott's kindness continued as long as John Ballantyne lived, to provide for him a constant succession of similar advantages at the same easy rate; and Constable, from deference to Scott's wishes, and from views of bookselling policy, appears to have submitted to this heavy tax on his most important ventures.'

But he obstinately refuses to see that Scott did not arrange these liberal commissions for John as his friend, but as his literary agent, in which capacity John seems to have shown some efficiency as well as zeal. Anyway, he pleased Scott, who was most concerned.

If they were able to arrange that this remuneration should be paid out of the publishers' share of the profits, it is a method to which no literary agent need object, and which all authors would approve today.

CHAPTER LXI.

The winter of 1816-17 was one of confused prosperity and want, with much unemployment, and consequently suffering, both in urban and rural districts. It is outside the scope of this book to attempt analyses either of the causes or conditions of this industrial chaos, but we have to notice, that, even through the severity of his own illness, and the pressure of work which was upon him during his intervals of recovery, Scott's correspondence shows that sympathy for those who suffered was preoccupying his mind continually; that he took upon himself the burden of relieving it in his own neighbourhood as a matter of course, and in a wholesale manner; and that in considering and facing its problems he showed a practical sagacity which a further century of experience, and an endless literature of sociology, does not enable us to excel, or perhaps equal, today.

In the course of a long letter to Robert Southey on May 9th, 1817, he deals with some severity with a scheme of employment upon public works which had been brought into operation in Edinburgh supported by a fund which had been raised through the private generosity of its citizens, and administered by a voluntary committee, and this criticism deserves the greater attention because it is sympathetic to all concerned. He recognises the generosity that has impulsed the project, and the 'yet more praise-worthy because most difficult exertions of those who superintend,' yet he thinks that the result has been 'full as much mischief as good'.

The scheme was organised on the reasonable premise that it must not be made sufficiently attractive to draw men away from other employment, or indifferent to obtaining it, and the scale of remuneration was fixed somewhat below the standard rates that were then current, with the addition of a compassionate allowance to those who had families. Scott observed the consequence to be that the scheme was regarded "partly as charity, which is humiliating," and "partly as an imposition in taking their labour below value," while there was a further opinion that it was 'a sort of half-pay, not given them for work, but to prevent rebellion,' and the consequence of these attitudes was the worst slacking that he had ever seen.

He remarks that it would be unreasonable to expect too much, because 'an individual always manages his own concerns better than those of the country can be managed,' which is an obvious truth that some of us are still unwilling to recognise, or to apply; but he lays down as a basic necessity of relief plans that they should be so contrived that the labourer will 'bring his heart and spirit to the work,' and he tells in some detail how he had contrived to reach this result.

When that winter came, there were about thirty men living around Abbotsford who were without employment, and he offered work to all of them in clearing, draining and planting the land he had bought. He says explicitly that it was not to be regarded as an act of charity on his part, for the work needed to be done, and it had been his ultimate purpose to carry it out; but he had thought of it as a gradual labour of many years, and the money had been very hard to find. We can easily believe that. Even for his income, and even if the printing and publishing enterprise had ceased, for the moment, to drain his purse, the support of thirty families month by month must have strained his resources, as he admits (without complaint) that it did: and the work on which the men were employed was not such as would bring any immediate return. But when his 'honest neighbours' were in need, what choice had he?

But he bears witness to a spirit the very opposite of that which prevailed at the relief works in Edinburgh. He had been shrewd enough to stipulate for piece-work wherever possible, and just enough to be careful that men should not undertake it, under the stress of want, at a price which would not give a fair wage for a good week's work. He observes that in a piece-work bargain it is always necessary to watch that 'the undertakers, in their anxiety for employment, do not take the job too cheap'.

Probably men recognised that his action, as he modestly says, was 'not altogether selfish,' and responded in the right way. There had been no slacking at Abbotsford.

At about the same time as he was corresponding with Southey on these matters, he was expressing himself to Morritt with a very radical vigour concerning the state of the artisans of Yorkshire and Lancashire, where the introduction of machinery was bringing fortunes to many manufacturers while the hand-workers starved, or were obliged to accept work at such wages as were offered, which were often no better than a subsistence minimum. He says truly that a Poor Law charity is no remedy for such conditions. Personally, he would go to any length to change them, even to the approval of a tax on manufacturers, to be levied according to the number of work-people they employed, and handed over to those whom they exploited, which even the Radical Committee at Manchester might have accepted as a sufficiently drastic remedy.

We have another view of his attitude regarding the obligations of those who control wealth or land in his correspondence at this time with his friend the Duke of Buccleuch, regarding the conduct of certain 'young blackguards' of Selkirk. The Duke's property included some beautiful and extensive woodlands on the banks of the Yarrow, and he had thrown the walks through these woods open to the inhabitants of Selkirk—and the inhabitants of Selkirk were destroying the woods. The Duke wrote to

Scott in evident anger, requiring him, in his office as Sheriff, to bring the culprits to justice, and expressing his intention of withdrawing a privilege which was being so grossly abused. There had, apparently, been some violent clash between the depredators and Hudson, the Duke's forester, for Scott alludes to the trouble as 'the disagreeable affair of Tom Hudson', in his reply.

As Sheriff, as a life-long friend, as a landowner himself in a smaller way, Buccleuch evidently assumed his sympathy and co-operation, and so far as the apprehension and punishment of those who transgressed were concerned, he received explicit assurances in reply. Neither was sympathy lacking: Scott can imagine 'hardly anything more exasperating' than the way in which the Duke's generosity had been received. But he will give no support to the threat that the privilege shall be withdrawn because some have abused it.

'I think,' He writes 'your Grace will be inclined to follow this up only for the purpose of correction, not that of requital. They are so much beneath you, and so much in your power, that this would be unworthy of you—especially as all the inhabitants of the little country town must necessarily be included in the punishment. After all, those who look for anything better than ingratitude from the uneducated and unreflecting mass of a corrupt population must always be deceived; and the better the heart is that has been expanded towards them, their wants, and their wishes, the deeper is the natural feeling of disappointment. But it is our duty to fight on, doing what good we can....''

He added a suggestion that the Duke might reach his purpose by an opposite road, if he would 'distinguish by any little notice such Selkirk people working with you as have their families under good order'.

That was his counsel to another, which is always easy to give. He showed how he would act himself on a later occasion, when people who were going to Selkirk began to trespass across the 'very centre' of his Abbotsford grounds, finding that they could shorten the distance by that invasion. He told Tom Purdie to put up a notice at the place where the trespassers entered. Tom did his best, but he spelt with an independent spirit. 'The Rod to Selkirk ' was the legend which ended the difficulty. You cannot trespass where you are invited to come. Scott told Captain Basil Hall that he would never prosecute a man for trespass, under any circumstances: he added that he had never known anyone to break his fences, or damage his growing trees

It was while Scott was writing to Morritt his opinion of those who exploited the labour of the poor that the news reached him that a shot had been fired at the Prince Regent, and he added a footnote to his letter: "I hear the Prince Regent has been attacked and fired at. Since he was not hurt (for I should be sincerely sorry for my fat friend), I see nothing but good luck to result from this assault. It will make him a good manageable boy, and, I think, secure you a quiet session of Parliament."

CHAPTER LXII.

The remainder of 1817 was mainly spent on the writing of *Rob Roy*, varied by a volume of *Border Antiquaries*, and a substantial portion of the *Annual Register*, in the publication of which Scott continued with a stubborn determination that would not admit defeat. He visited Loch Lomond and Glasgow to refresh his memory of the scenes with which the novel would largely deal, and when Washington Irving saw him at Abbotsford in August, he found him in apparently vigorous health, but the attacks of "cramp in the stomach" recurred at frequent intervals, and beyond a restricted diet, the physicians appear to have concentrated their prescriptions rather upon relief of pain than any radical cure. He was taking opium to render endurable the recurrent bouts of pain.

Yet, all the time, he was planning for the future with unabated courage. He laid the foundations of the house which he had resolved to build: he arranged the purchase of the adjoining house of Topsfield, with considerable additional land, and was able to offer it as a home to Adam Fergusson, his friend from boyhood, who now retired from the army on half pay, and came to reside there with his sisters. The name of the house was changed to Huntley Burn. The purchase brought into Scott's possession the whole field of the Battle of Melrose, and Thomas the Rhymer's Glen. It gave him more excuse to find occupation for William Laidlaw as steward of the estate, a position which was gradually established, though Scott appears to have found difficulty during the first year in advancing pretexts for the payments which he knew that Laidlaw's family required, and in overcoming his friend's reluctance; for he wrote to him in November arguing that 'this same account of Dr. and Cr. which fills up so much time in the world, is comparatively of very small value...it would be very silly in either of us to let a cheque twice a year of £25 make a difference between us....'

It is customary to represent Scott's purchases of land as an imprudent folly, but it is difficult to accept this view without reservations, especially if we look at things as they were, with no more recognition of the future than he himself could have had at the time. In itself, to create large sums of money by the writing of novels, and to invest them in landed properties is a road to affluence rather than to financial disaster. By purchasing Huntley Burn, and letting it to the Fergussons, he did not only gratify friends and obtain good neighbours. He got good tenants also, and the investment seems to have been sound enough.

But the foundations of the new house at Abbotsford foretold an expenditure that would increase with the years; the planting of the bare lands he bought might have a far-sighted wisdom, and might bring good wages into many homes where the pinch of poverty might otherwise have been felt, but was not of an immediately remunerative character; the obligations of hospitality as he understood them were an unceasing drain; and the cheques that William Laidlaw was so reluctant to take, the cheques for Weber at the York asylum, the cheques for the support of Daniel's nameless child, they are only those at which we have happened to glance among—how many?—others, that diminished his resources in a score of directions. Money would always be to him a power, not to hoard but to use. It was the chivalrous ideal by which he would live or die.

It may be said that even the purchase of freehold property was an imprudence, if not an impropriety, while money was owing from many borrowings on bills that were being indefinitely renewed. But, even on this point, there may be material misapprehension. The printing business was still being carried on with a good deal of capital which was provided by the bankers, or other commercial channels, and Scott was leaving it largely to the management of James Ballantyne with an easy—if we are to believe Lockhart, a too-easy—mind. But the successive sales of stock, and some of the large sums that Scott had been making by his pen, had been so applied that all the John Ballantyne bills which had been placed among friends, even those which Morritt had so freely offered to finance, appear to have been taken up. Only the overdraft on the Duke's guarantee was still outstanding, and as he finished *Rob Roy*, and felt that he had well earned the value of Constable's advances, he determined upon a bold move which would close the chapter of the publishing business for ever. He instructed John Ballantyne to open negotiations with Constable for a second series of *Tales of my Landlord* to be ready by the following midsummer.

> "I have hungered and thirsted," he wrote to John, "to see the end of those shabby borrowings among friends; they have all been wiped out, except the good Duke's £4,000—and I will not suffer either new offers of land or anything else to come in the way of that clearance. I expect that you will be able to arrange this resurrection of Jedediah, so that £5,000 shall be at my order."

That John had justified this confidence is shown by a note which Scott wrote to Buccleuch on January 7th, 1818: "I have the great pleasure of enclosing the discharged bond which your Grace stood engaged in on my account."

In fact, John had, in Lockhart's contention, gone far beyond his instructions. The details of the event, and Lockhart's comments upon them, in view of the charges which he made against John in regard to his conduct of the previous negotiation, are sufficiently curious to deserve the investigation of a separate chapter.

CHAPTER LXIII

Constable was in a good temper with himself and the world, and especially with his Abbotsford bargains. He had believed in *Rob Roy*. The Highland outlaw was a good subject for a novel, and one which he had been confident would be suitable to the author's genius. He liked it none the less because he had named it himself. James Ballantyne had been enthusiastic about the chapters as they had come into his hands. Constable could be bold, as we know, and he was usually bold at the right time. Now he adventured a first edition of 10,000 copies—an enormous quantity at that time—and the public bought them at once. He had to order the printing of 3,000 more. *Rob Roy* was going to earn a huge profit for its publisher, and much more for its author than the £1,700 which Constable had advanced already. It was a novel rich alike in background, in incident, and in character; and in Diana it had a more vivacious heroine than those of Scott's prose imaginations had so far been. Probably we may thank Charlotte for that. As Matilda is Williamina Stuart, fencing between her friendship with Walter Scott, and her growing love for Willie Forbes, Diana is with equal certainty, and bolder, clearer delineation, the Charlotte Charpentier that Walter Scott and Adam Fergusson first saw riding upon the Westmorland Hills.

Scott may be the poet of action, the novelist of adventure: to a superficial survey he may appear to be occupied with material things, but, in fact, his is a dream-world in which there is no physical dominance, and little physical reality. It is a world in which only spiritual values are taken seriously. To a generation saturated with the prolonged osculations of Hollywood, and avid for Warwick Deeping's sentimental hysteria. Scott's reticences are inexplicable both in kind and degree. Diana Vernon's gay fortitude gives way for an instant, as she leans from her horse in the darkness, and a tear falls on her lover's face.... You can't get much kick out of that! Perhaps not. But it may be your loss, all the same.

Scott's illness may have had its share in the tone and quality which divided *Rob Roy* from his earlier novels. Physical weakness and periods of convalescent exhaustion may clarify mental processes, and give leisure for imagination which it would otherwise lack. Anyway, the fact stood that *Rob Roy* was another evidence of variety in what might well seem to be an inexhaustible power, and from which, in fact, still further varieties of excellence, including the two greatest of the Waverley novels, were yet to come.

John was right in thinking that Constable would be keen to deal, and he planned a coup after his own heart. Scott had instructed John to procure £5,000. He had not specified how it was to be obtained, whether by further sales of stock, or by a contract for novels alone, but he had said definitely that Constable was to have the first offer. That being so, we can imagine how the purity of Lockhart's soul is shocked by the way in which John carried out his instructions. It is true that he did not approach any other publishers, and in the end he made a good bargain with Constable. He also got Scott the £5,000, and a good bit more. His sin was that he did not go straight to Constable and say: "I'm instructed to sell you the next series of *Tales of my Landlord*. Scott wants £5,000. Will you give it, and, if so, what for?" Instead of that he just talked about the new series of the *Tales* on which Scott was engaged. The last had been published by Murray and Blackwood. Instead of John going to Constable, an anxious Constable came to him. What were the terms on which Scott would give him the preference for the *Tales*, so that he should become his exclusive publisher? John invited him to bid high. It was not a question now of taking part of the John Ballantyne stock. It must be finally cleared. If Constable would do that, he could have the *Tales* on the usual profit-sharing terms. The wholesale value of the remaining stock was placed at £5,270.

Constable gave way. The stock was carted to his own premises. He signed the usual series of bills. There was the necessary interview at the bank. Constable's name stood high in the banking world of Edinburgh in 1814. So did that of Scott. The bills were discounted, and Buccleuch's guarantee was handed back.

Constable had bought a large stock of publications, on the realisation of which he would almost certainly lose. But in view of the profits which he was making from the Waverley novels, he could afford to do so. It was worth a large risk, even the certainty of a large loss, to draw Scott definitely into his own orbit, outside that of Blackwood and Murray—the two men in the trade whom he hated most: the two who had the impudence to bring out magazines in competition with his.

Lockhart is censorious over this transaction. He says that John had "acquitted himself with a species of dexterity not contemplated in his commission". He sheds a tear on Constable's desk concerning the unsaleable nature of that stock. On a previous occasion he asserts that John could easily have sold the whole stock to any of the publishers concerned, and that he deliberately betrayed his employer's interests for his own ends when he failed to make a sufficient effort to do so. Now he does the very thing that he was blamed for not attempting earlier, and which he was accused of scheming to avoid, and he is wrong again. Lockhart's path of righteousness is very narrow for John.

The accusation is, of course, utter nonsense in itself, as well as being destructive of that which had been made before. Scott's instructions to his agent were obviously confidential, and it was no part of his duty—might, indeed, have been a definite betrayal—to communicate them to Constable. He carried these instructions out both in letter and spirit, obtained what Scott required, and deserved, and doubtless received, his thanks.

Scott's letter of instructions leaves much latitude for negotiating how the required sum was to be obtained, but, in view of the profit-sharing system now in vogue between Constable and himself, he can scarcely have expected to secure immediate control of £5,000 without such a deal as John Ballantyne made.

Anyway, the stock was gone, and the firm of John Ballantyne & Co. had come to a final end. Scott reckoned that by nursing the stock, and the method of realisation which he had adopted, he had not merely avoided loss, but had closed his account with a final profit of about £1,000. His reckoning may not have been such as would be considered a satisfactory basis for an accountant's certificate, and the results, in any event, were due to his own value as an author rather than the intrinsic merits of the stock which he had been so largely responsible for creating. The credibility of such a result depends upon the way in which the Hanover Street expenses had been discharged, and the directions in which the heavy costs of bill-renewing had been debited. There would be other questions, such as that of the final adjustments of the loan to James at the start, which would affect the figure, but, considering the quantity of stock which had been dealt with by the John Ballantyne firm, if they finally secured a 10%, margin of profit upon the whole, it is not an impossible result. And, in any case, the printing office had had its usual scale of profit upon that immense turnover.

It had been an enormous blunder, and, whether by its own inevitability or John's mismanagement, it had brought Scott to the threshold of ruin on at least two occasions. But, as he posted back the Duke's guarantee, he could feel that, by his own energy and ability, as well as by his genius as a novelist, he had first sustained, and afterwards redeemed the position. For years he had thought of it as, at the best, a source of almost ruinous loss, and now, at last, it was a chapter in his life which was closed; and, almost miraculously, he was £1,000 to the good. Now he had only to write a couple more novels for Constable, and he would be a few thousand pounds more on the right side. Even if James were losing money at the Canongate works (which he did not suppose) he could hardly be doing so as fast as that. If Scott looked forward to the future with a confident courage, we may think that few men had a better right.

Yet we may observer that he had received a very large total during the last year in the form of Constable's bills. They had been easily discounted. Constable's name was good. His bills were always met to the day. He was the Napoleon of the trade. And the fact that he was making a fortune out of Scott's novels was not likely to make him less able to meet his obligations. Yet it is a fact that if he *should* fail, Scott might be called upon to repay all the money which the banks had given him so readily against the publisher's signature. It was a remote—it might seem an absurdly remote—possibility. It was a risk which the banks would take for a small percentage, and they usually knew what they were doing. It was no more than a business risk, such as all might take at times. But that Scott was not careless, even in regard to such remote contingencies, was shown by that instruction to John last year to see that Longman's own bill, rather than Constable's substitute, should be paid over to him.

CHAPTER LXIV

It was in August of this year (1817) that Washington Irving called at Abbotsford. He had a note of introduction from Thomas Campbell, which he sent down to the house with his card, and a line upon it saying he was on his way to inspect Melrose Abbey, and would it be convenient for Mr. Scott to receive a visit from him in the course of the morning? He sat in his chaise on the highroad above the house—'a vineclad cottage' he called it—waiting for the reply, and Scott came out himself, walking vigorously though lamely along the path, with the help of a heavy stick. Irving did not know of, nor apparently guess, those bouts of illness which were wearing down his strength at this time. He called out heartily how was Tom Campbell, before he reached the side of the chaise. Dogs frisked round him, greyhound and setter. Maida, the great staghound, walked gravely behind. Mr. Irving must come in and have breakfast. Mr. Irving excused himself. He had had it already. Then another would do no harm. It will be remembered that Scott had a habit of breaking the back of the day's work before breakfast. It was a late meal. Mr. Irving had a full programme to get through that day. It had been early with him.

He was soon in the breakfast room, meeting Mrs. Scott and the four children, who were all there. Sophia was nearly eighteen, with much of her father's intelligence, much of her mother's vivacity. Walter, two years younger. Anne, a girl of fourteen, quieter than her sister, Mr. Irving thought. Perhaps shyer would be the better word. And there was Charles, not yet twelve who was delegated to show Melrose to the visitor later in the morning, a duty which often fell upon him on behalf of the Abbotsford guests. It was a family which was seldom separated as yet. Its affections were strong and close. Scott had given up teaching the boys Latin since they left Ashestiel, but he had engaged George Thomson, the son of the minister of Melrose, as a tutor, and by this time, like Miss Miller, he was almost one of the household. He was a natural athlete, who was still good at single-stick or on horse-back, though he had a wooden leg—the result of a violent accident in boyhood, concerning the cause of which he had always maintained silence, so that the culprit had gone free.

Mr. Irving, thinking to stay hours, found that it would be days. Scott said the country could not be read like a newspaper, in a single morning. There would be a walk on the hills for the afternoon, and up the Yarrow tomorrow, and a drive to Melrose next day.

In the afternoon, Scott took him up to the hills. Irving says that he looked round in a "mute surprise". The hills were not very high: they were very bare. Scott saw that he was not greatly impressed. Irving paid an adroit compliment in the assurance that it had a greater charm to him than any English scenery, because of the mantle of romance in which Scott himself had clothed it. But that was no consolation to Scott. He loved that land far more than his own fame.

"It may be pertinacity," said he at length; "but to my eye, these grey hills, and all this wild border country, have beauties peculiar to themselves. I like the very nakedness of the land; it has something bold, and stern, and solitary about it. When I have been for some time in the rich scenery about Edinburgh, which is like ornamented garden land, I begin to wish myself back again among my own honest grey hills; and if I did not see the heather, at least once a year, *I think I should die!*"

They made Mr. Irving one of the family that evening, sitting in the room, now 'half drawing-room, half study,' where Scott had once worked in the window with a curtain behind his back. Now he read Mallory to the family for an evening recreation.

In the morning, wakened by the sound of voices, Mr. Irving looked out through a window of honeysuckle, to see Scott, already about directing the labour of the new house that he had commenced to build. Later in the day, he saw the old quarry at Kaeside, from which Scott was getting his own stone for his own house, and learnt incidentally that when he had been abroad he had brought back presents for all the men he employed, that each might know that he had not been out of his thoughts.

He left at length, marvelling not merely at the unexpected hospitality he had had from one who was of so great a fame, but at the appearance of leisure which Scott, in spite of his immense industry, was able to show to the world. Yet the burden of such entertainment fell very heavily upon him, and upon the whole family, as the years passed. Those who came with letters of introduction were always received as expected guests, and even those who made a merely unmannered intrusion upon the privacy of the home sometimes came off better than they deserved. It was a year later that Lockhart observed such an incident, when, on returning with Scott from a visit to

Dryburgh, they found two American callers of another pattern. They had arrived from Selkirk earlier in the day, enquired for Mr. Scott, and shown such annoyance when told that he was out that the servant had asked if they would like to speak to his mistress. They accepted this offer, and had so conducted themselves as to convey the impression to Charlotte that they were visitors of importance, so that she had entertained them for lunch, and she and the girls had had them on their hands all day. When Scott returned for dinner with his guests, they met him on his own doorstep with such assurance that he would have welcomed them in the presumption that Charlotte knew who they were, but suspicion had been a growing plant in her mind, especially since they had annoyed her by enquiring first as to Mr. Scott's age, and then what was her own? Now she interposed to suggest that they would like to take the opportunity of presenting their letters of introduction. The gentlemen said they had none. They were travelling on their own merits. Scott said politely that it was a long walk to Melrose, and the day was advancing: it would be wrong to detain them further. Visibly reluctant, they went.

Scott listened with amusement to Charlotte's indignant comments, and laughed her annoyance away. But his own mind was uneasy; he remarked that no traveller of respectability could ever be at a loss for such an introduction as would ensure his best hospitality. Half-an-hour after he broke out with: "Hang the Yahoos, Charlotte—but we should have bid them stay dinner." And then later to Captain Fergusson he was on the same subject in the local dialect: "For a' that, the loons would hae been nane the waur o' their kail."

CHAPTER LXV.

It is at this time that Lockhart's previous introduction to Scott was improved into a personal acquaintance, and Scott conquered the young lawyer of literary predelictions, as he conquered all who came under the immediate influence of his personality.

Lockhart, in his facile journalistic style, becomes almost lyrical in his praise:

> "At this moment, his position, take it for all in all, was, I am inclined to believe, what no other man had ever won for himself by the pen alone. His works were the daily food, not only of his country-men, but of all educated Europe. His society was courted by whatever England could shew of eminence. Station, power, wealth, beauty, and genius, strove with each other in every demonstration of respect and worship, and—few political fanatics and envious poetasters apart—wherever he appeared in town or country: whoever had Scotch blood in him, 'gentle or simple', felt it move more rapidly through his veins when he was in the presence of Scott. To descend to what many looked on as higher things, he considered himself, and was considered by all about him, as rapidly consolidating a large fortune:—the annual profits of his novels alone had, for several years, been not less than £10,000 his domains were daily increased—his castle was rising—and perhaps few doubted that ere long he might receive from the just favour of his Prince some distinction in the way of external rank, such as had seldom before been dreamt of as the possible consequences of a mere literary celebrity. It was about this time that the compiler of these pages first had the opportunity of observing the plain easy modesty which had survived the many temptations of such a career; and the kindness of heart pervading, in all circumstances, his gentle deportment, which made him the rare, perhaps the solitary, example of a man signally elevated from humble beginnings, and loved more and more by his earliest friends and connections, in proportion as he

had fixed on himself the homage of the great and the wonder of the world."

It was at the dinner table of Mr. Hall Drummond that Lockhart found himself next to the man who had the greatest reputation of any of the nation to which they both belonged, and experienced "a cordiality which I had not been prepared to expect from one filling a station so exalted".

Scott did not spread the feathers of his own genius for a young man to admire. He led the conversation to Mr. Lockhart's own opinions and experiences, as his way had been from a child. Mr. Lockhart had been in Germany, in Weimar. He had seen Goethe. He had plenty to tell which Scott was pleased to hear. When they left the table, Lockhart had been told that he would be expected one day at Abbotsford. Scott had added him mentally to that innumerable list of the young men of Edinburgh who were interested in literature, and for whom it was mere routine for him to provide.

A few days later Lockhart received a letter from Messrs. James Ballantyne & Co. It appeared that Mr. Scott's 'various avocations' had prevented him from writing the usual historical summary of the year for the Edinburgh Register, 1816, which would be due for publication in the autumn. It would be agreeable both to Mr. Scott and themselves if Mr. Lockhart would undertake it on this occasion.

We may suppose that he did not hesitate in accepting this opportunity. He saw Scott several times in connection with it while he was in Edinburgh, usually in the library behind the dining-room at North Castle Street, where Weber had once produced his pistols, and where Maida (who used to accompany his master on all the migrations between the city and Abbotsford) would now be stretched at the side of his chair, or rise to strike the door with an imperious paw if he required Scott to open it for his exit, when the cat would come down from his high security at the ladder-top to take the vacated place at his master's side .... But, however intimate he may become,

Lockhart warns us to expect no exposures of private confidence from him.

> "I never thought it lawful," he remarks in his sententious manner, "to keep a journal of what passes in private society, so that no one need expect from the sequel of this narrative any detailed record of Scott's familiar talk. What fragments of it have happened to adhere to a tolerably retentive memory, and may be put into black and white without wounding, any feelings which my friend, were he alive, would have wished to spare, I shall introduce as the occasion suggests or serves. But I disclaim on the threshold anything more than this; and I also wish to enter a protest once for all against the general fidelity of several literary gentlemen who have kindly forwarded to me private lucubrations of theirs, designed to *Boswellise* Scott, and which they may probably publish hereafter. To report conversations fairly, it is a necessary pre-requisite that we should be completely familiar with all the interlocutors, and understand thoroughly all their minutest relations, and points of common knowledge and common feeling, with each other. He who does not must be perpetually in danger of misinterpreting sportive allusions into serious statement; and the man who was only recalling, by some jocular phrase or half-phrase, to an old companion, some trivial reminiscence of their boyhood or youth, may be represented as expressing, upon some person or incident casually tabled, an opinion which he had never framed, or if he had, would never have given words to in any mixed assemblage—not even among what the world calls *friends* at his own board. In proportion as a man is witty and humorous, there will always be about him and his a widening maze and wilderness of cues and catchwords, which the uninitiated will, if they are bold

enough to try interpretation, construe, ever and anon, egregiously amiss—not seldom into arrant falsity. For this one reason to say nothing of many others, I consider no man justified in journalising what he sees and hears in a domestic circle where he is not thoroughly at home; and I think there are still higher and better reasons why he should not do so where he is."

It is an admirable sentiment, and though most of us could have said it more clearly in fewer words, we will not quarrel with it for that. Lockhart's style is his own, and has been admired. The qualification that the bounds of decency are only to be observed towards those whose feelings the one of whom we are writing would not wish to wound is a subtlety of ethics which we must not turn aside to explore. It is sufficient to observe that Lockhart forgot either his own resolution, or that both James and John Ballantyne were Scott's lifelong friends.

Yet Lockhart probably did have his conscious reticences and reservations, for he was a man who would see much, and overhear more. He was one of those who live in their surroundings, who are more conscious of their environment than themselves. Sight or sound or scent—he would be alert to every assault upon his senses, of whatever kind. Those who live in themselves, in the resources of their intellects, or the riches of their imaginations, tend to lose, or at least omit to exercise, the acuteness of their physical senses, except by an exertion of conscious will. Scott puzzled Lockhart in these ways. He was less quickly conscious than others of the approach of a haunch of overkept venison: could not (or so Lockhart accuses him) tell corked wine from sound, either by scent or taste. Lockhart thought him deficient in appreciation of music, concerning which we may come to a consideration of his own testimony.

He went out little in the evenings while in Edinburgh at this period of intermittent illness, unless it were occasionally to the theatre, or more often for a drive, if the weather were favourable. Now or then, he gave or attended a formal dinner. On Sundays it was customary to invite three or four intimate friends to dinner *en famille*, with whom the evening would be spent informally in reading and conversation. Scott sometimes read aloud on these occasions, and Lockhart, who was often one of the party, says that he read 'high poetry with far greater simplicity, depth, and effect, than any other man I ever heard'. His favourite selections were from Shakespeare, Crabbe, Joanna Baillee, Dryden, Johnson; occasional scenes from Beaumont and Fletcher; and, among contemporary poets, Wordsworth and Southey were conspicuous, and all Byron as it was published. James Ballantyne was frequently a member of the Sunday gatherings, and took his share in the readings; Constable less frequently. John Ballantyne is not mentioned.

But Lockhart saw something of John, if it were not in Scott's drawing-room at North Castle Street. The dual occupations of auctioneer, and literary agent to the best-seller of the day, appeared to have brought prosperity to John at this period. He was often abroad, making search in France or Belgium for the antique treasures which his sale-room offered. He had lived with his family on the premises in Hanover Street in the days when his salary had been £300 from a publishing business which did not pay: now, he had a villa by Trinity, near to the Firth of Forth, which he had 'invested with an air of dainty voluptuous finery'. It had gardens, not extensive in themselves, but so contrived as to conceal their limitations with 'trellised alley and mysterious alcove, interspersed among their bright parterres'. John Ballantyne was a small man, and had chosen a wife of a larger size, as small men frequently do. Lockhart makes this difference the basis for one of the quaintest innuendoes likely to be discovered in any biography. He says: "he had erected for himself a private wing, the access to which, whether from the main building or from the bosquet, were so narrow that it was physically impossible for the handsome and portly lady who bore his name to force her person through any of them."

It was as a guest that Lockhart observed and was able to record this sinister peculiarity. He went out to dinner, and Scott and Constable were there also. He did not ascertain, or does not record, whether a maid-servant was kept specially slimmed to enter the private wing, or whether John cleaned it himself. But, of course, it may never have been cleaned at all.

The house which Scott made momentarily respectable by his presence had mirrors also, and portraits of actresses—Peg Woffington among them, and Kitty Clive. "Every actor or singer of eminence" who visited Edinburgh would be invited to its "Paphian arbours". "Here Braham quavered, and here Liston drolled his best—here Johnstone and Murray and Yates mixed jest and stave—here Keen revelled and rioted—and here the Roman Kemble often played the Greek from sunset to dawn." It is a dreadful tale. Lockhart sometimes gives us figures which we are able to check, with surprising results. But we can check nothing here. Once again, we must believe what we will.

But if we doubt John's depravity, Lockhart has a supporting anecdote. John, as we know, went to Paris on business. Paris, as we know, is a singularly wicked place. A certain Calvinistic bookseller of Edinburgh also had to go there on business, had John's address (how carelessly given!) and called upon him about buying a book. John was out, but the bookseller was invited to see 'madame' and taken up to a room where a lady was in bed, and several others—men and women—were there also. Shamelessly, they ate and drank. The good bookseller 'ran out o' the house as if I had been shot. What judgement: will this wicked world come to! The Lord pity us!'

Scott was not complaisant to vicious follies, and Lockhart was puzzled because he laughed at this joke.

In the intervals of squeezing into his private wing, John was fond of riding to hounds. When he went to his Princes Street auction room, he rode on a milk-white hunter, and ascended the rostrum in the half-dress of a sporting club—'a light-grey frock, with emblems of the chase on its silver buttons, white cord breeches Land jockey-boots in Meltonian order'. John's greyhounds used to come into Edinburgh behind the hunter, and Maida knew so well his master's habit of attending John's sales when the Court of Session rose, that he would go in advance to join the other dogs where they waited outside the auction rooms.

When John drove, he drove tandem, mounted on a bright-blue dogcart. That is about the last of his sins at this period. It is a slightly redeeming feature that his horses were named after Scott's novels, and his dogs after characters therein.

We may recognise Lockhart as a picturesque rather than an impartial witness, and still conclude that John Ballantyne's heirs were unlikely to live in idleness on anything he would leave.

Of James Ballantyne, whose acquaintance Lockhart made practically at the same time through his visits to North Castle Street he gives a widely different account. It appears that James invited him to his own house almost immediately they met, and he accepted the opportunity. He gives this description:

> "James Ballantyne then lived in St. John Street, a row of good, old-fashioned, and spacious houses. adjoining the Canongate and Holyrood, and at no great distance from his printing establishment. He had married a few years before the daughter of a wealthy farmer in Berwickshire—a quiet, amiable woman of simple manners and perfectly domestic habits: a group of fine young children were growing up about him: and he usually, if not constantly, had under his roof his aged mother, his and his wife's tender care of whom it was most pleasing to witness. As far as a stranger might judge, there could not be a more exemplary household, or a happier one; and I have occasionally met the poet in St. John Street when there were no other guests but Erskine, Terry, George Hogarth, and another intimate friend or two, and when James Ballantyne was content to appear in his own true and best colours, the kind head of his family, the respectful but honest school-fellow of Scott, the easy landlord of a plain comfortable table."

George Hogarth, a lawyer by profession, a man of reputed culture and author of a History of Music, was James's brother-in-law. At Scott's invitation, he had drawn up the documents which had released James from the partnership liabilities to clear the way for his sister's marriage; Scott's selection of him being good evidence of the liberality of his treatment of James, and of a personal confidence which he had no reason to regret.

Lockhart's account of James in this instance is not free from the usual tone of contempt, and the phrase "respectful *but* honest" may deserve a smile, yet it is not unkindly, nor derogatory in its broader outlines. The fact is that, in his treatment of James, there is such recurrent inconsistency that it would be easy to select half-a-dozen passages by which it would appear that James was of admirable character and exceptional abilities, and half-a-dozen others which give an opposite evidence. There is none of this inconsistency in the treatment of John. He is attacked on every possible occasion, and accused of every possible delinquency. If a stone can be flung in his direction, neither improbability nor inconsistency will be allowed to prevent its flight.

The cause of this difference may be that Lockhart always disliked John—and it is a likely guess that John was not fond of him. But Lockhart received hospitality and kindness from James during these years of prosperity, when their sequel was an unguessed, and would have seemed an incredible thing, and the impressions formed at that time will not leave his mind. The result is that while he caricatures John with a steady merciless consistency, that leaves him at last with the aspect of a monkey rather than a man, his James Ballantyne is neither successful caricature nor consistent portrait. It is at the worst an impossibility, at the best a blur.

It is also worth notice that while his bitterest representations of John were contained in the original *Memoirs of Sir Walter Scott*, he was comparatively reticent or restrained in his attacks upon the elder brother, until his accuracy in what he had said was intemperately challenged by the James Ballantyne Trustees, when he made the random counter-charges of a cornered man.

Lockhart's opportunities of observing James were not limited to the semi-domesticity of a private dinner party. He was invited to the christening dinner of the new novel which came out at this midsummer, to get which Constable had taken the whole of that Hanover Street stock. It was the *Heart of Midlothian*. Scott had given about six months of work as continuous as his health had allowed, and with little else to distract his mind. If Constable had paid high, he had got good value returned.

Now there was a congregation of Edinburgh celebrities, literary and social, at the printer's house, to welcome another novel by the author for whom James had invented the title of the Great Unknown.

Lockhart can describe a feast, and especially its drinking features, in a spirit which Dickens himself might not think unworthy. The turtle and venison were 'aldermanic' on this occasion: the ale was 'potent', the Madeira 'generous'. Scott Was present, quietly amused, and watchful of that thin cloak of incognito which he would not drop. There was the usual loyal toast, as the solid fare (or what was left of it) was removed, and then one that, James said: "shall never be omitted in a house of mine—that of Mr. Walter Scott".

When this had been drunk, and Scott briefly replied "with some expressions of warm affection" to James, Mrs. Ballantyne retired, and then "James rose once more, every vein on his brow distended, his eyes solemnly fixed on vacancy, to propose, not as before in his stentorian key, but with bated breath, in the sort of whisper by which a stage conspirator thrills the gallery— '*Gentlemen, a bumper to the immortal author of Waverley*'". It is a little difficult to understand how or why James distended so many veins when he spoke in a low voice, but, otherwise, the scene is realistic enough, with the 'cool demure fun' on Scott's face as he joins in the applause and listens to James returning thanks for the anonymous author, who would experience 'the proudest hour in his life' when informed of the reception which the toast had met.

And then James, too adroit to let discussion arise in Scott's presence from that hilarious assembly, started a song 'in a style which would have done no dishonour to almost any orchestra', and so the convivial evening went on with song and wine until Scott and Erskine, with any other 'clerical or very staid personage that had chanced to be admitted, saw fit to withdraw'.

That was the signal for claret and olives to be cleared away. Broiled bones took their place, with a 'mighty bowl' of punch, and after James had had several glasses of this beverage (but Lockhart may not have been in a condition to count accurately at this hour, and we need not take this aspersion too seriously) he was persuaded to read from the proof sheets the dialogue in the new novel which he thought best of all.

In this atmosphere, James read in such a style that 'the effect it produced was deep and memorable', the scene in Richmond Park between Jennie Deans, the Duke of Argyle, and Queen Caroline. We may agree that James made a good choice.

And after that they all drank again to the Great Unknown, and James recited the last words of Marmion (which was the closing ritual on these occasions) and everyone went home as best they could—and the *Heart of Midlothian* was published when they woke up, or perhaps earlier.

CHAPTER LXVI.

The Court of Session rose, and Scott, whose health had shown some improvement during the summer days, went back to Abbotsford to superintend the building of his new house, with the happy knowledge that the *Heart of Midlothian* had exceeded even his own successes. He had a genius which rose to its opportunities. Perhaps no great writer of fiction has been so dependent upon the spiritual qualities of the tale which he has to tell. To Scott, a poor theme meant a poor novel, but a poor theme would always be, and was particularly at this period of physical weakness, an unlikely choice.

It is a common superficial folly to represent him as the novelist of pageant rather than reality, of silk and steel, or even of pasteboard and tinsel; but here a young woman comes to us in a peasant's shawl, without wealth, without beauty, without intellect or culture, and by simple force of character, by the spirit in which she faces tragedy, she reduces those decorations of life to their essential triviality. If she were with us in the flesh today, she would be a woman, through the revelation of Scott's genius, that all would delight to honour. And so real is her presentation that it seems idle to say that she had less objective reality than any of those of her own time whose records are so much less vivid in actuality. We may tell ourselves that John Porteous lived, but that Jeanie Deans is an invented character, but we are not convinced. We feel that it is a fundamental falsehood. If God had not first created Jeanie Deans, the genius of Scott would have been unable to do so afterwards. She is the spirit of the Lowland peasant at its noblest possibility, as only Scott could have understood and revealed it. For Scott's mind searched everywhere for nobility. If he found it most easily in the glamour of the past, he did not therefore cease to seek, or fail to find it, in the life around him.

The *Heart of Midlothian* might well be received with enthusiasm in Edinburgh. It was the last and greatest chapter in the epic series of verse and prose by which its author revealed Scotland to herself, as well as to the outer world.

Leaving the loud chorus of applause with which the book was received, he went back to Abbotsford, to another dream of less enduring nobility—the house which he had designed in his mind, and which, had it been possible, he would doubtless have built with his own hands. But the days when he had made the dining-table for Lasswade, even the days when he had laboured among the masons on the first alterations at Abbotsford, were gone now, and for ever. Yet though he could not labour himself he had contrived that the house should be, as far as possible, the work of his neighbours' brains, and his neighbours' hands. He discovered talents of mason and carpenter among the local work-people which, under his directions, rendered him comparatively independent of imported assistance. Now one wing of it approached completion. In a few weeks it would be possible to migrate to some of the new rooms. The expense of building was heavy, and that of furnishing was Still to come. They would have been heavy even had Scott been one to make hard bargains, which was not his way. There must be a deal with Constable for another book. There would be no difficulty about that. Especially not now that there was no more old stock for disposal, and with this last book being so great a success. He must contract at once for ten thousand copies. That would mean good profits for the author, and good printing orders for the Canongate works. The old money troubles were over now—surely over for ever. But for this battle against ill-health, the recurrence of this terrible internal pain, the skies would have been of unbroken blue....

In September, Mr. Cadell came to Abbotsford. Being Constable's partner, he was in the secret of the authorship of the novels. He found Scott in better health. He was so busy upon the house-building, and the plantations, and the laying out of the new gardens, that Cadell wondered when he had time to think. But he said that he did that in the mornings, before he rose, and while he dressed, and if he would write for a few hours afterwards, the words came quickly enough. There would be no difficulty about another novel—no difficulty, and no delay. The subject had been chosen last year, before he had realised that *Midlothian* would be so long a tale. There would be no difficulty about the contract either. Everything went smoothly now that the nightmare of the stock was an ended dream.

Scott was building a new dyke at this time to keep back the Tweed at times of flood from his lower land. He had built one before, but it had been swept away in a night. He was building more strongly now. We do not make the same mistake twice, be it in conflict with financial forces or river flood.... Not the same, perhaps. But the wrong roads are many, and are most easily taken when we are oversure of the way.

Scott was laying out a new bowling green also, with a quiet seat for himself, where he might rest in the evening hours. He had chosen that spot because it was near the window of the room where Peter Mathieson, the coachman, had evening prayers with his family when the day's work was done. Lockhart thought that Scott was not fond of music. He was not an expert in the gymnastics of sound. He agreed about that. He was always quick to agree as to his own deficiencies. But he liked to sit by himself where he could hear the singing of the evening psalm from Peter's window.

It was early in the following month that he gave a dinner to half-a-dozen friends to celebrate the opening of the new dining-room. It was not yet ready for occupation, and the meal was laid in the little room in the cottage, into which all must be crowded as best they could, but there was to be dancing afterwards in the new room, which would be lit up for the first time.

The significance of the occasion was increased by the fact that two of the guests had been friends of Scott's boyhood days, with whom he had kept up an intimacy of correspondence, but whom he had not seen for many years. These were Lord Melville (he had been Lord Melville's son in the old days), and Captain Adam Fergusson, so long abroad in the wars, and now to be settled with his sisters at Huntley Burn, whom Charlotte remembered also as Scott's companion of the happy days of Gilsland when first they met. Scott of Gala came also and other neighbours not too distant to return home when the evening's celebration was over, for the guest-rooms of Abbotsford were still unready for occupation, and the accommodation of the old house was very limited, both above and below. But the little separate cottage, called the chapel, had two bedrooms, and Scott had heard that young Lockhart and John Wilson were taking holiday at Windermere, and had written to them to stop at Abbotsford on the way back, and to be there by October 8th, for their own good.

His object was to introduce them to Lord Melville who, as he told them once, was 'the great giver of good things' at

Parliament House, and whom it might be of advantage to them to know. It was a time when careers—or at least, their opportunities—were largely dependent upon such patronage.

Now they walked with the older men round the plantations, and by the half-built dyke, and watched Maida forget his dignity to join the terriers in useless chasing of the fleeter hares that swarmed on the unploughed land.

Fourteen or fifteen people had to be accommodated in a room that ten would crowd, but Charlotte managed it somehow, so that space was left for the servants to wait, and Lockhart (who was critical of such things) approved both service and company. He had not previously seen Scott in such buoyant spirits, nor been present at a gayer dinner.

It was eaten to the sound of John Bruce's bagpipes. John of Skye was a hedger-and-ditcher who had found service at Abbotsford, and Scott, learning that he could play the pipes, had dressed him in full Highland costume for this occasion. Now he paraded outside the window, and added music to the merriment within.

There was a turret already risen at the western end of the half-built mansion, and after dinner those who were young and vigorous, and such of the elders as did not know what they were about to do, accepted Scott's invitation to ascend it for the enjoyment of the moonlit view. He led the way himself, though he must apologise for the stairs, which were dark and narrow and very steep, and there were enough who followed to crowd the little platform, and look down upon the beauty of the moonlight-softened scene, and the distant ruin of Melrose, clear and white against the dark background of the Eildon hills...and the piper played *Lochaber no more* from the shadows beneath the tower.

After that, there was dancing in the new dining-room, for which the piper played, and there were none but joined, except Scott himself and the lame tutor Thomson, who must stand aside and look on. After that there was a song or two: *Johnnie Cope* from Captain Fergusson, and *Kenmure's on and awa'* from the girls, and then they must all join hands in a circle for the final chorus:

> "Weel may we a' be,
> Ill may we never be,
> God bless the King and the good companie."

And after that they went home.

Lockhart, sleeping in the 'chapel' bedroom, was waked before seven by the sound of his host's voice. He looked out through the latticed window to see Scott and Tom Purdie in conference. They had a rough sketch of the 'Blue Bank' at Toftfield—a field of clay that Scott was resolved to drain. He was up no later for the merriment of the night before. He did not seem like a sick man.

When he came in to breakfast two hours later he ate well of kippered salmon, and cut freely at the brown loaf which was beside his plate. Those who saw him at breakfast might think him to be a man of great appetite, but, in fact, doing some hours' work before it, as his way was, he had come to make breakfast the principal meal of the day. Lockhart had noticed in Edinburgh, (where his breakfast appetite may not have been equal to that of Abbotsford) how little he ate at dinner, and how singularly little (to Lockhart's mind) he seemed to care what it might be.

The post-bag came in while the breakfast proceeded, with a weight of contents which caused Lord Melville to wonder what was happening at the moment, but Scott said that it was no more than the usual infliction. He had good friends who helped him with the franking of envelopes, and the post-office was kind, but his bill for letters alone was £150 a year, and as to parcels—he told a tale in illustration against himself.

He had carelessly opened a parcel one morning, never doubting that it was franked—for who in his senses would send such a weight of matter unless under that customary protection?—and had been appalled to find that it was a MS. play from a lady in New York who thought that, if he would write a prologue and do a few other necessary things, he might place it with Constable to her great advantage—and, of course, with the manager at Drury Lane. A hurried glance at the cover showed that he had been debited £5 odd by the Post Office for this parcel, but he had broken the seal, and there was no more to be said.

Yet, in spite of this lesson, he was equally careless with another parcel a fortnight later, to find to his horror that it was a second copy of the same play. The lady had considered the risks of tempest and the uncertainties of our earthly life, and had sent a second copy to make sure that her treasure should not be lost....

So Scott dispersed his guests to such pleasures as the country gave, and disappeared with his morning correspondence till one o'clock, when he emerged with a dozen letters written in his own hand for the post, and a coach-parcel addressed to James, which an urchin at the toll-gate fielded as they drove out to see Melrose in the afternoon, and carried into the adjoining pot-house, to wait the coach. The careful Lockhart considered how thin was the disguise of the Great Unknown, which might be exposed by any unscrupulous stranger who should break the seal of one of those daily parcels which were so randomly handled.... And how many might be willing to do it—or even to steal such a priceless packet!—of the endless tourists who lounged around Abbotsford and Melrose now? For they had driven past two loaded chaises, drawn up at the gate, and waiting for a glimpse of Scott if he should be coming out, and at the side of the road (it being before the era of photography) there were men who sketched.... But Scott left Lockhart to do the worrying. His day's work was done. He threw the packet to the urchin who may have caught so many before, and drove on to Melrose and Dryburgh Abbey to show his guests what their beauties were.

CHAPTER LXVII.

Charles Charpentier was dead. He had died in his Indian exile, leaving a wife, but no children. He left considerable property—spoken of as £30,000 to £40,000—to his wife during her life, and then to his sister's children. Scott thought of this money with some satisfaction. It was an added security for his children, if the inspiration of his novels should cease, and his income with it. He felt that he would embark on his dreams of improving Abbotsford with more confidence than before. But he did not want the children to take the news in the wrong way. He would not have them overvalue money, or the power it brings. He suggested that their mother had the first right. So she had, they said generously; she could have all if she would.

Scott thought he could provide for their mother himself, but he was pleased by the way they spoke. They could not know that that money would never be more than a mirage to them. None of them would see it. Charles Charpentier's widow would outlive them all. But who could have guessed that then?

Charlotte had not seen her brother since he sailed for India twenty years ago. We might think that his death would mean little to her. But she did not feel it like that. He had been her one link with a dead past—a past that was private to her own mind. His letters had been the one thing that kept it alive. Now it was utterly gone. The home in southern France that was a childhood's dream. Her dead parents. Her only brother, who was dead now. She had no relative left alive. There had been an uncle—a colonel in the Russian army—but news of him had ceased many years ago. Doubtless he was dead.

Walter could not console her now, for they were people—it was a life—he had never known. Now it was so utterly gone, and these memories that none could share—it was like being dead while you still lived. For with all the gay courage with which she had faced the changes of life, Charlotte knew that she was an exile here. She would be exiled from his memory when he was dead. He might have no complaint of her, or she of him, but afterwards it would always be said that he had not chosen the right wife. She did not care (overmuch) for his books, though she had a great pride in all that he did. She did not pretend to care for the derivation of a burn's name. Why should she? She was a daughter of southern France. Of a land she would never see. With memories that there was no one alive to share. For two days she lay taking consolation from none. Scott wrote about it to Morritt on the third day. He understood well enough. It was a grief that he saw that he could not share. He had never seen her brother. That was the cry of her distress. What could such a death be to him?

But on that day she had regained her courage, her self-control. She was coming downstairs again.

Biography is most often unfair to those whose lives surrounded the genius on which it dwells. They are the furniture of his life. It is intolerable that they should disturb or frustrate it. They should understand what they are for. They are thrust into a publicity which they have done nothing to challenge, and they are regarded only in relation to an orbit which is not theirs. It is obvious that their own lives should be subordinated to that of the genius who was their parent, or whom they married or bore. If they fall short of understanding that, they are execrated for the failures which they are shown to be.

But Charlotte did not fail. She married a man of a foreign race, and a poet of genius, which is a sufficiently difficult combination for any woman to undertake. She was handicapped by the fact that he had contracted an earlier love which he could never—which, indeed, he did not desire to forget. Yet she did not fail him in any way. She gave him pleasure and peace. She showed no jealousy of his genius, which is a common experience of such marriages. She showed no jealousy of his very numerous women friends. She ruled his home well, and in the spirit which he preferred. In her own sphere, she was as generous as he. She was loyal to him in every circumstance and relation of life.

She had her reward in a love which grew closer as the years

passed, and a comradeship which was no less real because there were some things which they did not fully share. She made a very fortunate marriage, and requires no sympathy. But she requires a more difficult thing—justice, which she has not had.

CHAPTER LXVIII.

The thought of Charles Charpentier's fortune, which might be his children's at any time, may have encouraged Scott to regard his substantial professional income, and the almost fantastic profits that his novels brought, as money which he could spend with a freer hand than he would otherwise have done, but he was not insensible of the future, nor reckless in regard to his present commitments.

It may have been owing to the extent of his current expenditure upon the building of the new house, to which it is commonly attributed, that he now entered into a negotiation with Constable regarding the copyrights which he had retained in his own name; but it is more probable that it was induced by consideration of the uncertainty of his own life, and a desire to lease his estate in a settled form. Cramp in the stomach did not sound a very formidable name to give the seizures to which he had become intermittently liable, and he had survived several already. He had found that, as soon as it had time to take effect, opium would do much to deaden the pain. He was not one to give way to morbid fears. The moment that the symptoms ceased, he would be his usual buoyant resolute self. But his courage was of the kind that would look facts in the face, and he knew that he was weakening and ageing under these attacks, that were always recurring and for which no one could offer him any radical cure.

It is most probable that he looked death in the face when he made the bargain with Constable which was expressed in a formal bond, the terms of which were agreed in December, and which was executed in February, 1819.

Up to this date, he had retained all or part of the copy rights of some of the poems, and part of the copyright of some of the novels. Now he made them over to Constable for a total consideration of £12,000. The money was not to be paid at once, and the copyrights were not to be legally assigned until, or as far as, the money was paid. Scott protected himself in this way, even against the possibility of Constable's insolvency, of which no one thought at that time. But it was a definite undertaking to buy at a settled price. It removed that portion of his estate from the hazards of incompetent bargaining, or a change of literary fashion which might reduce their value. Scott was adventurous by disposition, and immensely generous both by principle and inclination, but he never showed lack of business ability in regard to any matter which engaged his attention seriously.

He had had separate occasion to review the solidity of his financial position during the last few months owing to an intimation which had come to him some months earlier with the usual initial informality, that the Prince-Regent would be pleased to confer on him the rank of baronet, if he would be pleased to accept it. His correspondence shows that he was dubious about this distinction, which he was clear-sighted enough to see would be a burden rather than an advantage financially, not only to himself, but potentially to his children. There was a prolonged delay before he gave such a reply that the invitation could be formally issued, but in the end he accepted, as men usually do.

But though he signified his acceptance, the actual assumption of the honour was delayed, for, as the winter had come, the attacks of illness had resumed their violence, and increased their frequency. He spent these months in Edinburgh as usual, and continued his duties of Clerk of Session as often as heath allowed; he was even seen at the theatre more than once, where *Rob Roy* was performed in February, and had a run of forty-one nights, but his condition was such that he delayed the commencement of the projected novels, contenting himself with historical and antiquarian essays in his better intervals, and when the Court rose in March, and he was able to leave for

Abbotsford, his state of health was a subject of anxious conversation among his friends.

He went home with the resolution that the novels—for he had more than one in his mind at this time—should not be longer delayed, let his health be what it would. He called on Laidlaw's services again to take down from his dictation, and then on John Ballantyne also. John left his business in Princes Street, and the pleasure (whatever it might be) of squeezing through the narrow door in his Trinity villa, to spend long periods at Abbotsford at his patron's call.

It seems an expensive method of dictating, but the day of professional stenographers had not come. The writing had to be rapid and accurate, for Scott would dictate fast, especially when he came to a passage of dialogue, or a scene of special animation, and it must be intelligently transcribed.

John said that he used to start in the morning with a dozen pens laid out for use, so that he should not risk having to pause to mend a quill when the narration was in full flow. Scott lay on a couch at this time, the sentences of dictation often broken with groans of pain, but there were times (John said) when he would forget his physical weakness in the excitement of climax, and pace rapidly up and down the room as he dictated, in the different voices of the characters, the conversation which he conceived.

Toward the end of the vacation, Lockhart had an invitation to spend a few days at Abbotsford, and rode out with John, who had warned him of the rapid change which illness had made since he had seen Scott only a few weeks before, but he found it to be far more than he had supposed. His clothes hung loosely on a frame that had lost its flesh, his face was haggard and yellow, his hair, which had been slightly tinged with grey, had turned almost snow-white during those weeks of agony.

But his eyes had even more than their old brilliancy, his greeting was cordial, his spirits good. He came to the table at dinner, though his diet was rice-pudding only, with toast and water to follow. He talked of his illness as a battle that he had fought and won. He said that there had been a time when he had feared that it was affecting his brain, and he had tried whether he could translate an old German ballad, as a test to reassure himself. They could see what he had done. Sophia went for the script.. She and William Laidlaw had taken it down between them during one day of incessant pain. He read the *Noble Morringer*. It is a wonderful translation, by any standard, worthy to be placed among the best of his ballads. It has a gaiety of tone which is an amazement for a composition under such conditions. When he found that his guests praised it freely, he said it should go into the new Register.

Certainly, his illness had not weakened his mind. But he had tired visibly as he read the poem, and he said he would go to bed. Later, when the family were retiring, his illness returned acutely, and Dr. Scott was hastily summoned. For some hours his groans could be heard even at some distance from the house. The only 'remedy' that was attempted at this stage was hot baths, with opium to relieve the pain.

Lockhart resolved that he would leave in the morning. It was no time to inflict a guest on that house. But as he was dressing, before seven, Scott tapped on his door, and came in, looking better than the night before. He said he mustn't think of leaving, for after last night he was sure of three days' respite at least. He wanted to ride out, to get rid of that accursed laudanum. He would finish his morning's dictation to John, and they would all go to Selkirk together. Not do twenty miles after last night? He had done forty under similar circumstances a week ago. There was an election on, and Buccleuch, who was ill and gone abroad with Adam Fergusson, was relying upon him to see it through.

So, by eleven o'clock they set off, John on the milk-white steed of which we have heard before, and Scott on Sybil Grey, an active cob, on which he cantered briskly to catch up his companions after telling them to ride forward when he stopped at the Sheriff's office in Selkirk.

Thin and white-haired he might be, but he seemed in good health enough as they rode by Philliphaugh, and he must describe the battle when Montrose was beaten at last. For he was busy on *A Legend of Montrose* as well as the *Bride of Lammermuir*, and would have them both ready for publication by midsummer, unless he were a dead man before that.

And the next day they rode out again over Bowden Moor and beyond, canvassing doubtful voters, as he had promised to do, and with results with which he was well content.

And the day after that, having done with the election, they went over the Eildon hills and within sight of Smailholm Tower, and elsewhere, and that night he had the cramp, as they called it, again, though not so badly as before. And Lockhart left him next morning dictating to John, and talking cheerfully of what he would do when he was in Edinburgh; but his own thought was that he might have seen Scott for the last time.

A few days later Scott had the news that Buccleuch was dead at Lisbon, and he wrote to Fergusson, who was bringing home his remains: "I have had another eight days' visit of my disorder, which has confined me chiefly to my bed. It will perhaps shade off into a mild chronic complaint—if it returns frequently with the same violence, I shall break up by degrees, and follow my dear chief. I thank God I can look at this possibility without much anxiety, and without a shadow of fear."

He wrote to Southey also, a long letter commenced on April 4th, in the course of which he said:

> "I have gone through a cruel succession of spasms and sickness.... I have been seized with one or two successive crises of my cruel malady, lasting in the utmost anguish from eight to ten hours. If I had not the strength of a team of horses, I could never have fought through it.... I did not lose my senses, because I resolved to keep them, but I thought once or twice they would have gone overboard, top and top-gallant. I should be a great fool, and a most ungrateful wretch, to complain of such inflictions as these. My life has been, in all its public and private relations, as fortunate

perhaps as was ever lived up to this period; and whether pain or misfortune may be behind the dark curtain of futurity, I am already a sufficient debtor to the bounty of Providence to be resigned to it. Fear is an evil which has never mixed with my nature, nor has even unwonted good fortune rendered my love of life tenacious...."

But there is an undated postscript to this letter which says:

"Another ten days have passed away, for I would not send this Jeremiad to tease you, while its termination seemed doubtful. For the present
"The game is done—I've won, I've won,
Quoth she, and whistles thrice."

He travelled back to Edinburgh for the new Session, but an attempt to return to his duties at the Court proved beyond his capacity. He was in bed there for several weeks: still in bed when the new novels were published, and those who read them supposed them to be the last that he would ever write.

The knowledge of his condition had spread by this time wherever a newspaper penetrated through the world that knew him. The two tales were received in the atmosphere of this consciousness, and would have escaped any severity of criticism had they been much worse than they were. They were good enough, but we have to forget Scott at his best before we can praise them freely. They are both significantly short, and the genius of Scott at his best needed a large canvas. *A Legend of Montrose* does not rise to its opportunities. Under other circumstances of composition, it might have been one of his greatest novels. The *Bride of Lammermuir* has always been a disputed book. To some it is dull and unreal; others have placed it high, or even highest on the list of Scott's romances. Probably, preference for the species of tale it tells has deranged their judgement. But the doubt is the condemnation. Had it been written with the intellectual vigour and imagination of the *Heart of Midlothian*, its tragedy would have left no doubt in our minds. It was composed under such conditions that its author read it without memory of its contents, and turning each page in fear of what nonsense he might discover upon the next. He fortified himself with the thought that he could trust James not to have let anything dreadful pass, and he ended with the thought that it might do well enough with a friendly public. In this verdict he showed sounder judgement than some who have praised it since. Had it been the work of an unknown author, it is doubtful whether it would have attained popularity, or been remembered at all today. It may be easy to find points on which we can praise it, but the truth is a better thing.

The fact was that the severity of his illness had been too great to enable him to imagine with continuous power. Previously, it had had the effect of giving him an increased leisure for composition, perhaps an increased consciousness of the spiritual values of life. Hence the *Heart of Midlothian*. Now he had been too ill, and too exhausted, for successful effort. The determination that the books should be written had carried him through, but this obstinate courage had

"ill supplied
"The stream of life's exhausted tide,"

and the results are as we see them to be.

There had been times during their composition when his own resolute courage had thought it better to face the fact that he could not live, than to continue the struggle. Sophia remembered one evening in June when he called the family together, thinking that he would not live through the night, and addressed them in words of confident faith and exhortation, telling them to leave him at last that he might "turn his face to the wall". But after that he slept very long, and the next day the doctors spoke with a new hope. They thought that there was a change in his condition, to whatever weakness he had been reduced. They spoke of a crisis past.

Passers-by glanced at the house in North Castle Street with its muffled knocker from day to day expecting to see a house of death, but he did not die. When the session ended, he was well enough, and we can suppose how willing, to be moved to Abbotsford. The attacks did not return with their old severity. Very slowly he was regaining strength. He had already commenced a new novel before he returned to Abbotsford, where the masons were still at work, and the house grew, as did the plantations round it.

CHAPTER LXIX.

As Scott's health came slowly back in the summer days, he dictated a new novel to Laidlaw—not that which he had commenced in the period of severe illness. He was dissatisfied, uncertain, about that. He had thrown it aside. A new and fortunate imagination had invaded his mind.

He might be weak and unable to get about for more than a few hours of the day, but he was buoyant of mood and clear of brain. He knew that he was doing a good thing. James thought the same. There was a growing enthusiasm in the Canongate office as the chapters came, one by one, on the coach from Abbotsford, and were prepared for the press.

In fact, as his health returned, Scott approached the peak of prosperity and reputation. It was a height such as few can even approach, and from which it would not be easy to fall.

Yet during this year, when his own sun rose higher, as though it would never set, the shadows of the mutability of earthly things fell thickly across his path. For twenty years, strong affection and settled judgement had combined to keep his children closely around him. Now Walter must go. At seventeen, he was gazetted ensign to the 18th Hussars, stationed in Ireland. Sophia's interest in John Lockhart, and his in her, pointed to another separation that could not long be delayed. The home that had been founded in the Lasswade cottage was commencing to break apart. These were signs of a new flowering, rather than the falling of ruined leaves, but December brought its sorrows of a different kind. Vigorous and clear of intellect to the last, Scott's mother died. Her half-brother, Dr. Rutherford died. Her half-sister, Christian Rutherford, died. All within three weeks. Christian had been sister to Scott, rather than aunt. There was a close affection between them of forty years. He had griefs enough this December when *Ivanhoe* came out, and the flame of his reputation rose to its fullest height.

His own health was largely restored by this time, and he had even thought to mount a battle-charger again. For the unrest in the industrial districts of Scotland had become so great that the talk of revolution was in every mouth. Volunteer regiments for the preservation of public order were being raised in all parts of the country. Scott of Abbotsford and Scott of Gala consulted together for the peace of their own district. There were a hundred names sent in of men in his neighbourhood who would join a sharpshooter regiment if he would act as its colonel. Then the political skies cleared for the time, and the project was put aside. Scott had ordered a charger of the kind he rode in the old Yeomanry days, though he cancelled this before an actual purchase took place.

As to the novel, being of a new kind, he had been bent on the adventure of another anonymity. For this reason it had been printed in a new setting, on better paper than had been used for the Waverley series. It was to be a three-volume publication, at the increased price of 10/- each—thirty shillings the set. And he was so sure of success on this occasion, name or no name, that he had stipulated for the first edition to by larger than ever.

At the last moment, Constable had protested against the folly of anonymous publication, and Scott had given way, but he was probably right in thinking that it would have made no difference. England had welcomed the Scottish novels, but not as she welcomed *Ivanhoe*. They had had immense sales, but not such as were now recorded. Twelve thousand sets at thirty shillings—eighteen thousand pounds the public handed to the trade for these books, and demanded more.

There will always be those who dispute pre-eminence between *Ivanhoe* and the novels of Scottish life, in which the element of imagination is less, and that of observation more. It is a problem without solution, because they have different excellences of which there can be no common standard of measurement. We may discuss it till we tire, but praise and preference will go together at last.

There have been those who have criticised *Ivanhoe* because it is not an accurate portrait of life in England in the days of King John. They have also said that Cedric was not a man's name. Perhaps not: but it is now. Minds of that order will think that the Scottish novels are of a better kind.

But there are others to whom that order of criticism has no meaning. To them, if it could be shown that King John or Richard had never lived, that there had never been such a time at all, Ivanhoe would be even a greater wonder than it is now.

From whatever materials, Scott has created a living world. It is the marvel of his genius that he had made three separate successes, of which no two include or imply the third. The author of the *Lady of the Lake* had produced a poem of the highest order, and his place in the world's literature was secure over all changes of fashion, while the language lasts, but he might have written that poem and been incapable of producing *The Heart of Midlothian*. Similarly, the author of that novel had won his rank in the realms of fiction, but it contains no evidence that its author could project his imagination into the atmosphere in which *Ivanhoe* is conceived.

It is equally true that the author of these three works of highest imagination might have been incapable of such lyrics as are scattered among them and his other romances in verse and prose, and had he published these lyrics and ballads separately as the whole work of his life, he would have won a place in English poetry which would have been both high and secure. And by this four-fold strength he is entrenched upon the heights, beyond the challenge of mediocrity.

It has been objected that the plot of *Ivanhoe* would have been more interesting had its hero and Rebecca defied their environment, and eloped together. It would certainly have made it nearer to the pattern of tale which is approved today; but to Scott it would have been an impossible thing for a hero to do, being without heroism. We say that we must be true to ourselves and, it we cannot be true to others, it may be all that remains. It is the last ditch. But Scott's ideals were different. For a man to break faith with a woman who loves him, and whom he is pledged to marry, may be prudent, for all its baseness. It may even be wise. But it would not have occurred to Scott to call it a romantic action.

There are details in the plot of the novel which outrage probability. They belong to the possibilities which are as unlikely as truth itself, which the careful novelist should avoid. They belong to Scott's method of constructing his plots en route. A different habit would have prepared the Templar for his final exit with some earlier evidence of a bad heart.

The resurrection of Athelstan was James Ballantyne's contribution, and an evidence of Scott's complaisancy. But we may doubt whether he would have been so complaisant had he not enjoyed exercising the ingenuity which the alteration required.

The book does not depend upon plot, but upon the splendour and vividness of its scenes and characters. A reader accustomed to let a dozen modern novels drift every month across the mind's surface, leaving no trace, would find it hard to read the scene in Friar Tuck's hut and forget it with the same facility.

CHAPTER LXX.

Ivanhoe was followed within less than three months by another novel which will not endure comparison. The *Monastery* had been commenced with, or before, *Ivanhoe*, and continued intermittently. A few chapters had been set in type even before the publication of: the other novel. They were set in the usual style of the Waverley series, as it was intended that this should be announced as the next novel by that author, while *Ivanhoe* should be put forward as the work of a new candidate for public favour, 'Lawrence Templeton'. That idea had been abandoned, but it was too late, even had it been desirable, to arrange to bring out the *Monastery* in the ornate style of *Ivanhoe*, and at its higher price. Longmans had the London publishing of this book. Constable could not complain. He was making a small fortune out of *Ivanhoe*, for which there was a sustained demand. Longmans could place important printing orders with James, which he was glad to have. They could not be entirely ignored.

But the book itself failed, as it deserved to do. It had a large sale, but those who read it were not pleased. It had good features, of course, as anything which Scott wrote would be sure to have, but in its broad effect it was dull, and, at times, silly; it was an immense contrast to *Ivanhoe*. Constable may have been well content that it had Longman's name on the cover. He had his own idea as to the next book that Scott should write for him. It should be about the Armada. Scott so far agreed that he said he would give him a book about Elizabeth. But the scene must be Kenilworth. Scott liked to work either by pure imagination, or on scenes that he knew. He had inspected Kenilworth twice—the second time with some care. He had a tale in his mind. It should be called *Cumnor Hall*. Constable said, why not call it *Kenilworth*? James objected that that would ruin the best book ever written. Worth a kennel! What a name! But Scott sided with Constable. *Kenilworth* it should be. Constable almost felt that he was writing these anonymous Waverley novels himself. He had named one of them previously. Now he had suggested a period and christened the book as well. There was only the remaining detail of writing it, which Scott could attend to quite competently. He promised that it should be out before the end of the year. But before he began it, he must go up to London for the formal acceptance of the title which had been offered him more than a year ago by the Regent who was now King. And he must be back before April was over, for Sophia was to be married to John Lockhart, and Scott shared the superstitious objection to a marriage in May.

He planned to visit London as soon as the Court rose, and before then there must be a hurried week-end visit to Abbotsford, for he had a vacant secluded cottage on his property, beyond Huntley Burn, which could be improved into a summer residence for John and Sophia. They would commence on a slender income, which does young people no harm, but he would do nothing to hinder the marriage. His own observation of life was too sound, his own experience too bitter, for there to be any doubt of that.

It was probably the first week-end that the weather had permitted that six-hours drive to Abbotsford, with any probability that they would be able to inspect the cottage on the following day, for the winter had been one of exceptional severity, with a depth of snow which forbade all rural occupations, and had lain unthawed during the previous month.

For on January 19th, Scott had been writing his letter of instructions to Laidlaw, which seems to have been a weekly custom when he was in Edinburgh, unless he could get down for the week-end, and had sent him £60 for current expenses, with this concluding paragraph:

> "It makes me shiver in the midst of superfluous comforts to think of the distress of others. £10 of the £60 I wish you to distribute among our poorer neighbours so as may best aid them. I mean not only the actually indigent, but those who are in our phrase 'ill aff'. I am sure Dr. Scott will assist you with his advice in this labour of love. I think part of the wood-money, too, should be given among the Abbotstown folk if the storms keep them off work, as is like."

And a week later he sent another cheque for £50, with an added note of anxiety as to the condition of the people around

Abbotsford under such climatic conditions. "Do not let the poor bodies want for a £5 or even a £10 more or less." It is clear that it would never be easy for Walter Scott to be rich while there was a need around him that was unrelieved.

The allusion to the 'wood-money' in the first letter is interesting, because it shows how early this fund had been instituted. Several years later he explained to Captain Basil Hall that his energetic and systematic forestry had resulted in the production of large quantities of fire-wood which he would willingly have given, but that he had doubted the wisdom of... general charity. ("I very, very rarely" he had assured Captain Hall, "give anything away"!) So he had put a nominal price on the timber, which people really liked better. They carted it off without any uncomfortable feeling of obligation, and the money they left behind was paid into a fund which was handed over to Dr. Scott, with private instructions to charge against it his attendances upon Scott's poorer neighbours, so that they might have equal advantages with the most affluent.

But the snow had gone, and the weather was fine enough on this Saturday afternoon in February when he came to Court with his week-end clothes under his gown; and when the morning's work was over, the carriage was waiting outside, with Peter on the box, and as many of the family as it would hold, beside himself and John and Sophia, crowded inside, and they drove off to Abbotsford....

The next morning, John Ballantyne and Constable rode in to breakfast. Business still seemed to be flourishing with John, and his spirits were as irrepressible as ever, though he had the look of a sick man. He was very thin, and had trouble with his lungs. But he was of the usual ceaseless activity, and the expenses of his Trinity residence had not prevented him taking a hunting-box in the Leader valley, near Abbotsford, to which Constable came as his guest.

As to John's sources of income at this time, we get some light in a letter which Scott wrote to him during the previous autumn, when young Walter went up to London to get his officer's outfit, and Scott had been too ill to go with him. John was in London at that time: looking round for articles that he could buy cheaply and auction at higher prices in Edinburgh, and with a probable eye upon the publishers also, on behalf of the printing business.

Walter was staying with Miss Dumergue, and Scott would like John to look after him while in London, where he would be strange and shy, and particularly to oversee the cost of his outfit, some of the items of which seemed needless in themselves or extortionate in their cost. Scott adds that he wants John back in Edinburgh as soon as possible. He is short of money, and wants to fix up the contract for *Ivanhoe*, which is nearing completion, and he hints that if John is not on the spot to handle the negotiation it may not be easy to get that liberal percentage for him which Constable had been accustomed to pay.

John's regular business was that of an auctioneer of antiques and curios, in which he had established himself with substantial success, but he was also making a good income as Scott's literary agent, and in return for those easily-earned commissions, Scott regarded him—and he was evidently more than willing to be regarded—as at his disposal for any matter, business or private, in which he required his aid, whether it were to negotiate a printing order in London, or to act as his amanuensis at Abbotsford.

Now John drove in for breakfast in the early winter dawn. He was like Scott in preferring a horse to a carriage-seat, but he had Constable as his guest, and the publisher was a man of a different build. The day's programme had been arranged before the parties left Edinburgh, and John had fixed a place and time where his groom would meet him with Old Mortality, that milk-white hunter of which we have heard already.

But, being Sunday, Scott must first read prayers, and one of Jeremy Taylor's sermons, to guests and household, and then, while it was still before noon, the whole party set out for the two-mile walk to the cottage which was to be the young couple's future home, taking Huntley Burn on the way.

Two miles is not far, but it was a rough road. There were

hillocks to be climbed, and ravines to be descended, and Scott, lame and still half-invalid though he might be, set a pace which was far from easy for the corpulent city publisher to maintain beside him. Lockhart remembered Constable stopping to wipe his forehead with the remark that it wasn't every author who should lead him a dance like that.

Indeed, Lockhart remembered all the events of that day very vividly, as well he might; it was a happy occasion for him, in itself and in that which it promised for future days, and though we may suppose that Sophia had her share of attention, it did not prevent the words of others being heard, the actions of others being recorded, in a retentive memory.

They stopped at Huntley Burn, where the Misses Fergusson comforted Constable with a good lunch, and then went on to inspect the cottage, and hold counsel upon the alterations which would be needed, and which Tom Purdie who was of the party (with the inevitable dogs—even Maida had come down to week-end at Abbotsford) received instructions to put in hand.

It may have been the happy association of the day which caused Lockhart to describe John Ballantyne's part in a manner which, though not free from the element of caricature which was probably unavoidable with him towards those whom he disliked, is none the less convincing because it is almost kindly.

> "Johnny Ballantyne, a projector to the core, was particularly zealous about this embryo establishment. Foreseeing that he should have had walking enough ere he reached Huntley Burn, his dapper little Newmarket groom had been ordered to fetch Old Mortality thither, and now, mounted on his fine hunter, he capered about us, looking pallid and emaciated as a ghost, but as gay and cheerful as ever, and would fain have been permitted to ride over hedge and ditch to mark out the proper line of the future avenue. Scott admonished him that the country-people, if they saw him at such work, would take the whole party for heathens; and

clapping spurs to his horse, he left us. 'The devil's in the body,' quoth Tom Purdie; 'he'll be ower every yett atween this and Turn-again, though it be the Lord's day. I wadna wonder if he were to be ceeted before the Session.'—'Be sure, Tam,' cries Constable, 'that you egg on the Dominie to blaw up his father—I wouldna grudge a hundred miles o' gait to see the ne'er-do-weel on the stool, and neither I'll be sworn, would the Sheriff.' 'Na, na,' quoth the Sheriff, 'we'll let sleeping dogs be, Tam.'"

It is a curious sidelight on the Scottish sabbatarianism of the period that it should have been considered even a half-jocular possibility that a visitor might be disciplined by the local minister for the crime of jumping gates on his host's estate. The Dominie was, of course, George Thomson, the tutor of the Scott boys, who was a son of the Melrose minister of that name.

It is significant that, in this one-day truce of his post-mortem animosities, Lockhart gives us a more convincing portrait of John Ballantyne than in any dozen of the onslaughts which he makes upon him. He is a 'projector to the core', alert with suggestions for the alterations of cottage and garden, though they are nothing to him, and with an irrepressible activity, even though he looked the sick man that he surely was. We get a glimpse of the sanguine spirit, the desire to do, to create, the restless irrepressible audacities, which, joined to a fine capacity for personal loyalty and a genuine love of art or beauty in any form, endeared him to Scott, who was an exceptionally sane judge of his fellow-men, and explain the words he spoke as, a year later, he walked away from John Ballantyne's grave: "I feel as if there would be less sunshine for me from this day forth".

But now John rode his own way, and the rest of the party walked back to Abbotsford, the young couple gay with hope, happy in the coming idyll of their own lives, and Scott, conscious that his strength would never last again as once it did, leaning on Tom Purdie's shoulder—his "Sunday pony" he took to calling him in these days—as he must learn to do increasingly in the years to come.

CHAPTER LXXI.

It was in the month following this expedition to Abbotsford that Scott at last went up to London to formally receive the title which was to be conferred upon him, Charlotte remaining in Scotland to superintend the preparations for Sophia's wedding, which had been fixed for the end of April, and for which Scott had, of course, undertaken to return.

It may not have been without weariness for him to experience, and it would surely be wearisome to record, the glittering crowds among whom he feasted and talked, and who jostled each other for introductions to the greatest poet and (who could doubt the authorship of those novels now?) the greatest novelist of the day. The letters which he wrote during this period are of the usual pattern, full of interest in the well-being of those he loved, gently protesting at times that fuller news was not sent to him, discussing presents promised or to be thought of, and ballasted with anecdotes and comment which is always shrewd, and almost always kindly.

He wrote to James of a sharp quarrel which had arisen between the houses of Longmans and Constable, regarding the terms on which his novels were to be marketed, in regard to which he had resolutely refused to take sides; he added that he would not willingly place his novels otherwise than with Constable now, except for one reason. "Had we not been controlled by the narrowness of discount, I would put nothing past him." It is an evident deduction that Scott had as many of Constable's bills on his hands, after the completion of the *Ivanhoe* deal, as he could find channels in which to discount them. *The Monastery*, coming out so soon after, could only be productive of immediate money by placing it with another publisher. That there should be need to consider such a point, after the sum obtained for *Ivanhoe*, is evidence of how closely expenditure followed the footsteps of income, unless it were the case that Constable was already finding it necessary to renew older bills as they fell due, in which case Scott would have an increased weight of these documents for his bankers to carry, of which there is no evidence at this period, though it is likely enough. But, in observing this, it is fair to remember that Scott was printer as well as author. Publishers paid with long-dated bills for the books themselves, at this period, as well as for the author's copyright, so that money had to be raised on these documents for the heavy wages-lists and other outlays that the printing of these large editions required. Under such circumstances, it might seem no more than prudence to obtain some variety in the signatures upon these long-dated documents.

"You say nothing of John," Scott added, in a postscript to this letter, "yet I am anxious about him." John's friends seem to have been more alarmed than he was himself by the physical symptoms of recent months.

In a letter to Charlotte of about the same date, Scott mentions his plan of completing Abbotsford on a scale appropriate to the new dignity he had undertaken, which would furnish him "with a handsome library, and you with a drawing-room and better bedroom, with good bedrooms for company, etc. It will cost me a little hard work to meet the expense, but I have been a good while idle".

The 'idleness' must have been that of last year's illness. It had not been of recent months. *Ivanhoe* had been published in December: the *Monastery* in March, when this letter was written. Two more novels were planned to be out before the year should end. Beside Constable's pet idea, *Kenilworth*, Scott was already resolved upon a sequel to the *Monastery*. His reason was characteristic. It is usually the most popular books for which sequels are written—and they usually fail: Scott was going to write a sequel now because he recognised the book to be a failure, and he would not admit defeat. It was not that he thought the public verdict perverse, and hoped to bring it to his own view. His correspondence shows that he agreed. The *Monastery* was an uninteresting book. Very well. He was not going to admit failure. He would continue the tale, and turn defeat into victory. It was a decision which reason hesitates to approve. It was magnificent, but it was not war.

The decision to enlarge the Abbotsford plans was unfortunate, as we can see now. It was not the cost of the building alone, it was the entertaining of the ceaseless visitors who would come from all parts of the world during the next five years, and be entertained in Scott's unstinting way—unstinting, not only of money but of his own priceless time—which would be made possible by those added rooms. All this was involved: and adequate or more than adequate as Scott's income might appear to be for all possible demands that might be made upon it, yet it was a fact that money was being spent very promptly as it came in: it was a fact that the publishers' payments were in the form of bills for which Scott might be able to obtain cash, but which cash he would be liable to be called upon to refund if at any time they should fail, which is always a commercial possibility, however remote it may seem: it was a fact that the printing business, however active and prosperous it might now be, was working on a capital which was supported by bills in the same way: and it was a fact also that the printing business was largely occupied in production of Scott's own books, which did not make its prosperity any the less real while the publishers met their engagements to it, but did place Scott in the added jeopardy that, if these publishers should fail, he stood to lose not only as author, but as printer also. It did not increase the probability of such an event, but it doubled the severity of its consequences, if it should occur.

And though there were years of prosperity to come, and new triumphs to be recorded, yet the tide was at its full—may, even now, however slightly, however imperceptibly, have been on the turn....

Lockhart makes an assertion, and an accusation on this point which should not be passed unnoticed. It deserves at least the courtesy of a considered analysis, for he is a shrewd observer, and often worthy of attention if he be neither dealing with figures, nor suffering from Ballantynes on the brain. He says:

> "I cannot conclude without observing that the publication of *Ivanhoe* marks the most brilliant epoch in Scott's history as the literary favourite of his contemporaries. With the novel which he next put forth, the immediate sale of these works began gradually to decline; and though, even when that had reached its lowest declension, it was still far above the most ambitious dreams of any other novelist, yet the publishers were afraid the announcement of anything like a falling-off might cast a damp over the spirits of the author. He was allowed to remain for many years under the impression that whatever novel he threw off commanded at once the old triumphant sale of ten or twelve thousand, and was afterwards, when included in the collective edition, to be circulated in that shape also as widely as *Waverley* and *Ivanhoe*. In my opinion, it would have been very unwise in the booksellers to give Scott any unfavourable tidings upon such subjects after the commencement of the malady which proved fatal to him—for that from the first shook his mind; but I think they took a false measure of the man when they hesitated to tell him exactly how matters stood, throughout 1820 and the three or four following years, when his intellect was as vigorous as it ever had been, and his heart as courageous; and I regret their scruples (among other reasons), because the years now mentioned were the most costly ones in his life; and for any twelve months in which any man allows himself, or is encouraged by others, to proceed in a course of unwise expenditure, it becomes proportionately more difficult for him to pull up when the mistake is at length detected or recognised."

Now so far as sales did fall off, and if, and so far as, anyone did conceal the fact from him who was principally concerned, it was beyond defense. But in estimating the importance of this point we must observe that there certainly was no steady downward movement, such as would have been a clear and unmistakable warning, which could have been indicated to Scott *before* the last acre of the Abbotsford estate was bought, and the last stone laid of the edifice which would make curtailment in future a very difficult programme to carry out; and, further, that though it would be easy for any of us to avoid disaster if we could see three or four years ahead, and Scott, like the rest of us, would have found it very useful to be able to do so, even such prescience might have modified rather than averted the course of events, which would have been largely beyond individual control.

Lockhart's second opinion, "that it would have been very unwise in the booksellers, etc.," is partly at variance with the facts as they did occur, and otherwise hypothetical, and there it may be left. As to whether Scott's malady "from the first shook his mind" anyone may read the journal of those final years and form his own judgement. The general opinion might be that few have ever met disaster with clearer minds, or more unshaken fortitude.

But I think Lockhart is always disposed to magnify the extent to which Scott was oblivious of his environment or ill-informed concerning it. I think Scott was clearly and accurately aware of most of these circumstances, and had he been informed most completely, even to the last months of his life, nothing might have been worse—and very little might have been different.

However these things might have been, had they been other than they were, the fact is that Sir Walter Scott came back from London in time for his daughter's wedding, confident of recovered health, and of the plenitude of his mental powers. He had no thought of financial shadow, either near or far. He was making money with almost magical ease, and money to him was a power to use, not to hoard.

> "The only gold he ever stored
> Inlays his helm, and hilts his sword."

If we lose sight of that attitude, we are searching an enigma to which we have lost the key.

Lockhart sees the masons gathering for the new wing of Abbotsford, and the reflection that they are to be paid with the profits of *Kenilworth*, which is not half-written as yet, vexes his timid conventional mind. It is an imprudent thing. Most of us would agree to that. But, to Scott, it would make the enterprise of that new wing a more attractive, a more adventurous thing. He would dream *Kenilworth*, and the dream would turn into solid stone. Can the world give a greater magic than that? And it was so little, so easy a thing to do! He thought—it might be better to say, he knew—that the writing of books is no great matter of which to boast. Smaller men may swell with pride at a lyric's praise. But Scott measured all by the sky's height.

Did he never think as he walked over the plantation by which he was bringing beauty to barren hills, "There was a year when I was nearly ruined in May, and I was nearly ruined again in August, but I won both of those fights, *and in the July between I bought this land up to the Caulshields Loch*"?

There may have been many men who have been nearly ruined in March, and again in May. Doubtless there are also those who have overcome such perils and steered at last to a good port—but how many are there who bought wide lands in the month between? But those battles were over now. Over, also, that harder battle against disease—the fight that was almost lost.

Triumphs were easy now. There was nothing left but to ride a friendly bout against fate with a blunted spear.

So he went back to Edinburgh in good spirits for the Spring Session. He did his work at the Court with his usual thoroughness. He made good progress with the two novels. At the end of May he wrote to Walter in Dublin:

> "I have bought the land adjoining to the Burnfoot Cottage.... It cost £2,300...there is a good deal of valuable fir planting...still I think it is £200 too dear. Mr. Laidlaw thinks it can be made worth...."

Two months later he wrote to his brother Tom in Canada. He gave all the news, as his way was. He was happy about his daughter's marriage:

> "Lockhart seems everything I could wish.... They are to spend their vacations in a nice little cottage, in a glen belonging to this property, with a rivulet in front, and a grove of trees on the east side to keep away the cold wind."

Tom's eldest boy (another Walter) was to come to Abbotsford. Tom was not exactly a poor man now, but Sir Walter was proposing to pay all the charges of completing his nephew's education, and starting him on any career he might choose. Tom wanted him to take up accountancy, which was at that time in Scotland a branch of the legal profession. Scott replied at length on this point. It would be to the advantage of many sons if all parents should study this letter. He says that a parent who has established a sufficiently sympathetic relation with his son can almost always influence him to adopt the profession which he (the father) thinks most suitable, and, for that reason, he should be the more careful to consider the boy's proclivities rather than his own wishes. He adds:

> "Walter would have gone to the bar had I liked, but I was sensible (with no small reluctance did I admit the conviction) that I should only spoil an excellent soldier to make a poor and undistinguished gownsman. On the same principle, I shall send Charles to India, not, God knows, with my will, for there is little chance of my living to see him return....

He will not promise to influence or coerce the boy towards any profession he does not choose, or for which he does not think him suitable, but, apart from that; "When you send him here I will do all that is in my power to stand in the place of father to him, and you may fully rely on my care and tenderness." It was a promise well kept.

CHAPTER LXXII.

In the autumn, Mr. and Mrs. Lockhart were easily persuaded that Abbotsford had some residential advantages over the Chiefswood cottage, and they came there on a long visit.

Then, and afterwards, Lockhart had intimate and continual opportunities of watching the internal economy of a house that was assuming some of the attributes of an international hotel, and, in spite of his journalistic vice of verbosity, the picture he gives deserves to be reproduced in his own words:

> "The humblest person who stayed merely for a short visit, must have departed with the impression that what he witnessed was an occasional variety; that Scott's courtesy prompted him to break in upon his habits when he had a stranger to amuse; but that it was physically impossible that the man who was writing the Waverley romances at the rate of nearly twelve volumes in the year, could continue, week after week, and month after month, to devote all but a hardly perceptible fraction of his mornings to out-of-doors occupations, and the whole of his evenings to the entertainment of a constantly varying circle of guests. The hospitality of his afternoons must alone have been enough to exhaust the energies of almost any man; for his visitors did not mean, like those of country-houses in general, to enjoy the landlord's good cheer and amuse each other; but the far greater

proportion arrived from a distance, for the sole sake of the Poet and Novelist himself, whose person they had never before seen, and whose voice they might never again have an opportunity of hearing. No other villa in Europe was ever resorted to from the same motives, and to anything like the same extent, except Ferney; and Voltaire never dreamt of being visible to his *hunters*: except for a brief space of the day—few of them ever dined with him, and none of them seem to have slept under his roof. Scott's establishment, on the contrary, resembled in every particular that of the affluent idler, who, because he has inherited, or would fain transmit political influence in some province, keeps open house—receives as many as he has room for, and sees their apartments occupied, as soon as they vacate them , by another troupe of the same description. Even on gentlemen guiltless of inkshed, the exercise of this sort of hospitality upon this sort of scale is found to impose a heavy tax; few of them, now-a-days, think of maintaining it for any large portion of the year: very few indeed below the highest rank of the nobility—in whose case there is usually a staff of led-captains, led-chaplains, servile dandies, and semi-professional talkers and jokers from London, to take the chief part of the burden."

Now, Scott had often in his mouth the pithy verses—

"Conversation is but carving:—
Give no more to every guest,
Than he's able to digest:
Give him always of the prime,
And but little at a time;
Carve to all but just enough,
Let them neither starve nor stuff;
And that you may have your due,

Let your neighbours carve for you"—

and he, in his own familiar circle always, and in other circles where it was possible, furnished a happy exemplification of these rules and regulations of the Dean of St. Patrick's. But the same sense and benevolence which dictated adhesion to them among his old friends and acquaintance rendered it necessary to break them when he was receiving strangers of the class I have described above at Abbotsford: he felt that their coming was the best homage they could pay to his celebrity, and that it would have been as uncourteous in him not to give them their fill of his talk, as it would be in your every-day lord of manors to make his casual guests welcome indeed to his venison, but keep his grouse-shooting for his immediate allies and dependants.

> "Every now and then he received some stranger who was not indisposed to take his part in the *carving*; and how good-humouredly he surrendered the lion's share to anyone that seemed to covet it—with what perfect placidity he submitted to be bored even by bores of the first water must have excited the admiration of many besides the daily observers of his proceedings. I have heard a spruce Senior Wrangler lecture him for half an evening on the niceties of the Greek epigram; I have heard the poorest of all parliamentary blunderers try to detail to him the *pros* and *cons* of what he called the *Truck system*; and in either case the same bland eye watched the lips of the tormentor. But, with such ludicrous exceptions, Scott was the one object of the Abbotsford pilgrims; and evening followed evening, only to show him exerting for their amusement, more of animal spirits, to say nothing of intellectual vigour, than would have been considered by any other man in the company as sufficient for the whole expenditure of a week's existence. Yet this was not the chief marvel: he talked of things that interested himself, because he

knew that by doing so he should give most pleasure to his guests. But how vast was the range of subjects on which he could talk with unaffected zeal; and with what admirable delicacy of instinctive politeness did he select his topic according to the peculiar history, study, pursuits or social habits of the stranger! And all this was done without approach to the unmanly trickery of what is called *catching the tone* of the person one converses with. Scott took the subject on which he thought such a man or woman would like best to hear him speak—but not to handle it in their way, or in any way but what was completely, and most simply his own:—not to flatter them by embellishing, with the illustration of his genius the views and opinions which they were supposed to entertain—but to let his genius play out its own variations for his own delight and theirs, as freely and easily, and with as endless a multiplicity of delicious novelties, as ever the magic of Beethoven or Mozart could fling over the few primitive notes of a village air....

"...It is needless to add, that Sir Walter was familiarly known long before the days I am speaking of, to almost all the nobility and higher gentry of Scotland; and consequently, that there seldom wanted a fair proportion of them to assist him in doing the honours of his country. It is still more superfluous to say so respecting the heads of his own profession at Edinburgh: *Sibi et amicis*—Abbotsford was their villa whenever they pleased to resort to it. and few of them were ever absent from it long. He lived meanwhile in a constant interchange of easy visits with the gentlemen's families of Teviotdale and the Forest; so that mixed up with his superfine admirers of the Mayfair breed, his staring worshippers from foreign parts, and his quick-witted coevals of the Parliament-House—there was found generally some hearty home-spun laird, with his dame, and the young laird—a bashful bumpkin who, perhaps, did not soar beyond his gun and pointer—or perhaps a little psuedo-dandy, for whom the Kelso race-course and the Jedburgh ball were Life and the World. To complete the *olla podrida*, we must remember that no old acquaintance, or family connections, however remote their actual station or style of manners from his own, were forgotten or lost sight of. He had some even near relations, who, except when they visited him, rarely if ever found admittance to what the haughty dialect of the upper world is pleased to designate as society. These were welcome guests, let who might be under that roof; and it was the same with many a worthy citizen of Edinburgh, habitually moving in an obscure circle, who had been in the same class with Scott at the High School, or his fellow-apprentice when he was proud of earning three-pence a page by the use of his pen. To dwell on nothing else, it was surely a beautiful perfection of real universal humanity and politeness, that could enable this great and good men to blend guests so multifarious in one group, and contrive to make them all equally happy with him, with themselves, and with each other."

And when the boredom of this continual hospitality passed the bounds of endurance, or would have left even less than the minimum of time which he required for his own work, Scott would escape on some pretext of visiting a distant part of his estate, and ride over to Chiefswood, where he could be sure of quiet and where Sophia kept a dressing-room at his disposal for writing purposes. Here at times, also, especially in summer days when out-door picnicking would be possible, the more intimate guests of Abbotsford would be brought, or they would be taken to Huntley Burn, the inhabitants of castle, farmhouse, and cottage invading each other with little ceremony, and with what ever retinue.

They were happy, fortunate days, and Charlotte proved herself adequate to the control of this growing mansion with its incessant cosmopolitan hospitality; and yet she, and Sir Walter also, may have had the happier times in their first carefree days in the simplicity of the Lasswade cottage. Perhaps now it was the life at Chiefswood rather than at Abbotsford which wisdom might be disposed to envy.

But the cottage at Lasswade had fulfilled its vital purpose: the nest was emptying, though the cottage might be a mansion now. Charles had gone to Lampeter, to continue his studies there. Only Anne was left at home.

CHAPTER LXXIII.

As a picture of the successful exercise of the rites of hospitality on an extended scale, Lockhart's description may be interesting, and in some respects admirable enough. Certainly, it is without discredit to the man who received the international invasion. and neither repelled nor allowed it to overwhelm him. His apparent leisure may still appear wonderful, when its explanation has been observed, but that explanation obviously lay in his habit of retiring at a reasonable hour, and doing early morning work while his guests slept.

We may also observe that the exercise of hospitality on such a scale is a costly thing. The profits of the Waverley novels were very large, but so also was the number of those, both inside and around Abbotsford, who were living upon them.

We get another glimpse of this expenditure at the end of the year, when about a hundred of the children of the men employed on the estate danced to the bagpipes at the Hogmanay Festival, and got a meal, and a penny each when they went home. And Scott looked on, happily enough no doubt, but with a feeling of disquiet that, for no sufficient reason that he could see, he should be so much better off than they. "I declare to you, my dear friend," he wrote to Joanna Baillie, "that when I thought the poor fellows who kept these children so neat, and well-taught, and well-behaved, were slaving the whole day for eighteen-pence, or twenty-pence at the most, I was ashamed of their gratitude...."

But money was coming in fast at this time, and there seemed no need to be over-careful of the rate at which it was passed on to others. For Scott had done what he proposed *The Abbot* had been published in September, and *Kenilworth* appeared in the closing weeks of the year.

The Abbot, being a sequel of the *Monastery,* was published in the same style, and through the same channel—Longmans—as the previous book. It might have been wiser to make Mary Stuart the subject of a quite independent novel, but Scott largely justified his determination that the sequel should redeem the previous failure. It had, and deserved, a much better reception, and a larger sale.

Kenilworth was published by Constable in the more ornate style, and at the advanced price of *Ivanhoe*, and it rivalled, if it did not outshine, its success. The turn of the tide, if such there were, is still very hard to see.

And after the publication of *Kenilworth* there can have been no immediate reaction, for there was a pause of unusual length—nearly twelve months—before the next novel appeared. *Kenilworth* had been published in December, 1820. *The Pirate* appeared slightly earlier in December, 1821.

The earlier part of the year had not been entirely barren of literary output. John Ballantyne had recently conceived a project of publishing a series of the novels of a past generation, under the general title of The Novelist's Library. This was to be a private venture of his own, and Scott had promised to help him by writing lives of the novelists concerned as introductory matter. He did some of these, and some other miscellaneous work during the early part of the year, but the fact was that he went to London as representative of the Clerks of Session, who were interested in a bill before the House to relieve them of some of their more laborious and less responsible duties, and this business kept him in town for some months. It may be doubted whether he ever worked as well in London as when in Edinburgh or at Abbotsford. When he got back, Adam Fergusson was married in April, leaving his sisters at Huntley Burn, and taking Gattanside, in the next parish; and in June, more to his own surprise than that of his friends, John Ballantyne died.

Scott took Lockhart to see him during his last illness, and his description of that visit has his customary sharpness of vision with less than the usual bitterness:

> "John's deathbed was a thing not to be forgotten. We sat by him for perhaps an hour, and I think half that space was occupied with his predictions of a speedy end, and details of his last will, which he had just been executing, and which lay on his coverlid; the other half being given, five minutes or so at a time, to questions and remarks, which intimated that the hope of life was still flickering before him—nay, that his interest in all its concerns remained eager. The proof-sheets of a volume of his Novelist's Library lay also by his pillow; and he passed from them to his will, and then back to them, as by jerks and starts the unwonted veil of gloom closed upon his imagination, or was withdrawn again. He had, he said, left his great friend and patron £2,000 towards the completion of the new library at Abbotsford—and the spirit of the auctioneer virtuoso flashed up as he began to describe what would, he thought, be the best style and arrangement of the bookshelves. He was interrupted by an agony of asthma which left him with hardly any sign of life; and ultimately he did expire in a fit of the same kind. Scott was visibly and profoundly shaken by this scene and sequel."

Lockhart repeats a tale that Scott told him as they walked away from the funeral, of how he had once known the dead man give a cheque for £5 or £10 to a poor student of divinity whom he had noticed in his auction room. John remarked to the young man that he looked ill, and receiving an affirmative answer, said, with his usual jocularity, as he passed him the unexpected cheque, that it would prove beneficial if taken on an empty stomach.

Scott gives that as his last memory of the man who certainly worshipped him, and whom he had called his friend—that, and the thought that there would never be so much of sunshine in his life again. But Lockhart will not leave without dealing a final kick at the coffin.

> "I am sorry," he says. "to take leave of John Ballantyne with the remark that his last will and testament was a document of the same class with too many of his *states* and *calendars*. So far from having £2,000 to bequeath to Sir Walter, he died as he had lived, ignorant of the state of his affairs, and deep in debt."

It is a fact that John did not leave a sufficient estate to allow of the payment of the £2,000 legacy, and that so far was Sir Walter from thinking of, or desiring to receive it, that he was considering soon afterwards the possibility of continuing the Novelist's Library for the widow's benefit. There is also a vague suggestion that Scott may have discharged some of his debts, but it is indefinite in itself, and might have arisen (if it had any basis at all) from his payment of obligations incurred by John as agent on his behalf. It may be agreed that had John been insolvent Scott would have been very likely to take such a course, but, in fact, the statement that John died 'deep in debt' appears to be no more than one of Lockhart's rhetorical flourishes.

At the time of John's death he was so far either from anticipating that event, or conscious of financial trouble, that he was engaged in the conversion of some old houses that he had bought at the end of the Kelso High Street into one mansion, which was to be named Walton Hall, and enable him to take up a stately residence in his native town. He might be of a naturally gay or even mercurial disposition, but at the time of serious crisis with the John Ballantyne bills he is said on more than one evidence to have been ill with worry. He had now been 'on his own' for several years, and that his spirits would have been high enough to overcome his physical weakness, and left him energy for this new building enterprise, had he really been 'deep in debt' is an obvious improbability. But when we examine his sources of income we observe that they would all cease at his death, and a half-finished mansion may not be a very saleable asset to leave behind.

It is no unforgivable crime to die poor, even if it be John Ballantyne who commits the offence but the real sting of the paragraph quoted is the innuendo of the allusion to 'his states and calendars'.

Lockhart charges him elsewhere with the faking of 'States' or Balance Sheets, but the accusation breaks down utterly on examination. By 'calendars' he meant lists of obligations (specifically, Bills payable) which require to be honoured during a forth-coming financial period. There is evidence that both Scott and James Ballantyne relied upon John for the keeping of such records over long periods in connection with both the publishing and printing firms. Had he been carelessly inaccurate the consequences would have been too disastrous for it to have been possible to retain him in such a position. Had he been deliberately so, it would have been evidence that he was *non compos mentis*. Is there the slightest evidence that he ever made a single mistake in these documents at any time, or of any kind?

But in this final attack, over his grave, upon the man with whom he had been on terms of apparent cordiality, Lockhart preserves an outward decency of expression. He professes perfunctory sorrow that he should have to make accusations, which there was no reason to do. When he had been convicted of other inaccuracies, he repeated the charge, such as it is, with an altered vocabulary, which shows what his true feelings were. He says (Letter to Sir Adam Fergusson, p. 64, footnote)—

> "In how far John had deceived himself as to his pecuniary status, I cannot undertake to guess. That, situated as he really was, death should have arrested him in the midst of constructing a splendid villa on the Tweed, and that he should have penned legacies when he could leave nothing but debt to be discharged by his friends—even these circumstances are sufficiently in keeping with the whole of this person's history."

We may observe an obvious inaccuracy of rhetoric in the statement that "he could leave nothing but debts". Lockhart has told us of a half-built house. Had he been substantially insolvent, it is likely that there would be more and different evidence than a vague statement that Scott paid his debts, and such evidence Lockhart would have been glad to produce. The expression "this person's" as a substitute for "his", which is all that the construction of the sentence requires, shows temper, for which there should have been no occasion had he conducted his investigation in a judicial spirit.

John made an estimate of his position, for his own guidance, shortly before his death, in which he valued his assets at £5,000 against liabilities of £2,000. As a 'going concern' this was probably accurate enough, and gave no cause for anxiety to a man who was making a large income, as he must have been doing at this time, and was living within it, or he would not have reached that position.

CHAPTER LXXIV.

A few weeks after John Ballantyne's death, Scott was in London again, this time for the King's coronation, and it was not till he got back to such limited peace as Abbotsford gave that the *Pirate* appears to have made a steady and regular progress. William Erskine, who, it will be remembered, had been one of the party with whom Scott had visited the scene in which this tale is laid, and who, in his official capacity as Sheriff of the Orkney and Shetland islands, was otherwise familiar with those localities, came with his two daughters (his wife had died two years earlier) to stay at Abbotsford, and gave the assistance of his own knowledge to Scott's limited notes or uncertain memories. Keenly interested as he always was in the progress of these novels, he appears to have taken an exceptional 'constant and eager delight' in the creation of one which dealt with the locality he represented. He would commonly, during this summer holiday period, get from Scott at breakfast the sheets which he had written in the early morning and take them over to Chiefswood for the pleasure of reading them to the Lockharts, where we are assured that 'tender affection and admiration, fresh as the impulses of childhood, glistened in his eye, and trembled in his voice'. Lockhart does not record his own emotions at these ceremonies (he is usually more detailed and picturesque regarding those of others) nor what Sophia thought of being called from her housework in the middle-morning to sit under a tree listening to an emotional rendering of one of her father's chapters, but we may conclude that William Erskine enjoyed the job. With the impulse of his admiring society, the book grew. But it had been an unusually long time in process of composition, and that was not a good sign. Neither was it favourable that Scott should have come to divide his attention between it and some fictitious letters which he was endeavouring to write in the style of the seventeenth century, which with a sudden wisdom, he threw aside to commence a novel against the same background. He made considerable progress with this before he wrote the *Pirate's* concluding words, and that was a good omen in one direction, for he had never yet written two novels at once without making one a success of the first order.

The programme of building advanced this year more rapidly than the novels. Scott had come back from his spring visit to London with complete plans for the final wing, and the work had only been delayed by his refusal to allow the demolition of the porch of the old cottage until the roses and jessamines had ceased to flower. Then, on a late-autumn Sunday, having come from Edinburgh for the purpose, he removed the roots of the creepers to Chiefswood, and planted them with his own hands around the entrance to his daughter's cottage.

It is in dealing with this period of an abundant prosperity, and very heavy expenditure, that Lockhart makes a statement regarding Scott's income and reasonable expectations which requires notice because it is loosely false, both in fact and inference and is a major example of the distortions with which he gradually blurred what in itself is both a simpler and a nobler tale.

It was in November of this year that Scott made a further agreement with Constable regarding the copyrights which had been created since his previous comprehensive sale, and Lockhart makes it occasion for this statement:

> "Sir Walter concluded, before he went to town in November, another negotiation of importance with this house. They agreed to give for the remaining copyright of the four novels published between December 1819 and January 1821—to wit, *Ivanhoe, The Monastery, The Abbot,* and *Kenilworth*—the sum of five thousand guineas. The stipulation about not revealing the author's name, under a penalty of £2,000, was repeated. By these four novels, the fruits of scarcely more than twelve months' labour, he had already cleared at least £10,000 before this bargain was completed. I cannot pretend to guess what the actual state of his pecuniary affairs was at the time when John Ballantyne's death relieved them from one great source of complication and difficulty. But I have said enough to satisfy every reader, that when he began the second, and far the larger division of his building at Abbotsford, he must have contemplated the utmost sum it could cost him as a mere trifle in relation to the resources at his command. He must have reckoned on clearing £30,000 at

least in the course of a couple of years by the novels written within such a period."

It might not be difficult to prepare an approximately accurate statement of Scott's financial position at this time, and it would certainly show him to have been substantially solvent, with a very large income, which his expenditure did not equal; but no one with a knowledge of what accountancy is will needlessly indulge in such estimates. Ascertained figures are sufficiently difficult to handle justly. We may agree that Lockhart was wise, in not 'pretending to guess' in that direction, and we may pass with a moment's wonder the suggestion that John Ballantyne's death relieved Scott's pecuniary affairs from 'one great source of complication and difficulty'. Lockhart does not explain what he means, and no one else is likely to have that ability. It is no more than a random stone cast backward upon a grave. But the major figures he gives, both the £10,000 and the £30,000 are utterly fallacious, and double the annual profits that Scott received, or could reasonably have expected to receive, from his novels at any period. It is absurd to assert, because four novels were published within fourteen months, that they were written within such a period, and Lockhart has himself given detailed and conclusive contrary evidence. By a parity of reasoning, if a man have pains at regular intervals, and one is at four and the next at eight, he has two in four hours, and as there are twenty-four hours in the day he must have twelve pains a day. The production of the novels was irregular, but never greatly exceeded two a year, and averaged less. During the year when Scott is discredited with these absurd calculations (which he would certainly never have made) his output was one.

The estimate of these figures is as random as were the assertions that the popularity of the novels declined after *Ivanhoe*, and that Scott ought to have been made aware of this circumstance. *Ivanhoe* and the *Monastery* were published almost together, and the *Monastery* was the nearest thing to a failure he had yet had. *Kenilworth* and the *Abbot* were issued in the same bracketed way. Lockhart's own testimony is that *Kenilworth* was as successful as *Ivanhoe*, and that the *Abbot* was better received than the *Monastery*. The next novel—*The Pirate*—was yet to come. What evidence of declining popularity call be extracted here?

Nothing beyond a very vague estimate of the annual profit which Scott was making from his novels, or which he could reasonably expect in future, could have been made then, or is possible now, but the figure could have been most reasonably placed at between £6,000 and £7,000. With his salaries and other sources of income he may have approached £10,000, against which we have to place the fact that the outlay upon the development of the Abbotsford estate (apart from the house and grounds) must have exceeded the immediate receipts, though it was not foolishly expended, and was increasing the annual value of the property.

Scott's position was that he was making a large income with fantastic ease, that he was living well within it, even after allowance has been made for his almost endless generosities, and was developing an estate by a method which looked ahead rather than to immediate returns, and which was likely to render it of permanent and increasing value.

While living well within his income, as he appears to have done, without exception during the whole of his life, he was not saving to any great extent, which it was not his nature to do, or, at least it was not his nature to plan cautiously to such ends. He was confident rather than cautious by disposition, a lover of hazards, but not therefore one incompetent in business or other relations of life. Such a combination of qualities would have come to earth at the first ditch.

The weakness of his position lay in the fact that an income from literature must always be precarious (though on this point he justified his confidence in his own capacity); and in the fact that he was taking payments from his publishers in longdated bills, not only for his literary work, but for the actual manufacture of the novels at the Canongate Press.

Must we, after a survey of the whole position, as it then was, convict him of imprudence in enlarging Abbotsford, or continuing the printing business, as Lockhart asks us to do? To answer this question we must return our regard to the affairs of James Ballantyne & Co., which we have left very much to themselves since James asked to be relieved of his partnership about five years ago.

It may be remembered that Scott had generously given him the right to resume the position which he had vacated, if, at any future time, he should think it to be to his advantage. Now he made a formal application to be reinstated in partnership.

If we would regard these events in a correct perspective, the significance of this application cannot easily be exaggerated. Now that the publishing firm was dead, and its liabilities ended, the printing business was the most vulnerable side of Scott's financial position, and it was there, several years later, that the line broke. James had been left in sole authority, and with comparatively little supervision during the last five years. He should know, if anyone did, what the position was, and the nature of the responsibility which he would assume. It was a step which proved, in the end, disastrous to him. Was that end one which a good business man should have foreseen at this time, or did it arise from future causes which were beyond the possibilities of human foresight? Was James himself, and, if so, to what extent, responsible for the position of this business at this date, or for the events that followed?

All these were points of acute controversy between Lockhart and the Ballantyne trustees, and either side would have been capable of spoiling a good case with bad advocacy. Their charges and counter-charges are a wild chaos of baseless calumnies and recriminations; their figures, and their deductions from them, are nightmares of improbability and inconsequence. Can we disentangle sufficient facts to get the position clearly and simply stated?

We have the clear fact that after this five-years arrangement James felt sufficient confidence in the business to desire to resume his partnership, and that he thought the profits to be such that it would be to his advantage to do so; and we have the further and even more significant fact that George Hogarth was again consulted, and was the legal instrument of reconstituting the partnership which he had previously considered it essential to terminate in his sister's interest.

We have the fact also, that Scott was sufficiently satisfied with the method in which James had managed the business to commence a new partnership with him, and this was quite voluntary on his part, for, as we shall see, there had been sufficient errors of default, if not of commission, on James's part to give Scott solid legal ground for refusal, had he desired to take that course.

As to the competence of the parties, Scott was a barrister, trained in a lawyer's office at a time when law and accountancy were a single profession. He showed on several occasions the ability to grasp and analyse even intricate financial problems which a barrister is expected to have, and which could reasonably be expected from his professional training, and intellectual capacity. The large-handed way in which he dealt with money, and his habit of regarding his income as a fund for the support of endless relatives and friends, and for all indigent people within a five mile radius of where he lived, or with whom his voluminous correspondence might acquaint him, was a defect (if such we call it) of character, not of intellect, and its results were incidentally augmented by the fact that Charlotte's generosities were of a similar liberality.

James always said frankly that he did not like figures. His interest in his business was on its practical side. But it does not appear that he was incompetent, if he would discipline himself to the work.

When the principle of a new partnership was agreed, the evident course on both sides would have been to have entrusted John with the preparation of the accounts on which it would be based. It is improbable that this should have been the case, after several years experience of a man who, according to Lockhart, could not or would not draw up a list of forthcoming bills accurately, yet so it was. But, while the negotiation was in its preliminary stage, John died.

A fortnight before his death, on June 3rd, 1821, when it was evident that his assistance would not be available, James wrote a letter to Scott of which this is the concluding portion:

> "With some unwilling foreboding that this might happen, and that John might be unable to assist us in our approaching arrangement, I have been studying the whole affairs of the concern with all the attention I could exert; and, as generally happens to persons of good sense, I have found that what others can accomplish I can accomplish too. I am very sure that in one week I shall he able to produce a statement which, subject to your amendments, may prove a very sufficient foundation for a new contract between us. I do not pretend to think that I can make out a balanced account which would brook an accountant's examination; but that happily you do not exact; and have kindly allowed for the former negligence, which renders that altogether impracticable. But I am pretty confident that I can show how the concern stands with the world—what it owes, and what is owing to it; I can show what is the value of its present stock; I am ready to agree to any terms you can propose for me; and most zealously trust (*and you will see that I will not fail*) to keep everything betwixt us in future as regularly as the affairs of the Weekly Journal. Still, therefore, I look forward with hope and confidence to be useful to myself, my family, and you. I am sure this is yet in my power, and I think you will believe it is. I may venture to say that I have never been idle but, on the contrary, most active and assiduous in those parts of my business which I liked—trusting most absurdly to others to attend to the most important departments which I did not like.

> Henceforward I shall trust to myself alone, and I really have no doubt that I shall manage everything as correctly as is my duty. With the deepest respect and gratitude.—J. B."

The admissions in this letter are not the less serious because they are so frankly made. It is clear that the books had been badly kept. James had been absorbed in the production department, and had entrusted the accounts to others; without even exercising sufficient supervision to see that the work was properly done. It is evident also that during these very busy and prosperous years Scott cannot have exercised a strict control, or required exact periodic accounts to be presented to him, as he had in earlier years. Doubtless, he had asked for them. Doubtless, they had been promised. But the busy days had gone by and they had not been completed for him. Yet at times some estimated figures there may—indeed, must—have been, for Scott makes an incidental allusion to having drawn 'the profits' during these five years.

James had been a salaried manager. His remuneration had been £400, which had afterwards been raised to £500. It was substantially less than he had been accustomed to spend, and he was still paying interest on some amounts of borrowed capital, and on a bank overdraft. He was editing a weekly newspaper, for which he received a salary of £200, and Scott had agreed that that should be outside the business, as his separate income. Scott had also made an arrangement with him by which a percentage of the profits of each of the novels was written off that capital debt of £3,000, as a remuneration for his services in correcting the proofs, and it had been reduced to £1,800 in this way. This has some of the aspects of a gift, as James's salary already covered such services, but James had no other substantial source of income. Unless by his labour, how was it to be repaid at all? By this arrangement, Scott reduced it in accordance with the advance of his own prosperity.

Beyond these, his wife had some means, though, considered

as income-producing capital, they were not large. James has described her as a frugal manager. They lived in substantial comfort, though without ostentation. While John rode his white hunter, or drove tandem with a liveried groom up to the auction-room door, James was content with a sober cob: while John had his villa at Trinity, and his rising mansion at Kelso, James was content with the quiet respectability of his St. John Street residence.

Yet, though we can acquit him of personal extravagance, if Lockhart's indictment that he habitually drew from this business much more than he was entitled to do can receive no better reply than that he does not prose his case, and that any figure he gives without verification is almost certainly wrong, and if, in fact—as is quite possible—James was innocent at this time of any such excessive expenditure—the fault is his own. He was in sole control of the business, and he failed to balance his cash.

Everyone with any experience of book-keeping knows that, if a cash book is to be accurately balanced, it must be written up, and its totals watched, with continual regularity.

James had written to his brother a few months before to this somewhat astonishing effect:

> Oct. 31st 1820.
>
> On checking your note of bills with my bill-book I find the following do not appear there:
>
> 1821 Jan. 4th—£876
> 23rd
> Acceptance for Cash Lent—£500
> \-\-\-\-\-\-\-
> £1376
> \-\-\-\-\-\-\-
>
> For the first you say you find funds: but, as they both ought to go regularly through my books I will

thank you to furnish me with a state of the particulars of these bills, as drawer, acceptor, endorser, date, and time. When I reflect how many bills I have paid for Sir Walter Scott on verbal orders or mere notes, which I thought no more about, I absolutely quake for the aspect under which I might be considered were he to die. Thousands upon thousands might be brought against me; and all I could say would be, "Well, gentlemen where are they? My manner of life is well known—I have not spent them; my cash accounts are open—they are not there." Of late I have been more careful; but even yet I am sure there are some of his transactions which I am called upon ultimately to pay which have never appeared in my books, and which if rigidly scrutinised would make an ignorant accountant like me stand upon character alone. Many is the hours vexation and alarm this gives me."

It sounds incredible, but we owe the production of this letter to the Ballantyne Trustees, who put it forward as evidence of the reckless manner in which Scott drained the business for his private purposes! He drew so many items that the poor manager had not time to enter them in the cashbook as he paid them out! It is the paradox of that controversy that when we examine Lockhart's charges against James they break down so completely that we are prepared to deliver a verdict of not guilty without troubling the witnesses for the defense; but when they insist on putting their evidence forward, we find that it is not such a clear case as it had appeared to be....

After the receipt of James's letter, Scott went into the affairs of the business with him direct. It was becoming too evident that John's assistance would never be available, and Scott was not content to leave James to produce the account at which he aimed, and start a new partnership on such a foundation. During the next fortnight there were many conferences, at the end of which time Scott had decided to admit James as a partner again, and had outlined the conditions, but he had stipulated that the agreement should not take effect for twelve months. There was to be that probationary period, at the end of which time proper accounts were to be prepared by independent accountants, as was actually done when the time came. On June 15th, 1821—the day before John died—Scott wrote the following letter:

"Dear James,

It appears to me that the contract betwixt us may be much shortened by an exchange of missive letters, distinctly expressing the grounds on which we proceed; and if I am so fortunate as to make these grounds distinct, intelligible, and perfectly satisfactory in this letter, you will have only to copy it with your own hand, and return me the copy with your answer expressing your acquiescence in what I have said, and your sense of the justice and propriety of what I have to propose as the result of our investigations and conferences.

It is proper to set out by reminding you that upon the affairs of the printing house being in difficulties about the term of Whitsunday 1816, I assumed the total responsibility for its expenditure and its debts, including a salary of £400 to you as manager; and on condition of my doing so, you agreed that I should draw the full profits. Under this management, the business is to continue down to the term of Whitsunday next, being, 1822, when I, considering myself as fully indemnified for my risk and my advances, am willing and desirous that this management shall terminate, and that you shall be admitted to a just participation of the profits which shall arise after that period. It is with a view to explain and ascertain the terms of this new contract, and the relative rights of the parties to each other, that these missives are exchanged.

First, then, it appears from the transactions of our former copartnery that you were personally indebted to me in the year 1816 in the sum of £3,000, of which you have already paid me £1,200, by assigning to me your share in the profits of certain novels; and as there still remains due at this term of Whitsunday the sum of £1,800, I am content to receive in payment thereof the profits of three novels, now contracted for, to be published after this date of Whitsunday 1821. It may be proper to mention that no interest is imputed on this sum of £3,000; because I account it compensated by the profits of the printing-office, which I have drawn for my exclusive use since 1816; and, for the same reason, such part of the balance as may remain due at Whitsunday 1822, when these profits are liable to division under our new contract, will bear interest from that period.

Secundo. During the space betwixt Whitsunday 1816 to Whitsunday 1822, I have been, Imo, At the sole expense of renewing the whole stock of the printing office, valued at £1,700; 2do, I have paid up a cash-credit due at the Bank of Scotland, amounting to £500; and 3tio, I have acquired by purchase certain feus affecting the printing-office property, for the sum of £375—which three sums form altogether a capital sum of £2,575, for one half of which sum, being £1287. 10. 0, sterling, you are to give me a bill or a bond, with security if required, bearing interest at 5 per cent. from the term of Whitsunday 1822.

Tertio. There is a cash-credit in your name as an individual with the Royal Bank for £500, and which is your proper debt, no part of the advances having been made to James Ballantyne & Co. I wish my name withdrawn from the obligation, where I stand as a cautioner, and that you would either pay up the account, or find the Bank other caution.

The above arrangements being made and completed it remains to point out to you how matters will stand between us at Whitsunday 1822, and on what principle the business is after that date to be conducted.

Primo, At that period, as I will remain liable personally for such Bills of the Company as are then current (exclusive of those granted for addition to stock, if any are made subsequent to this date, for which we are mutually liable) and exclusive also of such debts as were contracted before 1816, for which we are also mutually liable) I shall retain my exclusive right of property to all the several funds of the Company, book debts, money, bills, or balances of money, and bills in bankers hands for retiring the said current bills, and indemnifying me for my advances; and we are upon these terms to grant each other a mutual and effectual discharge of all claims whatsoever arising out of our former contract, or out of any of the transactions that have followed therefrom excepting as to the two sums of £1,800 and £1,287. 10. 0. due by you to me as above mentioned.

Secundo. The printing-office, the house in Foulis Close, and all the stock in trade, shall from and after the term of Whitsunday 1822 be held a joint property, and managed for our common behoof, and at our joint expense; and on dissolution of the partnership, the partners shall make an equal division of all balance that may arise upon payment of the copartnery debts affecting the same.

Tertio. In order to secure a proper fund for carrying on the business, each of us shall place in Bank at the aforesaid term of 1822 Whitsunday, the sum of £1,000 (to form a fund for carrying, on the business until returns shall come in for that purpose)—I say the input to be £1,000 each.

Quarto. The profits of every kind after Whitsunday 1822 (excepting works in progress before that period, and going on in the office) shall be equally divided. It being now found from experience that the influence and patronage which it is in my power to afford the concern is of nearly the same advantage as your direct and immediate exertion of skill and superintendence.

5to. Respecting books which have been begun before the term of Whitsunday 1822, but not finished till afterwards. I propose, after some consideration, the following equitable distinction. Of all such works as, having been commenced and in progress before Whitsunday 1822, shall be published and sent out of the office before Lammas in the same year, I shall draw the profit; repaying the concern one half of the calculated wages expended per sheet or otherwise on the said works, subsequent to the term of Whitsunday. On the other hand, the profit of all such works as, having been commenced before Whitsunday 1822, shall not be published or delivered till after Lammas in the same year, shall be divisible between us in terms of the new copartnery; you in that case repaying me moiety of such wages and expenditure as shall have been expended upon such sheets or volumes previous to Whitsunday 1822.

6to. I think it would be highly advisable that our drafts on the business (now so flourishing) should be limited to £500 per annum, suffering the balance to go to discharge debt, reinforce our cash accounts, add to stock in case it is thought advisable, until circumstances shall authorise in prudence a further dividend.

It is almost unnecessary to add that there must be the usual articles about the use of a firm, etc. But the above are the peculiar principles of the new copartnery, and I should be desirous that our mutual friend Mr. Hogarth, your brother-in-law, and a man of business and honour, should draw up the new copartnery, coupling it with a mutual discharge. He will be a better judge than either you or I of the terms in which they should be couched to be legally binding: and being your connection and relative, his intervention will give to all who may hereafter-look into these affairs the assurance that we have acted towards each other on terms which we mutually consider as fair, just, and honourable.

The letter which I wrote to you at the time of your marriage in 1816, or about that time, explained completely the conditions on which I then undertook the management of the printing office, so far as cash matters were concerned; and, as they were communicated to Mr. Hogarth, he will recollect their tenor. In case they are preserved. I think you will find that they accord with what I now propose, and are in the same spirit of regard and friendship with which you have always been considered by, Dear James, Yours very truly,

Walter Scott."

The letter bore this postscript:

"Mr. Hogarth will understand that though the mutual discharge of our accounts respectively cannot be perhaps effectually executed till Whitsunday 1822, yet is not our purpose to go back on these complicated transactions, being perfectly satisfied with the principles of arrangement above expressed. So that if it should please God that either of us were removed before the term of Whitsunday 1822, the survivor shall not be called to account upon any other principle than those which we have above expressed, and which I, by the writing hereof, and you by your acceptances declare are those by which we intend these affairs shall be settled: and that after full consideration, and being well advised, we hereby for ourselves and our heirs renounce and disclaim all other modes of accounting whatsoever.

Walter Scott."

It is possible to place various interpretations upon the postscript to this letter, but its significance becomes reasonably clear when we consider the circumstances with which it dealt. Scott was the sole legal owner of the business. The death of his manager could not have embarrassed him with any necessity of explaining their financial relations. The deed of dissolution by which that position was created five years ago was in the supposed interests of James's wife, and prepared by her brother. Neither could it be of great importance to Scott to have the exact amount of James's liabilities to him settled beyond the possibility of dispute in such an eventuality. It was certain that, if James died within the year, he would have little to leave, and Scott was not the man to worry his mind about such a remote contingency, nor to press a claim under such circumstances.

But if Scott should die—and he had had warning enough that his constitution was not invulnerable—and his manager had the task of explaining a cash book which was far from balancing to unsympathetic executors, it might be a more serious matter. We are reminded of the warning that Scott had given at the time of the trouble over the Alexander Ballantyne bill.

If this be its interpretation, it was an act on Scott's part to safeguard James from any possible consequences of his inability to give a satisfactory account of his stewardship, chivalrous in its conception, and particularly so in its wording. It made no imputation on James whatever. It was a letter he could show to anyone. But it was a free pardon also, issued in advance, if any charge should subsequently be made against him.

It is fair to say that it is capable of another explanation, equally creditable to Scott, and not reflecting by implication upon James in the same way. There were at this time a large number of the firm's bills in circulation. The nature of these bills, and the circumstances and consideration for which they had been issued, and for whose benefit, are problems which we now approach. If, as the Ballantyne Trustees asserted, and Lockhart denied, they had been discounted for Scott's private assistance, it is theoretically possible that there might be circumstances or accounts relating to them which James might have found it difficult to explain, now that John was dying, if Scott also were dead. It is mere theory, without supporting evidence, and much less probable than the explanation previously suggested, but it is a possibility which it is only fair to observe.

On June 22nd 1821—a week after Scott's missive letter was written, the interval being sufficiently explained by John's intervening death—James returned it with this acceptance endorsed upon it:

> "I hereby agree to the propositions contained in the prefixed letter; and am ready to enter into a regular deed founded upon them, when it shall be thought necessary.
>
> James Ballantyne."

CHAPTER LXXV.

It may be convenient to conclude the consideration of the circumstances of this new partnership by going forward at once to the spring of 1822, though it will be necessary to revert subsequently to some earlier incidents.

A deed of partnership was drawn up by George Hogarth, on the terms of Scott's letter of June 15th, 1821, and executed on April 1st, 1822. It was evidently at Scott's insistence, and by an independent accountant, that new books were opened, and the financial relations of the new partners clearly set out. Nothing could be clearer in themselves than are the conditions of the deed, or the opening of the accounts in the partnership books, and it is evident that the whole circumstances of the position must have been known not only to James Ballantyne but to George Hogarth also. Yet is it in regard to one of these accounts, or rather the interpretation that should be placed upon it, that the controversy between Lockhart and the Trustees reached its bitterest issue. There was incompetence, intemperance, and prejudice on both sides, and it is easy to show that either was wrong; but to find the truth is a harder thing.

This is the account in question:

State of Debts due by and to Sir Walter Scott.

The amount of bills payable, now current,
and to be provided for by him—£33,954 1 13
The amount of Bills Receivable is—£6,097 1 81
Outstanding Printing Accounts—£488 9 9

Balance on Sir Walter Scott's A/C—£2,052 1 42

£6,586 7 10—£36,007 5 5*

Sum due by James Ballantyne for which
he has granted an assignment of his Life
Assurance Policy.—£2,524 11 8—£9,110 1 96

£26,896 5 11

[* By an evident printers' error this figure is £36,077. 5. 5. in the Ballantyne pamphlet.]

There is nothing puzzling or unusual in the construction or itemising of this account: it is the amount of the liabilities for which Scott accepted personal responsibility which is surprising, and for which two contrary explanations were advanced with equal confidence and unnecessary vehemence.

It will be remembered that Scott proposed, in his letter of June 15th, 1821, to accept personal responsibility for all the debts of the business, *except* such as had been incurred prior to the previous dissolution of partnership. This distinction is, evidently based upon the fact that Scott was reinstating James in the half-possession of the assets of the business, other than bookdebts, *as they then were*, only debiting him with a half-charge for the additions thereto, and this exception, only loosely logical as it was, is shown by other accounts to have been observed. It supplies an argument for excluding the possibility that these bills had any connection with the old John Ballantyne & Co. issues, and, in any event, those bills ought to have been extinguished, for the whole of the stock was now sold.

Lockhart finds no difficulty in supplying an explanation. He asserts as a fact that this extraordinary total represented the mismanagement and extravagance of James Ballantyne during the previous five years, and that Scott, with a splendid generosity, took it upon himself to give James a clean start, and a fresh chance, on his promising to behave better in future. He makes a number of statements which are either disputable or demonstrably false, and then concludes (letter to Sir Adam Fergusson, p. 83) 'I have already shown that the outstanding bills at the date of the contract were not his' (Scott's) 'private debts, but were merely assumed till the Company's profits should clear them off. Their amount was £36,000.'

But he had not shown it at all. Nor does he appear to observe that if the liability had been incurred in that way, and it had been agreed that it should be discharged from future profits, it is extremely improbable that the account would have been entered on the ledger by an independent accountant in this form; nor would it have been properly reduced by an item which was a personal debt of James to Scott, unless Lockhart would have us believe that this huge sum was to be charged to Scott's share of the profits alone; and, if so, why? On Lockhart's contention, it would be an absurd adjustment of such a deficiency.

Indeed, its amount makes this explanation inherently incredible. After allowing for the fact that the assets of the business, other than its book debts, had been increased, And were, apart from this figure, transferred to the new partnership (subject to some minor qualifications) in an unencumbered form, it still remains that James's deficiency must have accumulated at the rate of at least £4,000 a year, up to a total of £20,000.

If this had not been urged as a fact by Scott's biographer, it would hardly deserve the formality of refutation. But its amount presented no difficulty to him. He advanced two evidences in its support. He pointed to the item on the account "Sum due by James Ballantyne etc. £2,524. 11. 8." and boldly asserted that this was (part of) a fresh deficiency created by James, even during the interval for which Scott had stipulated before the new partnership was commenced. If that were true, it would be supporting evidence of the strongest kind; and it might well have been that after such an interval, and the deaths of all the parties concerned, it might have been impossible to prove the falsehood of this assumption. But—*magna est veritas*—the actual composition of this figure was still on record. This is how it was made up:

£s.d.
Balance of £3,000 as agreed due in 1816, still outstanding—1,800 0 0
Add half-cost of Scott's additions to assets, as set out in his letter of June 15th, 1821, and in the partnership deed—1,287 10 0

3,087 10 0

Less credited by Scott to James for his agreed
share in the sale of the *Pirate* copyright—562 18 4

Balance due—£2,524 11 8

The liberal reward to James for his services on the *Pirate* MS. is an interesting evidence of the large-handed liberality with which Scott treated those who were associated with his prosperity, but as an evidence of extravagance on the part of James it fails utterly. Not a penny of the sum passed through his hands. It is no more than a bookkeeping entry.

But Lockhart brought forward another amount which does, at first, have a more sinister appearance. He said that, in addition to the £2,524, when the partnership was commenced, there was found to be a deficiency of £1,629 on the cash book, and that the opening of the new books included a ledger account charging James with this amount.

Had these two sums been beyond explanation, there would have been a *prima facie* case for convicting James of doing away with over £4,000, beyond his proper remuneration, even in what we may describe as his probation year, and so Lockhart would have us believe; and there would have been no more to be argued over than whether a hopeless fool had gone into a second partnership with a hopeless knave, or they were no worse than two fools in the same boat. But once more the truth wins. How Lockhart could have justified the way he abstracted and interpreted these figures, or his blindness to what it was not convenient to see, or in what category he places himself by this accusation, it is not necessary to determine. But the fact is this. The cash book in which this balance appeared was not the trade cash book, but a separate one which James kept to record sums which passed through his hands on Scott's behalf; and the accountant who opened the new books did not bring this sum into the account we were previously considering for a reason which was carefully explained in the *vidimus* to which Lockhart had access, and from which he quoted. The explanatory note is this:

> "As this cash book was merely a state of transactions between Sir Walter Scott and Mr. Ballantyne, the above balance is due to Sir Walter, but as it arose in a

great measure from the accidental circumstance of the transactions, on the day they closed, having left a considerable sum in Mr. Ballantyne's hands, which would speedily be extinguished by further transactions of Sir Walter Scott's account, the above balance is carried to the credit of Sir Walter, and the debit of Mr. Ballantyne in the books opened for the new concern."

That is to say, it was not money which James had collected from business funds and misappropriated, as Lockhart alleged, to his own use, but money provided by Scott and entrusted; to James for specific payments to be made on or after April 1st, and for which purposes it was properly in his hands on that date.

It may be asked for what purposes it had become necessary to have such a separate cash book, and this may be best considered after hearing the widely different allegations made by the Ballantyne Trustees regarding the origin of this £36,000 of floating bills. But it may be useful to observe at this point, and to bear in mind, that Scott's three adventures in anonymity—one as poet, and two as novelist—had created a position by which he could not collect a large part of his own income in his own name.

James Ballantyne & Co. disposed of the copyrights of the works of anonymous authors, and, in the first instance, must receive the proceeds of such transactions. This position had been modified since Constable had been taken into full confidence, but was still applicable to transactions with Longman, Murray, Blackwood, or other publishers.

Finally, in discussing Lockhart's explanation as to the genesis of these bills, we may consider Scott's own deliberate entry in his Journal nearly four years later (20th Jan. 1826):

"I have been far from suffering from James Ballantyne. I owe it to him to say that his difficulties, as well as his advantages are owing to me."

It is a generous voluntary testimony, written not for living eyes, but for those who were to come after. It reads somewhat like the postscript of the 'missive' letter—as though Scott were aware of facts which might incline the scale (even beyond the point of equity) to a different judgement. It may be the act of one who throws a cloak over a friend's failing: who says: "if I forgave, cannot others forget?" We know that Scott could be a good friend.... Or it may be no more nor less than the bare justice of literal fact.

But one thing is sure. Scott could have felt no occasion or inclination to make such record had the facts at this time and afterwards been as Lockhart would have us believe.

The Ballantyne Trustees gave an absolutely different explanation of the existence of these bills, and were as confident as Lockhart in their assertions. The bills were really nothing to do with the business at all. Scott, they said, used the credit of the firm to discount them, and the money for his private objects—that is, for the purchase of land.

Having asserted this as a fact, without supporting it with any evidence, they went on to found some disputable theories upon it. They said:

> "If Sir Walter Scott had never been connected with James Ballantyne in business, but had contented himself in extending his patronage to his old schoolfellow, it would have been infinitely better for both parties. Mr. Ballantyne would, in that case, have realised a respectable fortune; and Sir Walter would have escaped the temptation presented by the facilities of a mercantile co-partnership to raise money for the purchase of lands for which he had not otherwise the means of paying.
>
> "Sir Walter Scott's embarrassments, and the consequent embarrassment and ruin of his partner, arose, as we have just stated, from his extensive purchases of land before he had realised money to pay for it: and

> from his making a free use of the name of the Company (with the consent of his partner, of course) to meet the payments for these purchases—a proceeding which led to a series of bill transactions with Constable & Co, which, on the failure of that firm, brought ruin both on himself and on Mr. James Ballantyne."

Even assuming the premise that the Trustees set up, there are gross inaccuracies in these paragraphs.

In the first place, Lockhart had not, in his original life of Scott, made any allusion to the dissolution of partnership in 1816 or its renewal in 1822. He had ignored these events entirely. He may not have done this with deliberation. They were not material to the narrative in the form in which he presented it. But the Trustees in this first pamphlet dealt affirmatively with the events of this period, and preserved a corresponding silence. It is difficult to avoid the conviction that they thought Lockhart might be unaware of the break in the continuity of the partnership, and did not intend to disclose it.

Even in the passage quoted, there is an evident lack of candour in the construction of the argument, because at the time when these bills were issued, no question of a partner's consent could arise, for James was a manager only.

Beyond this, it is not a fact that the renewals of these bills, under whatever circumstances they were created, was the sole or even a major cause of the resulting catastrophe, as we shall observe in its due place. And it is almost wild hypothesis to say that Ballantyne, if he had traded alone, would have 'realised a respectable fortune'.

One change of circumstance in human life must, as the years pass, involvle a myriad others, utterly beyond calculation; but if we are to consider seriously the hypothesis of there having been no partnership, and everything else having occurred on parallel lines, then James would have been printing the *Waverley* novels (or how else would he have made a fortune through Scott?), he would have been printing them for Constable; he would have been paid with Constable's bills; Constable would have obtained all possible credit from him in the last difficult years; Hurst, Robinson & Co. would have failed; then Constable would have failed, and it is at least improbable that James would have survived; *whoever* printed the Waverley novels must have sustained a ruinous loss when Hurst, Robinson & Co. suspended payment, and that suspension was utterly remote from the existence of these bills.

But without admiring the superstructure of theory and reproach which the Trustees built upon this foundation, we may still ask, had that foundation itself any solidity? What, in fact, did these bills represent?

Lockhart has given us his assertion, and has supported it with evidence which will not endure examination. The Trustees have given us their assertion, and have supported it with no evidence at all, relying upon its plausibility. To a superficial examination it seems a simple, probable thing. Scott was anxious to buy the land around Abbotstord. He did buy it largely. Bills were, in fact discounted for large amounts while he was in sole possession of the business. It is far more plausible to say that he used the money for the purchase of the land he desired than that James used it to such amounts in profligate private expenditure, and that Scott then took over the liability thus created, and rewarded him with a new partnership. The trouble is that this plausibility decreases on closer examination.

Let us see first what these purchases of land were. We will accept Lockhart's own figures. He gives the total expenditure upon the purchase of Abbotsford, and the adjoining properties, as £29,083 from 1811 to 1821 inclusive, and he adds that the largest expenditure on building and planting took place *after* these dates.

It is a large sum. But we must deduct from it the first £4,200, because we know the sources from which that money came. We know also that buildings and freehold lands are forms of property on which money can be more easily and more cheaply borrowed than commercial bills. That was (almost) as true then as it is now. It would seem improbable that Scott, under any financial circumstances, would have preferred to raise the whole of such an amount on bills rather than to mortgage the properties, or obtain an advance from his bankers by depositing the deeds. But if we allow that he might have had such a preference (which is negatively supported by the fact that the deeds must have been his unencumbered property a few years later), and go on to the supposition that he raised the money by discount of these Ballantyne bills, we find that we have only changed one difficulty for another. For what then became of his income from other sources?

During this period his receipts from professional salaries and his wife's estate had approached £2,000 a year. He had also been making a huge income from his literary work. What became of this latter income if the whole or even the bulk of his investments in landed property were raised by discounting what were practically his own bills? It becomes a problem so insoluble that we may conclude with some confidence that the premise is false.

It is also contradicted by various subordinate evidences. There are frequent allusions in his earlier correspondence to his own freedom from debt, apart from the complications of the publishing and printing businesses; after the completion of the disposal of the publishing stock, these allusions cease, but there are occasions when he mentions that he is needing money, and always in relation to the dates at which payments for his novels could be arranged. When large amounts are received for them he is affluent: in the intervals he is not. If he had been raising £25,000 in a few years for his own purposes by the simple method of discounting his own bills, these peaks of prosperity and plains of depression would have been comparatively levelled.

There is also an extreme absence of documentary evidence to support the assertion that the Ballantyne Trustees made. Had Scott been putting this huge total of bills into circulation for his own purposes during the period when James was manager, everything must have been done through him, and there must have been frequent correspondence concerning it.

The Trustees put forward overwhelming evidence that Scott kept in regular touch with the finances of the business, which Lockhart had been foolish enough to deny, but on this point they advanced only one utterly inconclusive letter, in which Scott made an appointment to meet James in relation to one of his purchases of land, but for what exact object he does not say. Even if it were for the receipt of money in connection with the discount of a bill (of which there is not the remotest suggestion) it would prove nothing, because John or James collected publishers' bills for the anonymous novels, and they may well have been discounted through the firm's bankers. Yet the production of this letter is of a real significance, because it shows that the Trustees had searched and had failed to find.

But the central objection to the interpretation which they placed upon the existence of these bills is that we can see that Scott had a large income from other sources during the period in question, the allocation of which becomes inexplicable. It is a subordinate objection, but falls, as every evidence does, into the same scale, that there is no record of any objection being taken by George Hogarth, no discussion in correspondence, no allusion in Scott's missive letter to the existence of such ultra-commercial transactions. Everyone takes these bills in silence, and as a matter of course. It is a position open to several interpretations, but it does not help that of the Trustees.

Yet the bills were a fact. It is more than possible that they are an enigma to which we have lost the key: that there is some unguessed explanation which we shall never know, as to the nature of which we have no guide but the character of those concerned; and if this be thought an improbable suggestion, let us consider how easily it might have happened that Lockhart's plausible and confident assertion that those items of £2,524 and £1,629 represented James's defalcations in a single year would have been beyond the disproof of any remaining evidence, and would have appeared so certain that it would have seemed a mere perversity to dispute it.

Yet, it is possible, and better than no explanation at all, that the truth may be midway between the diverse explanations which were put forward by contending prejudices.

We have to rule out the possibility of the inclusion of any liabilities which were originally created prior to the dissolution of partnership, because they were explicitly placed in another category both in the missive letter and the partnership deed, and this alone shows how dangerous conjecture may be, for apart from this evidence, we might have confidently attributed the creation of at least part of this liability to that period; but it remains a possibility that Scott may have made some use of the credit facilities of the firm to complete the amounts which he paid for the properties he acquired: that James may have drawn, during the five years, considerably more than he was entitled to do: and that the business had been conducted by him with such financial laxity that considerable losses or leakages had occurred and had been covered by this easy method—easy in busy prosperous-seeming days—of increasing the floating acceptances of the firm. When we remember that the *net* amount which has to be explained, after allowing for the value of the otherwise unencumbered business assets, is not more than £20,000, and that, before the era of limited liability companies, the issue of such bills was a normal financial expedient, we may recognise that we are as near to a reasonable explanation as we are likely to get.

If Scott were offered a property, say, for £5,000, and had £3,000 in hand, he might feel that he could safely and reasonably borrow the balance on the commercial credit of the business, and keep the deeds in his own desk.

If the total of bills (which James had the legal power to issue on behalf of the actual owner of the firm) had grown beyond any proper explanation that he could furnish—and this imputation is not groundless in view of the anxious letter to John which the Trustees so naively published, the protestation of better bookkeeping in future in his letter to Scott, and the suggestion of indemnity which is implicit in Scott's postscript to the missive letter—we have a position which Scott might have accepted, however unsatisfactory, in a spirit of generosity and forgiveness, and allowed liabilities to be charged to himself at the formation of the new partnership for which he was already legally liable, and which James, even if he were in default, had no means of paying, without subjecting him to a penurious scale of living which Scott, in a time of personal prosperity, would have been very reluctant to do. If we accept this midway explanation, we can understand George Hogarth's silence and acquiescence. Five years earlier, he and his father had insisted that James should resign his partnership, as they supposed, in the interests of his intended wife. This course had proved needless, and detrimental if not disastrous to James. The financial storm which had appeared to threaten had passed over. A great fame had come to his partner, and a period of prosperity which James had lost his title to share. If Scott were willing to reinstate him now, and if he had to admit to George that his books would not balance, and he could not account for the full amount of the bills which he had put into circulation, but that Scott had agreed to accept the position as it should be ascertained to be without probing the past, it was unlikely that George would propose to do so. Scott had said that they could debit those bills to him. It was the utmost that James could hope, and more than he was entitled to claim. Let the past lie.

It may be all wrong, and yet as near the truth as we are ever likely to get.

It has, at least, more probability than either of the contending explanations which it compromises rather than denies.

All we certainly know is that it was on this basis that the new partnership was commenced.

CHAPTER LXXVI

The Pirate was published in December, 1821. It was a clear year since the last novel had appeared. It had a good title. It was well-enough received. It had good features, as any novel by Scott would be sure to have. It has its lovers today, who place it high on the Waverley list. At times it has a sombre vigour: at others it is nearly dull. Its humour is like the sunlight of a pallid day. Its background is less clearly conceived than are those either of the novels in which he told of familiar scenes, such as the *Heart of Midlothian*, or such as *Ivanhoe*, where his imagination moved in a clear space. Memory and imagination are bad yoke-fellows, and Scott never did his best work when he drove them in equal harness. They should be driven tandem, if at all; and then it may be difficult to keep their heads in the same direction. If Scott had never visited the Orkneys, the *Pirate* might have been a more vivid romance to those who are under the same disadvantage.

It was followed by the *Fortunes of Nigel* at the end of May. Constable had been building himself a country house in Fifeshire in these affluent days, but a breakdown in health had been followed by medical advice that he should go south for a time, and he was living near London. If it were a fact, as Lockhart states, that the sales of the Waverley novels showed some diminution at this time (of which there is little evidence, apart from his assertion), then it is true that Scott was not well served by his publisher, for Constable's letters only boasted increasing triumphs.

It was Sunday when the smack *Ocean* sailed in from Leith, and tied up at the London docks. At one A.M. on Monday the bales were being hauled out of her holds, and by 10.30 a.m. 7,000 copies had been dispersed to the trade. Constable saw people reading the book as they walked the streets. So he wrote. Scott had promised to write something for Miss Joanna Baillie at this time, for a miscellany which she was preparing for publication, to assist a literary friend in indigent circumstances. The call of charity is responsible for most of his worst work. He sent her the dramatic sketch, Halidon Hill.

Robert Cadell, Constable's partner, heard of it, and offered £1,000 for the copyright, which Scott accepted. When Constable heard of it, he wrote warmly approving the bargain. He gave (bills for) the £1,000. He suggested that Scott should supply him with a similar sketch once a quarter at the same price. Lockhart thinks he had lost his head at this time. But if he had, Scott hadn't. He ignored the offer.

We need not take Lockhart's reflections on Constable too literally at this period. Lockhart judged by results. Constable is to fail in business in four years time, and already he is being dressed for the part.

But Lockhart's explanation of his alleged condition of mental instability is too quaint for omission. He says that Constable's corpulent body was now suffering from 'a threatening of water on the chest', for which doses of foxglove had been prescribed. The result of this treatment was that the whole world was a rosy dream, in which innumerable Waverley novels went into editions of incredible size. Let all takers of digitalis beware.

It was, we are told, under the influence of this curious form of intoxication that he sent Scott a summary of the reprints which he had recently had occasion to order from the Ballantyne Press.

> " "A new edition of Sir W. Scott's Poetical Works" in 10 vols. (miniature)—5 000 copies
> "Novels and Tales," 12 vols ditto—5,000"
> "Historical Romances," 6 vols ditto—5,000"
> "Poetry from Waverley, etc." 1 vol. 12mo.—5,000"
> Paper required 7,772 reams
> Volumes produced from Ballantyne's press—145,000!"

Lockhart does not suggest that these figures were incorrect, nor that Constable was placing orders beyond the requirements of the trade, and these omissions leave his outburst in a somewhat unconvincing condition. But as a matter of cool business argument, if the earlier books were being bought to this extent, the copyrights were extremely valuable, and we can understand Constable's anxiety to acquire them absolutely. To do this, he had to bid high, and reach a figure at which Scott would he willing to take cash down (or perhaps bills down would be a more accurate expression) for an absolute sale. And 'cash down' and 'bills down' may have seemed to both of them at this time, and even to their bankers, to be very similar things.

But if we are to understand the position fairly, we must ignore this talk about digitalis and swelled heads, and consider the credits which such figures as those above quoted must have involved. The Ballantyne Press was producing hundreds of thousands of books which were all charged to one firm—Constable & Co. That firm was re-selling them to many retail booksellers in Scotland, but mainly to its London agents, Hurst, Robinson & Co., who distributed them, mostly on long credit terms, to the English book-trade. So long as Hurst, Robinson & Co. met their engagements regularly, all would be well. The James Ballantyne & Co. bills, about which Lockhart and the Trustees disputed so acrimoniously, would not matter at all. And Hurst, Robinson & Co. had the reputation of being at this time (and were in fact) a very wealthy firm.

As to Constable, he had built up a splendidly successful business. As a going concern, he was a prosperous, even a wealthy man. Scott may have been his best author, but he would have had a large business had he never touched a *Waverley* novel. His weakness was that his business had grown so fast and so far that it had gone beyond the support of its original capital. It was carried on almost entirely by bills. Bills to Ballantyne & Co., and half-a-score of other printers: bills to Scott and other authors: bills from Hurst, Robinson & Co., for many thousands of pounds: even accommodation bills at times exchanged with friendly firms when a strain came. But it was a prosperous, profit-making firm, seemingly impregnable in its strength—while Hurst, Robinson & Co. met their engagements, as they surely, surely would.

It is under these circumstances that Lockhart asks us to glance at Constable's home in Fifeshire, with this comment: "Alas! For 'Archibald Constable of Balniel' also, and his overweening intoxication of worldly success, Fortune had already begun to prepare a stern rebuke."

Lockhart can be rather sickening at times.

CHAPTER LXXVII

However opinion may divide upon the merits of the *Pirate*, those of *Nigel* are well agreed. It dealt with a period of English history of which Scott had an enormous knowledge, which was not confined to its domestic or international politics or its prominent figures, but included social conditions, and religious and intellectual interests. He did not have to read up in preparation for this novel, consciously storing his mind, as he had done for *Old Mortality*, nor was he concerned by any vexed question of historical equity. The period was too remote for the excitement of living passions: his own knowledge too well assimilated for the process of digestion to delay his imagination, which moved freely, both in this novel and the subsequent *Peveril*, constructing a world as real as that of *Ivanhoe*, and with a far nearer approach to the re-creation of an actual past. It showed again, as had the *Heart of Midlothian,* the freedom and domination of his imagination when applied to a period outside the radius of feudal romanticism, with which what he wrote was most strongly, and is still too narrowly associated in the popular mind, and sometimes by the superficialities of literary criticism. The reception of *Nigel* and its sales were such that the ebb of the tide which Lockhart asked us to observe a year earlier is still very hard to see. It seems rather to rest at flood.

And at this time, in the full tide of his prosperity, Scott became the inspiration of a national gesture which may be described as the burial service of the Jacobitism which he was supposed to favour. No Hanoverian prince had entered Scotland, except or since when the Duke of Cumberland had conquered at Culloden, and left behind him a hated name. But the Cardinal of York was dead, and the restoration of the Stuarts no longer anything more than a sentimental dream. If all the races of Scotland, all creeds, and all political parties, could be united in giving enthusiastic welcome to the Hanoverian king, a bitter quarrel of centuries would be consigned at last to a quiet and final grave. But was it a possible thing?

Unfortunately, George IV was not one about whom it was easy to be enthusiastic. Tories showed an outward loyalty, and spoke their thoughts in the privacy of the club-room: Whigs gave theirs in the public press.

If there were one man who could organise and unite Scottish prejudices and Scottish jealousies, and overcome Scottish disaffection, so that such a visit would be an assured success, it was Sir Walter Scott. He believed it possible, and that it ought to be attempted. In correspondence with the King, he brought him to the same view.

The visit was arranged, and the task of organising the reception, with its processions, receptions and banquets, was thrown, largely by formal resolution and in practice almost entirely, upon Scott's shoulders. It was a gigantic labour of detail, and a feat of diplomacy at which no other could have succeeded. To marshall the chieftains of the Highland clans in an order of precedence which was in itself defensible, and which they would all accept without drawing of dirks, or going sulking home, was alone an unattempted dexterity which might have been regarded as impossible had not Scott achieved it, and he was probably the only man who would have ventured on such an enterprise.

But Scott could do what no other would have attempted with prudence. Burns had represented the Lowland-Scotsman to the world that admired his poetry in the guise of a profligate sot. Scott had interpreted Scotland, Highlands and Lowlands both, in nobler, broader and truer portraiture, and to an ever wider audience. He may have been the man at this time who was of the most fame in the world: that he was first in Scotland and Scottish hearts, there can be no doubt at all.

And beyond this popularity, he had exceptional qualifications for the organisation of such a reception. He was known to all, and of a universal friendship. He had powers of persuasion and conciliation which have been rarely equalled. He had the unusual combination of qualities which is essential to the successful organiser on a large scale—he could plan with imagination, and then could give his mind to the endless details on which the large outlines depend.

The King was entertained at Dalkieth House by the boy-Duke of Buccleuch, and there was a crowded fortnight of banquets, receptions and processions, in which, for the first time in recorded history, Scottish men from all parts of the kingdom appeared united, not only in a common loyalty, but a common friendship. Having been done successfully, it may seem to have been a simple thing, but it had been of the nature of audacious experiment, which only Scott would have adventured, only Scott could have persuaded the King to attempt, and only Scott could have brought to its triumphant end.

The Home Secretary, Mr. Peel—afterwards Sir Robert—addressed a letter to him on the King's departure:

> "The king has commanded me to acquaint you that he cannot bid adieu to Scotland without conveying to you individually his warm personal acknowledgements. His Majesty well knows how many difficulties have been smoothed, and how much has been effected by your unremitting activity, by your knowledge of your countrymen, and by the just estimation in which they hold you. The King wishes to make you the channel of conveying to the Highland chiefs and their followers, who have given to the varied scene which we have witnessed so peculiar and romantic a character, his particular thanks for their attendance, and his warm approbation of their uniform deportment."

As a fact, there was a little feeling among Edinburgh citizens that the picturesqueness of the Highland clans had been rather too prominent. They counted populations and discussed importances. But Scott's instinct for pageant and the management of men had both been justified by the event.

Sir Robert Peel related, long afterwards, how he had had occasion to walk up the High Street on the day of the King's progress from Holyrood to the Castle, before the procession passed, Scott accompanying him, to see whether some arrangements for the reception were complete. Mr Peel said: "You will never get through in privacy." Scott said to that: "They are all absorbed in loyalty." But it was an occasion on which Scott was wrong. They walked through a roar of cheers "from one extremity of the street to the other." "Never," Sir Robert bore record "did I see such an instance of national devotion expressed."

To the eyes of all around him, except those who were most intimate, it must have seemed that few men were so enviable as Sir Walter Scott at this time. He had the world's gifts at his feet. Fame and honour and wealth were supported by recovered health and domestic felicity. He had the land that he most loved in his own possession: day by day its plantations grew towards the beauty that he had dreamed to give it. The last wing of Abbotsford rose, and while the masons' trowels rang on the stones, the portions already finished were "like a cried fair" with the crowding of many guests. It was some weeks after the King had gone back to England before the last of those who were entertained in this connection had climbed into their carriages and left Abbotsford to no more than its normal bustle.

Yet while the festivities were at their height, and Scott was the life of the whole, he was distracted by a personal sorrow, in the death of William Erskine, his lifelong, and in some relations, his most intimate friend.

It is difficult to know William Erskine: Lockhart's caricature intervenes. He represents him as a man who lived in a state of perpetual tears. With a curious lack of variety, and violation of probability, he represented William Laidlaw in the same monotony of occupation. When Scott offered him Kaeside, Lockhart could hear him sobbing twenty years away.

There are evidences which profoundly modify, if they do not refute, the accusations of moral and physical weakness which Lockhart made against William Erskine; but it appears to have been true that he was of a particularly gentle and sensitive disposition.

For a long time, he had had a private dissatisfaction with the moderate recognition in the public service which had come to him as the reward of family connections and his own merits. Scott had shared this feeling, and had been indefatigable in urging his claims to higher office. It was only at the beginning of this year that his representations had succeeded, and Erskine had been elevated to the Bench, and the title of Lord Kinneder conferred upon him.

He had only enjoyed this office a few months when his health failed. The reason which is given for this certainly goes far to justify Lockhart's invertebrate presentation. He is said to have died of grief because his name was involved in a baseless scandal. He took to bed, and the physicians bled him white. It was a method which appears to have been frequently successful in prolonging the lives of apoplectic lawyers, but as a remedy for mental depression it failed. Scott observes, with his invincible tolerance, that the treatment may have been necessary, but it certainly increased the patient's weakness. William Erskine died.

Scott must attend his funeral in the midst of one of the busiest days of the celebrations. Up to then, with that capacity to use time as though it were of unlimited amount for which he had such amazing faculty, he had been sitting 'day and night' at his friend's bedside, while every moment of his time seemed to the outer world to be given to the elaborate organisation for which he had accepted responsibility. Lockhart, who went with him to the funeral, says that he never saw him in such a state of dejection as he was when they parted in the street, and he was turning again to the scenes of gaiety in which there could be no place for private grief.

Scott found a spare moment to write to his eldest son with the news of Erskine's death:

> "It would be rather difficult for anyone who has never lived much among my good country-people to comprehend that an idle story of a love intrigue, a story alike base and baseless, should be the death of an innocent man of high character, high station, and well advanced in years. It struck into poor Erskine's heart and soul, however, quite as cruelly as any similar calumny ever affected a modest woman—he withered and sunk. There is no need that I should say peace be with him! If ever a pure spirit quitted this vale of tears, it was William Erskine's. I must turn to and see what can be done about getting some pension for his daughters."

The last sentence is characteristic.

It is a detail of the occupations of this period that George Crabbe, a poet for whom Scott had always felt and expressed a high measure of admiration, and whose works he could probably have quoted as fully as their author himself, selected this time of the King's visit to appear at North Castle Street, where Scott put him up and found space and time to entertain the somewhat precise and bewildered old gentleman in the midst of the crowding distractions of the time.

It is not surprising that, as the crowds withdrew and the noise died, Scott found that he had exerted himself beyond the limit of his own strength. He lay exhausted and ill for some days, while correspondence accumulated upon him from a hundred directions. Everyone who had helped to make the King's reception successful now expected some reward of title or patronage, and who but Sir Walter could put it forward in such a way that it would not be ignored in Whitehall?

We can suppose with what patience he answered, with what

discretion he put forward such pleas as might be reasonably advanced; but he had a larger claim to advance for others, a more personal desire to plead on his own behalf. He made a formal written request that the peerages forfeited in consequence of the insurrection of '15 and '45 might be restored, so that the last memory of the old divisions, the last bitterness they had left, might be ended. It was a petition which was soon afterwards granted, giving many noble families in Scotland a cause for gratitude to him; granted also—after some years of unavoidable delay—was his own plea that Mons Meg should be returned to its place on the Edinburgh battlements.

It is worth a moment's reflection, for it is an incident of revealing quality, that Scott's one great political achievement (apart from the equally characteristic *Malachi* letters, to which we have still to come) was a battle in the cause of peace.

It is equally characteristic that when he was putting forward so many claims, and might have asked for himself almost anything that he would, his only request of a personal nature was for the restoration to Edinburgh of its famous cannon. For himself he asked nothing at all.

Yet, it might be questioned, what could he have asked that was not already his? Honours and wealth and fame had come to him already, and by a better way. Not by inheritance, or a blundering chance, but by the quality of his own work. He had the joy of that work, and the consciousness that it was of a good kind, doing evil to none. He had domestic happiness also, such as is seldom gained with the world's more spectacular blessings. If he were of an easy faith, thanking God for a good world, was it much to boast? If he were generous to others, was it much to praise?

CHAPTER LXXVIII.

Peveril of the Peak was published in January 1823, and was received with less enthusiasm than had been the recent experience. It was criticised with justice for the faults which it had, and less than adequately praised for its compensating excellences. Fenella is not an exact parallel of the White Lady, but she is similar in being a somewhat unearthly character, and she fails in the same way. She is unconvincing; and her unreality affects the flavour of the whole book.

But the fact was that Scott had set a standard which was almost impossibly difficult to maintain. The *Waverley* novels have certain features of unity which distinguish them from all other works of the kind. They are inimitable; and had one been left till this day in undiscovered manuscript everyone would recognise it for what it would be, even though it might be as far from any other as is *Ivanhoe* from *Guy Mannering*. But while they maintained a separate standard of excellence, they also showed a wide divergence among themselves, and it is these differences—this newness—which had been the occasions of their greatest separate triumphs. The *Heart of Midlothian* had been unexpected: so had *Ivanhoe*: so had *Nigel*. There is little in *Waverley* itself to foretell any of these books.

Peveril would have been a greater success had not *Nigel* preceded it. It was too nearly of the same pattern to astonish: criticism found its voice.

Large as the sale was, it showed a reduction on other recent figures. Lockhart has cast Constable for the part of an infatuated man, rushing obstinately upon his fate: he has completely lost his head over the *Waverley* novel sales, and undertakes wild liabilities in an utterly reckless way. *Quos Deus vult perdere, prius dementat*. Such is the picture he gives us, but he gives us facts also, and these have a different front.

A year or two ago, Constable had contracted with Scott for four novels, for which he had boldly given bills in advance of their production. Now he had had two of them—*Nigel* and *Peveril*, and the third was promised for the spring. We know that Constable was making a large annual profit at this time. His partner, Cadell, puts it at about £10,000, of which he says that Constable drew £4,000. We know also that the financing of the huge business from which these profits grew was carried on mainly by means of the discount of bills. More than from any other single source, this large profit came from handling the works of Sir Walter Scott. To retain him was vital prudence. To do this by means of advance agreements and the obligation of longdated bills, was the obvious method under the circumstances of the case. Now the existing agreement was approaching its end, but Constable did not press for, nor even propose another. He sat back and watched.

Lockhart has alleged in condemnation of those concerned, and in an exculpation of Scott for which there is no need, that he suffered a decline in popularity which was concealed from him during these years. *Peveril* is the first book in regard to which such a decline can be demonstrated, and it is not easy to discover that such concealment was attempted.

It is Lockhart's own witness that Scott was informed by Constable himself when he thought the first reception of the next novel *Quentin Durward*, to be disappointing, and Scott was writing to Ballantyne about it immediately:

"The mouse who only trusts to one poor hole
Can never be a mouse with any soul."

There was no concealment: he knew at once. And he was so alert to such indications that he was already thinking of abandoning fiction, and adventuring on a different line of literary work. As a fact, he had had doubts himself concerning *Peveril*. He had written to Terry in the previous October, expressing fears both as to the state of his own health, and its possible effect on the book, which are of dual significance. In an expression of uncertain implications he mentioned apoplexy. It is reasonably supposed that the illness which is known to have laid him up for a week or two in that month may have given him some warning symptom which he concealed from those who were nearest to him. If that be so, there was, for a time, a complete recovery. Leaving *Peveril* to sink or swim as it would, he pushed forward with his French romance. He was trying a cast with a novel of a fresh kind. When he heard that it was coldly received, it must have been disconcerting, though he took it easily.

As to the future, Constable showed caution. He did, indeed, make an offer, and came to terms, for the purchase of the moiety of the copyrights in the last four novels which Scott had retained. He purchased these outright, giving bills for five thousand guineas. But as for further agreements, he was inclined to pause.... And then the scene changed again.

The tide, which had shown some signs of recession, rose again to full flood. London might have seemed cold to *Quentin Durward*, but Paris was wild with enthusiasm. London flared up, somewhat late, to the height of the Paris fire. For the last time, a *Waverley* novel was hailed as a fresh achievement of the first rank: a new peak in the range. From this time, we are dealing with a day in which there may still be sunny hours, but the high noon is passed.

CHAPTER LXXIX.

St. Ronan's Well was published in December, and its reception was sufficiently cordial in Scotland, but colder in London, as it deserved to be. It can be praised well enough, if we chose the right words with care, but by the standard of the *Waverley* novels it is a poor thing. The novelty of the conception was good. Had it succeeded fully, it would have added a new triumph to the series. To describe the life of a contemporary; Scottish watering-place, and make it the scene of tragedy of a modern kind, had it been done in a manner comparable with that of the *Antiquary* or *Ivanhoe, Nigel,* or the *Heart of Midlothian*, would have added a different excellence to those of the existing gallery, but the book would not have endured such a comparison, even had it been left unmutilated. James Ballantyne read some chapters and raised a wail of protest. There was an episode (he said) which the public would not endure. After some argument,

Scott gave way. He tore up twenty-eight pages, and wrote a different version. It was the solitary incident of his life for which a biographer can attempt no apology, beyond recognition of the fact that all men have their weak moments, their weak moods. All we know of those twenty-eight pages is that in them Clara Mowbray's false marriage was consummated, while in the revised ending it is not. The difference is fatal to the plausibility of the final tragedy. It is a kind of alteration which Scott would not have made—for instance—in the *Heart of Midlothian*, nor in any book which he had imagined with a sufficient energy. In fact, by doing it, he condemned himself and the book together.

It is true that the actual change is without violation of probability, but the sequel becomes comparatively inconsequent. It has the irritation of a needless tragedy, and Clara not only goes mad at a provokingly inopportune moment, when she had only to remain quiescent for a few further hours for everything to have been happily adjusted, but she has already alienated the reader's sympathy by never seeming quite sane.

In short, Scott allowed James Ballantyne's opinion to spoil a book which was quite easy to spoil. It was not only criticised with some severity: the trade found the large number of copies which had been distributed were in excess of their requirements. The sale of the *Waverley* novels had been raised to a total which it was almost impossible to sustain permanently, and though it was still at a great height, the weakening of the position was apparent. The success of *Quentin Durward* had required the impulsion of foreign favour, and now the ground recovered had been lost again.

But Scott, as usual, had another novel in preparation: and, as usual he put it on the market the more quickly when he became aware that the line of battle wavered. Six months later, *Redgauntlet* appeared.

The position of *Redgauntlet* in the *Waverley* gallery is somewhat anomalous, and it is not difficult to understand that its first reception was hesitant rather than enthusiastic or hostile. It approaches more nearly to autobiography than do any of the others, and has a unique interest in that consequence. Few would place it among the first six: perhaps fewer still would place it in the lower half of the list. It cannot be considered as a new triumph. It held rather than advanced a retreated line. But the position which it entrenched was still of a great strength.

For the summer of 1824 Scott put fiction aside. He had made a profitable contract for re-editing a second edition of the Swift volumes which had cost much labour in earlier years: he allowed himself much time also to design and superintend the fittings and furnishings of Abbotsford, from which the masons and carpenters were at last withdrawing. Charlotte ruled in the drawing-room, but the remainder of the house was completed to his own preferences, and largely to his own designs. He spent much time also in the plantations, where the quick-growing larches were evidence of the years that had passed since he had purchased the strip of land which had been known at that time as Cartly Hole. He spent much time with Tom Purdie during these summer days, as the pressure of many visitors allowed. His health seemed to be re-established. He liked to show Tom that he could still use an axe with the vigour and accuracy of earlier years.

His literary output showed a tendency to slacken, though the difference might not be great. He had been drawn into serving on many Committees and Public Boards during the months when he was in Edinburgh, and even his energies had their limits, as had the hours of his day. Had the current of life continued smoothly, it may be questioned whether there would have been so much of achievement in the following years—even whether those years might have been longer, as is the usual facile presumption. But this year was without omen of approaching evil. There were financial responsibilities to be watched: credits to be renewed. But the position was controlled without difficulty. His income was large: his credit good. If the expenditure at Abbotsford had become heavy—as it had—and if fittings and furnishings and decorations might levy an even more liberal tribute than that of the masons and carpenters of earlier years, yet it was not beyond the reasonable expenditure that such an income allows. The drain of Scott's endless generosities was best known to himself. At the worst, another novel could always be written, and a few additional thousands provided. Indeed, for several years past, it had not been necessary to write it. If further funds were needed, it would be sufficient to sign a contract to provide one at a future date, and Constable's bills would be accepted and the banks would discount. And had Constable refused, other publishers would have crowded forward to take his place. But who had a better claim to be preferred? Who would give more liberal terms? Who was more solidly established than he?

It might even have been argued that it would be needless to enquire into the financial stability of any publisher who should deal regularly with the *Waverley* novels: the fact that he had the contract for them would in itself be sufficient to establish him on an impregnable financial rock.

And the contracts were kept: the bills received their value. If Ballantyne intimated that he had presses for which work was required, the daily packets of copy would come from Abbotsford or North Castle Street, and in due course there would be more bills to be drawn—Constable's again—for the printing of eight or ten thousand books; and the books would be shipped at Leith for the London docks, and would be scattered among the trade, and the public would buy, and thousands of pounds would flow inwards, to enable bills to be paid off, and make way for others to be drawn and discounted against the novels of future days....

It was a year of domestic rather than literary event. The year of the final arrangement of the new library at Abbotsford: the year of Maria Edgeworth's visit: the year that Charles went to Oxford—the idea of Indian exile having been gladly abandoned as fortune smiled:—the year that ended with the news that Tom had died in Canada. More than all these, it was the year of Walter's engagement to Lady Fergusson's niece, Miss Jobson of Lochore. This last was a fact of many consequences, and Abbotsford blazed at Christmas with the splendour of a ball given in Miss Jobson's honour. It was the first time since its completion that it had been thrown open to such festivities—it was the last time also that all its splendid rooms would be open for the reception of visitors until it would be for the funeral of its creator, though that event would be eight years away. But who could guess those things now?

Jane Jobson was a quiet loving girl. We see in a later generation that the Scotts can still choose their wives well. She was also an heiress of great wealth. There was a marriage contract to which her guardians' signatures must be affixed. There must be wealth for wealth. They had stipulated that Sir Walter should settle Abbotsford upon his eldest son. It was not an unreasonable suggestion. Title and land should go together. Sir Walter made no difficulty about that; nor, we may be sure, did Charlotte. The six-foot soldier was her favourite child.

It was a happy marriage, and must have been a joy to Walter's parents, as much, almost, as to himself. Scott had let him go into the army with an evident reluctance. He knew what army life was among the officers of those days. He had given his son the freedom of his own preference, but his constant letters to him when he was first stationed in Dublin and the nature of their contents, shows how keen his anxiety, how wise his influence had been. They are letters which, like that to his brother Tom on the nature and permissible extent of parental influence and authority, are conspicuous for that quality of sympathetic insight which explains Lord Cockburn's remark that Sir Walter Scott's sense was more wonderful than his genius. They show that the loving intimacy with which he had always treated his children had had that most difficult and rarest of rewards—he had retained his son's confidence and his own authority.

Walter wrote freely and frankly of the life in the officers' mess which he had joined. He gave particulars regarding some of those whom he had made his friends which did not have the effect which he had anticipated on his father's mind. He was told that their conduct was discreditable, and he should avoid such intimacies.

Walter protested that they were men whose friendship it was

an honour to have. They were received in the best houses in Dublin.

His father replied that that was impossible, because houses which received them showed, by so doing, that they were not the best. He advised his son to observe that discreditable conduct is not condoned by insobriety, because men do not change their natures when they drink. Vicious proclivities are exposed, not originated, by alcohol.

Walter is discouraged from criticising the Irish Governor, even in correspondence. The duties or deficiencies of governors do not concern him. Let him concentrate on the qualities which good subalterns require.

He is encouraged to be generous, but never wasteful with money. His necessities are liberally but not loosely supplied. A small bill which he left unpaid when moving from town to town, and which came to his father's hands, occasioned a sharp rebuke. It was an omission beyond excuse.

Any deviation from the self-evident standards of personal chastity and rectitude in his own relations with women (which his father would not easily believe), whatever might be the standard of other officers, would occasion his *extreme displeasure.*

It is as creditable to son as to father that such correspondence could be continued with an affectionate freedom, and that rebuke or criticism did not discourage a further confidence.

On the father's side it exhibits his constant attitude, the aloofness of a personal integrity which is yet all things to all men, and the creed which places conduct before all other considerations either of gain or pleasure....

Captain Basil Hall, an indefatigable diarist, was at Abbotsford when this ball was given. He was not on terms of any intimate friendship with the family—he did not even grasp its occasion, or recognise that Jane Jobson was the guest of honour; but his observations may not be lessened in value from the detachment of the position from which they were taken.

"Last night," he wrote, "there was a dance in honour of Sir Walter Scotts's eldest son, who had recently returned from Sandhurst College, after having passed through some military examinations with great credit. We had a great clan of Scotts. There were no less than nine Scotts of Harden, and ten of other families. There were others besides from the neighbourhood—at least half-a-dozen Fergussons, with the jolly Sir Adam at their head. Lady Fergusson, her niece, Miss Jobson, the pretty heiress of Lochore...."

The gathering of that 'great clan of Scotts', in the mansion of the man who had made their name as immortal as English speech, and the good fellowship that Abbotsford gave to its neighbours of all degrees, may have occasioned the direction in which Captain Hall led the conversation when Scott had leisure to walk with him (as of course he had) over the land.

He learnt something of Scott's theories of the ways in which wealth should relieve surrounding poverty without the humiliations of charity: of the wood-fund for secret medical charges which must have grown now to substantial figures: of the importance of avoiding prying into the affairs or habits of those who are indigent, or of insulting them with unasked advice: of the freedom with which everyone was allowed to trespass on the Abbotsford land.

"'I make not a rule to be on intimate terms,' he told us, 'with all my neighbours—that would be an idle thing to do. Some are good—some are not so good, and it would be foolish and ineffectual to treat all with the same cordiality; but to live in harmony with all is quite easy, and surely very pleasant. Some of them may be rough and *gruff* at first, but all men, if kindly used, come about at last, and by going on gently, and never being eager or noisy about what I want, and letting things glide on leisurely, I always find in the end that the object is gained on which I have set my heart, either by purchase or exchange, or by some sort of compromise by which both parties are obliged, and good-will begot if it did not exist before—strengthened if it did exist.'—I have never seen any person on more delightful terms with his family. The youngest of his nephews and nieces can joke with him, and seem at all times perfectly at ease in his presence—his coming into the room only increases the laugh, and never checks it—he either joins in what is going on or passes. No one notices him any more than if he were one of themselves. These are things which cannot be got up."

The wedding took place in Edinburgh at the beginning of February. Scott settled Abbotsford, with all its land, upon his eldest son, subject to a right to charge it up to £10,000 if he should at any time have occasion to do so. Lockhart was present when the marriage-contract containing this provision was signed, and his memory of Sir Walter's words was that he said, as he laid down the pen:

> "I have now parted with my lands with more pleasure than I ever derived from the acquisition or possession of them; and if I be spared for ten years, I think I may promise to settle as much more again upon these young folks."

Was it a reasonable anticipation at this time, on the very threshold of catastrophe? Or was it the infatuation of a self-deluded man? Or was it even the dishonest action of one aware of a doubtful solvency who thus attempted to alienate his substantial assets from his creditors' grasp?

The question has been raised and must be faced, because it goes to the root of any judgement of Scott's character either for probity or business judgement. It must be considered in the light of facts to which we have still to come. For the moment we may observe that it was done in a very public way. There can have been few people of importance in Edinburgh who were not aware of the nature of the settlement. It appears also, and is significant, and in some aspects may seem surprising, that the whole of the Abbotsford properties were un-encumbered by any existing charge.

We may think that, if Scott's circumstances were embarrassed, or his credit strained, the news of such a settlement would produce pressure from various quarters, and might even promote an otherwise avoidable crisis, but there is no evidence of such sequel. On the contrary, a few weeks later, Scott was able to raise the large sum of £3,500 to purchase his son a commission in the King's Hussars—a loan of £5,000 being negotiated through George Hogarth with another member of that family.

The circumstances under which this purchase was undertaken may be worth a glance. They increase the evidence that Scott was not aware of any present or approaching financial shadow, and show that the expenditure was somewhat different from a random extravagance.

Mrs. Jobson was an elderly widow, and Jane was her only child. She had resolutely opposed the marriage unless Lieutenant Scott would resign his commission, and settle down at Lochore. She did not want to lose her daughter's society: she urged the hardships and uncertainties of barrack life. But on this point Sir Walter had been equally resolute. He would never agree that his son should degenerate to the idle life of a fox-hunting squire. Relatives and friends uniting their pressure upon her, Mrs. Jobson had reluctantly given way.

But, in any direction that was not inconsistent with his own welfare, Scott had been anxious to placate the old lady's objections, which were not entirely groundless. The accommodation that might be available for a subaltern's wife in any Irish town in which Walter's regiment might be stationed, would not be attractive to a young girl who had been used to the sheltered luxuries of Lochore.

A commission in the King's Hussars meant living in London instead of Dublin or Limerick, and the status of a Captain's was very different from that of a Subaltern's wife.

Scott's letters at this time, both to Walter and Jane, show that the girl's happiness in the strangeness of her new life was constantly in his thoughts, and the very price of the commission is evidence of how highly the difference of social life was valued.

It appears that there had been an offer on the part of Jane's Trustees to find at least part of the purchase money if Scott should consider it more than he was able or willing to pay, for in a letter to Walter (27 th April, 1825) he says that he had "written to Edinburgh to remit the price as soon as possible," and adds, "I can make this out without troubling Mr. Bayley; but it will pare my nails short for the summer and I fear prevent my paying your carriage, as I had intended."

Sir. Isaac Bayley was one of Jane's trustees. Scott had written a previous letter advising her of the kind of carriage that she should purchase, but without hinting that he had thought of the bill being sent to him. The statement that he had 'written Edinburgh to remit...as soon as possible,' exposes the fact, to which there will be occasion to return, that he was treating James Ballantyne & Co. very much as his bankers at this period. He frequently sent James instructions to settle lists of trades-people's accounts, or would sometimes give them notes of authority to apply to him for the money. This may not have been an unnatural procedure, under a variety of financial circumstances, which must be the subject of later consideration. The mere fact of this procedure being adopted does not imply that he was drawing upon the business beyond the total of amounts which it collected on his behalf, which is enough to say of it in this place. The refusal to allow part of the price of the commission to come from the Jobson estate shows that he was reasonably confident in the sufficiency of his own resources: the wording of the intimation does not suggest that he was reckless in such expenditure, or incurred it without calculation.

The remainder of this letter to Walter is of a further significance. He says that "Nichol is certainly going to sell Faldonside." That was an adjoining property. He was asking £40,000—a price which, under any circumstances, Scott would not pay. But, apart from that, how did Walter and Jane feel about it? It mattered more to them than to him. He adds:

> "I think I could work it all off during my life, and also improve the estate highly; but then it is always a heavy burden, and I would not like to undertake it unless I were sure that Jane and you desire such an augmentation of territory. I do not intend to do anything hasty, but, as an opportunity may cast up suddenly, I should like to know your mind."

This suggestion may be regarded variously, according to the final judgement which must be rendered as to what Scott's financial position really was at this time, and whether we accept Lockhart's assertion that (whether culpably or not) he was allowing himself to be kept in ignorance of it, as to which we may have to conclude that he was as fully aware of it as it was in his power to be, or in that of James Ballantyne to have informed him.

It is sufficient of observe here that it adds to the overwhelming weight of evidence that he was not aware of any advancing shadow, and that he was still confident in his power to use his pen for the earning of a further fortune.

But there is one question which is fundamental when we consider the prudence of these successive land purchases, which are commonly represented as having been of a disastrous kind.

In suggesting that he might devote the remainder of his life to the earning of enough money to purchase this further estate, Scott says that he thinks he could 'improve it highly'. Did he really add greatly, by his methods of planting and cultivating, to the value of the land he bought, or was this also the self-delusion of an infatuated man? The question is fundamental, because, though it may be possible for even a wealthy man to become embarrassed by ill-considered purchases of land which he is incompetent to handle properly, it is difficult to establish the proposition that a man who makes very large sums (as Scott did) by literary work is acting imprudently by investing it in land, if he be of competence and industry to increase its value greatly, and this difficulty is not substantially reduced if we allow that such properties were acquired somewhat in advance of the dates at which the whole amounts of the purchase moneys had been fully earned. If Scott really managed and developed the estates, which he purchased from the huge sums which he made from his writings, in a profitable way, and if he was ultimately ruined, we must look elsewhere for the cause.

This question leads us back to Captain Hall's diary. It is the record of a man who was an eyewitness at Abbotsford, an acute and curious observer, not sufficiently intimate to be called a friend and who wrote down what he saw and heard each evening while it was fresh in his mind. He saw Abbotsford and the Scott family at the peak of their apparent prosperity, and their most lavish expenditure. He walked over the estate with Scott and others on at least two occasions, on one of which—it is a proof of Scott's physical vigour and energy at this period—the Captain records that they must have covered 'five or six miles'.

In the course of these walks he made three specific observations. He saw a property which the tenant-farmer had vacated at the time it came into the market, and Scott bought it. Scott had turned the better half of the land into a plantation, his theory being that few crops are so profitable as timber for those who have patience to wait its growth, and that less satisfactory results are achieved owing to the custom of planting it only on the worst land. Timber requires and repays the use of the best land it can have. Now the tenant farmer was back again. The wind-screen of the young plantation had proved so valuable (possibly with other improvements of which Captain Hall did not hear) that he had agreed to pay the same rent for the half that he previously paid for the whole.

There was another farm for which Scott had suggested to his tenant that a dressing of lime on a generous scale would be beneficial. Finding that the man would not incur the expense he had told him to do it all the same, and to deduct the cost from the rent. At the end of the year the man had paid the full rent, saying that the results of following Scott's advice had been such that he could not honestly make any deduction.

But the Captain's third observation was not hearsay, but of an ocular kind. There was a wood of which Scott had bought the half five years earlier. The part which he had controlled had been thinned and pruned, while that which the owner had retained had been left to go its own way. Captain Hall says that it appeared almost incredible that five years should have produced so great a contrast. The trees in Scott's portion were not only well-proportioned and producing valuable timber, they were 'twice the height' of those in the neglected wood. The second of these observations is particularly illustrative of that quality in Scott's character which was most baffling to those of alien minds, and the controlling nature of which Lockhart did not sufficiently appreciate. If Scott saw land that was needing lime, he would regard it as of the first importance that it should have it, and of second importance to consider who would pay for it, or benefit. It was not that he was at all indifferent to his own profits: the difference was not absolute but relative. He hated waste or disorder of any kind, as liberal natures always do. If he saw a need it was his instinct to help first, and to consider afterwards who would pay the bill. He would not willingly pay £4,000 for land that was worth £3,000, but if he had no better choice, he would be happier in doing that and raising its value to £3,500 by intelligent industry, than if he had bought land for £3,000 that was worth £4,000 and allowed it to fall in value to £3,500 by neglect, though to a meaner mind the difference might seem to be against himself to the extent of some hard work and £1,000.

He gave help to all those in need with whom he came in contact as a natural necessary thing, and if some adjoining land were degenerating or undeveloped his instinct would be keener to go to its rescue than if it were already receiving sufficient care....

Captain Hall's observations were not confined to the land. On December 29th, 1824, he had a careful look round the house, and that evening he made this entry:

> "All is in good order, and an air of punctuality and method, without any waste or ostentation, pervades everything. Everyone seems at his ease; although I have been in some big houses in my time, and amongst good folk who studied these sort of points not a little, I don't remember to have met with thins better managed in all respects."

This may be regarded as a certificate of excellence for Lady Scott, even more than Sir Walter; and it is high praise, for it is to be remembered that this was not a great house of established traditions and long-ordered service, but one which they had built up almost literally with their own hands, and adapted for the entertaining of people of all nationalities and every social grade.

There was an indication of what that burden of hospitality had become in the notices which Captain Hall observed to be displayed at the inns in Selkirk and Melrose, warning people that they could not be received at Abbotsford without invitation or previous arrangement. It was a breakwater which had become inevitable after a point was reached at which the whole family were becoming entirely occupied in showing strangers over the house and grounds, a condition obviously intolerable on a day when sixteen unauthorised parties had stopped their carriages at the gate.

Captain Hall noted shrewdly that however much money the novels were bringing in, he doubted whether much was being saved; but he entered another conclusion which was of equal truth: "I should suspect that when the author of *Waverley* sets his shoulder to any wheel, it must be a devilish deep slough if it be not lifted out."

He could not guess the depth of the slough which was to test the shoulder of the Author of *Waverley* scarcely twelve months ahead.

CHAPTER LXXX.

Walter and Jane went from Edinburgh for a three weeks holiday at Abbotsford, and then to join his regiment at Dublin. Scott remained in Edinburgh, as was usual at this time of year, busy with two new novels. He had thought of a period and new lands for imagination to conquer. He would write a series of romances, under the general title *Tales of the Crusades*, and in accordance with his frequent custom he was writing two of them more or less side by side: they were to be called *The Betrothed* and *The Talisman*.

They were making rapid progress, too, in the midst of legal duties, and multifarious distracting interests. Scott was Chairman of a Gas Company at this time, which aimed to supplant candles with a new illuminant, and here we have occasion to see how provokingly difficult it is to classify him in the clear and final manner with which the public likes to regard its celebrities. Abbotsford had been panelled with old oak, and decorated with ancient armour, showing its creator to be a man obsessed by the past: one who must dislike change: who looked back with regret. But in building it he had inserted specimens of a wild untested innovation: a crack-brained invention of pneumatic bells. Any sane person could have told in advance that they would not act. Lockhart would have seen it at once. In the end, they had to be taken out, and sensible wires substituted, such as the experience of our ancestors has shown to be the right thing. But when poets design houses what better can you expect?

That was not all. The completed Abbotsford was illuminated in a new way. It had a private plant for the manufacture of coal-gas. Opinions differed about the result. There was no doubt there was enough light; but it was said that women looked old and haggard in the merciless glare. Some thought that the excess of light must be bad for the eyes. They prophesied that the use of glasses would increase, as it did.

Yet Scott was right in thinking that candles would be supplanted by coal-gas. As Chairman of the Gas Company that aimed to illuminate Edinburgh, as a pioneer of progress who installed a flaring jet over his desk; in North Castle Street, we observe him to be a farseeing business man.

Yet, that is not the whole tale. The Gas Company did not succeed. After years of struggle to overcome a general prejudice against the invention it advocated, and the competition of a rival company, it failed to get the Parliamentary power it required. In the end, it was wound up. Others reaped where it had sown too early for its own crop to survive. Scott lost the money he had invested. After all, we had better call him a fool; especially as the failure was so largely his own fault. He was the one man on the Board with political influence in London which might have got the Bill through, and he declined to use it, let his colleagues urge as they might. The Bill must go through on its own merits, if at all. He would not use his influence with the Government in London to force upon his fellow-citizens in Edinburgh an installation which they did not want, even though he thought it a good thing, and to have done so would have been his own gain. So, in the end, the Gas Company closed its doors....

Scott had scarcely raised and paid away the £3,500 which was the price of his son's commission in the London regiment when he had another demand for help of sufficiently large amount to deserve a separate mention. Daniel Terry, jointly with Frederick Yates, another comedian very popular at the time, had an opportunity of acquiring the lease of the Adelphi Theatre in London, and Terry appealed for help, either by loan or guarantee, both to Scott and James Ballantyne. Neither of them regarded it as a desirable investment. Scott knew the hazard of all adventures in the theatrical world, and had a particular doubt of Daniel Terry's fitness for such a management. But he had made Terry his friend and confidant for several years. He had been associated with him in connection with the staging of more than one of the *Waverley* novels. It was not easy for him to refuse a friend under such circumstances. But his correspondence with Terry shows something very different either from a facile willingness, or a selfish reluctance to give the needed assistance. He is frank with his friend as to his own financial engagements. Cash, to such an amount as is required, he is unable to spare. A guarantee must be given, but he must first be satisfied that the project has a reasonable business chance of success. He goes into this question in much detail. Long letters were exchanged, and many queries were asked and answered. There is one letter in particular which Lockhart characterises as being 'when considered with reference to the time at which it was written, and the then near, though unforeseen, result of the writer's own commercial speculations, as remarkable a document as was ever penned'.

Perhaps it was, though perhaps not quite for the same reasons which were in Lockhart's mind when he wrote. Indeed, it is an abuse of language to say that Scott was engaged in any 'commercial speculations', though he was subject to some commercial hazards, at this time.

The letter is one to which anyone who is adventuring upon theatrical enterprise might well give a week's thought. It deals with penetrating sagacity alike with the broader principles of sound commercial enterprise, and the special difficulties of theatrical finance and successful management, as well as with the estimates of this particular venture. It is a letter that Lockhart could not have written just because he could never have embarked on the bold hazard of a publishing venture, and still less, when the whirlpool of disaster threatened to suck him in, could he have trimmed helm and sail with the skill and courage which would have cast anchor at last in a quieter sea. His comment is as though one should say: "How can this man teach another to guard his life in the fight? He shows the scar of a wound. More than that, he may be wounded again in a year's time."

Probably Lockhart's special astonishment is aroused by the fact that Scott wrote in explicit condemnation of the practice of obtaining capital by means of accommodation bills. It would have been far more surprising, after his observations and experiences of the past fifteen years, had he failed to see the defects of that system of capitalisation. It would not have occurred to him to modify the expression of any judgement he might have formed lest it might appear to reflect upon his own business ability, whether past or present. Besides, he might have said to Daniel Terry with truth, though he would be unlikely to do so, that what he might do himself with reasonable safety would be more perilous for one who had less legal and commercial knowledge, and far interior resources, whether of money, of intellect, or of character, to retrieve an error.

However these things may have been, Scott did finally agree to give a guarantee of £1,250 in Terry's support, and though he wrote plainly that he would not influence James to take a similar risk, the printer also helped his friend with a guarantee for about half that amount.

The incident is a conclusive evidence that at this date—May, 1825—not only the name of Walter Scott, but that of James Ballantyne, which was given upon a separate guarantee, was considered good for a substantial credit in banking circles, and that not merely in the routine support of his own business or commitments, but for a separate responsibility which might have been refused on several grounds, without reflection on his solvency, had it been considered prudent to do so.

In the course of this correspondence with Terry, Scott wrote about his own expenditure and resources with a deliberate frankness. He could not spare a large sum in cash, for expenditure upon the marriage of his eldest son and the purchase of his commission had been very heavy. Besides the £3,500 for the commission, he mentions that he had given presents to the bride 'jewels and so-forth becoming her situation and fortune' which had cost him £500, and that £1,000 'at least' had gone in providing Walter with a good horse and much else, so that he should have a clear start for his marriage, on the very moderate income (£400) which was all the financial reward of that £3,500.

Scott added: "I am a sharer to the extent of £1,500 on a railroad, which will bring coal and limes here at half-price, and double the rent of the arable part of my property, but is dead outlay in the meantime, and I have shares in the oil-gas, and other promising concerns, not having resisted the mania of the day, though I have yielded to it but soberly; also, I have the dregs of Abbotsford House to pay for—and all besides my usual considerable expenditure, so I must look for some months to be put to every corner of my saddle."

"The mania of the day"—the idea that a concluded war brings automatic prosperity to an exhausted nation—which had led to so much wild financial adventure in the commercial world, was to bring ruin to many thousands before the conclusion of the year in which he wrote. Who could be sure of escape when the storm would break?

It is in one of the long letters which Scott wrote to Walter and Jane at this period, giving endless news of events at Abbotsford and Lochore, and endless, though never fussy, advice for the conduct of their own lives, that there comes an ominous allusion—not the first in his correspondence—to the health of John Hugh, Sophia's child.

Born (somewhat prematurely, it was said) eight months after marriage, he had been a cause of frequent anxiety. Now he was getting better from a bad cough. Had it been whooping-cough? No one was quite sure. But, anyway, it was better now.

Scott's affection for this first grandchild seems to have been particularly strong, even for one who had much affection to give. And the child was easy to love, being intelligent, and responding in loving ways through his pathetically shortened life, of which there were still some years to be. But he had no physical vigour. From whatever cause, Lockhart could not give his wife robust children. We are reminded of his naive astonishment that Scott could have lived decently before his own marriage. The thought may do injustice to the biographer, but who is to blame for that?

CHAPTER LXXXI.

The Betrothed was sent to the Ballantyne Press, and set up chapter by chapter as it proceeded, in the method which had usually been adopted with these novels, and as James prepared its pages for the press he expressed his feelings upon the narrative, as it had become his habit to do.

Often, in the past, Scott had been encouraged by the enthusiasm of his printer; often he may have benefited by criticism, or by his attention being directed to obscurity or omission in those rapidly-written sheets: sometimes, as in the mauling of the plot of *St. Ronan's Well*, he was misled by a fatuous importunity. But James's criticism was generally sound enough, and it came from a man whose loyalty was beyond question—a man who was prepared and anxious to praise.

But there was no praise on this occasion. Chapter after chapter came under review and went into type, and he said monotonously that the book was a disappointment. So it was. It was not bad in any affirmative way. It was just dull. It never sank below its level of dullness, nor rose above it. Incidentally, it supported Scott's objection to a revealing title—or, at least, to one which is first adopted, and has to be written up to. As it proceeded, it became evident that it had little to do with Crusaders in that capacity.

Scott knew it to be a failure. It was a depressing realisation, for, so far as this period is concerned, Lockhart's suggestion that the decrease in the sales of the *Waverley* novels (such as it was) had been concealed from their author is obviously untrue. He was so watchful of such signs, and so sensitive to their implications, that he was considering seriously, as he had done before at a similar indication, the advisability of abandoning fiction entirely for a new field of literary enterprise. But more than once before he had found fresh triumph by breaking new and unexpected ground. This he had resolved to do again in what should be a final effort. There was prudence in this resolution, as there was courage in the renewed attempt. The *Waverley* novels had a large continuing sale. It would do no good to their author's reputation, little good to his pocket, and harm to them, for him to add to their number a succession of inferior examples. He had set up a standard of achievement below which he could not afford to fall.

His own judgement confirming Ballantyne's reluctant pessimism, he took the bold resolution of suppressing the book entirely, at a time when it was approaching completion. But it was not surprising that James demurred to that drastic remedy. With the exception of its concluding chapters, the book had not merely been set up, the sheets of a complete edition were already printed, according to the method by which he contrived that publication should follow almost immediately on the writing of the last chapter of one of these novels. There was hesitation, Lockhart records, with his incurable journalistic looseness, in consigning the huge piles of printed sheets 'to the flames'.

Scott had in fact, got another tale developing in his mind, of a greater promise. It might recover the lost ground, which *The Betrothed* certainly never would. He sent James the opening chapters of *The Talisman.*

James read them and did not respond to their author's mood. It would be little use to have the great loss and delay of suppressing *The Betrothed*, if the substitute were of the same brand. So he wrote.

Scott was roused to protest in reply: "is it wise to mend a dull overloaded fire by heaping on a shovelful of wet coals?" He had invariably agreed with James's criticisms before, but he felt differently now. Yet this criticism may neither have been wrong in itself nor unfortunate in its effects. The book does move heavily in its opening chapters. But as it advances its paragraphs shorten, its animation increases. James felt the change and was quick to congratulate. As the book progressed, the old enthusiasm revived. Here might be another success to equal the splendour of those that the past had seen.

Then there came a disconcerting rumour that the sheets of *The Betrothed* had been stolen, and that it was to be printed in Germany. James suggested that the two books should be issued together, and the quality of *The Talisman* would be sufficient to distract attention from its companion's deficiencies. Scott agreed reluctantly, in view of that rumour of piracy, that it would be the best course, though, he said, he would rather have written two novels than those concluding chapters. In that spirit he finished it, and the two books appeared together.

This singular recipe for the selling of a dull book may appear questionable in itself, and has never become a popular precedent in the trade; but, in all the circumstances, it may have been a wise decision, and it was justified by its results. The two books appeared together in June, and *The Talisman* had an instant popularity, such as few of its predecessors had surpassed. People were too busy praising it to have many words to waste on the sister-story, which had no evident defects to draw the lightning of criticism. It is the usual fate of dullness to be disregarded. It might have been expressly written for the part it played.

CHAPTER LXXXII.

It is one of Lockhart's most curious features as a biographer that he constantly supplies materials for the destruction of his own assertions.

It was shortly before the publication of the *Tale of the Crusades* that he was present at dinner one Saturday evening at Abbotsford, on an occasion when James Ballantyne and Constable were the only other guests. The conjunction of these two, and the fact that Scott had no one else there except his son-in-law, who was regarded as one of the family, is evidence that the meeting was of the nature of a business conference. However long, and in some ways intimate, might be Scott's associations, in different degrees, with these two men their relations always maintained a measure of business formality. James said, at the end of his life, that he had never taken the liberty of visiting Abbotsford without formal invitation. Constable and Scott, while recognising qualities, each in the other, which had their due measure of admiration and approval, were never entirely congenial. The old days of difference might be almost forgotten, their scars barely visible now, but Constable might still be disposed to aggrandise his own importance as a publisher, his own services to the author on whom his prosperity so largely depended.

Lockhart has represented Constable as almost insanely intoxicated by the huge sales which Scott's writings now commanded: he has represented him and Ballantyne (somewhat inconsistently) as conspiring to deceive their author as to their declining popularity. When this meeting took place, the success of *The Talisman* was an event of the following month. It was nearly a year since *Redgauntlet* had been a respectable, but unexciting success. The interval of publication had been unusually long. The success of the *Tales of the Crusades* could be no better than a hopeful guess. It is evident that both Scott and Constable had been considering what the position would be if they should meet a cold reception. They did not regard such a possibility with dismay. They were both confident capable men. But they were both of the temperament which is too cautious not to plan in advance against the possibilities of failure, and too adventurous not to plan in audacious ways.

They met now with different plans in the minds of each, which they would endeavour to mould into one shape, and which were equally based upon the presumption that it might prove impossible to maintain the sales of new Waverley Novels indefinitely at the prevailing level.

When the ladies withdrew from the dinner-table, the four men were left alone—Sir Walter, Constable, Ballantyne and Lockhart. We have Lockhart's account of the conversation that followed. It is the record of a witness who was sometimes unscrupulous in adding intention to recollection, who became hostile to two of those who were present on this occasion between the time of his observation and that on which he recorded his memory, and who was of a natural incompetence in commercial matters. But it is the only witness we have.

"After dinner," he says, "there was a little pause of expectation, and the brave schemer suddenly started *in medias res*, saying "Literary genius may, or may not, have done its best; but the trade are in the cradle." Scott eyed the florid bookseller's beaming countenance, and the solemn stare with which the equally portly printer was listening and pushing round the bottles with a hearty chuckle, bade me "Give our two *soncie babbies* a drap mother's milk." Constable sucked in fresh inspiration, and proceeded to say that, wild as we might think him, certain new plans, of which we had all already heard some hints, had been suggested by, and were in fact mainly grounded upon, a sufficiently prosaic authority—namely the annual schedule of assessed taxes, a copy of which interesting document he drew from his pocket and substituted for his *D'Oyley*. It was copiously diversified, "text and margent" by figures and calculations in his own handwriting, which I for one might have regarded with less reverence, had I known at the time this 'great arithmetician's' rooted aversion and contempt for all examination of his own balance-sheet. He had, however, taken vast pains to fill in the number of persons who might fairly be supposed to pay the taxes for each separate article of luxury, armorial bearings, hunters, racers, four-wheeled carriages, &c &c; and having demonstrated that hundreds of thousands held, as necessary to their comfort and station, articles upon articles of which their forefathers never dreamt, said, that our self-love never deceived us more grossly than when we fancied our notions as to the matter of books had advanced in at all a corresponding proportion. "On the contrary," cried Constable "I am satisfied that the demand for Shakespeare's plays, contemptible as we hold it to have been, in the times of Elizabeth and James, was more creditable to the classes who really indulged in any sort of elegance then, than the sale of *Childe Harold* or *Waverley* is to this nineteenth century."

"Scott helped him on by interposing, that at that moment he had a rich valley crowded with handsome houses under his view, and yet much doubted whether any laird within ten miles spent ten pounds per annum on the literature of the day. "No," said Constable, "there is no market among them that's worth one's thinking about. They are contented with a review or a magazine, or at least with a paltry subscription to some circulating library forty miles off. But if I live for half-a-dozen years, I'll make it as impossible that there should not be a good library in every decent house in Britain as that the shepherd's ingle-nook should want the *saut poke*. Ay, and what's that?" he continued, warming and puffing; "why should the ingle-nook itself want a shelf for *the novels*?"—"I see your drift, my man," says Sir Walter— "You're for being like Billy Pitt in Gilray's print—you want to get into the salt-box yourself." "Yes," he responded (using a favourite adjuration)—"I have hitherto been thinking only of the wax lights, but before I'm a twelvemonth older I shall have my hand upon the tallow." "Troth," says Scott, you are indeed likely to be 'The grand Napoleon of the realms of *print*'."—"If you outlive me," says Constable, with a regal smile, "I bespeak that line for my tomb-stone, but, in the meantime, may I presume to ask you to be my right-hand man when I open my campaign of Marengo? I have now settled my outline of operations—a three-shilling or half-crown volume every month, which must and shall sell, not by thousands or tens of thousands but by hundreds of thousands—ay! by millions! Twelve volumes in the year, a half-penny of profit upon every copy of which will make me richer than the possession of all the copyrights of all the quartos that ever were, or will be, hot-pressed! Twelve volumes, so good that millions must wish to have them and so cheap that every butcher's callant may have them, if he pleases to let me tax him sixpence a week!"

"Many a previous consultation, and many a solitary meditation, too, prompted Scott's answer.—"Your plan," said he "cannot fail, provided the books be really good; but you must not start until you have not only leading columns, but depth upon depth of reserve in thorough order. I am willing to do my part in this grand enterprise. Often of late, have I felt that the vein of fiction was nearly worked out; often, as you all know, have I been thinking seriously of turning my hand to history. I am of opinion that historical writing has no more been adapted to the demands of the increased circles among which literature does already find a way, than you allege as to the shape and price of books in general. What say you to taking the field with a with a Life of the *other* Napoleon?" "

There are several statements here which must be accepted with caution if at all. The suggestion that Constable had a 'rooted aversion and contempt for all examination of his own balance-sheet' condemns itself by its own excess. Besides, the book-keeping department of Constable's business was in the hands of his partner, Robert Cadell, who, Lockhart asserted subsequently, when setting up his witness against that of the Ballantyne Trustees, was one of the best business men in the world. He may not have been that, but he was certainly capable of accurate accountancy, and, during Constable's illness, and long absences in the south, he was in entire charge of the Edinburgh office, and in financial control of the business. There is not a shred of evidence that Constable's books were badly kept, or that any subsequent disaster can be attributed to such negligence.

Printer and publisher were invited to continue their visit over Monday, when the discussion was resumed in detail during a long drive to Smailholm and Dryburgh Abbey, "both poet and publisher," Lockhart says, "talking over the past and future course or their lives, and agreeing, as far as I could penetrate, that the years to come were likely to be more prosperous than any they had yet seen."

Before Constable left, a detailed plan had been agreed by which a cheap monthly series was to be started, to consist of alternate reprints of the *Waverley Novels* and new historical works by their author. The first volume was to consist of one halt of *Waverley*, the second of the commencement of a Life of Napoleon. *Waverley* was to be completed in three further parts and followed by other new historical works, alternated with re-prints of the novels in the order of their original publication.

The impetus of the new series was to be supplied by this Life of Napoleon, for which, with a sound publishing instinct, Constable anticipated an enormous demand. The closeness with which Scott had followed the historical events through which he had lived, his prodigious memory, his imagination, and his ability to arrange and analyse evidence rendered him peculiarly fitted for the task he had undertaken, but it was one which obviously could not be done with finality or completeness until much documentary material should be disclosed that he could not hope to reach.

Yet the generation that is alive will not refuse to receive such information as is available, if it be well presented, because their children will be better served. A Life of Napoleon by such an author would be of an assured quality, and would have an assured sale. Constable undertook to obtain material for it, and proceeded to do so with an instant energy. Books, pamphlets and newspapers in wholesale quantities were collected from all parts of Europe, and delivered in wagon-loads at North Castle Street, and as Scott commenced the actual writing of the book it became immediately apparent to all concerned that the original idea must be abandoned. Four of those small cheap projected volumes would not avail to contain the work that was in progress now. The decision was taken to publish it separately, first in four volumes of the full library size, and then in an ever increasing number, as the extent of the ground which such a work must cover was more adequately realised.

Meanwhile, it was found that the original plan could not, in any event, have been put into immediate execution. The quantities of the existing editions of the Waverley novels which were still in the hands of the trade proved, on enquiry, to be more considerable than had been supposed. For a cheap issue to be taken up with the proper enthusiasm it was necessary that time should first be allowed for this stock to be sold off. Then the urgency of the enterprise was reduced, as it was seen that the *Tales of the Crusades* was a success. After all, the Waverley novels need not be looked upon as a series that neared completion. And Constable still thought that the success of the *Miscellany*, as he had christened his new idea, depended mainly upon the inclusion of the *Napoleon*. Let that come out first in a full-dress form—such was the final decision—and a second edition could form part of the cheaper series, which must be deferred accordingly.

Confident in the present, and looking for greater successes in the years to come, so they agreed their plans.

CHAPTER LXXXIII.

In the early part of July, a month after the *Tales of the Crusades* had been successfully published, the Napoleon had made at least a substantial commencement. Scott was then intent upon an Irish holiday. He had promised to visit Miss Edgeworth in her own land. He wanted to see Walter and Jane in their Dublin home. He wanted to see the country. It was decided to postpone the actual setting up of Napoleon until he should return, when it should be commenced in earnest. He blamed himself afterwards for the time which this holiday occupied. Had he known, had he exerted himself to the swift production of another novel—so he thought, but it would have made no difference. It may be that had he been given a full knowledge of all that destiny had prepared for the next six months he might have had ability, and would certainly not have lacked energy or courage to turn the lightning aside, but the mere writing of another novel, or three for that matter, the mere provision of an additional five or ten thousand pounds, would have made no difference at all.

As it was, a carefree party of three—himself, and Lockhart, and Anne—took carriage to Glasgow and there put it on to the packet's deck, and sailed for Belfast. The next six weeks were spent in wandering across Ireland and returning by different routes, and then sailing from Dublin to Holyhead, and driving home through North Wales and the lakes of Westmorland.

There was a long pause with Miss Edgeworth at Edgeworthstown; and a shorter one at Windermere on the way home.

The little party had expected a friendly reception from the Protestant gentlefolk of the country, and a ready hospitality. Beyond that there had been a doubt. The Irish peasant was not expected to be familiar with the Waverley novels, and the feeling of the Catholics in general might not have been over-cordial. Catholic emancipation was then an acute political issue, and Scott had publicly opposed it. It was not only that he doubted its political wisdom at that time; he considered it to be a foolish attempt to heal a sore with an ineffectual remedy. He said with forceful metaphors that Ireland's real grievance was the exactions of the absentee landlords, for whom he had a bitter contempt. While that evil continued, no measure of Catholic Emancipation would do any good, and, doing no good, it might do actual harm. Yet when it became clear that such a measure would be passed he condemned the Bill because it did not go far enough. He said that if it were done at all, it should have been with a more generous equity.

Now while the controversy was acute and bitter, there might well have been an element of coldness, if not of hostility, among those to whom he was something more than a vague name.

Such doubts there might be. But except among the friends to whom he journeyed, Scott did not expect that the passing of his inconspicuous carriage would attract any notice at all. It was a repetition of the mistake which once drew upon himself the louder plaudits of the Edinburgh crowd than would greet the King at a later hour.

He had not adequately understood his immense reputation or his universal popularity, which may have exceeded anything in the world's history which poet or novelist had won during his own lifetime. It might be only occasionally that he would be personally recognised in the London crowds. In Edinburgh or Selkirkshire, everyone was his friend. But in Ireland his coming was an event. Celebrities who visited it were few and separate, and the whole of the population was aware of such a presence, though it might not always stir them to cheers.

Scott found that he drove through shouting crowds. If he made a call in a Dublin Street, it would be hard to start the horses again amid the pressure of the cheering mob. From high and low, from Catholic and Protestant, from town and country, there was the same cordiality of reception, the same attitude of respectful homage. It was a triumphal procession rather than a private visit.

In Dublin, he had the pleasure, for the first time, of being entertained at his son's table.

Lockhart records how greatly he was moved to sorrow and indignation by the contrast of luxury in the occasional mansions of Southern Ireland, and the squalid misery that surrounded them, and it is, doubtless, a truthful witness. Yet there is a significant difference between Lockhart's account, and the notes on the same subject that Scott made in his Journal a few months later. Lockhart pours indignant intemperate words into a single scale. No strength of feeling or sympathy would ever destroy Scott's sense of equity or the impartiality of his judgement. He wrote:

> "There is much less exaggeration about the Irish than is to be expected. Their poverty is not exaggerated: it is on the extreme verge of human misery; their cottages would scarce serve for pig-styes, even in Scotland and their rags seem the very refuse of a rag-shop, and are disposed on their bodies with such ingenious variety of wretchedness that you would think nothing but some sort of perverted taste could have assembled so many shreds together. You are constantly fearful that some knot or loop will give, and place the individual before you in all the primitive simplicity of Paradise. Then, for their food, they have only potatoes, and too few of them. Yet the men look stout and healthy, the women buxom and well-coloured.
>
> "I said their poverty was not exaggerated; neither is their wit—nor their good humour—nor their whimsical absurdity—nor their courage....
>
> "There is perpetual kindness in the Irish cabin: butter-milk, potatoes, a stool is offered, or a stone is rolled that your honour may sit down and be out of the smoke, and those who beg everywhere else seem desirous to exercise free hospitality in their own houses. Their natural disposition is turned to gaiety and happiness; while a Scotchman is thinking about the term-day, or, if easy on that subject, upon hell in the next world—while an Englishman is making a little hell of his own in the present, because his muffin is not well roasted—Pat's mind is always turned to fun and ridicule. They are terribly excitable, to be sure, and will murther you on slight suspicion, and find out next day

that it was all a mistake, and that it was not yourself they meant to kill at all at all."

He noted that there was 'courtesy as well as wit' in the retort of a ragged peasant to whom he handed a shilling, and should have had an unproducable sixpence change: "May your Honour live till I pay you!"

We may wonder how many of such sixpences he left behind, and under what variety of circumstances, when we read that this tour 'cost me upwards of £500, including £100 left with Walter and Jane'. It is a large sum to be spent in less than two months, during almost the whole of which time the party were being entertained by others, and by one who had resolved to 'pare his nails' very closely during the next few months. A more prudent man might have gone home with the best part of that £500 still in his pocket-book. We may suppose that he did not regard poverty with a closed hand. We may praise him for this, if we will; but there is not much cause. Being received as a prince, it is natural to act as a prince would. It is always more blessed to give than to receive. He had the easier part.

When a man is conscious that he can make £5,000 in a few weeks, any time that he will by writing a book about noble living to live nobly may not be a very difficult thing.... He could not know that the devil's voice was heard about this time in the courts of Heaven: *"Doth Job serve God for naught?"*

CHAPTER LXXXIV.

The little party stopped for a few days on the way back, at Storrs, off the shore of Windermere, to be entertained by its owner, Mr. John Bolton, a Birmingham engineer, whom Scott had met first in London on an occasion when Allan Cunningham heard of an exchange between them which was not of the friendliest. Scott overheard a remark of John Bolton—not addressed to him—that Scots and rats could be found in all places, and with his quick reaction to any slight on his country, he interposed to say: "Mr. Bolton, you should have added *and a Brummagem button*". The engineer turned round to the interrupter and replied seriously, with an equal pride in his own place: "We make something better than buttons in Birmingham—we make steam-engines, sir".

Mr. Bolton was the owner of the Birmingham mint of that day. Scott liked him for the courage he had shown on the occasion when there had been an armed attempt of robbery of his gold ingots, which he had resisted without asking the police for help, and when his porter had been shot dead by the thieves.

Now he was using his Windermere house to give Canning and Scott an opportunity of meeting, which they had both desired. Wordsworth came also. It seems that Mr. Bolton entertained well. Lockhart who shared the privilege of that hospitality, becomes lyrical in its praise. He almost forgave his host the degrading fact that he was a business man. The whole passage deserves quotation, if only for the unconscious humour with which he patronises the far abler and more important man who received him into his house because he was the son-in-law of his friend:

> "It has not, I suppose, often happened, to a plain English merchant, wholly the architect of his own fortunes to entertain at one time a party embracing so many illustrious names. He was proud of his guests; they respected him, and honoured and loved each other; and it would have been difficult to say which star in the constellation shone with the brightest or the softest light. There was 'high discourse' intermingled with as gay flashings of courtly wit as ever Canning displayed; and a plentiful allowance, on all sides, of those airy transient pleasantries, in which the fancy of poets however wise and grave, delights to run riot when they are sure not to be misunderstood. There were beautiful and accomplished women to adorn and

enjoy this circle. The weather was as Elysian as the scenery. There were brilliant cavalcades through the woods in the mornings, and delicious boatings on the lake by moonlight; and on the last day, 'the Admiral of the Lake' presided over one of the most splendid regattas that ever enlivened Windermere. Perhaps there were not fewer than fifty barges following in the Professor's radiant procession, when it paused at the point of Storrs to admit into the place of honour the vessel that carried kind and happy Mr. Bolton and his guests. The bards of the Lakes led the cheers that hailed Scott and Canning: music and sunshine, flags, streamers and gay dresses, the merry hum of voices, and the rapid splashing of innumerable oars made up a dazzling mixture of sensations as the flotilla wound its way among the richly-foliaged islands, and along bays and promontories peopled with enthusiastic spectators."

With that naive lack of humour which makes Lockhart so fascinating to those who can read him in the right mood, this egregious paragraph, in which the feelings of the guests towards each other are so carefully differentiated from that which they can cultivate for 'kind and happy' Mr. Bolton, is shortly preceded by an anecdote of how Scott had rebuked a member of his family for using the word 'vulgar' was an adjective of contempt. He had pointed out that the word meant nothing but common, and the best things, by God's mercy, are all of a vulgar kind.

CHAPTER LXXXV

A short visit to Southey, a few days with Wordsworth and his daughter, completed the Westmorland pause, and the holiday party drove back to Abbotsford.

"Without an hour's delay," Lockhart records his observation, Scott "resumed his usual habits of life—the musing ramble among his own glens, the breezy ride over the moors, the merry spell at the woodman's axe, or the festive chase of Newark, Fernilee, Hangingshaw, or Deloraine; the quiet old-fashioned contentment of the little domestic circle, alternating with the brilliant phantasmagoria of admiring, and sometimes admired, strangers—or hoisting the telegraph flag that called laird and bonnet-laird to the burning of the water, or the wassail of the hall. The hours of the closet alone had found a change. The preparation for the *Life of Napoleon* was a course of such hard reading as had not been called for while 'the great magician', in the full sunshine of ease, amused himself, and delighted the worlds by unrolling, fold after fold, his endlessly varied panorama of romance.

"He had now to apply himself doggedly to the mastering of a huge accumulation of historical materials. He read, and noted, and indexed with the pertinacity of some pale compiler in the British Museum; but rose from such employment, not radiant and buoyant, as after he had been feasting himself among the teeming harvests of Fancy, but with an aching brow, and eyes on which the dimness of years had begun to plant some specks, before they were subjected again to that straining over small print and difficult manuscript. It was a pleasant sight when one happened to take a passing peep into his den, to see the white head erect, and the smile of conscious inspiration on his lips, while the pen, held boldly, and at a commanding distance, glanced steadily and gaily along a fast-blackening page of *The Talisman*. It now often made me sorry to catch a glimpse of him, stooping and poring with his spectacles, amidst piles of authorities—a little note-book ready in the left hand, that had always used to be at liberty for patting Maida."

There may be something beyond Lockhart's journalistic love of contrast in the picture which he elaborates of the burden of Scott's Napoleonic labours, but we must not take it too seriously. Lockhart was always too fond of writing with tears in his eyes. At the most, it was a kind of work of which Scott had done a great deal in earlier years. Both as editor and biographer, he was used to the discipline of mind which research requires and his memory rendered it easier to him than to most of those who undertake such biographies. Besides, it was done entirely at his own choice. Constable would have been content with a short work, such as Scott could have written in three weeks from the resources of his own mind, with no more precaution than to delegate an assistant to verify names and dates. The whole idea had been Scott's from the first, and it was by his preference that the bulk grew. Nor was he working, at this time, at a killing pace. Tom Moore, paying him a long-hoped-for visit, and being fortunate enough to find him almost alone with Charlotte and Anne, did not find that he made any difficulty about giving him a leisurely companionship both of field and fireside. The visit belongs rather to Moore's biography than our present subject. Scott got on well with him, as he did with all the combative poet race: they might quarrel among themselves, but not here.

"All the world," Moore wrote "might admire him in his works, but those only could learn to love him as he deserved who had seen him at Abbotsford." "Kindness and gentleness" were the qualities which impressed Tom Moore's mind most strongly, as he observed Sir Walter in his own family. But that such qualities were worn without weakness, we may observe from another incident of this autumn, when Mrs. Coutts, the banker's widow, perhaps the richest woman of the time, drove up to the gates of Abbotsford. She was touring Scotland. She had met Scott incidentally years before. She claimed some remote kinship, with the aid of one of those complicated pedigrees which are dear to the Scottish heart. She had solicited and received an invitation, and was an expected guest.

Before the banker married her, she had been a comedy actress. Now she had control of millions. The day when she would be Duchess of St. Albans was still ahead. But though she had left the stage, the comedy continued. She travelled with many servants. She took a doctor because she might fall ill on the road. But, being a prudent woman, she saw that he might fall ill at the same time. Therefore she took two. The rest of her retinue was on the same scale.

But Mrs. Coutts was not inconsiderate. She left four carriages and sixteen horses at Edinburgh, with the sections of her staff which they had contained. Three carriages, each drawn by four horses, pulled up at the gates. Mrs. Coutts, the Duke of St. Albans and his sister, two physicians, two lady's maids, a companion, and an assortment of other 'menials of every grade' alighted from them. There is no record of what Lady Scott said. It happened that Abbotsford was full at the moment with a party of high-born guests. When the accommodation for the invaders had been arranged, we may guess that some of these earlier arrivals were less comfortable than they had been before. The ex-comedy-actress was tolerated for her wealth to her face, and joked at her behind her back, in the London society from which she came. And the joke was a nuisance here.

Scott observed the conversation at dinner and was not satisfied. The ladies rose and left the men at table according to the ugly custom of the time. But Scott cut this sitting unexpectedly short. With the minimum of interval, he led the way to the drawing-room.

He observed what was going on for a few moments, and then quietly asked the Marchioness of Northampton, 'the youngest, gayest and cleverest, who was also the highest in rank' among his guests, to step out into the hall, where he told her plainly that he knew it was the custom in London to attend the balls and fetes which Mrs. Coutts gave, and to cold shoulder her on other occasions. Fine people would do shabbiness for which beggars might blush. But Abbotsford had different standards. He had mentioned two days ago that Mrs. Coutts would be coming, and those who were not prepared to treat her with courtesy should have left before she arrived.

The Marchioness was a daughter of Mrs. Maclean Clephane of Torloisk. Scott had known her from childhood. (Whom did he not know?) In fact, she had been his ward. He knew the right way to influence her now. They went back into the drawing-room together, and the Marchioness was soon singing a song for Mrs. Coutts's particular pleasure. Half-an-hour after, a happy woman was telling comic anecdotes of her early theatrical experiences and all went amicably until she left three days later.

This incident is additionally curious because of Lockhart's laboured and elaborate comments upon it. He says that some silly people might suppose that Scott only acted in this way because his guest was a wealthy woman, which would be unjust, as Scott treated every guest, of whatever wealth or poverty or social status, with equal consideration. Possibly there are people sufficiently silly or sufficiently incapable of understanding a character such as Scott's, to form such an opinion but are they worth two pages of refutation?

And the most curious thing is that in his muddled verbiage Lockhart actually makes several attacks upon Scott which his own biographical records are sufficient to refute about a hundred times over.

"I dare not deny," he says, "that he set more of his affections, during the great part of his life, upon worldly things, wealth among others, than might have become such an intellect." But we are not to blame Scott for this (alleged) weakness overmuch, because of the influences (whatever they were) to which he was exposed in the 'plastic period'. If we were to tabulate and believe, all the 'influences' to which Lockhart attributes Scott's actions from youth to age, we might decide that he had no more individuality than a composite photograph.

If Scott were really one who cared over-greatly for 'worldly ' wealth, his biographer should say so plainly, without equivocation, or twaddle about plastic periods. And having said so, he should not go on to assert that he valued wealth mainly as a means to helping others; and rank far more than wealth; and rank so little that he took so little interest in it apart from the pleasure or advantage it gave to other members of his family, that he accepted a title for 'the pleasure which his wife took, and gaily acknowledged that she took, in being My Lady', and refused a Privy Councillorship, because he did not care for a title which was merely personal to himself. It is logically possible for Lockharts first assertion to be true or for there to be truth in those that follow, but they are mutually destructive.

The assertion that Scott at any period of his life, however plastic, cared over-much for money, even though it be made (and then elaborately denied) by his own son-in-law scarcely merits reply. As Scott himself suggested in his letter to Lord Byron, the conduct of his life makes refutation too easy.

"The circumstances of the King's visit in 1822," Lockhart observes, at the commencement of his final and most fatuous paragraph on this subject ,"and others already noted, leave no doubt that imagination enlarged and glorified for him many objects to which it is very difficult for ordinary men in our generation to attach much importance; and perhaps he was more apt to attach importance to such things, during, the prosperous course of his own fortunes, than even a liberal consideration of circumstances can altogether excuse. To myself it seems to have been so; yet I do not think the severe critics on this part of his story have kept quite sufficiently in mind how easy it is for us all to undervalue any species of temptation to which have not happened to be exposed."

Lockhart's real grievance concerning this episode of the King's visit appears to have been that, being a Lowland Scot, he thought the Highlanders, by Scott's decision, were too prominent in the processions. That Scott's use of his 'fat friend', George IV, as an instrument to reconcile not only English and Scottish differences, but many latent internal animosities, was an act of bold political wisdom which only he would have had the audacity to conceive, and the personal influence, energy and courage to carry through to success, Lockhart scarcely seems to have understood.

CHAPTER LXXXVI

It may be remembered that, in Scott's correspondence with Daniel Terry, earlier in the year, he had alluded to a prevalent wave of speculation in business circles as a 'mania' into which he had only ventured with a sober moderation.

It was in fact, a post-war boom, such as was experienced a century later, which ended in a similar depression, though the catastrophe was, for a time, more stoutly resisted, and was far more disastrous when it came, for reasons which do not concern us except so far as they are necessary to elucidate the events with which we are dealing. There was, at this period, no law of limited liability, such as prevails today, and which, apart from speculations on margins (which are gambling, transactions disconnected with legitimate business) enables even the largest of commercial vessels to founder with no more than a distributed loss, such as may not involve a single shareholder in financial ruin. Such vessels may founder with far less effort to save them than would be made if every shareholder, however small, were responsible for their debts to the limit of his own possessions, and to the risk of a personal bankruptcy. Indeed, the shareholders who would then have been making frantic efforts to keep them afloat, may now send them under with a parting kick. The idea of the limitation of joint-stock liability grew out of the disasters of the decade with which we are dealing, but the rope it threw was of no benefit to those who were drowned already.

Having assured themselves and each other that the world had entered upon an era of automatic and ever-increasing prosperity, men made investments under conditions of unlimited liability which seem to us fantastic in their disproportionate hazards, even though we make allowance for the fact that the larger measure of individual freedom which prevailed in Britain a century ago bred a bolder and more adventurous population. But their actions were of the nature of an infectious insanity, and the risks taken may not have been more reckless, and miscalculations no greater, than were those that built up the stock-exchange boom in the United States a few years ago.

But the fact of this unlimited liability of every stockholder, and the prevalence of the system of bill-finance, which bound people together in another way, deferred and aggravated the catastrophe, until the position of the great banks themselves became precarious, and they must destroy their customers as they struggled desperately for their own survival....

Immediately on the conclusion of his Irish holiday, Lockhart left for London on personal business, and found himself surrounded there with a restless talk of commercial disaster that he says frankly he was not competent to understand. He was a lawyer by training, and then a journalist by profession. Lawyers deal with, and are amongst the first to hear of financial difficulties: journalists hear and talk of the affairs of publishing houses, with which they have many associations. It was not wonderful that Lockhart heard gossip around him which he understood sufficiently to disturb his mind. It was said that several publishing houses were on the verge of failure. There were rumours even about the great firm of Hurst, Robinson & Co. Lockhart knew of them as being Constable's London agents, and the distributors of the Waverley novels. He wondered how much loss it would mean to Constable if they should go down. When he heard Constable's name also mentioned as one who was swimming against the current, he considered that his failure might cause Scott to lose the price of a novel (his thoughts did not go beyond that), and he very properly wrote to Sir Walter with a report of the rumours that had reached his ears.

He received a confident letter in reply. Constable was 'rooted as well as branched, like the oak'. Let who would fall in London, Edinburgh had nothing to fear. Lockhart read, and dismissed the matter with an easy mind.

If Scott had communicated these rumours, and if he had received bold assurances from the publisher which went somewhat beyond his real feelings, we must not blame Constable without reservation. It is said that a pack of hungry wolves will devour one of their number which is maimed or wounded. Commercial custom was of a similar standard. Even today, we do not provide a hospital, or even a system of first-aid, for a business in difficulties. There is only the wasteful slaughterhouse of the Official Receiver. To show a wound, in the conditions that prevailed in the autumn of 1825, was to ask to be torn to pieces immediately. Constable said stoutly that all was well with him though all London should fail. Scott wrote in the same tone. Doubtless Lockhart repeated the thing he read. Adverse rumours would be somewhat discounted in consequence, somewhat reduced....

But Lockhart had not been long back at Chiefswood when he had a letter from a barrister friend in Lincoln's Inn, Mr. William Wright, who was a friend of Constable also. He said it was reported in London that Constable's banker had 'thrown up his book' .

The rumour, if true, would be of an uncertain gravity. The relations between banker and customer were rather different in several ways a century ago from what they are now. They were usually more personal in character. There were actually some country bankers who never dishonoured a cheque. They might close the account of an unsatisfactory customer, but so long as they were his agents, his honour was theirs. Such bankers accepted customers with discretion, and the mere fact of having an account with them was a substantial reference.

The large London and Edinburgh banks were not so widely different in their practices from the Joint-stock banks of today, but Constable's account was a large and valuable one, which no bank would lightly lose. On the other hand, no bank would have been likely to retain his custom without giving substantial discount facilities, even if there were no unsecured overdraft. If he had been asked to remove his account, it might be a disastrous sign. If, on the other hand, it were the case of a man conscious of his own strength resenting some lack of accommodation in the assurance that other bankers would give him more generous treatment, it might be of a different significance.

It was five in the afternoon when Lockhart read the letter. He rightly thought that it was a report of which Scott ought to know. He got out his horse at once, and rode over to Abbotsford.

He found Sir Walter taking his ease before dinner. His day's work was done. There had been a time when, having finished writing before this hour, he would have been toiling among the masons at the building of the house where he now sat, enjoying a weak glass of whisky and water, and a cigar, of which he had recently taken to smoking rather too many. He was at ease with himself and the world. Since he came back from Ireland, and had heard how well the *Talisman* was selling, he had decided on alternating the *Napoleon* with work on another novel. He liked best to have two books on hand together in that way. He could always turn aside to the other, if imagination tired of the one, or material halted. He had commenced *Woodstock* of which he thought he could make a good thing. Constable, impressed by the *Talisman* sales, had been very willing to contract for it, though he had said prudently that they would agree for this book alone. He would not again risk contracting for several novels ahead, and incurring further liabilities on long-dated bills.

Scott felt that he might have been unjust to his own powers when he told Tom Moore, a few weeks ago, "they have been a mine of wealth to me but I find I fail in them now. I can no longer make them so good as at first". After all, he was not dead yet.

And though he might not work with the masons now, he could still use an axe with ease, as Tom Purdie observed when they went out together. For the plantations grew, and there was much thinning to be done, and Sir Walter would do his share with the axe, or a bit more. He might find a need to lean on Tom's shoulder at times, if he should walk far, but there was no weakness in his arms when the axe swung. If he dozed now before dinner, after that afternoon's walk, few men had a better right.

He roused himself when Lockhart was announced, and took Mr. Wright's letter to read. Lockhart watching his face, saw no sign that he was disturbed.

He handed back the letter with his usual look of tranquil good-humour. He said he had no doubt the report was false. If Constable's account were to be had, there would be a pretty decent scramble among the London bankers to get it. He went on placidly with his cigar.

Lockhart rode back to Chiefswood with a relieved mind. Sir Walter sat thinking quietly while the sound of the horse-hooves died on the road. Then he got up. He told Charlotte that, he thought he would go over to see Constable. There was a matter of business he would like to talk over with him. Peter had better get out the carriage. He drove to Poulton without stopping, and got there just as Constable was going to bed.

The next morning, before Lockhart was up, he heard the sound of wheels, and looked out of his window to see a carriage below, with Peter Mathieson on the box. Scott descended, yawning, having waked when the carriage stopped. He went to join his grandson, who was feeding the ducks on the stream. It appears that Lockhart's family got up earlier than he. Lockhart talks about a 'fleet of ducklings on the brook,' but as it was October we may be content to conclude that he did not take much interest in domestic poultry. It is such little slips that are frequent with Scott's biographer, and make it difficult to give faith to his circumstantial narratives. He was a journalist, rather than a deliberate liar; but the practical difference is not great.

Scott told Sophia that he would stay for breakfast. He seemed in good spirits, though tired. When his son-in-law appeared he told him frankly that he had been more disturbed by Mr. Wright's letter than he had been disposed to reveal. He had gone to see Constable at once, and an hour's conference with him had re-assured his mind. Constable had been definite that the report concerning his bankers was false (as, in fact, it was).

Scott would prefer that nothing should be said at Abbotsford about this. He had not told Lady Scott or Anne of the reason for his sudden visit to Poulton.

After that there was a merry breakfast, and then Scott, who had told Peter not to wait for him, walked home through the woods, with Lockhart for company, and leaning on his shoulder, which he seldom did at this time with anyone other than Tom Purdie, but this morning he was in an exceptionally happy and affectionate mood.

Lockhart went back to talk to his wife. It was evident to both of them that her father must have been very much disturbed by the idea that Constable might be in financial difficulties. Sophia suggested that such an event might have very serious consequences for Mr. Ballantyne. She thought that such circumstances would trouble her father almost as much as though the loss were personal to himself. They agreed that this was a likely explanation. Lockhart says: "we well knew that James was his confidential critic—his trusted and trustworthy friend from boyhood." That is the actual statement of a man who was building up an elaborate structure of needless falsehood on the basis of his emphatic assertion that James was not trustworthy, and had never been so. He writes so randomly that he sometimes tempts us to wonder whether he was quite sane. He adds this:

> "But that Sir Walter was, and had all along been James's partner in the great printing concern, neither I, nor I believe, any member of his family, had entertained the slightest suspicion prior to the coming calamities which were now 'casting their shadows before'."

We may accept Lockhart's assurance that neither he nor Sophia were aware of the partnership at this time, but, beyond that, the statement is palpably false. There are few things more certain than that Charlotte had been in her husband's confidence from the first. It would be easy to demonstrate that the partnership must have been known to dozens of people (probably hundreds) at this time; and that some of them had known it for many years. Such a secret (even if it were desired to keep it as such, of which there is not a single item of evidence! is no secret at all.

That Sophia was not aware of it proves nothing. She had been five years old when the partnership was commenced. What interest at any time, is she known or likely to have taken in her father's business affairs? Still less does it prove anything that Scott had not felt it necessary or had occasion to mention it to his son-in-law. Lockhart was not a man with whom any intelligent person would go into counsel on business matters. And Scott was not a man who chattered about himself or his affairs. His letters show that he was not reticent, in the sense of concealment, about his financial circumstances. He wrote to several people, and under various conditions, with a frank precision. But his letters are mainly occupied with abstract interests, or the affairs of those to whom he wrote; and there is much evidence that his conversation was of the same pattern.

We may accept as an unsurprising fact, that, in October 1825, Lockhart and his wife did not know that her father was a partner in the firm of James Ballantyne & Co., and on this slender basis has been built up one of the great myths of biography.

Scott was also Ballantyne's partner in the *Edinburgh Weekly Journal*. Lockhart happened to know this, because he had been incidentally present at a conversation between them which had disclosed it, neither making any pretence of secrecy. But for this accidental circumstance, he would have been ignorant of that also and been able to provide us with an additional mystery.

CHAPTER LXXXVII.

It was in November 1825 that Sir Walter procured a thick quarto vellum-bound book, with a good lock, and commenced the habit of keeping, a daily journal. To anyone who did as much desk-work as he, and wrote with such swift precision, it was no great task to make entries in such a book either long or short as time and inclination led, sometimes two or three times a day, and continuing, with some considerable gaps, as long as he had strength to hold a pen, and sight to guide it.

The thousand pages of the book became, from this date the most reliable guide to the events that follow, and any other biography must be of a supplementary and explanatory kind. He commenced this Journal with a resolution, to which he adhered, not to alter or erase anything which he might enter, in whatever mood, or however it might be falsified by succeeding circumstance. It is here only, apart from two or three dozen lines in his poems, two or three paragraphs in his novels, and occasional passages in private correspondence, that he partially overcomes an habitual reticence, and reveals himself in his own words. It is one of the few books of its kind which are worth reading.

At the time when he made the first entry—November 20th—he held a position such as few men have ever reached. He had one of the greatest fames that have ever come to a man during his own life, and it had come in a good way, without violence or crime, or the ruin of others; it was a fame that was sustained without anxiety, and provoked no foes. He had joy in his work, which was done with ease, so that he had much leisure in later hours for the outdoor occupations he loved, and for social intercourse. He had domestic happiness, such as comes to few who give themselves to the winning of the world's more glittering rewards. He may not have had great wealth, to which he would have attached no value, but he had found that money came to his call with a magic ease, and he had used it to gain control of the land he loved, and very freely for the help of others in a hundred needs. Publicly and privately, there can have been few men in the world's history who, in their own life-times, have been more honoured or better loved. It might seem that there was nothing more than either Earth or Heaven could give. Was it wonderful if he faced life, as Job had faced it in his prosperity, with an aspect of courage, and a confident faith

Who could have guessed that he was on the threshold of the moment when everything but his own fortitude would be swept away?

At this moment, he was saddened only by one change, which had no aspect of disaster. Chiefswood was emptying. Lockhart was going to London, with Sophia and his family—going permanently, to take up the editing of the *Quarterly Review*, left vacant by Gifford's death. It was a reward, in part, of Lockhart's own ability, in part of Scott's exertions on his behalf. It had not been easy to arrange. Lockhart's unscrupulous uses of his pen in the earlier *Blackwood* days were remembered against him. He was better adapted to be an editor than a novelist, at which he had made several unsuccessful attempts. He reverenced grammar. But that he would never have had this position had he not been Scott's son-in-law, is a certain thing. The idea seems to have originated with Canning, either before or during the meeting at Storrs, when he questioned Anne about her brother-in-law's opinions and qualifications. Murray gave Lockhart a contract for the position when he saw him in London, and then, when protests came from members of the Government and others about the reputed character of the new editor, he sent Benjamin D'Israeli to Edinburgh to ask Scott's assistance in smoothing the difficulty. D'Israeli saw Lockhart, and talked of the matter as still in suspense. Scott was roused on his son-in-law's behalf. He wrote Murray with some stiffness, in his legal vein. Murray replied in haste that D'Israeli should have gone direct to him, and not to Lockhart at all. All that were needed were confidential letters from Scott to endorse the opinion that Lockhart was the right man. So a letter went to Southey and another to Heber, and the storm fell. It meant a salary of £1,200, and extra payment for special articles. If Lockhart could hold the appointment successfully (as he did) he had a life-provision from the magazine which Scott had done so much to found.

There was no disaster in that, but the days when Scott would ride through the woods to escape from the crowded hospitalities of Abbotsford to the quietness of that little upstair room, where he could work in peace till Sophia would give him breakfast or lunch, and he would relax to talk and games with Johnnie Hugh, were over for ever.

Two days later there was a letter from Constable, and the shadow of financial ruin fell definitely across his path. He did not write as he had spoken a few weeks earlier, when he had given assurance that all was well. He said that Hurst, Robinson & Co., were in financial difficulties, and it was essential to give them support, for he would be ruined if they should fail. He would be coming tomorrow to discuss what could be done. That day Scott entered in his Journal:

> "Here is a matter for a May morning, but much fitter for a November one. The general distress in the city has affected H. & R., Constable's great agents. Should they go, it is not likely that Constable can stand, and such an event would lead to great distress and perplexity on the part of J. B. and myself. Thank God, I have enough at least to pay 20/- in the pound, taking matters at the very worst. But much distress and inconvenience must be the consequence. I had a lesson in 1814 which should have done good upon me, but success and abundance erased it from my mind. But this is no time for journalising or moralising either.... If *Woodstock* can be out by 25th January it will do much and it is possible... "

Having made that entry, his mind left his personal concerns very easily; he went on to write of other persons and other things. And then he remembered that he had an engagement to dine with David Boyle in Charlotte Square, and went there to discover that he had made a mistake of memory—the engagement was for the next week—and returned "well pleased, not being exactly in the humour for company, and had a beef-steak".

The next day Constable came. His partner, Robert Cadell,

was with him, and James Ballantyne, and they were anxious men. But Constable was of a resolute mind to meet a crisis which he did not minimise, and confident that it would be overcome.

For some time past, Constable explained, Hurst, Robinson & Co., had been placing him in a serious financial difficulty. Owing to causes which they had, at first, represented as quite temporary, they had been renewing, instead of meeting their bills, so that the total had grown. The bulk of the proceeds of the *Waverley* novels passed through their hands. They also owed him large sums in respect of other publications. He always gave them a very large credit. Their name was good, and he could discount their bills for very large amounts. But those amounts were not unlimited. Every new transaction meant further bills being issued, and their discountable value depended upon some of the older ones being paid off.

There had come a time when Constable had said that he could not renew further. He could not digest bills to a larger total. Some of those that would soon be falling due *must* be met without renewal. Then let him help to tide them over the emergency with accommodation bills. If they had some with his name upon them, they would find means to raise the money on such documents, and their floating bills to him would be reduced accordingly.

Constable might not have liked to do this, but what alternative had he, except immediate ruin? The complicated structure of bills payable and receivable by which his business was carried on had always been a subject of watchfulness and anxiety, but, so far, he had ridden and controlled it successfully. Since Hurst, Robinson & Co., had been taking these continually extending credits, it had become like a nightmare dream. Yet, even so, he felt strong enough to handle it successfully, providing that Hurst, Robinson & Co. should maintain their credit with the banking world. But if that should fail—it had been easy to go cold at the thought.

He had seen that the bills for which they asked must be given. Into whatever depth of difficulty the great firm might be slipping, he must pull with all his weight upon a rope which he could not cut. He had given the bills.

But now it had gone further than that. A time had come when bills were of no avail. Both they and he had exhausted their discounting facilities. Their credit shook. They had written to him that there were large obligations approaching which they must have help to meet, not in bills but in cash.

It was the kind of conference which was being held in business circles in every commercial quarter. Failure followed failure. About three weeks later, one of the great London banks itself would collapse in ruin.

What was to be done? Constable was in no doubt about that. Hurst & Robinson must be supported at any cost. He had already raised a large sum, which was on its way to London now. If Scott would take the same view, all might yet be well. It was not of Scott's nature, nor is it clear that it would have been wiser on the knowledge that they then had, to take a different attitude. When the conference broke up, he wrote in his Journal:

> "Constable has been here, as lame as a duck on his legs, but his heart and courage as firm as a cock. He has convinced me we will do well to support the London House. He has sent them about £5,000, and proposed we should borrow on our joint security £5,000 for their accommodation. J. B. and R. Cadell present. I must be guided by them and hope for the best. Certainly to part company would be to incur an awful risk."

Why should it have been an awful risk to part company? The answer requires some examination into the affairs of the printing business, which would be a shorter and simpler matter if Lockhart had not obscured it with a flood of voluble explanations of which some are mere nonsense, and others deserve no worse criticism than to observe that they are untrue. Let him speak for himself first.

It will he remembered that Lockhart charged James

Ballantyne with recklessly extravagant drawings from the first partnership business, prior to the time when John was employed upon its accounts. He does not make that specific allegation in this place but charges James with negligence in more general terms, from which cause he suggests that the business had been in continual financial difficulty from its earlier days. He goes on:

"The necessity of providing some remedy for this radical disorder must very soon have forced itself upon the conviction of all concerned, had not John introduced his fatal enlightenment on the subject of facilitating discounts, and raising cash by means of accommodation-bills. Hence the perplexed *states* and *calendars*—the wilderness and labyrinths of ciphers, through which no eye but that of a professed accountant could have detected any clue; hence the accumulation of bills and counter-bills drawn by both bookselling and printing-house and gradually so mixed up with other obligations, that John died in utter ignorance of the condition of their affairs. The pecuniary detail then devolved upon James; and I fancy it will be only too apparent that he never made even one serious effort to master the formidable array of figures thus committed to his sole trust.

"The reader has been enabled to trace from its beginning the connection between Constable and the two Ballantyne firms. It has been seen how much they both owed to his interference on various occasions of pressure and alarm. But when he, in his overweening self-sufficiency, thought it involved no mighty hazard to indulge his better feelings, as well as his lordly vanity, in shielding these firms from commercial dishonour, he had estimated but loosely the demands of the career of speculation on which he was himself entering. And, by and by, when advancing by one mighty plunge after another in that vast field, he felt in his own person the threatenings of more signal ruin than could have befallen them, this "Napoleon of the press"—still as of old buoyed up to the ultimate result of his grand operations by the most fulsome flatteries of imagination—appears to have tossed aside very summarily all scruples about the extent to which he might be entitled to tax their sustaining credit in requital. The Ballantynes, if they had comprehended all the bearings of the case, were not the men to consider grudgingly demands of this nature, founded on service so important; and who can doubt that Scott viewed them from a chivalrous attitude? It is easy to see, that the moment the obligations became reciprocal, there arose extreme peril of their coming to be hopelessly complicated. It is equally clear, that Scott ought to have applied on these affairs, as their complication thickened, the acumen which he exerted and rather prided himself in exerting, on smaller points of worldly business, to the utmost. That he did not, I must always regard as the enigma of his personal history. But various incidents in that history which I have already narrated, prove incontestably that he had never done so; and I am unable to account for this having been the case except on the supposition that his confidence in the resources of Constable and the prudence of James Ballantyne was so entire, that he willingly absolved himself from all duty of active and thorough going superinspection.

"It is the extent to which the confusion had gone that constitutes the great puzzle. I have been told that John Ballantyne, in his hey-day, might be heard whistling for his clerk, John Stevenson (often alluded to in Scott's correspondence as *True Jock*) from the *sanctum* behind the shop with, "Jock, you lubber, fetch ben a sheaf o' stamps". Such things might well enough be believed of that hare-brained creature; but how sober solemn James could have made up his mind, as he must have done, to follow much the same wild course whenever any pinch occurred, is to me, I must own incomprehensible. The books were kept at the printing-house; and of course Sir Walter (who alone in fact had capital at stake) might have there examined them as often as he liked; but it is to me very doubtful if he ever once attempted to do so; and it is certain that they were *never balanced* during the latter years of the connection. During several years it was almost daily my custom to walk home with Sir Walter from the Parliament-House, calling at James's on our way. For the most part I used to amuse myself with a newspaper or proof-sheet in the outer room, while they were closeted in the little cabinet at the corner; and merry were the tones that reached my ear while they remained in colloquy. If I were called in, it was because James, in his ecstasy, must have another to enjoy the dialogue that his friend was improvising—between Meg Dods and Captain MacTurk, for example, or Peter Peebles and his counsel.

The reader may perhaps remember a page in a former chapter where I described Scott as riding with Johnny Ballantyne and myself round the deserted halls of the ancient family of Riddell, and remarking how much it increased the wonder of their ruin that the late baronet had kept 'day-book and ledger as regularly as any *cheese monger in the Grassmarket*'. It is nevertheless true, that Sir Walter kept from first to last as accurate account of his own *personal* expenditure as Sir John Riddell could have done of his extravagant outlay on agricultural experiments. I could, I believe, place before my reader the sum-total of six-pences that it had cost him to ride through turnpike-gates during a period of thirty years. This was, of course, an early habit mechanically adhered to: but how strange that the man who could persist, however mechanically, in noting down every shilling that he actually drew from his purse, should have allowed others to pledge his credits year after year, upon sheafs of accommodation paper, without keeping any efficient watch—without knowing, any one Christmas, for how many thousands he was responsible *as a printer in the Cannongate*!

"This is sufficiently astonishing—and had this been all, the result must sooner or later have been sufficiently uncomfortable; but it must be admitted that Scott could never have foreseen a step which Constable took in the frenzied excitement of his day of pecuniary alarm. Owing to the original habitual irregularities of John Ballantyne, it had been adopted as the regular plan between that person and Constable, that, whenever the latter signed a bill for the purpose of the other's raising money among the bankers, there should, in the case of his neglecting to take that bill up before it fell due, be deposited a counter-bill, signed by Ballantyne, on which Constable might, if need were, raise a sum equivalent to that for which he had pledged his credit. I am told that this is an usual enough course of procedure among speculative merchants; and it may be so. But mark the issue. The plan went on under James's management, just as John had begun it. Under his management also—such was the incredible looseness of it—the *counter bills*, meant only for being sent into the market in the event of the *primary bills* being threatened with dishonour—these instruments of safeguard for Constable against contingent danger were allowed to lie uninquired about in Constable's desk, until they had swelled to a truly monstrous 'sheaf of stamps'.—Constable's hour of distress darkened about him, and he rushed with these to the money-changers. And thus it came to pass, that, supposing Ballantyne & Co. to have at the day of reckoning obligations against them, in consequence of bill transactions with Constable, to the extent of £25,000, they were legally responsible for £50,000.

"It is not my business to attempt any detailed history of the house of Constable. The sanguine man had, almost at the outset of his career, 'been lifted off his feet', in Burns's phrase, by the sudden and unparalleled success of the Edinburgh Review. Scott's poetry and Scott's novels followed: had he confined himself to those three great and triumphant undertakings, he must have died in possession of a princely fortune. But his 'appetite grew with what it fed on', and a long series of less meritorious publications, pushed on, one after the other, in the craziest rapidity, swallowed up the gains which, however vast, he never counted, and therefore always exaggerated to himself. Finally what he had been to the Ballantynes, certain other still more audacious 'Sheafmen' had been to him. Hurst, Robinson & Co. had long been his London correspondents: and he had carried on with them the same traffic in bills and counter-bills that the Canongate Company did with him—and upon a still larger scale. They had done what he did not—or at least did not to any culpable extent: they had carried their adventures out of the line of their own business. It was they, for example, that must needs be embarking such vast sums in a speculation on hops! When ruin threatened them, they availed themselves of Constable's credit without stint or limit—while he, feeling darkly that the net was around him, struggled and splashed for relief, no matter who might suffer so he escaped! And Sir Walter Scott, sorely as he suffered, was too plainly conscious of the 'strong tricks' he had allowed his own imagination to play, not to make merciful allowance for all the apparently monstrous things that I have now been narrating of Constable."

It may occur to anyone on reading these explanations that they are rather more numerous than the occasion requires. It may be considered also that if they were substantially true it would have been more probable, at this period of financial panic, that the improvident firms of Ballantyne and Constable would have been appealing to Hurst, Robinson & Co. for assistance rather than dispatching money to London, in such sums as we have seen already, to assist their agents more urgent need. But the picture which Lockhart gives, though radically misleading, and in the idea of Sir Walter's negligence definitely false, contains the proportion of truth which makes a lie most poisonous, and cannot therefore be passed without some consideration.

The anecdote about Jock and the 'sheaf of stamps' may be dismissed as nonsense. To finance a business by means of the discounting of bills is only possible by careful forethought and exact accounting. It is an anxious process at the best, and there is sufficient evidence that John Ballantyne felt it to be so. No one could have gone through his experiences with the publishing business, and continued to regard such obligations with levity, if he had been sufficiently foolish at any time, which is improbable.

The allegation that John 'introduced this fatal entanglement' might or might not be a serious one, but it would be waste of space to discuss it, for it is untrue. The system of raising capital by means of bill-discounting was used by James Ballantyne & Co. before John came to Edinburgh.

The various aspersions upon Constable's character and business capacity may contain a percentage of truth, but are very randomly expressed, and cannot be regarded as a judicial pronouncement. The earlier transactions between Constable and the Ballantyne firm have been sufficiently explained to show that they were founded on business considerations and mutual interests, and though his better feelings may have also been exercised there is no occasion to talk about 'lordly vanity' or 'over-weening self-sufficiency' in this connection.

He did all that he undertook at those times, and neither vanity or folly can properly be charged against him.

The tale about Constable's misuse of 'counter-bills' may also be dismissed as a groundless slander. The James Ballantyne Trustees gave it the lie direct. They said that no such bills were ever left in Constable's hands, and that this lurid statement is imagination on the part of Scott's biographer. Their testimony is not always reliable, but they had no particular reason for defending Constable, or denying the tale, if it were true. Beyond that, it contains a number of improbabilities. Bills have dates. Even if such a pile of accumulated documents were still current, they would be so drawn that they would be very quickly due, if they were not so already—unless they had been deposited in blank, which is a wildly unlikely thing. To discount bills which will fall due almost immediately, and for which the acceptors do not expect to have to provide, is about as short a cut to his own ruin as a man can take. Also, had it been possible to save the position by means of such discounting, it is certain that Constable would have asked for the assistance they offered, and almost certain that it would have been given in documents more appropriate than these old alleged ones would have been likely to be.

Finally, no such explanation is needed. Accommodation bills provide, in the first instance, capital for both of those who exchange them. The natural result is that either becomes liable for twice the amount he receives. That is a position which results automatically, and is probably all the leaven of fact that Lockhart's assertion contains.

If these things be false, what remains? To answer this question it is necessary to clear away another misstatement.—That Scott really left anyone to pledge his credit year after year, upon sheafs of accommodation paper, without keeping any efficient watch, or knowing for how many thousands he was responsible in the Canongate business. It may be held to increase the extent of Scott's responsibility for the position in which he stood, and it certainly alters its character from that in which Lockhart attempts to dress it, but we are concerned only with the truth. Scott knew, from month to month, all about the liabilities of the printing-business, and Lockhart was well aware of this when he wrote these mendacious paragraphs. There was a certain book, bound in red morocco, which at this time, and for many previous years, had been sent to Scott every month, and which would contain a list of all the bills and other obligations, including estimates of the wages for which provision must be made during the coming month, together with estimates of the resources which would be available. This book had certainly been in regular use during John's lifetime, and it is extremely probable that the system had been instituted by Scott after he found that he had not been promptly and fully informed of the difficulties of the publishing business, and to prevent the possibility of the recurrence of such a position.

Challenged on this point, Lockhart admitted that he was familiar with the book, but he declined to withdraw his assertion of Scott's ignorance of the finances of the Ballantyne business. He said that the book was not a 'private' one of Sir Walter's, because the Jock of whom we have heard used to take it backwards and forwards between Abbotsford and the printing-office, and that he had examined it without finding that it contained anything in Scott's writing.

The first of these statements is important, because it supplies additional evidence of how little secrecy there was regarding Scott's interest in—and, indeed, control of—the printing business, but otherwise they are no more than the futile wrigglings of a convicted liar.

Strong as is the evidence of this book, it is only complementary to that of Scott's own letters to James, for he did not merely give a casual or doubtful attention; he used to write his detailed instructions as to the financial dispositions required by the obligations which it disclosed.

The first transaction with Constable of considerable magnitude of which there is a detailed record, and which was purely of an accommodation character, occurred early in July 1819. It will be remembered that Scott had been suffering from severe illness during the earlier part of that year, which reached a crisis in June, at which period his friends hardly expected his recovery, and there were times when he himself lost hope, if not courage, in the extremities of weakness and pain.

On July 5th of that year James Ballantyne & Co. handed Constable & Co. a series of bills totalling £3,160, and received a series from them differing in amounts and dates, but of an exactly similar total.

Such a transaction might be primarily for the accommodation of either party, but, in such a case, it was usual for the one that sought the assistance to give bills for a slightly larger amount, as payment for the risk taken and the trouble involved. The fact that the bills were for an exactly similar total, and other circumstances of the transaction, suggest that it was a mutual convenience, and that both firms were in need of additional capital, or of paying off similar obligations previously incurred, for which they hoped to provide by this means.

It might be supposed that, Scott being as ill as he was, this transaction was arranged by John and James, whether legitimately or not, without Scott's knowledge, or, at least, without his active participation. But the fact is that it was done with his full knowledge, and, though he had been too ill to leave his room a fortnight before, he appears to have been in firm control of the major operations involved.

On July 26th he received from James a long and detailed report of the obligations of the coming month, with a suggested scheme for financing them. He replied in equal detail, giving an amended scheme, with an alternative variation due to the fact that he thought James had overlooked a bill 'Veitch £1,000' for which provision should be made during August.

He also declined to allow the renewal of a bill of Constable's for £423, which he detected among the list, or of two for £424 and £425 during the following months, which related to that final purchase of stock in 1817, and which had been renewed up to this date.

His letter on this point is sufficiently characteristic to

deserve quotation. He thought that James was ignorant of, or had forgotten, what these bills originally represented, and that Constable's office was taking advantage of his oversight. Under such circumstances he had a habit of using plain words. He says:

> "Constable's people ought not to have asked for a renewal of this bill: it was a catch at your ignorance of the transaction."

And he enclosed a letter which could be shown to them, on the point. In regard to the two further bills for £424 and £425, he wrote:

> "The two bills were renewed in April last when they were beyond credit, and when, by-the-by, I paid the discount, which is still due to me by Messrs. Constable. You will not, therefore, renew either of these bills. But if Messrs. Constable want any accommodation of the same kind which they very frankly grant us, you will of course be ready to oblige them. But to discount their bills and get them the money, having so much of their paper, cannot be expected. I request you to lose no time in explaining this, in case Messrs. Constable should be relying on this, which, however, ought not to be the case, John's explanation having been explicit."

This letter is typical of the business attitude which Scott usually displayed in his letters. It is firm in resisting any attempt to gain advantage by manoeuvre, and chivalrous in its deliberate generosities. Other letters of later dates might be quoted in equal illustration of the control which Scott exercised over these financial transactions, but this is of particular importance, because it shows not only that the system of mutual accommodation was in operation as early as 1819, but that Scott considered that there was an obligation of honour to oblige Constable in that way if a request should be made. It is, indeed, an explicit instruction to his manager (as James then was) to be ready to do so if requested.

It is obvious, from a letter written to James from Abbotsford a week later, that there was more difficulty than had been anticipated in distributing this £3,160 of bills in such a way that the full benefit could be obtained, and that, till *Ivanhoe* should materialise, it was essential to do so. And it appears that this difficulty had in some way obstructed the purchase of the paper for *Ivanhoe*, and that the printing of the opening chapters had been delayed in consequence, for Scott wrote:

"August 2, 1819.

Dear James,

I observe your unpleasant dilemma, out of which I trust to help you. It is indeed at the unpleasant alternative of anticipating funds designed for the end of the month and the beginning of next; but the thing cannot be helped. What is perhaps worst of all is the delay of the paper for Ivanhoe—had I known of it!—but this avails little now.

Upon receiving this, you will restore to Mr. Constable the bills which you find difficulty in discounting. I will draw on him for £450, which I am pretty sure to get at Galashiels, and for £350, which I trust to get at Jedburgh. The former sum I trust to send you by Monday's post."

He added that Cowan (a paper merchant) must renew under the circumstances a bill for £220 which he had previously put on the list to be met, but that Cowan's accounts 'have been so regularly paid that he cannot refuse us such an accommodation'. It must stand till *Ivanhoe* could be got out, for which, "But for that blasted blunder about the paper, two months would be sufficient". (The estimate was too sanguine. *Ivanhoe* was not published until December 18th, and the delay of the paper in July can have had little, if any, influence upon that date.)

Scott did, in fact, discount the two substitution bills which he drew upon Constable at Galashiels and Jedburgh, and sent James the money.

It is clear from this correspondence (and other similar evidence might be detailed) that Scott controlled the major operations of the printing business. It is clear, also, that the proceeds of this £3,160 of accommodation bills was required, not for his personal use, but entirely for business purposes.

It may be observed that by this means the two firms obtained banking accommodation to a total of over £6,000, which would have been refused to either separately. The money was not required to fill a hole, but for the legitimate financing of two prosperous and expanding businesses. Otherwise the banks would not have found it at all. Our present system of financing by permanent limited-liability investments is much better, but we must not therefore condemn too readily the adoption of the methods of finance which were then available.

It may be further observed that, from the time when Scott took control of the finances, and had these estimates of the requirements of the coming month supplied to him, the credit of James Ballantyne & Co. was steadily maintained. Whatever might be the amount of its floating acceptances, they were always paid at maturity, and at this crisis of the affairs of the London firm (which collected the proceeds of the Waverley novels and Constable's other publications from the English trade, and from which source the main supplies of money should come) the credit of James Ballantyne & Co. was unshaken, and would have been maintained without difficulty, even in this worldwide crisis, had the business of Hurst, Robinson & Co. been controlled by a similar standard of prudence.

The fact that Scott kept in touch through all stresses of other work, and absences which were sometimes prolonged, with the major financial operations of the firm, does not, of course, imply that he was familiar with all its details, or that James might not have damaged it by negligence, or weakened it by extravagant drawings, though it does place some limit upon the amount which he was likely to be able to appropriate without explanation being required.

The fact that Scott had a habit, over many years, of treating the firm somewhat as his private bank, and referring his house hold tradesmen to it for payment, does admit of the allegation that he drew heavily—even too heavily—from it, but this remains an assertion without proof, and if it were really the case, and if James was unable to prove it, his own negligent bookkeeping is a matter for which no one but himself can be blamed.

As to the fact of Scott drawing on the business in this way, there is no doubt, and though Lockhart does not disclose it in his first biography, he did not dispute it, for it would have been impossible to do so.

As far back as 1820 there was a mercer in Edinburgh, a Mr. Blackwood, to whom Scott addressed this letter:

"October, 15, 1820.

Sir,

You will find beneath an order upon Mr. James Ballantyne to settle your account by payment or acceptance, which will be the same as if I did it myself. I could wish to be furnished with these bills before they exceed £50, for your convenience, as well as mine.

Your obedient servant,

Walter Scott."

The account to which this letter related had amounted to £218 before it was sent in, and this is not the only letter which shows that Scott liked his private accounts to be promptly rendered, and to give them a speedy settlement.

Approaching the period with which we are now concerned, we find that when the time arrived in 1825 at which the Scotts usually left Edinburgh for the summer vacation there was an accumulation of personal and household accounts incurred during the season, which Sir Walter wished to clear up before leaving. It appears evident that there was a difficulty in dealing with these, which arose from the fact that Constable was already straining the resources of the firm, by renewing bills rather than paying them—an inevitable result of the strain which Hurst, Robinson were putting upon him, which, so far, he had not disclosed.

It appears that Scott told James that he would be sending him a large batch of accounts for payment, and that James made such a reply that Scott decided to see Constable personally. After doing so, he sent this letter:

"July 8. 1825.

Dear James,

I was at Constable's yesterday and found all right. Cancelling all former orders, I send a list of accounts and payments to be made. Those to Isaac Bayley £176, and Leith Bank to my account should be made early. You will get the £2,000 on application."

He enclosed a batch of (mainly household) accounts for payment amounting to about £1,500.

Constable paid James £1,100 on that day, and £1,000 on the day following. These payments were on account of money due, not to the firm but to Scott personally, and were so credited to him against the required payments which James made during the following days. The total was somewhat increased by a letter from Lady Scott at the end of the week, evidently written as she was on the point of leaving:

"July 13th. 1825.

Lady Scott with best compliments to Mr. Ballantyne, takes the liberty of enclosing him two of Miss Scott's bills, which have omitted being added to her own, and might occasion some difficulty in the settling of them, as Misses Jollie & Brown are giving up business. Lady Scott has many apologies for giving all this trouble, and having also to request that, when he is so obliging as to settle her account with Mr. Pringle the butcher, that he would also settle her last account with him, that she may be quite clear with him. Lady Scott thinks that her second account will amount nearly to £40.

Castle Street,

Saturday morning."

On the following Thursday, in accordance with these instructions the dressmakers, who had already received accounts £91. 1. 7 and £65. 2. 7 a few days before, received a further payment of £96. 12. 6, and Pringle, the butcher, benefited by £38. 8. 8, Lady Scott's idea of the probable amount having been very accurate.

As this list of accounts (of which the final total was £1,666. 2. 5.) included another dressmakers' bill of £63 from the Misses Fergusson, we may conclude that Lady Scott and her daughter dressed well.

That was six months before the final catastrophe. We can only imagine with what difficulty Constable paid over that £2,100, but he must have been conscious that his indebtedness to Scott did not admit of the refusal of the required amount, and that he was already using the discounting facilities of the two firms to their full capacity, so that only cash would avail; and he was still showing a bold financial front to the world.

There remains the question of how far, if at all, the printing business had been weakened for the struggle which was before it by the extravagant drawings of either or both partners. The question is not of the first importance, for it could have made little ultimate difference to the course of events, nothing being clearer than that the embarrassment of the position did not commence at their end of the line, and that, at the other, it was uncontrollably bad; but it has been raised acutely, and therefore requires to be faced.

Lockhart repeats the charge against James Ballantyne which he made in reference to earlier periods. He says that, whereas James had undertaken, at the commencement of the new partnership, to draw no more than £500, he had, in fact, drained the business to this extent:

1822—£1,3396.9.
1823—£2,21915.7.
1824—£2,84219.8.
1825—£2,2963.5.
1826—£ 65310.0.

On this basis he calculated (somewhat inexactly) that James had overdrawn £7,581. 15. 5. and he attributed the difficulties with which we are now dealing largely to this extravagance, which would be inaccurate, even if his figures be correct, for which there is no separate evidence, and which the general character of his testimony on points of account does not enable us to accept with confidence.

But, even it the figures be so accepted, the charge against James Ballantyne is not pros ed. The profits of the business must have been very substantial during this period, and half of them were legitimately his. The arrangement to restrict drawings to £500 a year was subject to revision by mutual consent, and such consent may have been (and very probably was) exchanged during the years of prosperity.

The charge against James to which there is no defence is that, in spite of the promises he had given when the new partnership was commenced, his cash book had been unbalanced for several years, and the postings of its financial, as distinct from its commercial entries, were in arrears. Any accountant will understand how he had drifted into this position, and that it was not inconsistent with his having been able to supply the monthly lists of approaching liabilities and the estimated receipts, which enabled Scott to make the provisions in advance by which credit was systematically maintained during these years. We may conclude that estimates of profits must have been made in a merely approximate form, by deducting wages and expenses from the totals that the day-books showed.

To the charge of personal extravagance as it was made by Lockhart against James Ballantyne, in relation to the period of the new partnership, his Trustees retorted that Scott had drawn from the business to at least equal amounts, and they put forward an account which they had made up themselves to support this statement. They admitted that it was compiled of unposted items abstracted from the unbalanced cashbook, but they said that though James might have failed to post this book or add its columns, he had entered it accurately, and they offered to pay half the expenses, up to fifty guineas, if Lockhart would agree to having their account examined by an independent accountant, which offer he declined.

The totals of this account are:

1822-26. Amounts paid for Sir Walter Scott—£48,289 18 2.
"received £33,083 13 9."

Net Balance paid for him—£15,206 4 5.

It this account be true it would appear to show no more nor less than that he was drawing as heavily on the business as Lockhart alleges that James was doing, and that the total drawings were probably in excess of the profits made, but it is impossible to accept its figures with confidence. Many items are not particularised in such a manner that their nature is discoverable. One (May 23rd, 1823) is described as 'To Cash paid his Acceptance to Constable for paper of *Nigel*, £540. 5. 8.' There may be an explanation of why they should have considered this to have been Scott's personal liability, but it is difficult to imagine. If Constable supplied the paper on which *Nigel* was printed, he naturally required to be paid, and, with the financial methods prevailing, we can understand that he might like to draw a separate bill rather than allow the firm to deduct the amount from the printing account; but why on earth should it be regarded as Scott's personal liability?

The confusion is increased by the fact that the Trustees supplied a summary of this account, and that none of the items of that summary are so worded that they could possibly include such an item as this, though they agree with the total of the detailed account. But they do include these two items on following lines as debits against Sir Walter:

"Bills taken out of the circle by means of loans—£3,216.0.4.
Repayment of these loans—£3,240.0.1

One or other of these items (if they are accurately described) might properly be debited to Sir Walter's account. It is impossible to tell. To debit both loans *and* repayments seems absurd.

Incidentally, Scott is debited in this account for various sums remitted to Coutts for the purchase of Walter's commission. They total £5,349. 7. 3. including the cost of remitting. Both Scott and Lockhart put the cost of this commission at £3,500.

It is improbable that any accountant, after the death of those principally concerned, and in view of the state in which James had left his books, would have been prepared to certify any figure with confidence as showing the amount which Scott had drawn from the business during these years. It was most probably much less than the £15,000 alleged. James was in sole charge of the books which should have contained these records, and the responsibility for any doubt concerning it is certainly and entirely his.

But in estimating the position fairly, we must not lose sight of one fact to which Lockhart, in his anxiety to prove that Scott had an impossible ignorance, and James a culpability of incompetence, does not give a reasonable recognition. It was not the firm of James Ballantyne & Co. that was in difficulties; neither, primarily, was it that of Constable. If Hurst, Robinson & Co. had contrived to meet their obligations, there is no reason to doubt that the Edinburgh firms would have done the same without difficulty, even without the assistance of the large sums which were now raised by Scott and his business associates to send to London to assist the extremity there. To read Lockhart one might easily conclude that these Edinburgh firms, badly managed and recklessly financed over many years as he alleges them to have been, would be pulling down their London agents in their headlong fall. But the position is opposite. Hurst, Robinson & Co. are the ones who are slipping upon the rope. If it be true, as Lockhart says, that they had risked £100,000 outside their own business in a disastrous speculation in hops, it seems a sufficient fact alone to explain the pit into which the proceeds of the Waverley novels, and the money raised by discounting Constable's accommodation bills, had been drained away. Constable, in his turn, had had to ask Ballantyne and Scott to renew his bills when they should have been met, till they had grown to a huge total of liability from him to them. Latterly, he had been obliged to get them to give him their own bills also, so that he might use them to sustain the credit upon which their common stability depended. We are not concerned with the affairs of Hurst, Robinson & Co. except so far as they affect those with whom we are more immediately dealing, but if this hop speculation be a fact, it alone explains more than all Lockhart's suspicions and insinuations are sufficient to do—and he could hardly make the dead John or even the living James, responsible for that.

CHAPTER LXXXVIII.

The decision to give whatever support might be needed to Constable's London agents, left Scott with the sense of a danger past. It had been no worse than a warning that he should address his mind to the curtailment of the expenditure which, as we have seen, had been abnormally heavy during the year, and to disentangling his affairs, and those of the printing partnership, from Constable's perilous association. With a prudent effort, and in view of the large sums which his writings were always likely to command, it did not seem that it would be a very difficult enterprise, or one that would take over-long to do. Two days later he recorded his resolutions:

"No more building.
"No purchases of land till times are quite safe.
"No buying books or expensive trifles—I mean to any extent, and
"Clearing off encumbrances, with the returns of this year's labours:—
"Which resolutions, with health, and my habits of industry, will make me 'sleep in spite of thunder'."

It is easy to criticise the fact that he still failed to understand the magnitude of the crisis which faced him, but, in fact, he had no material on which to do so. He believed—as Constable did also—that Hurst, Robinson & Co. were a normally sound and solvent firm, driven into temporary difficulty by the financial blizzard which was raging across the world. To refuse assistance under such circumstances would have been as foolish as it would have been cowardly: having given it, it was a natural attitude for one of Scott's solid judgement and business capacity to consider the risks of such business entanglements, and to resolve that they should not be avoidably continued. When he wrote the above resolutions, Robert Cadell had just left his library in North Castle Street, probably having called to arrange the form and terms of the accommodation he had promised Constable two days before. Those details were calculated to provoke thought. He dined quietly with Charlotte and Anne, and the resolutions formed in his mind.

Two days later, he lent £300 on a second mortgage of doubtful value to a widow the affairs of whose son had come under his notice, having been embarrassed by a careless agent. He noted on this:

> "I have no connection with the family except that of compassion and may not be rewarded even by thanks when the young man comes of age. I have known my father often so treated by those whom he had laboured to serve. But if we do not run some hazard in our attempts to do good, where is the merit of them? So I will bring through my Orkney laird, if I can?"

CHAPTER LXXXIX.

Following the conference of November 23rd, and the dispatch to London of the funds with which the Constable and Ballantyne firms had resolved to support the credit of Hurst, Robinson & Co., there was an interval of three weeks, during which no further cause for anxiety was apparent. Scott's Journal during these days is occupied with domestic details, and some resolutions showing that while he was not nervously apprehensive of further evil, he was resolved to diminish both the risks and expenditures of future days.

> "Dined alone with my family," he writes of one evening. "I am determined not to stand mine host to all Scotland and England as I have done."

He even hardens his heart against one or two preposterous calls upon his charity that the postbag brought. A Danish captain, who required to go to Columbia, wrote that he had dreamed that Scott would find him the money, which occasioned the note: "I can tell him his dreams go by contraries".

But when his invertebrate literary friend—or perhaps acquaintance would be a sufficient word—R. P. Gillies, consults him about a financial crisis which is overwhelming him, after noting that "it would be useless to help him to money on such very empty plans," the Journal continues: "I offered him Chiefswood for a temporary retirement. Lady Scott thinks I was wrong, and nobody could less desire such a neighbour, all his affectations being caviare to me. But then the wife and children!"

There is only one note of despondency in the records of these weeks, yet they contain the foreshadowing of all the calamities which were to be the burden of the coming year.

He notes a secret fear as to Charlotte's health, "though I trust and pray she may see me out". Yet she seems outwardly well enough. She goes to the theatre with Anne. He parts with Lockhart and Sophia in confidence that his daughter will not fail her husband, or discredit her family in London circles; but to let his well-loved grandson go! "O my God! that poor delicate child, so clever, so animated, yet holding by this earth with so fearfully slight a tenure."

He records the first warnings of failure of his own physical and mental powers, and his characteristic reactions to them, which would hold them at bay for six further years of such toil as few men have undertaken, even in the energy of their youth. He had made a second mistake respecting a dinner engagement, and Charlotte undertook to watch these dates in future. He mislaid a draft for £750, a few minutes after it arrived, in a foolish manner which meant some hours of search for the precious document. He found it increasingly difficult to walk on a hard pavement, though he thought he would still be able to do five or six miles on the softer country soil when he should get back to Abbotsford. His eyesight was increasingly troublesome.

Yet he said stubbornly: "My health cannot be better," and on December 10th, being a rough wet day, he walked home through the rain and rather liked it, for "no man that ever stepped on heather had less dread than I of catch-cold, and I seem to regain, in buffeting with the wind, a little of the high spirit with which, in younger days, I used to enjoy a Tam-o'Shanter ride through darkness, wind, and rain—"

On December 14th, he heard such bad reports of commercial conditions in London that he turned his thoughts to borrowing the £10,000 with which the marriage-contract allowed him to charge the Abbotsford estate. He thought that, with such a sum in hand, he would be independent of difficulty. He made calculations which showed that in his own affairs he was 'certainly not less than £40,000 or nearly £50,000' on the right side. 'But the sun and moon shall dance on the green ere carelessness, or hope of gain, or facility in getting cash, shall make me go too deep again, were it but for the disquiet of the thing.'

But on December 17th, he was 'annoyed with anxious presentiments' as he anticipated the arrival of the London post. It was not that he had had any specific bad news, but the newspapers told of increasing financial panic in London. How were Hurst, Robinson & Co. riding the storm?

The next morning James came to North Castle Street with the news that Hurst and Robinson were reported to be failing, in which event Scott saw clearly that they would all be involved in a common ruin. If Hurst & Robinson went down, it seemed impossible that Constable should survive. If he went down, how could the printing business continue? All the proceeds of the novels themselves, all the cost of printing them, had been paid in Constable's bills. How could the money which had been received from the banks as they were discounted be returned when they should demand it? Much of the capital of the printing business, and of the publishing firm, had been found by the discounting of the bills they had exchanged for this purpose. How could Ballantyne & Co. hope to take up those they had under discount themselves, and provide also for those on which Constable's capital had been raised? Then there was that £5,000 bond which had been signed to relieve the position three weeks ago. It was a mere fraction of the gross liability which confronted them.

It is not surprising that Scott found himself unable to continue his work on *Napoleon* that day. He wrote at great length in his Journal. Facing the fact, as his way was, he told Charlotte at once, and was met with incredulity. In the evening, hope came again.

The thoughts which he wrote down that day were not all accurate anticipations. He did not foresee consequences without miscalculation. Yet the entries themselves on that and some succeeding days are better than any comment upon them:

> "*December* 18th. Ballantyne called on me this morning. *Venit illa suprema dies*. My extremity is come. Cadell has received letters from London which all but positively announce the failure of Hurst & Robinson, so that Constable & Co. must follow, and I must go with poor James Ballantyne for company. I suppose it will involve my all. But if they leave me £500, I can still make it £1,000 or £1,200 a year. And if they take my salaries of £1,300 and £300, they cannot but give me something out of them. I have been rash in anticipating funds to buy land, but then I made from £5,000 to £10,000 a year, and land was my temptation. I think nobody can lose a penny—that is one comfort. Men will think pride has had a fall. Let them indulge their own pride in thinking that my fall makes them higher, Or seems so at least. I have the satisfaction to recollect that my prosperity has been of advantage to many, and that some at least will forgive my transient wealth on account of the innocence of my intentions, and my real wish to do good to the poor. This news will make sad hearts at Darnick, and in the cottages of Abbotsford, which I do not nourish the least hope of preserving. It

has been my Delilah, and so I have often termed it; and now the recollection of the extensive woods I planted and the walks I have formed, from which strangers must derive both the pleasure and profit, will excite feelings likely to sober my gayest moments. I have half resolved never to see the place again. How could I tread my hall with such a diminished crest? How live a poor indebted man where I was once the wealthy, the honoured? My children are provided: thank God for that. I was to have gone there on Saturday in joy and prosperity to receive my friends. My dogs will wait for me in vain. It is foolish—but the thoughts of parting from these dumb creatures have moved me more than any of the painful reflections I have put down. Poor things. I must get them kind masters; there may be yet those who loving me may love my dog because it has been mine. I must end this, or I shall lose the tone of mind with which men should meet distress.

I find my dogs' feet on my knees. I hear them whining and seeking me everywhere—this is nonsense, but it is what they would do could they know how things are. Poor Will Laidlaw! poor Tom Purdie! this will be news to ring your heart, and many a poor fellow's besides to whom my prosperity was daily bread.

Ballantyne behaves like himself, and sinks his own ruin in contemplating mine. I tried to enrich him indeed, and now all—all is gone. He will have the 'Journal' still, that is a comfort, for sure they cannot find a better Editor. *They*—alas! who will *they* be—the *unbekannten Obern* who are to dispose of my all as they will? Some hard-eyed banker; some of those men of millions whom I described. Cadell showed more kind and personal feeling, to me than I thought he had possessed. He says there are some properties of works that will revert to me, the copy-money not being paid, but it cannot be any very great matter, I should think.

Another person did not afford me all the sympathy I expected, perhaps because I seemed to need little support, yet that is not her nature, which is generous and kind. She thinks I have been imprudent, trusting men so far. Perhaps so but what could I do? I must sell my books to someone, and these folks gave me the largest price; if they had kept their ground I could have brought myself round fast enough by the plan of 14th December. I now view matters at the very worst, and suppose that my all must go to supply the deficiencies of Constable. I fear it must be so. His connections with Hurst & Robinson have been so intimate that they must he largely involved. This is the worst of the concern; our own is comparatively plain sailing.

"...I am so much of this mind, that if any one would now offer to relieve all my embarrassments on condition I would continue the exertions which brought it there, dear as the place is to me, I hardly think I would undertake the labour on which I entered with my usual alacrity only this morning though not without a boding feeling of my exertions proving useless. Yet to save Abbotsford I would attempt all that was possible. My heart clings to the place I have created. There is scarce a tree on it that does not owe its being to me, and the pain of leaving it is greater than I can tell. I have about £10,000 of Constable's, for which I am bound to give literary value, but if I am obliged to pay other debts for him, I will take leave to retain this sum at his credit. We shall have made some *kittle* questions of literary property amongst us. Once more, 'Patience, cousin, and shuffle the cards.'

"Anne bears her misfortune gallantly and well, with a natural feeling, no doubt, of the rank and consideration she is about to lose. Lady Scott is incredulous, and persists in cherishing hope where there is no ground for hope. I wish it may not bring on the gloom of spirits which has given me such distress. If she were the active person she once was that would not be. Now I fear it more than what Constable or Cadell will tell me this evening, so that my mind is made up....

"*Half-past Eight*. I closed this book under the consciousness of impending ruin, I open it an hour after, thanks be to God, with the strong hope that matters may be got over safely and honourably, in a mercantile sense. Cadell came at eight to communicate a letter from Hurst & Robinson, intimating they had stood the storm, and though clamorous for assistance from Scotland, saying they had prepared their strongholds without need of the banks. This is all so far well, but I will not borrow any money on my estate till I see things reasonably safe. Stocks have risen from—to—a strong proof that confidence is restored. But I will yield to no delusive hopes, and fall back. My resolutions hold.

I shall always think the better of Cadell for this, not merely because his feet are beautiful upon the mountains who brings good tidings, but because he showed feeling—deep feeling, poor fellow—he who I thought had no more than his numeration table, and who, if he had had his whole counting-house full of sensibility, had yet his wife and children to bestow it upon—I will not forget this if I get through. I love the virtues of rough and round men; the others are apt to escape in salt rheum, sal-volatile, and a white pocket-handkerchief. An odd thought strikes me: when I die will the Journal of these days be taken out of the ebony cabinet at Abbotsford, and read as the transient pout of a man worth £60,000, with wonder that the well-seeming Baronet should ever have experienced such a hitch? Or will it be found in some obscure lodging-house, where the decayed son of chivalry has hung up his scutcheon for some 20s. a week, and where one or two old friends will look grave and whisper to each other, 'Poor gentleman', 'A well-meaning man', 'Nobody's enemy but his own', 'Thought his parts could never wear out', 'Family poorly left', Pity he took that foolish title'? Who can answer this question?

What a life mine has been! half educated, almost wholly neglected or left to myself, stuffing my head with most nonsensical trash, and undervalued in society for a time by most of my companions, getting forward and held a bold and clever fellow, contrary to the opinion of all who thought me a mere dreamer, broken-hearted for two years, my heart handsomely pieced again, but the crack will remain to my dying day. Rich and poor four or five times, once on the verge of ruin, yet opened new sources of wealth almost overflowing. Now taken in my pitch of pride, and nearly winged (unless the good news hold), because London chooses to be in an uproar, and in the tumult of bulls and bears, a poor inoffensive lion like myself is pushed to the wall And what is to be the end of it? God knows. And so ends the catechism.

December 19th. Ballantyne here before breakfast. He looks on Cadell's last night's news with more confidence than I do; but I must go to work be my thoughts sober or lively. Constable came in and sat an hour. The old gentleman is firm as a rock, and scorns the idea of Hurst & Robinson's stopping. He talks of going up to London next week, and making sales of our interest in (*Woodstock*) and *Boney,* which would put a hedge round his finances. He is a very clever fellow, and will, I think, bear us through .

December 21st. ...Things are mending in town. and H & R. write with confidence, and are, it would seem, strongly supported by wealthy friends. Cadell and Constable are confident of their making their way through the storm, and the impression of their stability is general in London. I hear the same from Lockhart. Indeed, I now believe that they wrote gloomy letters to Constable, chiefly to get as much money out of them as they possibly could. But they had well-nigh overdone it."

The renewed hope, after the shadow of ruin had come so closely upon him, caused a feeling of physical buoyancy on the next day, and an ability to labour which saw the completion of about twenty-four pages of the *Napoleon*, and the composition of *Bonnie Dundee* in the later day. "Can't say," the Journal records, "what made me take a frisk so uncommon of late years, as to write verses of free will. I suppose the same impulse which makes birds sing when the storm seems blown over."

Unfortunately, 'seems' was the right word to use; yet, over Christmas, which was passed very quietly at Abbotsford, the hope held.

Before leaving Edinburgh on Christmas Eve, Scott wrote to Walter and Jane, telling them "of how things had been in the money market" as a peril past, but saying that he might still have to raise the £10,000 on Abbotsford to relieve the position.

Constable, always a good fighter, had been to him with a proposal that they should get out an edition of the *Waverley* novels, with new introductions and notes. He calculated that there would be a £20,000 profit on the whole enterprise. Scott could name his own terms.

So they drove to Abbotsford in good spirits enough, and on Christmas morning Scott made notes of all the work he would get through during the quiet vacation days, and then he was seized with a sudden violent pain, and a 'deadly sickness' that followed, and sent in haste for Clarkson, the surgeon at Melrose, who diagnosed gravel, and there was no work for two days, after which he was able to write up his Journal again having slept twelve hours from exhaustion, after the pain ceased.

"I cannot expect," he wrote, "that this will be the last visit of this cruel complaint, but shall we receive good at the hand of God, and not receive evil?" And by the afternoon he was able to work again, and Sir Adam Fergusson came to dinner, and suggested that the verses written in Edinburgh a few days before would go well to the tune of *Bonnie Dundee*, which was a good thought.

The next day there was a letter from a gentleman named Campbell who had previously 'had an impulse' to request a loan of £50 for two years. Scott had 'felt no corresponding impulse,' and now had the pleasure of paying one-and-two-pence postage on the letter of abuse which was the frequent sequel of such refusals.

On December 30th the Journal records:

> Spent at home and in labour—with the weight of unpleasant news from Edinburgh. J. B. is like to be pinched next week unless the loan can be brought forward. I must and have endeavoured to supply him. At present the result of my attempts is uncertain. I am even more anxious about Constable & Co., unless they can get assistance from their London friends to whom they gave much. All is in God's hands. The worst can only be what I have before anticipated. But I must, I think, renounce the cigars. They brought back (using two, this evening) the irritation of which I had no feelings while abstaining from them. Dined alone with Gordon, Lady S., and Anne. James Curle, Melrose, has handsomely lent me £600; he has done kindly. I have served him before and will again if in my power."

The next day he took a 'good sharp walk,' the first time he had been able to do so since he arrived at Abbotsford, and felt better for it. In the evening, Colonel Russell and his sister came, and a tribe of Fergussons. They came to sit up for the New Year in the usual Scottish custom, but Scott felt so tired about eleven that he 'was forced to steal to bed'.

So the year closed.

CHAPTER XC.

The first fortnight of the new year passed happily and quietly at Abbotsford in the society of the Skenes and other of Scott's closer and older friends. It was a time of snow, into which he ventured with lengthening walks. There was one day of alarm when he could not work. 'To my horror and surprise I could neither write nor spell, but put down one word for another, and wrote nonsense.' But this trouble passed. Nor did he allow himself to be disturbed by letters from James, pointing out carelessness of style in the recent proof-sheets, and once the repetition of a long passage of history.

The deed that charged £10,000 on the Abbotsford property was signed and dispatched to Edinburgh. Its proceeds were to be used to strengthen the position of the printing business. Constable was supposed to be in London, fighting his own battles there. On January 5th Scott noted:

> "Got the desired accommodation with Coutts, which will put J. B. quite straight, but am a little anxious still about Constable. He has immense stock, to be sure, and most valuable, but he may have sacrifices to make to convert a large proportion of it into ready money. The accounts from London are most disastrous. Many wealthy persons totally ruined, and many, many more have been obliged to purchase their safety at a price they will feel all their lives. I do not hear things are so bad in Edinburgh; and J. B.'s business has been transacted by the banks with liberality...."

It was evident that there would be no difficulty with James Ballantyne & Co., if their associates were equally well managed and well supported.

But on January 14th, there is an entry of a different kind:

> "An odd mysterious letter from Constable, who is gone post to London, to put something to rights which is wrong betwixt them, their banker, and another moneyed friend. It strikes me to be that sort of letter which I have seen men write when they are desirous that their disagreeable intelligence should be rather apprehended than avowed. I thought he had been in London a fortnight ago, disposing of property to meet this exigence, and so I think he should. Well, I must have patience. But these terrors and frights are truly annoying.
>
> A letter from J. B., mentioning Constable's journey, but without expressing much, if any, apprehension. He knows C. well, and saw him before his departure, and makes no doubt of his being able easily to extricate whatever may be entangled. I will not, therefore, make myself uneasy. I can help doing so surely, if I will. At least, I have given up cigars since the year began, and have now no wish to return to the habit, as it is called. I see no reason why one should not be able to vanquish with God's assistance, these noxious thoughts which foretell evil but cannot remedy it."

Two days later the family drove back to Edinburgh. As usual on these occasions, they went first to Mr. Skene's on their arrival and had dinner there before going home to North Castle Street. They had a merry time. Skene said he had never seen Sir Walter in better spirits. But when he got home, he opened his letters and made this entry:

> "Came through cold roads to as cold news. Hurst & Robinson have suffered a bill of £1,000 to come back upon Constable, which I suppose infers the ruin of both houses. We shall soon see. Constable, it seems,

who was to have set off in the last week of December, dawdled here till in all human probability his going or staying became a matter of mighty little consequence. He could not be there till Monday night, and his resources must have come too late."

The next morning, very early, there came a verbal message to Mr. Skene asking him to go round to see Sir Walter as soon as possible. Thinking that his illness had returned, he went at once. It was seven, and the winter morning was still dark, when he entered the Castle Street library. Scott was at his desk, working by candle-light, surrounded by many papers. He held out his hand as his friend entered: "Skene, this is the hand of a beggar. Constable has failed, and I am ruined *de fond en comble*. It's a hard blow, but I must just bear up; the only thing that wrings me is poor Charlotte and the bairns." Such is Skene's memory. Actually, and as yet, Constable had not failed. But Scott's judgement was right. And now that the crisis had come, there was to be no hesitation, little of the moods which impulsed those long entries in the Journal a month ago. His courage rose to face the emergency.

It seemed, for the moment, as though he were infatuated with a false idea of his own ruin, which others knew to be groundless.

Sir John Hope and Sir Henry Jardine were sent to him by the Royal Bank of Scotland with an intimation that they were prepared to serve him. "The Advocate came on the same errand." Skene and Colin Mackenzie made offers of help. But he refused all alike. "Borrowing would but linger it out." Two days later, there were letters from Constable and from Hurst & Robinson direct. The last persisted still that they could weather the storm. They blamed Constable for not having come earlier. But Scott did not fail to see clearly what that returned bill must mean. His own resolution was fixed. He would assign all he had to his creditors. When he knew what the loss was, he would pay it off. It would be worth their while to give him time, for they could be paid in no other way.

On the 19th he wrote:

> "I feel quite composed, and determined to labour...I have finished about twenty pages of *Woodstock*, but to what effect others must judge. A painful scene after dinner, and another after supper, endeavouring to convince these poor dear creatures that they must not look for miracles, but consider the misfortune as certain and only to be lessened by patience and labour."

It was not wonderful that it seemed hard to believe.

The next day Sir William Forbes called: "the same kind honest friend as ever." Others came, and all on the same errand. "All anxious to serve me, and careless about their own risk of loss."

Scott had never lacked good friends. But his answer was the same to all. He would accept no help.

CHAPTER XCI.

What had been happening in London during these fatal days?

When Constable lowered his portly body from the London coach, he arrived, as we know, a week too late. Hurst & Robinson's bill to himself for £1,000 was in the act of being dishonoured and thrown back on his own bank. Would it have saved the position had he come earlier? It is hard to say. Probably for the moment, it would. If so, it must have been only to face a future of almost daily peril until fresh capital could be obtained, a more conservative policy gradually strengthen the position, or a different atmosphere of world-finance render credit easier to negotiate. Yet, looking at the solid nature of the three businesses with which we are dealing, the large profits they were making, and the fact that they had the goodwill of an author who might still prove to be an unexhausted goldmine, we may conclude that only time was required to restore confidence, and to fill the pit of deficiency which had been dug by Hurst & Robinson's unfortunate speculations.

It was a thought that must have maddened Constable as he sat hour by hour while the coach drove southward over the winter roads. They were all profit-making firms. It would be absurd, or worse, to subject them to the wasteful processes of liquidation. It would be needless, ruinous loss for all, and not least for the creditors in whose interests it would be asserted that it was done. But that was a position of daily occurrence then, as it is now. The creditors who break up a business by their impatience are themselves the sufferers, as some of them often deserve to be. They are like bees who die through their of their own stings.

Constable came late; and when he came he was ill. He was ill with anxiety, and physical weakness. He had been unfit to take such a journey in such weather. He stayed fretting in his hotel for two days, unable to move.

But while he was confined there he planned with a resolute and audacious mind. He knew that Hurst & Robinson were struggling against overwhelming odds. They were doing all that they could. He had asked aid from Scott and Ballantyne, and had had it with a generous hand. They had done their part. Now it rested with him.

There was one species of property that he had which was unencumbered, and which he rightly thought to be of enormous value—the unexhausted copyright of the *Waverley* novels. Suppose he were to go to the Bank of England, explain the emergency, and ask for a loan upon them, throwing his other copyrights, including the Encyclopaedia Britannica, and his part-ownership of the Edinburgh Review, into the scale? He judged rightly that it would be useless to ask for such a loan from any other of the London banks on such security, in the financial panic that was prevailing. He judged also that the Bank of England would not be likely to do anything unless they were assured that it would thoroughly establish the position. Suppose he were to ask for a loan of £200,000, and get half that amount?

Anyway, it was worth a try. The Bank of England—even the Government—might be willing to avert the threatened failures. The failures in the City during the last few weeks were so many already. And Sir Walter's was a magic name. If only he were here! He knew him for a man as resolute, as audacious, and yet of sounder judgement than himself.

Together they might have done much.

But Constable had done much himself by his own courage and his own wits since he had opened a second-hand bookshop in a side street of Edinburgh. His idea might fail now, but it was worth a throw. If Scott were not here to back up the plan, there was his son-in-law, young Lockhart. He disliked Lockhart: his self-sufficiency and conceit. When we remember Lockhart's surprise that he could have the manners and appearance of a gentleman, we cannot blame him for that. But, at the crises of life, personal differences are forgotten. Surely Lockhart could not refuse to come with him on such an errand, even though he might not be much use, and would be a poor substitute for his father-in-law at the best.

He had sent a note to Lockhart as soon as he arrived in London, asking him to come to the Adelphi hotel were he was staying, and we have only Lockhart's account of the interview that resulted. He heard Constable explain in detail a position with which he had not been fully familiar, and learnt for the first time how heavily Scotts interests were involved. He says that Constable used a violence of language at times which roused his 'wonder and commiseration'. But he himself was a dumb dog. He had no encouragement to give, no counsel to offer. He refused his aid without hesitation, and, in the light of all that happened afterwards, he remained complaisant over that refusal. He says:

> "To be brief, he requested me to accompany him as soon as he could get into his carriage, to the Bank of England, and support him (as a confidential friend of the Author of *Waverley*) in his application for a loan

of from £100,000 to £200,000 on the security of the copyrights in his possession. It is needless to say that without distinct instructions from Sir Walter, I could not take upon me to interfere in such a business as this. Constable, when I refused, became livid with rage. After a long silence, he stamped on the ground, and swore that he could and would do alone. I left him in stern indignation."

Lockhart thought it 'needless to say' that he refused. Perhaps, to those who knew him, it was. Yet what harm to Sir Walter's interests, under any conceivable circumstances, could it have done to have given Constable the support he asked? He would be unable to pledge the copyrights, except so far as he could show that they were his property, and any money he might raise would serve to relieve a position in which Scott's fortune and honour were involved. Scott had shown Lockhart, by that early morning call at Chiefswood, how much he was concerned at a mere rumour detrimental to Constable's credit.

We may doubt the possibility of successful effort, the commercial atmosphere being what it was, and the liabilities what they were. We cannot blame Lockhart that he proposed no remedy. His condemnation is that he declined to try. He contributed his 'stern indignation'!

Constable, swallowing his contempt, saw him again two days later.

He said that, if £20,000 could be raised quickly in Edinburgh, he could still save the position. Would Lockhart write to Scott, urging that this should be done? With more justification than in his previous attitude, Lockhart would 'promise nothing but to acquaint Scott immediately with his request, and him with Scott's answer'. What was the use of that? Constable knew how to use a pen. The result was 'another scene'. At such a time, Lockharts rectitude must have been very difficult to endure.

Lockhart's view was that a man could only get in a ditch by his own fault. Men like himself, who are prudent enough to have parents of means, and walk cautiously ever afterwards, will keep clear of the mud. He remarks sapiently that if Constable had confined himself to his great successes, such as the Edinburgh Review, the Encyclopaedia Britannica, and the exploiting of Scott's works, he would have come to a different end. It sounds a simple recipe, though even then the result is not sure, for Hurst and Robinson would still have failed, and it is impossible to judge how he would have endured the loss that he must have suffered; and Lockhart is very vague about what his publishing errors were. No publishing business can be carried on without mistakes being made, and certainly not one which is as boldly enterprising, and as successful as Constable's had been up to this time. And when a tide of financial disaster sweeps across the world, it is often the ablest and most enterprising—those who are in the forefront of the battle—who are the first to be overwhelmed.

CHAPTER XCII.

Lockhart says that Constable 'lingered on' in London, 'fluctuating between wild hope and savage despair, until, I seriously believe, he at last hovered on the brink of insanity'.

We may call this an error of memory, or a picturesque invention, or what we will, but it cannot be true. It was on the 14th of January that Scott received Constable's letter saying that he was going to London. It was on the 23rd—only nine days later—that he called upon Scott at North Castle Street. He cannot have been in London for more than five days, including the two during which he was unable to move from the hotel, and it seems clear that, immediately after his second interview with Lockhart, he decided that if the £20,000 which (he thought) would save the position were to be raised in Edinburgh, he must not depend upon letters, but must return himself to inspire and engineer the operation. That Scott could have raised that, or a much larger sum, had he been persuaded to attempt it, there is no doubt at all. It is useless speculation to consider whether he would have attempted it, had Hurst & Robinson's bill not been dishonoured, and had it seemed possible that credit could still be maintained. Had he once decided upon such a course, he would, in all probability, have carried it through to a final triumph, for the three threatened firms were essentially sound, profitable concerns, with very valuable assets, which liquidation was about to waste.

But when Constable got back to Edinburgh, he found that he was too late again. Cadell had decided, in his absence, that the game was up; and the action taken by Ballantyne & Co., on that first morning when Scott and James met, had made recovery of the position an almost impossible thing. For that day there had been bills of Ballantyne & Co. coming up at the bank for payment, amounting to some thousands of pounds. There was money in hand to meet them, as a result of the £10,000 charge which Scott had given upon the Abbotsford estate. Having to make a prompt decision, Scott and James had agreed that they ought to stop payment instead of letting further money be paid away. It was a position in which all creditors should be treated equally. It may have been a wise, and was in some respects a courageous decision, but it must have been fatal in its results to any effort to carry on subsequently.

Constable, not without reason, attributed the position which faced him on his return largely to Cadell's attitude. Had Cadell maintained his own courage, had he even maintained silence about Hurst & Robinson's bill, the whole position would have been different. Why on earth did he tell James about that?

Cadell pointed to the bill-book. Why not recognise facts? They could no longer expect the bank to take H. & R.'s bills, and without being able to use them, how could they meet the obligations that were before them? A violent quarrel resulted.

In most battles, men are not really defeated by their enemies. Lacking sufficient courage for victory, they defeat themselves— often when their enemies would themselves be in flight, if the line were held for another hour.

Constable thought of Cadell as one who defeats himself,

and who had betrayed the partnership trust. Cadell thought that Constable showed an obstinate folly in refusing to face the truth. Constable went to see Scott.

He was certainly not insane at that interview. He 'seemed irritable, but kept his temper under command'. He gave Scott the impression that he meant to find some means of re-establishing his position, and leaving Cadell out. He was rather staggered when Scott expressed his legal opinion that the unfinished *Woodstock* and *Napoleon* would revert to himself, the contracts lapsing with the impending failures. But Scott had formed his own plans by this time, and those copyrights were the strength of his position, both for attack and defense.

Constable wanted to know whether they would still be working in alliance. He said he was utterly ruined unless Scott would stand by him now. Scott gave a friendly reply, and was frank about his own plans; but he would give no pledge. He thought the quarrel with Cadell a mistake. 'I will help him, I am sure, if I can,' Scott wrote that night, 'without endangering my last cast for freedom.'

For Scott had made his plans, and had already done much during the last six days. He had assigned his estate to his lawyer, Mr Gibson, and two other lawyers of good standing in Edinburgh, as his Trustees, and a meeting of his creditors and those of Ballantyne & Co. had been convened for the 26th, at which there would be proposals to be put forward on his behalf.

He had had a week of bad health, being unable to find sleep until towards morning, when it came heavily, and was followed by a reluctant awaking, and a despondency in which he would be glad that his mother, and his 'almost sister' Christy Rutherford, and Will Erskine were dead. But after that 'more dutiful' thoughts would return. If he had weak moments, they were not such that others could see them. He showed a quiet and resolute face to the world. But as accounts were examined, and Cadell assured him that there was little to be hoped from the realisation of Constable & Co.'s assets, he abandoned hope for the moment that he would ever see Abbotsford again. It was a bitter thought. 'Yet,' he wrote, 'I feel neither dishonoured nor broken down.'

He had formed two resolutions. He would do so many pages of writing every day, be the quality what it might, and at whatever physical cost. It might be a poor chance, but if he could not do that, and imagination respond, there was none at all. For he was determined to attempt that the debts should be paid with his own hand.

Resolutely, he refused all the offers of help, whether large or small, that were pouring in. They were from many sources, of very various amounts. There was an anonymous one of £30,000 from a 'high quarter' in London. Mr. Pole, a music teacher who had taught his daughters the harp, offered his life's savings— £500 or £600. But he refused them, large and small alike. 'I will involve no friend,' he wrote down his resolution 'either rich or poor.' And his resolute courage had its influence upon others, and its reaction upon himself. For he heard the voices of Lady Scott and Anne talking merrily in the drawing-room on the day that Constable called, and it did him good to hear them....

And one morning he sent a note over to Skene, asking him to walk with him after lunch, for Skene was a good friend for such a time, and he knew that he could lean on him as he did on Tom Purdie, should his strength fail. And when they parted Skene wrote down what he could remember of their conversation.

Scott had told him of his resolution to attempt to pay his debts and rebuild his fortune with his own hand, but 'I much mistrust my vigour, for the best of my energy is already expended'. He spoke of the day when he had been unable to control his hand to write the words that he would. Then he had been in mortal fear that his mind was going. But that fear had passed. Had he not good cause to be thankful for that? "Few," he said, "have more reason to feel grateful to the Disposer of all events than I."

Scott's refusal to accept the many offers of assistance that poured in upon him during this week, and subsequently, may seem, to a superficial view, inconsistent with the financial adventures of earlier years.

In the aggregate, these offers would have been sufficient to have enabled him to control the whole position. He could have re-established both the Ballantyne and Constable firms and have set about the work of repayment in a secure leisure, fortified by the profits of the businesses that he would have saved. Twenty years earlier, it is at least probable that he would have taken that course. In earlier days, he had accepted loans from his friends. More than that, he had asked. There was that £4000 guarantee from Buccleuch. In fact he had borrowed money almost as lightly as he had lent it—with the difference that it had been repaid. But at those times he had been confident in himself. He must borrow, now, if at all with a different doubt. And under such circumstances a man who will drain the pockets of relatives and friends to pay his debts does not save his own honour, he only shows he has none to lose.

Scott's judgement, almost always sound, whether for himself or others, told him that there was not one chance in ten, but that he was facing his last and greatest defeat. It was at that thought that his spirits rose. For weakened in body and saddened in mind though he might be, his spirit was still that of one to whom it had seemed a natural thought that

"if the path be dangerous known,
The danger's self may lure alone."

But he saw that he must enter the arena alone. Let others sit back and watch, though it were to see nothing better than an old man's fall. A man who was old—and tired. But yet one whose courage endured: in whom the spirit of romance was young.

And having resolved in this way, he was not wholly unhappy, nor quite ashamed. For the feelings of those who face the worst fate that the world can deal are different from the terrors of those who run.

CHAPTER XCIII.

The creditors met on the 26th. Sir William Forbes was in the chair. He was the head of the largest private bank in Edinburgh, and it was very deeply involved. So, though not so heavily was the Royal Bank of Scotland. But Sir Walter, who had decided not to attend the meeting, had had a talk with two of their Directors in the morning and their attitude was agreed in advance.

Thirty years ago, Willie Forbes had captured the girl whom Scott had wooed for five years, and Scott had declined to make it a cause of quarrel between them. Now Sir William Forbes held his future in his hands in a different way—a way that would have seemed incredible even three months ago.

Mr. Gibson explained the position to the assembled creditors. Sir Walter, finding that bills which were payable to himself, and which he had placed under discount, were not being met, had been advised to assign his whole estate into the hands of trustees for the benefit of his creditors. It was open to them to agree to the deed, or to throw the estate into bankruptcy.

He explained that there was a marriage settlement, made less than twelve months ago, the effect of which was that the creditors would not be able to pay themselves by selling Abbotsford. They would be entitled to let it during Sir Walter's life. They would be entitled to collect the rents of the estate during the same period. At Sir Walter's death, it would pass absolutely to his eldest son.

Apart from the life-rents of Abbotsford, there was the house in North Castle Street, which had been Sir Walter's property for many years, and its contents. There were some shares of no very great value. There were the assets of the printing business, of which the other partner, Mr. Ballantyne, had decided that he must submit to a personal bankruptcy.

Altogether, a few thousands could be promptly realised.

But the liabilities were a very large total. There were bills which Constable had given to Sir Walter for his literary work, which had been renewed and added to, till they had reached a very large amount. There were financial bills which had provided the capital for the printing business. There were large exchanges of bills with Constable for his support and that of Hurst, Robinson & Co. There was one bill of the latter firm which was in the hands of Ballantyne & Co.'s bankers. All these bills had been discounted, and Sir Walter was liable upon them as drawer, endorser, or as a partner in the printing firm. Their total was over £100,000. (The gross total of liabilities was finally settled at £130,000, of which the partnership business of Ballantyne & Co. was responsible for £117,000, and £13,000 were Sir Walter's separate debts.)

Sir Walter's offer was to pay these debts in full. He had his official salaries, on which (or less) he was prepared to live. He thought that, in five or ten years, he could earn enough with his pen to clear every claim that could be made upon him.

As to that, he was already engaged upon a life of Napoleon, and a novel, from which he hoped that a sum would be realised sufficient to make a substantial distribution before the year closed.

Mr. Gibson having concluded his statement, a discussion followed. On the larger half of the liabilities, Constable & Co. were primarily, and on a much greater proportion they were legally, liable. Sir Walter's ultimate responsibility, and the creditors' risk of ultimate loss, would depend largely upon what Constable could pay—and that, again, would depend upon Hurst, Robinson & Co., who had not yet legally failed, and still talked of carrying on. There was a doubt here which no discussion would clear away.

There was another point for Mr. Gibson to explain. Scott had made contracts with Constable for the two books he was now writing. There would almost certainly be a claim upon these from Constable's estate. But, as the books were not yet complete, he thought that it could be resisted successfully, and he could promise them the proceeds. That was, if they accepted Sir Walter's offer. You cannot compel an author to finish writing a book.

The marriage settlement naturally came up for discussion. Being made less than a year ago, it was at least possible that it could be upset, if it could be shown that Sir Walter was actually insolvent when it was executed. If they should accept the offer now made, they might be throwing away the real prospect of payment for no more than an old man's dream.

As to that, Mr. Gibson pointed out that it might be very difficult to set up that Sir Walter was insolvent a year ago. If these bills were properly met, he would not be insolvent now. And the matter had passed out of Sir Walter's hands. He was not holding back Abbotsford from his creditors. He placed it at their disposal as long as his life should last. But, beyond that, it had become a matter for the Trustees of the Marriage Settlement, who would certainly fight in the interests of Mrs. Walter Scott. There were several trustees, including some of the most prominent men in Edinburgh. The settlement had been publicly known at the time, and no creditor had taken any motion against it. It had been entered in the Record Office, in the usual way.

Sir William Forbes, in the chair, did not encourage talk of contesting the settlement. He thought Sir Walter's offer should be accepted. The representative of the Royal Bank said the same. In the end, a resolution to that effect was passed unanimously.

Looking back, we can see that it was a wise resolution for themselves, as generosities often are. Yet, at the time, it may have worn a different face. Those who met in Edinburgh were, for the most part, Scott's personal friends, as, indeed, all Edinburgh was. Yet when large amounts are involved, and men have their own difficulties in mind, they may forget much. And this plan of paying off such a sum by future earnings had a wild sound. They all knew Sir Walter as a man of inexhaustible courage and energy, but he was obviously ageing. He had been white-haired ever since that illness of years ago. He had been seen two days back—the first time he had been out since his ruin was public talk—with Mr. Skene. He had walked slowly, leaning on the shoulder of the younger man. He might be good yet for some years at the Clerks' table in the Court of Session; but as to paying these debts—wouldn't it be better to face the inevitable with an immediate bankruptcy, and get it over? Wouldn't it be better for him?

Apart from that, if the creditors stood firm that it should be payment or bankruptcy, there might be help from many quarters and in forms that Sir Walter could not refuse. There might even be a public subscription.

Looking at the position as it then was, we may conclude that the unanimity of that resolution arose less from a balancing of selfish interests than from a common desire to do that which Sir Walter wished. Its atmosphere was reflected in the cheerful tone with which Mr. Gibson told the news when he hurried to North Castle Street at the termination of the meeting.

Scott had not stopped working during the last few days. Thirty-eight pages of *Woodstock* had been sent over to James to be set up. But he had been unable to sleep. Now he knew what was before him; and he wrote that night that he thought that he would sleep well, as he did.

His Edinburgh creditors were his friends still. But London creditors might be differently influenced, and their decisions were still to come.

The next day he drew £325 for his official salary, and asked Mr. Gibson's consent to send £200 to Abbotsford to deal with essential payments there. He enclosed it to William Laidlaw with a letter of instructions to make immediate economies, but to carry on till his Trustees should decide what was to be done.

He arranged with Charlotte that she was to have £12 a week, which must have seemed a small sum after the expenditure of recent years, and set himself resolutely to the task of filling up the financial pit that evil circumstance or his own folly had opened before his feet.

CHAPTER XCIV.

The first day of February brought a joint letter from Walter and Jane. They put Jane's fortune at Scott's disposal to use as he would. It was an almost anticipated offer, but roused him to an unusual extremity of expression. 'God Almighty forbid!' he wrote, as he recorded the intended generosity.

He was working so rapidly on the conclusion of *Woodstock* that he reckoned that he was earning for the estate at the rate of £1,000 a week, if the book should sell as well as did those that preceded it. Actually, this was to prove an underestimate. The first volume of *Napoleon* was completely printed. Conscious of these results, and in a state of some mental exhaustion from the amount of work he was doing, he felt almost indifferent when he heard that a second, more formal meeting of creditors had accepted his offered settlement.

From the balance of salary left in his hands, he sent £35 to Charles at Oxford, with a letter urging economy, which would not be disregarded. Charles was a boy you could trust. He found time to write to his nephew Walter, Tom's son, who was also on his hands, and now graduated as a lieutenant of Engineers. He wrote to William Laidlaw to come to Edinburgh to discuss the future management of Abbotsford with the Trustees. There was the question of the home farm, which he thought should be given up.

> "With our careless habits," he wrote, "it were best, I think, to risk as little as possible. Lady Scott will not exceed with ready money in her hands; but calculating on the procedure of a farm is different, and neither she nor I are capable of that minute economy. Two cows should be all we should keep. But I find Lady S. inclines much for the four. If she had her youthful activity, and could manage things, it would be well, and would amuse her. But I fear it is too late a week."

A few days later he had to face one of the practical difficulties of the assignment that he had made, and his resolution not to accept assistance from others. His nephew Walter had an appointment in Bombay, and, since he had taken charge of him at Abbotsford, he had paid all his expenses. He went to see John Gibson, and borrowed the required amount, £240, from him, to be returned in the spring. "I wish I could have got this money otherwise," he wrote, "but I must not let the orphan boy...miscarry through my fault."

Following this, there came Sir Patrick Murray, one of the Barons of the Court of Exchequer, to see him, with a proposal that he should be made a Judge of the Court of Session. The Lord Justice Clerk, and Abercromby, his friends from school days, would exert their combined interest to secure that position for him. But he declined this on several grounds. He had neglected the study of law, and was unfit; he intended to continue the writing of fiction, which he thought would be inconsistent with the dignity of such a position. Underneath this offer, he could see the conviction prevailing among his friends that he was a ruined man. The talk of paying off that huge total of debts was no more than a fantastic dream, such as might find its home in a romancer's mind. Practical friends talked among themselves of what best could be done. "I can see," he wrote, "people think me much worse off than I think myself. They may be right; but I will not be beat till I have tried a rally, and a bold one."

Yet the offer vexed his mind somewhat on the next day, on the afternoon of which William Laidlaw arrived. They went together over the wages list of Abbotsford, and struck off the names of many, keeping only 'active, young and powerful men'. He showed no mercy in this, for it was a duty to the Trustees that the estate should be made to pay, and Laidlaw must understand the new conditions of service; but he recorded a vow that night that he would 'contrive to make it easy for the sufferers'.

As it was, Laidlaw's interview with Gibson next morning was not an easy one. In fact, Abbotsford was not a proposition to be easily handled under the new circumstances. He came back to North Castle Street to report that the conditions under which he was to carry on had been arranged, but that Mr. Gibson had said that if it were anyone but Sir Walter Scott, he would have disposed of the whole affair.

Two days later, Scott had an offer from a manufacturer of patent medicine to share the profits of the invention, if he would lend it his name and blessing. He sent a polite refusal—"for what purpose can anger serve?" He also sent a further £40, from the slender balance of salary which was left in his hands, to his nephew Walter, as the £240 had proved insufficient for his passage and equipment.

There was kindness from many during these days, but little encouragement for Scott's resolute optimism. There were such 'loads of game' sent in by Mr. Scope and C. K. Sharpe that Lady Scott's gratitude 'became ungovernable' and they must be asked to dinner. They came on February 14th, just four weeks after the return to Edinburgh, and the receipt of the news of ruin which had been waiting there. They were the first visitors to be entertained since that day, and likely to be the last, for as they arrived the sale-bills were fixed to the house. Cadell had called earlier, depressed by difficulties in getting such trustees appointed for his firm's estate as would realise its assets with intelligence. The stock, like the liabilities, was very large. He foresaw the wasteful realisation that actually occurred. Scott saw that any hope he had felt that Constable's estate would substantially relieve the weight of obligations he had taken up must be abandoned. Cadell was not likely to be in very good spirits. He had been in sanctuary in Holyrood for the past week, the Royal Bank having taken process to arrest him for debt, which had only just been retired. And the total result was a day on which not a line was written. This was not only from lack of spirits; it was because Scott could not get the right idea for ending the book. He liked best to write without the harness of a settled plot: to spin a web first, and then think of a way by which it could be broken through. Now he must pause in contemplation of his own dilemma. And while he did so, James Hogg came for advice and help. He said he needed £200, which Scott was reluctantly unable to give.

CHAPTER XCV.

It was after dinner, immediately following the visit of the Ettrick Shepherd, that Mr. Gibson called on Sir Walter bringing bad news. The Royal Bank of Scotland had been considering the Marriage Settlement. They did not propose that any action should be taken to set it aside, but they thought it was the duty of Scott's Trustees, either by friendly agreement or a suit at law, to secure some modifications of its provisions, so that the estate could be handled more freely. In particular, they thought that the library, which must be worth a large sum, should be sold.

Scott listened, and said at once that he could not agree.

There were two opposite points of view here, which, considered separately, appear about equally reasonable. Scott had assigned his possessions to his creditors. What is the point or meaning of that, if they are not to be realised for their benefit? The Royal Bank felt that they had done all that could be reasonably asked in assenting to the assignment that Scott had proposed.

Their action may have been influenced by the fact that the financial position of Constable & Co. was being gradually disclosed as far worse than had been anticipated. This meant that the Bank had to face another very heavy bad debt, and it also meant that there would not be much dividend from Constable's estate for the benefit of Scott's creditors. The mood to which they had come was shown by the extremity of their recent action against Cadell.

Ultimately, the debts of Hurst, Robinson & Co. were proved at £300,000, and those of Constable & Co. at £256,000. It must not be understood that we can add £117,000 to these figures and obtain the gross liabilities of the three firms in that way as being £683,000. A creditor holding a bill with all three names upon it would claim against the three estates. Hurst, Robinson & Co. ultimately paid about £18,000 in dividends to its creditors: Constable & Co. paid £35,000 in spite of the fact that their assets were realised in a very hurried and wasteful way, probably not amounting to a quarter of their fair value. The ratios of liabilities and dividends show where the real weakness had been.

Facing such losses, the Royal Bank felt that they must do what they could for their shareholders and themselves. Scott was a lawyer, and when he signed the deed he should have expected that his library would have to go. If he wanted to retain it, let him make arrangements to buy it in.

Scott knew the law well enough. He had been prepared for the possibility of this position arising ever since he had signed the deed. He had thought already of buying in the library, if he were made bankrupt. He had good friends enough, at a pinch, to enable him to do that. But he was resolved that it should be as a bankrupt that he should do it, if at all. If he resolved upon bankruptcy, he would be free in future to use his pen as he would, or to lay it down. If he were to undertake to write off that burden of debt, he must have reasonable conditions in which to work, and the library was an essential thing.

He told Gibson to give the Royal Bank an instant ultimatum. If they took the sword of the law, he said, he would take the shield. If they thought that, being bankrupt in fact, he was afraid of the name, they would soon have something to learn.

He was willing to give up the North Castle Street house. They could sell his life-long possessions there. That was reasonable enough. But he required an assurance that his library would not be touched, or he would apply for a sequestration at once.

The next morning, Mr. Gibson discussed the position with another of the Trustees, Mr. Alexander Monypenny, who had been originally nominated by the Royal Bank. He was a stranger to Scott, they not having met until he had called at North Castle Street to introduce himself after the deed had been executed, though Scott had known his father, and subsequently some of his brothers.

Mr. Gibson came again in the evening with a somewhat better report. Mr. Monypenny had expressed himself personally as being 'decidedly in favour of the most moderate measures and taken burthen on himself for the Bank of Scotland proceeding with such leniency' as would give 'some time and opportunity to clear these affairs out'.

It was not the most explicit of surrenders, but Scott had been debating in his mind whether he had been right or wrong, and he now resolved that he ought to accept the measure of concession which Mr. Monypenny's attitude implied. He remembered that he was 'a man of perfect honour and reputation', and that he himself had 'nothing to ask which such a man would not either grant, or convince me was unreasonable'.

He went on to a very penetrating self-analysis, which the incidents of his life are sufficient to illustrate continually:

> "I have, to be sure, some of my constitutional and hereditary obstinacy; but it is in me a dormant quality. Convince my understanding, and I am perfectly docile: stir my passions by coldness or affronts, and the devil will not drive me from my purpose. Let me record, I have striven against this besetting sin. When I was a boy and on foot expeditions, as we had many, no creature could be so indifferent which way our course was directed, and I acquiesced in whatever anyone proposed; but if I was once driven to make a choice and felt piqued in honour to maintain my proposition, I have broken off from the whole party, rather than yield to anyone. Time has sobered this pertinacity of mind; but it still exists, and I must be on my guard against it."

He remembered that Alexander had at one time been in a business partnership with Colin Mackenzie, and that Colin spoke well of him. He told John Gibson that he was satisfied to rely on Mr. Monypenny's equity of decision. So the storm blew over.

CHAPTER XCVI.

At this moment, when Scott analysed so acutely the stubborn core of his outwardly pliable nature, he was to give evidence of it in an unexpected direction, and to enter the political arena for the second time, and to as victorious, though not so important, an issue as when he had reconciled his country's external and internal animosities by the device of the King's visit three or four years earlier.

The tornado of financial disaster which had swept over the country during the winter, and by which Scott himself had been ruined, had caused the Government to propose certain measures of legislation which might, at least, mitigate the severity of such calamities. It proposed, in particular that the power to issue their own notes, which had been general to English and Scottish banking houses, should be entirely removed, and that only the Bank of England should be allowed to continue a restricted circulation of notes of £5, and upwards.

The proposal may have been wise in itself, though it was something less than a radical remedy for the evils which had occasioned it, but there was a natural resentment among Scottish bankers at a measure which proposed to reduce their prestige and profits, and a wider national reluctance to assent to a financial reform which must ultimately reduce the relative importance of Edinburgh as a banking centre.

It was the latter aspect of the matter which stirred in Scott's mind the passionate resentment which was so quickly aroused by any attempt of the London Government to reduce the separate privileges of the sister-kingdom. He contributed to the *Edinburgh Weekly Journal*, which Ballantyne edited, three *Letters of Malachi Malagrowther*. These letters aroused the Scottish opposition to a point of resistance that no government could ignore. The replies which Croker wrote in the *London Courier* might be convincing to an impartial reader, but they had little effect upon the crowded meetings of protest which were being held all over Scotland, or the size of the resulting petitions which were delivered at Westminster. The Government bent to the storm, and the provisions of the bill were limited in their application to the English banks.

Scott's Journal shows that he wrote these letters with some doubt and reluctance. He reflected that he would 'offend his English friends without propitiating one man in Scotland'. It might also seem that he was 'making himself of too much importance', to attempt interference with a financial measure of this kind. He saw the humour also, on the day when John Gibson brought him the formal deed which assigned his possessions to his creditors to sign, that he, who had proved himself unable to manage his own affairs, should be taking those of Scotland into his charge.

Yet he saw other consequences as the days passed, and the excitement grew. He was before his countrymen in another aspect than that of an insolvent debtor. He knew that the popular mind cannot conceive of a man in two characters at once, and he liked the change. The Edinburgh banks were also aware of the unexpected championship, which certainly repaid them a thousandfold for any consideration which they had shown to him. They were urgent for the letters to be published in pamphlet form, ordering 500 copies in advance when it was arranged for Blackwood to do this.

But Lockhart wrote anxiously from London. The letters had greatly disturbed the Government. Scott was of their own party. Many of its members were his personal friends. They had not expected it from him. Melville was particularly incensed, forgetting a life-time's friendship in his anger. He felt the position more acutely because he was the man to whom Scotland looked to defend her national interests. That there should be such an attack upon a measure to which he had given his assent was as though he were directly accused of having sold the pass.

Scott took these things with a quiet philosophy, declining all individual quarrels, and writing personally to Croker in a way which averted any danger of a breach with one whose friendship he would have been sorry to lose. He had done that at which he aimed, and he must leave it to time to soothe any irritations that it had occasioned. He had been easily reconciled to the delay which this diversion had occasioned in the completion of *Woodstock*, because he was still watchful as to any claim being made upon it on behalf of Constable's estate, and he reflected cheerfully that while it remained unfinished the game remained in his own hands.

Lockhart had written that there were many in London, the King included, who were anxious to do something to assist him, so the talk went. Lockhart thought that interest could be made to secure an appointment as Baron of Exchequer at an early date. It was a position of which Scott had thought at times, even before this disastrous reversal of fortune came. Its duties were less onerous than those of a Clerk of Session: its dignity was much greater: it would mean an extra £1,000 a year.

But he reflected that the *Letters of Malachi* would hardly have prepared the ground favourably for such an application to be put forward, and a—stronger argument—there was Sir William Rae, who would otherwise be the natural choice for the first vacancy that would occur. He resolved that he would not allow his name to be put forward for a possible *tour de force* in London which would over-ride Sir William's natural preferment. Let things go on as they were.

CHAPTER XCVII.

By the beginning of March the position was so far clarified that it had been resolved that the family should return to Abbotsford when the Court rose.

It appeared to Scott's Trustees, as to himself, the most reasonable course to take. There could, of course, be no return to the lavish expenditure of previous days. It would be rather as caretaker than owner that he would re-enter the house of his own designing. But it is evident that such a house, which would become his son's at any moment that he should die, would not be easy to let.

If Lady Scott were willing to return—? Charlotte was quite willing for that. She was, in fact, mortally ill, which she refused to admit. She had, at this time, only twelve weeks before her of rapidly weakening life, but she carried on with the same courage, if not the same gaiety of spirit, with which she had first faced the strangeness of this cold Northern capital nearly thirty years ago. Up to now, she had deceived even Scott as to her real condition, though she can hardly have deceived herself to the same degree. He was often anxious and careful about her health, but still thought or hoped that she might live longer than he. Loyally, through these weeks of trouble, she had done her part, falling in with everything that was proposed. Now the plan was that the family should live entirely at Abbotsford. The North Castle Street house would be sold, and there would be no family migrations to Edinburgh in future, two or three times a year. Scott was to find lodgings for himself during the months when the Court was sitting.

So it was agreed, and there was packing, and turning out of many papers, and reading of old letters before they went to the final flames, and sorting of such things as might be taken to Abbotsford and saved from the sale. It was a bitter experience for Scott, who would not readily part with anything that he had once loved. He asked Charlotte about many trifles, pictures and 'trumpery' things, as he called them, that they had valued once when they had set up housekeeping together, and was secretly wounded because she always replied in the same way. Let it go. She didn't mind about that.

There had been no difficulty about money during these weeks. Now that entertaining had ceased, Charlotte had found no difficulty in paying the current expenses with the twelve pounds that had been agreed between them. Scott had spent nothing on himself since they came to Edinburgh 'save two or three guineas for charity, and six shillings for a pocket-book', and he had given Charlotte £24 on the 22nd February, for the fortnight to come.

But, when early in March it became time to arrange for the removal, there was the fact to be faced that the next quarter's salary could not be drawn before the 20th. There was a gap to be filled somehow. But the *Letters of Malachi* came in useful here. It does not appear that Scott had received anything for contributing them to the *Weekly Journal*, but there would be profit to come from the publication of the pamphlet, the first edition of which was already exhausted. Blackwood paid £25 on account, and the difficulty was over. Scott reflected cheerfully that his money troubles were fewer, and more easily resolved, than in the days when he thought of himself as a wealthy man.

It was Friday, March 11th, when the Court rose, and his inclination had been to leave as quickly as possible for Abbotsford. He had no will to stay in a house which was already disordered by removal, and the impending auction. But Charlotte said she could not go. There were still things to be done. And she was reluctant for him to go yet. "I am glad," he wrote, "that Lady Scott does not mind it, and yet, I wonder, too. She insists on my remaining till Wednesday, not knowing what I suffer."

There is pathos, of a sort, in these two, each of a different courage, concealing their own troubles, and so, after a comradeship of thirty years, only partly understanding that which the other felt.

Charlotte had been slow to believe in the reality of the financial trouble. She had believed that there was nothing that her husband was not equal to turn aside. But she had faced it bravely when she had realised that it was something that could not be averted by an effort of will, or a brave word. She had her own trouble, which she had been trying, with an equal futility, to put aside in the same way. But she had been persuaded or had resolved, that she would face it before she left Edinburgh. She would see Dr. Abercrombie, who could be trusted to tell her the truth—or as near to that as a doctor will.

So Scott spent Sunday in a last sorting and packing of papers, which brought on the painful heart attacks of which he did not make overmuch, having being assured that they were nervous only; on Tuesday he had James to see him, to talk of proofs and take leave; and then he went out to say goodbye to Constable and Cadell, and walked up Princes Street with Mrs. Skene, whom he happened to meet, and went home feeling better in mind and body, and finished reading *Pride and Prejudice* for the third time, and reflected that Jane Austin had an art which he could never reach.

The next morning he went back to Abbotsford. He travelled with Mrs. Mackay, the housekeeper, and one of the maids, for Charlotte said that she had still matters that must have attention before she left, and she would follow him on Sunday and till then she would keep Anne for company. But his spirits rose again as he approached the place that he had made to be what it was, and was met by 'the tumult, great of men and dogs, all happy to see me'.

He spent the next day pleasantly enough, out walking in fine spring weather from one to four, calling on the ladies at Huntley Burn, and going through the plantations with Tom Purdie. Disaster had brought a congenial change of duties to Tom, for he was no longer to be responsible for the farm. He was to give his whole time, with a lessened staff, to the plantations, where, as was the case with his master, his strongest affections lay. What was to be kept of the farm was to be in the gardener's charge. If there were only three pages of *Woodstock* to be sent off to James in the morning, there was no need to worry about that, for, in the ease and quiet of an Abbotsford to which no visitors would be likely to come, that could easily be finished, and much progress could be made with the *Napoleon*, before it should be necessary to go back to Edinburgh.

But the 'ease and quiet' were broken when the post came. There were letters from Lockhart and Sophia to say, that John Hugh's illness had developed into a difficulty in walking. There were symptoms that the spine was affected, and he was visibly weaker. This contrasted with a cheerful letter which had said he was better only a week before. Sophia had taken him to Brighton, where Lockhart would join her at week-ends. But what hope was there in that?

> "The bitterness of this probably impending calamity is extreme. The child was almost too good for this world; beautiful in features; and though spoiled by every one, having one of the sweetest tempers as well as the quickest intellect I ever saw; a sense of humour quite extraordinary in a child, and, owing to the general notice which was taken of him, a great deal more information than suited his years.... The poor dear love had so often a slow fever, that when it pressed its little lips to mine, I always foreboded to my own heart what all I fear are now aware of."

He slept badly that night, having dreams of the sick child. It was a quality of his constitution that he did not dream at all unless he dreamt ill. If health were good and circumstances propitious, he would sleep placidly all the night to wake with an imagination that was active and clear, so that, by the time he had dressed in a leisurely way, the day's work of the mind was done, and there was only the slower toil of the pen to follow. But in times of trouble he would be vexed by evil dreams of a vivid quality, in which old griefs would return. He sat in his study without the heart to go out in the usual way, but Tom lingered outside the window, with their two axes in hand, and lured him forth at last, and they cut palings together. Tomorrow Charlotte and Anne would come. But Sunday morning brought a letter from Anne. Her mother had seen a doctor, and had been told that she was more seriously ill than she had supposed. There was talk of a new remedy being tried, and they stayed till Wednesday. 'A new affliction,' Scott wrote that night, 'where there was enough before; yet her constitution is so good that if she will be guided by advice, things may yet be ameliorated. God grant it! for really these misfortunes come too close....'

But the next letter from Anne was in a more cheerful tone, and when they arrived back on Wednesday evening, in time for dinner, Charlotte seemed better than he had feared to see her. It was, in fact, Anne who looked ill. 'On the whole,' Scott wrote that night, 'things are better than my gloomy apprehensions had anticipated.'

For Charlotte had been much her old animated self, and he had exciting news for her arrival. There was a letter from Lord Downshire's lawyer, saying that he believed that there were funds in Chancery belonging to Lady Scott, or her deceased brother, which might be recovered if proper instructions were given; and he must promise that he would write about it tomorrow. Charlotte had been advised to take digitalis—a remedy for many ills in the early part of the nineteenth century—and believed that she was already better in consequence. So he slept well that night, and made good progress with *Woodstock* next morning, and had a long vigorous walk in the afternoon, and wrote Mr. Handley, the London lawyer; and when Mr. Gibson came to Abbotsford unexpectedly, a week later, through a country whitened with unseasonable snow, and bringing colder news that neither Constable's nor Hurst's were likely to pay any considerable dividend, he was able to take the news indifferently, for *Woodstock* was finished at last.

If Hurst and Constable were likely to do little to discharge that gross total of half-million of debt, there was the more cause to show that the assignment that Sir Walter Scott had executed was not equally illusory. The convincing evidence would be the sale of *Woodstock* at a good price. It was arranged that Mr Gibson should go on to London at once, to dispose of the copyright. If Hurst, Robinson & Co. were in a position to handle the book, and could find cash to pay for it, they were to have the first chance; otherwise it must go elsewhere.

Mr. Gibson, looking frail, and complaining of the bitter weather, went southward by the London coach. Scott wrote, in his Journal:

> "It is being too confident to hope to insure success in the long series of successive struggles which lie before me. But somehow I do fully entertain the hope of doing a good deal.—
> He walked and wrote, poor soul, what then?
> Why then he wrote and walked again."

CHAPTER XCVIII.

It was March 30th when Mr. Gibson took the London coach, and with such eagerness was the privilege of being Scott's future publisher sought, and with such celerity was the bargain made, that letters were at Abbotsford within five days, both from Gibson and James, announcing that *Woodstock* was sold. The bargain included the printing of the first edition, and was for a total price of £8,228. It was, as Scott noted, an extraordinary amount to be realised by three months' work, and he pushed forward the *Napoleon* with a strengthened hope. Another such bargain, and there would be no small reduction in that total of liabilities which confronted him. Perhaps, in four or five years....

Thinking of that successful sale, it was easier to forget the day when he had ceased work because the page would not keep steady before his eyes, and the one when the pain in his back had rendered one position intolerable....

They would have been quiet, busy, happy spring days after the snow went, with still a month before there must be a lonely return to Edinburgh, but for a growing anxiety as to Charlotte's health. Every day it became more difficult to maintain the fiction that she was not worse, though both she and Scott appear to have been stubborn in their determination to do it.

With the admission of illness which her reluctant visit to Dr. Abercombie had made, she had relaxed sufficiently not to get up till midday, and the quietness of Abbotsford, to which no visitors now came, except a few intimate neighbouring friends, must have been beneficial.

On April 13th the Journal records that she 'seems to make no way, yet can scarcely be said to lose any'. The next day Scott went to a friend's funeral at Kelso, and after that the course of events may be best told by the following abstracts:

> "*Apl.19th.* Returned last night from the house of death and mourning to my own, now the habitation of sickness and anxious apprehension. Found Lady S. had tried the foxglove in quantity, till it made her so sick she was forced to desist. The result cannot yet be judged. Wrote to Mrs. Thomas Scott to beg her to let her daughter, Anne an uncommonly sensible, steady and sweet-tempered girl, come and stay with us a season in our distress, who I trust will come forthwith .
>
> Two melancholy things. Last night I left my pallet in our family apartment, to make way for a female attendant, and removed to a dressing-room adjoining, when to return, or whether ever, God only can tell. Also, my servant cut my hair, which used to be poor Charlotte's personal task. I hope she will not observe it.
>
> *Apl. 20th.* Lady Scott's health in the same harassing state of uncertainty. Yet on my side with more of hope than I had two days since.
>
> *Apl. 21st.* This day I entertained more flattering hopes of Lady Scott's health than late events permitted. I went down to Mertoun.... Had the grief to find that Lady Scott had insisted on coming downstairs, and was the worse for it. Also a letter from Lockhart giving a poor account of the infant. God help us! earth cannot.
>
> *Apl. 22nd.* Lady Scott continues very poorly. Better news of the child.

Apl. 23rd. Lady Scott is certainly better, and has promised not to attempt quitting her room.

Apl 25th. Lady Scott was better yesterday, certainly better, and was sound asleep when I looked in this morning.

Apl. 26th. Lady Scott continues better, so the clouds are breaking up.

Apl. 27th. Lady Scott continues better, and, we may hope, has got the turn of her disease.

Apl. 28th. Found Lady Scott obviously better, I think, than I had left her in the morning."

So, as April ended, hope rose. And, apart from Charlotte's illness, things were going well enough. An article on Pepys for the *Quarterly* had brought a draft for £100 from its new editor, which was an important addition to the quarter's income. Lockhart's first number of the review occasioned a shrewd note in the Journal, which he must have read subsequently, though it did him no good:

"No man can take more general and liberal views of literature that J.G.L. But he lets himself too easily into the advocatism of style, which is that of a pleader, not a judge or critic, and is particularly unsatisfactory to the reader."

But Lockhart was not seeking advice, which he felt himself more competent to give. A fortnight later there is this entry:

"J.G.L. kindly points out some solecisms in my style, as 'amid' for 'amidst', 'scarce' for 'scarcely'. 'Whose' he says, is the proper genitive for 'which' only at such times as 'which' retains its quality of impersonification. Well! I will try to remember all this, but after all I write grammar as I speak, to make my meaning known, and a solecism in point of composition, like a Scotch word in speaking is indifferent to me."

Lockhart could not easily understand the self-confidence that did not seek a guiding authority, nor the stability which was unperturbed by his strictures. It might have seemed a strange idea to him that what Scott wrote today would be likely to be right tomorrow....

The news of *Woodstock* was good. The money it had realised was a tribute to Scott's past popularity rather than its own merits; if it should encounter public coldness or critical hostility, the payment might be the last of its kind. But it was received well; its sales, if not phenomenal, were satisfactory, even by the high standards of the past. Its success offset the news that, after many delays, and much talk of reconstruction, Hurst, Robinson & Co. had definitely given up the fight. It was news for which Scott was quite prepared, and to which he had become almost indifferent; but, for Constable, it was the end of a last hope. He had finally quarrelled with Cadell, and they were both trying to re-establish themselves in separate businesses, without much support either of capital or credit, and both hoping that some arrangement might be made with Scott which would enable them to publish for him again. If he should trust either in future, Scott was disposed to prefer the younger man. As to Constable, he pondered whether, or how much, he knew of the real weakness of Hurst, Robinson & Co. when he had drawn him into giving the support during the last fatal weeks which had added so greatly to the liabilities which he was now striving to repay—even how much he might have known or guessed earlier in the year, when he was renewing and exchanging bills with the printing business in ways by which so much of this same liability had been created? It was a question to which no certain answer could be given then: to which no certain answer can be given now. Lockhart answered it with confidence, in words of sweeping contemptuous condemnation. We may prefer those of

Scott, who had been ruined by that confidence, and who had the better right to be bitter. He wrote:

> "Constable is sorely broken down.
> 'Poor fool and knave, I have one part in my heart
> That's sorry yet for thee.'
> His conduct has not been what I deserved at his hand, but I believe that, walking blindly himself, he misled me without *malice prepense*. It is best to think so at least, unless the contrary be demonstrated. To nourish angry passions against a man whom I really liked would be to lay a blister on my own heart."

CHAPTER XCIX.

May came, with only ten days remaining before Scott must return to Edinburgh. The *Napoleon* had made good progress since *Woodstock* was finished, and as he walked among plantations to which the new leaves came he hardened his heart to the resolution that he would yet win them back to his own possession.

But it was becoming increasingly difficult to maintain the fiction that Charlotte was better than the day before. The Journal reads from this date:

> "*May 1st*. My Cousin, Barbara Scott of Raeburn, came here to see L.S. I think she was shocked with the melancholy change. She insisted on walking back to Lessudden House, making her walk 16 or 18 miles, and though the carriage was ordered she would not enter it.
> *May 2nd*. I wrote and read for three hours, and then walked, the day being soft and delightful; but alas! all my walks are lonely from the absence of my poor companion. She does not suffer, thank God, but strength must fail at last. Since Sunday, there has been

a gradual change—very gradual—but, alas! for the worse. My hopes are almost gone.

May 3*rd*. Mr. Handley has actually discovered the fund due to Lady Scott's mother, £1,200...at a happier moment, the news would have given poor Charlotte much pleasure, but now—it is a day too late.

May 4*th*. On visiting Lady Scott's sickroom this morning I found her suffering, and I doubt if she knew me. Yet, after breakfast, she seemed serene and composed. The worst is, she will not speak out about the symptoms under which she labours.

May 6*th*. The same scene of hopeless (almost) and unavailing anxiety. Still welcoming me with a smile, and asserting she is better.

May 10*th*. Tomorrow I leave my home. To what scene I may suddenly be recalled, it wrings my heart to think.

May 11*th* (Edinburgh). Charlotte was unable to take leave of me being in a sound sleep, after a very indifferent night. Perhaps it was as well—an adieu might have hurt her; and nothing I could have expressed would have been worth the risk...."

So these two parted, without leavetaking, who had met, thirty years before, from such different beginnings, on the hills of Westmorland.

For the first time in his life, Scott entered an Edinburgh in which he had no home. At first, when he saw that the house in North Castle Street must be given up, he had thought of taking rooms at a club. Then the Skenes had offered him hospitality. But he had refused that, because his necessity was not of a season, but would be, as he supposed, of a permanent kind. The days when the family had migrated three times a year between Abbotsford and Edinburgh, with a retinue of servants, horses and other domestic animals, were over for ever. He wanted no more now than rooms where he could have his books, and the quiet that would be needed for uninterrupted work. He took lodgings with a Mrs. Brown, 6, North St. David Street, while the bills TO SELL still hung in the empty North Castle Street windows, for the tide of fashion had moved westward since Charlotte and he had taken it a quarter of a century earlier, and it had become a house for which it would not be easy to find a buyer.

Scott would rather have spent the afternoon quietly when he arrived in Edinburgh. He was in a mood to be alone with his thoughts. But James had asked him to dine with him *en famille*, and the invitation, kindly meant, could not easily be refused. James's home had been sold up like his own, and he had removed himself and his growing family to a small house in the suburbs. The printing works were being carried on by the Trustees now, and James was manager at a salary which he must make sufficient for his reduced establishment. His fortunes were still linked to those of Scott, for the printing of *Woodstock* and *Napoleon* had been keeping the works busy, and Scott's practice of having the pages set up as he wrote them made it practically obligatory upon any publisher who took the copyright of a book to take the printed volumes from the same source.

So Scott wrote up his Journal when he arrived, with the record of that parting that sleep had hindered, and added his resolution to keep the engagement, let his feelings be what they might. "I will not yield to the barren sense of helplessness which struggles to invade me."

And when he came back he had his reward in being able to write: "I passed a pleasant day with honest J.B., which was a great relief from the black dog which would have worried me at home. We were quite alone."

The rooms did not seem to be bad of their kind. The people were 'civil' and apparently attentive.... But that was a minor matter, for Scott was supplying his own service. He brought a maidservant, and the butler, Dalgleish, who had been on the list of those who were to go, but had refused his dismissal, protesting that he would stay at whatever wages or none. So Scott was not without service of a faithful kind; but in his own spirit he was as lonely as when he lay beneath the storm, a laughing baby in the heather of Sandy-Knowe, though he would not laugh at the lightning now.... He had been two days in Edinburgh when there came a letter to say that Charlotte was dead....

There has been previous occasion to remark a disposition on the part of Scott's biographers to do less than justice to Charlotte Charpentier, and, in particular, to represent her as the makeshift substitute for the ideal partner whom Scott had loved, but had failed to win.

There is a common shallowness of judgement which will always idealise the frustrated in contrast to the consummated attraction. Either might in theory contain the greater potentialities of passion, of sympathy, or of understanding; but the fact that the one should fail through the impulse on either side being unequal to the conquest of circumstance, or the power of subjecting the other, is argument, though less than proof, of its comparative deficiency.

That which would follow the fruition of the first attraction can be a surmise only: that which follows the second is a tested thing. And in the case of Walter Scott and Charlotte Charpentier it was one that endures inspection, and defies criticism. Charlotte married a man of alien race, and widely different interests from her own: he was a dreamer and a poet. Neither the individual nor the institution of marriage can be subjected to many severer tests. It was a marriage which did nothing to obstruct, but obviously fostered the development of his own genius. It brought many years of happiness to these two who gave each other a most loyal and unswerving love.

Even the differences of their interests may be exaggerated, for they were both lovers of the open air, and of country life: they were alike in love of order, and in generosity of disposition. They were alike in love of the home they had united to form, and the children it brought; and whether in the town house, the Lasswade cottage, or the country mansion, Charlotte proved herself equal to the exceptional requirements of the partnership into which she had entered.

As to Scott's own feelings, they are best shown by a few further abstracts from his Journal during the fortnight following the news of his wife's death:

> "(*Abbotsford*) *May 16th*. When I contrast what this place now is with what it has been long since, I think my heart will break. Lonely, aged, deprived of my family—all but poor Anne—an impoverished and embarrassed man, I am deprived of the sharer of my thoughts and counsels, who could always talk down my sense of the calamitous apprehensions which break the heart that must bear them alone.... I wonder how I shall do with the large portion of thoughts which were hers for thirty years. I suspect that they will be hers yet, for a long time at least.
>
> *May 17th.* Yet would I not at this moment renounce the mysterious yet certain hope that I shall see her in a better world, for all that the world can give me...I remember the last sight of her, she raised herself in bed, and tried to turn her eyes after me, and said, with a sort of smile, "You all have such melancholy faces." They were the last words I ever heard her utter, and I hurried away, for she did not seem quite conscious of what she said. When I returned, immediately before departing, she was in a deep sleep. It is deeper now. This was but seven days since.
>
> *May 23rd.* ..... It seems still as if this could not be really so. But it is so—and duty to God and my children must teach me patience.
>
> *May 24th.* Slept wretchedly, or rather waked wretchedly all night, and was very sick and bilious in consequence, and scarce able to hold up my head with pain. A walk, however, with my sons, did a great deal of good; indeed, their society is the greatest support the world can afford me. Their ideas of everything are

so just and honourable, kind toward their sisters, and affectionate to me, that I must be grateful to God for sparing them to me, and continue to battle with the world for their sakes, if not for my own.

May 26th. I will go to town on Monday, and resume my labours.... Were an enemy coming upon my house, would I not do my best to fight, although oppressed in spirits, and shall a similar despondency prevent me from mental exertion? It shall not, by Heaven!...I cared not to carry my own gloom to the girls, and so sat in my own room, dawdling with old papers, which awakened as many stings as if they had been the nest of fifty scorpions. Then the solitude seemed so absolute—my poor Charlotte would have been in that room a score of times to see if the fire burned, and to ask a hundred kind questions.

Well, that is over—and if it cannot be forgotten, must be remembered with patience.

May 27th. A sleepless night. It is time I should be up and be doing, and a sleepless night sometimes furnishes good ideas. Alas! I have no companion now with whom I can communicate to relieve the loneliness of these watches of the night. But I must not fail myself and my family—and the necessity of exertion becomes apparent.

May 29th. Today I leave for Edinburgh this house of sorrow.

Edinburgh. May 30th. This has been a melancholy day, most melancholy. I am afraid poor Charles found me weeping. I do not know what other folks feel, but with me the hysterical passion that implies tears is of terrible violence—a sort of throttling sensation—then succeeded by a state of dreaming stupidity, in which I ask if my poor Charlotte can actually be dead. I think I feel my loss more than at the first blow.

> *May 31st.* The melancholy hours of yesterday must not return. To encourage that dreamy state of incapacity is to resign all authority over the mind, well I have been wont to say—
>
> "My mind to me a kingdom is."
>
> I am rightful monarch, and, God to aid, I will not be dethroned by any rebellious passion that may rear its standard against me.... Wrote this morning a memorial on the Claims which Constable's people prefer as to the copyrights of *Woodstock* and *Napoleon*."

The news of their mother's death had brought Walter and Charles, from Dublin and Oxford, to their father's side. Sophia, with a second child only just born, was unable to come. In view of her condition, Violet Lockhart, with a doubtful wisdom, had concealed the fact of her mother's illness from her, until the news of the death made it unavoidable to disclose the truth. Under the circumstances, Lockhart felt that his place was at his wife's side.

Anne's health had given way after her mother's death. Long fainting-fits before, and at the funeral, had added to the trouble of the household. Her cousin Anne, who had come to help in nursing her mother, was now to stay at Abbotsford for the time as a companion for her. The boys went back to their respective duties. Scott settled down to work in his Edinburgh lodging.

While he worked on *Napoleon* he had to deal with the half-anticipated legal difficulty over the copyrights which had first been sold to Constable & Co. That had been the first call to battle which had enabled him to resist the lethargy of grief, as the above-quoted abstract from the diary shows.

It was a legal point of great importance to Scott and his creditors, for if he could establish his contention that the copyrights were still his, the sale of *Woodstock* and the various amounts which had been realised from his other assets, including the contents of the North Castle Street house, and the debts due to James Ballantyne & Co., were now sufficient, Mr. Gibson calculated, to pay a first dividend of 6/- in the £, with the aid of another substantial sum to come when *Napoleon* should be finished. It made the prospect of paying off the huge total seem an almost possible thing—but if the proceeds of *Woodstock* were to go to Constable's creditors, from which only a fraction would be returned for Scott's own claims on that estate—and if the proceeds of *Napoleon* were to go by the same road—then the result of the year's work might be little better than a vain beating of the air. And the Napoleon was proving an immense labour. It had grown far beyond the scope of the ideas of either Constable or himself when they had held confident counsel together less than a year ago. It moved forward—even rapidly. Its bulk grew. More slowly, the years of *Napoleon's* life advanced, until he was now upon 'the victorious chess-board of Italy'. But as it advanced, its end seemed further away. The labour of its production, the price at which it could be published, the probable profits, were continually increasing estimates. Scott had been rightly determined that if he completed this book for the payment of the avalanche of liabilities which had descended upon him, it should be his own creditors, rather than those of Constable & Co., who should reap the benefit. When he shook himself free for a moment from the lethargy of grief, his first thought had been to prepare a statement of the case as he saw it to be, and though, when the time came a few days later for a conference on the subject with the Trustees, he records that he had been so distracted by other thoughts that he would probably have overlooked the appointment had not Gibson sent a note of reminder, yet he may not have been found wanting when the moment came, for his record is that he left the legal gentlemen confident in the strength of the case he put before them:

> "I think I know how our profession speak when sincere. I cannot interest myself deeply in it. When I had come home from such a business I used to carry

the news to poor Charlotte, who dressed her face in sadness or mirth as she saw the news affect me.... I passed a piper in the street as I went, and could not help giving him a shilling to play *Pibroch a Donuil Dhu* for luck's sake—what a child I am!"

For the next fortnight he worked as perhaps even he had never worked before, in the effort to win self-control, if not forgetfulness, and with the urge of the stubborn resolution which he had formed before this grief had clouded his mind. "My head aches," he recorded once, as he laid down the pen, "my eyes ache—my back aches—so does my breast—and I am sure my heart aches, and what can Duty ask more?" And when, on the 17th of June, he left to face a long week-end at Abbotsford, the third volume of *Napoleon* was complete.

The two Annes met him at Torsonce, giving a pleasant surprise, and when he had hardened his resolution to re-occupy his now-empty room, and walked next morning through the summer woods which owed their being to him, the old fighting spirit gathered strength again.

"The young woods," he wrote, "are rising in a kind of profusion I never saw elsewhere. Let me once clear off these encumbrances, and they shall wave broader and deeper yet. But to attain this I must work.... Wrought very fair accordingly...."

He 'wrought very fair' indeed, for he went back to Edinburgh five days later carrying with him a hundred pages of a new tale, and by the end of the month the deathless spirit of adventure was reawakened, and a new plot of anonymity was commenced.

James Ballantyne and Robert Cadell came to dinner together at Mrs. Brown's apartments, and though we have Dalgleish's evidence that Scott lived an abstemious life at this time, it is recorded in his own Journal that the evening saw the disappearance of one bottle of champagne, one of claret, and a glass or two of port among the three, with a glass each of whisky-toddy to complete the conviviality.

But it was primarily a business conference. Under the circumstances under which insolvent printer, insolvent publisher, and insolvent author met, it might be called a council of war.

The bargain made was this. Scott was to write a series of Tales which he was to send to Cadell, who would publish them anonymously under the title of *Canongate Chronicles*, or the *Canongate Miscellany*. Cadell was to employ the Ballantyne works to do the printing, and was to pay all charges thereon. He was to make Scott a cash advance of £500 upon this work, half of which was to be paid in time to return the money which Scott had borrowed from Gibson to equip his nephew for India when it should fall due in the autumn. Scott promised, in view of the responsibility that Cadell was taking, that, if the publication fell unregarded from the press, some steps—presumably leading to his admission of authorship—should be taken to call public attention to it.

But having made this bargain, he turned back to *Napoleon*, which must be his main occupation till it should be finished. He would complete the fourth volume, and then have a change with the Canongate book. He worked to such purpose that the fourth volume was finished by the middle of August, by which time he was back at Abbotsford, with Charles, and Walter and Jane, and Jane's mother come to increase the diminished family circle, to which no strangers intruded now. But he did not turn to the *Canongate Chronicles* then, for his mind was full of the Treaty of Amiens, and the fifth volume of *Napoleon* was commenced as the fourth was ended.

Youth asserted itself around him, as it always must, and there was music again in the large half-empty rooms, and he looked on, and was happy for his children, and sad for the vacant place which they could forget more easily than he. And they drove out to Drumlanrig, and climbed the Yarrow, and ascended the Birkhill path, where there was a good road; but there was an old woman in a herdsman's cottage who remembered how he had crossed the hills and bogs twice with Charlotte in a wheeled carriage, long ago, when there had been no road at all. And he knew it was true, "but, on my soul, looking where we must have gone, I could hardly believe I had been such a fool. For riding, pass if you will; but to put one's neck in such a venture with a wheeled-carriage was too silly."

The summer months, with summer hours spent in the open air, in a quieter social atmosphere than Abbotsford had provided in previous seasons, and with many short expeditions among neighbouring friends, was not without its hours of quiet happiness, and the freedom from invading guests enabled work to proceed to the limit of the daily 'task' of pages which he had set himself, to be a constant yoke while his health should endure it.

There was no trouble from the outer world, except that Mr. Gibson wrote in some anxiety respecting the Constable claim. It had been agreed to submit it to arbitration, and it appeared that (at least as far as the proceeds of *Woodstock* were concerned), the Arbitrator did not consider it quite as simple a case as it had been hoped that he would be disposed to do. Also, there had been a disconcerting hint of caution in reference to a project which Scott had formed of visiting London later in the year. There was a firm of money-lenders, there, Abud & Sons, creditors of Hurst, Robinson & Co., who held Ballantyne bills for £1,500, and who had not agreed to the deed. It might not be wise to venture into England while that matter stood as it did.

Napoleon had advanced very rapidly during these months. James had said that seven volumes would be necessary—had even suggested that it looked as though it would mean eight in the end, of which Scott was not willing to think. After all, he had passed Jena now. Napoleon was at the height of his power. There might be less space needed for his closing years.

And there had been some progress with the *Chronicles,* too; though Scott had, at times, a shrewd doubt as to whether he could write fiction now with the old vivacity of imagination. But that was not sufficient cause to avoid the attempt. 'In literature,' he reflected stoutly, 'as in love, courage is half the battle.'

So the long vacation drew to its end, and it was agreed that Anne should come back to Edinburgh with him, for cousin Anne had left, called away by another illness, and it would be best for both that they should be together now. So Anne and Jane and Mrs. Jobson went to Edinburgh to find suitable accommodation. Mrs. Brown's lodging had been accepted cheerfully. Even the secrecy of the Journal contained no grumble against it, till the day had come when it could be left. Then there was a hint that it had been no better than a dirty hole. Where-ever Scott went in the autumn, he did not mean to return there.

And then, early in the autumn, the difficulty about going to London was cleared away. Abud & Sons, though they still sat on the fence, and would not agree to the deed, had written that they would take no hostile steps for four or five weeks, if Sir Walter wished to visit England for such a period. And Longmans (Mr. Gibson wrote) had offered £10,500 for the *Napoleon*. It was a magnificent sum, showing there had been no rashness of optimism in Constable's earlier estimate that it would be worth £10,000. And the fifth volume was finished now.

Also, Cadell sent the second instalment of the £500 deposit which he had agreed to pay on the *Canongate Chronicles*. It was in English bills and money, such as would provide conveniently for the journey.

Everything pointed southward. Scott had come to a point in the *Napoleon* at which it was important to obtain sight of many State and other records which would be available there. But he was curiously reluctant to go. He was clearly in an overworked condition which could continue at its regular task, but could not easily rouse or reconcile itself to a different effort.

> "I am downhearted," he wrote, "at leaving all my things, after I was quietly settled; it is a kind of disrooting that recalls a thousand painful ideas of former happier journeys."

And the effort showed that there was no margin of safety in the degree of health which had left his Journal clear of any record of illness during the summer months. He wrote on the next day:

> *Oct. 11th.* We are ingenious self-tormentors. This journey annoys me more than anything of the kind in my life. My wife's figure seems to stand before me, and her voice is in my ears—"Scott, do not go." It half frightens me. Strong throbbing at my heart, and a disposition to be very sick. It is just the effect of many feelings which have been lulled asleep by the uniformity of my life, but which awaken on any new subject of agitation. Poor, poor Charlotte! I cannot daub it further. I get incapable of arranging my papers too. I will go out for half-an-hour. God relieve me!
>
> "I quelled this *hysteria passio* by pushing a walk toward Kaeside and back again...."

But the fluctuations of mood, the moments of weakness, which the Journal showed, were seldom allowed to become apparent to those around him, and still less often to deflect the course which courage or judgement willed him to take. He returned from the walk still suffering from the confusion of mind that disabled him from finding or arranging the papers which he must sort before he could leave for such a journey. So he gave it up at last, and went out to a parting dinner with some neighbours at Kippielaw. But the next day's entry is short and definite.

> "*Oct. 12th.* Reduced my rebellious papers to order. Set out after breakfast, and reached Carlisle at eight o'clock at night."

CHAPTER C.

The next six weeks were spent in London and Paris, with Anne for company. It was a journey fruitful in its immediate object. The Government offered free access to the state-papers of the Foreign Office: statesmen and soldiers offered their diaries: the Duke of Wellington promised a regular correspondence: much material was obtained in Paris by enquiry and conversation.

Socially, it enabled many old acquaintances to be renewed, and some new ones made. The Morritts were visited at Rokeby on the way to London, which was approached through Grantham and Biggleswade. Tom Moore, Rogers, Joanna Baillie, Allan Cunningham, Sir Thomas Lawrence, the Duke of Wellington, Lord Melville, the old friend of Charlotte's family, M. Dumergue, and a hundred others of public repute or private friendships welcomed and entertained them.

There was an invitation from the King to spend an afternoon with him at Windsor at the Forest Lodge, and Scott contrived to record the real kindness of a man so naturally uncongenial with a discretion which is free from insincerity. "I am sure," he wrote, "such a man is fitter for us than one who would long to head armies, or be perpetually intermeddling with *la grande politique*."

There was an 'April-weather' meeting with Sophia, whom he had not seen since she had left for London a year ago, when her mother had been alive, and he had just returned, at the height of an apparent prosperity, from the tumultuous reception of his Irish visit. There was John Hugh, little better or worse, 'looking well, though the poor dear child is kept always in a prostrate position;' and there was a gathering of the most eminent physicians, apparently by Scott's energetic interposition, around his couch, with no better result than that they agreed, with a learned solemnity, that there might be something wrong with his spine which could not be cured, but it was more likely that it could, though they didn't say how, except that sea or country air was better than that of the town.

And there was a visit to Daniel Terry, and the Adelphi Theatre, which, it will be remembered, Scott's guarantee had enabled him to acquire. And they went to the play there, and had the pleasure of seeing a crowded house, by which it might be thought that Daniel was doing well. But the theatre was badly ventilated, and the heat so great that Anne, who was very subject to fainting, was taken ill, and had to be carried into Daniel's house, which was contrived in a little space at the rear of the theatre 'like a squirrel's cage'.

And in Paris, besides the King, and a hundred French celebrities, Scott met the American author, Fennimore Cooper, who proposed a plan by which (he thought) the piracy of Scott's works in the United States might be circumvented by registering them as the property of an American citizen. Nothing came of that; but Scott, who liked and admired Cooper, wrote of him that night: "This man, who has shown so much genius, has a good deal of the manner, or want of manner, peculiar to his countrymen." And the Journal came to be published at last, and 'manners' was printed for 'manner', and it was supposed that Scott had made a reflection on the American people of that time which he did not imply.

Apart from the direct object of the expedition, and the pleasure which Anne took in such a holiday, it had a direct result in a promise from Sir Thomas Knighton, on the King's behalf, that a post should be found for Charles in the Diplomatic Service, which was good news to give, when they returned through Oxford, and Charles was able to entertain his father and sister in his college rooms.

Also, there had been some talk with French publishers in Paris about selling the translation rights of *Napoleon*, but there was not much in that, for the price proposed was no more than a hundred guineas, and even that was checked by a suggestion that this right had been sold already, though it was not clear who could have done it, unless it had been Constable & Co. at an earlier date.

So they came back by Cheltenham, where they saw Mrs. Thomas Scott, and then through the industrial Midland district, stopping at Birmingham and Manchester, and hearing dismal prophesies of the miseries and disorders that the coming winter would be likely to bring.

It was three in the morning when they got home, for they had been faced by heavy snow after leaving Manchester, and had made a forced march of the remainder of the way, taking 'two pairs of horses over the Shap Fells...and by dint of exertion reaching Penrith to breakfast'. Then they drove on till they found their own horses at Hawick, and so completed the journey, which the snow might have blocked by a later day.

It had been an expensive expedition. Of the £200 with which Scott had set out, he could count only £8 in his purse when he alighted at Abbotsford. He noted against this loss of money that he had gained:

> "in health, spirits, in a new stock of ideas, new combinations, and new views. My self-consequence is raised, I hope not unduly, by the many flattering circumstances attending my reception in the two capitals, and I feel confident in proportion. In Scotland I shall find time for labour and for economy."

There could be no pausing at Abbotsford. His duty lay at the Court of Session, from which he had been absent too long already. He spent the day of arrival packing a load of books which were to be carted to Edinburgh, and reflecting that the home of his building was still best to his own mind. "I have seen in my travels none I liked so well." And the next morning, after breakfast, they set out again, and though there was delay at Fushie Bridge, where all the horses had gone to the smithy to be rough shod, they got into town about eight, and drove to No. 3, Walker Street, a furnished house which had been taken for them, and which Walter and Jane, who were staying with Mrs. Jobson in Edinburgh, had made ready for their reception.

CHAPTER CI.

The record of the next seven months—until the midsummer of 1827—is one of concentration upon the *Napoleon*, for which other work was almost entirely laid aside, and a continual struggle against ill-health. Scott had a constitution which required, and was accustomed to, exercise, and his physical infirmities were increased at this time by severe attacks of rheumatism, which settled most obstinately in the knee of his sounder leg....

It was recognised in January that the *Napoleon* could not easily be compressed into seven volumes, and an eighth was added, with Longmans' assent. The effect of this, and of a bold decision to increase the quantity of the first edition, was that the author's immediate return was increased to a total of £18,000. Lockhart estimates that, with £8,000 from *Woodstock* and a valuation of £1,000 upon the portion of *Canongate Chronicles* written during the year, that Scott had earned by his pen a total of £28,000 within eighteen months. There is some inaccuracy here, as a proportion of this sum was for the manufacture of the books themselves, but the substantial result remains, and is a sufficient cause for wonder if all its circumstances be considered. His private expenditure was supplied during this period by a resolution of the Trustees to refund him the cost of travelling to secure materials for the biography. It is characteristic that, during the last days of completing this book, a new project was undertaken. The last words of *Napoleon* were written on June 10th. It had been on May 24th. that 'a good thought came into my head'. A week later he was discussing with Cadell the financial basis on which a series of historical tales for children might be produced, and on June 7th, he had fixed up a contract with him by which he was to receive £787. 10. 0 upon the first 10,000 copies of these *Tales of a Grandfather*.

But the record of this period is best given in the form of some brief abstracts from the Journal. It should be understood that the 'pages' of work to which allusion is sometimes made were large close-written sheets, each equal to several pages of a printed book.

>Dec. 17th. This was a day of labour, agreeably varied by a pain which rendered it scarcely possible to sit up.
>
>Dec. 18th. Almost sick with pain, and it stops everything.
>
>Dec. 21st. In the house till two o'clock nearly. Came home corrected proof-sheets, etc., mechanically. All well, would the machine but keep in order, but 'The spinning wheel is auld and stiff.' I think I shall not live to the usual verge of human existence. I shall never see the threescore and ten, and shall be summed up at a discount. No help for it, and no matter either.
>
>Dec. 24th. To add to my other grievances I have this day a proper fit of rheumatism in my best knee. I pushed to Abbotsford, however, after the Court rose, though compelled to howl for pain as they helped me out of the carriage.
>
>Dec. 27th. Still weak with this wasting illness, but it is clearly going off. Time it should, quoth Sancho. I began my work again which had slumbered betwixt pain and weakness. In fact, I could not write or compose at all.
>
>Dec. 28th. Stuck to my work.
>
>Jan. 2nd. I had resolved to mark; down no more griefs and groans, but I must needs briefly state that I am nailed to my chair like the unhappy Theseus.
>
>Jan. 7th. Wrought till twelve, *then sallied and walked with Skene for two miles*; home and corrected proofs, and to a large amount.

Jan. 8th. Slept well last night in consequence I think of my walk, which I will, God willing, repeat today.

...Afterwards I walked to the Welsh pool, Skene declining to go, for I

"...not over stout of limb,
Seem stronger of the two."

Jan. 9th.... Here blows a gale of wind. I was to go to Galashiels to settle some foolish lawsuit, and afterwards to have been with Mr. Kerr of Kippilaw to treat about a march-dike. I shall content myself with the first duty, for this day does not suit Bowdenmoor.

Went over to Galashiels like the devil in a gale of wind, and found a writer contesting with half-a-dozen unwashed artificers the possession of a piece of ground the size and shape of a three-cornered pocket-handkerchief. Tried to 'gar them gree,' and if I succeed, I shall think I deserve something better than the *touch of rheumatism*, which is like to be my only reward.

Jan. 10th. Enter rheumatism, and takes me by the knee. So much for playing the peacemaker in a shower of rain.

Jan. 12th. All this day occupied with camomile poultices and pen and ink. It is now four o'clock, and I have written yesterday and today ten of my pages—that is, one-tenth of one of these large volumes—moreover, I have corrected three proof-sheets. I wish it may not prove fool's haste, yet I take as much pains too as is in my nature.

Jan. 17th. (*Edinburgh*). Another proper day of mist, sleet, and rain, through which I navigated homeward. I imagine the distance to be a mile and a half. It is a good thing to secure as much exercise.

Jan. 23rd . I have got a piece of armour, a knee-cap of chamois leather, which I think does my unlucky rheumatism some good. I begin, too, to sleep at night, which is a great comfort. Spent this day completely in labour...."

Jan. 28th. Continued my reading with the commentary of the D. of W. If his broad shoulders cannot carry me through, the devil must be in the dice. Longman and Company agree to the eight volumes. It will make the value of the book more than £12,000. Wrought indifferent hard.

Jan. 30th.... By a letter from Gibson I see the gross proceeds of *Bonaparte*, at eight volumes are—

£12,600. 0. 0.
Discount, five months, £210. 0. 0.

£12,390. 0. 0.

I question if more was ever made by a single work or by a single author's labours, in the same time. But whether it is deserved or not is the question.

January 31st. ...Wet to the skin coming from the Court.... Dined at the Bannatyne Club, where I am chairman.

February 1st. I feel a return of the cursed rheumatism. How could it miss, with my wetting? Also feverish, and a slight headache. So much for claret and champagne. I begin to be quite unfit for a good fellow. Like Mother Cole in the *Minor*, a thimbleful upsets me—I mean, annoys my stomach, for my brains do not suffer. Well, I have had my time of these merry doings.

"The haunch of the deer, and the wine's red dye
Never bard loved them better than I."

But it was for the sake of sociality; never either for the flask or the venison. That must end—is ended. The evening sky of life does not reflect those brilliant flashes of light that shot across its morning and noon. Yet I thank God it is neither gloomy nor disconsolately lowering; a sober twilight—that is all.

February 3rd. There is nought but care on every hand. James Hogg writes that he is to lose his farm, on which he laid out, or rather threw away the profit of all his publications.

Then Terry has been pressed by Gibson for his debt to me. That I may get managed.

I sometimes doubt if I am in what the good people call the right way. Not to sing my own praises, I have been willing always to do my friends what good was in my power, and have not shunned personal responsibility. But then that was in money matters, to which I am naturally indifferent, unless when the consequences press on me. But then I am a bad comforter in case of inevitable calamity; and feeling proudly able to endure in my own case, I cannot sympathise with those whose nerves are of a feebler texture.

February 7th. Wrote six leaves today, and am tired—that's all.

March 1st. At Court until two—wrote letters under cover of the lawyers' long speeches, so paid up some of my correspondents, which I seldom do upon any other occasion. I would sometimes let letters lie for days unopened, as if that would postpone the necessity of answering them. Here I am at home, and to work we go—not for the first time today, for I wrought hard before breakfast. So glides away Thursday 1st.

March 3rd. Very severe weather, came home covered with snow. White as a frosted-plum-cake, by jingo! No matter; I am not sorry to find that I can stand a brush of weather . .

March 4th.... Sir Adam came, and had half an hour's chat and laugh. My jaws ought to be sore, if the unwontedness of the motion could do it. But I have little to laugh at but myself, and my own bizarreries are more like to make me cry. Wrought hard, though—there's sense in that.

March 5th.... I think today I have finished a quarter of vol. viii., and last. Shall I be happy when it is done?—Umph! I think not.

March 9th.... We were detained till half-past three o'clock, so when I came home I was fatigued and slept. I walk slow, heavily, and with pain; but perhaps the good weather may banish the Fiend of the joints.

March 11th.... James Ballantyne dined with us. He kept up my heart about *Bonaparte*, which sometimes flags; and he is such a grumbler that I think I may trust him when he is favourable. There must be sad inaccuracies, some of which might certainly have been prevented by care; but as the Lazaroni used to say, 'Did you but know how lazy I am!'

March 12th. (*Abbotsford*). Away we set, and came safely to Abbotsford amid all the dullness of a great thaw, which has set the rivers a-streaming in full tide. The wind is wintry, but for my part

"I like this rocking of the battlements."

I was received by old Tom and the dogs, with the unsophisticated feelings of goodwill.

March 13th.... Had a pleasant walk to the thicket, though my ideas were olla-podrida-ish, curiously checkered between pleasure and melancholy I have cause enough for both humours, God knows. I expect this will not be a day of work but of idleness, for my books are not come. Would to God I could make it light thoughtless idleness, such as I used to have when the silly smart fancies ran in my brain like the bubbles in a glass of champagne—as brilliant to my thinking, as intoxicating as evanescent. But the wine is somewhat on the lees. Perhaps it was but indifferent cider after all. Yet I am happy in this place, where everything looks friendly, from old Tom to young Nim.

After all, he has little to complain of who has left so many things that like him.

March 15th.... I drove over to Huntley Burn with Anne, then walked through the plantations, with Tom's help to pull me through the snow-wreaths. Returned in a glow of heat and spirits. Corrected proof-sheets in the evening.

March 18th. Took up *Boney* again. I am now at writing, as I used to be at riding, slow, heavy, and awkward at mounting, but when I did get fixed in my saddle, could screed away with anyone. I have got six pages ready for my learned Theban tomorrow morning.

March 21st. Wrote till twelve, then out upon the heights though the day was stormy, and faced the gale bravely. Tom Purdie was not with me. He would have obliged me to keep the sheltered ground. But, I don't know—

"Even in our ashes live our wonted fires."

There is a touch of the old spirit in me yet that bids me brave the tempest.

March 22nd. Yesterday I wrote to James Ballantyne, acquiescing, in his urgent request to extend the two last volumes to about 600 each. I believe it will be no more than necessary after all, but makes one feel like a dog in a wheel, always moving, and never advancing.

March 25th. Hard work still, but went to Huntley Burn on foot, And returned in the carriage. Walked well and stoutly—God be praised!—and prepared a whole bundle of proofs and copy for the coach tomorrow; that damned work will certainly end some time or other. As it drips and dribbles out on the paper; I think of the old drunken Presbyterian under the spout.

March 28th.... I did not work longer than twelve, however, but went out in as rough weather as I have seen, and stood out several snow blasts.

April 5th. Heard from Lockhart; the Duke of Wellington and Croker are pleased with my historical labours; so far well—for the former, as a soldier said of him, "I would rather have his long nose on my side than a whole brigade." Well! something good may come of it, and if it does it will be good luck, for, as you and I know, Mother Duty, it has been a rummily written work. I wrote hard today.

April 6th. Do. Do. I only took one turn about the thickets and have nothing to put down but to record my labours.

April 7th. The same history occurs; my desk and my exercise. I am a perfect automaton. *Bonaparte* runs in my head from seven in the morning till ten at night without intermission. I wrote six leaves today and corrected four-proofs.

April 8th. Ginger, being in my room, was safely delivered in her basket of four puppies; the mother and children all doing well. Faith! that is as important an entry as my Journal could desire. The day is so beautiful that I long to go out. I won't though, till I have done something. A letter from Mr. Gibson about the trust affairs. If the infernal bargain with Constable go on well, there will be a pretty sop in the pan to the creditors; £35,000 at least. If I could work as effectually for three years more, I shall stand on my feet like a man. But who can assure success with the public?

April 9th. I wrote as hard today as need be, finished my neat eight pages, and, notwithstanding, drove out and visited at Gattonside. The devil must be in it if the matter drags out longer now.

April 10th. Some incivility from the Leith Bank, which I despise with my heels. I have done for settling my affairs all that any man—much more than most men—could have done, and they refuse a draught of £20, because, in mistake, it was £8 overdrawn. But what can be expected of a *sow* but a *grumph?* Wrought hard, hard.

April 11th. The parks were rouped for £100 a year more than they brought last year. Poor Abbotsford will come to good after all. In the meantime it is *Sic vos non vobis*—but who cares a farthing? If *Boney* succeeds, we will give these affairs a blue eye, and I will wrestle stoutly with them...."

April 14th. Went to Selkirk to try a fellow for an assault on Dr. Clarkson—fined him seven guineas, which, with his necessary expenses, Will amount to ten guineas. It is rather too little; but as his income does not amount to £30 a year, it will pinch him severely enough, and it is better than sending him to an ill-kept jail, where he would be idle and drunk from morning to night. I had a dreadful headache while sitting in the Court—rheumatism in perfection. It did not last after I got warm by the fireside.

April 15th. Delightful soft morning, with mild rain. Walked out and got wet, as a soverign cure for the rheumatism. Was quite well though, and scribbled away.

April 20th. A surly sort of day. I walked for two hours, however, and then returned chiefly to *Nap*. Egad! I believe it has an end at last, this blasted work. I have the fellow at Plymouth, or near about it. Well, I declare, I thought the end of these beastly big eight volumes was like the end of the world, which is always talked of and never comes.

April 27th. ...I have been a little nervous, having been confined to the house for three days. Well, I may be disabled from duty but my tamed spirits and sense of dejection have quelled all that freakishness of humour which made me a voluntary idler. I present myself to the morning task, as the hack-horse patiently trudges to the pole of his chaise, and backs, however reluctantly, to have the traces fixed. Such are the uses of adversity.

April 29th. ...I wrote all the morning then cut some wood. I think the weather gets too warm for hard work with the axe, or I get too stiff and easily tired.

May 12th. ...Walked with my cousin, Colonel Russell, for three hours in the woods, and enjoyed the sublime and delectable pleasure of being well—and listened to on the subject of my favourite themes of laying out ground and plantation.

May 14th. To town per Blucher coach, well stowed and crushed, but saved cash, coming off for less than £2; posting costs nearly five, and you don't get on so fast by one-third. Arrived in my old lodgings here with a stouter heart than I expected.

May 24th. Rather too many dinner engagements on my list. Must be hard-hearted. I cannot say I like my solitary days the worst by any means. I dine, when I like, on soup or broth, and drink a glass of porter or ginger-beer; a single tumbler of whisky and water concludes the debauch. This agrees with me charmingly. At ten o'clock bread and cheese, a single draught of small beer, porter, or ginger-beer, and to bed.

May 26th. I went the same dull and weary round out to the Parliament House, which bothers one's brains for the day. Nevertheless, I get on. Pages vanish from under my hand, and find their way to J. Ballantyne, who is grinding away with his presses. I think I may say, now I begin to get rid of the dust raised about me by so many puzzling little facts, that it is plain sailing to the end.

June 7th. This morning finished *Boney*. And now, as Dame Fortune says, in Quevedo's Vision's, *Go, wheel, and the devil drive thee*. It was high time I brought up some reinforcements, for my pound was come to half-crowns, and I had nothing to keep house when the Lockharts come. Credit enough to be sure, but I have been taught by experience to make short reckonings.

...I arranged with Mr. Cadell for the property of *Tales of a Grand-father*, 10,000 copies for £787. 10. 0.

June 9th. Corrected proofs in the morning.

June 10th. Rose with the odd consciousness of being free of my daily task.... Fortunately my thoughts are agreeable; cash difficulties, etc., all provided for, as far as I call see, so that we go on hooly and fairly. Betwixt (now) and August 1st. I should receive £750, and I cannot think I have more than the half of it to pay away. Cash, to be sure, seems to burn in my pocket. 'He wasna gien to great misguiding, but coin his pouches wouldna bide in.' By goles, this shall be corrected, though!"

Within a week of the last proof-sheets being corrected, *The Life of Napoleon Bonaparte*, in eight large close-printed volumes, was in the hands of the booksellers.

CHAPTER CII.

The Life of Napoleon Bonaparte is in some respects, if not Scott's greatest, yet, considered as a feat of intellect, his most marvellous work. His own feeling was expressed, a few weeks after its publication, in conversation with Mr. J. L. Adolphus, to whom "he said, in a quiet but affecting tone, 'I could have done it better, if I could have written at more leisure, and with a mind more at ease.'" But in breadth of imagination, in mastery of a thousand details, in balance and equity of presentation, it is in the foremost rank of the world's biographical or historical works. Almost all historians, almost all biographers, may be classified as writing either with the warmth of prejudice, or in a spirit of cold-blooded impartiality. It is the peculiar excellence of the *Napoleon* that it is alive with an impartial sympathy. It deals with the world-events of half a century, and with a myriad of characters, many of whom were still alive at the time. It was written without access to many records and documents which were subsequently available. For this reason it has been superseded by later works, but its broad conclusions are unshaken. It became a mine of information and guidance for later historians.

It is of such bulk, and of such a nature, that it might be supposed to be the work of a decade, if not of a lifetime. It was not merely written during two years of financial disaster, broken health, crushing personal sorrow, and other occupations, it was written from end to end without alteration or revision, as perhaps no such work ever was before or will be again, the chapters being set up in type and printed, one by one, as they came from the author's hand.

It was attacked, on publication, from every side, as such a book would be certain to be. The attacks cancelled each other. They died down, and the book stood.

There was one serio-comic episode in connection with General Gourgaud, who had been on Napoleon's staff at St. Helena. He had been active in representing in France that Napoleon had been harshly treated at St. Helena. Scott discovered at the Foreign Office private reports from this man to the English Government of a directly contrary character. He referred to this inconsistency in the *Life* and Gourgaud burst into excited denials. Thereupon, Scott published his authorities. There was talk of a challenge from the furious Frenchman. Scott expressed a good-humoured readiness to oblige him, and actually went so far as to engage William Clerk to act as his second in the encounter, but the General contented himself with a verbal bluster.

Immediately following the completion of this work, Scott paid a short visit to Charlton, in company with Sir Adam Fergusson, William Clerk, and a number of other friends of earlier years, "all in the humour to be happy, though time is telling with us all." They went to St. Andrews together, and Scott, for the first time in his life, found himself left behind when there was a turret-stair to be mounted. They climbed St. Rule's Tower, while he sat on a grave-stone below, lamenting rheumatism, and reflecting that "I think this is the first decided sign of acquiescence in my lot". His mind went back to when he had been there thirty-four years before, and carved Williamina's name "in Runic characters on the turf beneath the castle-gate, and I asked why it should still agitate my heart," but his friends came down from the tower, and the foolish idea was chased away.

Returning to Edinburgh, he turned attention again to the *Canongate Chronicles* and the *Tales of a Grand-father*, both at once as his way was, but with some relaxation of the pressure at which he had worked till the *Napoleon* was finished; and as the Lockharts had come north, to take a summer holiday at Portobello, he went there about every second day, and tried the *Tales* on his grandson (who was somewhat stronger now, giving a short-lived hope that he would out-grow his weakness), so that he could be sure that he had the right tone for such a work, and when the session closed and he was able to get back to Abbotsford, the Lockharts came also, and John Hugh was found to be strong enough to sit on a pony, and they went rides together in a sedate way, for Scott had found a horse that he could contrive to mount, and that would bear him safely.

Sybil Grey had been sold, after an attempt to take a jump which would once have been easy alike to horse and rider had resulted in a dangerous spill, but Douce Davie was a horse of another colour—in fact, dun, with a black mane. Douce Davie had a great and singular reputation. He had belonged to a laird who was always drunk when he went home at night, and he was so expert in balancing that his master might lurch as he would without falling from the saddle, every movement would be so intelligently anticipated, so skilfully countered. When his owner died, it was anticipated that the whole countryside would compete for so useful a quadruped, and it was perhaps the greatest tribute ever paid by Selkirkshire to its beloved Sheriff that on it becoming known that he desired the purchase, all competition ceased, and he was able to buy at his own price.

Scott was cheered at this time by the news that Gibson had nearly £40,000 in hand or in sight for distribution among the creditors, only awaiting the result of the arbitration upon the Constable claim. He calculated also that he could see a sufficiency of the smaller sums which he was making at this time by miscellaneous writing for his own use, and the manner in which he interpreted his resolutions of future economy is illuminated by a Journal entry which says:

> "A distressing letter from Haydon; imprudent, probably, but who is not? A man of rare genius. What a pity I gave that £10 to Craig! But I have plenty of ten pounds sure, and I will make it something."

In July, Constable died. He is said to have succumbed to the weight of his misfortunes, but his health was already ruined by self-indulgence. He died at fifty-two, and Scott had written of him as "the old gentleman" in an earlier year. Yet his death was probably hastened by the strain and grief of the events which had destroyed his business, scattered has assets for a fraction of their proper value, and left him poor and discredited. He may have found an additional cause for depression in the fact that Scott had preferred Cadell to himself in the recent publishing arrangements which he had made, but there was no ill-feeling underlying this arrangement, and it is improbable, had he lived, that Scott would have refused him some share in his future favours. But, in any case, he had brought the position upon himself, having forced the quarrel upon Cadell by which they were parted, at a time when it was of the first importance that they should have held firmly together. Scott may have felt an obligation of equity, as well as a greater confidence in the energy of the younger man. But his final feeling is best expressed in his own words:

> "Constable's death might have been a most important thing to me if it had happened some years ago, and I should then have lamented it much. He has lived to do me some injury; yet, excepting the last £5,000, I think most unintentionally. He was a prince of booksellers... he knew, I think, more of the business of a bookseller in planning and executing popular works than any man of his time.... I have no great reason to regret him, yet I do. If he deceived me, he also deceived himself."

The paragraph appears to state the position with equitable moderation. Lockhart's random allegation that Scott was ruined by the Ballantynes will not endure examination and would probably never have been suggested by anyone but himself. To say that Constable ruined Scott has a more literal accuracy, but to say that it was by *his fault* would be to go much further, and would be more disputable. Ultimately, they were all ruined by Hurst, Robinson & Co.'s failure. The bulk of Scott's income, the bulk of the gross turnover of the printing works, a large part of Constable's turnover, all came through Hurst, Robinson & Co.'s hands, and should have been paid over by them. The whole disaster was fundamentally due to their default. But Constable was the one who had chosen them as his agents, who conducted all financial and other transactions with them, and who assured Scott from time to time that all was well, when he had good reason to doubt it. Hurst, Robinson & Co. had acted with most culpable imprudence in their speculations, but, if they could be heard in their own defense, they would call themselves the victims of a world-wide financial crisis—and a fall in the price of hops.

Scott blamed Constable specifically for persuading him to

undertake the final £5,000 of responsibility, which added that amount to his liabilities, without any gain whatever. It was, at the worst, an error of judgement, by a man whose instinct was to fight, and who saw that the alternative was a final ruin. Scott did *not* blame him (as is commonly said) for the £10,000 which he raised on the security of Abbotsford shortly after the signing of the £5,000 bond. He would not have thought of doing so, for the £10,000 was intended, and was applied (so far as it was paid out at all) to the reduction of the Ballantyne & Co. liabilities. But the fact that he had so raised, and so applied it, did enable him to say that the catastrophe was not due in any degree to himself or to the printing business. Had Hurst, Robinson & Co. and Constable & Co. continued to meet their liabilities, there is not the smallest doubt that James Ballantyne & Co. and Sir Walter Scott would have done the same.

Almost immediately after Constable's death, the arbitration regarding the copyrights was substantially decided. The earlier ones were declared to be the absolute property of the Constable estate, but those of *Woodstock* and *Napoleon* to belong to Sir Walter Scott. This was a victory for Scott's Trustees, and Scott called himself a feather-headed gull because the good news kept him awake in the night. He reflected that he could now clear off about a third of his debts. And as to the other two-thirds? Well, he was in no worse health than he had been a year ago. "Tomorrow I will resume on the *Chronicles*, tooth and nail."

So he resolved; but we may doubt whether his heart was ever in these tales in a continuous or embracing way. There are passages, and one or two characters, one or two scenes, which are of the authentic *Waverley* pattern, but if the bulk of *The Surgeon's Daughter*, the *Highland Widow*, and the *Two Drovers* were consumed in the same fire, would their author's reputation be any lower, the work he has left be appreciably diminished? Doubtless, he was conscious of this approach to failure, and James made no secret of his feelings when he came, with George Hogarth, to talk business at Abbotsford. James missed the old glitter, the old pageantry of the historical romances. He pleaded for something more in the same style. Scott thought he under-estimated the importance of novelty. He had not made his greatest successes in the past by imitation of earlier efforts, but by bold adventures upon difficult backgrounds.

Whichever were right, their difference was irrelevant. The trouble was not in the themes, but in the quality of the telling, which was not sustained at a high level, though it might be reached occasionally. It would be wrong to say that Scott could not write a short story. *Wandering Willie's Tale* is a classic of its kind. But it was a bad sign when a longer effort showed a tendency to finish early. Scott's method of composition, which did not work to a set plot, but let it develop as the inter-play of characters, and the invention of incident led, resulted in a tale which spread vigorously, as a plant grows, if it were from a seed of sufficient vitality, and nourished by a sufficient vigour of imagination. The fault with these *Canongate Chronicles* was that they were the driven work of a tired brain. Reading them, James might well doubt himself if the debts could be ever paid. *Woodstock* and *Napoleon* had realised an immense sum, but the novel had been projected and partly written before the crisis came, and the biography was a special, unrepeatable thing.— Now, on the return to the fiction which had supplied the steady golden fountain of the past—well, James couldn't imagine that there would be any enthusiasm about these tales. Scott may have felt the same doubt; but what use was there in regarding that? They were the way out. Besides, he had contracted to write them. He thought of that £40,000 already in Gibson's hands, and

"Fresh vigour with the hope returned."

He went at them 'tooth and nail'.

There is no doubt—it is his own testimony—that the desire to free his beloved Abbotsford from the control of strangers was a driving force at this time, which would renew its strength as he walked through the woods that he had caused to be. He was already, as his power recovered and his hope grew, reasserting his will as to the spirit in which the estate should be administered—a standard of high efficiency, with very liberal treatment of those who served it. William Laidlaw, when the first fury of the storm descended, had been turned out of Kaeside, and his salary stopped. Scott had agreed to this at the time; but that fund now in Gibson's hands, the larger half of which had been produced by his own subsequent toil, and was of the nature of a gift to his creditors, gave him a good right to dictate the terms on which he should continue to serve them. The Laidlaws would soon be back in their former home.

But if we recognise that the desire to ransom Abbotsford from alien control was a driving and inspiring force at this time, we must not therefore conclude that Scott's attitude regarding the discharge of his liabilities had been determined by this consideration. We must observe that his decision had been the same from the first, and at a time when it had not been clear to his own mind that he would be able to return to Abbotsford at all, nor even, in the shock of the first realisation of ruin, that he would desire to do so.

In broad outline, the record of this closing period of his life is one of a stubborn continual effort, which met with undespairing courage the implacable verdict of the years. Brain and body failed beneath the efforts by which the fund in Gibson's hands was augmented, and it was hard to guess on which side victory would lie at the last. Looked at in outline thus, it is a sombre heroic tale, but it would be wrong to think of it as being without its periods of quiet happiness, its times that were free from any sense of physical disability or discomfort. The record of such a Journal as Scott wrote during these years may be the best indication of his fundamental feelings, but there is much of happiness there, as well as of sorrow and ever-increasing physical infirmity, and the courage that overcame. There is evidence of a different kind, but a no less certain value, in the observations of others, at times which were free from the self-consciousness that the entering of such a Journal requires.

Mr. J. L. Adolphus came to see him this autumn. His

previous visit to Abbotsford had been in 1824 when Scott was at the height of his prosperity. His credential had been the *Letters to Richard Heber*, in which, apart from the discussion of their authorship, the *Waverley* novels had received one of the best criticisms and appreciations that they are ever likely to have. Now he was asked to stay three days in a house to which few visitors came. Scott recorded that it was a "very agreeable" visit. "He is a modest, as well as an able man."

Mr. Adolphus has left us his own impression of that visit, which he had approached with "painful and anxious" apprehensions of the changes which adversity might have produced. He says that these feelings "gave way at once to the unassumed serenity of his manner. There were some signs of age about him which the mere lapse of time would scarcely have accounted for; but his spirits were abated only, not broken; if they had sunk, they had sunk equably and gently. It was a declining, not a clouded sun." He went on:

> "One morning a party was made to breakfast at Chiefswood; and anyone who on that occasion looked at and heard Sir Walter Scott, in the midst of his children and grandchildren and friends, must have rejoiced to see that life still yielded him a store of pleasures, and that his heart was as open to their influence as ever. I was much struck by a few words which fell from him on this subject a short time afterwards. After mentioning an incident which had spoiled the promised pleasure of a visit to his daughter in London, he then added—"I have had as much happiness in my time as most men, and I must not complain now." I said, that whatever had been his share of happiness, no man could have laboured better for it. He answered—"I consider the capacity to labour as part of the happiness I have enjoyed"."

It was about this time that he recorded the depression produced by 'my loneliness, and the increased disability to walk,' and gave complement to Mr. Adolphus's observation, when he wrote:

> "I generally affect good spirits in company of my family, whether I am enjoying them or not. It is too severe to sadden the harmless mirth of others by suffering your own causeless melancholy to be seen; and this species of exertion is, like virtue, its own reward; for the good spirits, which are at first simulated, become at length real."

The summer quietude at Abbotsford was briefly interluded by a visit to Glasgow, and several friends in its neighbourhood.

Edinburgh, taken on the way, gave opportunity for a call on Gibson, who had the welcome news that the firm of Dickinson (papermakers, of London) would be satisfied with 10/- in the £ on the bills they held. Scott noted on this:

> "These debts, for which I am legally responsible, though no party to their contraction, amount to £30,000 odd. Now if they can be cleared for £15,000 it is just so much gained. That would be a giant step to freedom."

It was Hurst & Robinson's debt, and Dickinson's would, of course, receive additional dividends from their and Constable's estates, so that the difference which their offer made would be nearer £10,000 than £15,000; but even so, it was a substantial reduction in the confronting total, and good cause for a cheerful holiday.

There was good hope, too, in a project which had been in Constable's mind, and which Cadell was maturing—that of an edition of the complete Waverley novels, to which Scott should write new introductions and notes. It will be remembered that a plan to bring them out in a cheaper form had been put aside because there were still substantial quantities of existing editions in the hands of the trade. Now Cadell thought that these stocks would nearly be exhausted. He said that, at his own shop, he sold a novel or two, and two or three *Napoleons* almost every day, and his stocks must soon be replenished from London. His brothers were now supporting him with ample capital. It was a large project, needing careful planning, and with some copyright difficulties at the threshold, but it had the possibilities of a great success.

Scott stayed the night at 10, Walker Street, which he now hired when in Edinburgh, and observed for the first time that, by some ironic chance, some of his old Castle Street furniture had found a resting place in the house. It gave him 'rather queer feelings.... I remember poor Charlotte and I having so much thought about buying these things. Well, they are in kind and friendly hands.'

The next morning he drove to Glasgow, with his one-time ward, the young Marchioness of Northampton, for company, whom he had once rebuked at Abbotsford for lack of respect for his guest, and the journey was made pleasant by her kindness and vivacity. After that, there were many invitations on arrival to be refused or accepted, and a few happy days with George Cranston (Lord Corehouse) and other friends of earlier days at Corehouse Castle, with a return to Abbotsford a week later, and the final comment:

> "Thus ends a pleasant expedition among the people I like most. Drawback only one. It has cost me £15, including two gowns for Sophia and Anne; and I have lost six days' labour. Both may be soon made up."

The next day he was on the bench at Selkirk, and fined a man for assault. "He pleaded guilty, which made short work." Crimes of assault and violence, mostly of a political character, were becoming very common over all the country, and the agitation for a reform of the franchise threatened the foundations of the existing order.

CHAPTER CIII.

Lockhart, recording the experiences of the visit which Sophia and he paid to Abbotsford during this autumn of 1827, throws a pleasant light upon the conditions of its new economy:

> "I admired," he says, "the manner in which all his dependents appeared to have met the reverse of his misfortunes—a reverse which inferred very considerable alteration in the circumstances of every one of them. The butler, Dalgleish, had been told, when the distress came, that a servant of his class would no longer be required—but the man burst into tears, and said, rather than go he would stay without any wages. So he remained—and instead of being the easy chief of a large establishment, was now doing half the work of the house, at probably half his former salary. Old Peter, who had been for five-and-twenty years a dignified coachman, was now ploughman in ordinary, only putting his horses to the carriage upon high and rare occasions; and so on with all the rest that remained of the ancient train. And all, to my view, seemed happier than they had ever done before.
>
> "...All this warm and respectful solicitude must have had a salutary influence on the mind of Scott, who may be said to have lived upon love. No man cared less about popular admiration and applause; but for the least chill on the affection of any near and dear to him he had the sensitiveness of a maiden. I cannot forget, in particular, how his eyes sparkled when he first pointed out to me Peter Mathieson guiding the plough on the haugh: "Egad," said he, "auld *Pepe*"

(this was the children's name for their good friend)—"auld *Pepe's* whistling at his darg. The honest fellow said, a yoking in a deep field would do baith him and the blackies good. If things get round with me, easy shall be Pepe's cushion"."

At the beginning of October, there was another brief interlude in the routine of work, when Scott accepted, with some reluctance, an invitation from Lord and Lady Ravensworth to meet the Duke of Wellington at Ravensworth Castle, and to attend a grand dinner in the Episcopal Castle at Durham. He returned to make rapid progress with the *Tales of a Grand-father*. On one day he wrote the equivalent of forty pages of print. "But then the theme was so familiar, being the Scottish history, that my pen never rested."

A few days later, he received a letter from Lady Jane Stuart, Williamina's mother, with whom he had had no communication since he had ridden away from Invermay when her daughter had finally refused him, thirty-one years ago.

Lady Jane, now a widow of seventy-four, wrote that there were some ballads in Scott's handwriting in an album of Williamina's which a friend was anxious to print. Would he give permission? He replied with a request that he might see the album.

Lady Jane, in a second letter, made clear the warmth of affection which she had always felt for her daughter's wooer, and which thirty years had not been sufficient to weaken. The letter is of the kind which whoever finds should place quietly upon the fire, as an obviously personal and private document, but it has been printed already.

> "Were I to lay open my heart," she wrote, "(of which you know little indeed) you would find how it has and ever shall be warm towards you. My age encourages me, and I have longed to tell you. Not the mother who bore you followed you more anxiously

(though secretly) with her blessing than I! Age has tales to tell, and sorrows to unfold."

Scott's Journal-record of the receipt of this letter reads:

"A surprise amounting nearly to a shock reached me in another letter from L.J.S. Methinks this explains the gloom which hung about me yesterday. I own that the recurrence to these matters seems like a summons from the grave. It fascinates me. I ought perhaps to have stopped it at once, but I have not nerve to do so! Alas!—alas!—But why alas? *Humana perpessi sumus.*"

The beginning of November brought trouble of a different kind.

It will be remembered that when Scott had been desirous of visiting London it had been necessary to obtain an undertaking from Messrs. Abud & Sons, one of Hurst Robinson & Co.'s creditors, that they would not use the opportunity for any legal process. They had consistently refused to assent to the Assignment which Scott had made. They said they required payment, or desired bankruptcy.

On the last day of October, when Scott says that he was 'merrily cutting away,' among his trees, Mr Gibson suddenly appeared at Abbotsford with the news that Messrs. Abud were taking action in the Scottish court.

The law of imprisonment for debt was simpler, being less hypocritical, than it is now; but it was used, then as now, as a form of legal blackmail by which money could often be extracted from a debtor's friends. Messrs. Abud had chosen their time well. They had waited till there was a good sum in Mr. Gibson's hands, and a distribution was about to be made.

As they had not assented to the Deed, they had no claim to any part in that distribution. But their rights of legal action remained. Let Mr. Gibson distribute the money among other creditors, if he would. Meanwhile, Scott should find himself in a debtor's prison. What was the remedy? Let their account be paid in full. It had been £1,500 originally. Interest and costs had brought it up to nearly £2,000 now.

There were three courses from which a choice must be made. Scott could cut the knot at any time by consenting to bankruptcy, and this was the course which Mr. Gibson was disposed to advise. Scott had, by his industry after the date of the financial catastrophe, created a fund from which a dividend of 6/- could be paid. He had done enough for honour. It could always be said that he would have continued that course, had not Abud's action rendered it impossible.

Or their debt might be paid in full from the funds in hand, if the other creditors would agree.

Or, finally, he might defy them to do their worst, which would be to confine him in the Canongate jail, till they got tired of such a barren remedy, and agreed to take their place with the other creditors.

To escape the last evil, he might withdraw to the Isle of Man, as his brother Tom had done when in a similar difficulty, or take sanctuary in Holyrood, for the Church still had this privilege of protection against the inhumanity of the law.

Scott's Journal shows that his first impulse was to accept Mr. Gibson's advice: to give up the fight and consent to bankruptcy, unless the creditors should resolve to relieve him of the difficulty by giving preferential payment to these pertinacious pursuers. But the entries that follow during the week before, in response to a letter from Gibson, he went to Edinburgh, show a hardening of resolution, of which he scarcely seems himself aware until his decision forms itself. He had some changes of mood. He waked in the night, and lay two hours in feverish meditation, resulting in the reflection that 'it is no purpose being angry with Ehud or Ahab, or whatever name he delights in. He is seeking his own; and thinks by these harsh measures to render his road to it more speedy.

Three days later he concludes that

"Our hope, heavenly and earthly, is poorly anchored, if the cable parts upon the strain. I believe in God, who can change evil into good; and I am confident that what befalls us is always ultimately for the best."

But it would be a profound misjudgement of Scott's character to suppose that this mild reflection indicates that he is now in a mood to surrender. He concludes his entry with the resolution that: "If I can prevent it, he shall not take a shilling by his hard-hearted conduct."

In fact, he had resolved, as Mr. Pickwick did on a later day, that he would end his days in the Canongate Jail rather than be defeated by such manoeuvres. The next morning he put his papers in order, congratulated himself that the First Series of the *Chronicles of the Canongate* had been completed two days ago, and 'firm as a piece of granite' (but for Anne's doleful looks) he set out for Edinburgh.

CHAPTER CIV.

Things seldom happen according to plan, except on the battlefield, and then most often only by the mendacity of bulletins. Scott arrived in Edinburgh to find that the scene had changed.

The Trustees, being lawyers, and as much interested as himself, though from a different angle, in frustrating this interference in an arrangement by which the assenting creditors were already benefiting very largely, had been examining Messrs. Abud's judgement. The interest which had been charged to Hurst, Robinson & Co. was certainly calculated with liberality. If usury could be established, the judgement would be worthless, as against Scott, in the Scottish courts. Anyway, if evidence could be obtained sufficient to allow of a case being entertained, it would mean delay. It was resolved that the attempt should be made. Cadell was despatched to find Robinson, and gather material for the application. Scott's judgement, on leaving the conference, was that, as far as he was concerned, the danger was past.

> "This much I think I can see, that the trustees will rather pay the debt than break off the trust, and go into a sequestration. They are clearly right for themselves, and I believe for me also. Whether it is in human possibility that I can clear off these obligations or not, is very doubtful. But I would rather have it written on my monument that I died at the desk; than live under the recollection of having neglected it.... Were I shirking exertion, I should lose heart, under a sense of general contempt, and so die like a poisoned rat in a hole."

The twelfth of November—fourteen days after the issuing of the process which had started Mr. Gibson hurrying to Abbotsford—was the date on which Abud & Sons would be able to obtain their committal of Sir Walter, unless it could be stayed by the legal process in contemplation, and, under the circumstances, he decided not to go back to Abbotsford. He was not intending to return to Walker Street. Mrs. Jobson had a more comfortable furnished house, 6, Shandwick Place, which the family were anxious that Sir Walter should have while in Edinburgh. It was a consideration which, with that £40,000 in hand, and the hope of future favours, the Trustees could not refuse. They had agreed to pay £100 for the house for the four months that the Court would be sitting, and, from this time, it was Scott's regular residence when in the city. He now made an easy arrangement, by paying an extra £5, that he could have immediate possession. He had brought a man servant, John Nicholson, with him, who got fires in the house, and 'all snug' while he slept one night with his friend, John Home, and wrote to Anne that he should not be returning to Abbotsford.

No. 6, Shandwick Place was opposite to Maitland Street, from which address Lady Jane Stuart had written, and on the same day (Nov. 6th.) that Scott took possession he asked Mrs. Skene to accompany him to make a call upon her. Lockhart says that Mrs. Skene said afterwards that the result was 'a very painful scene'. The Journal contains no more than the brief entry: 'I waited on L.J.S., an affecting meeting.'

There is no better evidence of the depth and tenacity of Scott's affections than the profound mental disturbance which was occasioned by the renewal of this acquaintance. The fact—mere coincidence though it was—that Sir William Forbes called in the evening, being concerned about the Abud matter, and anxious to give counsel and sympathy, could do nothing to turn Scott's mind from the duel in which Sir William had defeated his hopes thirty years before. The Journal shows how warmly he appreciated the attitude of the man with whom his friendship had survived the severest of all possible tests, but he cared nothing for Abud now.

He rose next morning with a determination not 'to leave the mind leisure to recoil on itself,' and commenced the essay on *Ornamental Gardening* which subsequently appeared in the Quarterly. But he found himself blocked almost at once by the need for books of reference which were not available in this new house which he had entered before his time. At that, he made an attempt to commence a second series of the *Chronicles*, but the starting of a new tale, on which the imagination was slow to move, did not supply the kind of labour which might have enabled him to control his thoughts. He gave up the attempt at last, and walked over to make another call on Lady Jane, of which he has left his own record:

> "I went to make another visit, and fairly softened myself, like an old fool, with recalling old stories till I was fit for nothing but shedding tears and repeating verses for the whole night. This is sad work. The very grave gives up its dead, and time rolls back thirty years to add to my perplexites. I don't care. I begin to grow over hardened, and like a stag turning at bay, my

naturally good temper grows fierce and dangerous. Yet what a romance to tell, and told I fear it will one day be. And then my three years of dreaming and my two of waking will be chronicled doubtless. But the dead will feel no pain."

He worked steadily for the next two days, and then:

"Nov. 10th. Wrote out my task and little more. At twelve o'clock I went to poor Lady J. S., to talk over old stories. I am not clear that it is right or healthful indulgence to be ripping up old sorrows, but it seems to give her deep-seated sorrow words, and that is a mental blood-letting. To me these things are now matter of calm and solemn recollection, never to be forgotten, yet scarce to be remembered with pain."

Yet he was glad to remember (this being Saturday) that he had an invitation to spend the week-end with Sir William Rae, where society might assist him to bring these haunting memories under control. And so he went to St. Catherine's, and after prayers next morning he sauntered about with Sir William, exchanging recollections of the old days of the Yeomanry regiment which they had been united to raise, and then drove over to see Lord Melville and his family in the afternoon, and came back through the early November twilight beneath a sky of topaz and vermilion that glowed above the amethysts of the Pentland Hills.

CHAPTER CV.

On Monday morning it was necessary to return to Edinburgh to face Abud & Sons' action, on the delaying of which Scott's immediate liberty depended, and his spirits rose almost to gaiety as the moment of crisis came.

"I cannot say," he wrote, "I lost a minute's sleep on account of what the day might bring forth; though it was that on which we must settle with Abud in his Jewish demand, or stand to the consequences. I breakfasted with an excellent appetite, laughed in real genuine easy fun, and went to Edinburgh, resolved to do what should best become me."

He got back to Shandwick Place to find that Anne was there, and Walter also awaiting him. How Walter had heard of the coming trouble does not appear. Perhaps Anne, who had taken the news of her father's coming jeopardy more quietly than might have been expected, had been using an urgent pen. Anyway, Walter had got sudden leave, and hurried to Abbotsford and then on to Edinburgh in time to be on the scene at the day of crisis.... And then there was the realisation that the crisis was postponed again, and neither Walter's military assistance, nor that of Jane's money would be required.

Mr. Gibson had had an anxious time, for Cadell had not returned, and the affidavit from Robinson, on which he had relied to support his application, was not available. Yet, without that, he had obtained the suspension that he required.

And in the afternoon, which would have been an hour too late, there was a letter from Cadell, enclosing another from Robinson, who would do all that might be required.... Abud would have to prove to the Court of Session that his usury had not been beyond the limit of Scottish law, and, until he should have done this, his teeth were drawn.

It may be convenient to follow this incident to its end, rather than to revert to it on a later page. It might be thought, after the result of this preliminary skirmish, that Abud & Sons would have been in a mood to abandon the fight, and join the other creditors, rather than contest such an action in Edinburgh. But they proved to be of a more obstinate temper. They not only fought: they won. They secured from the Edinburgh court, which would certainly have preferred to render a different decision, a verdict that they had not burdened Hurst, Robinson & Co. with an excessive usury.

After that, Sir Walter was informed that an arrangement had been made by which the debt would rank with those of the other creditors, and the trouble was over. He did not know, until after the death of Sir William Forbes, that this was not the result of any legal compromise. Sir William had bought the debt, paying Abud's claim and costs in full, to a total of nearly £2,000.

It deserves chronicle that this was not the only instance in which friends who had offered direct assistance, which Scott had refused to accept, had facilitated, without his knowledge, the operation of the scheme of settlement on which his heart was set.

Abud & Sons had not been the only creditors who had declined to assent to the deed, in the shrewd opinion that a different attitude might result in a full and much speedier settlement.

Three of the Clerks of Session, who had been his life-long friends—Colin Mackenzie Sir Robert Dundas, and Macdonald Buchanan—had united in the provision of a secret fund from which such debts were bought up. Only Mr. Gibson knew that they had become the actual creditors, in place of those whose names appeared on the schedule of liabilities. Sir Walter Scott never knew this. All his life, he had good friends.

CHAPTER CVI.

The next day Cadell came. He was in good spirits at his successful chase of the elusive Robinson, but on another matter he had heard a disturbing report.

The sale of the *Waverley* copyrights, together with most of those of the poems—in fact, of all that had been purchased by Constable, or which remained the property of Scott's estate, had been fixed for Dec. 19th. It had been agreed that the amount realised should be held until the Arbiter's award should be fully given, but that nothing could be gained by further delaying the sale.

Cadell had come to a clear agreement with Scott as to the terms on which a new edition of the novels should be produced, but this was dependent upon the copyrights remaining under their control. The amount which they would realise at such an auction could only be vaguely guessed, but it had been hoped that it would not be beyond their capacity to arrange it, and that it was a matter in which the Trustees could be induced to co-operate. Now, talking among the trade in London, Cadell had realised that the competition for these copyrights might be more serious than he had anticipated.

So fresh reckonings were made and plans were discussed anew. Scott planned in a bold way, as he always would. It did not follow that he was wrong. He had projected great plans in the past, and had been equal to their realisation. There was to be a new complete edition say—thirty volumes. Suppose one were published each month, in an edition of 5,000? He reckoned that there should be a clear £10,000 profit within three years, after all costs had been paid. Work for James's presses: profit for Cadell's publishing business: and £10,000 for his own creditors—less whatever the copyrights would cost—and the copyrights would be a continuing asset. He would write new introductions and notes to earn that £10,000 for his estate. 'I must urge these things to Gibson,' he noted; 'for, except these copyrights be saved, our plans will go for nothing.'

There were further conferences during the following weeks of a rather complicated kind. Gibson was persuaded that the scheme to purchase the copyrights was sound, and that they must be secured at 'almost any' price. The other Trustees were disposed to concur.

The position was simplified by the formal issue of the Arbiter's final award, which was substantially in favour of Scott's estate. It cleared the way for the distribution of the money now in the bank. A meeting of creditors was held on Dec. 4th, at which a dividend of 6/- in the £ was voted, together with the thanks of the meeting for the successful efforts which Sir Walter had made.

There was the right atmosphere, and a concrete plan. Cadell had contracted for a second series of the *Canongate Chronicles*, and had offered to pay £4,000 cash down, which he was in a position to do. Scott was to hand this sum over to the Trustees, and they were to apply it, so far as might be required, toward the purchase of a half-share in the copyrights. Cadell was to finance the other half of a purchase which was to be jointly made.

Cadell might be supposed to be about the last man who would do anything to disturb the smooth working of this programme, yet disturb it he did, after anxious consultations with James, finally writing a letter to him, which it was agreed that he should send on to Scott with a covering letter of his own. He was, in fact, in a very difficult position, confronting a choice of evils.

The first volume of the *Canongate Chronicles* had been published a few weeks earlier, and had been received in a lukewarm way. The intention of anonymity had been abandoned by Scott's own decision, for a reason which he gives at some length in his Journal, and which shows that he had less than his usual confidence in the quality of these volumes. He had considered that if the publication should pass unnoticed, and it should subsequently become necessary to stimulate sales by announcing the authorship, criticism would be certain to defend its previous indifference by asserting that the fault was in the *Tales* themselves—that they showed a declining power—even though that should not be a true explanation.

There is substance in this argument, and it was certainly the wiser course to publish in his own name, but it was not one which would have entered his mind ten or twenty years earlier, nor would it have had a decisive weight at this time had he faced the event with the consciousness that a new *Ivanhoe* or *Midlothian* was being launched on its career of triumph.

Anyway, published in his name they had been, and criticism was cold, and the sales were poor. That was not all. A considerable proportion of the MS. of the second series had been supplied, and James and Cadell were of one mind about it. It was worse than the first.

They both saw that if, as this MS. appeared to indicate, Scott's power as a novelist had declined, it became all the more important that the copyrights should be secured, and that he should be occupied upon the notes and introductions which he, and only he, would be competent to write. It would become an absolutely vital matter for James (who was aiming to re-establish himself in the ownership of the works) that the printing of whatever new editions of the Waverley novels might be required should come into his hands, if there should be no more new ones to keep him busy.

Yet, even so, Cadell was not willing to pay £4,000 for a MS. of less than doubtful value, even though the money might be applied in a direction which he desired. He would do better to keep it in his own pocket, and buy the copyrights (if that should become necessary) entirely himself. Not that he desired to do this. He appears to have acted honourably in a very delicate position.

So the letter to James was written, and James sent it on to Scott, making his own agreement clear. In fact, *My Aunt Margaret's Mirror*, which was the (subsequent) title of the commencing tale of the second series, was not worth printing.

The letters were awaiting Scott when he came back from Court on December 11th. He had been in a particularly happy and confident mood since the meeting of creditors on the 4th. The long-drawn dispute over the ownership of the copyrights was ended; and the method of their purchase had been arranged. The *Tales of a Grandfather* had been finished, and he had a well-founded confidence in their success. His health was better than it had been last winter.

Beyond these things, after a period of hesitation, he had got a theme for a new novel which pleased his mind. Not one of these stop-gap tales, but one on which his genius could expand in its old prodigal style. The germ of it had come to him in the form of an anecdote he had heard a few weeks ago. Now he saw it in a setting of time and place in which it could be brought to a natural flower. And it had the spiritual theme that his genius required before it could rouse itself to the exercise of its full capacity. It was the latest and most difficult lesson that Scott's comprehensive sympathies had enabled him to learn—that a man may be a physical coward, and yet not deserve contempt. He had conceived the idea of the *Fair Maid of Perth*. Two days ago he had recorded: "I set hard to work, and had a long day with my new Tale."

From this mood he was violently roused by the reading of Cadell's letter. Promptly adjusting his mind, he wrote back that afternoon, saying that he would release him from the contract, rather than that further loss should be incurred. He noted:

> "I can shift for myself amid this failure of prospects; but I think both Cadell and J. B. will be probable sufferers."

It appears that Cadell and J.B. thought the same. They received Scott's letters, and read them with consternation. Cadell had got all he asked, and more than he had a right to expect. He was offered at once the cancellation of the contract, without argument or condition. He was released from an obligation to pay £4,000 on a doubtful bargain; and having got that release, he was at once aware that that was not what he had been wanting at all.

In their hearts, neither James nor Cadell had believed—or would be willing to believe—that the old power, the old glamour, had gone; that they were asking gold from an exhausted mine. They had called out in their distress, as a man calls to a god, and had expected that a different provision would be made, which would equal their need.

Meanwhile, Scott had been considering the position. In his own heart he knew that the first series of *Canongate Chronicles* had experienced the reception it deserved. He had been watchful for several years to detect any slackening of his power of writing fiction. He was not one who would easily admit defeat, but he would always face facts. If it were now as it seemed to be well, he must find another method of victory. He wrote that morning:

> "December 12th. Reconsidered the probable downfall of my literary reputation. I am so constitutionally indifferent to the censure or praise of the world, that never having abandoned myself to the feelings of self-conceit which my great success was calculated to inspire, I can look with the most unshaken firmness upon the event as far as my own feelings are concerned. If there be any great advantage in literary reputation, I have had it. and I certainly do not care for losing it.
>
> "They cannot say but what I *had* the *crown*. It is unhappily inconvenient for my affairs to lay by my (work) just now, and that is the only reason why I do not give up literary labour; but, at least, I will not push the losing game of novel-writing. I will take back the sheets now objected to, but it cannot be expected that I am to write upon return. I cannot but think that a little thought will open some plan of composition which may promise novelty at the least. I suppose I shall hear from or see these gentlemen today; if not, I must send for them tomorrow. How will this affect the plan of going shares with Cadell in the novels of earlier and happier days? Very much, I doubt, seeing I cannot lay down the cash. But surely the Trustees may find some mode of providing this, or else with cash to secure these copyrights. At any rate, I will gain a little time for thought and discussion."

He made no mistake in supposing that he might "hear from or see these gentlemen today". They had spent the morning in anxious conference, and in the afternoon they were side by side on the doorstep at Shandwick Place. They entered with a waving of white flags, a bending of abject knees. They had convinced themselves that they hadn't said anything—or, if they had, they hadn't meant it at all; and when Scott told them that he was disposed to lay fiction aside for six months or twelve, having plenty of other literary work on hand, or which he could obtain, they were voluble in protest. Such an interval, they exclaimed (it was no longer than that which had preceded the publication of *The Pirate*) would raise public anticipation to such a pitch of intensity that no book which might then appear could be sufficient to satisfy it! What they had really *meant* (whatever they might have said) was no more than that a deletion of part of the *introduction* to the second series might improve the volume for which it had been intended! "So," Scott wrote that night, "the word is 'as you were'."

So the word might be, but the fact was different. Scott was too sensible to disregard a warning the truth of which was echoed in his own mind. He threw *My Aunt Margaret's Mirror* aside. He treated *The Laird's Jock*, which was to have followed, in the same way. When the next three volumes of the *Canongate Chronicles* should appear, they would be occupied by a single novel—*The Fair Maid of Perth*.

CHAPTER CVII.

When Scott quieted that friendly rebellion of publisher and printer by telling them that he could find plenty of occupation for his pen without resorting to fiction, he spoke no more than was plainly true. He had been writing some well-paid review articles in the midst of the occupations and distractions of recent months, and it was only the next day that the London post brought two substantial offers such as it was a frequent necessity to decline with the degree of courtesy that their substance might merit. And even in these mental and financial extremities, he could not break himself of the habit of doing charities with his pen.

His unstable, thriftless acquaintance, R. P. Gillies, always a shameless beggar, as those who waste their own substance most often are, had already successfully solicited a free article for a review which he had been founding. Recently, in an effort to keep it alive, he asked for another. Each of these requests may be compared to soliciting a gift of £100, at which price Scott could have sold them easily. In view of the position in which he was known to be placed, the requests were entirely impudent. The second did move him, to whom it was so natural to give aid to others, to a momentary indignation. "I am pulling for life," he noted, "and it is hard to ask me to pull another man's oar." But the other man got his oar pulled, all the same.

There was another incident of about this time, which belongs to the same category. Years before, under circumstances which have been detailed at greater length than their interest merits, Scott had drafted two sermons for a nervous protégé who desired to enter the ministry, but who had not used them. Now, this man, Huntley Gordon, wrote that he was in desperate difficulties, which it would require £180 to relieve. It must have been an exceptional morning when Scott opened his letters without becoming better acquainted with someone's financial troubles than he had been on the previous day. Mr. Gordon did not ask for a loan. He wanted permission to sell the sermons, which he thought would realise enough to relieve his difficulties.

Scott's first inclination was to refuse. He knew that the price of the sermons would be conditional upon the appearance of his name upon them—

> "and that is at present out of the question. People would cry out against the undesired and unwelcome zeal of him who stretched out his hands to help the ark with the best intentions, and cry sacrilege. And yet they would do me gross injustice; for I would, if called upon, die a martyr for the Christian religion...."

It was a causeless humility, for there are few men who have ruled their lives more closely to the vital principles of

Christianity; but it is indicative of the inferior status of imaginative literature a century ago, if not absolutely, yet as compared with religious writings. It was about a quarter of a century later that Tennyson approached the priest's dominion in a similar spirit of diffidence.

> "Urania speaks with darkened brow
> 'Thou pratest now where thou art least.
> This faith has many a purer priest,
> And many an abler voice than thou.'
>
> And my Melpomene replies,
> A touch of shame upon her cheek,
> 'I am not worthy even to speak
> Of thy prevailing mysteries.'"

A world-famous novelist or poet of today would be more likely to expect gratitude from the churches, if he should use his pen to preach their religion, or support their doctrines.

But Scott's reluctance to appear before the public as a writer of sermons gave way as he considered the urgency of Huntley Gordon's debts, and, a few days later, he wrote

> "Dear Gordon,
>
> As I have no money to spare at present, I find it necessary to make a sacrifice of my own scruples to relieve you from serious difficulties. The enclosed will entitle you to deal with any respectable bookseller. You must tell the history in your own way as shortly as possible. All that is necessary to say is that the discourses were written to oblige a young friend. It is understood that my name is not to be put in the title-page, or blazed at full length in the preface. You may trust that to the newspapers.

> Pray do not think of returning any thanks about this; it is enough that I know it is likely to serve your purpose. But use the funds arising from this unexpected source with prudence, for such fountains do not spring up at every place of the desert. I am, in haste, ever yours most truly,
>
> WALTER SCOTT."

The issue appears from a Journal note six weeks later—January 25th, 1828.

> "Huntley Gordon has disposed of the two sermons to the bookseller Colburn for £250—well sold I think-and is (sic) to go forth immediately. The man is a puffing quack; but though I would rather the thing had not gone there, and far rather it had gone nowhere, yet, hang it! if it makes the poor lad easy."

On February 29th, there is a note that the proofs had been passed for the press: "A foolish scrape, but what could I do? It involved the poor lad's relief from something very like ruin."

The 'puffing quack' was, of course, not Huntley Gordon, but the publisher, who was not one who had a reputation for the publication of sermons; but the *Religious Discourses* were soon in a second edition, and had a large sale .

But apart from such generosities, Scott had ample opportunities of using his pen to profit, without the writing of fiction. On the morning after Cadell and Ballantyne called, there was a letter from Lockhart saying that Murray would contract for a book on Landscape Gardening on whatever terms Scott might consider satisfactory. It would have been congenial work, as is shown by his essays on that and kindred subjects. Scott's knowledge of landscape gardening and arboriculture was only obscured by more popular aspects of his many-sided genius. But his thoughts were fixed continually upon the remaining balance of debt which must be cleared, if ever, in the few remaining years of life which, his judgement told him, were all that he could hope to have. It was a race against time. Well-paid editorial work, or such sums as could be made by essay-writing of any kind, might be affluence for others, but they were of no use to him.

In the same spirit, but with a readier decision, he refused an offer which came this same morning from the publisher of the *Religious Discourses*, Colburn, that he should edit the Garrick papers, and preface them with a biography, for which £1,000 had been refused already, and for which he could now have any price he would like to ask. 'My name,' he said, 'would be only useful in the way of *puff*, for I really know nothing of the subject. So I will refuse; that's flat.'

And having decided to decline these alternative occupations, his mind went back to the doubt of whether he could still write such fiction as would command the old sales, and he ended with these reflections:

> "Having turned over my thoughts with some anxiety about the important subject of yesterday, I think we have done for the best. If I can rally this time, as I did in the Crusaders, why, there is the old trade open yet. If not, retirement will come gracefully after my failure. I must get the return of the sales of the three or four last novels, so as to judge what style of composition has best answered. Add to this, giving up just now loses £4,000 to the trustees, which they would not understand, whatever may be my nice authorial feelings. And moreover, it ensures the purchase of the copyrights—i.e. almost ensures them."

A couple of days later there was a call from Cowan, one of the Constable Trustees. Alexander Cowan, the paper merchant, was of a friendly disposition. It was he who assisted James Ballantyne by becoming the medium through which the printing business was ultimately purchased from Scott's Trustees, and became James's own property. But his present business was one in which his interests and Sir Walter's were not at one. For the benefit of the Constable estate, he wished the *Waverley* copyrights to be sold at the highest possible price: he was aware that Cadell and Scott were aiming to buy them. Whether there would be competition from the London trade, or to what height it might go, could be no more than guessed. Now the Trustees had to agree on a reserve price. It was a delicate negotiation, for, if there were no serious competition, the reserve would be the price at which they would be knocked down to Cadell's bid: on the other hand, it might make the whole proceeding abortive to fix it higher than Cadell and Scott were prepared to go. This 'upset' price had been tentatively fixed at £4,750.

Scott followed his usual business method, which was at once frank, bold and capable. He said he was anxious that the copyrights should not be lost. They were worth more to him than to anyone else, because he held the more recent ones, and only he could re-issue the works in a complete edition. He was willing that the reserve should be increased. He named £5,500. This could be considered a firm offer, on one condition. If that amount were not reached at the auction, there should be no private bargaining afterwards. The sale should be made to Cadell and himself at that price.

The condition attached to the offer, though it made no ultimate difference, might easily have been of a vital importance, as the event proved; and the fact that Scott foresaw so clearly the probable course that the sale would take, may be commended to the consideration of those who think they can supply a key to the enigma of his life by the assertion that he was of less than average business capacity.

Mr. Cowan accepted the offer, and Scott was left to think over the new responsibility which he was proposing to undertake. That night he summarised his thoughts in this cautious and yet confident paragraph:

"This speculation may be for good or for evil, but it tends incalculably to increase the value of such copyrights as remain in my own person; and, if a handsome and cheap edition of the whole, with notes, can be instituted in conformity with Cadell's plan, it must prove a mine of wealth, three-fourths of which will belong to me or my creditors. It is possible, no doubt, that the works may lose their effect on the public mind; but this must be risked, and I think the chances are greatly in our favour. Death (my own, I mean) would improve the property, since an edition with a Life would sell like wild-fire. Perhaps those who read this prophecy may shake their heads and say, "Poor fellow, he little thought how he should see the public interest in him and his extinguished even during his natural existence." It may be so, but I will hope better. This I know, that no literary speculation ever succeeded with me but where my own works were concerned; and that, on the other hand, these have rarely failed. And so—*Vogue la galère!*"

CHAPTER CVIII.

The copyrights were not destined to be bought in at the reserve figure. There were a number of publishers present who had travelled from London with the determination to purchase, and who did not intend that a thousand pounds, more or less, should deter them. If they had heard that Cadell was in the market, they had probably heard also the "upset" price, which might be taken to indicate the height to which he was prepared to go. It looked as though they might have to pay anything up to £6,000, and, huge as the figure sounded, they were prepared to do it; or more, if necessary. The real competition seemed likely to be among themselves, when Cadell should be left behind.

So they thought, and when the bidding passed the reserve they were not deterred. "They came on briskly, four or five abreast." The bidding passed £6,000. It passed £7,000. More slowly, it went up to £8,000. But Cadell had not ceased to bid. At £8,400 the copyrights were knocked down to him. Hurrying from the auction-room, to take the news to Scott, he encountered him in the street, on his way to the Bannatyne Club. He had been delayed in setting forth by the visit of a young lady who would not give her name, but who desired his advice in dealing with an uncle and aunt with whom she lived. He recorded this casual incident in a novelist's life in his Journal that night, together with particulars of the old friends (the Abercrombys, and Buchanan of Cambusmore) with whom he dined. But of that purchase of copyrights he did not know what to write. He must consider it till the following day.

It was no use blaming Cadell. There was a sufficient answer to that in the fact that the copyrights could be sold at a profit forthwith, if the price should be thought too high. For the position had developed exactly upon the lines which Scott had visualised in his talk with Cowan, though on a higher level. No one had thought before the auction of such a price being reached. They had gone up, hundred by hundred, rather than lose that which they had each come resolved to buy, and had hesitated at last at the £8,400 at which the hammer had come down. But when they thought it over, and realised that Cadell had been bold enough for such a purchase, they wished that they had bid more. Rather than go back defeated to London, they would give him a profit upon a transaction which might, perhaps frighten him by its magnitude in the cold blood of the following day. So they went to Cadell to know at what price he would sell.

But he did not want to sell. Neither did Scott, who thought it over, and decided that it was a good day's work.

> "I think the loss would have been very great had we suffered these copyrights to go from those which we possessed.... Even if they were worth only £8,400 to others, they were £10,000 to us. The largeness of

the price, arising from the activity of the contest, only serves to show the value of the property.... On the whole, I am greatly pleased with the acquisition."

Having recorded a considered opinion, which time has justified Scott reviewed his position. How far was he from a final victory? If the copyrights had been fairly valued, those which he possessed personally, including *Napoleon*, must have a large value also. He estimated a gross total of £24,200. His life was insured for £20,000. He added a valuation of books, plates and other property. In addition to that 6/- in the £ already paid, he reckoned that his death at any moment would place £50,000 at the disposal of his creditors. He concluded:

"There will still remain upwards of £35,000. Heaven's arm strike with us, 'tis a fearful odds, yet with health, and continued popularity, there are chances in my favour."

He went to dine with James Ballantyne, in the little suburban house into which he and his family were now crowded. It was a happy day for James. The purchase of those copyrights meant several years of busy profitable work for him. It meant a recovery of something of the old prosperity, from which the old worries would have been pruned away. It meant that he would be able to leave about £5,000 to his family at his death.

The next day, Scott returned to the subject in his Journal:

"Called at Cadell's, who is still enamoured of his bargain, and with good reason, as the London booksellers were offering him £1,000 or £2,000 to give it up to them. He also ascertained that all the copies with which Hurst & Robinson loaded the market would be off in a half year. Make us thankful! the weather is clearing to windward. Cadell is cautious, steady, and hears good counsel; and Gibson quite inclined, were I too confident, to keep a good look-out ahead."

On December 24th, having stayed a few days at Arniston, on the way from Edinburgh, Scott returned to Abbotsford, which he had left only six weeks before with his mind upon the alternatives of bankruptcy or a debtor's prison. He considered that his financial position might already have been on the way to re-establishment, had he then consented to bankruptcy, for which he would have had good excuse in the eyes of all.

> "But," he reflected, "I could not have slept sound, as I now can.... I see before me a long, tedious and dark path.... If I die in the harrows, as is very likely, I shall die with honour.... And so I think I can fairly face the return of Christmas day."

The old lavish Abbotsford hospitality might be impossible now, but there was a gathering of neighbours, and a few old Edinburgh friends—William Clerk, and the Lord Chief Baron, and the Lord Chief Commissioner, and some ladies, both old and young, so that there was a Christmas party full of mirth and harmony.

And two days later, there was a good letter from Cadell. It said that the *Tales of a Grandfather*, which had just been published, were going so well that he would like a revised or extended edition to be prepared at once.

So Scott turned to this congenial work while his guests went off to an inspection of Dryburgh Abbey—a regular feature of a visit to Abbotsford, from which he would excuse himself, since Charlotte had been buried there; and, when the last day of the year came, he was able to contrast it with that of twelve months earlier in a spirit of cheerfulness, if not of optimism.

> "...though I am still on troubled waters, I am now rowing with the tide, and less than the continuation of

my exertions of 1827 may, with God's blessing, carry me successfully through 1828, when we may gain a more open sea, if not exactly a safe port. Above all, my children are well. Sophia's situation excites some natural anxiety, but it is only the accomplishment of the burthen imposed on her sex. Walter is happy in the view of his majority, on which matter we have favourable hopes from the Duke of Wellington. Anne is well and happy. Charles' entry upon life under the highest patronage, and in a line for which I hope he is qualified, is about to take place presently.

For all these great blessings it becomes me well to be thankful to God, who in his good time and good pleasure sends us good as well as evil."

Sophia was expecting her third and last child, which was born early in January. Charles was entering the diplomatic service, to a career which was to continue honourably for fourteen years, when it would be ended by fever at Teheran.

CHAPTER CIX.

The demand for the *Tales of a Grandfather* was so much beyond anticipation that Cadell proposed to distribute the printing of a second edition among three firms, of which Ballantyne was, of course, to be one; but this suggestion was met by Scott with an emphatic veto. "I will not have poor James Ballantyne driven off the plank to which we are all three clinging."

It was a generous metaphor, the plank being entirely his, but it may be doubted whether there was much practical disadvantage from the decision, for James could do rapid work when the need came.

The news generally was good; Longmans, always reticent with information, admitted that *Napoleon* was going well. Confident in control of the copyrights, Scott began, in the intervals of other work, the preparation of notes for the great edition which was contemplated. Cadell thought it worth while to order 1000 copies of *St. Ronan's Well* to be printed-immediately, on the presumption that they would be sold before the announcement of the collected edition would spoil the market. Scott settled to the completion of *The Fair Maid of Perth*. He did this with some reluctance. He would have preferred to be engaged on revision of *Napoleon*, if he could have persuaded himself that another edition of the *Life* was an immediate requirement, and though he worked with an unremitting diligence he was not always satisfied with the result. James was silent, which he interpreted as disapproval, thinking he only waited to be asked, to express his disfavour. "But he may wait long enough, for I am discouraged enough."

When the criticism came, it was not welcomed. James said the characters were too monotonously Ossianic, which Scott disputed. When James objected to the death of Oliver Proudfute, Scott said that he was outrageous, and he would alter nothing. He had 'a humour to be cruel'. Cadell was better satisfied. He thought James was too hard on the book.

Cadell had good reason to be content. He told James that he had balanced his books, and showed from £3,000 to £4,000 to the good. Not a profit in book-debts, or doubtful bills: he had cash in the bank. As he had confined his publishing to Scott's own work, it was news to please them all three. It was a good augury for the *Magnum Opus*, as Scott called the new comprehensive edition which was in contemplation.

Scott rejected more than one offer of well-paid editorial work at this time, including one of from £1,500 to £2,000 annually if he would take charge of the *Keepsake*, an annual volume which was beautifully produced, but filled with literary trash of a sentimentally popular kind. And though he politely declined this doubtful honour, he sold *My Aunt Margaret's Mirror* to the *Keepsake* proprietors for £500, so it didn't go absolutely to the waste-paper-basket after all.

The weather was bitterly cold during the first two months

of the year in Edinburgh, and Scott had some return of rheumatism with swelling of his better knee, but otherwise he had little reason to complain of his health, or he did not record his troubles.

With the close of the season, he returned as usual to Abbotsford, where the *Fair Maid* was finished, for good or evil, on March 29th, and on the same afternoon Mr. Cadell, with James and Alexander Ballantyne, got down from the Edinburgh coach, and that evening a comprehensive scheme of action—and of work for Sir Walter, including the immediate starting of a new novel—which Cadell had outlined in a previous letter, was discussed in detail.

Cadell wanted the new edition of the novels, from *Waverley* to *Woodstock*, to be published in thirty-two volumes, at 5/- each, or £8. 0. 0. for the set. He proposed that they should be well produced with good frontispieces, and on a scale which would involve expenditure of anything from £4,000 to £8,000 before any return could be expected. To reconcile the Trustees to this outlay, and to provide the required funds, he offered to contract for three further novels, at £4,200 each, to be delivered at intervals of six months, and to make advances against this contract in cash, sufficiently to enable the *Magnum Opus* to be put in hand at once, or as soon as Scott should have the introduction and notes for the first volume ready.

There was a sharp difference of opinion between Cadell and James as to the quality of *The Fair Maid of Perth*. James's opinion was 'low'. That of Cadell was 'equally uppish'.

Scott thought James the better judge, but he recognised that the book was not the kind which he was quickest to appreciate. Cadell's opinion was more gratifying to an author's ears. Anyway, if the man who was to find the money was content to offer a fortune for three more of the same brand, and it was the one remaining purpose of Scott's life to earn it, the refusal could not come from him. He listened to a 'a long discourse' from Cadell, elaborating his scheme, and wrote to Gibson recommending its adoption.

It is not necessary to doubt that Cadell was genuine in his praise of *The Fair Maid of Perth*. He was backing up his opinion with his own cash, which was a good test. Yet, we may observe that he had much to incline him to the adoption of that opinion, and the course of action which he proposed. He owned a half-share of the copyrights. It was as important to him as to Scott that the new edition should be brought out. Scott could not finance it. Neither could James. The Trustees would be strange specimens of their kind if they would be prepared to do so. Only Cadell remained. If he had to find the money he could not easily do better than to stipulate for works of fiction against it. He had learnt already that Scott would be quickly willing to cancel a contract which was not satisfactory to the other side. A new novel from him was a valuable property, at the worst. At the best, it was an incalculable thing. It might be a gold-mine, indeed.

And, in fact, the one just finished deserved something better than the gloomy looks which James turned in its direction. There were passages in it in which imagination rose to the old vigour, the old vividness. It could not be said against it that it was a dull book. Yet its light was that of a setting sun. Scott had known the highest joy of humanity, the joy of work, to a degree which few men have been blessed to equal. But he did not now talk of the joy of work. He spoke of the daily task, counting the pages done.

Cadell went back to Edinburgh with James and Alexander feeling that he had done good business. Scott felt the same. He wrote:

> "The Ballantynes and Cadell left us in high spirits, expecting much from the new undertaking, and I believe they are not wrong. As for me, I became torpid...I was main stupid, indeed, and much disposed to sleep, though my dinner was very moderate."

It was only a fortnight ago, when overworking upon the conclusion of the book, that he had had a return of 'that vile palpitation of the heart—that *tremor cordis*—that hysterical passion which forces unbidden sighs and tears,' which had troubled him before, but seemed to have been overcome during recent months. How long—and to what further purpose—would courage and stubborn will drive the tired brain, and control the exhausted body?

Three days later, with Anne for company, he set off for London.

CHAPTER CX.

The visit to London, which meant a delay of two months before there could be an active commencement of the ambitious programme which had been agreed, was undertaken with reluctance, and for a number of reasons, each of which might have seemed separately insufficient. For its results, we have the advantage of a summary in the Journal, entered on the day of departure from London, which affords curious illustration of how large was the number of 'other men's oars' which Scott would still find occasion to pull.

> "1st. I have been able to place Lockhart on the right footing in the right quarter, leaving the improvement of his place of vantage to himself as circumstances should occur.
>
> 2nd. I have put the Chancery suit in the right train, which without me could not have been done.
>
> 3rd. I picked up some knowledge of the state of existing matters, which is interesting and may be useful.
>
> 4th. I have succeeded in helping to get a commission for James Skene.
>
> 5th. I have got two cadetships for the sons of Allan Cunningham.

> 6th. I have got leave to Andrew Shortreed to go out to India.
>
> 7th. I have put John Eckford into correspondence with Mr. Loch, who thinks he can do something for his claim.
>
> 8th. I have been of material assistance to poor Terry in his affairs.
>
> 9th. I have effectually protected my Darnick neighbours and myself against the new Road Bill.
>
> Other advantages there are, besides the great one of scouring up one's own mind a little and renewing intercourse with old friends bringing one's-self nearer in short to the currency of the time.
>
> All this may weigh against the expenditure of £200 or £250, when money is fortunately not very scarce with me."

Most of these items require no explanation. The Chancery suit was for the recovery, for his children's benefit, of the sum of Charlotte's money which had now been located in the hands of that Court.

Scott had arrived in London to receive the unexpected news that though the Adelphi Theatre, of which he had assisted Daniel Terry to obtain control, was (said to be) doing well, Terry himself was in a condition of total bankruptcy. It was a severe loss to one to whom money had become a serious consideration, for he had helped Terry to the extent of £500 in cash, in addition to the larger guarantees which would fall due during the next two years; but that was his least concern. He had hurried to Terry's solicitor on hearing the news to see what succour might still be possible. He examined the books, and decided that nothing could be done to defeat the crisis. It was an accumulation of old debts which had been his friend's undoing, 'with principal and interest accruing, and all the items which load a falling man'. The catastrophe occasioned an entry in the Journal which requires a pause of consideration:

> "It is written that nothing shall flourish under my shadow—the Ballantynes, Terry, Weber, Nelson, all came to distress. Nature has written on my brow, "Your shade shall be broad, but there shall be no protection derived from it to aught you favour"."

Considering the number of people whom Scott had been active to help during the last half-century, it was beyond reasonable expectation that they would all have subsequently become wise and prosperous citizens, especially as so many of them had been first encountered when fallen beside the way. In the three (otherwise different) cases of Weber, Nelson and Terry, habits of personal dissipation were, in differing degrees, responsible for their final catastrophes. The inclusion of Nelson's name is almost fantastic, he having been a man to whom, when 'down and out', Scott gave secretarial employment, and who left him of his own will to take up some form of military service, after which he was reported to have fallen ill, as a result of his own irregularities, and to have died in a Liverpool hospital. It will be seen, from a consideration of these cases, including that of Weber, how much—or how little—may be implied by the inclusion of Ballantyne's name in such a lamentation. But it is worth observation that Constable's name is not here. Constable had been utterly ruined by the same catastrophe from which Ballantyne was now emerging to a recovered prosperity. Had Scott recognised any measure of responsibility for his troubles, he could hardly have thought of Ballantyne without thinking also of the major tragedy. But Scott, who was always ready both to accept responsibility and to impute blame to himself, never did this, even in the self-revealing privacy of his own Journal. Neither did he write a single line to defend himself from such an imputation. It does not appear to have ever occurred to him that it could be made.

Yet it had been made, at the time of Constable's failure, in a letter from Sir James (then Mr.) Gibson-Craig, to Miss Edgeworth, of which Scott would not be likely to hear, and it has been repeated more or less uncertainly since, largely on the assertion which that letter contains, though an examination of it is sufficient to show that it would be deserving of little credence, even if we were not in possession of a more complete knowledge of the whole circumstances than Sir James was ever likely to have had the opportunity of acquiring.

Sir James alleged to Miss Edgeworth, in reply to a letter from her asking for information regarding Sir Walter's difficulties, that, to his own knowledge, Constable *in anxiety to save Scott* had commenced to exchange accommodation bills with him as far back as about 1813, which had produced, as it could not fail ultimately to do, the ruin of both.

It was the letter of a man who was antipathetic to Scott, and who probably had little liking for him. Sir James was of the opposite political party, which does not imply much in itself, for Scott had many friends in their ranks, but there is a significant note in his Journal at a time when (under a plan that came to nothing) the Directors of the Gas Co. elected Mr. Gibson-Craig and himself to represent them jointly in London:

> "Agreed to go to parliament a second time. James Gibson and I to go up as our solicitors. So curiously does interest couple up individuals, though I am sure I have no objection to Mr. James Gibson-Craig.'

It is an entry which, coming from Scott, implies more than it says. But Sir James's letter might still be true, though it were not written with a friendly pen. In fact, it contained that percentage of truth which a lie needs, but no more.

It is doubtless true that Scott and Constable exchanged accommodation bills in 1813, but it is obvious that anxiety to help Scott could not have necessitated a transaction of that nature. Constable might give bills with such an object: he could only take them to help himself. Actually, the transactions of 1813 had scarcely anything to do with the catastrophe of 1826.

Sir James, in his letter, omitted to give Miss Edgeworth the two fundamental facts of the position which are of an invincible quality, and which the persistent distortion to which it has been subjected make it necessary to emphasise and repeat.—That the final catastrophe did not occur through any act or default either of Constable, Ballantyne, or Scott, but through the failure of Constable's London agents to meet their engagements; and that, when this crisis came, Constable was found to be indebted to Scott personally, as well as to the printing house, for very large sums, and not Scott to him. Had Hurst, Robinson & Co paid their debts, Constable could have paid his; and had he paid his, Scott could have done the same with no difficulty at all. It may seem needless to repeat this after what has been said previously, but we are dealing with a lie that dies hard....

In Scott's decision to make this journey to London, he had been influenced, or at least encouraged, by the prospect of seeing his children and grandchildren, very probably for the last time, in a happy and complete assembly; for, besides the Lockharts, who were now living at Regent's Park, Walter and Jane were in London, stationed at Hampton Court, and Charles was living with the Lockharts. But that which might have been an occasion of glad re-union was darkened by a relapse in the condition of Johnnie Hugh, which co-incided with Scott's arrival in London. In a last vain effort to save the life of a slowly-dying child, Sophia took him to Brighton, and her father and Anne were left in a house from which its mistress, and all its gaiety had departed....

The 'New Road Bill' was one which was then in the hands of a Parliamentary committee. Its provisions would have taken a turnpike road through one of Scott's own fields, and swept away the dwellings of a number of cottagers at Darnick, who had a strong preference for remaining in their own homes. We may observe one of the first motions of the tide of parliamentary government which has since risen, in the course of the intervening century, to the destruction of all individual freedom, and the substitution of the servile comforts and securities of bureaucratic control. Even then, it is unlikely that anyone would have listened to the protests of the Darnick cottagers, or that they would have had enough manhood to make a useless effort to defend their homes. But Scott appeared before the committee on their behalf, and the officious road-makers discovered that they could go by a different way....

As to the old friends with whom Scott was able to renew acquaintance during this six-weeks' holiday in London, merely to record their names would be to show how vain it would be to attempt to follow him into all his friendships. To make a list of all who were most prominent, or most deserving of prominence, in art, in science, in religion, in civil government or military affairs, would be to arrive at the same place by a shorter path. He encountered, in more than casual meeting, the Duke of Wellington, Mr. Robert Peel, Sir James Macintosh, Lord John Russell, Samuel Rogers, Coleridge, Tom Moore, the Wordsworths, Tom Campbell, Joanna Baillie, Dr. Phillpotts, Morritt, Sir George Phillips, Theodore Hook, Sir Thomas Lawrence, Sydney Smith, the Duchess of Kent, the child-princess Victoria ('she is fair, but does not look as though she would be pretty'), and a host of others from whom it would be arbitrary to make selection, and tedious to detail. The old difference with Lord Holland was so completely forgotten that, on Scott visiting Holland House, Lady Holland prevailed upon him to stay the night, which he would usually be reluctant to do.

He met Mrs. Arkwright, and heard her on several occasions, experiencing as much delight "as sound could ever give me" from that lady's singing.

Scott had a love of music—particularly of vocal music—which may easily be misrepresented, and has been denied. Yet of the fact there is no doubt. Music, by his constant desire, was a regular feature of the evenings at Ashestiel and at Abbotsford, where cards seldom appeared. When Sophia married, Anne practised an art in which she was less naturally proficient, so that her father might not be deprived of hearing his favourite songs; her own preference being for foreign instrumental music.

But, in common with most poets, he had little appreciation

of music merely as a demonstration of vocal or instrumental gymnastics. This is a natural distinction, because poetry, though it aims in a kindred way to produce intricate and sustained beauties of sound, does this to the definite end of expressing its content more adequately than is possible by inferior prosaic constructions.

Music attempts the same end by a lower road. It may rouse the heights and stir the depths of emotion, but it is still a beast's cry, rather than a man's speech. Yet, if it cannot be equally articulate, it can at least try.

Wedded to words, it has reached its highest possibility but it is not an equality of marriage, or, if it he so, it is an equality which can be reached by submission only. Music must subordinate itself to words as a condition of its final triumph. If it will do this, there may be something greater begotten from such a union than either alone can give.

This may not be a complete statement of the case. Certainly, no musician would allow it to be so. But, whether consciously or not, it is the poet's attitude, with the few exceptions of those (such as Milton or Campion) who are musicians also. Scott expressed it when he praised Mrs. Arkwright for 'marrying music to immortal verse', and added that most people place them on separate maintenance....

He had wandered down England by a winding road, taking Carlisle, Penrith, Tamworth, Stratford, Warwick, and the beauties of Buckinghamshire on the way, that he might show them to Anne, and doubtless for his own pleasure also, but he returned in impatience for Abbotsford, doing more than a hundred miles a day on the Great North Road, which he called the dullest in England, and solacing its monotony by reading the first volume of Napier's *War in the Peninsular*, which had just been published. He could observer that it was not free from error, but noted that the defence of Sir John Moore (to whom his own *Napoleon* does less than justice) was 'spirited and well-argued'. He read also Lockhart's *Life of Burns*, concerning which he made a very disputable note in his Journal.

> "He has judiciously slurred over his vices and follies; for although Currie, I myself, and others, have not said a word more on this subject than is true, yet as the dead corpse is straightened, swathed, and made decent, so ought the character of such an inimitable genius as Burns to be tenderly handled after death. The knowledge of his vicious weaknesses or vices is only a subject of sorrow to the well-disposed, and of triumph to the profligate."

It is a curious judgement, because it advocates that which was contrary to his own method, the kindliness and penetrating sympathy of which was never allowed to pervert the truth, or obscure it. To understand might be to forgive, but it was not to deny. Even the sterner Dante was not more uncompromising in calling evil by its own name, though it had made its dwelling in those who were loved and admired on other grounds. Indeed this very note, which he must at least have half-intended to leave to posterity, is a defiance of that which it expressly condones.

Even if we accept with sympathy the idea that we should treat with a tender reticence the vices of one to whom we are so deeply in debt, it is of an obvious futility, for no probing into the events of any poet's life can reveal him so justly, or so deeply, as he will have done already by his own work; and a complete collection of the verse of Robert Burns exposes him, both in his baseness and his nobility, as nakedly as the most unreserved of biographies could ever do. How far, if at all, such a life should be written, or is worth writing, is another matter and Scott's proposition is, at least, of a better quality than is the practice to which much modern biography has fallen—that of seeking diligently for dirt, even when it is not there.

CHAPTER CXI.

They stopped one night at Rokeby, and left after breakfast, reaching Carlisle in the dusk of a rainy evening. It was a well-known road to Scott, who had ridden or driven it under many varying circumstances. He had halted here sufficiently long on the way south to visit the Cathedral, so that he might stand on the spot where he had married Charlotte more than thirty years before. Now he fought against the sombre memories of the past, and the realisation of his own decay in animal strength and mental energy, as the rain fell without, and he would gladly have pushed on in the early morning to the expected welcome of Abbotsford; but he had to wait to secure a certificate from the parish register, to support the claim in the Chancery Court, and it was approaching noon before they left the Carlisle walls, and pushed on rapidly enough for a late lunch at Hawick, and to rouse the joyful barking of the dogs as they drove through the gates of Abbotsford, in the late dusk of the long June day.

For the two months that Scott had been away, he had scarcely written a line for publication, or corrected twenty pages of proof-sheets. He had spent the time in congenial friendly intercourse, and a rigid moderation of physical indulgence, and though it had not been without its sorrow, it had been a time of peace to mind and body, such as he had not often experienced. He recorded, as he looked back, that the two months had passed without a single attack of the depression of spirits against which he was so often obliged to struggle, or the *tremor cordis* which was its resulting physical penalty. He waked to spend one idle happy day in the plantations he loved.

> "I waked to walk about my beautiful young woods with old Tom and the dogs. The sun shone bright, and the wind fanned my cheek as if it were a welcoming. I did not do the least right thing, except packing a few books necessary for the completion of the *Tales*. In this

merry mood I wandered as far as Huntley Burn, where I found the Miss Fergussons well and happy: then I sauntered back to Abbotsford, sitting on every bench by the way.... I cannot afford to spend many such days nor would they seem so pleasant."

The next day he went on to Edinburgh....

The brief happiness of these June days of 1828, and the measure of recovered health which they record, suggest what difference of vigour and longevity might have resulted had Hurst, Robinson & Co.- not speculated in hops. Different they would doubtless have been. Happier, probably. Better is a harder word.

The first morning in Edinburgh was cheered by Cadell's presence at breakfast, with the news that the *Fair Maid of Perth* was going well. Yet Scott knew the truth of the lessening of his intellectual vitality, and it was with courage rather than confidence that he wrote that night:

"A disappointment being always to be apprehended, I too am greatly pleased that the evil day is adjourned, for the time must come—and yet I can spin a tough yarn still with anyone now going."

There was good news also of the *Tales of a Grandfather*, for which the demand continued. This meant financial ease in personal expenditure, for there was now a vaguely agreed plan that he should give the proceeds of his major fiction, and of the editing of the new projected edition, to the Trustees, and support himself and the reduced Abbotsford establishment on his official salaries, and the bye-products of his pen, of which the *Tales* had provided an unexpectedly liberal fund. It was this revenue, and the fact that Cadell's rejection of *My Aunt Margaret's Mirror*, and *The Laird's Jock* had left him free to sell the serial rights of these two tales to the *Keepsake*, which had enabled him to finance the London holiday with a quiet mind, and to indulge in at least a shadow of the generosities which had been one of the major pleasures of earlier years. He had arranged a system of dealing with his accounts similar to that which he had had with Ballantyne in the old affluent days. They were sent to Cadell, who paid them for him, and debited them against the royalties which the *Tales* were earning. But Cadell kept his books with care. Three days after they had breakfasted together:

> "Cadell rendered me report of accounts paid for me, with vouchers, which very nearly puts me out of all shop debts. God grant me grace to keep so!"

Mr. Gibson had called in the meantime, and though the Trustees were disposed to some argumentative reluctance concerning the scale of the proposed expenditure upon the *magnum opus*, yet it was evident that they only required firm handling to be brought to heel. And Scott, refreshed with rest and animated with new hope, set steadily to work again.

On June 6th, he 'wrought both before and after dinner, and finished five pages, which is two above bargain.' It may be well to mention again that these 'pages' amounted each to several of type. June 7th, being Saturday, was 'another working day, and nothing occurred to disturb me'. On Sunday, he did five sheets again.

On Monday, he 'laboured till one', when he was obliged to go out on business errands. The record of the next five days, when the Court was sitting, is grouped together in a single entry, such as his Journal had not previously contained:

> "June 10-14. During these five days almost nothing occurred to diversify the ordinary task of the day, which, I must own, was dull enough. I rose to my task by seven, wrought it out in the course of the day, far exceeding the ordinary average of three leaves per day. I have attended the Parliament House with the

most strict regularity, and returned to dine alone with Anne."

On June 17th, there is this ominous entry:

"Violent rheumatic headache all day. Wrought, however. But what difference this troublesome addition may make on the quality of the stuff produced truly I do not know. I finished five leaves."

On the next day:

"My head aches...well, I have finished my task, and have the right to sleep if I have a mind."

The headache continued, as did the work, during the following day, and on the next he "scribbled very lustily", and then went to Court. On his return:

"Wrote when I came home, both before and after dinner—that's all, I think. I am become a sort of writing automaton, and truly the joints of my knees, especially the left, are so stiff and painful in rising and sitting down that I can hardly help screaming—I that was so robust and active. I get into a carriage with great difficulty. My head, too, is bothered with rheumatic headaches....

June 20th.—My course is still the same.

June 22nd.—Wrought. Had a note from Ballantyne complaining of my manuscript, and requesting me to read it over. I would give £1,000 if I could; but it would take me longer to read than write...I will look at his proof, however, and then be quiet and idle for the rest of the evening...."

After the plain warning of the manuscript which James was unable to interpret, Scott took things more easily for a couple of days, though he wrote many letters: "So on the whole I am no bad boy."

The next day he again did more than the allotted 'task' which he now aimed to put forth with a monotonous regularity. A few days later he was recording the return of the rheumatic headaches, and on the 8th of July the Journal abruptly ceased until the January of the following year.

CHAPTER CXII.

Lockhart spent the Christmas of 1828 at Abbotsford. With the commencement of the new year, there came a quiet, congenial little group of other visitors—Morritt and his niece, Skene, and Sir James Stewart of Allanbank among them, and the Fergussons and others were coming in frequently. Lockhart thought that 'except that he suffered from rheumatism' Sir Walter was well in health. How he felt himself was (as we shall see) a somewhat different matter.

He had had six months of hard, monotonous work, for the results of which he must wait in doubt, (except only that he had added much to the *Tales of a Grandfather*, and that these children's tales were proving to be a mine of unexpected richness), and in the depression of this unrelieved alternation of the Courtroom and his own desk, his Journal had lain neglected from day to day, till he had lacked heart to enter its arrears, and had let it cease.

Much had been done upon the *magnum opus*, from which so much was hoped, but there was much more still to do. It was nine months since the contract had been signed with Cadell for three further novels at six-monthly intervals, against which the funds were to be provided to finance the major enterprise, but no novel had been delivered.

It was a day of deep snow early in January when Scott's

guests sat in the library at Abbotsford, and he gave them the proof-sheets of about half a new novel to read. He went into the next room, to his own work, but came in at intervals as the morning passed, to enquire how they liked the tale.

With the old boldness of conception, he had chosen a new period, a new background; and with the old fertility of invention he was constructing a good tale. It had moved forward slowly, for the *magnum opus* was an immense and urgent work, and he had often felt more inclined to pursue it than to add to the manuscript of the novel, but it was about half done now, and he felt, rather doubtfully—well, that it might be worse.

"All," Lockhart assures us, "were highly gratified with those vivid and picturesque pages." Both Morritt and Stewart gave particular approbation to the descriptions of Swiss scenery, with which they were familiar, but which their author had never seen. Naturally, Scott was pleased by the praise. Lockhart says that he had never seen him more gently and tranquilly happy.

'Tranquil' is a significant word. It is not one which would have occurred to anyone to apply to Scott in earlier years, even for his serener moods. The praise given to this first half of *Anne of Geierstein* seems to have been quite genuine, though it was not coming from impartial critics. The pleasure it gave may have shown the depth of the doubt in its author's mind.

Scott had hesitated about resuming his Journal at the commencement of the year. When his guests left on January 10th, and there would still be three days before he must return to Edinburgh, he overcame his reluctance, and opened it again. He did not record that he had had any happiness, tranquil or otherwise, during the past three weeks. He wrote:

> "I cannot say I have been happy, for the feeling of increasing weakness in my lame leg is a great affliction. I walk now with pain and difficulty at all times, and it sinks my soul to think how soon I may be altogether a disabled cripple. I am tedious to my friends, and I doubt the sense of it makes me fretful.

> Everything else goes off well enough. My cash affairs are clearing, and though last year was an expensive one, I have been paying debt. Yet I have a dull contest before me, which will probably outlast my life...."

In fact, the six-months interval had been sufficient to show how certainly the night was falling. There is not only the increasing failure of physical powers: there is less capacity for concentration, less ability to perform long hours of literary labour, though the will is unweakened, and drives forward with a remorseless monotony.

On the 13th, Scott travelled back to Edinburgh over frozen roads, and the next day he recorded:

> "This morning I got back some of the last copy, and tugged as hard as ever did Soutar to make ends meet. Then I will be reconciled to my task, which at present disgusts me...Lockhart dined with us, which made the evening a pleasant but an idle one. Well! I must rouse myself.
> "Awake! Arise, or be for ever fallen."

A few days later, he went with Lockhart on a two days' excursion to Milton, to see a new property that William Lockhart had purchased there. The fight against a growing disability to walk abroad was being undertaken with the same obstinate spirit that calculated the remaining balance of mental energy against the total of debts that were still unpaid.

> "During this excursion, I walked very ill—with more pain, in fact, than I ever remember to have felt—and, even leaning on John Lockhart, could hardly get on.
> January 24th.—Heavy fall of snow.... The day bitter cold. I went to the Court and with great difficulty

returned along the slippery street. I ought to have taken the carriage, but I have a superstitious dread of giving up the habit of walking, and would willingly stick to the last by my own hardy customs.... My hands are so covered with chillblains that I can hardly use a pen—my feet ditto.

January 26th.—I muzzed on—I can call it little better—with *Anne of Geierstein*. The materials are excellent, but the power of using them is failing. Yet I wrote out about three pages sleeping at intervals.

January 29th.—I wrote only two or three pages of *Anne*. I am as one

"who in a darksome way
Doth walk with fear and dread."

But walk I must, and walk forward too, or I shall be benighted with a vengeance."

So *Anne* moved forward with effort enough, and at no great pace, though there was a day at the beginning of February which saw eight pages done—and the second volume finished. The momentary sense of recovered power made the work pleasant again; and though there were several days of violent headache to follow, there was some reduction in the disability of the lamer leg, and on the 19th, it being an execrable day "half sleet, half rain, and wholly abominable", he walked round by the North Bridge, and "faced the weather for two miles".

He had a settled determination to finish *Anne* before the time should come, in the middle of March, for returning to Abbotsford, and had the encouragement of the knowledge that the heavy expenditure of money and time upon the *magnum opus* was to be justified by results. A preliminary prospectus, sent out by Cadell to the trade, had resulted in such a total of orders that it was resolved that the quantity of the first edition should be increased from 7,000 to 10,000 copies—for which the price to the public would be £80,000.

So he worked on with a fresh hope, and had a feeling of unworthy irritation when he found that his manuscript of *Anne* was being sent to the printers somewhat more rapidly than proofs were coming back to him, and learnt that it was because James was neglecting business on the pretext of his wife's illness. James 'had a nature to indulge apprehensions of the worst'. To neglect business on such excuse was an amiable weakness, for which it was quite easy to feel contempt. But two days later he heard that Mrs. Ballantyne was dead.

The first effect of his wife's death on James Ballantyne was that he broke down completely. Scott realised this probability, for he noted:

> "With his domestic habits the blow is irretrievable. What can he do, poor fellow, at the head of such a family of children! I should not be surprised if he were to give way to despair."

James was unable to attend the funeral, and he came to Shandwick Place a few days later in a mood suggestive of religious mania, to announce that he was retiring to the country to await his end.

He had at this time acquired possession of the printing business, to which he had admitted his brother Alexander to partnership, and was re-establishing his commercial position, with the essential assistance of the orders which were being placed with him for the *magnum opus*, and Scott's other publications.

To enable him to arrive securely at this position it had been essential for him, according to the Scottish law of that time, to obtain letters of consent from his creditors to the discharge of the sequestration of his estate. Such letters, if there be sufficient goodwill or business interest to obtain that they be written at all, are about as valuable as tombstones for authentic evidence of character; yet there may be significance in their omissions or in the assertions which they contain; and in view of Lockhart's allegations against James Ballantyne, it is interesting to observe the kind of documents with which he was able to support his application.

That from Scott himself, worded with an appropriate formality, reads:

> Dear Sir,
>
> I am favoured with your letter, and, so far as I am concerned, give my consent with great pleasure to your discharge, being satisfied that, in all your transactions with me, you have acted with the utmost candour and integrity. I am, dear sir,
>
> Your most obedient servant,
>
> Walter Scott.

From a firm of Edinburgh bill-discounters, he received this:

> Sir,
>
> We deeply regret that you should have been exposed to such great affliction from an over-confidence in others, knowing, as we do, that your integrity and correct business habits should have led to a far different result.
>
> We have much pleasure in signing your discharge, accompanied by our best wishes for your continued prosperity. We remain, dear sir,
>
> Your very obedient servants,
>
> Alex. Allan & Co.

If James had really brought a flourishing business to ruin by a career of reckless extravagance, in which he had deceived and cheated his partner and defrauded his creditors, they are remarkable letters to have been written under whatever circumstances.

It is a curious fact that Cadell experienced much greater difficulty than Ballantyne in obtaining the discharges which he required, probably because there was money among his relatives that it was hoped to reach; and, even at this time, the Old Bank were still standing out, and Scott had to use the argument that Cadell's ambiguous position, while proving to be of no profit to them, was detrimental to his own (Scott's) interests, to influence them in the right direction.

But now James was to give Scott a degree of trouble which had no relation to finance. The melancholia which threatened to overwhelm him was a form of weakness against which Scott would have made a better fight than the printer was likely to do, and he was too clear-sighted not to recognise with some contempt the mixture of egotism and cowardice which religious mania requires for sustenance. For the moment, and under the immediate influence of the stronger man, James 'bore his distress sensibly' in Scott's phrase, continuing at his desk, and rewarding Scott's efforts in his own way by writing a letter to Cadell in which he expressed the decided opinion that *Anne* was no better than unprintable rubbish. Cadell sent the letter to Scott, who called him into immediate conference. The result was a decision to put the book aside for a few weeks, and then approach it again with a fresh mind. Cadell said that nothing could be lost by that, for it would have been a mistake, even had it been ready, to publish it while the Catholic Emancipation struggle was at its height.

That was a question which was agitating the country with an extremity of bitterness which it is no longer easy to realise. After a hesitation which may have shown practical sagacity beyond that of the policy of either of the political parties which were divided on this issue, Scott had decided to give the measure his support, and had signed a petition to Parliament in its favour. Peel wrote to him: "The mention of your name as attached to the Edinburgh petition was received with loud cheers."

Scott's view was that it was a demand of justice which must be granted, and must be done generously, but he had no belief in the argument of its advocates that it would pacify Ireland. He thought that the absentee landlords were the major political evil there. Now he wrote:

> "I am not confident that the measure will disarm the Catholic spleen. And not entirely easy at finding myself allied to the Whigs, even in this instance, where I agree with them. This is witless prejudice, however."

So it was agreed to put *Anne* aside for a few weeks, and Scott went to Abbotsford, and turned to review-articles, and the *magnum opus*, and miscellaneous writing, and found that, though his strength might have diminished, he could still make better efforts at walking on the softer country paths than he had been able upon the streets of Edinburgh. It was April 14th when he noted that he

> "set a stout heart to a stay brae, and took up *Anne of Geierstein*. I had five sheets standing by me, which I read with care, and satisfied myself that worse had succeeded, but it was while the fashion of the thing was new. I retrenched a good deal about the Troubadours, which was really *hors de place*. As to King René, I retained him as a historical character. In short, I will let the sheets go nearly as they are, for though J.B. be an excellent judge of this species of composition, he is not infallible, and has been in circumstances which may bias his mind. I might have taken this determination a month since, and I wish I had. But I thought I might strike out something better by the braes and burn-sides. Alas! I walk along them with painful and feeble steps, and invoke their influence in vain. But

my health is excellent, and it were ungrateful to complain either of mental or bodily decay."

But no reflection could alter his feeling towards the unfinished novel, which was now one of actual hostility. "I don't know why or wherefore, but I hate *Anne*. I mean *Anne of Geierstein*, the other two Annes are good girls."—It should have been mentioned before this that his niece (Tom's daughter) was now living at Abbotsford again, as a companion to the daughter who was giving up her youth to her father's care, and was only destined to survive him by a few months.

Yet, having recommenced upon the book, he completed it stubbornly: "Whether I succeed or not, it would be dastardly to give in." It was finished on April 29th, and published by the middle of May. Both Scott and Cadell watched its advent with minds which were prepared for failure, but, in fact, it was well received. It had taken twelve months to write, and had been the product of prolonged mental effort, as its texture shows. Had the same time and care been bestowed upon it five or ten years earlier, it might well have had its place among the very first of the *Waverley* novels. As it was, Scott's utmost efforts could not make it more than a respectable member of that goodly company. It begins flatly, and ends in a dull way, but there are better pastures among its very numerous pages....

While Scott was at Abbotsford, he had bad news of James, who showed a disposition to neglect his business entirely for the contemplation of his religious uncertainties. James never owed more to Scott at any time of his life than he did now for the letters he received in which, in Scott's own phrase, the earlier pity gave place to anger, till he sent at last an ultimatum which brought James back to the desk which he should not have left.

Having been persuaded to return, he was roused to alarm by finding that Cadell was on the point of placing orders for part of the *magnum opus* elsewhere, and wrote in haste to Scott to interpose on his behalf, as he had done at similar issues before. But Scott thought it best to send him a stiff reply that 'he must be his own friend, set shoulder to the wheel, and remain at the head of his business'....

The funeral of Lord Buchan took Scott this April into Dryburgh Abbey, where he had not been since Charlotte was buried there, and which he had not thought to enter again till he should be laid beside her. A consideration of the records of Lord Buchan, and some other of the Erskine family led him to make a note in his Journal that "it is saving not getting which is the mother of riches". But it is possible to observe a result without admiring the process from which it comes. There had been an occasion, eighteen months before, when Scott had been in conversation with the Lord Chief-Commissioner, as they returned from an enquiry respecting Lord Melville's collar-bone (which he had had the misfortune to break), and the L.C-C. had quoted a dictum of Sir Gilbert Elliot: "No chance of opulence is worth the risk of a competence." Scott recorded it with this pregnant comment: "It was not the thought of a great man, but perhaps that of a wise one."

Scott might admire caution or thrift: there might even be occasions on which he would deliberately observe them. But he worshipped at other shrines.

CHAPTER CXIII.

The days that saw the completion of *Anne of Geierstein* had brought an offer from Sir James Macintosh of £1,000 for a one-volume history of Scotland to be included in Longmans' Encyclopaedia. It was a work which Scott felt could be completed in a few weeks, and from the resources of his own mind, and after a short pause of consideration he wrote accepting the offer. He actually commenced the work before the conclusion of *Anne*, and before the contract had been formally ratified.

The notes he makes in reference to this offer show how difficult he found the task of restricting expenditure, with perhaps some lukewarmness in those around him towards his more economical proposals, it being the common knowledge of all that they made no difference except to the total of the Trusteeship Fund.

> "It is the sum I have been wishing for, sufficient to enable me to break the invisible but magic circle which petty debts of myself and others have placed around me. With common prudence I need no longer go from hand to mouth, or what is worse, anticipate my means. I may also pay off some small shop-debts &c belong to the Trust, clear off all Anne's embarrassments, and even make some foundations of a provision for her.... If fine, within six weeks I am sure that I can do the work and secure the independence I sigh for. Must I not make hay while the sun shines? Who can tell what leisure, health, and life may be destined to me?... I have been of late in a great degree free from wafered letters, sums to make up, notes of hand wanted, and all the worry of an embarrassed man's life. This last struggle will free me entirely, and so help Heaven it shall be made!... Besides my large debts, I have paid since I was in trouble at least £2,000 of personal encumbrances.... I really believe the sense of this apparently unending struggle, schemes for retrenchment in which I am unseconded, made me low-spirited, for the sun seems to shine brighter upon me as a free man."

So he took a walk, with the help of Tom Purdie's shoulder, and turned in earnest to the writing of the one-volume history which became a two-volume one in the end, appearing in the Cabinet Cyclopedia, and bringing in £1,500 in place of the smaller amount of the original bargain.

With his more personal financial necessities relieved by this contract, Scott went back to Edinburgh to learn from Cadell that the labour upon the *magnum opus* was not being made in vain. Orders continued to come in, and the quantities of the first printing were being increased at every estimate. It would be tiresome to record these figures as they were revised and extended. It was on May 20th that Cadell came to breakfast, and submitted calculations from which it appeared that in the course of three or four years there must be a gross profit of not less than £50,000 to divide. If that were so, ten years of life and work would see the end of every confronting difficulty. Scott noted cheerfully that it might be too soon for the counting of chickens, but that they were certainly chipping the shell.

The collected edition was to be issued in monthly parts, of which eight appeared during this year. The first printing of *Waverley* was increased from 7,000 to 10,000, then to 12,000, and on June 5th to 15,000 copies. Calculations of divisible gross profit in sight rose to £18,000 a year on that day.

It became a matter of urgent importance to secure the copyrights of poetry which were still in the hands of Longmans and Murray, so that the edition should be extended into a complete and unencumbered property.

Murray held a fourth share of *Marmion*. Being approached, he declined to place a value upon it, but, with a fine generosity, he gave it back to its author.

Longmans were willing to deal, but they had a substantial stock of books on hand. They said that they would hand these over, and surrender their copyrights, for an inclusive payment of £8,000. There was some delay over the conclusion of this bargain, which required a rather difficult understanding between Scott and Cadell as to the apportionment of any resulting deficiency. Cadell made a proposal which Scott rightly rejected as unfair to himself. Then, with equal shrewdness and goodwill, Cadell agreed to leave the matter for Scott himself to decide when the loss upon the stock (if any) should have been ascertained. In the end, Longmans came down to £7,000, to be paid in bills at from one to three years, Cadell being free to realise the stock in the meantime. So the bargain was made—a fair one on either side.

Scott had Cadell to dinner on June 5th, the two Annes having gone out for the evening, and it was the delivery of letters during this meal which caused the final decision to increase the printing of the first volume to 15,000 copies. They sat calculating fortunes, and discussing the purchase of those remaining copyrights, and when Cadell got up to go Scott remembered that his pocket was empty, and that he was without any instant means of refilling it, and had to borrow ten pounds.

He had been staying quietly at home for a day or two before this, under his doctor's urgent orders, for he had had some fresh symptoms of physical trouble since his return to Edinburgh, with attacks of hemorrhage, for which cupping had been prescribed, and appeared to be a satisfactory remedy; for, after a quiet week in his own rooms, and one or two gentle strolls in the gardens of Princes Street, he made a note on June 10th: "My complaint quite gone," and took his place at the Court of Session again that day. On June 12th there was an apparent necessity that the first printing of *Waverley* must be increased to 17,000—a 'monstrous number'—and as Scott was leaving for a week of recuperation at Abbotsford, he heard that it was to be 3,000 more.

He returned to Edinburgh, where he was expecting Charles, with Sophia and her children—including John Hugh, who still got weaker, but did not die—to arrive by one of the new steamboats. Cadell came to breakfast again on the first morning, looking overworked, and saying that he had actually ordered new steel plates, though those which were now in use were supposed to print up to 30,000 without deterioration.

There is no evidence that there was any relaxation of work at this period, during which the Scottish history was on hand and the editing of the *magnum opus* was always able to provide occupation for what might otherwise have been a leisure hour, but it is significant that there was no talk of completing the contract for the three novels, of which only one had been supplied. It is evident that such undertakings could not be commenced again in the old confident spirit, nor pursued with the rapid ease of more vigorous days. If Scott thought of such an enterprise now, it was as of a labour of doubtful issue. He hesitated and deferred.

Cadell may have hesitated too. Why should he stake another £4,200, when the last amount had seemed to be so hazardously risked, and hardly, as it were, dragged with difficulty over the borderline of success? Besides, he was more than busy with orders for the new editions. And there was no longer need for a novel-fund with which to finance these printings. In every way, the torrent of orders which was pouring in tended to sweep away the thought of that dormant contract.

So Scott went back to Abbotsford at the Session's end, well content with the progress of his affairs, talking of better health since he had recovered from that disconcerting attack of a month ago, and happy in the company of children and grandchildren, in a circle from which Walter only was absent....

Visitors were beginning to come to Abbotsford again now, though not in the old numbers, nor with the old half-invited freedom. Mrs. Hemans came this July. Scott liked her, and her talk of her five children. She was 'a clever person, and has been pretty'. Sophia and the Annes were more critical. They said she was too 'blue'.

She went a walk with Scott, and discoursed to him upon the peculiar melancholy attached to the words 'no more'. He agreed about that. He should have replied by reciting *Where shall the lover rest?*, or *A weary lot is thine*, but he re-acted differently. He gave her one of his inexhaustible anecdotes. It was of a man who had ridden home over Cockenzie sands, with his wife behind him. Being drunk, she fell off the pillion into the arms of the advancing tide. Being in the same condition he arrived at Prestonpans before he noticed his loss. When he returned with neighbours, they found her with the waves lapping her mouth, while she murmured drowsily: 'No mair! I thank you kindly, not a drap mair.'

The two poets each talked after their own kinds, and the subject of *no more* was comprehensively considered in all its aspects. They returned amicably from their walk together— 'dined in family, and all well'.

Mr. Hallam came to Abbotsford also, during this autumn,

bringing his young son Arthur. We might know more of this visit but, after Mrs. Hemans left, the Journal abruptly ceased. On July 20th Scott wrote: "A rainy day, and I am very drowsy, and would give the world to—."

But he left the sentence unfinished, and what he wished we shall never know.

CHAPTER CXIV.

The curtain did not fall after that cryptic entry, but the shadows gathered during the autumn. One by one actors and audience are leaving, and the stir of departure draws attention, rather than the last scenes upon the darkening stage.

In October, rather suddenly, Lady Jane Stuart died. It was, to Scott, the close to what he regarded as the major grief of his life, for he had developed a habit of calling at 12, Maitland Street when in Edinburgh, and talking of those events of which only they two were alive to know—for Sir William Forbes had died a year earlier.

Tom Purdie also died as October ended. "There is a heart cold," Scott wrote to William Laidlaw, "that loved me well." Tom had even read the *Waverley* novels—'our books'—as he called them from love of their author, and had not been unrewarded, for he said they sent him to sleep as nothing else could.

Now there had come a day when he felt unwell, being out with his master at the time, and when the weather broke into storm Scott told him to leave him, and hurry home, which he refused to do. The next morning he got up without complaint, went to the table, and sat with his head resting on his arm.... His daughter spoke to him, and found that he was dead....

The sales of the new edition continued to increase, and by December they had reached a monthly total of 35,000. Scott talked no more of fiction, but he was busily occupied with further *Tales of a Grandfather*, which also seemed to be an unbottomed mine, though of a smaller yield. And he had on hand also a series of *Letters on Demonology and Witchcraft* for Murray's *Family Library.* Working to the limit of physical power, and counting always the length of his remaining days against the reducing total of debt for which provision must still be made, he went on until the middle of February (1830), when there came a day on which he attended Court as usual, and found a lady waiting his return whose father's Memoirs he had promised to look through and prepare for the press.

He took the MS. from her, and sat silently for half-an-hour, as though occupied with the papers before him. Then he tried to rise, failed, and sat down. He made a second effort, and walked unsteadily to the drawing-room, were Anne and Violet Lockhart were sitting, and fell forward across the floor.

Later, he wrote to Walter:

> "Anne would tell you of an awkward sort of fit I had on Monday last: it lasted about five minutes, during which I lost the power of articulation, or rather of speaking what I wished to say. I revived instantly, but submitted to be bled, and to keep the house for a week, except exercising walks. They seem to say it is from the stomach. It may or may not be a paralytic affection. We must do the best we can in either event. I think by hard work I will have all my affairs regulated within five or six years, and leave the means of clearing them in case of my death...I feel, thank God, no mental injury, which is most of all to be deprecated. Still, I am a good deal failed in body within these two or three last years, and the *singula praedantur* come by degrees to make up a sum. They say 'do not work', but my habits are such that it is not easily managed, for I would be driven mad with idleness."

For the time, it seemed that Scott recovered almost absolutely from this attack. He submitted for a considerable period to the strictest diet of 'pulse and water' which the medical faculty was accustomed to prescribe (rather late in the day) for such conditions; and, as had happened in the sequel of more than one previous illness, his constitution responded to the treatment, and, being compulsorily slowed down, it appeared to renew its strength. When he went about again, people noticed little difference in his appearance. The dreaded word paralysis, the disease of which father and brother had died, was scarcely whispered, even in his own family, was only half-admitted to his own mind.

Three months later, when about to return from Abbotsford to Edinburgh, he opened his Journal again, and commenced regular entries. They give no immediate evidence of failing health—indeed show more of serenity and vigour than is in the record of some previous periods. On May 24th he 'walked in very bad day to George Square from the Parliament House'. And he was still writing incessantly, under the pressure of the old urgency:

> "Wrought with proofs &c at the *Demonology*, which is a cursed business to do neatly. I must finish it though, for I need money...I was frightened by a species of fit which I had in February, which took from me my power of speaking. I am told it is from the stomach. It looked woundy like palsy or apoplexy. Well, be it what it will, I can stand it."

But the next day records his intention to retire from the long-held office of Clerk of Session. There was a projected reform by which the number of these clerks was to be reduced from six to four, giving a favourable opportunity for superannuation, and though it must mean some reduction of income, there was the cost of the Edinburgh house to be put against that, and 'I think the difference will be infinite in point of health and happiness'. The *magnum opus* was still going well, and 'if this can last for five or six years longer we may clear our hands of debt'.

So he still laboured, calculated, planned; doing three hours work in the morning before he left for the Court ('God bless that habit of being up at seven! I could do nothing without it.'), and recording the results with a general cheerfulness, and filling his Journal for the most part with the affairs of others, and reminiscence and anecdote, but with the strain showing clearly at times, as in the brief following entries:

> June 12th.—A day of general labour, and much weariness.
> June 13th.—The same may be said of this day.
> June 14th.—And of this, only I went out for an hour and a half.

and then, two days later, there comes the result of this concentration in the more cheerful note:

> "June 16th.—I wrought this forenoon till I completed the 100 pages, which is well done."

And that night he went to the theatre to see Fanny Kemble play *Isabella*, as he had surely earned the right to do, but had a sense of exhaustion next day, which kept him half-reluctantly at home, not caring much for the play that would be on that night, but remembering that Miss Kemble ought to be supported, because she had given 'her active support to her father at his need'. So he rested at the fire-side, and feeling better as the evening advanced, he turned to work again, and wrote three pages before he went to bed, blaming himself that he had 'lost a day' by the morning's headache.

He went home at the commencement of the long vacation, still in uncertainty as to whether it would be necessary for him to return to Edinburgh, but his application was formally granted a few weeks later, the salary of £1,300 being reduced to a retiring allowance of £840. Sir Robert Peel offered, on behalf of the Government, to add a pension sufficient to cover the difference, but Scott, after discussing the matter with his Trustees, rightly refused this. He was receiving an adequate retiring allowance, and was making a large income, however he might feel obliged to apply it. Such a pension would have been without moral justification. It would have been accepting a donation from the national purse toward the debts which he was still resolute that no one should assist him to pay.

The Lockharts came to Abbotsford that summer, and observed that there were more visitors coming than there had been during the previous year. Scott seemed in good spirits, for the most part, though of an obviously reduced vitality. He ate abstemiously, according to the strict medical directions he had received. He wrote regularly, and continued at his desk for as long hours as ever, but with more evident signs of fatigue as the evening came. He was cheered by the news that, though the issue of the novels had reached the point at which some of those which had been less popular on publication were appearing, yet the sales were maintained—were even increased. The Trustees, on whom he had been urging for some time the payment of a second dividend, had agreed to this, and the debts were to be reduced by a further 3/- in the £ before the year closed.

He contrived (Lockhart thought) to entertain his guests so that they saw little change, but his mouth would twitch uncontrollably at times when he was agitated, and this was noticed when he was reading letters from James Ballantyne, for the printer would hint that the quality of the copy he was receiving was not quite what it had once been.

Tom Purdie's shoulder was no longer available for the daily walks among the plantations, but Scott could still ride Douce Davie, if he were helped to mount, and he often did so in the summer weather, amid a retinue of grandchildren and others on ponies and donkeys. And William Laidlaw—back at Kaeside since Tom died—would be walking beside him to take instructions regarding the care of the woods.... And in the autumn, when he was back in Edinburgh (for he did not actually cease attendance at the Parliament House till the middle of November) he told Cadell that he was writing another novel.

After that, the first chapters of *Count Robert of Paris* began to arrive on James Ballantyne's desk. It was a difficult position, both for printer and publisher. Neither of them was able to believe in the book. Yet, when they talked it over together, they could not say definitely that Scott's power had failed. There were times when his mind seemed as clear, his intellect as vigorous as ever. Could they tell him that he was no longer fit to write? James tried to get over the difficulty by arguing that he had chosen a hopeless period, concerning which a popular success would be impossible. Scott read the letters, and his mouth twitched, and he went back to his desk. It was a good tale, let James say what he would, and he was not dead yet. But he knew that he sometimes spoke with difficulty: that he sometimes wrote the wrong word.... And in November he had another slight stroke.

In younger, more self-confident days, he might have rejected James's remonstrances, as he had done more than once before, and continued on his own way, but now the doubt in his own mind and the urgent warnings of his physicians united to discourage the effort of his failing powers. On December 8th he had a letter from James which caused him to write to Cadell proposing to abandon *Count Robert*, and cancel the contract. He wrote to James also:

> "Having never supposed that any abilities I ever had were of a permanent texture, I am glad when friends tell me what I might be long in finding out myself. Mr. Cadell will show you what I have written to him. My present idea is to go abroad for a few months, if I hold together as long. So ended the fathers of the novel—*Fielding and Smollett*—and it would be no unprofessional finish for yours—W. S"

Cadell and Ballantyne read their letters, and were not happy. They consulted together, and decided to go over to Abbotsford, with what programme is less than clear, but they wisely deferred the journey till a meeting of creditors, which had been convened for the 17th to approve the further dividend, should have been held. When they went on the next day they were able to take the news that not only had the dividend been approved, but that the creditors had unanimously passed a resolution restoring to Sir Walter the 'furniture, plate, linens, paintings, library, and curiosities of every description' at Abbotsford, in recognition of 'his most honourable conduct, and in grateful acknowledgement for the unparalleled and most successful exertions he has made and continues to make for them.'

Scott had actually had this information before they arrived, in a letter from Mr. George Forbes, who had succeeded his brother, Sir William, as Chairman of these meetings. They found him in better spirits, and apparently in better health than they had expected. He was satisfied to talk business that evening, and it was not until they met in the library next morning that they found that they had a fresh trouble to face.

It had been one of their first desires at this time, and that of his own family, to keep him clear of the political arena, where the storm of the Reform agitation was at its height. It was not easy to do, for he was not of a disposition to stand aside from a fight of whatever kind, and he could not be ignorant that he had an enormous personal influence, as had, indeed, been demonstrated only two months before, when it had become known that the Government had offered the hospitality of Holyrood to the dethroned king, Charles X.

The refugee was not popular in Edinburgh, which had given him an earlier asylum, and personal and political animosities had combined to threaten him with a hostile reception. But Scott had issued an appeal in the press from "one who was leaving his native city never to return as a permanent resident," and who was "proud of distinctions received from his fellow citizens," that the ancient reputation of Edinburgh for hospitality should not be disgraced, and discords and animosities had sunk to silence at his desire.

Now he told Ballantyne and Cadell that, whether it were right or wrong, he had decided to accept their verdict, and, for the time, he had laid *Count Robert* aside, but he was not therefore admitting, nor was he conscious of, any failure of mental power. The political situation demanded the attention of every patriotic mind. He had been occupied during the past week with another *Epistle of Malachi*, dealing not with currency but with the more vital political issues which now divided the country. He gave Ballantyne the essay to read.

It is extremely difficult to judge fairly of what followed, because the subject of the discussion is not before us. James, with diffidence, opposed its publication.

Cadell spoke more plainly. He said (doubtless in politer language) that Scott did not understand the subjects on which he wrote, that he was behind the times, and, finally, that such an expression of his political views would do nobody any good, and the *magnum opus* a great deal of harm.

Lockhart states that a 'scene of a very unpleasant sort' followed this declaration. Scott would not give way, and the immediate issue was a compromise. The name of Malachi and the idea of a pamphlet were to be dropped, and the article was to appear anonymously in Ballantyne's newspaper.

In due course, James sent the proofs, which he had annotated with many arguments and objections. Scott read them, pondered the matter, and threw the whole thing on to the fire.

Cadell afterwards wrote to Lockhart that Sir Walter 'never recovered' from this incident, for which he blamed himself. Lockhart assumes that this self-condemnation was causeless. He says that Cadell 'did only what was his duty by his venerated friend; and he did it, I doubt not, as kindly in manner as in spirit'. All this may be true but, without knowledge of what the essay contained, how can we—or how could Lockhart—have material on which to judge? The only three whose witnesses we have on the matter—Ballantyne, Cadell, and William Laidlaw—were all Scott's political opponents. The pamphlet was an attack upon their own convictions, and they were not likely to admire its arguments. Had it been in favour of the policy of Lord Grey's government, they might have thought better of its quality, or that it would not be beyond human ingenuity to strengthen its weaker clauses. It is also apparent that Cadell's idea (which was probably groundless) that its publication would injure the sale of the novels, ought not to have influenced the decision. and Scott would certainly not have been moved by such a fear.

There is nothing in the general standard of Scott's literary output at this time to suggest that he was mentally incapable of writing a political pamphlet of a high standard. It was a very grave responsibility for his friends, who were also his political opponents, to take, to oppose its publication in such a spirit as to raise the doubt of mental instability in his own mind, and it is not surprising that Cadell did not feel very comfortable about it afterwards. Yet he may have had the courage to do the right thing in a difficult position. We cannot tell. But we may be sure that neither his opposition, nor that of James, would have prevailed but for that knowledge in Scott's own mind that his speech was sometimes difficult to control, that his hand would not always write the word which he had meant it to do. And so there came that moment, whether of insight or despair, when he destroyed the MS. which his friends condemned.

After that, the history of *Anne of Geierstein* was repeated. Cadell and Ballantyne combined to say that they had condemned *Count Robert* too hastily. Why not go on with it in a quiet way? There would be no hurry about completing it while men's minds were distracted by politics, as they then were.

CHAPTER CXV.

It is no part of our present subject to consider the political conditions of Europe at this time, except as far as is necessary to enable us to understand Scott's attitude towards them, and the degree to which they darkened his closing days.

We look back at the record of the last century, we observe the forces which overcame, and we may conclude that they were of an invincible strength, so that resistance was foolish, and condemnation vain. But their aspect was different then. Nor is it possible for us to do more than guess what might have happened had they been controlled by a different wisdom.

Yet even those who are best satisfied with the course of the prevailing current may recognise that its smoothness was largely due to those who were unmoved by the surrounding clamour, who thought more of the brake than the steering-wheel.

Scott saw France and Belgium in revolution, and his own country sick with social disorders and discontents. There were tales of riot and violence from every quarter. Men clamoured for a wider franchise, as the remedy for every evil. Scott doubted that bad government could be so easily turned into good, and feared that the last state might be worse than that which he lamented around him. He watched politicians who dodged and compromised and gave way to the storm.

His own opinion was that those on whom the responsibility lay should have the courage to govern, and that they should do it in such a spirit, and with such wisdom, as would bring content to a prosperous land. He saw the beginning of the exodus from rural to urban life, and the squalor of the new slums, and he recorded his opinion that it was an evil thing. A healthy population, he said, should be distributed over the land. Who can say that his fears were not justified by the appalling conditions of the towns of the next half-century? Who can say that a government, however autocratic, animated by such a spirit as his, would not have averted many of the worst features of the coming industrial slavery, as the polling-booth proved incompetent, or too slowly competent to do?

Now, as Christmas approached, he had a reluctant duty to perform at the Selkirk Court. A new Act had been passed to foster the salmon fishing in the Tweed, and to this end it had been considered necessary to repress poaching with severe penalties. The fact was that poaching had been practically permitted for many years, and the Tweed salmon-fishing was being rapidly destroyed in consequence. To protect the spawning fish during the close season was an essential condition of any improvement.

Scott did not disagree about that; but when he heard that six men were in custody charged with destroying the fish, and were to be brought before him on December 23rd, he recorded his opinion that he 'would have counselled the matter to be delayed a little season'. He thought that there was trouble enough at that time, without making more. There was a 'reform' meeting to be held in Selkirk on the same day.

He saw that, to many of those who would be there, reform meant no more nor less than 'the privilege of obeying such laws as please them'. His own political sagacity would have concentrated attention upon the major social evils of the moment, and let the poaching go on. But, all the same, and first of all, he would have order in Selkirkshire so long as he were its sheriff.

On December 20th, he had noted 'the constant increase of my lameness: the thigh-joint, knee-joint, and ankle-joint,' and the next day he had walked "with great pain in the whole limb, and am at every minute, during an hour's walk, reminded of my mortality".

But on the 23rd he was on the bench of the Selkirk court, tried the six men, and convicted four. As the decision was given, one of the convicted men made a sudden rush from the dock to the door, and would have escaped, but that Scott alone had foreseen his purpose and left the bench so quickly that, in spite of all his lameness, he was first at the entrance. For a moment, before slower-witted men had run forward to help, sheriff and prisoner confronted one another in the narrow doorway. 'Never!' an onlooker heard the Sheriff say, 'unless it be over the body of an old man.' But the prisoner would not lift his hand against the man who had sentenced him, and was secured in a moment. It is pleasant to know that he broke away successfully at a later hour.

CHAPTER CXVI.

"If I were worthy, I would pray God for a sudden death." So Scott wrote on the first of January, 1831. He had calculated that he had already secured that the final purpose of his life was reached, and that, with £30,000 of profit to come from the publications now proceeding, more than £20,000 of insurance money which his death would make available for his creditors, and £10,000 that might be raised on the remaining value of the copyrights, the payment of the balance still outstanding would, at his death, become a speedily possible thing.

With this feeling in his mind, and with a dread that he might at any time be incapacitated from speech or motion, though life should continue, he went into Edinburgh at the end of January, with the purpose of consulting his physicians there, and making the will which he had deferred till there should be something tangible to leave.

He had ascertained in correspondence with Walter that he would be able, and would prefer to make some monetary provision for Charles and his sisters, rather than that the library and other effects at Abbotsford should be realised for their benefit, and he now left them to Walter, subject to the payment of £1,000 to Sophia, and £2,000 each to Charles and Anne. Beyond that, all his copyrights and other properties were to be devoted to the payment of his debts, and the residue, if any, was to be for the benefit of his children equally.

He had been obliged to take this journey alone, Anne being too unwell to accompany him, and, for the first time in his life, he must put up at an hotel in his native city; but, next day, Cadell appeared on the scene, and persuaded him to accept the quieter hospitality of his own home. That was a fortunate thing, for the deep snow through which Scott had driven from Abbotsford was followed by a further fall, making the roads impassable, and for ten days he was weather-bound in Cadell's house in Atholl Crescent.

The time was not lost, for the physicians resorted to further bleeding and other remedies, which appear to have been justified by their results, for he returned to Abbotsford with a clearer mind, and without the giddiness which had been annoying him before he set out.

He had also got an ingenious mechanical contrivance made for the resting of the lamer leg, which gave great relief for a time, though not permanently.

He had been very quiet at Cadell's, retiring each morning to continue *Count Robert*, and resting during the later day, with the company of a single friend to dinner—Skene, or Thompson, or William Clerk—and had ventured out to dinner twice through the snow in a sedan chair.

So he went back feeling better, but with an increased consciousness of infirmity, for he had been using Laidlaw at Abbotsford as an amanuensis, and when he had been obliged to resume writing himself, he had been aware of an increased difficulty in controlling the pen....

The next three months were spent quietly at Abbotsford, while *Count Robert*, among other literary occupations, made progress which was steady, if not rapid. The days passed in a monotonous regularity, of which a complete picture is given in one Journal entry:

> "March 16.—The affair with Mr. Cadell being settled, I have only to arrange a set of regular employment for my time, without over-fatiguing myself. What I at present practice seems active enough for my capacity, and even if I should reach the threescore and ten from which I am thrice three years distant or nearer ten, the time may pass honourably, usefully and profitably, both to myself and other people. My ordinary for action runs thus—Rise at a quarter before seven: at a quarter after nine breakfast, with eggs, or in the singular number at least: before breakfast private letters &c.; after breakfast Mr. Laidlaw comes at ten, and we write together till one. I am greatly helped by this excellent man, who takes pains to write a good hand, and supplies the want of my own fingers as far as another person can. We work seriously at the task of the day till one o'clock, when I sometimes walk—not often,

however, having failed in strength, and suffering great pain even from a very short walk. Oftener I take the pony for an hour or two and ride about the doors; the exercise is humbling enough, for I require to be lifted on horseback by two servants, and one goes with me to take care I do not fall off and break my bones, a catastrophe very like to happen. My proud promenade a pied or a cheval, as it happens, concludes by three o'clock. An hour intervenes for making up my Journal and such light work. At four comes dinner—a plate of broth or soup, much condemned by the doctors, a bit of plain meat, no liquors stronger than small beer, and so I sit quiet to six o'clock, when Mr. Laidlaw returns, and remains with me till nine or three quarters past, as it happens. Then I have a bowl of porridge and milk, which I eat with the appetite of a child. I forgot to say that after dinner I am allowed half a glass of whisky or gin made into weak grog. I never wish for any more, nor do I in my secret soul long for cigars, though once so fond of them. About six hours per day is good working, if I can keep at it."

It was a few days before this entry that Scott had received an offer from Robert Cadell of £6,000 for a half-share of the copyrights of the later novels (those from *St. Ronan's Well* onwards) which were still entirely his own property. The intention was that the whole series should then be owned on equal terms, which might have some advantages of convenience, but Scott rejected the proposal after two days consideration, for reasons which there is no need to detail, but which show that he had no disability to analyse a business proposition in an exhaustive and logical manner. Nor were his physical infirmities sufficient to keep him away from a Jedburgh meeting at which it was proposed to pass public resolutions against the policy of the Whig Government.

He appeared on the platform there, but his speech was only

partly audible, and was shouted down by an influx of 'unwashed artificers' who had burst into the Court House. He resumed his speech after a time, and was shouted down again. Then he proposed a resolution which no one heard. He turned, a few minutes later, as he left the platform, to face the hisses of the audience. We may see in it, if we will, the old order facing the new, but the difference was deeper than that. "*Moriturus vos saluto*," he said, audibly to those around him, as he bowed farewell to the shouting mob.

CHAPTER CXVII.

It was a fortnight after the Jedburgh meeting that James Skene went on a visit to Abbotsford, taking with him his son, a young man of twenty-one, who afterwards held the position of Historiographer Royal for Scotland. Lord Meadowbank and his son, and Colonel Russell and his sister, were there also.

Lockhart says that Scott, "feeling his strength and spirits flagging," was "tempted to violate his physician's directions, and took two or three glasses of champagne, not having tasted wine for several months before. On retiring to his dressing-room he had a severe shock of apoplectic paralysis, and kept his bed under the surgeon's hands for several days."

That is a circumstantial account, and Lockhart is definite that it was at the dinner at which he entertained Lord Meadowbank, and in an endeavour to be adequate to his duties as host, that this alleged indiscretion took place. The only objection which need be made is that it cannot possibly be true. It is disproved by Scott's Journal, which broke off, with his illness, two days after the dinner in question, and by the quite separate record of Mr. Skene's son.

There may still be some different basis of fact for Lockhart's account—or there may not. His journalistic looseness, and his habit of filling in deficiencies of fact with guesses to which he gives a circumstantial plausibility, are maddening to anyone who may be tempted to place reliance upon him. To check Lockhart is almost always to find him wrong, and we are left to think what we will of a hundred statements which he gives in the same way, and which are beyond verification.

Young Skene recorded his memory of this visit, and it supports the Journal dates. He remembered the dinner, at which Mr. Pringle was also present (which the Journal confirms) and the carriage-drive up the Yarrow, when Sir Walter got out, and walked up the side of the river, 'pouring forth a continuous stream of anecdotes, traditions, and scraps of ballads' as he leaned on his arm.—Lord Meadowbank having gone on circuit that day.

The dinner was on Thursday evening. The walk was on Saturday. It was on Sunday morning that Sir Walter did not come down to breakfast, sending a message that he had caught cold, but at a later meal he came down and sat silently, without eating. Then he roused himself, and told an anecdote with much humour. There was a short interval of silence, after which he told it again. When he commenced it for a third time, Anne motioned her guests to rise from the table, and persuaded her father to return to his own room.

The next day, at the doctor's suggestion, the Skenes left. He said that Sir Walter was seriously ill, and the house must be kept as quiet as possible. There was the usual process of bleeding, the usual interval of lying quiet, and a week later he was able to write with an unsteady hand in his Journal: "I think I will be in the Secret next week, unless I recruit greatly."

But the next entry was more cheerful:

> "I walked out, and found the day delightful...I have been whistling on my wits like so many chickens, and cannot miss any of them. I feel on the whole better than I have yet done."

The next day Walter appeared, having got leave on hearing of his father's illness, but Sir Walter said that he was recovered. He went back to *Count Robert of Paris*.

Sophia came with the children a few days later and then Lockhart joined his family, and they settled at Chiefswood for the season, of which Anne must have been glad.

On May 7th, *Count Robert* was within a page of being finished, and the same day there was a 'formal remonstrance' from Cadell and Ballantyne against the portion of the third volume which had reached their hands.

> "I suspect," Scott noted, "their opinion will be found to coincide with that of the public; at least it is not very different from my own. The blow is a stunning one, I suppose for I scarcely feel it. It is singular, but it comes with as little surprise as though I had a remedy ready. Yet, God knows I am at sea in the dark, and the vessel leaky, I think, into the bargain...I will right and left at these unlucky proof-sheets, and alter at least what I cannot mend...I have suffered terribly, that is the truth, rather in body than in mind, and I often wish I could lie down and sleep without waking. But I will fight it out if I can.... My bodily strength is terribly gone; perhaps my mental too?"

But on the days that followed, the weather was 'uncommonly beautiful', and though 'very weak, scarce able to crawl about without the pony' he turned his thoughts again to the thinning of plantations, and, finding that his head swam when he took up those hateful proof-sheets, in what he knew to be a dangerous way, he resolved to put them aside, and see what could be done with *Count Robert* when he should feel able to work again.

But there could be no peace for Sir Walter while there was still power of mind or muscle in the exhausted body. The day of the elections of 1831 was approaching.

On May 13th he was knocked up at midnight 'to sign a warrant against some delinquents'. He heard after that the officers of the law were pursued by a mob from Galashiels for many miles, but lodged their prisoners at last in Jedburgh Castle. What levity of mis-government, his Journal asked, could have brought a peaceful and virtuous population to such a pass? All the elections, it was said, were being held amid the shouting of violent mobs.... And on the 18th there was the polling-day at Jedburgh, and he said that he must be there.

There were about half a hundred freeholders of Roxburghshire in whose hands the election of the county member lay. The opinions of most electors were known in advance, and the result could usually be foretold with certainty, under the conditions of such a limited franchise. But the widespread determination that this franchise should be extended was being supported by a large body of opinion within the privileged ranks of those who had it already. The remainder of the population could influence results only by making it as difficult as possible, by arguments of stone and stick, for any voter who did not show the reform colours to fight his way to the polling-place.

In Roxburghshire there was no doubt that Henry Scott of Harden would secure election, and he had himself joined in the efforts which were made by Scott's family to persuade him to keep away from the scene of contest.

On the previous evening, it was thought that these endeavours had been successful, but Lockhart, coming down at seven next morning, with the intention of riding to Jedburgh, was told that Sir Walter had countermanded his horse, and ordered the carriage for both. The carriage was at the door already, and Scott was waiting impatiently to set off.

They entered Jedburgh through a riotous crowd, and drove with some difficulty to the Shortreeds' house. Stones were thrown at the carriage as it passed, and some fell harmlessly within it. Robert Shortreed, who had led the way of the first Liddesdale raid, nearly forty years ago, had been dead for two years past, but he had left sons, and with a young Shortreed on one side, and Lockhart on the other, Sir Walter set out on foot for the hustings.

The crowd had gathered from all the county to make trouble for those who did not wear the reform colours. A thousand weavers from Hawick paraded the streets in an organised body of rowdyism, only held in check from the grosser forms of violence by the two troops of dragoons who were drawn up, a silent menace, on Ancrum Bridge.

Scott was too well known not to be recognised: he moved too slowly not to gain the full attention of the mob: the mere fact that he did not wear the Whig colours invited insult. There was a cry of 'Burke Sir Walter' as the three pushed their way slowly through the cursing, jostling crowd: from a window a woman spat. Yet he gained the platform at last, and appeared to speak, but even those who were nearest could hear nothing through the roar of the mob.... As the hours passed, the condition of the streets became more menacing, and when the election was over the leaders of both parties united in their efforts to get him safely out of the town.

One of the leading Whigs, Captain Russell Elliot, R.N., owned a villa at the rear of the *Spread Eagle*, and offered its hospitality, which was reached by some back alleys, such as were too frequent a feature of the Scottish towns of that day. Peter Mathieson brought the carriage there by a twisting route. Joseph Shillinglaw, a Darnick carpenter, got some of his cottage neighbours together to form a rearguard, and in this protection, and with no worse experience than the shower of stones which came over the heads of his protectors, Sir Walter drove out of Jedburgh for the last time. He noted that evening:

> "The day passed off with much clamour and no mischief. Henry Scott was re-elected—for the last time, I suppose. *Troja fuit*. I left the borough in the midst of abuse, and the gentle hint of *Burke Sir Walter*. Much obliged to the brave lads of Jeddart"

The Selkirkshire election was two days later, and his family made no attempt to dissuade him from driving into Selkirk on that occasion, for he was still Sheriff of the county, and it was his duty to go....

There was a man in Selkirk that morning who was conspicuous among the mob that jostled a voter who strove to make his way to the polling-booth. Conscious that the crowd had fallen quiet, he looked round to see the Sheriff descending slowly and painfully from his carriage.... He was coming toward him through the silent, watchful crowd.... Now the Sheriff's hand was upon him.... The man made no effort to escape. Scott called for a constable, and gave instructions that he should be locked up. There might be no dragoons in Selkirk, but there were special constables, men he could trust, whom he had sworn in for that day. While he was Sheriff, he would have order in his own county, though there were chaos in all the world beside.

It may not be a barren thought to consider how far that incident justified his own theories, his own ideals. He had kept order in Selkirk through thirty difficult years, and was still able to do so, by the powers of courage, justice, and love.

CHAPTER CXVIII.

The excitement of the election died, and Scott, now remaining quietly at Abbotsford, with occasional short visits to his closer friends, found his health improve somewhat, in what could be no more than a final flicker, as the June days lengthened.

He turned his mind to the thought of creative work again, and, with a pale imitation of the spirit of the old buoyant vigorous years, when he would find it sufficient recreation to turn from one novel to another, and back again as the overcrowding imaginations competed, he did not immediately complete *Count Robert*, but commenced the telling of another tale, *Castle Dangerous*, which had been in his mind ever since he outlined it in his *Essay on Chivalry*, twenty-seven years before. He wrote to Cadell, informing him of his new occupation, but said that he should not take James, nor, perhaps Lockhart, into his confidence on this occasion. Let them think that he was doing no more than to finish *Count Robert* in a drawling way.... Yet he found that he must tell Lockhart, for he doubted his memory of the topography of the tale, and must have his company to visit Lanarkshire. And when it came to the point of commencing to put the book into type, he decided that James must know also, for, though there had been a shadow of estrangement between them during recent months, he could not bear to wound his friend with the ultimate knowledge that he had given work to another printer.

Lockhart thinks, with probability on his side, that Scott had been hurt by some of James's strictures upon *Count Robert of Paris*, but it might be wrong to assume that this feeling was a dominating impulse towards the intended secrecy.

Scott was proposing to himself to make a last test of his failing powers, and he might reasonably feel that he would prefer to do it without the discouragement of a running fire of depreciatory criticism. He intended to do the best he could, and if it were failure he would know soon enough.

But there was probably a deeper motive still in that love of adventure which was fundamental to Scott, which Lockhart could never understand, and to which he alludes from time to time with a most causeless apology. It underlay the procession of anonymities with which Scott, from time to time, had thrown aside the protecting shield of past prestige, and would needlessly risk the financial harvest, for which, to the superficial observer, it might seem that his work was done.

To take a risk for a risk's sake, was, to Lockhart's mind, an almost incomprehensible thing. He searches diligently for the concealed motive which he feels that there must be, and if he cannot find it, imagination supplies the deficiency. To understand his attitude, we may turn to the adulatory paragraphs of his closing chapter, and observe the nature of the one spot which he feels that he must admit upon the sun of Sir Walter's excellence which he describes as his 'initiation in the practice of mystery a thing at first sight so alien from the frank, open, generous nature of the man, than whom none ever had or deserved to have more real friends.' He continues thus:

> "The indulgence cost him very dear. It ruined his fortunes—but I can have no doubt that it did worse than that. I cannot suppose that a nature like his was fettered and shut up in this way without suffering very severely from the 'cold obstruction'. There must have been a continual insurrection' in his 'state of man'; and, above all. I doubt not that what gave him the bitterest pain in the hour of his calamities was the feeling of compunction with which he then found himself obliged to stand before those with whom he had through life, cultivated brotherly friendship, convicted of having kept his heart closed to them on what they could not but suppose to have been the chief subjects of his thought and anxiety in times when they withheld nothing from him. These, perhaps, were the 'written troubles' that had been cut deepest into his brain. I think they were, and believe it the more, because it was never acknowledged."

How even Lockhart could 'believe it the more because it was never acknowledged', unless he would have believed it less if it had been, we need not waste space to consider, because this is no more than an empty concluding flourish to a paragraph of baseless nonsense.

Scott may, or may not, have 'ruined his fortunes' by being a partner in a printing business, but that ruin was not occasioned, nor materially affected by the fact (so far as it may have been a fact at all) that many people were ignorant of that partnership. That there is not the faintest trace in his correspondence at the time, or in the privacy of his Journal, of any compunction whatever on any such grounds, nor even of there being any grounds for such compunction, is exactly what we should expect to find. If Scott wished to talk or write to his friends about his own affairs, so he would, and often with great frankness, but it would not have crossed his mind that he was under an obligation to do so.

Lockhart's curious assumption that our neighbours have a natural right to know what we are doing, and that there is a taint of moral turpitude in any deliberate privacy, is an illogical fiction of weaker and smaller minds, finding its extreme illustration in the half-witted criminal who makes himself a nuisance to the community by insisting upon the confession of some ancient half-forgotten misdeed.

But just as Lockhart believes the more in his assumption because he can observe no evidence in its support, so he is able to strengthen his conviction that Scott was disposed to lean upon others even from the fact that he now made a deliberate attempt to avoid their interference. It sounds a difficult proposition to maintain, but what he says is:

> "Sir Walter's misgivings about himself, if I read him aright, now rendered him desirous of external support, but this his spirit would fain suppress and disguise even from himself."

So Scott decided to go his own way, and whether it were in an effort to disguise from himself his desire to do otherwise, or from a less childish motive, we may each think as we will. And when Lockhart arrived at Abbotsford after an absence of a few weeks in London, he showed him the earlier portion of *Castle Dangerous*, and asked him to accompany him by carriage to the Douglas country. He also mentioned that he should let James print the book, but should not invite his opinions upon it. In fact, he spoke in accordance with his first letter to Cadell on this subject. He was making a deliberate and possibly final test of his remaining powers, and he did not intend that it should be subject to disconcerting criticism as it proceeded.

This attitude of mind is confirmed by Lockhart's witness that, during their journey together,

> "He seemed constantly to be setting tasks to his own memory. It was not as of old, when, if anyone quoted a verse, he, from the fullness of his heart, could not help repeating the context. He was obviously in fear that this prodigious engine was losing its tenacity, and taking every occasion to rub and stretch it. He sometimes failed, and gave it up with *miseria cogitandi* in his eye. At other times he succeeded to admiration, and smiled as he closed his recital."

It was in the third week of July that this carriage journey was made from Tweed to Clyde, renewing some old acquaintances on the way, obtaining the required topographical details, and ending at the home of William Lockhart, where a neighbour, who was too old a friend of Scott's to be denied—Elliot Lockhart of Cleghorn—came over to see him.

Elliot Lockhart had had an attack of paralysis some time previously, but had made a good recovery. He made this visit the occasion of a convivial evening, at the end of which he left with the understanding that Scott would look in upon him at Cleghorn on the way back.

But next morning there came a messenger with the news that he had had another stroke after he got home and was in no condition to see anyone.

Lockhart thinks that Scott took this incident as a warning to himself, as he well might. He had agreed to stay two days longer, but he now asked William Lockhart to lend him horses, so that he could start home at once.

> "We started accordingly, and, making rather a forced march, reached Abbotsford the same night. During the

journey he was more silent than I ever before found him; he seemed to be wrapped in thought, and was but seldom roused to take notice of any object we passed. The little he said was mostly about *Castle Dangerous*, which he now seemed to feel sure he could finish in a fortnight."

Putting everything else, even his Journal, aside, he did in fact finish that book and *Count Robert* within a month of that date, and, having done them, he rested, as he had previously declined to do. The thought of wintering abroad, which had been in his mind for several years, now became a definite plan. If anything could yet prolong life, and restore a sufficient degree of health to make it worth having, it was agreed that it was the climate of Italy.

The fact that Charles was now attached to the British Legation at Naples made that destination a natural choice; and when Captain Basil Hall heard of the plan he wrote privately to the First Lord of the Admiralty, with the result that the Government offered to place a frigate at Sir Walter's disposal for the outward voyage.

For the next six weeks—until the last days of September—he rested quietly at Abbotsford, making no effort to commence any new literary labour, and allowing the idea to prevail that he would spend the winter abroad in the same idle way, but, all the time, the plan of a new romance must have been forming. He would go to Malta on the way to Naples. If the more genial climate could do all that was hoped, there should yet be another Waverley novel. *The Knights of Malta* should be its name. Meanwhile he must rest as placidly as he could, and conserve his remaining strength. This change of climate was the last hope—but hope of what? Life meant work to him.

So he rested and planned. And Lockhart observed that he was 'always tranquil, sometimes cheerful'.

He had a few guests during these weeks—old intimate friends, for the most part—and the Lockharts being at Chiefswood, the two families used to dine there or at Abbotsford on alternate days.

The artist Turner came to see him at this time, in Cadell's company, in reference to the illustration of the poems in the collected edition, and was entertained for a few days. He was taken to see Dryburgh Abbey, in the old routine of Abbotsford guests, Skene and Lockhart, with Scott himself, making up the party; but Scott found that he was still unable to enter the place where Charlotte was buried, and his friends had the good sense to leave him alone outside.

Cadell had arranged that the printing of the two last novels should not be commenced till Scott should sail, so that his correction of the proofs, and any alterations he might like to make could be undertaken at leisure. He also came to Abbotsford to discuss questions in relation to the Trust accounts, and to arrange for the provision of funds which would be needed for the journey, and for the maintenance of Abbotsford while Scott would be absent. Lockhart thought that "he probably strained a point to make things appear still better than they really were. He certainly spoke so as to satisfy his friend that he need give himself no sort of uneasiness about the pecuniary results of illness and travel".

That may be true. Cadell's conduct throughout in the business transactions of these last years (from which he made a fortune for himself) was exemplary. But it is difficult to observe that there was any occasion for straining points. The truth was good enough, and there were ample resources for the expenses in question.

Lockhart goes on to make a more serious statement which has been frequently quoted without the comment which it deserves. He says:

> "It was about this time that we observed Sir Walter beginning to entertain the notion that his debts were paid off. By degrees, dwelling on this fancy, he believed in it fully and implicitly. It was a gross delusion

but—neither Cadell nor any one else had the heart to disturb it by any formal statement of figures."

Such evidence, coming from a biographer who wrote of that which was under his own observation, cannot be lightly challenged. Yet there is substantial documentary evidence to discredit it. To some of this we must come in its own place, and it is sufficient here to observe that if at any time before his death Sir Walter thought that his debts were fully and literally discharged it was a mistake. But it could not properly be described as a gross delusion, for the battle was practically won.

We have seen from a Journal entry previously quoted that he had estimated that he had already made such provision that *at his death, and with the assistance of the insurance monies that would then fall due,* it would be possible for the debts to be cleared, and that conviction doubtless enabled him to relax his efforts without self-reproach at this time. But this was not the delusion of a brain-sick man. It was a sound business estimate, as the event proved.

He may have spoken in general terms at this time as of a struggle already won, without going into explanations with a son-in-law who did not understand business, and who appears to have been blandly unconscious of his deficiencies in that direction. It is the kindest suggestion as regards Lockhart which can be made, in view of the evidence which is to come, but the essential point of accuracy is that whatever Scott may have thought or imagined, there could be no gross delusion on the part of anyone in thinking or speaking of those debts as paid. There was only the difference of actual payment, or of provision having been made therefor.

CHAPTER CXIX

As the day of departure from Abbotsford drew near Scott decided to resume his Journal, apparently with the feeling that there would be more of interest to record during his journey than had been the case during the monotony of his recent days.

He re-commenced it with an undated entry, probably written about the middle of September, which does not suggest that he had been conscious of any improvement in his general state of health, nor that he was under any delusions respecting the condition of his financial affairs. This is what he wrote:

> "I have been very ill, and if not quite unable to write, I have been unfit to do so. I have wrought, however, at two Waverley things, but not well, and, what is worse, past mending. A total prostration of bodily strength is my chief complaint. I cannot walk half a mile. There is, besides, some mental confusion, with the extent of which I am not, perhaps, fully acquainted. I am perhaps setting. I am myself inclined to think so, and like a day that has been admired as a fine one, the light of it sets down amid mists and storms. I neither regret nor fear the approach of death if it is coming. I would compound for a little pain instead of this heartless muddiness of mind which renders me incapable of anything rational. The expense of my journey will be something considerable, which I can provide against by borrowing £500 from Mr. Gibson. To Mr. Cadell I owe already, with the cancels on these apoplectic books, about £200, and must run it up to £500 more at least; yet this heavy burthen would be easily borne if I were to be the Walter Scott I once was; but the change is great. This would be nothing, providing that I could count on these two books having a sale equal to their predecessors; but as they do not deserve the same countenance, they will not and cannot have such a share of favour, and I have only to hope that they will not involve the *Waverley*, which are now selling 30,000 volumes a month in their displeasure."

There is no suggestion here that he thought that the debts were paid. Had that been the case, the Trust would have been wound, or winding, up and the question of 'borrowing' from Mr. Gibson would not arise. We may observe also that Scott had a clear opinion as to the quality of the last two books he had written, and there is an implication that he had cancelled his contract with Cadell in consequence, and had substituted an arrangement much more favourable to the publisher by which his remuneration would depend upon the sales of the books. The result of this was that instead of drawing 4,000 guineas against the manuscript in the old way, he 'owed' £200 to Cadell, which might have to be increased to £500 against the uncertainty of these sales, and he could not regard the expense of the winter in Italy with entire equanimity until he should know what the sales of these books, which were not to be published until after his departure, would be.

This entry was made in September, at the very time at which Lockhart says the 'gross delusion' began to be observed. We cannot place it later, because Scott left Abbotsford on September 23rd, and Lockhart did not accompany him beyond London. We shall see that later entries in the Journal show the same clear grasp of the financial position, and the entries, which were continued with frequency and approximate regularity during the winter months, *do not contain a single line to suggest that he was under such a delusion at any time.*

CHAPTER CXX.

A 'long and painful journey' to London did little to encourage a course, which, if it would ever have been radically beneficial, was being tried too late. Scott observed during this journey that the weakness of his limbs was 'palpably increasing', and though he doubtless assisted his own condition by the cheerful courage with which he endured it, yet he was not of the disposition which deceives itself with an easy optimism. No one could undertake a forlorn hope with a cooler valour, but few would judge it more accurately for its likely end: 'have not warm hopes of being myself again'.

So he came to London for the last time—to a city that was 'in a foam with politics', to see the windows of the Duke of Wellington's house smashed by a mob which made lawless havoc of London when the second Reform Bill was thrown out, and to be told that the christening of the new heir to the Buccleuch dukedom must be postponed because it was not considered safe for the King to drive through the streets of London.

During his last days at Abbotsford the Wordsworths had come for a final visit; on his way to London he had paused a day at Rokeby to say what was to be a last farewell to his lifelong friend there; one by one, as he remained in London during the next three weeks, old friends came to him at the Lockharts' house in Regent's Park. He went out two or three times to breakfast, but made no further effort to dine abroad.

Doctors gathered around him, and withdrew for consultation. When they returned, his chair was withdrawn to a shadowed corner of the room. They spoke favourably; and he told them that he had not wished them to see how he would take their verdict: "I feared insanity, and I feared you."

Dr. Robert Fergusson gives this description of his appearance on his arrival in London. It is the witness both of a physician and a friend:

> "The alterations which had taken place in his mind and person since I had seen him, three years before, were very apparent. The expression of the countenance and the play of features were changed by slight palsy of one cheek. His utterance was so thick and indistinct as to make it very difficult for any but those accustomed to hear it to gather his meaning. His gait was less firm and assured than ever; but his power of self-command, his social tact, and his benevolent courtesy, the habits

of a life, remained untouched by a malady which had obscured the higher powers of his intellect."

The 'higher powers of his intellect' might be obscured by the physical weakness which had assailed them, but the soul, the individual, which is separate from the brain and muscle which it controls, was the same which had laughed at the lightning in the heather of Sandy-Knowe, and overcome with stubborn courage in those childhood years the infirmity of the dragging limb.

We do not understand the nature of the ordeal of these closing years if we emphasise the sometime 'muddiness of mind' of which Scott was conscious when he tried, not only to weave new fancies within it, but to translate them to written form. For the most part, his mind was clear, and though it might be a diminished force, it was still of a great activity. His Journal throughout the winter shows no sign of any mental confusion whatever. But the writing of the palsied hand is very hard to decipher. His speech must have been often difficult to understand. When he tried to walk by himself he could only move with a painful slowness; yet he would not cease the attempt, and when, on the way to Portsmouth, his carriage stopped to change horses at Guildford, he descended unobserved and was nearly knocked down by a stage-coach in the narrow street.

The tragedy of such existence is not that of insanity, it is that there is still active life in the isolation within, though the blinds fall; and with Scott there was still a restless intellectual vigour which he restrained with difficulty under the urgent medical advice he had received. But he restrained it with a different purpose than that of those who advised him. They thought only of prolonging life; he thought only of using that life to some further purpose, apart from which possibility, to conserve it would be a vain thing. He thought that he might yet add one more to the Waverley novels that men would be glad to have. Or, if the hope was faint, the indomitable purpose held. And who can doubt that he was right in this, and his physicians wrong? Wrong, even though their advice might have somewhat prolonged his years? He did not want to exist, but to live. And as he obeyed them during those weeks in London, writing only a few final notes for the *magnum opus*, an introduction to *Count Robert*, a few pages in the Journal, a few letters to friends, he was strengthened to this control by that faint enduring hope that the Italian climate might yet restore him, not to a prolonged passivity, but to ride out a final tilt with fate before the darkness fell.

CHAPTER CXXI.

The *Barham* (Captain Pigot) lying at anchor at Portsmouth, had few companions, for the most part of the fleet was making the voice of England audible amid the disorders of Europe by a demonstration of force in the Baltic. She was one of the finest frigates in the service, and exceptional in her accommodation by the standards of those days, for she had once been a seventy-four, and cut down to a frigate of fifty guns when the peace left England with a larger line-of-battle fleet than she was likely to need again, and at a time when battle-ships did not become obsolescent as rapidly as they do now.

Yet the accommodation was crude and cramped enough, and the discomforts more than an invalid landsman would lightly face, as the *Barham*—after some delay owing to adverse weather, during which Scott had remained in readiness to embark at the *Fountain Inn*, and the naval officers had shown Anne and Jane the sights of Portsmouth (for Walter had got a long leave, and he and his wife were of the party)—moved slowly down the channel, wooing uncertain winds, and then took to 'terrible tossing' as she passed Plymouth, and would beat southwards for Finnisterre against a rising gale.

For three days they tossed vainly, with the Lizard and Land's End always in sight through the squalls. On the fifth day out Scott kept "the deck the whole day, though bitter cold". It was nine o'clock of the November night before he turned in to his coffin-like berth; and next morning, having overcome the sickness of the earlier days, though the night had been 'far from voluptuous', he established himself in the after-cabin to read, and write as well as he could, with the plunging of the ship and the unsteadiness of his own hand.

After that, there came fair but variable winds, and the frigate set her course and made good progress enough, and so continued until the Bay of Biscay was left behind, so that they passed Lisbon during the night when they had been a fortnight out; after which the weather changed again to the southwest, and it was three days more before, with the wind 'in gentle opposition, like a well-drilled spouse', they wore slowly toward Gibraltar, and Scott felt his heart 'beat faster and fuller' as they passed the battle-sites of St. Vincent and Trafalgar, though with the humility of one who had not been accounted physically worthy to share the struggle; and the older sailors told of the battles in which they had taken part, but which were already no more than hearsay to the younger members of the crew.

Was he better already in the milder air? The officers thought he was. He thought himself that his spirits were better, that he could write more easily. "The difficulty will be to abstain from working hard, but we will try". So he recorded, after writing to Cadell to catch the Gibraltar mail. The spirit of discovery and adventure stirred again, and whatever benefit there might be in the milder air he 'would put up with a good rough gale which would force us into Tangiers and keep us there for a week'.

But the winds continued light and variable, so that they glided quietly along the barren African coast, a greater mystery then than it is now, and saw a French schooner of eighteen guns tacking backwards and forwards as it blockaded Oran, and had a good view of the high white, incurving crescent of buildings which was Tangiers, looking less formidable than its reputation, and passed the cape where the Mediterranean fleet used to trade for cattle in those endless war-years when it blockaded Toulon, and then came to the lower Tunisian coast, and watched for an appearance of Arabian cavalry, and saw nothing more formidable than a red cow. And at this time, the winds being light, they were passed by the steam mail-packet which had left Portsmouth at the same time as themselves, and was destined to beat them by a day or two, which, in better weather, it would have been unable to do.

And on November 20th, when they had been nearly a month out, they sighted Graham's Island, a product of submarine volcanic disturbance which had appeared above the sea about four months before, and was destined to disappear a few days later. It was already greatly diminished in extent, and its substance was so loose and soft that those who trod it must be prepared to sink 'to the knee' at each difficult step, but Scott would not content himself without landing upon it, and finding progress impossible to one of his weight and infirmity, he mounted upon the shoulders of a willing seaman, and proceeded almost to the top of the Island. He sent a very long letter to Skene, descriptive of this natural curiosity, with one of the largest blocks of lava which he could find, for the information of the Royal Society; and neither this letter, nor the long entries in his Journal during the voyage, show any failure of observation, confusion of thought, or inability to describe with the old vividness, or the old power. It is only the writing which is hard to read.

So he landed at Malta, and after some strictness of quarantine (for there was an active dread of cholera at the time) he settled in Beverley's Hotel in the Strada Ponente.

It is difficult to suppose that he could have gone to any part of the English-speaking world and not found himself among friends. Here Sir John Stoddart, who will be remembered to have called at Lasswade about thirty years ago, was the Chief Judge: Colonel Bathurst, the Lieutenant-Governor, had often met him before leaving his father's home: William Erskine's (Lord Kinnedder's) eldest daughter was now the wife of an officer of the garrison, Captain Dawson: his old friend, John Hookam Frere, was now a permanent resident.

On the day after landing, while still in the confines of Fort Manuel, which the courtesy of the Governor had substituted for the ordinary quarantine quarters, he had studied the architecture of the town sufficiently to get a new idea for extending Abbotsford "by a screen on the west side of the old barn, and with a fanciful wall"; and the next day, in the quietude of those quarantine walls (but he was allowed to receive visitors of consideration so long as they kept at a yard's distance from members of his party, and many came) he recorded:

> "I am getting on with this *Siege of Malta* very well. I think, if I continue, it will be ready in a very short time, and I will get the opinion of others, and if my charm hold I will be able to get home through Italy—and take up my old trade again."

But when quarantine was over, there was much pressure of hospitality, and much carriage-driving to survey the land, and libraries to be viewed, and church vaults to be descended; and at the end of that time Captain Pigot said that he was sailing for Naples, and would Sir Walter like to be taken on there?

And though it would mean delay in receipt of the expected letter from Cadell, which was to tell how the new novels were going, and what funds would be available from that source, which Scott was anxious to have, he decided that the offer of free transportation was too good to be declined; and no more had been done for the *Siege of Malta*, beyond the collection of some old legends and some old prints.

It was Christmas Day at Naples when Sir Walter and his party were released from a week's quarantine there, and went ashore to establish themselves in an apartment of the Palazzo Caramanico which had been taken for their reception. There was the 'great joy' of seeing Charles again; and there were acquaintances to be renewed or formed with many English residents 'of most of whom' Scott noted that he had some knowledge already.

By the 26th December, the absence of the expected letter, or any remittance from Cadell, was becoming an active anxiety. The money which Scott had brought with him had been rapidly disappearing, as money in his hands had always been likely to do, and he noted now:

> "Walter has some money left, which we must use or try a begging-box, for I see no other resource, since they seem to have abandoned me so."

But the crisis cannot have been very acute, for after this rather querulous sentence there is no allusion to any financial need till the mail came a fortnight later, and anxiety ended.

Cadell wrote cheerfully about the novels, which had not been long published when he wrote, on December 2nd., and made it clear that there would be no occasion to worry about remittances. "I think," Sir Walter noted, "£200 a month, or thereby, will do very well, and it is no great advance."

By this time he had written a large part of *The Siege of Malta*, and felt more confident of its success than had been the case with the two previous novels. The book was never published, and Lockhart brushes it aside with the remark that it is 'hardly to be deciphered with any effort', but he dismisses the Journal of this period in the same way, and that writing has been deciphered since, and does not show any lack of clear thinking or narrative power.

Early in January, Scott was busy with the contents of the libraries and museums of Naples, to which the King had given him unrestricted access. He had found an old copy of Sir Bevis of Hampton, and engaged an amanuensis to transcribe it for him.

On the 26th he had another letter from Cadell, in greater detail than before, announcing that *Count Robert* and *Castle Dangerous* had succeeded beyond expectations. At least, so the Journal records; and Sir William Gell noted that on the morning when the letter arrived, Scott called upon him in a mood of

THE LIFE OF SIR WALTER SCOTT | 745

unusual elation, saying: 'I could never have slept straight in my coffin till I had satisfied every claim against me; and now,' turning to a favourite dog of Sir William's, 'my poor boy I shall have my house and my estate round it free, and I may keep my dogs as big and as many as I choose without fear of reproach.'

Lockhart says that in talking in such a manner Sir Walter 'was haunted with a mere delusion, on the origin of which' he would 'form no guess'. It is difficult to understand what he means, unless it be that no such letter arrived, which is against probability. The entry in the Journal for that day shows no lack of clear thinking, though it may be sanguine in spirit. This is what he says:

> January 26. This day arrived (for the first time indeed) answer to last post end of December, an epistle from Cadell full of good tidings. *Castle Dangerous* and *Sir Robert of Paris*, neither of whom I deemed seaworthy, have performed two voyages—that is, each sold about 3,400, and the same of the current year. It proves, what I have thought almost impossible, that I might right myself. But as yet my spell holds fast. I have besides two or three good things on which I may advance with spirit, and with palmy hopes on the part of Cadell and myself. He thinks he will soon cry *victoria* on the bet about his hat. He was to get a new one when I had paid off all my debts. I can hardly, now that I am assured all is well again, form an idea to myself that I could think it was otherwise.
>
> And yet I think it is the public that are mad for passing those two volumes: but I will not be the first to cry them down in the market, for I have others in hand, which, judged with equal favour, will make fortunes of themselves. Let me see what I have on the stocks—
>
> *Castle Dangerous* (supposed future Editions)—1,000

Robert of Paris—1,000
Lady Louisa Stuart—500
Knights of Malta—2,500
Trotcosianae Reliquiae—2,500

I have returned to my old hopes, and think of giving, Milne an offer for his estate.

Letters or Tour of Paul in 3 vols—3,000
Reprint of Bevis of Hampton for Roxburghe Club
Essay on the Neapolitan Dialect

Now, whatever criticism may be made upon these reflections, they are not those of one who had deceived himself in the previous September into thinking that his debts were paid in full, and had ever since (as Lockhart explicitly asserts) been getting this idea more firmly fixed in his mind. It is obvious both that he knew that they were not paid, and that Cadell made no mystery of the true position in his correspondence. He had not yet bought the hat, though he thought that he might soon be able to do so.

Nor did Scott deceive himself as to the quality of the last two books. He thought the public were mad to receive them as well as they had done.

Nor can we say that his estimate of the proceeds of these or of future books if he should be able to write them, was unreasonably optimistic. Cadell had given him £4,200 for *Anne of Geierstein* and had not regretted the bargain. He estimates that the *Knights of Malta* may bring in £2,500.

Yet he did regard it as substantially true that the success of the *magnum opus* had relieved him from the burden of debt, and that if he could still make money by fiction with the old magical ease he would be able to fulfil the dream of many years by adding Faldonside to the Abbotsford estate. We have come to a dream that is no bolder nor wilder than had been many of earlier days, but we have come at last to one which will not come true.

The Knights (or Siege) of Malta would not be published, would earn nothing; the other books on the list would be no better, or less than that; the new idea to go on to Rhodes and write a romantic poem there would be all imagination, and nothing more. Lockhart looks at these dreams and sees only a 'painful' thing. Why would he not sit quietly by the fire, and drowse till his life should end? Why did he not realise that he was so soon to die? Simply because he was not Lockhart, but Walter Scott; and he would have thought such an end, accepted in such a spirit, to be a more 'painful' thing.

Yet he did not deceive himself as to his physical peril, for it was only in the previous entry that he had parodied Wordsworth:

"For as my body's growing worse
My mind is growing better".

And as to the 'gross delusion' about the debts, let us have the facts as they finally proved to be. This is Lockhart's account:

> "In the winter succeeding the poet's death, his sons and myself, as his executors, endeavoured to make such arrangements as were within our power for completing the great object of his own wishes and fatal exertions. We found the remaining principal sum of commercial debt to be nearly £54,000. £22,000 had been insured upon his life; there were some monies in the hands of the trustees, and Mr. Cadell very handsomely offered to advance to us the balance, about £30,000, that we might without further delay settle with the body of creditors. This was effected accordingly on the 2nd day of February 1833; Mr. Cadell accepting as his only security, the right to the profits accruing from Sir Walter's copyright property and literary remains, until such time as this new and consolidated obligation should be discharged."

This position was allowed to continue until the death of Sir Walter's eldest son, fourteen years later, on which we may have Lockhart's account also:

> "Mr. Cadell then offered to relieve the guardians of the young inheritor of that great name from much anxiety and embarrassment by accepting, in full payment of the sum due to himself, and also in recompense for his taking on himself the final obliteration of the heritable bond, a transference to him of the remaining claims of the family over Sir Walter's writings, together with the result of some literary exertions of the only surviving executor. This arrangement was completed in May 1847; and the estate, as well as the house and its appendages, became at last unfettered."

Now the plain facts half-concealed in this verbiage are that Sir Walter *was* right in estimating that his exertions during the last five years had been sufficient to provide for the payment of all his liabilities (in strict English, most of them were not debts) at his death, and that the final settlement resulted also in the removal of the £10,000 mortgage upon the Abbotsford property. It must be added, and it is no disparagement of Robert Cadell to say, that the three executors—Lockhart and Scott's two sons—were no match for him in a business deal. When the final bargain was made, Lockhart was the only surviving executor. If the real value of the copyrights which were still the property of the estate was exactly the same as the balance of the mortgage upon the property, it was an extraordinary coincidence. It was the kind of bargain which executors make, and people who are acting for themselves very seldom do. The estate which Scott left did not merely discharge in full the liabilities which had fallen upon him, it also provided a second fortune for Robert Cadell, in addition to that which Scott's own contracts had allowed and intended him to make.

CHAPTER CXXII.

It was early April 1832 when Scott gave up the intention to visit Rhodes, and decided to return to Abbotsford for the summer. About the reason for the abandonment of the Rhodes project there is no doubt. The intention had been formed some months earlier; for it was mentioned in an undated letter to Lockhart which cannot have been written long after the receipt of the news of the death of his grandson, John Hugh, which occurred in the previous December. The object was to collect material for a poem in the old six-canto style, the subject of which was to be a chivalrous legend connected with that Island. To Rhodes he would certainly have gone, on the invitation of his old friend, Sir Frederick Adam, who was then the Governor of the Ionian Islands, had he not been transferred to an Indian appointment, so that the frigate which he had promised could not be sent.

On hearing that, Scott altered his intention, and decided to go home. The picture that Lockhart draws—and it is right to remember that he had the advantage of hearing the accounts of Anne and Charles (who obtained special leave to accompany his father), is that of the desperate haste of a consciously dying man to reach his home while he yet lived.

He says further that the news of the death of Goethe, whom Scott had intended to visit on returning through Germany (which death occurred on March 22nd) "seemed to act upon Scott exactly as the illness of Borthwickbrae" (Lockhart of Cleghorn) "had done in the August before. His impatience redoubled; all his fine dreams of recovery seemed to vanish at once—'Alas for Goethe!' he exclaimed: 'but he at least died at home. Let us to Abbotsford.'"

There may be an element of fact in this presentation, but it must be modified by recognition of Lockhart's tendency to represent Scott as always being influenced by surrounding people and circumstances much more than he actually was, and by the Journal itself, which shows a substantially different mood.

> "April 15th. *Naples*. I am on the eve of leaving Naples, after a residence of three or four months, my strength strongly returning, though the weather has been very uncertain."

He goes on to record that he has packed two chests of books, and the means he is taking to get them safely home by sea (as they must have been beyond the capacity of the carriage in which the party would travel), and that is hardly the act of a dying man, or one who anticipates dissolution.

He also records that he had sent home the complete three volumes of the *Siege of Malta*, and the "letters by L.L. Stuart", in the charge of Lord Cowper's son; which shows how steadily he had worked, for he had rarely completed a novel (of whatever quality) in a shorter time.

After these notes he goes on to enter *in extenso* a Calabrian legend which he had heard on 'respectable authority' though he would not vouch for its truth.

On the morning after these entries were made, the party, consisting of Sir Walter, Anne, Charles, and two servants, started from Naples, but got no further than St. Agatha, for after breakfasting there, and driving about half a mile onward, a wheel came off the carriage. With sufficient difficulty it was conveyed back to that place, and the party had to put up with the wretched accommodation that St. Agatha could provide, till it could be repaired, and a new start made at seven of the following morning.

The day's journey was long and fatiguing. Scott attributed a severe headache to the bad air of the Pontine marshes through which the road lay. It was moonlight when they arrived in Rome. Charles had asked Sir William Gell to engage a lodging for their arrival, but had omitted to make any arrangement for obtaining its address. Anne had made the same request to another friend,

Mrs. Ashley, but had also made the same omission. They were in the absurd position of having two lodgings and not knowing the address of either. They drove about in the moonlight till they met with a servant (presumably of Sir William Gell's) who guided them to the lodging they needed. Scott entered a detailed record in his Journal of the scenes they passed, with a regret that he had been too tired to inspect the ancient chateau of Velletri when they rested there, as he would have liked to do. On arrival at their lodgings at last, he wrote: "We slept reasonably, but on the next morning—". And with that unfinished sentence the Journal ends.

CHAPTER. CXXIII.

Having arrived in Rome, the return journey paused. Scott was in good spirits, and confident in the hope that years of work and new successes were still before him. He believed that his health had been permanently improved by the Italian winter. He was glad to be returning to Abbotsford, but content to remain for a time in Rome, and its neighbourhood, where he was entertained by Mr. Edward Cheney (a close friend of the Maclean Clephanes, and so very ready to be his own) at a villa in Frascati, which had once been the residence of the Cardinal of York Regarding this delay at Rome, Lockhart says:

> "The certainty that he was on his way home for the time soothed and composed him; and amidst the agreeable society which again surrounded him on his arrival in Rome, he seemed perhaps as much of himself as he had ever been in Malta or in Naples. For a moment even his literary hope and ardour appear to have revived. But still his daughter entertained no doubt, that his consenting to pause for even a few days in Rome was dictated mainly by considerations of her natural curiosity."

There is sufficient difference between the tone and substance of this statement to prepare anyone familiar with Lockhart's inaccuracies for the fact that the duration of the stay in Rome was between three and four weeks.

On the 11th May, Rome was left, with the definite intention of returning to Abbotsford. Scott, we are told, was anxious to be home again, as can easily be understood, and seemed impatient to his younger companions, who would gladly have turned aside or lingered at a score of places.

> "His companions could with difficulty prevail on him to see even the falls of Terni, or the church of Santa Croce at Florence. On the 17th, a cold and dreary day, they passed the Apennines, and dined on the top of the mountains. The snow and the pines recalled Scotland, and he expressed pleasure at the sight of them. That night they reached Bologna, but he would see none of the interesting objects there:—and next day, hurrying in like manner through Ferrara, he proceeded as far as Monselice.'

Yet the 'hurried' journey had occupied eight days on the road to Venice, where there was a four-days' pause, during which Scott insisted on descending into the dungeons beneath the Bridge of Sighs, though it was an 'exceedingly painful' effort; and it was actually June 5th when he entered a bookseller's shop at Frankfort, and a shop assistant, hearing English voices, but not knowing who the party were, offered them some views of Abbotsford.

Up to this point, although we are assured that Scott had been in such haste that 'though in some parts of the journey they had very severe weather, he repeatedly wished to travel all the night as well as the day', yet the dates are conclusive in proof that the journey had been taken in a quite leisurely manner, with many pauses besides that at the Frankfort shop, unless Europe was a substantially larger continent than it is now.

But it had become evident by this time that the fatigues of travel, the changes of climate, the uncertainties of diet, or other obscurer causes, were proving gravely detrimental, and it is probable that a consciousness of this physical condition caused a natural impatience and anxiety as the weeks passed and the endless-seeming journey continued.

More than once, we are told, his servant Nicholson, who had been instructed in the art of bleeding, had attempted that remedy before, on the evening of June 11th, when descending the Rhine and in the neighbourhood of Nimeguen, he had a further stroke of paralysis. He rallied sufficiently to be able, and to insist upon resuming his journey on the next day, and was transferred two days later from the Rhine boat to an English steamer at Rotterdam.

The party arrived in London without having been able to advise anyone of their coming, owing to the speed at which the journey had been completed (showing incidentally that, till that stroke decided the matter, it had been the intention to linger, even over the final stages) and they drove to an hotel in Jermyn Street.

Within a few hours Dr. Fergusson was with him. Other doctors followed. They decided that he was unfit to be moved again, and for three weeks he lay in a condition between life and death in the St. James's Hotel.

Dr. Fergusson's account is this:

> "When I saw Sir Walter, he was lying in the second floor back room of the St. James's Hotel, in a state of stupor, from which, however, he could be roused for a moment by being addressed, well then he recognised those about him, but immediately relapsed. I think I never saw anything more magnificent than the symmetry of his colossal bust, as he lay on the pillow with his chest and neck exposed . During the time he was in Jermyn Street he was calm but never collected, and in general either in absolute stupor or in a waking dream.

He never seemed to know where he was, but imagined himself to be still in the steam-boat. The rattling of carriages, and the noises of the street, sometimes disturbed this illusion—and then he fancied himself at the polling-booth of Jedburgh, where he had been insulted and stoned. During the whole of this period of apparent helplessness, the great features of his character could not be mistaken. He always exhibited great self-possession, and acted his part with wonderful power whenever visited, though he relapsed the next moment into the stupor from which strange voices had roused him. A gentleman (Mr. Richardson) stumbled over a chair in his dark room—he immediately started up, and though unconscious that it was a friend, expressed as much concern and feeling as if he had never been labouring under the irritability of disease. It was impossible even for those who most constantly saw and waited on him in his then deplorable condition to relax from the habitual deference which he had always inspired. He expressed his will as determinedly as ever, and enforced it with the same apt and good natured irony as he was wont to use.

At length his constant yearning to return to Abbotsford induced his physicians to consent to his removal; and the moment this was notified to him, it seemed to infuse new vigour into his frame. It was on a calm, clear afternoon on the 7th July, that every preparation was made for his embarkation on board the steam boat. He was placed on a chair by his faithful servant Nicholson, half dressed, and loosely wrapped in a quilted dressing gown. He requested Lockhart and myself to wheel him towards the light of the open window, and we both remarked the vigorous lustre of his eye. He sat there silently gazing on space for more than half an hour, apparently wholly occupied with his own thoughts, and having no distinct perception of where he was, or how he came there. He suffered himself to be lifted into his carriage, which was surrounded by a crowd among whom were many gentlemen on horseback, who had loitered about to gaze on the scene. His children were deeply affected, and Mrs. Lockhart trembled from head to foot, and wept bitterly. Thus surrounded by those nearest to him, he alone was unconscious of the cause or the depth of their grief, and while yet alive seemed to be carried to his grave."

But who knows of what the mind is conscious under such conditions? He remained in that apparent passivity, letting others do as they would, throughout the voyage to Edinburgh, and in the hotel in St. Andrews Square, and on the first two stages of the carriage journey to Abbotsford, but he stirred and looked round as they turned into the Gala vale, and when 'his eye caught at length his own towers at the distance of a mile, he sprang up with a cry of delight'.

But the Tweed was in flood from a summer storm, and it was necessary to drive to Melrose, and cross by the bridge there, and (Lockhart says) it required the combined persuasions of himself and Nicolson and Dr. Watson, and sometimes their combined strength also, to restrain him from attempting to leave the carriage...and so they wheeled him at last into the Abbotsford dining-room, where he sobbed over the fawning dogs.

During the next few days there was an uncertain flicker of hope among those who watched, for he showed some revival of mental, if not of physical vigour, and a quiet happiness in being wheeled through the rooms and gardens that he had made to be what they were. He must be read to—from St. John's Gospel, and Crabbe—and clearly appreciated what he heard, though it seemed that well-known passages of Crabbe were regarded as though heard for a first time.

But if he had forgotten Crabbe, his thoughts must have gone back during these long silent weeks over a hundred things that are recorded here, and a thousand others that have gone from human record or memory now...and there came a day when he said that he must be wheeled to his desk, for he was well enough to begin writing again.

"Now give me the pen," he said, "and leave me a little to myself." So Sophia put it to his hand; but his fingers refused to close, and the pen fell.

He looked up with eyes from which the tears were falling. "Friends," he said, "don't let me expose myself...get me to bed."

For though there might still be the two months' detail of dying, he knew then that his life was done.

ABOUT THE AUTHOR

SYDNEY FOWLER WRIGHT (1874-1965) penned over seventy volumes of science fiction, fantasy, classic mysteries, historical novels, poetry, and non-fiction, many of them being published by the Borgo Press imprint of Wildside Press. Please visit his website at:

www.sfw.org

www.ingramcontent.com/pod-product-compliance
Lightning Source LLC
Chambersburg PA
CBHW021755220426
43662CB00006B/66